Microbial Protoplasts,
Spheroplasts
and L-Forms

Microbial Protoplasts, Spheroplasts and L-Forms

editor LUCIEN B. GUZE, M.D.

Chief of Staff for Research and Education,
Veterans Administration Center and
Associate Professor of Medicine,
Department of Medicine, University of
California, Los Angeles School of Medicine,
Los Angeles, California

THE WILLIAMS & WILKINS COMPANY
BALTIMORE 1968

Composed and printed at
The Waverly Press
Mt. Royal and Guilford Avenues
Baltimore, Md. 21202 U.S.A.

To

Patricia, Lorie, Barry and Julie Guze

with much love

The stimulus for this book was the conference "Microbial Protoplasts, Spheroplasts and L-Forms" sponsored by The Upjohn Company, Kalamazoo, Michigan, held at Brook Lodge, November 10–11, 1966.

Preface

Although microbial variants had been noted in the past, L-forms as such were first described and studied by Dr. E. Klieneberger-Nobel in 1935. Since that time L-forms have been found in almost every microbial species and have been produced by a variety of different manipulations. Many investigators have worked with these microorganisms, which have served as models for bacteriologists, immunologists, anatomists, biochemists, physicists and geneticists investigating many unrelated problems, some seemingly remote from the world of microbiology. In addition, clinicians and experimental pathologists have been increasingly interested in L-forms and the relation of these microorganisms to infectious diseases and various chronic illnesses of unknown etiology.

Because of these diverse research efforts by such a variety of scientific disciplines, it was appropriate to bring the investigators together for an exchange of experiences and ideas. Such an international meeting was planned and, with the generous support of The Upjohn Company, held in Kalamazoo, Michigan, on November 10–11, 1966.

From the onset, the importance of such an interdisciplinary meeting became apparent. A round table discussion dealing with definitions and terminology was held the first morning with representatives from several different scientific disciplines participating. In addition, there was considerable contribution from the general membership of the meeting. The time allotted for the discussion proved inadequate and the meeting was resumed that night. These discussions have not been included in this book, at the request of many of the participants, simply because they were so lengthy and inconclusive. Indeed, it was not possible to obtain any type of agreement as to definition or meaning of commonly used terminology. It was finally decided that each investigator should define the terms he used as specifically as possible, in the hope that in this way future workers would be able to interrelate findings from different laboratories.

It was the recommendation of many that the proceedings of the meeting be published. In addition to serving as a current progress report of ongoing research, it was hoped that much background material could be included to provide, in one place, a textbook-like source of information for interested persons. With this in mind, the participants were encouraged to expand their presentations. We believe this has resulted in much more complete discussions. At the same time, this has occasionally resulted in some apparent repetitions; in many instances, these were editorially left intact, since they provide important frameworks of discussion for an individual author's own work as well as usually affording nuances as viewed by different scientific disciplines.

Many individuals participated in the meeting and deserve special thanks. I am happy again to acknowledge the very generous support of Dr. Harold L. Upjohn and The Upjohn Company, who made it possible. Particular recognition of the contributions of Dr. Raymond M. DeHaan must be made: not only did Dr. DeHaan participate in the conception and planning of the meeting, but his arrangements at Brook Lodge made the meeting most pleasant. To the staff of Brook Lodge, and to Mrs. Janet Zuidema, all of us are pleased to give our thanks for their cooperation and for making us so welcome.

We had the wonderful help of capable session chairmen in the planning and conduct of the meeting; I would like to extend special thanks to them: Drs. Harry Gooder, Morton Hamburger, George Gee Jackson, Robert G. Petersdorf, A. Frederick Rasmussen, Jr., Milton R. J. Salton, and Claes Weibull. In addition, I would like to thank Dr. George M. Kalmanson for his help and advice during the planning of the meeting.

For help in the final preparation of this volume, I am happy to extend special thanks to Mrs. Martha Bascopé-Espada for her advice and valuable editorial assistance. I am grateful to Miss Frieda Dreyer for her very important efforts in checking the references cited.

To Mrs. Juanita Guedel, Mrs. Jauson Streeter and Mr. Donald Rittersbaugh go my deepest thanks for their loyal and continued help in this and many other endeavors.

LUCIEN B. GUZE

Contributors

*ADOLPH ABRAMS, Ph.D.
Professor of Biochemistry
Department of Biochemistry
University of Colorado School of Medicine
Denver, Colorado

*TSUNEHISA AMANO, M.D.
Professor of Immunology
Department of Immunology
The Research Institute for Microbial
  Diseases
Osaka University
Kitaku, Osaka, Japan

*MICHAEL F. BARILE, Ph.D.
Research Microbiologist
Division of Biologic Standards
National Institutes of Health
Bethesda, Maryland

CARL BARON, B.Sc.
Research Associate
Department of Biochemistry
University of Colorado School of Medicine
Denver, Colorado

*ABRAHAM I. BRAUDE, M.D.
Professor of Medicine
Department of Medicine
University of Pittsburgh
Pittsburgh, Pennsylvania

CARROLL BURRIS
Department of Bacteriology
Walter Reed Army Institute of Research
Washington, D. C.

*JUDITH CARLETON, A.B.
Junior Research Associate
Infectious Disease Division, Department
  of Medicine
University of Cincinnati College of
  Medicine
Cincinnati General Hospital
Cincinnati, Ohio

*PATRICIA CHARACHE, M.D.
Assistant Professor of Medicine
Johns Hopkins University and University
  of Maryland
Assistant Chief of Medicine
Baltimore City Hospitals
Baltimore, Maryland

*MORRIS COHEN, Ph.D.
Research Biologist
Veterans Administration Center
Los Angeles, California

RICHARD L. COHEN, M.S.
Department of Microbiology
University of Maryland
College Park, Maryland

*ROGER M. COLE, M.D., Ph.D.
Chief, Laboratory of Microbiology
National Institute of Allergy and Infectious
  Diseases
National Institutes of Health
Bethesda, Maryland

MARGARET J. CONOVER, B.A.
Research Assistant
Temple University School of Medicine
Philadelphia, Pennsylvania

*BERNARD D. DAVIS, M.D.
Professor and Head
Department of Bacteriology and
  Immunology
Harvard Medical School
Boston, Massachusetts

*STARKEY D. DAVIS, M.D.
Assistant Professor of Pediatrics
Department of Pediatrics
University of Washington School of
  Medicine
Seattle, Washington

*RAYMOND M. DEHAAN, M.D.
Medical Development
The Upjohn Company
Kalamazoo, Michigan

*Participant in the conference

ix

*ROSALYN A. DEIGH
Laboratory Technician
Department of Medicine
UCLA School of Medicine
Los Angeles, California

*LOUIS DIENES, M.D.
Honorary Physician
Massachusetts General Hospital
Boston, Massachusetts

*MONROE D. EATON, M.D.
Associate Professor of Bacteriology and
  Immunology
Department of Bacteriology and
  Immunology
Harvard Medical School
Boston, Massachusetts

*WOLFGANG EPSTEIN, M.D.
Associate in Biophysics
Biophysical Laboratory
Harvard Medical School
Boston, Massachusetts

*F. ROBERT FEKETY, JR., M.D.
Associate Professor of Medicine
Chief, Infectious Diseases Division
Department of Internal Medicine
University of Michigan School of Medicine
Ann Arbor, Michigan

*PHILIP C. FITZ-JAMES, M.D.
Research Associate
Medical Research Council of Canada
Professor, Departments of Bacteriology
  and Immunology and of Biochemistry
Medical Science Center
University of Western Ontario
London, Ontario, Canada

THOMAS C. FRANCIS, D.D.S.
Dental Surgeon
Oral Medicine and Surgery Branch
National Institute of Dental Research
Bethesda, Maryland

*EARL H. FREIMER, M.D.
Assistant Professor and Associate Physician
The Rockefeller University
New York, New York

DIETHARD GEMSA
Research Associate
Department of Pediatrics
University of Washington School of
  Medicine
Seattle, Washington

*CARL W. GODZESKI, Ph.D.
Research Associate
Lilly Research Laboratories
Eli Lilly and Company
Indianapolis, Indiana

*HARRY GOODER, Ph.D.
Associate Professor
Department of Bacteriology and
  Immunology
University of North Carolina School of
  Medicine
Chapel Hill, North Carolina

EDWARD A. GRAYKOWSKI, D.D.S., M.D.
Director, National Institute of Dental
  Research Unit
United States Public Health Service
  Hospital
San Francisco, California

*LAURA T. GUTMAN, M.D.
Research Instructor
Department of Pediatrics
University of Washington School of
  Medicine
Seattle, Washington

*LUCIEN B. GUZE, M.D.
Chief of Staff for Research and Education
Veterans Administration Center
Associate Professor of Medicine
UCLA School of Medicine
Los Angeles, California

*GARY J. HALLER, M.A.
Graduate Research Fellow
Department of Microbiology
University of South Dakota School of
  Medicine
Vermillion, South Dakota

*MORTON HAMBURGER, M.D.
Professor of Medicine and Director,
  Infectious Disease Division
Department of Medicine
University of Cincinnati College of
  Medicine and Cincinnati General
  Hospital
Cincinnati, Ohio

*BETTY A. HATTEN, Ph.D.
Instructor in Microbiology
Department of Microbiology
The University of Texas Southwestern
  Medical School
Dallas, Texas

*WILLIAM L. HEWITT, M.D.
Professor of Medicine
Department of Medicine
UCLA School of Medicine
Los Angeles, California

---

*Participant in the conference

*GLADYS L. HOBBY, Ph.D.
Chief, Special Research Laboratory
Veterans Administration Hospital
East Orange, New Jersey

*EARL G. HUBERT, M.A.
Research Microbiologist
Veterans Administration Center
Los Angeles, California

ANTOINETTE IANNETTA
Senior Laboratory Technician
Department of Pediatrics
University of Washington School of
    Medicine
Seattle, Washington

*GEORGE GEE JACKSON, M.D.
Professor of Medicine
Department of Medicine
University of Illinois College of Medicine
Chicago, Illinois

*BENJAMIN M. KAGAN, M.D.
Director, Department of Pediatrics
Cedars-Sinai Medical Center
and Professor of Pediatrics
UCLA School of Medicine
Los Angeles, California

G. Y. KAGAN, M.D.
Head, Laboratory of Mycoplasma and
    L-Form Bacteria
Gamaleya Institute of Epidemiology and
    Microbiology
Academy of Medical Sciences
Moscow, USSR

*GEORGE M. KALMANSON, M.D., Ph.D.
Section Chief, Internal Medicine
Veterans Administration Center
Assistant Professor of Medicine
UCLA School of Medicine
Los Angeles, California

*EDWARD H. KASS, M.D., Ph.D.
Director of Bacteriology and The Channing
    Laboratory
Boston City Hospital
Boston, Massachusetts

*OTTO E. LANDMAN, Ph.D.
Professor of Biology
Department of Biology
Georgetown University
Washington, D. C.

KATHLEEN LEE
Senior Laboratory Research Technician
Department of Medicine
University of Pittsburgh
Pittsburgh, Pennsylvania

*RAYMOND J. LYNN, Ph.D.
Associate Professor
Department of Microbiology
University of South Dakota School of
    Medicine
Vermillion, South Dakota

*JUDITH H. MARSTON, Ph.D.
Assistant Professor
Departments of Medicine and Microbiology
Baylor University College of Medicine
Houston, Texas

*H. H. MARTIN, Ph.D.
Professor of Microbiology
Institut für Mikrobiologie
Technische Hochschule
Darmstadt, Germany

*LIDA H. MATTMAN, Ph.D.
Associate Professor of Microbiology
Department of Biology
Wayne State University
Detroit, Michigan

RUTH G. McCANDLESS, B.A.
Physiologist
Veterans Administration Center
Los Angeles, California

ZELL A. McGEE, M.D.
Department of Internal Medicine
Vanderbilt University Hospital
Nashville, Tennessee

*JOHN Z. MONTGOMERIE, M.B.,
    M.R.A.C.P.
Research Associate
Veterans Administration Center
Los Angeles, California

*EDWARD A. MORTIMER, JR., M.D.
Professor and Chairman
Department of Pediatrics
The University of New Mexico School of
    Medicine
Albuquerque, New Mexico

*ROBERT G. E. MURRAY, M.D.
Professor and Head
Department of Bacteriology and
    Immunology
Health Sciences Center
University of Western Ontario
London, Ontario, Canada

*LOUIS H. MUSCHEL, Ph.D.
Professor, Department of Microbiology
University of Minnesota Medical School
Minneapolis, Minnesota

*Participant in the conference

*Bruce A. Newton, Ph.D.
External Staff of the Medical Research Council
Sub-Department of Chemical Microbiology
Department of Biochemistry
University of Cambridge
Cambridge, England

*Charles Panos, Ph.D.
Associate Member
Research Laboratories
Albert Einstein Medical Center
Philadelphia, Pennsylvania

*James T. Park, Ph.D.
Professor and Chairman
Department of Microbiology
Tufts University School of Medicine
Boston, Massachusetts

*Robert G. Petersdorf, M.D.
Professor and Chairman
Department of Medicine
University of Washington School of Medicine
Seattle, Washington

*Clarence S. Potter, Ph.D.
Research Chemist
Veterans Administration Center
Los Angeles, California

*A. Frederick Rasmussen, Jr., M.D., Ph.D.
Professor and Chairman
Department of Medical Microbiology and Immunology
UCLA School of Medicine
Los Angeles, California

*Richard B. Roberts, M.D.
Guest Investigator
The Rockefeller University
New York, New York

*Aser Rothstein, Ph.D.
Co-Chairman
Department of Radiation Biology and Biophysics
University of Rochester School of Medicine and Dentistry
Rochester, New York

*Antoinette Ryter, Ph.D.
Service du Photomicrographie
Institut Pasteur
Paris, France

*Milton R. J. Salton, Ph.D.
Professor and Chairman
Department of Microbiology
New York University School of Medicine
New York, New York

Stanley G. Schultz, M.D.
Associate in Biophysics
Biophysical Laboratory
Harvard Medical School
Boston, Massachusetts

Stephen J. Seligman, M.D.
Assistant Professor
Department of Medicine
UCLA School of Medicine
Los Angeles, California

*Gerald D. Shockman, Ph.D.
Professor of Microbiology
Temple University School of Medicine
Philadelphia, Pennsylvania

Jennie Siemienski, M.S.
Research Associate in Medicine
University of Pittsburgh
Pittsburgh, Pennsylvania

*Jack L. Strominger, M.D.
Professor of Pharmacology and Microbiology
Chairman, Department of Pharmacology
University of Wisconsin Medical School
Madison, Wisconsin

S. Edward Sulkin, Ph.D.
Professor and Chairman
Department of Microbiology
The University of Texas Southwestern Medical School
Dallas, Texas

J. Stuart Thompson, Ph.D.
Research Associate
Temple University School of Medicine
Philadelphia, Pennsylvania

*Marvin Turck, M.D.
Head, Division of Infectious Diseases
King County Hospital
Assistant Professor of Medicine
University of Washington School of Medicine
Seattle, Washington

Ralph J. Wedgwood, M.D.
Professor and Chairman
Department of Pediatrics
University of Washington School of Medicine
Seattle, Washington

*Claes Weibull, Ph.D.
Department of Microbiology
University of Lund
Lund, Sweden

*Participant in the conference

CAROL O. WILLIAMS, B.S.
Department of Bacteriology
Walter Reed Army Institute of Research
Washington, D. C.

RICHARD H. WINTERBAUER, M.D.
(formerly) Fellow in Medicine
University of Washington School of
   Medicine
Seattle, Washington

*RUTH G. WITTLER, Ph.D.
Chief, Mycoplasma Research Section
Department of Bacteriology
Walter Reed Army Institute of Research
Washington, D. C.

JOHN B. ZABRISKIE, M.D.
Assistant Professor
The Rockefeller University
New York, New York

*Participant in the conference

Acknowledgement

The following illustrations and tables (or the pertinent data) have been reproduced by permission of their original sources, as indicated in the respective captions. The Editor wishes to express his appreciation to the publishers and authors.

From *Annales de l'Institut Pasteur* (Paris): Figures 7.5B, 7.8, 7.9, 7.10.

From *Annals of the New York Academy of Sciences:* Figure 13.5.

From *Antimicrobial Agents and Chemotherapy:* Tables 17.1, 17.2, 28.1, 28.2, 28.4, 28.6.

From *Bacteriological Reviews* (American Society for Microbiology): Figure 11.10.

From *Biochemical and Biophysical Research Communications* (Academic Press, Inc.): Table 24.2.

From *Biochemistry:* Figures 13.1 (part), 13.3; Tables 13.1, 13.2.

From *Biochimica et Biophysica Acta:* Tables 13.3, 16.1; Figure 15.6.

From *Canadian Journal of Microbiology:* Figure 1.5.

From *Federation Proceedings* (Federation of American Societies for Experimental Biology): Figures 6.1, 6.2, 6.3, 6.4; Tables 6.1.

From *Folia Microbiologica* (Praha): Table 7.1.

From J. Holden (Ed.): *Amino Acid Pools* (Elsevier, Amsterdam): Figure 14.9.

From *The Journal of the American Dental Association:* Figure 45, *a* and *b*.

From *Journal of Bacteriology* (American Society for Microbiology): Figures 7.1, 7.3, 7.4, 7.6, 24.1, 24.5; Tables 1.1, 13.4 (part), 24.1, 46.3.

From *The Journal of Biological Chemistry* (The American Society of Biological Chemists, Inc.): Figure 14.8.

From *The Journal of Clinical Investigation:* Figure 43.1; Tables 43.1, 43.3.

From *The Journal of Experimental Medicine:* Figures 27.2, 27.3, 27.4, 27.5, 27.6, 37.1, 37.2, 37.3, 37.4, 40.1; Tables 27.3, 27.4, 37.1, 37.2, 37.3, 40.1, 40.2, 40.3, 40.4, 40.5.

From *Journal of General Microbiology:* Figure 16.1, Table 13.4 (part).

From *Journal of General Physiology* (The Rockefeller University Press): Figures 15.1, 16.2, 16.3, Table 13.4 (part).

From *The Journal of Immunology, Virus Research and Experimental Chemotherapy* (The Williams and Wilkins Co.): Figures 25.4, 25.5, 25.6, 25.7.

From *Journal of Infectious Diseases* (University of Chicago Press): Figures 21.1, 21.5; Table 21.1.

From *The Journal of Laboratory and Clinical Medicine:* Table 29.1.

From *Journal of Theoretical Biology:* Figure 7.5A.

From *Nature:* Tables 28.2, 28.4, 28.6.

From *Oral Surgery, Oral Medicine and Oral Pathology* (C. V. Mosby Co.): Figures 45.1D, 45.2 A, B, 45.4, 45.10.

From *Proceedings of the National Academy of Sciences of the United States of America:* Figures 6.5, 6.6, 6.7, 6.8, Table 33.2.

Contents

I.
MECHANISMS INVOLVED IN THE FORMATION OF PROTOPLASTS, SPHEROPLASTS AND L-FORMS

Milton R. J. Salton
CHAIRMAN

1

Bacterial Cell Wall Anatomy in Relation to the Formation of Spheroplasts and Protoplasts*

Robert G. E. Murray

UNIVERSITY OF WESTERN ONTARIO, HEALTH SCIENCES CENTER
LONDON, ONTARIO, CANADA

The purpose of this essay is to provide a structural framework for the discussions that follow. It is the normally rigid cell wall that must be removed completely to form bacterial protoplasts and that must be damaged in some specific way for it to become the elastic wall of a spheroplast. The associations of complex heteropolymers are susceptible to disruption, as is the polymeric backbone of some components, causing observable physical and anatomical changes. The anatomical disposition of the components is not random; they are layered concentrically, and the arrangement of these layers is usually consistent within the major natural groups of bacteria. The basis for variation in reaction to protoplasting or spheroplasting agents must rest, however, on both chemical and anatomical considerations which are now becoming appreciated. What I can say about this aspect of comparative anatomy can best be based

upon the authoritative and remarkable monograph by Prof. M. R. J. Salton,[55] and a fine essay by Prof. H. H. Martin[34] concerning bacterial protoplasts from a very different viewpoint. The reader should find them as useful as I have.

The cell wall is no mean component. Estimates of the cell wall contribution to the cell dry weight[55] range from about 5 to 35 per cent, varying with the organism; this sort of figure, as well as the thickness and complexity of the structure revealed in the modern techniques of electron microscopy, have added a very convincing dimension to the older awareness of a rigid structure surrounding a protoplast.[38, 40] One cannot overemphasize the tremendous impact of pictures, photo- and electron micrographs, in convincing a wide range of biologists to add a new anatomical dimension onto the rapidly elaborating biochemical and physiological framework.

It was not so long ago that Weibull,[64] following Salton's localization of the substrate for lysozyme, isolated protoplasts of *Bacillus megaterium,* demonstrating the spheres that could be preserved in a stabilizing environment. At that time the state of the art of fixing and embedding cells for sectioning and electron microscopy was

*The author is most grateful to Dr. B. K. Ghosh, Dr. S. Maier and Mrs. P. D. Glaister for discussions and for the provision of micrographs from our joint work. The electron microscopy of Mr. John Marak and the preparative work of Mrs. M. Hall have been invaluable. The consistent support of the Medical Research Council of Canada is gratefully acknowledged.

in its infancy and only the more massive structures, such as the cell wall, were open to reasonable resolution and to discussion of their dynamic implications. It gradually became clear that there was indeed a plasma membrane of much the same dimensions as that of plant and animal cells at the surface of the bacterial protoplasts,[24, 39, 50] and that this was very closely applied to and associated with the overlying cell wall in the bacteria.

The early work of Mudd and his associates[38] indicated that bacteria could be broken up, and that among the recognisable fragments were portions of cell walls; from the shapes and forms of these fragments they concluded that the walls were rigid and that their structure determined the characteristic shape of the organism from which they were derived. It is also clear from the earliest experiments with lysozyme that damage to the cell wall could lead to a loss of the characteristic shape of that cell.

The cell wall was obviously a critical component of both the shape and the division of the cell,[36] since the loss involved in protoplasting and the distortion involved in the development of L-forms seemed to preclude the possibility of normal cell division. The formation of a cell wall septum, a regional and anatomically exact synthesis of a diaphragm dividing the cell, was even more indicative of the morphogenetic challenge that now engages the interest of a large proportion of those working on the nature of the bacterial cell wall. Attention is further focused on new attributes by the increasing awareness that the cell wall involves complex extracellular synthesis of structure requiring organization, and that exoenzymes[30] have special properties and even functional arrest in the wall. The cell wall has thus become elevated in stature from an inert structure and an architectural adornment to a truly functional anatomical feature[42, 51] of bacterial cells, with some physiological and biochemical components which are distinct and segregated in the wall and unique to the cells having a procaryotic organization.[58] The combination of chemical dissection and electron microscopy now brings into focus the need to understand the arrangement of some of these components, which are indeed the substrates or targets involved in the formation of protoplasts and spheroplasts.

The General Profile and Associations of Gram-Positive and Gram-Negative Cell Walls

Gram-positiveness and Gram-negativeness has long been a distinctive and remarkably reliable feature for use in bacterial classification; it is a considerable relief to find that the distinction became no less clear as the biochemical and anatomical resolution improved.[55, 58] Indeed, the basic structure is remarkably constant and the two classes can nearly always be recognised on sight, given a reasonably resolved profile of a cross-section of the wall of the cell. In general, the Gram-positive type of cell (Figure 1.1A) shows a relatively thick and homogeneous component next to the plasma membrane, usually greater than 200 Å in thickness; this often has been the only element visible in the wall profile. In contrast, the profiles of the cell walls of Gram-negative bacteria are remarkably complex and consist of several obvious layers (Figure 1.1B). For some time confusion was compounded by a seeming similarity of the profile of the cell wall to the profile of the plasma membrane. It now becomes clear, however, that in the Gram-negatives, as well as in the Gram-positives, there is a common basic structure to be observed,[31] whether the species involved belongs within the swimming Eubacteria or among the gliding Myxobacteria, to cite some extreme examples. The common structure seems to approximate a two-part structure: an extremely thin, dense membrane, often as little as 30 Å in thickness and seldom much more than twice that, close to but not quite on the plasma membrane, and, outside this, a "double-track" of the order of 100–120 Å in thickness, which is continuous over the surface. It is this layer (it has been called the "plastic layer") that appears to relax and separate during the fixation process, so that a rather typical waved outline is given to the cell. Elaborations of wall structure occur,[8, 42] but they are nearly always external to these basic structures (Figure 1.1, C and D); and so, if the essential wall is removed, these outer layers will enclose a group of protoplasts.[43]

In virtually all cases (this now involves Gram-positive as well as Gram-negative instances), the wall structure is built up of concentric layers, each of which contains some characteristic polymer or an association forming heteropolymers, more or less sorted out in the layers.[34, 43, 46] This appears odd, for it would seem to be a process guaranteed to increase the problems of diffusing nutrients across such barriers to the cell and, since we must now think[23] in terms of columnar micelles of differentiated phases in membranes such as the plasma membrane, a peculiarly inept arrangement to allow the dynamic roles that they must play. Nature is as it is.

The cell wall is certainly in intimate relationship with the membrane that lies immediately beneath it, and we must assume that the plasma membrane plays a very direct role in the orderly and sometimes regional supply of components necessary to the building and maintenance of the cell wall. Cell division in Gram-positive and in many Gram-negative bacteria requires the synthesis of a cell wall septum which consists almost entirely of the innermost discernible layer (Figure 1.1C)[43] of the cell wall when that structure is layered at all. Some doubt has been expressed that the site of cell division is the place of major cell wall synthesis in the cell,[4] and I believe that this applies to the superficial layers of the Gram-negative cell wall. The layer that is involved in septum formation (the innermost layer) seems more likely to have a specific growing point, as would seem to be the case in staphylococci,[63] streptococci,[10, 11] and even in those Gram-negatives that are not commonly thought to form septa.[60] In all cases the newly formed septal wall is more susceptible to lysis,[63] and it is strictly this region (and the poles of rod-shaped bacteria, site of the *previous* division) that is most susceptible to autolysis and the initial damage induced by penicillin.[18]

The greatest elaborations of the underlying plasma membrane are found at the sites of septa and may be due to the production of more membrane of specialized synthetic capability in the place where it is needed. It is clear that these mesosomes, which Fitz-James[16, 17] named and suggested had functions, are substantial organelles derived from the plasma membrane. Some of them are quite specific anatomically, as Ryter & Jacob[52] have confirmed. Those in the region of cell septum formation do show some changes within 20 minutes of the administration of a sufficient dose of penicillin.[17, 18] All of these extrude or stretch into the peripheral membrane as the wall disintegrates and protoplasts are formed.[17, 19, 53]

There is usually a narrow "gap" between the innermost identifiable portion of the wall and the outermost identifiable portion of the membrane; it might be an artifact of preparation. However, where intrusions of plasma membrane occur, it is seldom that the two intruded lamellae come in contact with each other, although it is true that some membrane-derived vesicles can be collapsed to the point that the adjacent boundaries form a single line.[44] If there is a "gap" substance, it would seem likely that most of it belongs in terms of adherence to the plasma membrane. In some bacteria, strands of material bridging the "gap" and even vesicles (see Figure 1.2A) make this "no man's land" the more mysterious, and have led to the interpretation of a complex, tripartite plasma membrane.[15, 19] This zone may depend on the physiological state of activity of the cell. When cells are poisoned with penicillin[17] and converted into spheroplasts, there seems to be a widening and filling of this zone. This also happens in lysine-deprived *Escherichia coli*, studied by Knox and colleagues.[25] Observers of structure revealed by freeze-etching have noted that the external face of the plasma membrane commonly shows areas studded with some material substance.* Whatever the truth of

* W. de Boer (Institute of Microbiology, Delft, Holland): personal communication, 1966.

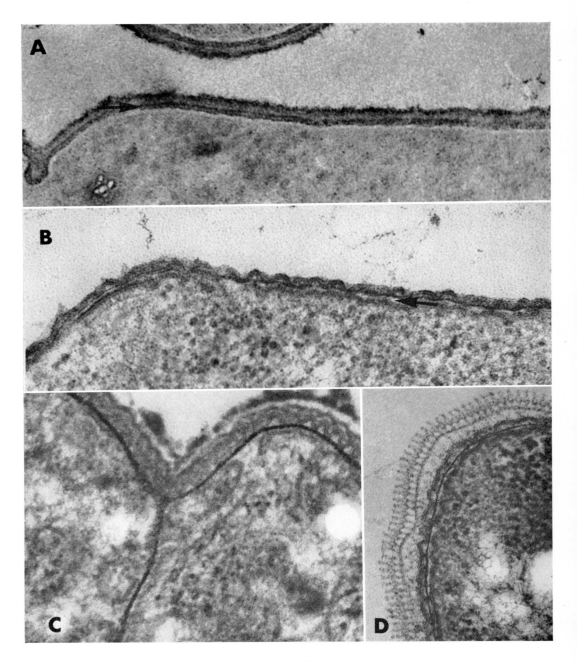

Figure 1.1. *A:* Example of Gram-positive (*Listeria monocytogenes*) cell wall in section: a dense, homogeneous, thick structure closely applied to the underlying plasma membrane; "gap" between cell wall and plasma membrane indicated by arrow ($\times$ 190,000). *B:* Example of Gram-negative (*Spirillum serpens*) cell wall in section: a very thin and dense layer with a loose "double track" layer on the outside; "gap" between cell wall and plasma membrane indicated by arrow ($\times$ 140,000). *C:* Wall profile of *Beggiatoa* sp., showing its complexity and the fact that the inner (mucopeptide) layer is the sole component of the cell wall septum ($\times$ 110,000). *D:* Another complex Gram-negative cell wall (*Lampropedia hyalina*) shows an elaborate outer structured layer (repeating units on a thin layer), which lies well outside the typical Gram-negative profile of the wall proper ($\times$ 110,000).

the matter may be, it is still hard to bridge the gap between the dynamic state of the living cell and the static representation of what can be fixed for embedding and sectioning.

FORMATION OF PROTOPLASTS FROM GRAM-
POSITIVES

B. megaterium and *Micrococcus lysodeikticus* remain the prime examples of organisms whose cell walls can be solubilized and removed. In neither case can the wall be considered to consist of mucopeptide only, yet the lysozyme substrate is sufficiently available to the enzyme to be readily degraded.[54] The wall substance seems to loosen and fray apart with rather rapid loss of the pieces into the surrounding medium. Yet it is almost certain that the cell wall of *B. megaterium* has two parts,[45] the outer 50 or 60 per cent of the thickness being easily removed with hot formamide (it seems to consist mainly of teichoic acid). The remaining inner 40–50 per cent of the 200–250 Å thickness of the wall consists of the mucopeptide. It would seem then that, in the case of *B. megaterium*, the lysozyme used in protoplasting has little difficulty in gaining access to the deep layer through the surface layer. The substrate is less readily available in many other species, e.g., *Staphylococcus*.

It might be expected that a single species of organism would be fairly constant in its response to enzymes such as lysozyme. Studies of *Listeria monocytogenes*, carried on in our laboratory, illustrate the fact that it is probably not so (Figure 1.2). Out of eight quite independent strains representing each of the four serotypes (Table 1.1), two were found to be very resistant to lysozyme (whether or not EDTA was present); of the remainder, although all were sensitive to lysozyme in various degrees, one was particularly so. It was found that a pretreatment of the lysozyme-resistant cells with lipase (steapsin) for a short time, without causing any visible defect, prepared the cells of all strains for a more complete action of lysozyme;[19] they were then almost quantitatively converted into protoplasts by that enzyme. One of the strains was remarkably sensitive to lipase alone, and sections (Figure 1.2D) showed that in this case, and on prolonged exposure of any of the strains to lipase, direct damage was done to the structure of the cell wall, an effect that was not accentuated by trypsin either before or when mixed with the lipase. This would seem to be a genuine intraspecific variation without morphological basis and not correlated with conventional serotypes (Table 1.1).

It is probable that the entire cell wall is not equally susceptible to enzymic destruction, and that the most recently synthetized part is more susceptible than the older, ripened part. This is indicated by the observations of Mitchell & Moyle[37] on protoplast formation from *Staphylococcus aureus*, where an autolytic enzyme cleaved the walls into hemispherical pieces because of the digestion and removal of the developing septum and the immediately adjacent wall portion.[63]

The lack of sensitivity of some Grampositive bacteria to the effective lysozyme may well be due as much to the complexity and nature of overlying layers of cell wall material as to some peculiar form of linking or of construction of the mucopeptide itself. An example of unsuspected complexity is provided by the wall of *Bacillus polymyxa*, which Nermut and I have studied recently in some detail.[46] This wall has a total thickness of approximately 250 Å and, if the sections are stained with either uranyl acetate or lead (or both), the wall appears to have a low density middle zone, unlike *B. megaterium*.[45] The inner dense portion is a little over 100 Å thick and the outer dense portion is approximately 80 Å thick (Figure 1.3D). The outer surface consists of a beautiful rectangular array, originally observed by Baddiley,[2] of squarish protein macromolecules with a spacing of approximately 100 Å, each of the component units being about 70 Å in diameter (Figure 1.3, A–C). The trypsin-sensitive outer layer can be taken apart (1% sodium lauryl sulphate for five minutes), or stripped off as a sheet (formamide at room temperature for five minutes, or 1% guanidine hydrochloride for 20 minutes). The

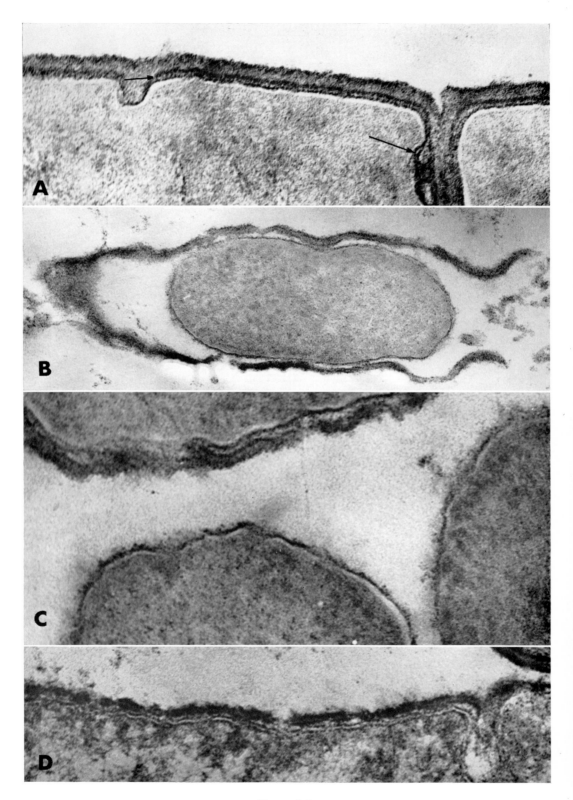

Figure 1.2

surface would thus seem to be linked to its substrate by hydrogen bonds. Sections of these treated cells (aldehyde fixed) show that the outer component is completely removed and that the remaining cell wall is only about 100 Å in thickness (Figure 1.3E). Like the intact cell wall, this residue, which we believe to be largely mucopeptide, is resistant to the effect of lysozyme. This particular species of *Bacillus* seems to offer an example of a kind of Gram-positive cell wall of unexpected complexity, which may in actual fact be rather common among at least *Bacillus* and *Clostridium*. In some ways there is considerable analogy to the general arrangement in *Streptococcus pyogenes*.[26]

LOCALIZATION OF THE MUCOPEPTIDE IN GRAM-NEGATIVES AND THE STRUCTURE OF SPHERO-PLASTS

The profile of the cell wall presented by Gram-negative bacteria is manifestly complex, consisting of a number of layers, and this is reflected[55] in the chemistry of the isolated walls, as well as in the retention of some wall layers in the surface of lysozyme- and penicillin-induced spheroplasts and natural "large bodies". The lack of the inner taut and relatively thin layer in spheroplasts and large bodies (compare E and F in Figure 1.4) and in isolated walls treated directly with lysozyme was indicative that the mucopeptide is probably located entirely in that layer.[43] As in the Gram-positives, this is essentially the only wall component taking part in the initial stages of septum formation and cell division;[60] as a result, the weakening of wall structure, whether due to external or internal effects, commonly shows first in central or polar areas.[32] Fortunately, for

TABLE 1.1*

Lysis of Strains of Listeria monocytogenes *Caused by Enzymes Singly and in Combination*

Strain	Serological type	Fall in Optical Density (%) after treatment with		
		Lysozyme	Lipase	Lipase and Lysozyme
79	1	70	8	80
118	4B	65	8	70
85	2	92	10	97
124	4B	63	6	71
109	4B	63	43	95
126	4B	60	8	72
42	1	25	6	75
81	3	24	18	76

* Data from Ghosh and Murray.[19]

simplicity's sake, the vast majority of Gram-negative bacteria have remarkably similar basic profiles.[31]

A somewhat special problem is presented by *E. coli* and its relatives among the enteric bacteria, whose profile has been represented until recently as a single dense-light-dense "unit" profile (Figure 1.4A); it is now not surprising that the profile of the spheroplasts was seemingly identical.[21] Detailed study of uranium and lead stained sections of normal cells by de Petris[13] and by our laboratory[43] showed that there was an inner component (Figure 1.4B) closely bonded to the inside of the apparent wall. Careful measurements of the minimum thickness of profiles of both the normal and spheroplasted *E. coli* (induced by either lysozyme-EDTA or with penicillin) show that the change during spheroplasting involves the loss of the innermost 30 Å (approximately) of the cell wall thickness (Figure 1.4C). This can also be observed directly using lysozyme alone on isolated

Figure 1.2. *A:* Normal cell wall of *Listeria monocytogenes* showing a septum, the beginning of a septum, the "gap" between wall and membrane, and some vesicles in the gap (arrows) (× 190,000). *B:* Release of a protoplast of *L. monocytogenes* following lipase-lysozyme treatment in a stabilizing medium[19] (× 110,000). *C:* A close view of the surface profiles of two *L. monocytogenes* protoplasts and a portion of wall damaged by lipase-lysozyme treatment; it appears probable that nearly all cell wall elements have been removed in protoplasting (× 200,000). *D:* Same cell walls as in *A–C,* but treated with lipase alone for two hours;[19] the start of the septum on the right is particularly damaged, but the entire wall is disrupted in many places (× 190,000).

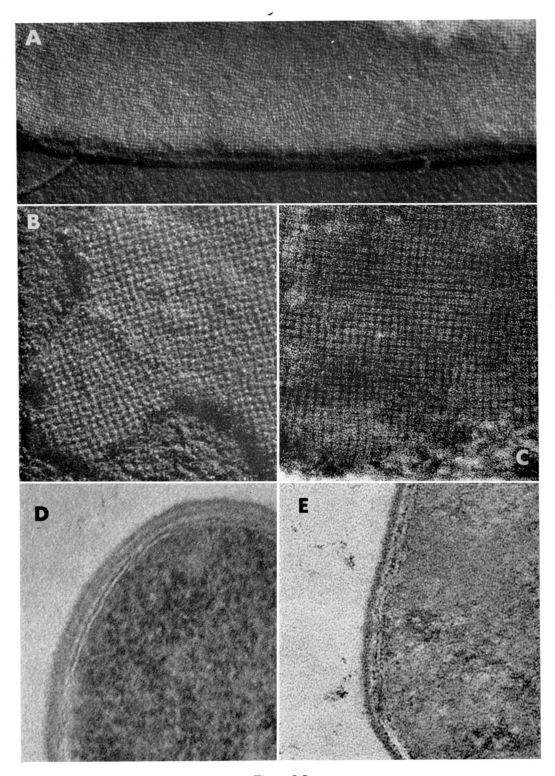

Figure 1.3

cell walls before embedding for sectioning and measurement.

The cell walls of *E. coli*,[60] *Nitrosomonas*,[44] and *Acetobacter*[9] have an unusual profile because the component layers of the cell wall tend to stay associated together, whereas in the vast majority of Gram-negative bacteria the outer "double-track" tends to separate during preparation from the underlying taut layer and produce a wrinkled profile. This may be due to the bonding of the protein granular layer of the rigid R-layer, which is interposed between the mucopeptide and the rest in *E. coli* and may have a more general distribution in nature. At first this profile was hard to correlate with the structure of the *E. coli* wall derived by Weidel and his co-workers (cf. Martin's review[34]) by a process of biochemical dissection followed by electron microscopy of shadowed preparations. There was no doubt that a series of layers could be stripped off from the cell; these were, from the outside inwards: lipoprotein, lipopolysaccharide, protein, and mucopeptide. The latter two components, making up about 21 per cent of the total weight of the wall, form the rigid or R-layer. The correlation of structure or profile with the component layers was difficult because the earlier studies of spheroplasts (in which the R-layer was supposedly damaged) and the seeming removal of the outermost "lipoprotein" components with a suitable detergent in low concentration did not, in fact, alter the profile noticeably. This latter component remains undefined but the profile in general can be compared[43] quite directly with the conclusions gained on biochemical grounds, so clearly set forth by Martin[34] (Figure 1.5).

In all the cases in which the mucopeptide had been removed, the loss was 20–35 Å; by measuring from the tables of the outer double-track one could conclude that the loss was entirely from the inner side of the stained components. De Petris,[13] on the other hand, favors the view that the mucopeptide portion is not visualized in the normal cell, and that the intermediate layer consists largely of a protein granular portion of the cell wall while the mucopeptide fills in the "gap", making a total wall thickness of the order of 150 Å. There is no doubt that de Petris showed a magnificent micrograph indicating the probable position of the protein granular layer in section, as well as showing triplet profiles, so it seems possible that the innermost part may still be the mucopeptide component.

The mucopeptide component of the cell wall of intact Gram-negative bacteria is then unavailable to the direct action of lysozyme and similar enzymes because the elaborate wall structures of the "plastic layers" are interposed between the mucopeptide and the environment. No doubt it will take an elaborate mixture of enzymes and reagents to prepare such walls for complete removal by dissolution. The "spheroplasting from without" has been largely accomplished following the prescription of Repaske.[48] Versene (EDTA) treatment allows penetration of the wall, probably by removing ionic crosslinks to form larger spaces for passage of the enzyme and by removing some lipopolysaccharide;[33, 34] yet the plastic layers seem to remain intact on the formed spheroplast. This implies that the plastic layers completely enrobe the mucopeptide and the cell. Bayer & Anderson[3] have used the most careful methods (cryostat preservation) and find that the surface of *E. coli* is furrowed with channels

Figure 1.3. *A:* The exterior surface of the cell wall of *Bacillus polymyxa*, demonstrated by shadowing with tungsten oxide; a regular rectangular array is visible over the entire surface (× 100,000). *B:* Shadowed preparation (tungsten oxide) of an isolated fragment of the surface layer shown in *A* (for methods see Nermut & Murray[46]); the individual units seem to be rough-surfaced (× 200,000). *C:* An isolated fragment of wall (as in *B*) prepared with uranyl acetate to give negative staining and definition of the units; each unit appears to have a few subunits (× 200,000). *D:* Section of glutaraldehyde-fixed *B. polymyxa*, stained with uranyl acetate; note the dense-light-dense profile of the wall (× 200,000). *E:* Companion to *D*, and prepared in the same way after treatment with formamide, which removes the structured surface layer; note the loss of the outer segment of the wall—only the inner dense component remains (× 200,000).

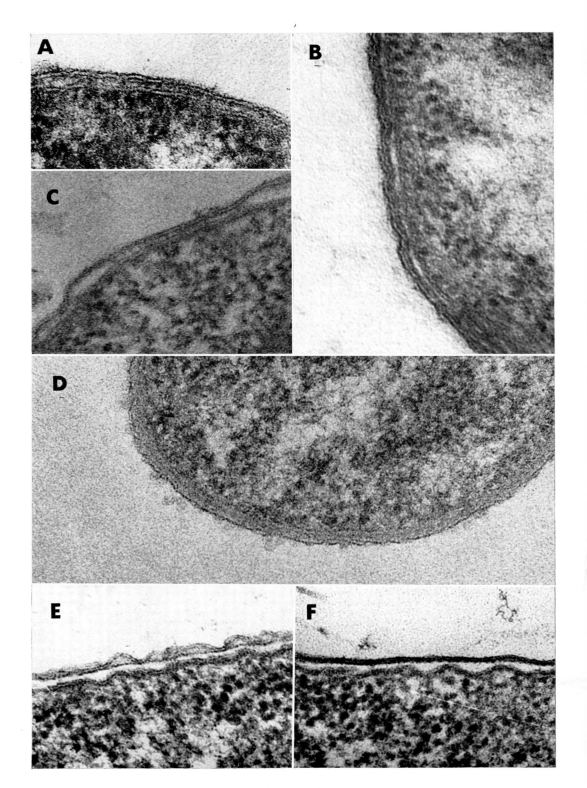

Figure 1.4

or grooves which penetrate, they believe, down to the protein part of the R-layer. If this is so one would expect that trypsin, which removes that layer, should prepare the cells for lysozyme action; this is not usually the case. Presumably some other substance is interposed or the channels are not quite as deep as is supposed.

An unusual form of natural spheroplasting is provided by the action of the bacterial parasite of Gram-negative bacteria, *Bdellovibrio bacteriovorus.*[61] The vibrio attaches to the host cell and practically immediately causes the cessation of motility of a flagellated host; usually in 5–30 minutes the host cell becomes a spheroplast. The parasite actually makes a hole in the cell wall of the host and slips inside;[59] this seems to be coincident in time with the spheroplasting and the loss, all over the cell, of the mucopeptide layer as a morphological entity. The gap in the wall is "corked" by the body of the parasite and the protoplast does not herniate through the hole before the wall is altered to a conforming elastic structure on the complete spheroplast. There is no evidence, as yet, of exoenzyme production by the parasite[56] and one must assume that it stimulates in some way the utilization or activation of host enzymes. Indicative is the finding in our laboratory by Huang and Robinson* that one *Bdellovibrio* strain will multiply in a heat-killed cell without causing the swelling or relaxation of the wall that it does in the living cell. This may be, then, a kind of "spheroplasting

* Unpublished data.

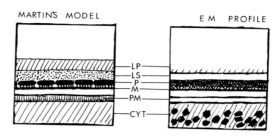

Figure 1.5. Diagram to summarize the correspondence between Martin's reconstruction[34] and the electron microscopic (EM) profile.[43] *LP:* Lipoprotein; *LS:* lipopolysaccharide; *P:* protein; *M:* mucopeptide; *PM:* plasma membrane; *CYT:* cytoplasm. The lipoprotein layer does not seem to be represented in the normal profile of *E. coli,* although it can be retained in other organisms (see Figure 1.6 E). (From Murray, Steed & Elson.[43])

from within" of which other forms are provided by incompetence in nutritionally deprived mutants.

It is indicated that the mucopeptide layer, seemingly conferring strength and form on the cell, is usually separated from the plasma membrane by a narrow "gap". The possibility exists that some kinds of bacteria may keep the rigid layer in even closer association with the plasma membrane, as reported with convincing supporting evidence by Pillot for *Treponema reiteri.*[47] The generality of this finding has not yet been tested, but some organisms appear to have a layer of moderate density attached to the outer table of the plasma membrane. In our experience this appearance is notable in the case of *Bdellovibrio,*[59] and has also been shown by Ritchie and coworkers[49] for *Vibrio fetus,* but in

Figure 1.4. *A:* Section through the cell surface of *Escherichia coli* B (fixed with osmium tetroxide, section stained with both uranyl acetate and lead), showing the commonly observed double-track wall and plasma membrane (× 200,000). *B:* Similar to *A*, but showing the now accepted tripartite profile of the cell wall of *E. coli;* the inner zone is considered to represent the site of the mucopeptide[43] (× 200,000). *C:* Section of a portion of a penicillin-induced spheroplast of *E. coli* showing the loose wall and the absence of the inner component of the tripartite wall (× 200,000). *D:* Section of *E. coli* B which was fixed with glutaraldehyde (5%), and washed in buffer before proceeding with the usual osmium tetroxide fixation and embedding; despite staining of the section with uranyl acetate, the layers are less distinct than in *B*, but smoother in outline and very closely applied to the plasma membrane (× 200,000). *E:* Section of osmium tetroxide-fixed and uranium plus lead-stained *Spirillum serpens* to show normal profile; note the very delicate mucopeptide layer (× 135,000). *F:* Section of a natural spheroplast of *S. serpens* showing the loss of the mucopeptide layer (compare with *E*) (× 135,000).

neither case has lysozyme digestion been done in such a way as to support the thesis.

The separation of wall layers during fixation and embedding that causes such unlikely looking wavy profiles is undoubtedly an artifact. The separations occur between mucopeptide and plastic layer in the case of most Gram-negative bacteria and between plasma membrane and the whole wall as a unit in the case of the Enterobacteriaceae. It is presented in most cases by prefixation with an aldehyde[12, 59] (Figure 1.4D), preferably glutaraldehyde, and addition of calcium and magnesium salts to the fixing environment. The possibility exists that the profound separations that can occur are due to a very localized autolytic[60, 65] process that is not prevented by the fixative employed. We have found that some strange divalent cations (e.g., zinc) in the fixing environment for Bdellovibrio, the most extreme example of wall loosening, lead to an almost smooth outline and coherent layers.

Apart from fixation, a major difficulty for the electron microscopist is that the cell wall has very little intrinsic contrast, perhaps because it is notoriously short of sulfur-containing amino acids and, indeed, of sulfur and phosphorus, so that there is very little natural scattering. The result is that practically all the contrast, and certainly all the differentiation of layers, has to be accomplished by the differential uptake of various metals in the form of metal salts which may be applied to the section as stains. Staining is not necessarily a very even or completely reproducible process, even though it is essential and remarkably effective.

SUPERFICIAL LAYERS AND WALL INTEGRITY

The mucopeptide component is less certainly identified in some marine and halophilic bacteria; indeed, there is some doubt of its really being possessed by some species.[6, 28] If it is not, these particular rod-shaped bacteria owe their strength and integrity to other components; Brown and coworkers[5, 6] have found no sign of the thin "intermediate layer" or of characteristic mucopeptide components in them. How-

ever, the marine pseudomonad studied by Buckmire & MacLeod[7] retains a chemically identifiable mucopeptide component as long as a sufficient concentration of Mg^{++} ion is present. As long as the mucopeptide is present, the wall and the plasma membrane remain close together in preparations of isolated walls, but they become definitely separated as soon as the mucopeptide goes into solution and the cell bursts. The halophiles, such as Halobacterium cutirubrum, studied by Kushner and his colleagues[27, 29] seem also to be without mucopeptide components, notably muramic acid, even when the whole culture is fractionated. The evidence in this case is strongly in favor of a wall consisting of protein, carbohydrates and lipids held together by ionic linkages; the monovalent cations serve in neutralizing the excess charge so that repulsive forces are minimized to allow close packing. Once the wall is stable the sodium requirement is spared by much smaller molarities (0.1 M instead of 2 M) of magnesium chloride. These would thus appear to be walls with a minimum of covalent bonds and crosslinking structures in addition to being anatomically deficient in mucopeptide.

The terrestrial organisms, which do not require large amounts of salt for integrity, have a wall structure that usually can only be disrupted entirely by a chemical or enzymatic attack; they are not damaged by suspension in solutions of low ionic strength. Yet it would now appear that these, too, have component layers that show evidence of being held together by charges, or that have polymers that are crosslinked by divalent cations. Versene (EDTA) has a bactericidal action on some organisms (e.g., Pseudomonas aeruginosa and Alkaligenes faecalis) and a direct effect has been observed on cell walls[14, 20] as well as on plasma membrane. In P. aeruginosa, Eagon and colleagues[14] showed very clearly EDTA-caused destruction of the mucopeptide layer, so this seems to be one good example of ionic crosslinkage.

The outermost layer of a number of Gram-negative bacteria consists of a close-packed hexagonal array of particles;[55] these are very regular and normally the units are about 80 Å in diameter and the repeat distance is about 140 Å. The halophiles are prominent possessors of this type of structure,[28] and the rules for integrity seem to be substantially those originally proposed by Abram & Gibbons[1] and elaborated by Kushner & Onishi[29] for the stability of the cell of a halophile. Very similar layers[22, 41] are possessed by many spirillums (including *Rhodospirillum*) and may be more widely distributed in nature. There is even one Gram-positive with just this type of surface (*Micrococcus radiodurans*[62]) and many species of *Bacillus* and *Clostridium* seem to have the rectilinear array of protein units of the type we have observed on *B. polymyxa*.[46] These, as with *Spirillum*, may well prove to be dispensible, inessential components.

The surface of *Spirillum serpens*, originally shown in all its elegance by Houwink,[22] has been studied in particular detail by the author[41] and his colleagues. It is clear that this structured layer (Figure 1.6) is on the outside of the "double track" of the plastic layer, and its components are very simply stripped from the underlying layer by low concentrations of highly polar substances, e.g., sodium lauryl sulfate in low concentration (0.01 per cent). Pamela Glaister, from our laboratory, has discovered* that this species shows a calamitous lysis when the stationary phase is attained in aerated fluid cultures, which is prevented by Ca^{++} but not by Mg^{++}, and which is accelerated by Na^+ or by EDTA addition. Curiously enough, this lysis is not exhibited by a mutant of the same culture which has lost the ability to form the superficial layer. Even stranger are the observations made with Maier and Glaister* on the structure of a variety of isolates of the same species, showing that the subunits can be arranged in at least three modes (see Figure 1.6, B–D). Crude chemistry indicates that this layer is mostly protein in nature and can be attacked by trypsin; the conditions of stripping and instability in culture indicate that

* Unpublished data.

it is held in place by no more than ionic bonds and that there is a specific requirement for calcium for this purpose. Since EDTA-lysozyme (not EDTA alone) causes the loss of the inner, mucopeptide layer and spheroplast formation, we must assume that some additional mechanism is involved in the lysis that occurs when Ca^{++} is depleted; this is further accentuated by the lack of calcium sensitivity of the mutant. Natural spheroplasting of *Spirillum* species is not unusual, and in these we have observed loss of the mucopeptide layer; whether or not the external layer is lost is unknown at the moment.

It is clear therefore that the Gram-negative bacteria possess layer upon layer of wall components, each probably containing distinct polymers or heteropolymers and exhibiting varying strengths of internal and external crosslinkages, which add to the complexity of the structural forces involved in strength and integrity. It is tempting to speculate that the specificity of the divalent cation requirements for wall integrity might show Mg^{++} to be needed for marine and strict halophilic organisms, and Ca^{++} for fresh-water and "terrestrial" organisms. This is probably not an absolute fact, since Eagon and colleagues[14] showed that ashed walls of a *P. aeruginosa* contained about equal quantities (0.06 per cent) of calcium and magnesium. This is apart from the probable requirement of all organisms for enough monovalent cation for the reduction of the total net charge of the complex polyanions making up the cell wall to a level consistent with close packing and the formation of whatever ionic, hydrophobic, hydrogen, or covalent bonding is needed for the structure. In any case, the balance of various cations is probably a very important consideration, not only for the purposes discussed but also for the activity of the wall enzymes necessary to "make and mend" processes. These enzymes seem to be either activated or inhibited by one or another of the divalent cations and appear to have replaced —S—S— linkages with Ca or Mg bridges.

Some variation of the plan of assembly

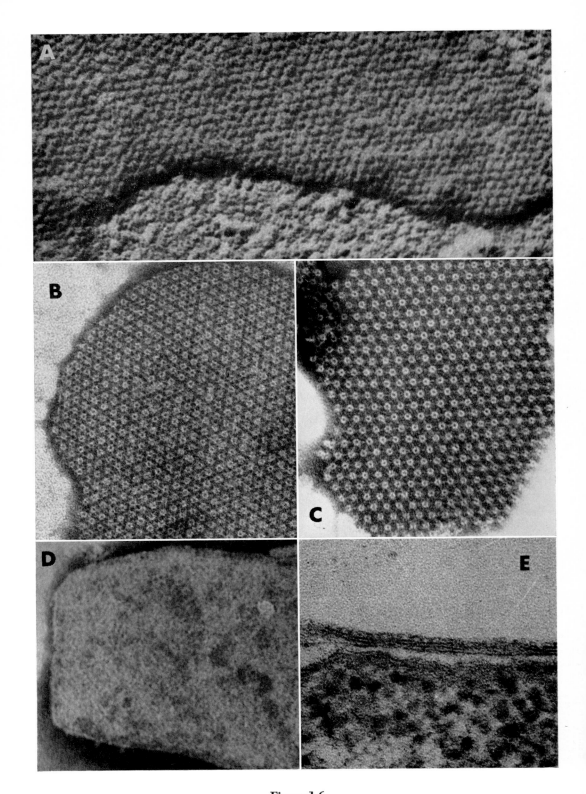

Figure 1.6

according to general environmental circumstances may be possible either as a consequence of solute changes in the aqueous environment, or as a consequence of changes in adjacent or nearby components which form the immediate environment of any one polymer. The latter condition could be genetic in origin, but could also involve unusual direct incorporation of a nutrient (e.g., amino acids, as shown by Shockman[57]) into wall structure.

PERSPECTIVE

The methods of morphology, both in classical and in biochemical terms, have developed to the point that the determination of the anatomical distribution of the major components is an attainable goal. As can be seen from the examples cited, the main success has attended the localization of mucopeptide. Biochemical fractionation and morphological identification of the elements with the sectional profile still have a long way to go. Even the most accessible and morphologically characteristic superficial layers have received scant biochemical attention because they have not been retained in the type of wall preparation generally used as a basis for chemical study. The interests of a group such as that meeting today focus strongly on the mucopeptide because it is an available target and methods of attack do exist, and because there is no doubt that strength and form is determined in most bacteria by this component and the polymers closely associated with it. Just the same, it is important to remember that it is seldom alone in its rigid state and that it is hard indeed to determine, as Rogers[51] and Weidel[66] and

their colleagues have tried to do, what is really involved in strength. For the moment, what we actually know about shape and about growth (i.e. addition of new wall for growth) comes within the realm of theoretical biology and awaits the stimulus of new approaches.

The presence of mucopeptide is a consistent but not an absolute trademark of a bacterium, even though it has the elements of a unique feature of the Procaryotae.[58] More examples of walled but mucopeptideless organisms are certain to be added to those already known. It is frustrating to the morphologist that current methods of electron microscopy do not necessarily distinguish these from their relatives which do have the component. This difficulty is particularly evident in the case of marine organisms with a fragile, weakly cross-linked mucopeptide, such as that studied by Buckmire & MacLeod,[7] in which the profile is not really distinguishable from that of the halophiles.

Morphology has a lot yet to learn about the hitherto unsuspected or virtually ignored components of the surfaces of many Gram-positive and Gram-negative bacteria. They may form as much as one-third to one-half of the total volume of the wall and are dispensable layers, since in some cases mutants or very close relatives without the structure have been found. What is involved in the genetics and the physiology of the loss of, let us say, the outer 100 Å of a total 250 Å is an open question. For those who wish to remove the wall or who wish to gain access to deeper layers of the wall, these specialized surfaces present special problems. Many of us have been surprised

Figure 1.6. *A:* Shadowed preparation (tungsten oxide) of a cell wall fragment from the VHA strain of *Spirillum serpens,* showing the regular hexagonal array of macromolecules in the surface layer. *B:* A negatively stained piece of wall (as *A*) made with phosphotungstic acid (pH 6.5), showing the complexity of the units and the Y-linkages joining the units. *C:* Preparation, similar to *B,* of a wall fragment of the MW6 strain of *S. serpens,* showing a variant arrangement of the surface structure; note that the units are directly linked and more widely spaced than those in *B;* another similar intraspecific variant shows half the space between the units. *D:* A wall fragment, prepared in exactly the same way as *B,* showing that the MW8 strain of *S. serpens* is "naked" and does not possess the structured surface layer. *E:* Section showing the profile of the VHA strain of *S. serpens,* in which the surface layer has remained intact due to an excess of calcium in both medium and fixative; note that the superficial layer shows a repeating structure (about 100 Å thick) of the same order of spacing as *A* and *B.* Magnification for *A–E,* × 200,000.

by how far away from the *visible* confines of the cell wall a tagged antibody or a particle such as methyl-ferritin is stopped.

The list of protoplastable or spheroplastable species grows all the time. Seldom is there any assessment of the intraspecific variability in sensitivity to this method. We certainly have found considerable variation to enzymic attack. One must suspect that a part of this blocking of activity may concern the highly organized superficial layers which are, we know, subject to mutation in terms of presence or absence, or of spatial arrangement of component parts, or in the exact nature of a component. There may be variations in more deeply set components (e.g., those *not* susceptible to removal by trypsin, or low concentrations of sodium lauryl sulfate) requiring a complex enzymic or chemical (e.g., EDTA) preparation for, let us say, the action of lysozyme. In the case of *L. monocytogenes* we have found a considerable intraspecific variation which has not yielded any morphological basis for selection of sensitive strains. What is left on spheroplasts as wall relicts must vary considerably according to the strain and the mechanism of induction.[35]

The final area of ignorance concerns the structure, function and content of that physiologically important zone that lies between the cell wall and the plasma membrane. There is no doubt that things happen there;[15, 18, 19, 25, 30, 65] it is also the place where the physiological *milieu extérieure* of the plasma membrane is defined. Disruption in this region seems to lead to profound changes, even if temporary, in the function of the membrane and to less defined effects in the intimate structure of the cell wall. We may have to return to considering the membranes as a physiological whole after a rewarding and profitable decade or two of separating them for study.

REFERENCES

1. Abram, D., and Gibbons, N. E.: The effect of chlorides of monovalent cations, urea, detergents, and heat on morphology and the turbidity of suspensions of red halophilic bacteria. *Canad. J. Microbiol.* **7:** 741, 1961.

2. Baddiley, J.: Teichoic acids and the bacterial cell wall. *Endeavour* **23:** 33, 1964.

3. Bayer, M. E., and Anderson, T. F.: The surface structure of *Escherichia coli. Proc. Nat. Acad. Sci. USA* **54:** 1592, 1965.

4. Beachey, E. H., and Cole, R. M.: Cell wall replication in *Escherichia coli*, studied by immunofluorescence and immunoelectron microscopy. *J. Bact.* **92:** 1245, 1966.

5. Brown, A. D., Drummond, D. G., and North, R. J.: The peripheral structures of Gram-negative bacteria. II. Membranes of bacilli and spheroplasts of a marine pseudomonad. *Biochem. Biophys. Acta* **58:** 514, 1962.

6. Brown, A. D., and Shorey, C. D.: The cell envelopes of two extremely halophilic bacteria. *J. Cell Biol.* **18:** 681, 1963.

7. Buckmire, F. L. A., and MacLeod, R. A.: Nutrition and metabolism of marine bacteria. XIV. On the mechanism of lysis of a marine bacterium. *Canad. J. Microbiol.* **11:** 677, 1965.

8. Chapman, J. A., Murray, R. G. E., and Salton, M. R. J.: The surface anatomy of *Lampropedia hyalina. Proc. Roy. Soc. London B* **158:** 498, 1963.

9. Claus, G. W., and Roth, L. E.: Fine structure of the Gram-negative bacterium *Acetobacter suboxydans. J. Cell. Biol.* **20:** 217, 1964.

10. Cole, R. M.: Bacterial cell wall replication followed by immunofluorescence. *Bact. Rev.* **29:** 326, 1965.

11. Cole, R. M., and Hahn, J. J.: Cell wall replication in *Streptococcus pyogenes. Science* **135:** 722, 1962.

12. Conti, S. F., and Gettner, M. E.: Electron microscopy of cellular division in *Escherichia coli. J. Bact.* **83:** 544, 1962.

13. de Petris, S.: Ultrastructure of the cell wall of *Escherichia coli. J. Ultrastruct. Res.* **12:** 247, 1965.

14. Eagon, R. G., Simmons, G. P., and Carson, K. J.: Evidence for the presence of ash and divalent metals in the cell wall of *Pseudomonas aeruginosa. Canad. J. Microbiol.* **11:** 1041, 1965.

15. Edwards, M. R., and Stevens, R. W.: Fine structure of *Listeria monocytogenes. J. Bact.* **86:** 414, 1963.

16. Fitz-James, P. C.: Participation of the cytoplasmic membrane in the growth and spore formation of bacilli. *J. Biophys. Biochem. Cytol.* **8:** 507, 1960.

17. ———: Discussion of: Fuhs, G. W., Fine structure and replication of bacterial nucleoids. *Bact. Rev.* **29:** 293, 1965.

18. Fitz-James, P., and Hancock, R.: The initial

structural lesion of penicillin action in *Bacillus megaterium*. *J. Cell Biol.* **26**: 657, 1965.

19. Ghosh, B. K., and Murray, R. G. E.: The fine structure of *Listeria monocytogenes* in relation to protoplast formation. *J. Bact.* **93**: 411, 1967.

20. Gray, G. W., and Wilkinson, S. G.: The action of ethylenediaminetetra-acetic acid on *Pseudomonas aeruginosa*. *J. Appl. Bact.* **28**: 153, 1965.

21. Hofschneider, P. H., and Lorek, H.: Studies on the residual cell wall structures of *E. coli* and *B. megaterium* spheroplasts and of L-forms of *Proteus mirabilis*. In: *Fifth International Congress for Electron Microscopy*, Vol. 2 (S. S. Breese, Jr., Ed.). Academic Press, New York, 1962: RR9.

22. Houwink, A. L.: A macromolecular monolayer in the cell wall of *Spirillum* spec. *Biochim. Biophys. Acta* **10**: 360, 1953.

23. Kavanau, J. L.: *Structure and Function in Biological Membranes*. Holden-Day, San Francisco, 1965.

24. Kellenberger, E., and Ryter, A.: Cell wall and cytoplasmic membrane of *Escherichia coli*. *J. Biophys. Biochem. Cytol.* **4**: 323, 1958.

25. Knox, K. W., Vesk, M., and Work, E.: Relation between excreted lipopolysaccharide complexes and surface structures of a lysine-limited culture of *Escherichia coli*. *J. Bact.* **92**: 1206, 1966.

26. Krause, R. M.: Antigenic and biochemical composition of hemolytic streptococcal cell walls. *Bact. Rev.* **27**: 369, 1963.

27. Kushner, D. J.: Lysis and dissolution of cells and envelopes of an extremely halophilic bacterium. *J. Bact.* **87**: 1147, 1964.

28. Kushner, D. J., Bayley, S. T., Boring, J., Kates, M., and Gibbons, N. E.: Morphological and chemical properties of cell envelopes of the extreme halophile, *Halobacterium cutirubrum*. *Canad. J. Microbiol.* **10**: 483, 1964.

29. Kushner, D. J., and Onishi, H.: Contribution of protein and lipid components to the salt response of envelopes of an extremely halophilic bacterium. *J. Bact.* **91**: 653, 1966.

30. Lampen, J. O.: Secretion of enzymes by microorganisms. *Symp. Soc. Gen. Microbiol.* **15**: 115, 1965.

31. Lautrop, H., Reyn, A., and Birch-Andersen, A.: A comparative electron microscope study of the cell walls of Gram-negative bacteria. In: *XIV Scandinavian Congress of Pathology and Microbiology; Proceedings*. Universitetsforlaget, Oslo, 1964.

32. Lederberg, J.: Bacterial protoplasts induced by penicillin. *Proc. Nat. Acad. Sci. USA* **42**: 574, 1956.

33. Lieve, L.: Release of lipopolysaccharide by EDTA treatment of *E. coli*. *Biochim. Biophys. Res. Commun.* **21**: 290, 1965.

34. Martin, H. H.: Bacterial protoplasts—a review. *J. Theoret. Biol.* **5**: 1, 1963.

35. ———: Chemical composition of cell wall mucopolymer from penicillin spheroplasts and normal cells of *Proteus mirabilis*. In: *Sixth International Congress of Biochemistry. Abstracts, I. Nucleic Acids*. Washington, D.C., 1964: p. 518.

36. McQuillen, K.: Bacterial protoplasts. In: *The Bacteria: A Treatise on Structure and Function. Vol. I: Structure* (I. C. Gunsalus and R. Y. Stanier, Eds.). Academic Press, New York, 1960: p. 249.

37. Mitchell, P., and Moyle, J.: Autolytic release and osmotic properties of 'protoplasts' from *Staphylococcus aureus*. *J. Gen. Microbiol.* **16**: 184, 1957.

38. Mudd, S., Polevitzky, K., Anderson, T. F., and Chambers, L. A.: Bacterial morphology as shown by the electron microscope. *J. Bact.* **42**: 251, 1941.

39. Murray, R. G. E.: Direct evidence for a cytoplasmic membrane in sectioned bacteria. *Canad. J. Microbiol.* **3**: 531, 1957.

40. ———: The internal structure of the cell. In: *The Bacteria: A Treatise on Structure and Function. Vol. I. Structure* (I. C. Gunsalus and R. Y. Stanier, Eds.). Academic Press, New York, 1960: p. 35.

41. ———: On the cell wall structure of *Spirillum serpens*. *Canad. J. Microbiol.* **9**: 381, 1963.

42. ———: The organelles of bacteria. In: *General Physiology of Cell Specialization* (D. Mazia and A. Tyler, Eds.). McGraw-Hill, New York, 1963: p. 28.

43. Murray, R. G. E., Steed, R., and Elson, H. E.: The location of the mucopeptide in sections of the cell wall of *Escherichia coli* and other Gram-negative bacteria. *Canad. J. Microbiol.* **11**: 547, 1965.

44. Murray, R. G. E., and Watson, S. W.: Structure of *Nitrosocystis oceanus* and comparison with *Nitrosomonas* and *Nitrobacter*. *J. Bact.* **89**: 1594, 1965.

45. Nermut, M. V.: The ultrastructure of *B. megaterium cell wall*. *J. Gen. Microbiol.*, in press.

46. Nermut, M. V., and Murray, R. G. E.: The ultrastructure of the cell wall of *Bacillus polymyxa*. *J. Bact.*, in press.

47. Pillot, J., Ryter, A., and Ginger, C. D.: La structure des treponemes. In: *IX International Congress for Microbiology; Abstracts of Papers* (V. M. Stakhanova, Ed.-in-Chief) Moscow, 1966: p. 60.

48. Repaske, R.: Lysis of Gram-negative bacteria by lysozyme. *Biochim. Biophys. Acta* **22**: 189, 1956.

49. Ritchie, A. E., Keeler, R. F., and Bryner, J. H.: Anatomical features of *Vibrio fetus:* electron microscopic survey. *J. Gen. Microbiol.* **43**: 427, 1966.

50. Robinow, C. F., and Murray, R. G. E.: The differentiation of cell wall, cytoplasmic membrane and cytoplasm of Gram positive bacteria by selective staining. *Exp. Cell Res.* **4**: 390, 1953.

51. Rogers, H. J.: The outer layers of bacteria: the biosynthesis of structure. *Symp. Soc. Gen. Microbiol.* **15**: 186, 1965.

52. Ryter, A., and Jacob, F.: Étude au microscope électronique des relations entre mésosomes et noyaux chez *Bacillus subtilis. C. R. Acad. Sci.* (Paris) **257**: 3060, 1963.

53. Ryter, A., and Landman, O. E.: Electron microscope study of the relationship between mesosome loss and the stable L state (or protoplast state) in *Bacillus subtilis. J. Bact.* **88**: 457, 1964.

54. Salton, M. R. J.: Cell wall of *Micrococcus lysodeikticus* as the substrate of lysozyme. *Nature* **170**: 746, 1952.

55. ———: *The Bacterial Cell Wall.* Elsevier, Amsterdam, 1964.

56. Shilo, M., and Bruff, B.: Lysis of Gram-negative bacteria by host-independent ectoparasitic *Bdellovibrio bacteriovorus* isolates. *J. Gen. Microbiol.* **40**: 317, 1965.

57. Shockman, G. D.: Unbalanced cell-wall synthesis: autolysis and cell-wall thickening. *Bact. Rev.* **29**: 345, 1965.

58. Stanier, R. Y., and van Niel, C. B.: The concept of a bacterium. *Arch. Mikrobiol.* **42**: 17, 1962.

59. Starr, M. P., and Baigent, N. L.: Parasitic interaction of *Bdellovibrio bacteriovorus* with other bacteria. *J. Bact.* **91**: 2006, 1966.

60. Steed, P., and Murray, R. G. E.: The cell wall and cell division of Gram-negative bacteria. *Canad. J. Microbiol.* **12**: 263, 1966.

61. Stolp, H., and Starr, M. P.: *Bdellovibrio bacteriovorus* gen. et sp. n., a predatory ectoparasitic, and bacteriolytic microorganism. *Antonie Leeuwenhoek* **29**: 217, 1963.

62. Thornley, M. J., Horne, R. W., and Glauert, A. M.: The fine structure of *Micrococcus radiodurans. Arch. Mikrobiol.* **51**: 267, 1965.

63. Virgilio, L., González, C., Muñoz, N., and Mendoza, S.: Electron microscopy of *Staphylococcus aureus* cell wall lysis. *J. Bact.* **91**: 2018, 1966.

64. Weibull, C.: The isolation of protoplasts from *Bacillus megaterium* by controlled treatment with lysozyme. *J. Bact.* **66**: 688, 1953.

65. Weidel, W., Frank, H., and Leutgeb, W.: Autolytic enzymes as a source of error in the preparation and study of Gram-negative cell walls. *J. Gen. Microbiol.* **30**: 127, 1963.

66. Weidel, W., and Pelzer, H.: Bagshaped macromolecules—a new outlook on bacterial cell walls. *Adv. Enzym.* **26**: 193, 1964.

2

The Formation of Spheroplasts by Immune Substances and the Reactivity of Immune Substances Against Diverse Rounded Forms*

Louis H. Muschel

UNIVERSITY OF MINNESOTA MEDICAL SCHOOL
MINNEAPOLIS, MINNESOTA

Bacterial cells may lose all or part of their walls under certain conditions. The remaining unit, consisting of the cytoplasm and its enclosed nucleus, is called a *protoplast,* but if there is doubt regarding the complete removal of the wall, then the term *spheroplast* is appropriate.[5] In this report, the former term will be used for the rounded forms of the Gram-positive organisms that are free of cell wall constituents, and the latter term for the rounded forms of Gram-negative bacteria that are not. Ordinarily, the loss of the cell wall results in an osmotically fragile spherical body which is lysed and therefore not observable, unless the lytic process is prevented or retarded by an appropriate stabilizing menstruum. A variety of solutes, including polyethylene glycol and sucrose in the range of 0.1 to 0.5 molar concentration, have been successfully employed to stabilize these spherical bodies.[26]

Two general methods are available for the preparation of spheroplasts or protoplasts. The synthesis of the cell wall may be interrupted by deprivation of an essential nutrient or the use of a specific poison. Thus, spheroplasts of *Escherichia coli* have been produced when diaminopimelic acid, a constituent of the cell wall, was absent in the growth medium of a mutant strain that requires this amino acid.[2] The use of specific poison may be illustrated by penicillin, which inhibits bacterial cell wall synthesis. Under appropriate conditions, growing cells of *E. coli* and *Salmonella typhimurium* have been transformed into spheroplasts by penicillin.[12]

The other general method for preparing spheroplasts depends upon the activity of suitable enzymes, such as lysozyme, upon the cell wall. The addition of lysozyme to suspensions of living cells of certain microbial species (*Micrococcus lysodeikticus, Sarcina lutea, Bacillus* sp.) results in a dissolution of the cell wall, while the bacterial protoplasm remains as a spherical body in the medium and soon lyses unless kept in 0.1–0.2 M sucrose or polyethylene glycol medium.[24] Although Gram-negative organisms are generally insensitive to lysozyme itself, various pretreatments of these organisms may render them suscep-

* This work was supported by grant No. AI-05454 from the National Institute of Allergy and Infectious Diseases.

tible to the enzyme. Washed and slightly starved cells of *E. coli* K-12 and *E. coli* B at pH 5 or pH 9 were converted to protoplasts by lysozyme.[29] In addition, treatment of several Gram-negative organisms with polymyxin B sulfate prior to lysozyme resulted in lysis or spheroplast formation.[25] The most interesting and biologically significant formation of bacterial spheroplasts results, however, from the combined activity of the complement (C′) system plus lysozyme. It was found that Gram-negative organisms susceptible to the immune bactericidal reaction mediated by C′ were lysed, or converted into spheroplasts, by the endogenous lysozyme present in serum or by the addition of egg white lysozyme to serum substances.[14] Previous studies by workers in Japan had shown that lysozyme accelerated the immune bactericidal reaction,[1] and later they also showed that it was involved in spheroplast formation.[11]

The similarity between the action of the C′ system and polymyxin suggested that their points of anatomical attack may be similar. It is well established that polymyxin damages the cell membrane of bacteria sensitive to this antibiotic. The action of C′ on the living bacterial cell was viewed as analogous, insofar as the anatomical site of injury was concerned, to the action of antibiotics that injure the cell membrane.[14]

This concept of the immune bactericidal reaction mediated by C′ suggested certain experiments to elucidate the reasons for the insusceptibility, particularly of Gram-positive bacteria, to the C′ system. To reduce the influence of the cell wall, bacterial spheroplasts and protoplasts prepared by the action of lysozyme or penicillin were subjected to the action of C′. It was anticipated that these structures might be analogous, or at least similar, to the erythrocyte in their reactivity to C′.

MATERIALS AND METHODS

FORMATION OF SPHEROPLASTS OF GRAM-NEGATIVE BACTERIA BY SERUM

The bacteria were obtained from stock cultures on agar slants, inoculated into 50 ml of penassay broth (Difco), and incubated for 16 hours at 37°C without aeration.[15] These cultures contained approximately 1×10^9 bacteria/ml, of which 0.1 ml was used as the inoculum. When subcultures of these organisms in penassay broth with three to four hours of incubation at 37°C were used, there was greater uniformity of results. Spheroplast formation was determined by observation of aliquots under a cover glass using an A O Spencer dark phase contrast microscope with a 97× objective and a 10× ocular. Bactericidal action of serum substances was determined by the quantitative growth assay method.[19]

For the quantitative determination of spheroplast formation from cells killed by C′, the procedure consisted of an initial incubation of the bactericidal reagents (antibody and complement) with the standard inoculum for one hour at 37°C. Then 0.6 ml of a sterile solution of 50% sucrose and 10% $MgSO_4$ was added to the 2 ml bactericidal reaction mixture,[19] and lysozyme added in different amounts, ranging from 0.1 μg to 100 μg per tube.[7] After incubation for an additional hour at 37°C, 0.5 ml of formaldehyde (37%) solution was added to stop the reaction and fix the cells. The ratio of spheroplasts to rod shaped forms was determined by counting 100 cells with the dark phase contrast microscope.

REVERSAL OF THE BACTERICIDAL REACTION BY MAGNESIUM

The quantitative photometric growth assay method[19] for the determination of the surviving organisms of the bactericidal reaction was used, except that the reaction of antiserum and complement with the test organism, *Salmonella typhosa* O901, was generally limited to 25 instead of 60 minutes.[17] The diluent for those experiments in which the effect of Mg^{++} was being studied was 0.146 M NaCl, instead of the usual diluent of 0.146 M NaCl and 0.003 M $MgCl_2 \cdot 6H_2O$. It was observed that the divalent cations of calcium and strontium formed a precipitate with the brain heart infusion broth (Difco) usually used for the cultivation of the test organism. Therefore, in testing the effect of salts of these ions, nutrient broth was used, and the surviving organisms were assayed by plate count on meat extract agar.

SERUM REACTIONS AGAINST SPHEROBLASTS AND PROTOPLASTS

Spheroplasts of *E. coli* B were prepared as follows: Twenty ml of a 20-hour culture in brain heart infusion broth were diluted 1:2 with fresh broth as a diluent.[18] After incubation for one hour at 37°C, the culture was centrifuged and the sedimented organisms resuspended in a stabilizing solution containing 0.8 M sucrose, 0.005 M $MgCl_2 \cdot 6H_2O$, 0.01 M NaCl, and sufficient bicarbonate to give a pH of 7.4. The solution was added until the optical density was lowered to 0.50. To 30 ml of this suspension, 1.2 ml of 0.1% solution of lysozyme (Worthington Biochemical Corp.) was added, and then 2.4 ml of a 4% solution of ethylenediaminetetracetic acid (EDTA). After 15 minutes at 37°C, over 80 per cent of the rod shaped forms were converted to spheroplasts. Spheroplasts of *Paracolobacterium ballerup* were prepared similarly. Penicillin spheroplasts of this organism were prepared as described by Lederberg[12] for *E. coli*.

B. subtilis 23 was grown for 18 hours on meat extract agar, and the organisms were suspended in 40 ml of brain heart infusion broth.[18] After incubation at 37°C for one hour, they were centrifuged and resuspended in the stabilizing solution to an optical density of 0.50. Then, 0.5 ml of a 0.1% solution of lysozyme was added and, after incubation for 30 minutes at 37°C, at least 95 per cent of the rod shaped forms were converted to protoplasts.

Different amounts of serum were added to 1.0 ml of the spheroplast or protoplast suspension. The total volume of the reaction mixtures depended upon the volume of serum tested and varied from 1.1 ml to 1.4 ml. The mixtures were appropriately diluted with the stabilizing fluid, and incubated at 37°C for 30 minutes. The number of intact protoplasts was determined by counting at least three fields with a phase contrast microscope and calculating the percentage surviving by comparison with control tubes without serum.

For the adsorption with bentonite, 6 mg of bentonite (American Colloid Co., Chicago, Ill.) were suspended in 1 ml of serum, and the suspension was incubated at 4°C for 30 minutes. The bentonite was removed by centrifugation.

RESULTS

PRODUCTION OF SPHEROPLASTS OF GRAM-NEGATIVE BACTERIA BY SERUM SUBSTANCES PLUS LYSOZYME

When 0.5 ml of undiluted, fresh guinea pig or human serum, 0.1 ml of 10% $MgSO_4 \cdot 7H_2O$, 0.1 ml of 50% sucrose, and 0.3 ml of 0.85% NaCl were added to 0.1 ml of cultures of the "rough" organisms, *E. coli* B or *S. typhosa* "Mrs. S.", the bacterial rods were converted to spheroplasts within a period of one hour at 37°C. Heat-inactivated (56°C for 30 minutes) serum was totally ineffective. In contrast, when cells of *S. typhosa* H901, a "smooth" organism, were used, no rounded forms were observed with the same method of treatment. However, a practically complete conversion of these cells to spheroplasts took place within one hour after the addition of guinea pig serum (absorbed with washed, heat-killed cells of *S. typhosa* H901, which resulted in the removal of its detectable natural antibody and lysozyme with retention of C'), *S. typhosa* O antiserum, lysozyme, and Mg^{++} (Table 2.1). The cells of the *S. typhosa* H901 culture lost their motility within 40 minutes, then swelled uniformly in all directions, and gradually assumed a more spherical shape with an apparent increase in density. The subterminal swelling of the bacterial rods and "rabbit ears" observed in the conversion of cells to protoplasts by penicillin[12] was not observed (Table 2.1). Heat-killed (60°C for 30 minutes) organisms were not changed to spheroplasts, but cells treated with ultraviolet light to prevent division were converted to spheroplasts in the same manner as viable cells. Although the egg white lysozyme concentration usually was 10 μg per ml (Table 2.1), as little as 1 μg of lysozyme sufficed for maximal spheroplast formation. Mg^{++}

TABLE 2.1

Formation of Spheroplasts of Salmonella typhosa *H901 by Serum Substances*

	Test tube*	Control tubes*				
	ml	*ml*				
Broth culture	0.1	0.1	0.1	0.1	0.1	0.1
S. typhosa anti-O[†]	0.1	0	0.1	0.1	0.1	0.1
Absorbed normal guinea pig serum[‡]	0.5	0.5	0	0.5	0.5	0.5
Lysozyme (1 mg/ml)	0.1	0.1	0.1	0	0.1	0.1
10% $MgSO_4 \cdot 7H_2O$	0.1	0.1	0.1	0.1	0	0.1
50% sucrose	0.1	0.1	0.1	0.1	0.1	0
Normal saline	0	0.1	0.5	0.1	0.1	0.1
Microscopic observation	Sphero-plasts	Motile rods	Motile rods, few clumps	Nonmotile	Ghosts	Sphero-plasts

* 60 min at 37° C prior to microscopic observation.
† 1:1000 dilution in normal saline.
‡ Absorbed with washed, heat-killed cells of *S. typhosa* H901.

and sucrose were added regularly to the system. The omission of added Mg^{++} led to the formation of large numbers of empty membranes or "ghosts". Omission of sucrose did not appear to diminish formation of spheroplasts, although it may have lessened their stability, since ghosts were noted occasionally in the absence of sucrose. Entirely comparable results were obtained when the reactions proceeded in the peritoneal cavity of the mouse instead of the test tube.[6]

THE BACTERICIDAL REACTION AND PROTOPLAST FORMATION

Since the conversion of cells of *S. typhosa* to the spheroplast form required antiserum and fresh normal serum in addition to lysozyme, it seemed likely that the bactericidal activity of the C′ system was involved in the reaction. The question was raised whether the bactericidal activity is a necessary prerequisite for the conversion of the cells to protoplasts or whether the organisms that survive are converted to spheroplasts. Additional experimental results strongly favored the former alternative. When the absorbed normal guinea pig serum was heat-inactivated or decomplemented by specific precipitate, such serum was ineffective in producing spheroplasts. Organisms treated with antibody and complement at 4°C instead of 37°C prior to lysozyme addition and subsequent incubation at 37°C with lysozyme were not killed nor converted to spheroplasts. Also, with limiting amounts of antiserum, an excellent correlation was obtained between the percentage of organisms killed with different amounts of antiserum as determined by the quantitative growth assay method[19] and the percentage conversion to spheroplasts. Moreover, cells of *P. ballerup,* an organism insusceptible to the bactericidal action of the C′ system, under the usual experimental conditions, were not converted to spheroplasts by *P. ballerup* antiserum, fresh guinea pig serum, and lysozyme with Mg^{++} and sucrose. Finally, when cells of *S. typhosa* H901 were first treated with lysozyme, they were not subsequently converted to spheroplasts by the action of antibody and C′. Thus, the evidence strongly suggests that the formation of spheroplasts by serum substances involves at least a two-stage process in which the bactericidal action of the C′ system exposes the lysozyme substrate that results in lysis or in spheroplast formation with stabilizing media.

REVERSAL OF THE BACTERICIDAL REACTION BY MAGNESIUM

Preliminary tests indicated that the addition of magnesium salts was capable of reversing the bactericidal action of serum. Accordingly, $MgSO_4$, giving a final concentration of 0.11 M was added to the mixtures of antiserum, complement and culture after 25 minutes. The surviving organisms were then assayed after an additional five minutes (Table 2.2). The results indicated that $MgSO_4$ is capable of partially reversing the bactericidal action of the C′ system. The greater survival in the control set with a 25-minute reaction period compared to the control set with a reaction period of 30 minutes indicated that the bactericidal reaction was not completed at 25 minutes, and that the reversal of the bactericidal reaction may have been effected while the reaction was still in progress in the absence of the added salt. The possibility that the $MgSO_4$ itself may have influenced the survival and growth of *S. typhosa* was excluded by additional control tubes. Lower concentrations of Mg^{++} (0.03 M $MgSO_4$) were almost as effective as 0.11 M, but a concentration as low as 0.01 M gave a scarcely detectable effect. Similar results were obtained with $MgCl_2$, but not with Na_2SO_4, indicating that the reversal of the bactericidal reaction may be attributed to Mg^{++}. The reaction period for these tests was 25 minutes. Additional tests indicated that the reaction was reversible after it had been in progress for as long as 50 minutes, but not after 100 minutes.

Many other substances tested over wide concentration ranges were not able to reverse the bactericidal reaction of serum. These included anticomplementary substances such as heparin, dicoumarol, sodium citrate, sodium oxalate and EDTA. Other materials also without effect were dextrose, sucrose, ovalbumin, gelatin, heated guinea pig serum, polyethylene glycol, sodium sulfate, ammonium chloride, strontium chloride and calcium chloride. Finally, concentrations of spermine phosphate and spermine tetrahydrochloride (10^{-3} to 10^{-5} M) were without effect in the reversal of the bactericidal reaction.

QUANTITATIVE RELATIONSHIPS BETWEEN THE BACTERICIDAL ACTION OF THE C′ SYSTEM AND LYSOZYME

The quantitative relationship between the killing of bacteria by the C′ system

TABLE 2.2

Reversal of the Bactericidal Reaction by Magnesium Ion

Antiserum	Complement	Per cent survival of *Salmonella typhosa* O901		
		Test with* 0.11 M $MgSO_4$	Controls (no Mg ion)	
			25 min†	30 min†
ml	*ml*			
2.6×10^{-6}	0.05	56	19	7
1.3×10^{-6}	0.05	96	57	17
None	0.05	100	100	100
2.6×10^{-6}	None	100	100	100
None	None	100	100	100

* Reaction period of 25 min, addition of $MgSO_4$, and assay of surviving bacteria after 5 min.

† Reaction time.

and their lysis by lysozyme remained to be determined. It had been established that organisms killed by the C′ system were quantitatively converted to spheroplasts by lysozyme, but it was not known whether these killed organisms were equally sensitive to lysozyme. Minimal amounts of antiserum and C′ were selected in order to kill 98–100 per cent of a standardized inoculum, and then the amounts of lysozyme required to convert 50 per cent of the killed cells to spheroplasts was determined. The results indicated an extremely wide degree of variation, ranging from no detectable amount (less than 1 μg) for *Vibrio cholerae* to 50 μg/ml for mouse and chimpanzee virulent *S. typhosa* Ty2.[8] *S. typhosa* Watson, which produces a smaller amount of Vi antigen than strain Ty2,[16] required only about 12 μg per ml, while the endpoint for *S. typhosa* strains O901 and R-2, which do not produce the Vi antigen, was less than 8 μg/ml. Thus, among stains of *S. typhosa* in which an association has been demonstrated between Vi content and normal serum resistance,[16] an additional association exists between Vi content or serum resistance and lysozyme resistance.

REACTIVITY OF SERUM AGAINST PROTOPLASTS AND SPHEROPLASTS

Spheroplasts of *E. coli* B prepared by the action of lysozyme and EDTA, and protoplasts of *B. subtilis* prepared by the action of lysozyme were subjected to the action of normal rabbit serum at 37°C. The *E. coli* B spheroplasts were disintegrated or ruptured by the untreated serum, but were apparently unaffected by heat inactivated (30 minutes at 56°C) serum. On the other hand, *B. subtilis* protoplasts were disintegrated by heated or unheated rabbit serum at 37°C (Table 2.3). In another similar experiment, human serum was almost as effective as rabbit serum against the *B. subtilis* protoplasts. Although the *B. subtilis* protoplasts in this and in several other similar experiments were slightly more susceptible to unheated serum, the predominant action of heat stable serum constituents unrelated to the C′ system made it difficult to study the effect of C′ on such forms.[18]

To elucidate the possible contribution of C′, however, sera were adsorbed with bentonite, which did not significantly reduce the titer of hemolytic C′, to reduce its protoplast lysing ability and to magnify any possible contribution of C′. Samples of the bentonite-adsorbed serum were decomplemented by heat (56°C for 30 minutes)

TABLE 2.3

Effect of Normal Rabbit Serum Against Escherichia coli *B Spheroplasts and* Bacillus subtilis *Protoplasts*

Amount of serum	Survival of Rounded Forms	
	Heated* serum	Unheated serum
E. coli B at 37°C		
ml	%	%
0.4	100	32
0.2	100	32
0.1	100	60
0.05	100	100
B. subtilis at 37°C		
0.1	0	0
0.05	10	0
0.025	13	10
0.0125	80	50
0.00625	100	100

* 56°C for 30 minutes.

or by treatment with an immune precipitate (ovalbumin-antiovalbumin). Both procedures resulted in a marked loss of protoplast-lysing ability. Whereas 0.2 ml of this sample of bentonite-adsorbed serum lysed about 70 per cent of the protoplasts, there was no detectable lysis with the decomplemented samples. This result provided evidence that the C′ system was capable of lysing *B. subtilis* protoplasts.

Since C′ is activated by an antigen-antibody complex, it seemed desirable to determine the need for antibody in conjunction with C′. Normal rabbit serum was adsorbed, therefore, with bentonite and with protoplasts of *B. subtilis*, the latter being used to adsorb "natural" antibody. The effect of heat inactivated rabbit antiserum, in conjunction with such doubly adsorbed sera as a C′ source, against *B. subtilis* was compared to that of a preimmunization serum sample. The antiserum showed a significantly greater effect. This result may be reasonably attributed to the presence in normal serum of heat labile natural antibody, which suffices for maximal sensitization of the *B. subtilis* protoplasts. Corroboration for this view came from the additional finding that, in contrast to the significant difference between the preimmunization specimen and antiserum when tested with C′ specifically adsorbed with *B. subtilis* protoplasts and with bentonite, no difference between these sera was observed when they were tested with C′ adsorbed with the cells of a heterologous organism, *S. typhosa* O901, and bentonite. In this experiment, normal antibody to the *B. subtilis* protoplast was not removed from the C′ source and apparently sufficed for maximal sensitization.

P. ballerup, when cultured at 37°C, is an organism which, under the usual testing conditions, is insusceptible to the C′ system.[20] Spheroplasts of *P. ballerup* prepared by treatment with penicillin had a sensitivity to fresh normal serum, however, comparable to that of similarly prepared spheroplasts of serum-sensitive organisms, *E. coli* B and *S. typhosa* O901. With an inoculum of about 1×10^8 spheroplasts of any of these organisms, and after an incubation period of one hour with different amounts of normal guinea pig serum, 50 per cent of the spheroplasts were lysed by about 0.20 ml of serum.

DISCUSSION

These studies have shown that the C′ system may render cells of Gram-negative organisms susceptible to lysis or spheroplast formation by lysozyme. Other processes, including exposure to an abnormal pH or polymyxin, also sensitize cells to the enzyme. The mechanisms of these actions are not known, nor is it clear whether the same mechanism operates in these diverse processes. An obvious explanation is that the mucopolysaccharide substrate of lysozyme is exposed by an abnormal pH, polymyxin, or the C′ system.

In immune hemolysis, the complexing of the antibody with antigens of the cell membrane initiates the C′ sequence with the cell membrane itself as the target of the C′ action. The entire process occurs sequentially in direct apposition to the cell membrane, and this probably insures maximal efficiency. "In a sense, the sensitized red cell surrounds itself with a halo of C′ activity." [28] By analogy with the immune cytolysis of erythrocytes or of nucleated mammalian cells, it may be postulated that the action of C′ upon sensitized Gram-negative bacteria is also directed against the cell membrane. The locus of the antigen-antibody complex which activates C′ is obviously on the surface of the cell wall, but the C′ target may be the cell membrane. It is well established that C′ mediated red cell lysis may result from the combination of antibody with surface antigens which may not be integral components of the red cells. [13] This fact suggests that the antigen-antibody reaction serves merely to concentrate C′ at a susceptible structure. Antigens of the cell wall or capsules of Gram-negative bacteria may act, therefore, like an adsorbed antigen on the cell membrane. In both hemolysis and bactericidal action, the damage that results in red cell lysis or bacterial cell death may result from membrane damage caused by an enzyme or C′, or by activation in the enzymes themselves.

This scheme of the immune bactericidal reaction requires, of course, that the cell wall of sensitive bacteria be permeable to one or more of the C′ component macromolecules. It is in accord with observations based on light microscopy of bacteria killed by the C′ system, which do not indicate any obvious structural distortion of the cells. Nonetheless, there is a loss of permeability control reflected by a loss of radioactivity from such bacteria labeled with P^{32} directly proportional to their loss of viability. [22] The action of Mg^{++} in reversing the action of the immune bactericidal reaction is also compatible with the bacterial cell membrane as the ultimate target of the C′ system. It is interesting to note that the action of C′, which requires a small concentration of Mg^{++}, may be partially reversed in the bactericidal reaction by the addition of larger amounts of that ion. Mg^{++} protects *Aerobacter aerogenes* and other Gram-negative organisms against the lethal effect of chilling, [23] and is effective in the stabilization of spheroplasts of Gram-negative bacteria (Table 2.1). These effects of the metal may be related to its effect in preventing the release of lipid residues of the plasma membranes, [27] thereby preventing a loss of permeability control by these membranes. Finally, pits (lesions) were observed by electron microscopy in the cytoplasmic membrane of *E. coli* as a result of C′ action. [3] These lesions showed striking morphological similarities to those found in erythrocyte membranes after an immune hemolysis reaction. [4]

As a result of membrane damage mediated by C′ and consequent killing of the bacteria, apparent lysis, or spheroplast formation in protective media, occurs only upon further enzymatic attack upon the cell wall mucocomplex by lysozyme. Crombie [7] has suggested that the increased accessibility of the lysozyme substrate results from the swelling of the cell as a result of water uptake after the loss of permeability control. Increased pressure upon the compact molecular structure of the cell wall might result, therefore, in its partial disruption and exposure of the mucopeptide substrate of lysozyme.

Quantitative studies of the relationship between the bactericidal reaction and lysis (or spheroplast formation) clearly differentiated the two processes. In addition, kinetic analysis of the conversion of spheroplasts to ghosts has also been performed by Davis et al.[9] Certain organisms, such as *V. cholerae*, are particularly susceptible to lysis, whereas other bacteria are rather resistant, although considerable differences are encountered among strains of the same species, as our results indicated with *S. typhosa* strains. The relatively virulent strains containing the Vi antigen are relatively resistant to lysis by lysozyme. It is tempting to speculate that this association is meaningful, but experimental investigation of this point has not been performed. The findings of Freeman, Musteikis & Burrows,[10] indicating that *V. cholerae* did not require detectable amounts of lysozyme for spheroplast formation, were confirmed. Perhaps the cell wall of *V. cholerae,* unlike the cell walls of Gram-negative enteric bacteria, requires an intact membrane to maintain its rigidity. Although data for *V. cholerae* are not available, the percentage of lipid in the cell wall of *Vibrio metschnikovii* is 11.2, and the percentage of polysaccharide is 12.3, while comparable percentages for *Salmonella gallinarum* are 22 and 28 respectively.[21] It is likely, therefore, that the cell walls of *Vibrio* species are less rigid and more easily ruptured. Other possible alternatives, however unlikely, include the activation of a cell wall autolytic process by C′ and the presence of bacteriolytic enzymes other than lysozyme which are not removable by the absorption procedures used to remove lysozyme.

These concepts regarding the mechanism of the immune bactericidal reaction suggested certain experiments to elucidate the reasons for the resistance of the Gram-positive bacteria to this reaction. Although certain members of the Gram-negative bacteria are also resistant under the usual experimental conditions, the general insusceptibility of the Gram-positive group to the C′ system provides one of the differential characteristics between the two groups of organisms. Since there are marked differences in the cell walls of these two groups of bacteria, experiments were performed with spheroplasts of resistant Gram-negative bacteria and with protoplasts of Gram-positive bacteria.

The results of these experiments have indicated that the resistance of Gram-positive bacteria to the C′ system is associated with their cell walls. Enzymatic removal of the wall of *B. subtilis* by lysozyme resulted in the conversion of the cells of that organism to protoplasts that are susceptible to the C′ system. These protoplasts are also susceptible, and to an even greater degree, to other serum substances unrelated to C′. Protoplasts of Gram-positive cells, like the whole cells of Gram-negative bacteria, treponemes, red cells, and nucleated cells, are therefore sensitive to the C′ system.

The C′ system may be assumed to act upon the bacterial cell's membrane in the manner in which the membranes of red cells and nucleated cells are attacked. The immune bactericidal reaction probably results from the activation of C′ by antigen-antibody complexes sufficiently accessible to the bacterial cell membrane causing membrane damage and cell death. The resistance of certain bacteria to the C′ system, however, may be associated with their cell walls, which protect the membrane. For example, *P. ballerup* is a Gram-negative organism which, under the usual experimental conditions, is resistant to the C′ system. Nevertheless, its penicillin spheroplasts were no more resistant than penicillin spheroplasts derived from C′ sensitive Gram-negative organisms. An obvious explanation for the resistance of some Gram-negative organisms to the C′ system is that those organisms possess cell walls that are anticomplementary, but supporting experimental evidence was not obtained.[20]

Similarly, protoplasts of *B. subtilis*, in contrast to the rod shaped cells from which they are derived, are also sensitive to the C′ system. Like resistant Gram-negative bacteria, the whole cells of *B. subtilis* are not anticomplementary; detectable anticomplementary activity was not noted, in experiments in our laboratory,* with 10^8 cells in a standard hemolytic system. The resistance of bacteria to the C′ system seems to be related, therefore, to their cell walls, which may be impermeable to one or more of the C′ components. Alternatively, the distance of the cell membrane from the activated C′ might be involved. The surface antigens of the cell, which constitute the locus of the antigen-antibody complexes that activate C′, may simply be too far removed from the susceptible membrane. The greater thickness of the cell wall of Gram-positive species compared to Gram-negative species may be significant. The wall of various Gram-positive species has a thickness of 150–800 Å, whereas the protoplasts of these organisms may have a thickness of only about 75 Å and the multilayered wall of Gram-negative organisms a thickness of 60–80 Å.[21] Since inhibition of the synthesis of cell wall mucopeptide by penicillin or the enzymatic breakdown of this material by lysozyme results in the conversion of C′ resistant to C′ sensitive cells, it seems likely that, in both Gram-positive and in Gram-negative C′ resistant bacteria, cell wall structures constitute the barrier to the action of C′. That the protoplasts or spheroplasts of both Gram-positive and Gram-negative bacteria are susceptible to C′ is in accord with this suggestion.

Finally, the role of the C′ system in the host's defense against microbial agents may be considered. Organisms such as *S. typhosa*, *Brucella* species, *Treponema pallidum*, and others may be destroyed by the immune bactericidal reaction. Specific immunity to typhoid fever probably depends on the presence of antibodies, but whether these act mainly by opsonization or by sensitization of the organism to the action of C′ is still doubtful. It is con-

ceivable that the action of the C′ system does not invariably result in a bactericidal effect, and that body fluids may provide protective substances that behave like Mg^{++} *in vitro*. The paradox of continued infection in diseases such as brucellosis or typhoid fever despite the presence of high levels of bactericidal antibody has been attributed generally to the intracellular growth of the microbes. An additional factor in the survival of these organisms may be related to the fact that the C′ system may result in bacteriostasis. Of course, some very effective antibiotics are bacteriostatic in their action, so that these considerations need not contradict the possible contribution of the C′ system to host defense mechanisms. On the other hand, it may help to explain certain stubborn infections with microbial persistence.

SUMMARY

Lysis of Gram-negative bacteria by serum, or their conversion to spheroplasts in a protective milieu, is dependent upon the bactericidal reaction mediated by the C′ system, plus the action of serum lysozyme. By analogy with mammalian cells lacking a cell wall, one may postulate that C′ provides the enzymatic attack that damages the membrane of a sensitive bacterium. Such a cell is capable of maintaining its structural integrity, but subsequent attack on the mucocomplex of its cell wall by lysozyme results in lysis or spheroplast formation. Moreover, organisms relatively sensitive to C′ tend to be sensitive to lysozyme.

Experimental results have indicated also that the resistance of Gram-positive bacteria to the C′ system is associated with their cell walls. Enzymatic removal of the cell wall of *Bacillus subtilis* by lysozyme resulted in the conversion of the cells of that organism to protoplasts that are susceptible to C′. Similarly, penicillin spheroplasts of C′ resistant Gram-negative organisms are as sensitive to C′ action as spheroplasts derived from C′ sensitive Gram-negative bacteria. It seems likely, therefore, that cell wall structures consti-

* Unpublished.

tute the barrier to the bactericidal action
of C'.

REFERENCES

1. Amano, T., Inai, S., Seki, Y., Kashiba, S.,
   Fujikawa, K., and Nishimura, S.: Studies on
   the immune bacteriolysis. I. Accelerating
   effect on the immune bacteriolysis by lysozyme-like substance of leucocytes and egg
   white lysozyme. *Med. J. Osaka Univ.* **4:**
   401, 1954.
2. Bauman, N., and Davis, B. D.: Selection of
   auxotrophic bacterial mutants through diaminopimelic acid or thymine deprival. *Science* **126:** 170, 1957.
3. Bladen, H. A., Evans, R. T., and Mergenhagen,
   S. E.: Lesions in *Escherichia coli* membranes after action of antibody and complement. *J. Bact.* **91:** 2377, 1966.
4. Borsos, T., Dourmashkin, R. R., and Hum-
   phrey, J. H.: Lesions in erythrocyte membranes caused by immune haemolysis. *Nature* **202:** 251, 1964.
5. Brenner, S., Dark, F. A., Gerhardt, P., Jeynes,
   M. H., Kandler, O., Kellenberger, E.,
   Klieneberger-Nobel, E., McQuillen, K.,
   Rubio-Huertos, M., Salton, M. R. J.,
   Strange, R. E., Tomcsik, J., and Weibull, C.:
   Bacterial protoplasts. *Nature* **181:** 1713,
   1958.
6. Carey, W. F., Muschel, L. H., and Baron,
   L. S.: The formation of bacterial protoplasts
   in vivo. J. Immun. **84:** 183, 1960.
7. Crombie, L. B.: *Quantitative Studies on
   Spheroplast Formation by the Antibody
   Complement System and Lysozyme on
   Gram-Negative Bacteria.* M.S. Thesis, Univ.
   of Minnesota, Minneapolis, 1966.
8. Crombie, L. B., and Muschel, L. H.: Quantitative studies on spheroplast formation by
   the antibody complement system and lysozyme on Gram negative bacteria. *Fed. Proc.*
   24: 447, 1965.
9. Davis, S. D., Gemsa, D., and Wedgwood, R. J.:
   Kinetics of the transformation of Gram-
   negative rods to spheroplasts and ghosts by
   serum. *J. Immun.* **96:** 570, 1966.
10. Freeman, B. A., Musteikis, G. M., and Bur-
    rows, W.: Protoplast formation as the
    mechanism for immune lysis of *Vibrio
    cholerae. Proc. Soc. Exp. Biol. Med.* **113:**
    675, 1963.
11. Inoue, K., Tanigawa, Y., Takubo, M., Satani,
    M., and Amano, T.: Quantitative studies on
    immune bacteriolysis. II. The role of lyso-
    zyme in immune bacteriolysis. *Biken's J.*
    2: 1, 1959.
12. Lederberg, J.: Bacterial protoplasts induced
    by penicillin. *Proc. Nat. Acad. Sci. USA*
    42: 574, 1957.
13. Mayer, M. M.: Immunochemistry. *Ann. Rev.
    Biochem.*, **20:** 415, 1951.
14. Muschel, L. H.: Immune bactericidal and
    bacteriolytic reactions. In: *Ciba Foundation
    Symposium on Complement* (G. E. W.
    Wolstenholme and J. Knight, Eds.). Church-
    ill, London, 1965: p. 153.
15. Muschel, L. H., Carey, W. F., and Baron, L. S.:
    Formation of bacterial protoplasts by serum
    components. *J. Immun.* **82:** 38, 1959.
16. Muschel, L. H., Chamberlin, R. H., and Osawa,
    E.: Bactericidal activity of normal serum
    against bacterial cultures. I. The activity
    against *Salmonella typhi* strains. *Proc. Soc.
    Exp. Biol. Med.* **97:** 376, 1958.
17. Muschel, L. H., and Jackson, J. E.: Reversal
    of the bactericidal reaction of serum by
    magnesium ion. *J. Bact.* **91:** 1399, 1966.
18. ———: The reactivity of serum against proto-
    plasts and spheroplasts. *J. Immun.* **97:** 46,
    1966.
19. Muschel, L. H., and Treffers, H. P.: Quanti-
    tative studies on the bactericidal actions of
    serum and complement. I. A rapid photo-
    metric growth assay for bactericidal activity.
    J. Immun. **76:** 1, 1956.
20. Osawa, E., and Muschel, L.: Studies relating
    to the serum resistance of certain Gram-
    negative bacteria. *J. Exp. Med.* **119:** 41,
    1964.
21. Salton, M. R. J.: *The Bacterial Cell Wall.*
    Elsevier, Amsterdam, 1964.
22. Spitznagel, J. K., and Wilson, L. A.: Normal
    serum cytotoxicity for P^{32}-labeled smooth
    Enterobacteriaceae. I. Loss of label, death,
    and ultrastructural damage. *J. Bact.* **91:**
    393, 1966.
23. Strange, R. E.: Effect of magnesium on per-
    meability control in chilled bacteria. *Nature*
    203: 1304, 1964.
24. Tomcsik, J., and Guex-Holzer, S.: Änderung
    der Struktur der Bakterienzelle im Verlauf
    der Lysozym-Einwirkung. *Schweiz. Z. allg.
    Path.* **15:** 517, 1952.
25. Warren, G. H., Gray, J., and Yurchenko, J. A.:
    Effect of polymyxin on the lysis of *Neisseria
    catarrhalis* by lysozyme. *J. Bact.* **74:** 788,
    1957.
26. Weibull, C.: The isolation of protoplasts from

Bacillus megaterium by controlled treatment with lysozyme. *J. Bact.* **66**: 688, 1953.

27. ———: The nature of the "ghosts" obtained by lysozyme lysis of *Bacillus megaterium*. *Exp. Cell Res.* **10**: 214, 1956.

28. Yachnin, S. Functions and mechanism of action of complement. *New Eng. J. Med.* **274**: 140, 1965.

29. Zinder, N., and Arndt, W. P.: Production of protoplasts of *Escherichia coli* by lysozyme treatment. *Proc. Nat. Acad. Sci. USA* **42**: 586, 1956.

3

The Formation of Spheroplasts by Leucozyme C, and the Destruction of Protoplasts by Phospholipase A

Tsunehisa Amano

THE RESEARCH INSTITUTE FOR MICROBIAL DISEASES

OSAKA UNIVERSITY

OSAKA, JAPAN

After Weidel and coworkers[17] found that the rigidity of bacterial cell walls was maintained exclusively by mucopeptide, which is the substrate of lysozyme, analytical studies were made of the possible participation of lysozyme in the spheroplasting activity of leucozyme C from guinea pig leucocytes on *Escherichia coli* B. The term *spheroplasts* as used here means osmotically labile, spherical cells still retaining somatic O antigen.[12]

Studies on plakin (anthracidal substance from blood platelets)[6] and on megacin A,[14] made it clear that the active substance of both plakin and megacin A was phospholipase A. Since heated Habu venom (HHV) contains phospholipase A[15] but no other phospholipases, comparative studies on these three phospholipase A's were performed on protoplast lysis of *Bacillus megaterium* KM. In addition, the effects of phospholipases C and D were also studied. These studies led us to examine whether the partial immunity of *B. megaterium* 216 M[+] to self-produced megacin A is retained in the protoplasts. The term *protoplast* is used here for the spherical body of strain KM because it is well known to be devoid of cell wall components. "Protoplast" is also used for strain 216, for which no analyses of surface components have been made.

MATERIALS AND METHODS

Bacterial Stains

E. coli B was grown at 37°C in Y-medium[1] with mechanical shaking, and harvested at the logarithmic growth phase.

B. megaterium strains KM, 216 M[+], 216 M[−] No.1 and No.2 were used to prepare protoplasts according to the method of Weibull.[16] Strain 216 M[+] is a producer of megacin A; 216 M[−] No.1 and No.2 are cured mutants.[14] All strains were grown in C-medium.[5] To wash the protoplasts by centrifugation, 50% sucrose containing Mg^{++} was placed at the bottom of the tube.

Preparation of Crude Leucozyme C and Lysozyme-Free Leucozyme C (LEC)

Leucocytes from guinea pig peritoneal exudate were washed with saline and then with distilled water and lyophilized. The powdered cells were homogenized (cold) in M/15 phosphate buffer (pH 7.5; 20 mg/ml) in a glass Potter-Elvejhem homogenizer. The homogenate was centrifuged for 15 minutes at 8700 G, and the resulting supernatant was used as crude leucozyme C. It was again centrifuged for one hour at 100,000 G. The pellets were resuspended in distilled water (20 ml per 1.0 g of starting lyophilized cells) by sonication, and kept in a bath at 0°C as LEC.

Assay System for LEC Activity

To 2.0 ml of the suspension (OD_{550} = 1.0) of washed *E. coli* B were added 1.5 ml of 50% sucrose, 0.5 ml of 100 μg/ml lysozyme and 0.5 ml of LEC. The total volume was adjusted to 7.0 ml by adding M/15 phosphate buffer or M/20 tris buffer, pH 7.5. The mixture was incubated at 37°C for 30 minutes unless otherwise stated. After incubation, three drops of 10% sodium deoxycholate were added to lyze the spheroplasts which had formed, and the difference in the optical density values (ΔOD) before and after deoxycholate treatment was taken as representing the amount of spheroplasts formed.

Preparation of Subcellular Fractions of Leucocytes

The subcellular fractions were obtained according to the method of Cohn & Hirsch.[3]

Phospholipase A Preparations

Plakin was prepared from the saline extract of horse blood platelets and purified as described by Higashi et al.[5] The anthracidal substance (= plakin) is assumed to be a phospholipase A.[6]

Habu (*Trimeresurus flavoviridis*) venom solution, 10 mg/ml, was heated at 100°C for 10 minutes at pH 5.0 and then neutralized (HHV). HHV contains only phospholipase A, as described by Wakui & Kawachi.[15]

Megacin A was prepared and purified as described by Ivánovics and coworkers[8, 9] and by Holland.[7] The preparation was further purified to give a single precipitation line on an Ouchterlony plate against the antisera to crude megacin A, and

megacin A was proved to be a phospholipase A.[14]

Estimation of Protoplast Lysis

To tubes containing 5.0 ml of protoplast suspension in 15% sucrose solution, a mixture of 0.3 ml of 50% sucrose solution, 0.2 ml of M/15 phosphate buffer (pH 7.4) and 0.5 ml of phospholipase A preparation was added. The tubes were incubated at 30°C with mixing by inversion at 10-minute intervals and, after mixing, the optical densities were read at 550 mμ in a Coleman universal spectrophotometer.

Phosphatidyl-Ethanolamine from the Ghost Membranes of B. megaterium

Phosphatidyl-ethanolamine (PE) was extracted from ghosts of *B. megaterium* with chloroform-methanol (1:2) and chromatographed on a thin layer of silica gel G with phenol - water - acetic acid - ethanol (8:2:1:1).

Miscellaneous Estimations

Phosphate was determined according to the method of Fiske & Subbarow,[4] and fatty acids were analyzed in a Hitachi-Perkin-Elmer gas chromatograph, model F6.

Chemicals

All the reagents used were of analytical reagent grade. Crystalline lysozyme was supplied by Dr. S. Shinka of our laboratory. Habu (*Trimeresurus flavoviridis*) venom was given by Dr. T. Kubo of our institute. Trypsin was a product from Mochida Pharmaceutical Co., Ltd. (Tokyo, Japan). Pronase was from Kaken Kagaku Kogyo (Tokyo, Japan). Adenosine triphosphate (ATP) was from Schwarz Bioresearch Inc. (New York). Adenosine mono- and diphosphate (AMP, ADP), cytidine, guanosine, and uridine triphosphates (CTP, GTP, UTP) and phospholipases C and D were obtained from Sigma Chemical Company (St Louis, Mo.). Egg yolk lecithin was obtained from Sumitomo Chemicals Co. (Osaka, Japan).

RESULTS

SPHEROPLAST FORMATION BY LEUCOZYME C

Indispensability of Lysozyme for the Activity of Leucozyme C

To find out whether the cooperation of lysozyme is indispensable for the spheroplasting activity of leucozyme C, studies were made to remove lysozyme completely from the crude leucozyme C preparation using gel filtration. The first protein peak contained a very weak spheroplasting activity and an almost undetectable lysozyme activity. The peak of lysozyme activity was found between the first and second peaks of the absorbency at 280 mμ. The pooled first peak components were again filtered through another column. Only the first peak was seen at the end of the void volume of the column and it was completely devoid of spheroplasting activity (Figure 3.1). It was centrifuged at 100,000 G for one hour and the precipitate was resuspended in distilled water by sonication. The suspension (LEC) was found to give stable spheroplasts only upon addition of lysozyme.

To study the effect of LEC plus lyso-

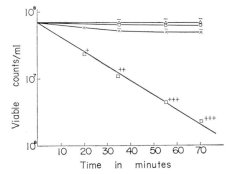

Figure 3.2. Effect of lysozyme on spheroplast formation by LEC. *Squares:* complete reaction mixture: 0.1 ml LEC, 0.1 ml lysozyme (100 μg/ml), 0.4 ml sucrose (50%), 0.2 ml *Escherichia coli* B (5 × 10^8/ml), 1.2 ml phosphate buffer (0.1 M). *Circles:* no lysozyme. *X:* no LEC. *Triangles:* no lysozyme or LEC in reaction system. Aliquots taken at intervals were examined for spheroplasts under a phase contrast microscope, and for viable counts by plating after destroying the spheroplasts by dilution with buffer. −: No spheroplast formation; +: about 33% of the bacteria converted to spheroplasts; ++: about 75% of bacteria converted to spheroplasts; +++: more than 90% of bacteria converted to spheroplasts.

zyme, viable counts were made by plating samples after destroying the spheroplasts formed with the buffer used as a diluent. The cells of *E. coli* B were converted to osmotically labile spheroplasts by LEC activity in cooperation with lysozyme (Figure 3.2).

Activation of LEC Activity by ATP and ADP

The enhancing effects of ADP, ATP and other triphosphates were found by chance. ATP, GTP, UTP and CTP could enhance LEC activity; ADP also did so to a lesser degree (Table 3.1). On the other hand, AMP had no activitating effect. As the purity of ADP was more than 97 per cent, the effect of ADP cannot be regarded as due to contamination of the sample with ATP. The effect of ATP and lysozyme without LEC was examined in the control, and no spheroplasts were formed.

These results led us to estimate ATPase activity of the LEC preparation following the method of Kielley.[10] The assay sys-

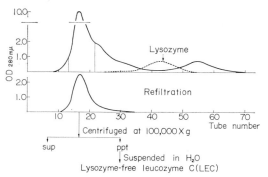

Figure 3.1. Gel filtration of leucozyme C preparation. Fifteen ml of leucozyme C preparation were passed through a Sephadex G-75 column (4 × 25 cm), equilibrated with 0.05 M phosphate buffer (pH 7.0). Fractions in the first OD$_{280}$ peak were pooled and passed through another Sephadex column. Fractions from the peak of the second column were pooled and centrifuged. The sedimented pellet was resuspended in 5 ml of distilled water by sonication (LEC).

tem consisted of LEC (0.5 ml), M/10 tris-buffer (0.5 ml), M/10 KCl (0.2 ml), M/100 $MgCl_2$ (0.1 ml), H_2O (0.5 ml) and M/100 ATP (0.2 ml). After incubation, 2 ml of 5% perchloric acid were added and the mixture was centrifuged. Inorganic P in the supernatant was determined. After 30 minutes of incubation only 14 per cent of the added ATP was hydrolyzed. When the amount of ATP used for the activation of LEC activity is considered, this result indicates that the activation effect of ATP cannot be explained by ATPase activity.

Effects of Metallic Ions on LEC Activity

Since lysozyme was indispensable for spheroplasting by LEC, LEC could be suspected to remove some metallic ions from the cell walls and to render them susceptible to lysozyme. If this were the case, some metallic ions added extraneously would inhibit LEC activity. To test this, varying concentrations of $CaCl_2$, $MgCl_2$, $CoSO_4$, $CdSO_4$, $FeSO_4$ and $FeCl_3$ were added to the system for assay of LEC activity. In this experiment M/20 tris-buffer at pH 7.5 was used. Fe^{+++} exerted the strongest inhibition (Figure 3.3); the inhibitory effect of the other ions were in the order: $Cd^{++} > Fe^{++} > Ca^{++} = Co^{++} > Mg^{++}$.

The preparation of LEC was preincubated with $CaCl_2$ at a final concentration of M/3000 and then the mixture was added to the assay system, in which the Ca^{++} concentration was lowered to M/21,000. If the LEC preparation plus lysozyme was directly incubated with bacterial

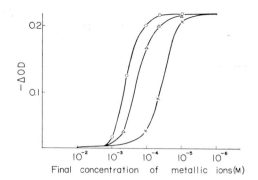

Figure 3.3. Inhibitory effects of metallic ions on spheroplast formation by LEC: Mg^{++} (circles); Ca^{++} (triangles); Fe^{+++} (X).

suspension in the presence of M/21,000 of Ca^{++} at the start, no inhibitory effect was shown by Ca^{++}. In this two-step incubation experiment, however, LEC activity was inhibited by Ca^{++}, and ATP could reactivate the inhibited LEC activity when it was added to the system at the second step (M/500 in final concentration). The same phenomenon was found in the case of Mg^{++}, and Fe^{+++} could inhibit LEC activity under the same conditions. However, ATP reactivated Fe^{+++}-inhibited LEC activity to a slight degree (Table 3.2). From these results it can be assumed that the inhibitory metallic cations can have some interaction with active particles of LEC and that Ca^{++} and Mg^{++} can be chelated by ATP, ADP and other triphosphates to give reactivated LEC.

In the next experiment, the effects of adding Fe^{+++} or Ca^{++} to the assay system during the action of LEC plus lysozyme were examined. The addition of Ca^{++} (M/3000 in final concentration) instantaneously inhibited the activity of LEC and no further increase of the spheroplasted cells was detected (Figure 3.4), whereas Fe^{+++} (M/5000 or M/10,000 in final concentration), the most powerful inhibitor in the above experiment, did not greatly inhibit the activity of LEC, and once the spheroplasting process started, it proceeded even after the addition of Fe^{+++} (Figure 3.4).

To see whether LEC particles were

TABLE 3.1

Activating Effect of ADP, ATP and other Nucleoside Triphosphates on LEC Activity

Nucleotide	Concentration	Activity ($-\Delta$ OD)
ATP	M/800	0.20
GTP	M/800	0.18
CTP	M/800	0.17
UTP	M/800	0.20
ADP	M/500	0.17
AMP	M/500	0.10
—	—	0.10

TABLE 3.2

Inactivation of LEC Activity by Preincubation with Metallic Ions and Reactivation by ATP

	First step						Second step*		
LEC *ml*	M/20 Tris buffer *ml*	CaCl₂ M/300 *ml*	MgCl₂ M/100 *ml*	FeCl₃ M/600 *ml*	Distilled water *ml*		ATP M/50 *ml*	Distilled water *ml*	Activity (−Δ OD)
0.5	0.2	0.1	—	—	0.2	Incubation, 37°C, 15 min	—	0.7	0.06
0.5	0.2	0.1	—	—	0.2		0.7	—	0.23
0.5	0.2	—	—	—	0.3		—	0.7	0.25
0.4	0.2	—	0.1	—	0.3		—	0.7	0.03
0.4	0.2	—	0.1	—	0.3		0.7	—	0.18
0.4	0.2	—	—	0.1	0.3		—	0.7	0.05
0.4	0.2	—	—	0.1	0.3		0.7	—	0.14
0.4	0.2	—	—	—	0.4		—	0.7	0.21.

* At the second step, total volume was adjusted to 7.0 ml.

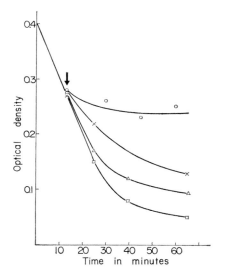

Figure 3.4. Effect of metallic ions on the protoplasting reaction by LEC plus lysozyme. The arrow indicates the time at which the ions were added. *Circles:* M/3000 Ca⁺⁺; *X:* M/5000 Fe⁺⁺⁺, *triangles:* M/10,000 Fe⁺⁺⁺; *squares:* no ion added.

freed from bacterial surfaces by the addition of Ca⁺⁺, the following experiments were performed. A preparation containing Ca⁺⁺, similar to that in the previous experiment, was left standing for 15 minutes and was centrifuged when no further increase of the spheroplasted cells could be detected. The supernatant was dialyzed and tested for LEC activity; no activity was found. A similar experiment was performed with cell walls of *E. coli* B. After incubation of LEC with the cell walls, Ca⁺⁺ was added, the tube was again incubated for 15 minutes, centrifuged, and the supernatant was dialyzed; no LEC activity was found in the dialyzed solution. Even M/400 EDTA could not liberate LEC particles into the medium.

No active uptake of Fe⁺⁺⁺ or Ca⁺⁺ by LEC could be found.

Physicochemical Properties of LEC

A suspension of LEC in distilled water was quite stable, and 80 per cent of the activity was retained even after heating at 100°C for 15 minutes, and at 0°C the full activity could be retained for ten days. The suspension was quite unstable in a solution of any electrolyte. The activity of LEC was not lost even after treatment with 8 M urea. It was destroyed by a proteolytic enzyme, trypsin or pronase, and by phospholipase A in HHV. DNase and RNase, however, did not affect it. The LEC-inactivating and phospholipase A activities of HHV were inactivated by heating at 100°C for 30 minutes at pH 11. These results suggest that the active particle consists of lipoprotein(s).

Distribution of LEC in Subcellular Fractions

Guinea pig leucocytes were fractionated according to the method of Cohn & Hirsch.[3] The LEC activity was found in both the microsomal and nuclear fractions, but not in the granular, mitochondrial or lysosomal fractions. The activity found in the nuclear fraction is chiefly due to the adsorption of microsomes on the nuclear body, for refractionation of the nuclear fraction resulted in the shift of most of its activity into the microsomal fraction.

The microsomal fractions of other organs of the guinea pig, such as the liver, spleen and lung, were examined, but only very weak activity was found in the lung and none in the other tissues. Ehrlich ascitic tumor cells were also examined with negative results.

LYSIS OF PROTOPLASTS OF *B. MEGATERIUM* BY PHOSPHOLIPASE A

Protoplast lysis by Megacin A

Lag periods were observed before the turbidity began to decrease; at low concentrations of megacin A, the duration of the lag period was roughly inversely proportional to the amount of megacin A added. The turbidity decreased immediately after the addition of large amounts of megacin A, however (Figure 3.5). Unlike the case with hemolysis, addition of phospholipid to the reaction mixture was unnecessary for the protoplast lysis, even when washed protoplasts were used. On the other and, the protoplasts were destroyed by neither phospholipase C from *Clostridium perfringens* even in the pres-

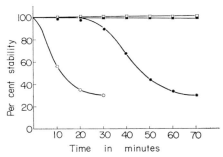

Figure 3.6. "Oxygen effect" on protoplasts with megacin A. *White circles:* 1500 units/ml, aerobic; *white squares:* no megacin, aerobic; *black circles:* 1500 units/ml, anaerobic; *black squares:* no megacin, anaerobic.

ence of added egg yolk lecithin, nor by phospholipase D from cabbage.

When tubes containing the protoplast suspension in a sucrose medium with added megacin A were left unmixed at 30°C, the turbidity of the suspension decreased more markedly at the top than at the bottom of the tube. Conversely, when the experiment was performed in a Thunberg tube under anaerobic conditions, the turbidity began to decrease evenly throughout the tube, and the lag period was much longer than that of an aerobic experiment with the mixture of the same composition (the oxygen effect), where the tube contents were mixed by inversion at ten-minute intervals (Figure 3.6).

Moreover, when azide (2×10^{-3} M), HCN (10^{-3} M) or CO was added to tubes under aerobic conditions with a constant amount of megacin A, the same prolonged lag periods were observed as in the anaerobic condition.

We have also demonstrated that both partially purified plakin and HHV bring about protoplast lysis in the same manner as megacin A. Both show a similar concentration-lag period relationship and also an oxygen effect.

Fatty Acid Analyses by Phospholipase A

Nine mg of PE, prepared from *B. megaterium* KM, emulsified in 5.0 ml of M/10 borate buffer, pH 8.0, were incubated at 37°C for two hours with 5.0 ml of HHV. After adding 37.5 ml of chloroform-meth-

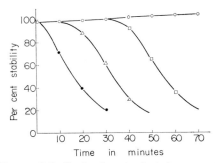

Figure 3.5. Lysis of protoplasts by megacin A. *Black circles:* 400 units/ml (final concentration); *triangles:* 200 units; *squares:* 100 units; *white circles:* no megacin A added. Optical densities were measured with a Coleman universal spectrophotometer.

anol (1:2), the mixture was centrifuged. The supernatant was dried *in vacuo*, and applied to a column of silicic acid (Merck: 8 g) and chromatographed first with ether and then with methanol. The ether fraction (1.7 mg), containing free fatty acids, and the methanol fraction (7.2 mg), containing lyso-PE, were separated. Fatty acids liberated from PE by HHV were mainly shorter than C_{15} acids, while those of lysoderivatives were mostly longer than C_{14} acids (Figure 3.7). Similar results were also obtained with phospholipase A of partially purified plakin (Figure 3.8).

Lysis of Protoplasts of Sensitive and partially Immune Strains of B. megaterium by Megacin A

Since the strain 216 M^+ is partially immune to self-produced megacin A, the difference in susceptibilities to lysis by megacin A was examined for protoplasts of the parent and M^- mutants. With intact cells, the M^- mutants, No.1 and No.2, are both 50 times more sensitive to the killing action of megacin A than the parent. The sensitivities of protoplasts of M^- to the lytic activity of megacin A were about 30 times higher than those of M^+ (Figure 3.9). Thus the differences in sensitivities of the protoplasts to the lytic action of megacin A were comparable to those of the intact cells. Trypsin could not enhance the lytic

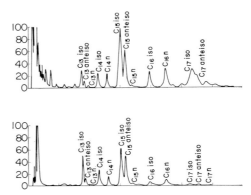

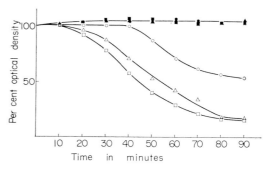

Figure 3.8. Gas chromatograms of fatty acids of membrane PE from *Bacillus megaterium* (*above*), and of those liberated from PE by plakin (*below*).

Figure 3.9. Lysis of protoplasts M^+ and M^- No. 1 and No. 2 by megacin A. *Upper curve* (black symbols): strains 216 M^+ (circles), 216 M^- No. 1 (squares) and 216 M^- No. 2 (triangles) without megacin A. The three *lower curves* (white symbols) show the effects of the amounts of megacin A indicated (in final concentration): strain 216 M^+ (circles) with 2000 units/ml; strain 216 M^- No. 1 with 200 units/ml (squares); strain 216 M^- No. 2 with 200 units/ml (triangles).

action of megacin A when both were added together to protoplasts of M^+.

The sensitivities of protoplasts derived from the three strains to the lytic action of HHV were about the same, however (Figure 3.10). From these results, the immunity is very specific for the self-produced phospholipase A.

DISCUSSION

As shown in Results, the spheroplasting activity of leucozyme C can be dis-

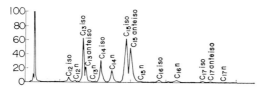

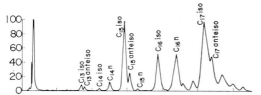

Figure 3.7. Gas chromatograms of fatty acids liberated from PE by phospholipase A of HHV (*above*) and of those found in the mixture of resulting lyso-PE and remaining PE (*below*).

tinguished as a two step reaction, (1) adsorption of active particles onto the surfaces of the sensitive organisms and removal of divalent cations from the surfaces of the bacteria, and (2) hydrolysis of mucopeptide by lysozyme contained in the leucozyme C preparation. It was difficult, however, to elucidate the mechanism by which the action of LEC occurred prior to that of lysozyme.

The keys to this problem were the inhibition by metallic cations and the activation by ADP, ATP and other nucleoside triphosphates. From these findings it was suspected that the active concentration of metallic cations by LEC particles was essential for LEC activity; this possibility was disproved by the very weak ATPase activity detected in the LEC preparation and negative results in active uptake of Fe^{+++} or Ca^{++}. The chief findings, which led us to assume that the binding of metallic cations is essential for LEC activity, were as follows: (1) LEC activity was inhibited by preincubation with a certain concentration of Ca^{++}, (2) the same amount of Ca^{++} did not inhibit the activity when directly added to the assay system, (3) when LEC activity was inhibited by preincubation with Ca^{++}, it could be reactivated by addition of ATP, and (4) no further increase of spheroplasts was observed after Ca^{++} was added during the action of LEC plus lysozyme. These findings led us to understand that the LEC particles chelate Ca^{++} and other cations from the bacterial surface and hence render the cell walls lysozyme sensitive.

The stability of the LEC preparation on boiling at 100°C for 15 minutes and its resistance to 8 M urea were unexpected results and forced us to reject the idea that the LEC activity was enzymatic. The LEC activity can be understood as a simple physicochemical reaction, namely chelation. The fact that the LEC activity can be destroyed by trypsin or phospholipase A suggests this agent to be a macromolecular complex.

The present studies also demonstrated that the LEC activity was localized in

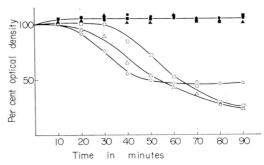

Figure 3.10. Lysis of protoplasts of M⁺ (circles) and M⁻ No. 1 (squares) and No. 2 (triangles) by 1:2000 HHV. *Upper curve* (black symbols): all three strains without HHV. *Lower curves* (white symbols): the respective strains with HHV.

the microsomal fraction of the leucocytes. The microsomes are derived from the cell membranes (including nuclear membranes) and endoplasmic reticula. Since endoplasmic reticula are not well developed in leucocytes, the microsomes of leucocytes can be assumed to be derived mainly from cell membranes and nuclear membranes.

As shown in Results, the relationship observed between the lag period and the dilution of phospholipase A added was an interesting phenomenon; a similar lag period was not obtained in the case of protoplast lysis by lipase or deoxycholate. The duration of the lag period was roughly inversely proportional to the amount of added phospholipase A, but the lysis proceeded at the same rate irrespective of the amount of enzyme. It seems reasonable to assume that lysophospholipids and free fatty acids are formed near to and on the surface of the protoplasts until their amount reaches a critical level, where the lysis of protoplasts can start. Lysophospholipids are highly active in the lysis of protoplasts as well as of erythrocytes.

Sheep red cells and protoplasts of *B. megaterium* KM behaved in ways quite dissimilar with respect to the phospholipases. Phospholipase A can lyze the protoplasts without added phospholipids, while it requires the addition of phospholipids to lyze red cells. Phospholipase C can directly lyze the red cells without extraneous phospholipids, whereas it cannot lyze the protoplasts even in the presence of added egg yolk lecithin. Phospholipase C from *C. perfringens* has been shown to hydrolyze PE only in the presence of lecithin.[2] As the protoplast membranes of *B. megaterium* KM contain PE but not lecithin,[6, 13] phospholipase C should have lyzed the protoplasts in the presence of egg yolk lecithin. However, this was not the case. These differences in sensitivities of the red cells and the protoplasts indicate the differences in their membrane structures.

Phospholipase D showed no effect on either the red cells or the protoplasts.

The "oxygen effect" observed during protoplast lysis is a phenomenon peculiar to phospholipase A. It seems improbable that the phospholipase activity itself is higher in aerobic than in anaerobic conditions. In addition, in the experiment using a cytochrome inhibitor, azide, HCN, or CO, there was also a very marked lag period even under aerobic conditions. On the other hand, Lehninger & Ray[11] found that the mitochondria from animal cells swelled under aerobic conditions and shrunk under anaerobic conditions even in a cell-free suspension. If the protoplasts also swell under aerobic conditions, it is conceivable that the susceptible sites become more exposed to the enzyme.

Immunity in bacteriocinogenic strains is a very interesting phenomenon. The results of this study showed that the partial immunity of the strain 216 M^+ is retained in protoplasts and that it is very specific to self-produced phospholipase A, for the three protoplasts of M^+, M^- No.1 and No.2, showed the same sensitivity to phospholipase A of HHV. In regard to the specificity of phospholipase A, there are two possible explanations: (1) these two enzymes differ in substrate specificity, (2) the structures of protoplast membranes of M^+ and M^- are different with respect to their accessibility to these enzymes. In this respect, the enhancing effect of trypsin on the lytic activity of megacin A, resistant to trypsin,[7] was studied, but no enhancement was observed. Further studies on a substrate level are in progress.

SUMMARY

The spheroplasting activity on *Escherichia coli* B of leucozyme C from guinea pig leucocytes was shown to consist of two components: the microsomal fraction of leucocytes (LEC) and lysozyme.

Metallic ions inhibited the activity, and ADP, ATP and other nucleoside triphosphates activated the reaction. The possible mechanism of the activity is understood as a metallic ion chelation by LEC and to the enzymic hydrolysis of mucopeptide by lysozyme. LEC was destroyed by digestion with trypsin or phospholipase A.

The protoplasts of *Bacillus megaterium* KM were lyzed by phospholipase A (megacin A, HHV and plakin). Characteristic phenomena were observed, namely lag periods before lysis and oxygen effect. The fatty acids liberated from membrane PE were of shorter carbon chains than those bound to lyso-PE.

The partial immunity of *B. megaterium* 216 M^+ to self-produced megacin A was still retained in the protoplasts, and it is very specific for self-produced phospholipase A.

REFERENCES

1. Amano, T., Inoue, K., Tanigawa, Y., Morioka, T., and Utsumi, S.: Studies on the immune bacteriolysis. XII. Properties of coccoidi-form bacteria produced by immune bacteriolysis. *Med. J. Osaka Univ.* **7**: 819, 1957.

2. Bangham, A. D., and Dawson, R. M. C.: Electrokinetic requirements for the reaction between *Cl. perfringens* α-toxin (phospholipase C) and phospholipid substrates. *Biochim. Biophys. Acta* **59**: 103, 1962.

3. Cohn, Z. A., and Hirsch, J. G.: The isolation and properties of the specific cytoplasmic granules of rabbit polymorphonuclear leucocytes. *J. Exp. Med.* **112**: 983, 1960.

4. Fiske, C. H., and Subbarow, Y. The colorimetric determination of phosphorus. *J. Biol. Chem.* **66**: 375, 1925.

5. Higashi, Y., Kurimura, T., Kuwahara, O., Ozaki, M., and Amano, T.: Studies on the role of plakin. X. Effect on membrane phospholipids. *Biken's J.* **6**: 111, 1963.

6. Higashi, Y., Saito, H., Yanagase, Y., Yonemasu, K., and Amano, T.: Studies on the role of plakin. XI. Demonstration of phos-

pholipase A in plakin. *Biken's J.* **9**: 249, 1966.

7. Holland, I. B.: The purification and properties of megacin, a bacteriocin from *Bacillus megaterium. Biochem. J.* **78**: 641, 1961.

8. Ivánovics, G., and Alföldi, L.: Bacteriocinogenesis in *Bacillus megaterium. J. Gen. Microbiol.* **16**: 522, 1957.

9. Ivánovics, G., Alföldi, L., and Nagy, E.: Mode of action of megacin. *J. Gen. Microbiol.* **21**: 51, 1959.

10. Kielley, W. W.: Mg-activated muscle ATPase. In: *Method in Enzymology,* Vol. II (S. P. Colowick and N. O. Kaplan, Eds.). Academic Press, New York, 1955: p. 588.

11. Lehninger, A. L., and Ray, B. L.: Oxidation-reduction state of rat liver mitochondria and the action of thyroxine. *Biochim. Biophys. Acta* **26**: 643, 1957.

12. Miyama, A., Ichikawa, S., and Amano, T.: Spheroplasts of colicine K producing *Esch-*

erichia coli K235 prepared by leucozyme C and by lysozyme. *Biken's J.* **2**: 177, 1959.

13. Mizushima, S., Ishida, M., and Kitahara, K.: Chemical composition of the protoplast membrane of *Bacillus megaterium. J. Biochem.* (Japan) **59**: 374, 1966.

14. Ozaki, M., Higashi, Y., Saito, H., An, T., and Amano, T.: Identity of megacin A with phospholipase A. *Biken's J.* **9**: 201, 1966.

15. Wakui, K., and Kawachi, S.: Some observations on the lecithinase of Japanese and Formosan snake venoms. *J. Pharm. Soc. Japan* **79**: 1177, 1959.

16. Weibull, C.: The isolation of protoplasts from *Bacillus megaterium* by controlled treatment with lysozyme. *J. Bact.* **66**: 688, 1953.

17. Weidel, W., Frank, H., and Martin, H. H.: The rigid layer of the cell wall of *Escherichia coli* strain B. *J. Gen. Microbiol.* **22**: 158, 1960.

4

Streptococcal Protoplasts and L-Form Growth Induced by Muralytic Enzymes*

Harry Gooder

UNIVERSITY OF NORTH CAROLINA SCHOOL OF MEDICINE

CHAPEL HILL, NORTH CAROLINA

Weibull[27] demonstrated that the action of lysozyme on *Bacillus megaterium* KM, in a hypertonic environment provided by sucrose or polyethylene glycol, released spherical structures termed protoplasts. The impressive amount of research on the anatomy and functional capabilities of these bodies has been reviewed by McQuillen[23] and also Martin.[20] It is now generally accepted that true protoplasts represent the internal cytoplasmic content of the bacterial cell, surrounded by the cytoplasmic membrane, free of all remnants of the cell wall. The various criteria useful for determining the absence of cell wall were listed by a group of workers in this field (see Brenner et al.[4]).

Klieneberger[14] reported the growth of soft protoplasmic forms from cultures of

* Supported in part by Public Health Service grants AI-04577 and GM-01138 from the National Institutes of Health, and by a contract (No. DR-49-193-MD-2352) from the U.S. Army Medical Research and Development Command under the sponsorship of the Commission on Acute Respiratory Diseases, Armed Forces Epidemiology Board.

The capable technical assistance of Mrs. Elizabeth Dayton is gratefully acknowledged. Appreciation is extended to the investigators who provided the microorganisms used in this study.

Streptobacillus moniliformis. Such growth was separated from the parent bacterial growth, and in pure culture consisted of soft protoplasmic elements without defined morphology. The growth no longer possessed forms recognizable as bacterial cells, nor did it revert to the bacterial growth form. The term L-form was applied to the characteristic colony formed by this growth on solid medium.[17] The use by Dienes[7] of penicillin to induce L-form growth possibly indicated the manner by which the soft protoplasmic forms were derived from bacterial cells, for penicillin was shown to interfere with the biosynthesis of the rigid mucopeptide layer of the bacterial cell wall. (See Park & Strominger[25] and related articles in this volume.) Examination of L-form cultures for the presence of bacterial cell wall constituents revealed that L-forms in general possess either very little or no cell wall mucopeptide material. The characteristic features of L-forms were reviewed by Klieneberger-Nobel.[15]

A common feature of protoplasts and L-forms was therefore the apparent absence of the constituents of the mucopeptide layer which confer rigidity on the bacterial cell. It was therefore of considerable interest to attempt to determine if protoplasts would develop, on suitable growth medium, into L-forms. Weibull[27] reported that the protoplasts of *B. megaterium* appeared to be incapable of forming colonies on solid media. In liquid media such protoplasts increased in size, optical density and dry weight, and some eventually formed a dumbbell shape.[22] The protoplasts did not revert to bacteria or give rise to a new protoplast population. Penicillin-induced protoplasmic bodies,[19] termed spheroplasts by McQuillen,[23] did give rise to L-forms and could revert to the bacterial form. Klieneberger-Nobel[15] therefore concluded that protoplasts and spheroplasts were not identical, in that the former could not give rise to L-forms, whereas the latter could.

Gooder & Maxted[10] prepared protoplasts of group A streptococci by use of a phage-associated muralytic enzyme found in a phage lysate of a group C streptococcus.[16, 21] The active lytic principle in the lysate has been purified by Barkulis and his associates[1] and shown to be an endoacetyl hexosaminidase. The group A streptococcal protoplasts were shown to be devoid of cell wall by chemical and immunochemical techniques, to be osmotically fragile, and to have lost phage receptor sites, so conforming to the criteria of Brenner and others.[4] When group A streptococcal protoplasts were inoculated into suitable media, typical L-forms developed even in the absence from the medium of any known selective or inducing agent for L-form growth. The L-forms grown from the protoplast inoculum, as well as those induced by penicillin, continued to demonstrate enzymic activities characteristic of the parent streptococcus.[8, 11] In many experiments, between 10 and 100 per cent of the colony forming units (cfu) of streptococci present in the original suspension gave rise to protoplasts which in turn developed into L-forms. Quantitation of streptococcal conversion is difficult because of the well-recognized mode of growth of this organism in chains. The advantage of using protoplasts in the induction of L-forms was the very high yield of L-forms obtained.

Freimer and associates[8] reported that the removal of penicillin from their growth medium allowed reversion of the L-forms, but Gooder & Maxted[11] found that the majority of the L-forms were stable immediately upon the development of the initial growth. The colonies were serially transferred through many subcultures without reversion and were ultimately adapted to give growth in liquid medium.

In a similar series of experiments, Landman & Halle[18] showed that protoplasts of *Bacillus subtilis* strain 168 (ind⁻), prepared by the action of lysozyme, grew as L-forms. The protoplasts were devoid of all cell wall when viewed in the electron microscope.[26] Quantitative recovery of the protoplasts as L-forms was reported and defined media for their propagation were developed. This allowed a study of medium constituents which would promote or inhibit the reversion of the protoplasts and L-forms to the bacillary state. The reversion was inhibited by certain D-amino acids, notably D-methionine, but was promoted by a change in the physical characteristics of the medium by the incorporation of gelatin in high concentration.

The known susceptibility of certain group D streptococci to phage lysins[3] and to lysozyme, and the preparation of protoplasts with such a system,[2] prompted an investigation of group D streptococcal protoplasts and their relationships to the parent coccus and derived L-form. The terms protoplast, spheroplast and L-form are used in this article in the sense as defined in the publications cited.

Materials and Methods

Bacterial Strains

Streptococcus faecalis F24 (ATCC 19634) was originally received by Dr. W. R. Straughn from Dr. E. L. Oginsky. Other workers prefer the designation of presumably the same strain, *Streptococcus faecium* F24 (Deibel, Lake & Niven[6]). The organism is a non-hemolytic group D enterococcus and is lysed by lysozyme. *S. faecalis var. liquefaciens* 31 (ATCC 13398) was received from the American Type Culture

Collection. *S. faecalis* E1 and many other strains of group D streptococci which will be alluded to only briefly were received from Mr. W. R. Maxted, Central Public Health Laboratory, Colindale, England. *S. faecalis var. zymogenes* 26C1a (D76) and the lytic phage active on this strain were received from Dr. A. S. Bleiweis.[3] *S. faecalis* GK was obtained from Dr. L. B. Guze.[12]

MURALYTIC ENZYMES

Crystalline egg white lysozyme was purchased from various commercial sources. The group D phage muralysin was prepared and concentrated as described by Bleiweis & Zimmerman.[3]

FORMATION OF PROTOPLASTS OF *S. FAECALIS* F24 AND *S. FAECALIS* GK

Protoplasts were prepared essentially by the method of Bibb & Straughn[2] with the modification of Gooder & King.[9] This method is summarized as follows: 18 hour (37°C) cultures of the appropriate strain grown in trypticase soy broth (Baltimore Biological Laboratory) were harvested by centrifugation and washed three times in distilled water. Mixtures of the washed cells and lysozyme were prepared in solutions of either pH 7.1 tris-chloride buffer (0.01 M) and sucrose (0.6 M) or pH 7.1 tris-chloride buffer (0.01 M) and polyethylene glycol (8%) (Carbowax 4000, Union Carbide Company). The final suspension contained 10^9 cfu streptococci and 200 μg of lysozyme per ml. The resulting mixture was incubated at 37°C for periods up to two hours, depending upon the individual experiment.

That protoplasts were formed was suggested by the following observations: For strain F24 the bodies remaining in suspension after lysozyme treatment (*a*) were osmotically fragile, (*b*) had lost over 90 per cent of the rhamnose normally present in the cell wall of the parent cell, (*c*) had retained over 75 per cent of the deoxyribonucleic acid normally associated with the cell, (*d*) had lost the serologically specific group D antigen thought to be located between the cell wall and membrane, (*e*) had

lost the specific recep tor sites for bacteriophage P13 (Brock[5]), and (*f*) showed no evidence of cell wall attachment when viewed in the electron microscope. For strain GK, only the osmotic fragility and rhamnose loss (over 95 per cent) were investigated.

PROTOPLASTS OF *S. FAECALIS VAR. LIQUEFACIENS* 31

These were prepared as described by Bleiweis & Zimmerman,[3] except that 0.1 M cysteine was added to the lysin preparation. They were not characterized further, since the original workers had demonstrated osmotic fragility, rhamnose release and loss of phage receptor sites.

VIABLE COUNT OF PROTOPLAST SUSPENSIONS

Ten-fold serial dilutions of 0.5 ml samples of the various protoplast suspensions were prepared. The diluent solutions were 0.01 M tris-chloride buffer pH 7.1 containing either 0.6 M sucrose or 8% polyethylene glycol as indicated in the individual experimental systems. Samples (0.05 or 0.1 ml) were removed from the dilution series and spread on the surface of solid growth medium by means of a bent glass spreader. In the majority of experiments the growth medium consisted of either tryptone soy agar (Oxoid) (designated LGA), or tryptone soy broth solidified with gelatin (designated LGG), containing, in addition, 0.5% glucose, 2% Seitz-filtered inactivated (56°C, 30 minutes) horse serum and, as appropriate, either sucrose or salts as osmotic stabilizers. The salts were usually NaCl (0.43 M) or NH_4Cl (0.43 M). Following inoculation the media were incubated for 2–7 days at 37°C if solidified with agar, or at 25°C if solidified with gelatin. The petri dishes were placed in plastic bags to retard drying of the medium. Streptococcal colonies and L-forms were distinguished by appearance. The identity of each colony type was confirmed by staining character using Dienes' stain and by replica plating or transfer to appropriate distinguishing media (blood agar, bile-aesculin agar).

RESULTS

INDUCTION OF L-FORMS OF *S. FAECALIS VAR. LIQUEFACIENS* 31 BY THE GROUP D PHAGE LYSIN

The cells from an 18-hour culture of *S. faecalis var. liquefaciens* 31 were sedimented by centrifugation, washed three times in 0.07 M phosphate buffer pH 7.0, and protoplasts prepared by treatment at 37°C for one hour with group D phage lysin (10%) in the presence of 0.6 M sucrose-0.07 M phosphate buffer pH 7.0 Table 4.1 records the results obtained when appropriate samples were plated on media suitable for growth of both the parent streptococcus and the L-form. In these experiments the growth medium LGA included 0.6 M sucrose as the osmotic stabilizer. In the absence of lysin or of cysteine, which are required for lytic activity, no L-forms developed. Under conditions which allowed protoplast formation, approximately equal numbers of L-forms and streptococcal colonies developed. The absence of any inducing agent in the growth medium is apparent, since no L-forms were seen except when the cells were treated with activated phage lysin. Such L-forms could be transferred by the agar-

TABLE 4.1

Induction of L-Colony Growth of Streptococcus faecalis Var. Liquefaciens 31 By Group D Phage Lysin

Additions to Streptococcal Suspension	Colony Count—cfu/ml	
	Streptococcus	L
None (control)	5 × 10⁸	n.s.
Cysteine (0.1 M)	5 × 10⁸	n.s.
Group D phage lysin	4.5 × 10⁸	n.s.
Group D phage lysin + cysteine (0.1 M)	10⁷	10⁷

n.s.: No L-forms seen from any of the dilutions plated.

Washed cell suspensions of strain No. 31 were treated with group D phage lysin in the presence or absence of cysteine for one hour at 37°C. Appropriate dilutions of samples from each tube were plated on media which allowed L-form and streptococcal colonies to develop (see text).

TABLE 4.2

Induction of L-Forms of Streptococcus faecalis F24 by Lysozyme

Additions to Streptococcal Suspension	Colony Count—cfu/ml	
	Streptococcus	L
Samples diluted in 0.01 M tris pH 7.1–0.6 M sucrose buffer		
None (control)	5 × 10⁹	n.s.
Lysozyme (200 μg/ml)	10⁶	2 × 10⁹
Samples diluted in 0.01 M tris pH 7.1.		
None (control)	5 × 10⁹	n.s.
Lysozyme (200 μg/ml)	5 × 10⁵	n.s.

n.s.: No L-forms seen from any of the dilutions plated.

Washed cell suspensions of strain F24 were treated with lysozyme (200 μg per ml) in 0.01 M tris-HCl buffer pH 7.1–0.6 M sucrose for one hour at 37° C. Appropriate samples were diluted in either 0.01 M tris-HCl buffer-0.6 M sucrose mixtures or in 0.01 M tris-HCl buffer alone. Determination of viable count from the diluted samples was on LGA medium containing 0.43 M NaCl.

block technique and appeared to be stable L-forms, but no systematic investigation was undertaken.

INDUCTION OF L-FORMS OF *S. FAECALIS* F24 BY LYSOZYME

Protoplasts were prepared from strain F24 by the action of lysozyme for one hour in the presence of 0.6 M sucrose as stabilizer. Appropriate dilutions of the protoplasts and control (no lysozyme) suspensions of streptococci were made in 0.01 M tris-HCl buffer pH 7.1 containing 0.6 M sucrose and samples plated on solid LGA medium containing 0.43 M NaCl. Approximately 40 per cent of the streptococcal colony-forming units were recovered as L-forms, while only 0.02 per cent survived as streptococci (Table 4.2). That the L-forms developed from osmotically sensitive protoplasts is apparent from the results of using a diluent in which the osmotic stabilizer, sucrose, was absent; in this case no L-forms were seen. Because

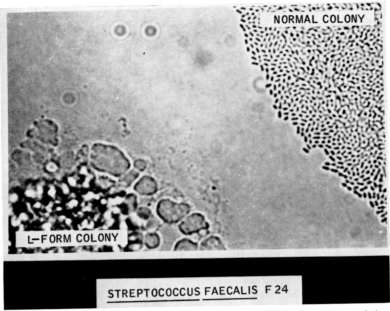

Figure 4.1. Edge of an unstained *Streptococcus faecalis* F24 colony and its L-form, grown from a protoplast suspension. ($\times$ 1280)

the presence of sucrose in the system rendered chemical analysis difficult, King[13] developed a similar system in which protoplasts were prepared and diluted in diluents containing 8% polyethylene glycol (Carbowax 4000). King[13] also investigated several parameters of this system, e.g., the optimal conditions for lysozyme treatment, chemical analysis of the protoplasts formed, and influence of different salts in the diluent and growth medium. These will be reported elsewhere.* The results of this investigation were a standard system in which lysozyme treatment of between 2 and 7 $\times$ 10^9 cfu of streptococci per ml in the presence of 8% polyethylene glycol for two hours at 37°C yielded protoplasts which fulfilled the criteria of Brenner and associates.[4] Cultivation of diluted samples of the protoplasts on LGA medium containing 0.43 M NH$_4$Cl usually yielded around 10 per cent of the original streptococcal count (cfu/ml) as L-forms. On more than 75 different occasions, between 10^7 and 5 $\times$ 10^9 L-form cfu/ml were induced from between 2 and 7 $\times$ 10^9 cfu strepto-

cocci per ml. At the appropriate dilution of the protoplast suspension, only a rare streptococcal colony would develop, surrounded by many L-forms. The two colony forms were easily distinguished without staining, by observation under ordinary light microscopy. Figure 4.1 shows the periphery of a streptococcus F24 colony and an induced L-form.

Other strains of group D streptococci were tested for lysozyme induction of L-form growth. *S. faecalis* (four strains), *S. faecalis var. zymogenes* (one strain), and *S. faecium* (one strain), all gave good yields of L-colonies. One strain of *Streptococcus durans* did not. Only one of these strains was studied extensively, so little can be said regarding the quantitative nature of the induction process. *S. faecalis* E1 was investigated in detail,[13] and it was shown in numerous experiments that, like strain F24, between 10^7 and 10^8 L-form cfu/ml were induced from 2 $\times$ 10^9 streptococcal cfu/ml. In this system protoplasts were not formed. Although the bodies resulting from lysozyme treatment were osmotically sensitive, it was seen by elec-

* J. R. King and H. Gooder, in preparation.

tron microscopy that remnants of cell wall were attached to the outside of the spheroplasts. Release of rhamnose from the streptococcal cell suspension never exceeded 70 per cent of the total present.

These results demonstrate that protoplasts and spheroplasts produced from group D streptococci can develop as L-forms. The remainder of this paper will consider some of the factors which affect the development and stability of the L-forms.

STABILITY OF L-FORMS DERIVED FROM PROTOPLASTS

L-forms of S. faecalis F24 and S. faecalis E1

Stability of L-forms refers to whether the L-form continues to propagate in the growth form on subsequent transfer in the absence of inducing agents or ultimately gives rise to bacterial growth of the original parent strain. Cultures which continue to transfer as L-form are stable, while those which revert are unstable. When blocks of solid medium, carrying L-forms grown from an inoculum of strain F24 protoplasts, were transferred to fresh medium, only a few colonies were found to revert to streptococcal growth. Selection of L-forms during initial subcultures quickly established a line of L-forms which did not revert during 100 succeeding subcultures. By reducing to zero the quantity of serum in the medium the line was established in a serum-free medium. After serial transfer for several months the L-form was then subcultured twice on medium consisting of Brucella broth (Albimi) containing 1% agar (Difco), 0.43 M NH$_4$Cl and 0.5% glucose. On succeeding subcultures the agar concentration was progressively lowered, and finally L-form growth was established in liquid medium. This culture has been maintained by regular subculture for over two years in liquid medium without reverting to streptococcal growth.

It was nevertheless of interest to compare the reversion rate of the initially induced L-forms of strains F24 and E1 when

TABLE 4.3

Frequency (%) of Reversion During 3 Routine Subcultures of Freshly Induced Streptococcus faecalis *L-Forms*

Strain	L-Forms Subcultured	Streptococcal Revertants Detected	Revertants %
F24L	2275	89	3.9
E1L	1001	185	18.5

Protoplasts of S. faecalis F24 and spheroplasts of S. faecalis E1 were deposited on routine L-form growth medium (LGA) containing 0.43 M NH$_4$Cl. Each petri plate grew 50–150 L-forms. The growth was replica-plated to similar plates of the same medium and, after growth developed, the process was repeated 3 times. Each subculture plate was in turn replica-plated to human blood agar medium and bile-aesculin medium to detect any typical streptococcal organisms which could form colonies.

subjected to normal subculture on solid medium. It was found that the initially induced L-forms could be subcultured by replica plating onto uninoculated L-form medium (LGA). Serial subculture was maintained in this manner through three passages from the original plate. Each subculture was also replica plated onto human blood agar medium and bile-aesculin medium to score any typical streptococcal colonies which developed. Approximately 4 per cent of the strain F24 colonies with the initial appearance of L-forms reverted, whereas 18.5 per cent of the initial E1 L-colonies reverted to the streptococcal form (Table 4.3). The majority of L-forms derived from group D streptococcal protoplasts were therefore stable L-forms following initial growth, a finding which parallels the experience with group A streptococcal protoplasts.[11] The L-forms derived from streptococcal spheroplasts were less likely to be stable.

L-forms of S. faecalis strain GK

In the early experiments with lysozyme-treated S. faecalis GK it was found that there was almost quantitative conversion of the streptococcal count to L-form. At this time the system for lysozyme treatment employed sucrose as an osmotic

TABLE 4.4

Differential Effect of Sucrose or NH_4CL as Osmotic Stabilizer on the Reversion of Strain GK

Treatment	Dilution	L-form medium with 0.43 M NH₄Cl			L-form medium with 0.6 M sucrose		
		Colony form, day of observation and count cfu/ml					
		GK(2)	L(4)	GKR(4)	GK(2)	L(4)	GKR(4)
Control	10^5	t.n.c.	n.s.	n.s.	t.n.c.	n.s.	n.s.
	10^6	253	n.s.	n.s.	219	n.s.	n.s.
	10^7	24	n.s.	n.s.	35	n.s.	n.s.
Lysozyme	10^5	25	t.n.c.	n.s.	3	t.n.c.	60
	10^6	n.s.	200	n.s.	n.s.	250	127
	10^7	n.s.	31	n.s.	n.s.	24	3

t.n.c.: Too numerous to count.

n.s.: No colonies of the appropriate morphology present.

Washed cells of *Streptococcus faecalis* GK were treated with lysozyme (200 µg/ml) for one hour at 37 °C in the presence of 0.01 M tris pH 7.1 and 8% Carbowax 4000 (polyethylene glycol). Dilutions of the protoplasts formed were made in similar tris-Carbowax solutions and samples plated on growth medium for L-forms (LGA) containing either 0.43 M NH₄Cl or 0.6 M sucrose. Colonies observed on the days indicated and scored by their appearance as streptococcal, strain GK (GK), L-form (L) or the peculiar 'kidney-shaped'' revertant colony containing both types of viable elements (GKR).

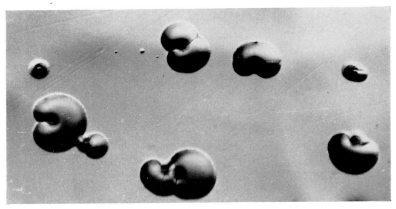

Figure 4.2. The "kidney-shaped" revertant colonies which appeared after 4 days incubation of medium inoculated with *Streptococcus faecalis* GK spheroplasts. See text for effect of medium composition. Small L-forms are also visible. ($\times$ 7)

stabilizer, and the growth medium (LGA) contained 0.43 M NH₄Cl. The L-forms selected for subculture were stable and no revertant colonies were noted on the original plate. If 0.6 M sucrose was substituted in the same growth medium (LGA), for the 0.43 M NH₄Cl, then revertant colonies of the original streptococcus developed. Table 4.4 records an experiment of this kind, which demonstrates the effect of change of osmotic stabilizer on the reversion of the induced L-form. A new colonial variant was noted on the fourth day of incubation of medium containing 0.6 M sucrose inoculated with protoplasts. The colonies were frequently "kidney shaped" and appeared to consist of streptococcal and L-form growth. Figure 4.2 depicts an area of a petri plate containing such a colony. On further incubation the L-form growth became surrounded by streptococcal growth. When the surface of the colony was scraped with the edge of a glass slide the streptococcal growth was removed, leaving the central portion of the colony, which had burrowed into the agar and contained granular elements typical of L-form growth. Figure 4.3 shows such a colony at higher magnification, seven days after protoplasts were inoculated. Such colonies are referred to as strain GK revertants (GKR) and were assumed to develop from GKL-forms. If the 0.6 M sucrose was not present in the medium, revertant streptococcal colonies did not develop, thus rendering it unlikely that the growth represented streptococcal cells which were present in the protoplast inoculum and which did not form colonies on the solid medium containing NH_4Cl. The results recorded in Table 4.4 show that not all the L-forms reverted on the medium containing sucrose. Thus this is not mass reversion of protoplasts or L-forms, but further experiments are necessary to rule out the possibility that this can be achieved.

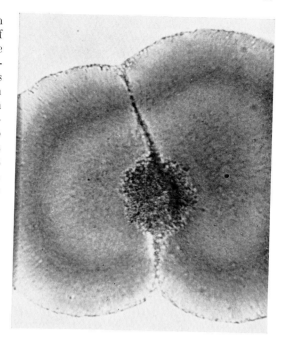

Figure 4.3. A revertant colony of *Streptococcus faecalis* GK spheroplasts after 7 days incubation. ($\times$ 58)

MASS REVERSION OF STREPTOCOCCAL PROTOPLASTS

Nečas[24] reported 100 per cent reversion, within 24 hours, of protoplasts of yeast which had been embedded in a growth medium containing gelatin. Landman & Halle[18] reported similar results with protoplasts of *B. subtilis*. They also reported an enhancement of the reversion rate by the use of stronger agar concentrations (up to 2.5%) than those normally used in L-form growth medium. Experiments in which lysozyme induced protoplasts of *S. faecalis* F24 were inoculated onto L-form growth medium (LGA) containing 0.43 NH_4Cl and 2.5% agar showed that these protoplasts also gave a higher reversion rate than that found with the usual 1% or 1.5% agar. This reversion rate rarely exceeded 15 per cent. It was noted that on medium with 2.5% agar the L-form growth was exceedingly difficult to distinguish from normal streptococcal growth. Both formed flat-surface colonies, and the L-form contained many granules with little of the normal fried-egg appearance. In order to test for reversion it was necessary to pick colonies or replica plate to selective media to distinguish the two colonial types.

On L-form medium solidified with gelatin (LGG) and containing 0.43 M NH_4Cl, both protoplasts of strain F24 and spheroplasts of strain E1 reverted quantitatively to the streptococcal state. The concentration of gelatin was critical, at least 15% gelatin (Difco) being necessary, the number of revertant colonies recovered increasing up to a maximum achieved at a level of 25% gelatin (Difco) (Table 4.5). Protoplast suspensions of strain F24 and spheroplast suspensions of strain E1 gave similar results.[13]

The bacterial count of streptococci unaffected by the lysozyme treatment was assumed to be less than 10^4 cfu/ml and the results show a high recovery rate, as streptococci, of streptococcal protoplasts. It was surprising that no L-forms developed on the medium containing the lower concentrations of gelatin. The addition of agar (up to 2.0%) to L-form growth medium containing 15% gelatin did

TABLE 4.5

Reversion of Streptococcus faecalis *F24 Protoplasts on L-Form Growth Medium Solidified with Gelatin*

Inoculum: Protoplasts prepared by lysozyme treatment of 2×10^9 cfu *S. faecalis* F24/ml.

Growth Medium		
LGA[1]	LGG[2]	LGG[3]
Agar 1.5%	Gelatin 15%	Gelatin 25%

Colony forming units per ml					
F24	F24L	F24	F24L	F24	F24L
$<10^4$	1.7×10^9	$<10^4$	n.s.	1.1×10^9	n.s.

n.s.: No L-forms seen from any of the dilutions plated.

S. faecalis F24 was treated with lysozyme (200 µg/ml) for one hour at 37° C in the presence of 0.01 tris HCl buffer pH 7.1 and 8% Carbowax 4000. Dilutions were prepared in a similar tris-carbowax solution and inocula from the appropriate dilutions plated on three different growth media:

LGA[1]—L-form growth medium containing 0.43 M NH_4Cl solidified with 1.5% agar and incubated at 37° C.

LGG[2]—L-form growth medium containing 0.43 M NH_4Cl solidified with 15% gelatin and incubated at 25° C.

LGG[3]—L-form growth medium containing 0.43 M NH_4Cl solidified with 25% gelatin and incubated at 25° C.

result in the appearance of L-forms. Similar results were seen by the addition of gelatin (up to 25%) to L-growth medium containing 1% agar (Table 4.6). Landman & Halle[18] suggested that the effect of gelatin on protoplast reversion was not due to nutritional or chemical factors but to physical characteristics of the gelling agent. The use of gelatin-agar mixtures allowed us to destroy the gelling capacity of gelatin by gelatinase but still utilize a solid medium for the testing of the growth characteristics of the *S. faecalis* F24 protoplasts. Although all the components of the gelatin-agar medium were present, when the gelling power of gelatin was destroyed by prior treatment with gelatinase it was found that the protoplasts did not

revert to streptococci, so indicating that the physical surroundings of the protoplast appear to control the manner of its subsequent development. The protoplasts of *S. faecalis* F24 would revert to streptococci in the presence of the high concentrations of gelatin, L-forms would not. Attempts were made by inoculating long established stable liquid cultures of the F24 L-form, and also by dragging agar blocks carrying stable L-forms across L-growth medium (LGG) containing 25% gelatin. In no case were any streptococcal colonies detected. L-forms, freshly induced from protoplast suspensions and allowed to develop into a colony, did not revert when transferred by the agar block technique or as a suspension to L-growth medium containing 25% gelatin. At the present time reversion on media containing high concentrations of gelatin appears to be a property of streptococcal protoplasts but not of stable streptococcal L-forms.

TABLE 4.6

Recovery of L-Forms and Revertant Streptococci from Streptococcus faecalis *F24 Protoplasts on Medium Solidified with Gelatin and Agar*

Inoculum: Protoplasts prepared by lysozyme treatment of 3×10^9 cfu *S. faecalis* F24/ml.

L-Form Medium Solidified with	Colony Count—cfu/ml	
	Streptococci	L-form
Agar 1%	n.s.	10^9
Agar 1% + gelatin 5%	n.s.	4×10^9
Agar 1% + gelatin 10%	6×10^7	5×10^8
Agar 1% + gelatin 25%	10^9	n.s.
Gelatin 15%	3×10^8	n.s.
Gelatin 25%	3×10^9	n.s.

n.s.: No colonies seen from any of the dilutions plated.

S. faecalis F24 was treated with lysozyme (200 µg/ml) for one hour at 37° C in the presence of 0.01 M tris-HCl buffer pH 7.1 and 8% Carbowax 4000. Dilutions were prepared in a similar tris-Carbowax solution and samples from appropriate dilutions plated on solid medium containing tryptone soy broth (Oxoid) with the addition of 0.5% glucose, 2% Seitz-filtered, inactivated (56° C 30 min) horse serum, 0.43 M NH_4Cl and either gelatin, agar, or mixtures of the two as indicated.

DISCUSSION

The overall pattern of the results obtained by treating the streptococcal cell suspensions with muralytic enzymes and the subsequent growth of the enzyme-damaged cells, as cultures of L-forms or streptococci, is summarized diagrammatically in Figure 4.4. Protoplasts were obtained with group A streptococci and phage-lysin, and with *S. faecalis* F24 and lysozyme. Spheroplasts were formed with *S. faecalis var. liquefaciens* 31 and phage-lysin, and with *S. faecalis* E1 and lysozyme. In all these varied systems, L-forms (containing thousands of viable units) were induced on appropriate soft agar medium (Tables 4.1 and 4.2). The characteristic growth of streptococci in chains renders the quantitative results expressed in terms of colony-forming units difficult to interpret in regard to a single streptococcal cell. Nevertheless, even when considering effects such as the initial de-chaining brought about by muralytic enzymes and the clumping of protoplasts, (with possibly an entrapped streptococcus) the systems still represent the recovery of a large number of L-forms from bacterial cell suspensions. The phage-associated lysins and lysozyme are enzymes with which, it is reasonable to suppose, bacterial cells come into contact during growth in natural environments. Enzymic induction of L-form growth may be one explanation for the appearance and isolation of spontaneously occurring L-forms. Maxted* has shown that it is possible to isolate L-forms from phage-infected streptococcal cultures. Pneumococcal L-forms have been isolated from autolysing cultures of pneumococci.†

All of the reported streptococcal systems are similar to the *B. subtilis*-lysozyme system[18] and support the concept that the change, from the normal bacterial mode of growth to the stable L-form, is accompanied by a persisting impairment in the ability of the L-form to synthesize the final morphological unit that is recognized

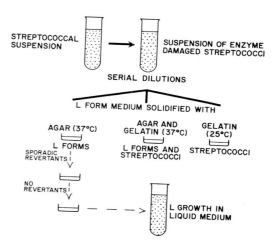

Figure 4.4. The general pattern of the interrelationships of group D streptococci and their stable L-form cultures. The dashed arrow indicates over 100 serial subcultures (as described in text).

as a cell wall. There are many functional steps in such a synthesis and disturbance of any one of these steps could result in the irreversible conversion of a bacterial cell to an L-form.[11] One of the more attractive hypotheses is that the process involves the interruption of a membrane-associated reaction sequence which resides in the mesosome.[18, 26] *B. subtilis* protoplasts and L-forms do not contain mesosomes.‡

A further similarity between the *B. subtilis* and streptococcal systems is the ability of the protoplasts of both organisms to revert to the parent bacterial form when inoculated onto a suitable growth medium solidified by strong agar or gelatin. The reversion rate of streptococcal protoplasts increases from less than 4 per cent on medium solidified with soft agar to approximately 15 per cent on medium of the same composition containing 2.5% agar. When agar is replaced by gelatin (25% or greater, depending on source), 50–100 per cent of the original streptococcal colony count is recovered (Table 4.5). It was extremely rare to find an L-form developing on the medium solidified with gelatin, but

---

* Personal communication.

† C. U. Mauney and H. Gooder, in preparation.

‡ See related articles by Drs. Ryter and Landman (pp. 110 and 319).

by the use of gelatin-agar mixtures both L-forms and streptococcal colonies could be recovered from protoplast suspensions (Table 4.6). The proportion of each colony type varied with the gelatin:agar ratio. Destruction of the gelling power of gelatin with gelatinase abolished the reversion process. These findings add support to the concept that reversion is promoted by the physical properties of the supporting matrix rather than by the chemical constituents of the medium.[18] Local environmental conditions on solid growth medium were previously shown to have a pronounced effect on whether or not L-forms developed from the protoplast inoculum.[11] Recent preliminary experiments extend these observations and suggest that the physical properties of the supporting medium are extremely important in determining whether L-form growth will be initiated from protoplasts. Streptococcal protoplasts do not develop as L-forms when inoculated on the surface of a cellulose filter (Millipore, 0.45 μ pore size) which is placed on a medium suitable for L-form development. If the filter is covered with a thin layer of agar, L-forms develop. Inoculation of the filters with stable streptococcal L-forms gives rise to L-form growth on the filter surface. Filters placed on the surface of medium previously inoculated with a protoplast suspension develop protoplasmic growth on the upper surface of the filter. The protoplast will apparently not pass through the filter, nor can it develop into an L-form in the absence of surrounding agar. The L-form will pass through the filter.*

The results obtained with lysozyme-treated S. faecalis GK grown on medium adequate for L-form formation indicate that it is possible to find chemical effects on the reversion process. In the presence of sucrose, revertant streptococci ultimately grew from the L-forms, but these mixed colonies were not seen in the presence of ammonium chloride (Table 4.4). Since other salts were not investigated, this may be a nonspecific salt effect on structures or enzyme reactions involved in the processes of reinitiating cell wall deposition and septation. D-amino acids prevent reversion of stable L-forms, but in this case there is evidence for inhibition of both cell wall formation and septation (see Landman & Halle[18]).

Streptococcal L-forms do not revert on the gelatin medium which promotes the reversion of streptococcal protoplasts. No explanation for this difference between the L-forms derived from protoplasts of B. subtilis and streptococci, respectively, can be offered at the moment. One possibility is that the complex medium used for streptococcal L-form growth contains an inhibitor which remains bound to the L-form inoculum. Alternatively, growth on this medium produces irreversible events leading to an impaired ability to resynthesize a normal cell wall.

The L-form finally adapted to liquid growth represents the end-product of a selection process carried out through hundreds of subcultures of stable L-form growth. The growth was adapted to liquid medium only with great difficulty and parallels previous experience with the group A streptococcal L-forms. The broth-grown cultures may represent selected mutants of the viable L-form granular elements whose genotype is considerably different from that of the original bacterial cell.†

SUMMARY

Streptococcal protoplasts and spheroplasts grow on soft agar medium as stable L-forms, but as streptococcal colonies on a similar medium solidified with gelatin. The change in both colony morphology and the structure of the viable units in these growth forms is influenced by the physical and chemical nature of the environment. The development of L-forms from bacterial cultures growing in natural environments may be expected to occur following induction by a wide variety of muralytic enzymes.

* H. Gooder and P. B. Wyrick, unpublished observations.

† See Wittler, p. 200.

REFERENCES

1. Barkulis, S. S., Smith, C., Boltralik, J. J., and Heymann, H.: Structure of streptococcal cell walls. IV. Purification and properties of streptococcal phage muralysin. *J. Biol. Chem.* **239**: 4027, 1964.
2. Bibb, W. R., and Straughn, W. R.: Formation of protoplasts from *Streptococcus faecalis* by lysozyme. *J. Bact.* **84**: 1094, 1962.
3. Bleiweis, A. S., and Zimmerman, L. N. Formation of two types of osmotically fragile bodies from *Streptococcus faecalis var. liquefaciens. Canad. J. Microbiol.* **7**: 363, 1961.
4. Brenner, S., Dark, F. A., Gerhardt, P., Jeynes, M. H., Kandler, O., Kellenberger, E., Klieneberger-Nobel, E., McQuillen, K., Rubio-Huertos, M., Salton, M. R. J., Strange, R. E., Tomcsik, J., and Weibull, C.: Bacterial protoplasts. *Nature* **181**: 1713, 1958.
5. Brock, T. D.: Host range of certain virulent and temperate bacteriophages attacking group D streptococci. *J. Bact.* **88**: 165, 1964.
6. Deibel, R. H., Lake, D. E., and Niven, C. F., Jr.: Physiology of the enterococci as related to their taxonomy. *J. Bact.* **86**: 1275, 1963.
7. Dienes, L.: Isolation of pleuropneumonia-like organisms from *H. influenzae* with the aid of penicillin. *Proc. Soc. Exp. Biol. Med.* **64**: 166, 1947.
8. Freimer, E. H., Krause, R. M., and McCarty, M.: Studies of L forms and protoplasts of Group A streptococci. I. Isolation, growth and bacteriologic characteristics. *J. Exp. Med.* **110**: 853, 1959.
9. Gooder, H., and King, J. R.: Growth as L colonies of protoplasts of *Streptococcus faecalis* F24. *Bact. Proc.*: p. 71, 1964.
10. Gooder, H., and Maxted, W. R.: Protoplasts of group A beta-haemolytic streptococci. *Nature* **182**: 808, 1958.
11. ———: External factors influencing structure and activities of *Streptococcus pyogenes.* In: *Microbial Reaction to Environment* (G. G. Meynell and H. Gooder, Eds.). Cambridge University Press, 1961: p. 151.
12. Guze, L. B., and Kalmanson, G. M.: Persistence of bacteria in "protoplast" form after apparent cure of pyelonephritis in rats. *Science* **143,** 1340, 1964.
13. King, J. R.: *Studies on L-Forms of Group D Streptococci.* Ph.D. dissertation, University of North Carolina, Chapel Hill, 1966.
14. Klieneberger, E.: The natural occurrence of pleuropneumonia-like organisms in apparent symbiosis with *Streptobacillus moniliformis* and other bacteria. *J. Path. Bact.* **40**: 93, 1935.
15. Klieneberger-Nobel, E.: L-forms of bacteria. In *The Bacteria, Vol. I: Structure.* (I. C. Gunsalus and R. Y. Stanier, Eds.). Academic Press, New York, 1960: p. 361.
16. Krause, R. M.: Studies on bacteriophages of hemolytic streptococci. I. Factors influencing the interaction of phage and susceptible host cell. *J. Exp. Med.* **106**: 365, 1957.
17. 'L-forms' of bacteria. *Nature* **179**: 461, 1957.
18. Landman, O. E., and Halle, S.: Enzymically and physically induced inheritance changes in *Bacillus subtilis. J. Mol. Biol.* **7**: 721, 1963.
19. Lederberg, J., and St. Clair, J.: Protoplasts and L-type growth of *Escherichia coli. J. Bact.* **75**: 143, 1958.
20. Martin, H. H.: Bacterial protoplasts—a review. *J. Theoret. Biol.* **5**: 1, 1963.
21. Maxted, W. R.: The active agent in nascent phage lysis of streptococci. *J. Gen. Microbiol.* **16**: 584, 1957.
22. McQuillen, K.: Bacterial protoplasts: growth and division of protoplasts of *Bacillus megaterium. Biochim. Biophys. Acta* **18**: 458, 1955.
23. ———: Bacterial protoplasts. In: *The Bacteria, Vol. I: Structure* (I. C. Gunsalus and R. Y. Stanier, Eds.). Academic Press, New York, 1960: p. 249.
24. Nečas, O.: Physical conditions as important factors for the regeneration of naked yeast protoplasts. *Nature* **192**: 580, 1961.
25. Park, J. T., and Strominger, J. L.: Mode of action of penicillin; biochemical basis for the mechanism of action of penicillin and for its selective toxicity. *Science* **125**: 99, 1957.
26. Ryter, A., and Landman, O. E.: Electron microscope study of the relationship between mesosome loss and the stable L state (or protoplast state) in *Bacillus subtilis. J. Bact.* **88**: 457, 1964.
27. Weibull, C.: The isolation of protoplasts from *Bacillus megaterium* by controlled treatment with lysozyme. *J. Bact.* **66**: 688, 1953.

5

The Mechanism by Which Penicillin Causes Conversion of Bacterial Cells to Spheroplasts

James T. Park

TUFTS UNIVERSITY SCHOOL OF MEDICINE

BOSTON, MASSACHUSETTS

One of the most remarkable properties of the penicillins (and the related cephalosporins) is their ability to convert bacteria to L-forms. With the discovery that penicillin interfered with cell wall murein (mucopeptide) synthesis, it was realized that the essential feature of conversion by penicillin involved loss of integrity of the wall. However, the exact mechanism by which penicillin brought about this loss of integrity was never really understood and has not been investigated. It certainly was never satisfactory to assume that a cell whose murein synthesis was blocked would, by its other metabolic activities, build up such a high internal pressure that it would explode. As other inhibitors of murein synthesis were discovered, it was found that, in spite of being excellent inhibitors, these antibiotics (bacitracin, vancomycin, ristocetin, oxamycin) were very poor agents for the production of L-forms. Thus, clearly, inhibition of murein synthesis is not sufficient explanation and there is something special about penicillin-like antibiotics. The purpose of my discussion is to suggest why the penicillins (and cephalosporins) are the most effective agents for the conversion of bacteria to their L-forms. A much better understanding of the structure of murein, of its biosynthesis, and of the mode of action of the antibiotics which interfere with murein synthesis has been obtained in recent years. I would like to summarize this new knowledge and then consider, in its light, what is special about penicillin.

The structure for a "typical" murein is shown in Figure 5.1. Its two essential features are:

1) It contains a polysaccharide consisting of alternating units of N-acetyl glucosamine and N-acetyl muramic acid linked β1–4, containing short peptides attached to the carboxyl group of the muramic acids. The peptides characteristically contain L-alanine, D-alanine, D-glutamic acid, and a dibasic amino acid such as lysine, diaminopimelic acid, ornithine, or 2,4 diaminobutyric acid.

2) The peptide chains are covalently linked to each other to form a net-like polymer. The crosslink is usually formed between the carboxyl group of D-alanine on one chain and the free amino group of the dibasic amino acid of another chain.

In some organisms, other amino acids are added to the amino group of the dibasic amino acid before the crosslink is formed. For example, in *Staphylococcus*, a peptide of five glycine residues is added to the epsilon amino group of lysine before the crosslink between chains is formed between D-alanine and the terminal glycine. Typically, about half of the potential cross links are formed, or at least are still intact, when the murein is isolated. In Gram-positive cocci the extent of crosslinking is often much greater than this.

The bacterial cell wall may be looked upon as one giant molecule of murein with other polymers either covalently linked or adsorbed to it. However, it is the murein which primarily maintains the integrity of the cell and it is now known that the crosslinks are essential for this structural function of murein.

A number of lytic enzymes are known which specifically attack either certain bonds in the peptide portion of murein or the amide bond between muramic acid and the peptide (cf. Petit, Muñoz & Ghuysen[4]). These enzymes can cause lysis of cells just as can lysozyme, which attacks the polysaccharide of the murein. Thus, the intact crosslinks are as essential as intact polysaccharides to preserve the integrity of the cell.

In the biosynthesis of murein, the final two reactions which concern us here are the polymerization reaction and the crosslinking reaction. The polymerization reaction forms the polysaccharide chains, with the short peptides attached to each muramic acid.[1] At this stage of the synthesis, these peptides terminate in -D-alanyl-D-alanine-COOH. The polymer formed by this reaction is an uncrosslinked murein. The crosslinking reaction is a transpeptidation in which the penultimate D-alanine is linked to the free amino group of the peptide from a neighboring chain with the release of the terminal D-alanine.[5, 6]

The penicillins and cephalosporins differ from the other inhibitors of murein synthesis in their point of attack: They interfere with the crosslinking reaction, whereas bacitracin, vancomycin and ristocetin block the polymerization reaction.[1, 3, 5, 6] Why, then, are the penicillin-like antibiotics, i.e., those that interfere with crosslinking, effective in producing L-forms,

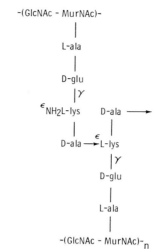

Figure 5.1. Structure of a typical cell wall murein. See text.

whereas the antibiotics which block murein synthesis by preventing the polymerization of the polysaccharide are not? When polymerization is stopped by bacitracin, vancomycin or ristocetin, the cell finds itself with an intact wall but without the capacity to produce more wall, and hence without the ability to grow and divide normally. Bacterial cells typically possess one or more enzymes which attack murein, i.e., autolytic enzymes. Depending on the quantity of such enzymes and their access to their substrate, cells inhibited by the above antibiotics may be converted to spheroplasts and would, therefore, have to replicate as L-forms or not at all. The fact that this series of events takes place with difficulty in the presence of bacitracin, vancomycin or ristocetin indicates either that the autolytic enzymes are not present in adequate amounts at the proper location or that these antibiotics have other effects on membrane function. It seems quite likely that at higher concentrations these antibiotics do interfere with membrane functions other than the polymerization reaction of murein synthesis. Further insight into this problem should be gained by attempting the conversion to spheroplasts and L-forms in the presence of the minimum growth inhibiting concentration of bacitracin, vancomycin or ristocetin.

With the penicillins and cephalosporins, the situation is significantly different. Even in the presence of a large excess of antibiotic, the cell continues to make murein. But it is uncrosslinked (i.e., defective) murein. If sufficient defective wall is made, and if the lytic enzymes required for cell division continue to be made and to function, the end result must be spheroplast formation. The recent observation of Chang & Weinstein[2] that inhibitors of protein synthesis prevented conversion of *Vibrio comma* to spheroplasts indicates that the cell's lytic enzymes are not indiscriminately available to attack its murein. The result would seem to suggest that newly formed lytic enzyme(s) is ordinarily delivered to the right place at the right time to achieve cell division without cell destruction.

SUMMARY

Penicillin-like antibiotics cause the bacterial cell to make defective wall, and at the same time allow lytic enzymes to be formed which can attack the existing murein. By this mechanism these antibiotics cause conversion of bacterial cells to spheroplasts.

REFERENCES

1. Anderson, J. S., Matsuhashi, M., Haskin, M. A., and Strominger, J. L.: Lipid-phosphoacetyl-muramyl-pentapeptide and lipid-phosphodisaccharide-pentapeptide: presumed membrane transport intermediates in cell wall synthesis. *Proc. Nat. Acad. Sci. USA* **53**: 881, 1965.
2. Chang, T.-W., and Weinstein, L.: Inhibitory effects of other antibiotics on bacterial morphologic changes induced by penicillin G. *Nature* **211**: 763, 1966.
3. Park, J. T.: Some observations on murein synthesis and the action of penicillin. *Symp. Soc. Gen. Microbiol.* **16**: 70, 1966.
4. Petit, J.-F., Muñoz, E., and Ghuysen, J.-M.: Peptide cross-links in bacterial cell wall peptidoglycans studied with specific endopeptidases from *Streptomyces albus* G. *Biochemistry* **5**: 2764, 1966.
5. Tipper, D. J., and Strominger, J. L.: Mechanism of action of penicillins: a proposal based on their structural similarity to acyl-D-alanyl-D-alanine. *Proc. Nat. Acad. Sci. USA* **54**: 1133, 1965.
6. Wise, E. M., Jr., and Park, J. T.: Penicillin: its basic site of action as an inhibitor of a peptide cross-linking reaction in cell wall mucopeptide synthesis. *Proc. Nat. Acad. Sci. USA* **54**: 75, 1965.

6

Enzymatic Reactions in Bacterial Cell Wall Synthesis Sensitive to Penicillins and Other Antibacterial Substances*

Jack L. Strominger

UNIVERSITY OF WISCONSIN MEDICAL SCHOOL
MADISON, WISCONSIN

A complex sequence of enzymatic reactions leads to the biosynthesis of the peptidoglycan of bacterial cell walls. Peptidoglycan synthesis occurs in three stages at three different sites in the cell. Antibiotics are known which interfere at specific points at each of these three sites.

The first stage of synthesis, the biosynthesis of the uridine nucleotide precursors, occurs in the cytoplasmic fraction of the cell (Figure 6.1). The end product of this sequence is the uridine nucleotide, UDP-acetylmuramyl-pentapeptide, discovered by Park & Johnson in 1949.[8] The antibiotic D-cycloserine interferes with this sequence and leads to the formation of bacterial protoplasts; it is a competitive inhibitor of two sequential reactions, catalyzed by alanine racemase and D-alanyl-D-alanine synthetase, which lead to the formation of the dipeptide.[10]

The second stage of wall synthesis occurs in the cell membrane. In this stage the two uridine nucleotides, UDP-acetylmuramyl-pentapeptide and UDP-acetylglucosamine, transfer their sugar fragments to a membrane-bound phospholipid to form disaccharide-pentapeptide attached to the phospholipid (Figure 6.2). Then a number of modification reactions occur, as a consequence of which a preformed unit of the cell wall is eventually synthesized. Finally, that preformed unit is transferred to introduce a new unit into a growing wall. Two antibiotics, ristocetin and vancomycin, interfere with the last reaction in this sequence, the transfer of the units to the growing wall.[1, 2] A third, bacitracin, also interfers in some manner with this reaction sequence.† Vancomycin and ristocetin at low concentrations (approximately the same concentration required to inhibit the growth of the organism) do not interfere with the synthesis of the lipid intermediates, but they do virtually completely eliminate the utilization of these intermediates for the introduction of new units into the wall (Figure 6.3). It is curious that ristocetin and vancomycin, which are potent inhibitors of this sequence, do not readily induce formation of spheroplasts of bacteria. They may have additional effects at the membrane site which, by inhibiting

*Supported by research grants from the U.S. Public Health Service (AI-06247) and the National Science Foundation (GB-4552).

† Bacitracin has been found to be an inhibitor of the following step in the reaction sequence.[9]

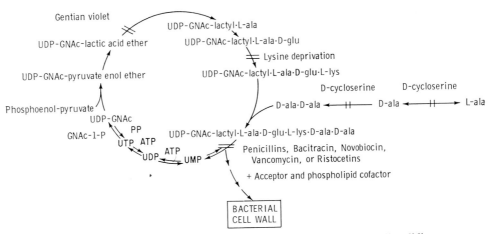

Figure 6.1. Biosynthesis of the uridine nucleotide precursors of the cell wall.[11]

protoplasmic growth, prevent spheroplast formation.

Finally, the last stage of wall synthesis is the crosslinking reaction, in which two peptidoglycan strands are crosslinked to each other with the elimination of the terminal D-alanine residue of the pentapeptide (Figure 6.4). This reaction occurs at the outer surface of the membrane, i.e., outside of the cell. At this site little or no ATP is available to catalyze synthetic reactions, and it may be for this reason that a transpeptidation evolved as a means of

catalyzing this bridge closing reaction. Several workers were led independently to the view that this reaction is the site of inhibition by penicillins and cephalosporins.[7, 12, 14] In thinking about what penicillins might do to this reaction it was recalled that, although a free carboxyl group in penicillins is not absolutely essential for their activity, this group greatly enhances their activity. The only free carboxyl group in the substrate is the carboxyl group of the terminal D-alanine residue, and it seemed possible that peni-

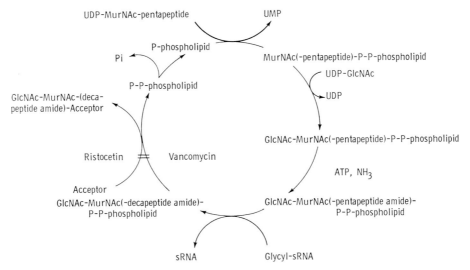

Figure 6.2. Utilization of uridine nucleotides for the biosynthesis of a linear peptidoglycan in *Staphylococcus aureus*.[11]

cillins might be structural analogs of the end of the pentapeptide chain.

Molecular models of the D-alanyl-D-alanine end of the chain and of penicillin (from its crystallographic structure) were built[12] (Figure 6.5). The β-lactam ring of penicillin (the highly reactive four membered ring) and the thiazolidine ring (the sulfur-containing ring) are almost at right angles to each other. The edge of the penicillin molecule as shown at the top of the figure has nearly the same conformation as does the backbone of D-alanyl-D-alanine at the end of the peptide chain. The highly reactive CO-N bond in the β-

lactam ring of penicillin occupies the same position as does the CO-N bond in D-alanyl-D-alanine. A mechanism for inhibition of the reaction by penicillins was therefore postulated (Figure 6.6). By analogy with other reactions of this type it was proposed that first a transpeptidase which catalyzed the crosslinking reaction would react with the end of the pentapeptide to form an acyl-enzyme intermediate with the elimination of D-alanine. This acyl-enzyme intermediate would then react with the free amino end of a pentaglycine chain in another peptidoglycan strand to form the crossbridge. If penicillins were analogs of the end of the peptide, they might also interact with transpeptidase. Since the CO-N bond of the β-lactam ring lies in the same position as the bond involved in transpeptidation, it might then acylate the enzyme and thereby inactivate it. A number of types of experiments with whole cells led to the conclusion that this was in fact the site of penicillin action.

The next step was to find a cell-free preparation which catalyzed the transpeptidation. It was found, not in *Staphylococcus aureus*, the organism in which cell wall synthesis had been studied for many years, but in *Escherichia coli*.[3, 5] There are in fact two terminal reactions in peptido-

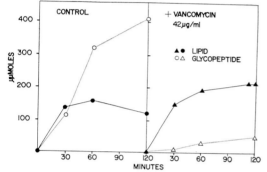

Figure 6.3. Effect of vancomycin on the biosynthesis of the lipid intermediates and peptidoglycan.[11]

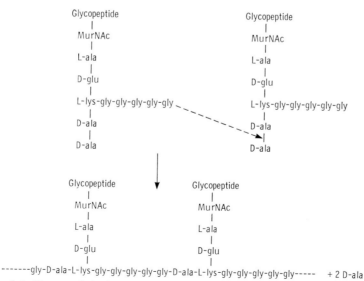

Figure 6.4 Closure of glycine bridges in *Staphylococcus aureus* by transpeptidation.

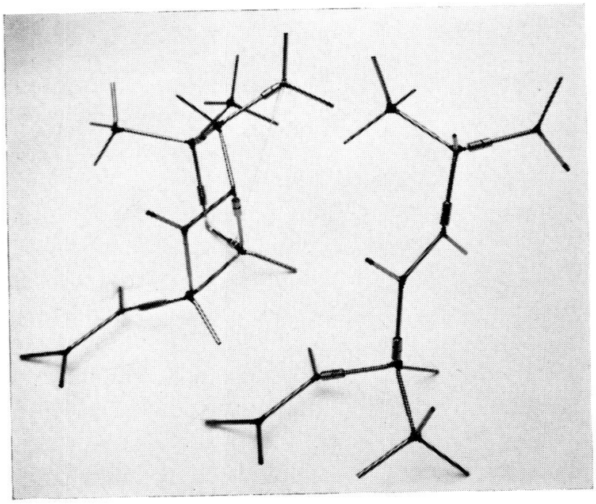

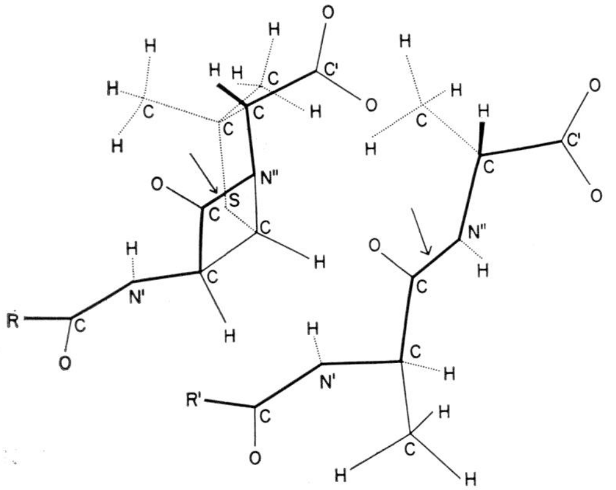

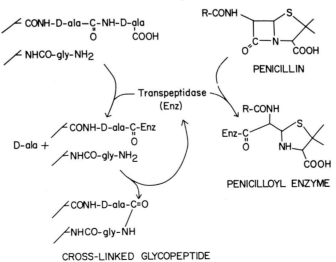

glycan synthesis in *E. coli* (Figure 6.7), the transpeptidation and another, catalyzed by a D-alanine carboxypeptidase which removes the D-alanine residue from the second strand. Presumably, the action of the carboxypeptidase limits the size of the peptide-linked oligomers in the cell wall of *E. coli* to dimers, a structural fact which had been demonstrated earlier in Weidel's laboratory.[13] In *S. aureus* no carboxypeptidase has been found, and the peptide-linked oligomers may be as large as decamers. Both the transpeptidase and the carboxypeptidase are inhibited by penicillins and cephalosporins.

With the uridine nucleotide substrate labeled in both of the terminal D-alanine residues, one of the ^{14}C-D-alanines was liberated during the course of the reaction as free alanine, while the other was incorporated into the polymer (Figure 6.8). In the presence of penicillin, the release of free alanine was eliminated and both alanine residues appeared in the polymer. A physical difference in the products formed in the absence or presence of penicillin was also evident. The crosslinked product formed in the control system was a highly water insoluble polymer which remained exactly at its point of application to the filter paper, while the water soluble polymer formed in the presence of penicillin spread on the paper so that it had a disc-

Figure 6.5. Dreiding stereomodels of penicillin (*above*) and of the D-alanyl-D-alanine end of the peptidoglycan (*below*).[12]

Figure 6.6 Proposed mechanism of inhibition of transpeptidase by penicillins.[12]

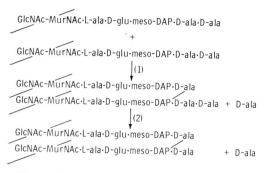

Figure 6.7. Reactions catalyzed by peptidoglycan transpeptidase (1) and D-alanine carboxypeptidase (2) in *Escherichia coli*.

like appearance (Figure 6.8). With increasing amounts of penicillin, increasing amounts of alanine were found in the polymer, until finally the amount found was doubled. In parallel, the liberation of alanine was progressively decreased and finally eliminated. All the penicillins and cephalosporins which have been examined had the same effects on this system.

The sensitivity data are summarized in Table 6.1. The growth inhibitory concentration for the organism studied is shown for four penicillin or cephalosporin preparations. The sensitivity of the transpeptidase to these substances, with one exception, exactly paralleled the growth inhibitory concentration. The important exception was penicillin G, which inhibited the enzyme at far lower concentrations than it inhibited growth of this organism. This fact may provide an explanation of Fleming's original observation that Gram-negative bacteria are much less sensitive to penicillins than are Gram-positive organisms. The insensitivity of the Gram-negative organisms is probably due not to any lack of the sensitive enzymes but to the fact that the antibiotic cannot penetrate to the site of these enzymes in the bacterial cell.

This fact is even more strikingly illustrated by the example of three other antibiotics, ristocetin, vancomycin and bacitracin, which inhibit the preceding step catalyzed by peptidoglycan synthetase. The intact cells of *E. coli* were virtually insensitive to these antibiotics, but the enzyme obtained from these cells was just

as sensitive to them as that same enzyme in *S. aureus*. These antibiotics must also be unable to penetrate to the site of the sensitive components in the intact cell.

The transpeptidase was irreversibly inactivated by penicillin. After inhibition, activity could not be recovered by treatment of the enzyme preparation with penicillinase or by washing out the penicillin. Another interesting property of the transpeptidase is that the reaction it catalyzes can be reversed to some extent by addition of D-alanine or of other D-amino acids, or by high concentrations of glycine, but it cannot be reversed by the addition of L-amino acids. D-amino acids and glycine are also known to induce formation of pro-

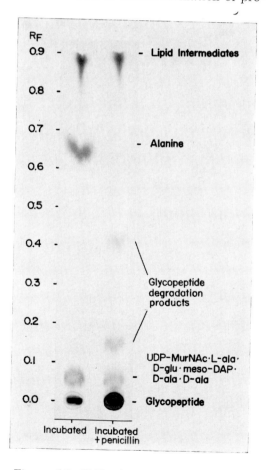

Figure 6.8. Utilization of UDP-MurNAc-L-ala·D-glu·Meso-DAP·[14]C-D-ala·[14]C-D-ala for peptidoglycan synthesis with *Escherichia coli* enzyme in the absence and in the presence of penicillin G.[5]

TABLE 6.1

Inhibition of Growth and Enzymes by Antibiotics*
(Escherichia coli)

Antibiotic	Growth	Concentrations Required for 50% Inhibition, μg/ml		
		Glyco-peptide synthetase	Glyco-peptide transpep-tidase	D-alanine carboxy-peptidase
Ampicillin	3	n.i.	3	0.04
Penicillin G	30	n.i.	3	0.02
Cephalothin	50	n.i.	50	1
Methicillin	1000	n.i.	1000	1
Ristocetin	1000	3	n.i.	n.i.
Vancomycin	100	10	n.i.	n.i.
Bacitracin	1000	40	n.i.	n.i.

n.i.: Not inhibited.
* Data from Strominger et al.[11]

toplasts and spheroplasts. This induction of spheroplasts is presumably due to reversal of the terminal crosslinking reaction in cell wall synthesis. Fibrous strands have been seen at the growing site in penicillin-inhibited bacteria by electron microscopy;[4] these fibrous strands are undoubtedly the uncrosslinked peptidoglycan which is formed in the presence of penicillin. Similarly fibrous material produced in the presence of D-amino acids has been visualized by electron microscopy;[6] again, this fibrous material presumably represents the uncrosslinked peptidoglycan strands which, in the presence of the D-amino acids, cannot be efficiently crosslinked.

Thus, the precise sites of inhibition of cell wall synthesis by penicillins, cephalosporins, D-cycloserine, vancomycin, ristocetin and bacitracin are now known, and the basis for the effect of D-amino acids on cell wall synthesis has been described. Inhibition at any of these sites might be expected to lead to formation of spheroplasts, provided that no other cellular process is simultaneously inhibited.

SUMMARY

Antibiotics interfere at three sites in bacterial cell wall synthesis. D-cycloserine is an inhibitor of the synthesis of a uridine nucleotide precursor of the cell wall. Ristocetin, vancomycin and bacitracin are in-hibitors of the phospholipid cycle which leads to the synthesis of a linear peptidoglycan from this precursor. Penicillins and cephalosporins are inhibitors of the terminal transpeptidation reaction in which the linear peptidoglycan becomes crosslinked to another strand.

REFERENCES*

1. Anderson, J. S., Matsuhashi, M., Haskin, M. A., and Strominger, J. L.: Lipid-phosphoacetylmuramyl-pentapeptide and lipid-phosphodisaccharide-pentapeptide: presumed membrane transport intermediaries in cell wall synthesis. *Proc. Nat. Acad. Sci. USA* **53**: 881, 1965.
2. Anderson, J. S., Meadow, P. M., Haskin, M. A., and Strominger, J. L.: Biosynthesis of the peptidoglycan of bacterial cell walls. I. Utilization of uridine diphosphate acetylmuramyl pentapeptide and uridine diphosphate acetylglucosamine for peptidoglycan synthesis by particulate enzymes from *Staphylococcus aureus* and *Micrococcus lysodeikticus*. *Arch. Biochem. Biophys.* **116**: 487, 1966.
3. Araki, Y., Shimada, A., and Ito, E.: Effect of penicillin on cell wall mucopeptide synthesis in a *Escherichia coli* particulate system. *Biochem. Biophys. Res. Commun.* **23**: 518, 1966.
4. Fitz-James, P., and Hancock, R.: The initial structural lesion of penicillin action in Bacillus megaterium. *J. Cell Biol.* **26**: 657, 1965.
5. Izaki, K., Matsuhashi, M., and Strominger, J. L.: Glycopeptide transpeptidase and D-alanine carboxypeptidase: penicillin-sensitive enzymatic reactions. *Proc. Nat. Acad. Sci. USA* **55**: 656, 1966.
6. Lark, C., Bradley, D., and Lark, K. G.: Further studies on the incorporation of D-methionine into the bacterial cell wall; its incorporation into the R-layer and the structural consequences. *Biochim. Biophys. Acta* **78**: 278, 1963.
7. Martin, H. H.: Composition of the mucopolymer in cell walls of the unstable and stable L-form of *Proteus mirabilis*. *J. Gen. Microbiol.* **36**: 441, 1964.
8. Park, J. T., and Johnson, M. J.: Accumulation of labile phosphate in Staphylococcus aureus grown in the presence of penicillin. *J. Biol. Chem.* **179**: 585, 1949.

* Only a few key references have been provided. Interested readers are referred to a recent review[11] for further references and details of the work described.

9. Siewert, G., and Strominger, J. L.: Bacitracin, an inhibitor of the dephosphorylation of lipid pyrophosphate. *Proc. Nat. Acad. Sci. USA* **57**: 767, 1967.

10. Strominger, J. L., Ito, E., and Threnn, R. H.: Competitive inhibition of enzymatic reactions by oxamycin. *J. Amer. Chem. Soc.* **82**: 998, 1960.

11. Strominger, J. L., Izaki, K., Matsuhashi, M., and Tipper, D. J.: Peptidoglycan transpeptidase and D-alanine carboxypeptidase: penicillin-sensitive enzymatic reactions. *Fed. Proc.* **26**: 9, 1967.

12. Tipper, D. J., and Strominger, J. L.: Mechanism of action of penicillins: a proposal based on their structural similarity to acyl-D-alanyl-D-alanine. *Proc. Nat. Acad. Sci. USA* **54**: 1133, 1965.

13. Weidel, W., and Pelzer, H.: Bagshaped macromolecules—a new outlook on bacterial cell walls. *Adv. Enzym.* **26**: 193, 1964.

14. Wise, E. M., Jr., and Park, J. T.: Penicillin: its basic site of action as an inhibitor of a peptide cross-linking reaction in cell wall mucopeptide synthesis. *Proc. Nat. Acad. Sci. USA* **54**: 75, 1965.

II.
MORPHOLOGY AND FUNCTIONAL CORRELATIONS IN PROTOPLASTS, SPHEROPLASTS AND L-FORMS

Claes Weibull
CHAIRMAN

7

The Morphology of Protoplasts, Spheroplasts, and L-Forms

Claes Weibull

UNIVERSITY OF LUND
LUND, SWEDEN

In this introductory presentation I have no intention of covering in full the vast field dealing with the morphology of protoplasts, spheroplast and L-forms. Rather, I would prefer to emphasize certain facts and problems. I shall also try to point out the sequence of events in this field, thus giving a kind of historical background to our present knowledge.

The most striking morphological characteristic that is common to protoplasts, spheroplasts and L-forms is that they all lack a rigid cell wall. They are thus soft, fragile and pleomorphic. A clear distinction between L-forms, on the one hand, and protoplasts and spheroplasts, on the other, cannot perhaps be made, but according to a widely accepted definition, L-forms should be able to grow and divide indefinitely, whereas protoplasts may, to some extent, increase in mass but are unable to divide.

The studies that demonstrated the possibility of isolating naked bacterial protoplasts from bacterial cells were clearly morphological in nature. Light microscopic observations, carried out independently by Tomcsik & Guex-Holzer[38] and myself,[43] revealed that the bacterial protoplasts assumed a spherical shape and that the cell wall disintegrated when cells of lysozyme-sensitive strains of *Bacillus megaterium* were treated with this enzyme in an isotonic or hypertonic medium. Subsequent investigations—analytical, electron microscopical, chemical, and immunological —showed that cell wall material was left in trace amounts, at the most, on the surface of the released protoplasts.[21, 44] The experiments performed with *B. megaterium* cells inspired similar studies on other, mainly Gram-negative bacteria. Spherical, osmotically fragile bodies were obtained also in these trials. However, it soon became evident that much of the cell wall material remained on the spheres derived from Gram-negative organisms. Such bodies were therefore named *spheroplasts*[22] to distinguish them from the naked protoplasts obtained from *B. megaterium*, a few other Gram-positive bacteria, and yeasts.[24]

As I mentioned, several lines of evidence showed that no more than trace amounts of wall material were left on protoplasts released from *B. megaterium* cells. This is perhaps most clearly evident from the appearance of electron micrographs of sectioned whole cells and protoplasts of this organism (Figures 7.1 and 7.2). It may also be mentioned that diaminopimelic acid (DAP), a typical cell wall constituent, could not be detected by chromatographic analyses of *B. megaterium*.[22] Similarly, no significant amounts of D-amino acids and rhamnose were found in protoplast membranes of *Streptococcus* species.[14, 36] Studies on the so-called "chemical anatomy" of Gram-positive bacteria thus agree with the morphological findings.

Another cytological characteristic of naked bacterial protoplasts is caused by the extrusion of the mesosomes during the degradation of the cell wall.[11] Thus, isolated protoplasts generally do not contain any mesosomes. These bodies are also extruded when whole cells are subjected to plasmolysis in the absence of lysozyme[29, 46] (Figures 7.1 and 7.3). The removal of the cell wall does not markedly alter the structure of the bacterial protoplasm in other respects.

When protoplasts released from *B. megaterium* cells are incubated in certain liquid media, they may synthesize proteins, nucleic acids and lipids, increasing about tenfold in mass.[8] The cell division process is inhibited, however, for reasons not yet clear. Recently, Fedorova[7] reported that *B. megaterium* protoplasts could grow and form colonies when incubated in a hypertonic, semisolid medium, but the colonies could not be transferred to fresh media. No colonies were formed when penicillin was included in the growth medium.

Electron microscopy clearly reveals the presence of cell wall remnants at the periphery of the spherical, osmotically fragile bodies which can be obtained from Gram-negative bacteria by treating cells with penicillin, with lysozyme and versene in combination, or by making use of metabolic disturbances in certain bacterial mutants[21] (Figures 7.4 and 7.5). Chemical and immunological studies have also shown that wall constituents such as mucopeptide(s), proteins and polysaccharides may be present in these bodies, the spheroplasts.[31]

The cytoplasmic membrane of Gram-negative bacteria seems to be folded in a

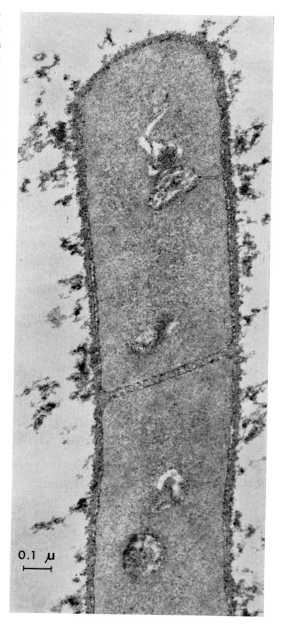

0.1 μ

Figure 7.1. Section of intact cell of *Bacillus megaterium*. Note the thick cell wall and the centrally located mesosomes (a connection between one of the mesosomes and the surface of the protoplasm can be seen). (From Weibull.[46])

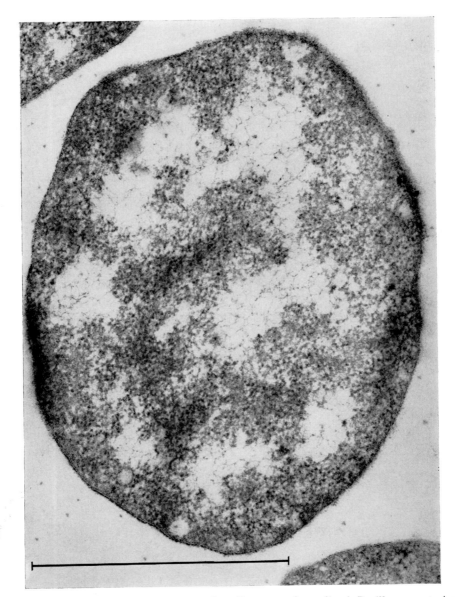

Figure 7.2. Thin section of a protoplast (lysozyme formed) of *Bacillus megaterium*, osmium fixed, uranyl and lead stained; scale marked: 1 μ. Note the peripherally located "unit membrane". (Courtesy of Dr. P. I. Fitz-James.)

rather simple manner. These organisms do not possess the well-defined mesosomes found in most Gram-positive bacteria. This would explain why the extrusion of mesosomes or mesosome-like bodies has been observed only in the latter organisms.

Many workers refer to the L-forms in two classes, stable and unstable. The unstable L-forms revert to the normal growth form when the inhibiting agent used for their production, usually penicillin, is removed from the medium. The stable L-forms do not revert when transferred to a medium free of the inhibitor.

This difference is reflected in the structure of the two types of L-forms: the stable ones possess only one "unit membrane" at their periphery[5, 40, 47] (Figure 7.6); the unstable forms have two peripheral membranes[5, 40] (Figure 7.7), the outer one probably representing the degraded wall and the inner one the cytoplasmic membrane. This assumption is in agreement with chemical data, according to which unstable L-forms contain considerable amounts of typical wall constituents, notably DAP and muramic acid.[31] Stable *Proteus* L-forms often contain DAP and muramic acid in small or moderate amounts, but it is doubtful whether these compounds are incorporated into high molecular weight polymers.[13, 23, 35, 49] No typical wall constituents have been demonstrated with certainty in streptococcal L-forms.[14, 16a, 35] Thus, spheroplasts are roughly similar to unstable L-forms with respect to the presence of wall constituents, and stable L-forms to protoplasts.

The protoplasm of L-forms is similar to that of normal bacteria, but the L-forms usually contain large vacuoles, and small bodies inside the vacuoles (Figure 7.6). The appearance of the small bodies often suggests that these bodies undergo division processes. It has therefore been assumed that they play an important role in the life cycle of the L-forms.[39] Filtration experiments indicate that the minimal reproductive units of the L-forms have a diameter of about 0.3 μ,[20, 26] but this value may be too low, since the L-forms are malleable and may be deformed during the passage through bacterial filters. Experiments in which L-forms were grown in slide cultures gave considerably higher values, 0.6 to 1.0 μ for L-forms of *Proteus*, *Staphylococcus*, and *Corynebacterium* strains.[45] Thus, according to these data, most of the granular forms seen in cultures of L-forms are non-viable. It should be emphasized, however, that the data obtained from filtration and slide culture experiments refer to L-forms existing free in the medium and not connected with or included within larger forms.

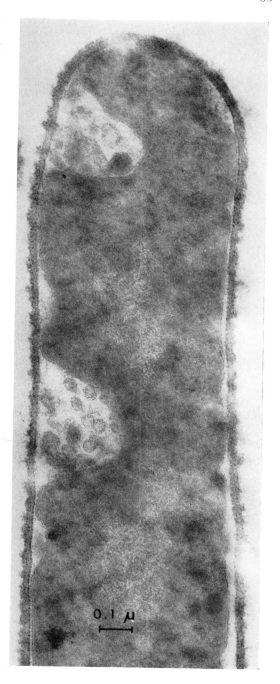

Figure 7.3. Section of plasmolyzed cell of *Bacillus megaterium*. Note the extruded mesosomes, which are located in pockets between the wall and the cytoplasmic membrane. (From Weibull.[46])

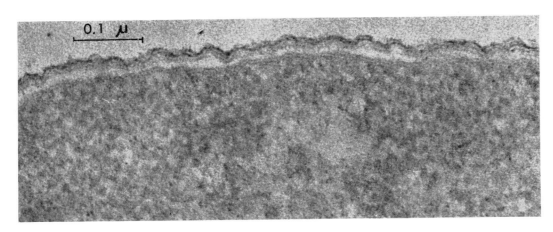

Figure 7.4. Section of peripheral part of a normal cell of *Proteus mirabilis.* Note the two surface layers: the multilayered cell wall and, underneath, the cytoplasmic membrane. The latter structure has the appearance of a "unit membrane". (From Weibull.[47])

Protoplasts, spheroplasts and L-forms share the characteristic of having no rigid cell wall with another bacterial group, the pleuropneumonia-like organisms (PPLO) or *Mycoplasma* (and a few other bacteria). The morphology of the PPLO has been vividly debated almost since the discovery of these organisms, which occurred at the end of the last century.[25] Some workers[4, 20] consider the fundamental morphological unit of the PPLO as granular or spherical, whereas others[15] find that they are basically filamentous organisms. If the PPLO are to be regarded as essentially round organisms, they are undoubtedly morphologically closely related to the L-forms. It could be mentioned that the L-form first isolated, that derived from *Streptobacillus moniliformis,* was for some time regarded as a PPLO by its discoverer, Dr. Emmy Klieneberger-Nobel.[19]

Since protoplasts, spheroplasts, and L-forms are fragile bodies which can be degraded by gentle means, they represent excellent starting materials for the isolation of various subcellular units. As Spiegelman and coworkers[37] described the isolation of nuclear bodies from protoplasts of *B. megaterium,* the protoplasts were suspended in a calcium-containing succinate-citrate buffer, the cytoplasmic membranes were dissolved with lipase, and the released nuclear bodies were isolated by centrifugation. Electron micrographs of drop preparations together with chemical data suggested that the isolated bodies consisted of a dense core surrounded by a gel of DNA. However, in later studies performed with sectioned material, the nuclear bodies were found to appear as fibrous masses without dense centers.[10] It was then assumed that the cores observed earlier represented remnants of mesosomes or lipid granules.

When protoplasts are shocked osmotically, they undergo a far-reaching lysis. The membranous structures left are often called "ghosts". Evidently these ghosts contain the peripheral, cytoplasmic membrane of the bacteria, but the extent to which they contain additional cytoplasmic structures or substances is hard to ascertain. Before the discovery of the mesosomes[9, 16, 41] it was often assumed that the ghosts represented reasonably pure cytoplasmic membranes. More recent studies show that the ghosts may actually represent a mixture of lysed mesosomes and cytoplasmic membranes.[32] Since the mesosomes probably consist of complicated invaginations of the cytoplasmic membrane, the two kinds of membranous matter may well have similar or identical properties.

Recent cytochemical studies,[34, 42] carried out on whole bacteria, suggest that they have to some extent different enzymatic characteristics. To my knowledge, a clear separation of mesosomes from the peripheral membranes has not been reported so far.

Membranous structures of the ghost type have been isolated from several lysozyme-sensitive bacteria by shocking protoplasts osmotically or by direct lysis of whole cells. The ghosts were separated by centrifugation from the bulk of the protoplasm. Preparations thus obtained consist essentially of "unit membranes" with varying amounts of adhering matter. The major chemical constituents of the membranes are proteins (40–70 per cent) and lipids (15–40 per cent). Smaller amounts of carbohydrates and RNA are frequently present. The membranes contain virtually all of the cytochromes, the succinic dehydrogenase and the NADH oxidase of the whole cells.

Perhaps the purest preparations of bacterial cytoplasmic membranes obtained so far are the ghosts isolated by Razin and associates[28] from the PPLO *Mycoplasma laidlawii*. It is of particular interest that these membranes could be converted by sodium lauryl sulfate to homogeneous subunits, which could be reaggregated to form membrane-like structures when transferred to a medium containing magnesium ions.

Preparations which essentially consist of fragments of cytoplasmic membranes can be obtained by disintegration of whole cells and subsequent differential centrifugation of the homogenates. The results, however, are highly influenced by the methods used for the disintegration of the bacteria, as is shown in Table 7.1. Since the succinic dehydrogenase in bacteria is generally considered as bound to the cytoplasmic membranes or its invaginations, the activity of this enzyme in a cell fraction can be used as a measure of the content of cytoplasmic membranes, whole or fragmented, in that particular fraction. It can thus be concluded that the cytoplasmic membranes of normal *Proteus* bacteria are extensively solubilized when these organisms are processed in the Ribi-Sorvall Cell Fractionator.[27] When the X-press of Edebo[6] is employed for the disintegration, the cytoplasmic membranes are less extensively fragmented; some of the mem-

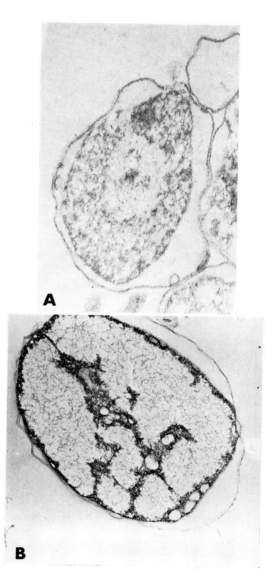

Figure 7.5. Spheroplast sections. *A: Escherichia coli,* ×51,000 (from Martin[21]). *B: Proteus mirabilis,* × 21,000 (from Tulasne, Minck & Kirn[40]). Note the two peripheral membranes (cf. Figure 7.4).

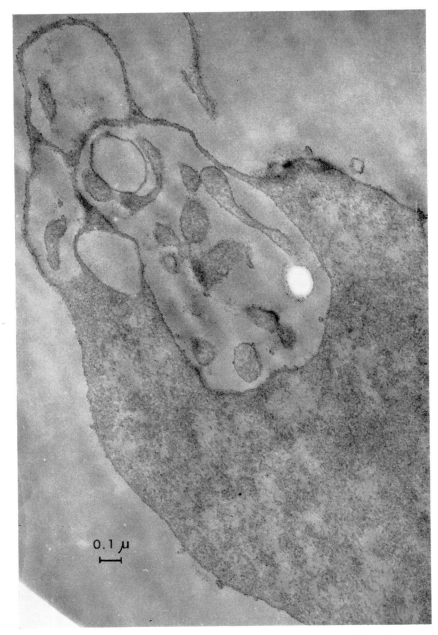

Figure 7.6. Section of a stable L-form (type A) of *Proteus mirabilis*. Note the "unit membrane" at the periphery of the L-form and the vacuoles with included bodies. (From Weibull.[47])

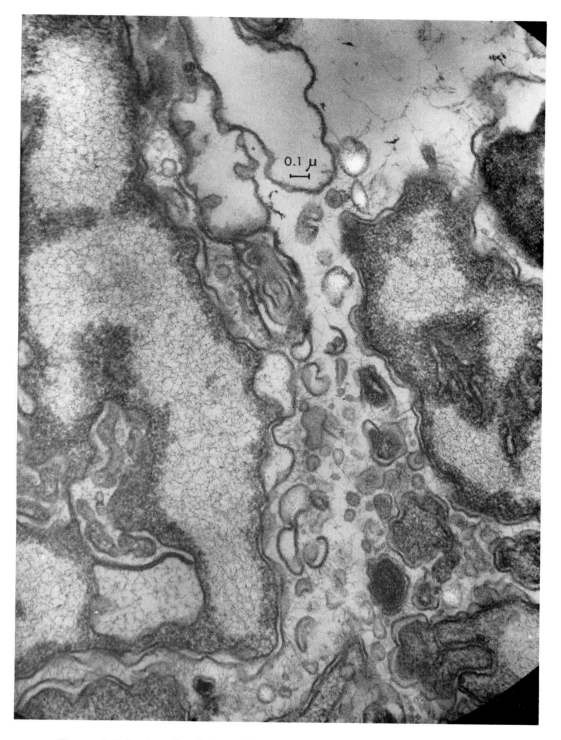

Figure 7.7. Section of an L-form of the B type (unstable) of *Proteus mirabilis*. Note the two membranes at the periphery of the L-form (cf. Figure 7.4). (Courtesy of Drs. S. Bullivant and L. Dienes.)

TABLE 7.1

Distribution of Succinic Dehydrogenase Between Sedimentable and Non-Sedimentable Fractions of Bacterial Homogenates

	Mode of Homogenization				
	Ribi-Sorvall fractionator		X-press		Osmotic shock
	Normal bacteria	L-forms	Normal bacteria	L-forms	L-forms
Sedimentable fraction	6	2	29	37	94
Non-sedimentable fraction	94	98	71	63	6

Three different methods of homogenization were used. The sedimentable fraction was obtained by centrifugation at 27,000 G for 45 min. The sum of the activities in a sedimentable and the corresponding non-sedimentable fraction was taken as 100. Three strains of *Proteus mirabilis* and their L-forms were studied. (Data from Weibull.[48])

brane fragments probably adhere to the cell walls. Similar fractions may be obtained after disruption of Gram-negative bacteria in the Mickle apparatus, as has recently been shown electron microscopically by Boy de la Tour and associates.[3] Table 7.1 also shows that the disintegration of L-form membranes is similar to that of the cytoplasmic membranes of normal bacteria in the two instruments employed. The ghosts obtained by osmotic lysis of the L-forms are easily sedimented.

Recent investigations have shown that close morphological and functional relationships exist between the cytoplasmic membrane and structures located in the rest of the bacterial protoplasm. Thus it has been demonstrated very clearly that the bacterial nucleus is connected at one point with a mesosome in *Bacillus subtilis* cells.[29] When the mesosome is extruded by plasmolysis, the nucleus becomes connected with the cytoplasmic membrane. Similar connections between the bacterial nucleus and the cytoplasmic membrane have also been found in cells of *B. mega-*

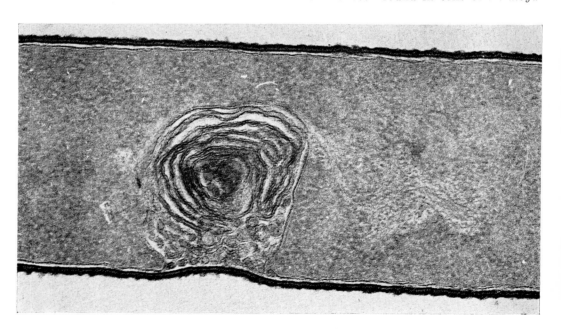

Figure 7.8. Section of normal cell of *Bacillus subtilis*, × 125,000. Note the connection between the nucleus and the mesosome. (From Ryter & Jacob.[29])

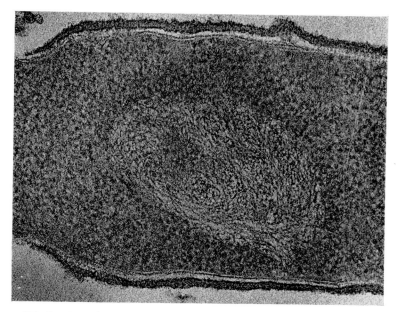

Figure 7.9. Section of plasmolyzed cell of *Bacillus subtilis*, × 100,000. Note the connection between the nucleus and the cytoplasmic membrane. (From Ryter & Jacob.[29])

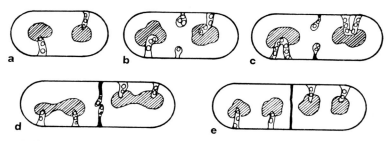

Figure 7.10. Schematic representation of the nuclear division in *Bacillus subtilis*. (From Ryter & Jacob.[29])

terium, Bacillus cereus and *Escherichia coli*.[12, 30] Separation of a bacterial nucleus into two daughter nuclei is probably initiated by growth of a well-defined region of the cytoplasmic membrane[18] (Figures 7.8, 7.9 and 7.10).

Connections between ribosomes, essentially polyribosomes, and the cytoplasmic membrane in bacteria have been demonstrated by several investigators.[1, 2, 17, 33] This indicates that the cytoplasmic membrane plays an important role in the protein synthesis in bacterial cells.

The study of protoplasts, spheroplasts and L-forms has undoubtedly increased our knowledge concerning various microbial groups. This study has also deepened our insight into the structure and function of the microbial and, especially, the bacterial cell. It has thus become clear that this cell is a more complicated and integrated structure than was believed about fifteen—or even five—years ago. The cell wall, the cytoplasmic membrane, the bulk of the cytoplasm, and the nucleus form a system, the functioning of which is a result of intricate relationships between its structural components. I am convinced that further morphological studies in protoplasts and related forms, carried out in combination with biochemical, biophysical and genetic studies, will continue to help us understand the structure and function of microorganisms at the submicroscopic and molecular levels.

REFERENCES

1. Abrams, A., Nielsen, L., and Thaemert, J.: Rapidly synthesized ribonucleic acid in membrane ghosts from *Streptococcus fecalis* protoplasts. *Biochim. Biophys. Acta* **80**: 325, 1964.

2. Aronson, A.: Adsorption of polysomes to bacterial membranes. *J. Mol. Biol.* **15**: 505, 1966.

3. Boy de la Tour, E., Bolle, A., and Kellenberger, E.: Nouvelles observations concernant l'action du laurylsulfate de sodium sur la paroi et la membrane d'*E. coli. Path. et Microbiol.* **28**: 229, 1965.

4. Dienes, L.: Controversial aspects of the morphology of PPLO. *Ann. N. Y. Acad. Sci.* **79**: 356, 1960.

5. Dienes, L., and Bullivant, S.: Comparison of the morphology of PPLO and L-forms of bacteria with light and electron microscopy. *Ann. N. Y. Acad. Sci.,* 1967 (in press).

6. Edebo, L. A new press for the disruption of micro-organisms and other cells. *J. Biochem. Microbiol. Tech. Eng.* **2**: 453, 1960.

7. Fedorova, G. I.: The formation of colonies from protoplasts of Bac. megatherium. *Zh. Mikrobiol. Epidemiol. Immunobiol.* 42(8): 36, 1965 (in Russian).

8. Fitz-James, P. C.: Cytological and chemical studies of the growth of protoplasts of *Bacillus megaterium. J. Biophys. Biochem. Cytol.* **4**: 257, 1958.

9. ———: Participation of the cytoplasmic membrane in the growth and spore formation of bacilli. *J. Biophys. Biochem. Cytol.* **8**: 507, 1960.

10. ———: Electron microscopy of *Bacillus megaterium* undergoing isolation of its nuclear bodies. *J. Bact.* **87**: 1202, 1964.

11. ———: Fate of the mesosomes of *Bacillus megaterium* during protoplasting. *J. Bact.* **87**: 1483, 1964.

12. ———: Discussion of: Fuhs, G. W.: Fine structure and replication of bacterial nucleoids. *Bact. Rev.* **29**: 293, 1965.

13. Fleck, J.: Étude chimique de la paroi de *Proteus* P 18 et de la forme L correspondante. *Ann. Inst. Pasteur* (Paris) **108**: 395, 1965.

14. Freimer, E.: Studies of L forms and proto-

15. Freundt, E. A.: Morphology and classification of the PPLO. *Ann. N. Y. Acad. Sci.* **79**: 312, 1960.

16. Glauert, A. M., and Hopwood, D. A.: A membranous component of the cytoplasm in *Streptomyces coelicolor. J. Biophys. Biochem. Cytol.* **6**: 515, 1959.

16a. Gooder, H., and Maxted, W. R.: Protoplasts of group A beta-haemolytic streptococci. *Nature* **182**: 808, 1958.

17. Hendler, R. W., Banfield, W. G., Tani, J., and Kuff, E. L.: On the cytological unit for protein synthesis *in vivo* in *E. coli*. III. Electron microscopic and ultracentrifugal examination of intact cells and fractions. *Biochim. Biophys. Acta* **80**: 307, 1964.

18. Jacob, F., Ryter, A., and Cuzin, F.: On the association between *DNA* and membrane in bacteria. *Proc. Roy. Soc. London B* **164**: 267, 1966.

19. Klieneberger, E.: The natural occurrence of pleuropneumonia-like organisms in apparent symbiosis with *Streptobacillus moniliformis* and other bacteria. *J. Path. Bact.* **40**: 93, 1935.

20. Klieneberger-Nobel, E.: *Pleuropneumonia-Like Organisms (PPLO) Mycoplasmataceae.* Academic Press, New York, 1962.

21. Martin, H. H.: Bacterial protoplasts—a review. *J. Theor. Biol.* **5**: 1, 1963.

22. McQuillen, K.: Bacterial protoplasts. In: *The Bacteria, Vol. I: Structure* (I. C. Gunsalus and R. Y. Stanier, Eds.). Academic Press, New York, 1960: p. 249.

23. Morrison, T. H., and Weibull, C.: The occurrence of cell wall constituents in stable Proteus L forms. *Acta Path. Microbiol. Scand.* **55**: 475, 1962.

24. Nečas, O.: The mechanism of regeneration of yeast protoplasts. II. Formation of the cell wall de novo. *Folia Biol.* (Praha) **11**: 97, 1965.

25. Nocard, E., and Roux, E. R.: Le microbe de la péripneumonie. *Ann. Inst. Pasteur* (Paris) **12**: 240, 1898.

26. Panos, C., Barkulis, S. S., and Hayashi, J. A.: Streptococcal L forms. III. Effects of sonic treatment on viability. *J. Bact.* **80**: 336, 1960.

27. Perrine, T. D., Ribi, E., Maki, W., Miller, B., and Oertli, E.: Production model press for the preparation of bacterial cell walls. *Appl. Microbiol.* **10**: 93, 1962.

28. Razin, S., Morowitz, H. J., and Terry, T. M.: Membrane subunits of *Mycoplasma laidlawii* and their assembly to membranelike struc-

plasts of group A streptococci. II. Chemical and immunological properties of the cell membrane. *J. Exp. Med.* **117**: 377, 1963.

tures. *Proc. Nat. Acad. Sci. USA* **54**: 219, 1965.

29. Ryter, A., and Jacob, F.: Étude au microscope électronique de la liaison entre noyau et mésosome chez *Bacillus subtilis. Ann. Inst. Pasteur* (Paris) **107**: 384, 1964.

30. ———: Étude morphologique de la liaison du noyau a la membrane chez *E. coli* et chez les protoplastes de *B. subtilis. Ann. Inst. Pasteur* (Paris) **110**: 801, 1966.

31. Salton, M. R. J.: *The Bacterial Cell Wall.* Elsevier, Amsterdam, 1964.

32. Salton, M. R., and Chapman, J. A.: Isolation of the membrane-mesosome structures from *Micrococcus lysodeikticus. J. Ultrastruct. Res.* **6**: 489, 1962.

33. Schlessinger, D., Marchesi, V. T., and Kwan, B. C. K.: Binding of ribosomes to cytoplasmic reticulum of *Bacillus megaterium. J. Bact.* **90**: 456, 1965.

34. Sedar, A. W., and Burde, R. M.: The demonstration of the succinic dehydrogenase system in *Bacillus subtilis* using tetranitro-blue tetrazolium combined with techniques of electron microscopy. *J. Cell Biol.* **27**: 53, 1965.

35. Sharp, J. T.: Amino sugars in L forms of bacteria and pleuropneumonia-like organisms. *J. Bact.* **86**: 692, 1963.

36. Shockman, G. D., Kolb, J. J., Bakay, B., Conover, M. J., and Toennies, G.: Protoplast membrane of *Streptococcus faecalis. J. Bact.* **85**: 168, 1963.

37. Spiegelman, S., Aronson, A. I., and Fitz-James, P. C.: Isolation and characterization of nuclear bodies from protoplasts of *Bacillus megaterium. J. Bact.* **75**: 102, 1958.

38. Tomcsik, J., and Guex-Holzer, S.: Änderung der Struktur der Bakterienzelle im Verlauf der Lysozym-Einwirkung. *Schweiz. Zschr. allg. Path.* **15**: 517, 1952.

39. Tulasne, R.: Les formes L des bactéries. *Rev. Immun.* (Paris) **15**: 223, 1951.

40. Tulasne, R., Minck, R., and Kirn, A.: Étude comparative, au microscope électronique, d'un *Proteus* et des forms L des types A et B correspondantes. *Ann. Inst. Pasteur* (Paris) **102**: 292, 1962.

41. van Iterson, W.: Some features of a remarkable organelle in *Bacillus subtilis. J. Biophys. Biochem. Cytol.* **6**: 515, 1961.

42. van Iterson, W., and Leene, W.: A cytochemical localization of reductive sites in a Grampositive bacterium. *J. Cell Biol.* **20**: 361, 1964.

43. Weibull, C.: The isolation of protoplasts from *Bacillus megaterium* by controlled treatment with lysozyme. *J. Bact.* **66**: 688, 1953.

44. ———: Bacterial protoplasts. *Ann. Rev. Microbiol.* **12**: 1, 1958.

45. ———: Size of minimal reproductive units of bacterial L forms. *Proc. Soc. Exp. Biol. Med.* **113**: 32, 1963.

46. ———: Plasmolysis in *Bacillus megaterium. J. Bact.* **89**: 1151, 1965.

47. ———: Structure of bacterial L forms and their parent bacteria. *J. Bact.* **90**: 1467, 1965.

48. ———: Localization of enzymes and endotoxin in *Proteus* L forms and in their parent bacteria. *Folia Microbiol.* (Praha) (in press).

49. Weibull, C., Bickel, W. D., Haskins, W. T., Milner, K. C., and Ribi, E.: Chemical, biological, and structural properties of stable *Proteus* L forms and their parent bacteria. *J. Bact.* **93**: 1143, 1967.

8

Morphology and Reproductive Processes of Bacteria with Defective Cell Wall*

Louis Dienes

MASSACHUSETTS GENERAL HOSPITAL
BOSTON, MASSACHUSETTS

HISTORICAL INTRODUCTION

Bacteria have well defined shape and size varying within narrow limits under the conditions which permit their survival and multiplication. They are, like most plant cells, enclosed in a rigid cell wall. It has been known since the earliest studies of bacteria that in some cultures they are pleomorphic,† larger than usual and irregular in shape, and that they sometimes develop into giant cells many times larger than the usual bacteria. In some species, such as *Streptobacillus moniliformis* and *Bacteroides*, the presence of these giant forms is regarded as a characteristic of the species. As multiplication of these large bodies was not observed and they seemed to play no role in the development of the cultures, they were regarded as involution or "dying forms". Their multiplication was observed first in *S. moniliformis*.[12] No bacteria were present in the colonies obtained from them, and the structure of the colonies and the morphology of the organisms in-dicated a striking similarity to the few species of *Mycoplasma* known at that time, the organisms of bovine pleuropneumonia and of agalactia. Somewhat later it turned out that similar colonies develop spontaneously in cultures of various bacteria and their development can be induced in many species by various artificial influences. The organisms in these cultures, which are usually designated as L-forms, are variable in size, and they are easily deformed or destroyed. This indicates that they do not have a rigid cell wall. In the filaments of *Proteus* it could be seen that their content herniates out, producing a large body which under appropriate conditions reproduces either the bacteria or the L-forms.

While this information on the L-forms was being accumulated, our knowledge of the structure of bacteria also increased. The cell wall was isolated and its chemical composition studied. It was observed that bacteria, after elimination of the cell wall by appropriate enzymes, continue to metabolize. They may increase in size and when transferred to solid media may produce L-forms. At first it was believed that the protoplasts so obtained from bacteria had no cell membrane. After development of the technic of thin sections for electron

* This research was supported by Grant AI-05625 from the National Institute of Allergy and Infectious Diseases.

† See author's Appendix (p. 84) for definition of terms used in this paper.

microscopy, it was apparent that the cell membrane and the inner structure of the protoplast and L-forms, insofar as we have information, are similar. Both protoplasts and L-forms need a certain amount of osmotic protection, which varies in different species, in order to survive and multiply.

The L-forms, however, cannot be regarded simply as multiplying protoplasts. Multiplication of the L-forms does not occur in the form of protoplasts, and one morphological element characteristic of the L-forms, the "elementary corpuscle", seems to be essentially different in structure from protoplasts. Neither can the L-forms be regarded as an example of extreme pleomorphism, for not only is their morphology changed, but also their mode of multiplication. The dividing line between pleomorphism and L-forms is the presence or absence of multiplication in the form of small soft granules which embed themselves into agar media. The large bodies produced in bacterial cultures are at the dividing line: something occurs during the development of large bodies which makes it possible for them to continue growth with altered morphology. My concept of the nature and definition of the L-forms is influenced by their similarity to *Mycoplasma*. This similarity starts with the change in the mode of multiplication.

According to this short historical review, bacteria surviving and multiplying with defective cell walls fall into two distinct groups, the pleomorphic bacteria and the L-forms, with the large bodies forming a connecting link between these two groups. Protoplasts are artificial products which do not take part, as such, in the growth of the cultures. Pleomorphism and transformation into L-forms represent in several respects increasing alteration of the cell. Spontaneous production of L-forms in a culture is usually preceded by pleomorphic growth and the agents producing transformation into L-forms, especially penicillin and glycine, also produce pleomorphism when applied in low concentrations. The basic alteration of the pleomorphic cultures has not been studied

and in the following discussion only a few references will be made to them.

Before discussing the morphology and reproduction of the L-forms it is necessary to indicate some of their properties which are often overlooked. One of these is that in several groups of bacteria two types of L-forms develop after exposure to penicillin; this was first observed in *Proteus*, and the types were designated as A and B. Two similar types develop in *Salmonella*, in *Escherichia*, and in hemophilic organisms; these types are distinct without transitional forms between them. The study of *Proteus* indicated that in Type B both the plasma membrane and the outer cell wall of bacteria are retained:[2] only the rigidity of the cell wall is lost; Type B remains sensitive to several phages,[19] and the culture contains some organisms that resume bacterial form immediately after elimination of the penicillin and continue to grow as such. In other respects the B type has the characteristics typical of L-forms: it is not sensitive to penicillin, but the bacteria recovered from it are fully sensitive; the colonies start to grow as small granules embedding themselves in the agar and their structure corresponds to that of the L-forms. The A type has a unit membrane corresponding to the plasma membrane of bacteria; it develops only on special media and colonies remain small; bacteria are reproduced from them rarely or not at all. The B type transplanted on the surface of agar may produce A type colonies. The A and B types do not correspond to "stable" and "unstable" L-forms. Both types reproduce bacteria for a period after isolation, and lose this property after long cultivation. It has not been thus far determined whether L-forms of other groups of bacteria immediately after isolation correspond to either of these types or are different from them. The tendency to return into bacterial forms usually is greatest immediately after isolation of L-forms and decreases with cultivation.

Another property of L-forms is that during long cultivation they may change markedly in morphology and in growth requirements. Sudden variations of the cultures may also occur. From the B type L-form of *Proteus* strain 52, six markedly different variants have been obtained. The old L-strains and variants are useful for certain purposes, but they do not give full information on the potentialities of L-forms. If the L-forms have any biological significance, this probably will be apparent soon after their isolation and not in the changed old cultures.

The morphology of L-forms differs from that of bacteria, as the organisms in the cultures of L-forms do not have a definite size and shape that remain constant under different conditions. There is a continuous variation in size from the elementary corpuscles to the large bodies, which may be up to 50 μ in size. Except for the smallest organisms, the shape varies from spherical to large irregular masses branching and extending in different directions. Both the possibility of growth and the size and shape depend to a large extent on the physical properties of the medium. One has the impression that in the presence of appropriate nutrients the L-form retains the tendency to enlarge, but the physical properties of the immediate environment of the organisms determine whether this occurs and in which form. Only the elementary corpuscles, and possibly also the fully developed large bodies, seem to have a specific role in reproduction; all other sizes and shapes seem to be essentially similar, and possess similar potentialities for development.

DEVELOPMENT OF L-FORMS FROM BACTERIA

Pleomorphism and growth into large bodies occur spontaneously in many bacterial species preceding autolysis of the culture. Such alteration of the cultures can be induced by such variable influences as exposure to certain amino acids, some antibiotics, salts of various metals (lithium, cadmium), antibodies, and cold.[8] This occurs in liquid as well as on various solid media. With few exceptions, growth of L-forms from bacteria has been observed only after they have grown to large bodies

either spontaneously or under the influence of inducing agents. With few exceptions, it was observed only on agar media of appropriate consistency or on membrane filters of appropriate pore size.[7] The mode of development from bacteria has been studied in several species: in *S. moniliformis*, *Escherichia coli*, and *Bacteroides* without inducing agents; in *Proteus*, *Salmonella* and *Bacteroides* under the influence of penicillin and glycine; and in the enterococcus and *Bacillus subtilis* after exposure to lysozyme[15] or to other enzymes. Figure 8.4A* illustrates the growth of irregular granules forming B type colonies from the large bodies. Their cell wall is continuous with that of the large body, and ribosomes and nuclear material are transferred into them. The successive steps starting with protoplasts will be illustrated with enterococci. The cocci in strain **9790** are almost all transformed to protoplasts under the influence of lysozyme (Figure 8.1A). Transferred to agar medium containing 3% NaCl, many protoplasts grow into large bodies (Figure 8.1B), and from them the small granules start to grow (Figure 8.1, C, D) and produce the L-colonies. After some growth, the cocci may be reproduced in the colonies (Figure 8.1G).

A similar development of L-forms from the large bodies has been observed in all species studied. In addition, another type of development occurs in *Proteus*[19] and *Salmonella* after exposure to penicillin: a small droplet extruded before marked growth of the bacillus grows into an L-colony.

Development of B type colonies from bacteria was observed with *Proteus* and *Salmonella* on hard gelatin media containing penicillin. The bacteria grow to very large bodies (Figure 8.3A), and some of these produce extensions in various directions on the surface (Figure 8.3B). In a few cases these irregular organisms segment into fractions and continue to multiply. No small granules are produced and the medium is not invaded.

In liquid media many bacteria exposed

* See representative illustrations at end of paper.

to penicillin grow to large bodies, but multiplication of these or production of viable granules does not occur. I observed only one case in which the large bodies produced from a strain of *Proteus* multiplied in successive transplants in a shallow layer of broth in glass flasks. The interpretation of this observation is doubtful because L-forms adhering to a glass surface continue to multiply submerged in broth.

Morphology, Structure and Reproduction of L-Forms

Immediately after isolation from bacteria, multiplication of L-forms as small granules has been observed only inside agar media of appropriate consistency. Figure 8.1D shows the extension of small elongated granules in strands inside the agar. Another photograph from the same culture (Figure 8.1E) shows that the granules can be much larger. As these granules grow only inside the agar, they can be seen only in thin sections with the electron microscope. In these, the cross-section of granules shows different sizes and shapes, the distribution of which varies in different cultures. From the distribution of circular, elongated and irregular forms in the section, some conclusions can be drawn about the actual shape of the organisms. For instance, in a section from the edge of a young *Proteus* A type colony, some of the larger organisms were long, oval or extended in several directions, and some were circular. The size was as large as 5 μ in length and 1.5 μ in width (Figure 8.4C). According to the shapes apparent in the micrographs, the actual shape of the majority of organisms growing at the periphery of colonies is an irregular branching mass extending in various directions. In the densely grown center of isolated agar colonies, the organisms are of more regular, usually elongated, shape.

The elementary corpuscles are characterized by small size, regular shape and high density. Their size varies continuously from about 0.1 μ up to the larger forms, and there is no sharp dividing line

separating them from the larger forms. Nuclear areas of increasing size appear in the center. Their number varies considerably in different parts of the colonies. In the young colonies studied, the greatest number of elementary corpuscles occurred at the growing edge of the colonies. In one area of a section made from the L-culture designated as LX,[2] 23 larger forms and 74 corpuscles increasing in size to 0.5 μ were counted. It is apparent from the micrographs that the elementary corpuscles grow from the surface of large organisms, occasionally more than one at the same time. The large number of circular forms of the corpuscles in the sections indicates that many of them are spherical. They are seen in short chains and filaments, and oval forms indicating sections of a filament. This probably means that elementary corpuscles grow and multiply in this form. The continuous transition in size and structure to the large bodies demonstrates that they grow into large organisms.

On hard media containing 3.5% agar, the transferred organisms grew to large size but no multiplication occurred. The same was observed on membrane filters with a pore size of 0.1 μ or less.

The extension of L-forms cannot be seen in membrane filters as clearly as in agar.[7] It occurs not in small granules but in branching irregular filaments or interconnected irregular masses, similar to those seen inside the agar. The size and shape are not determined exclusively by the structure of the filter because extension of different L-forms in similar filters is noticeably different. In well-developed colonies quite large round organisms are often seen. On the surface of membrane filters, the large bodies multiply by irregular growth and segmentation (Figure 8.2C) and the penetration of irregular growth into the pores of the filter is apparent (Figure 8.2D).

Immediately after isolation most L forms do not grow in liquid media. I obtained growth from A type L-culture of *Proteus*, *Salmonella* and *Bacteriodes* in broth containing 0.2% agar. The organisms in these cultures were in the form of large bodies, and multiplication of small granules was not apparent. Similar cultures developed also with 0.4% agar. Immediately after isolation, *Serratia* L-forms have grown in the form of large bodies in broth without the addition of agar[1] (Figure 8.1H). Young colonies of L-forms of streptococci and staphylococci gave very slight growth consisting mostly of vacuolated very large organisms (Figure 8.1L) and could not be maintained in successive transplants.[5] L-forms of diphtheroids grew well in the form of large bodies in broth containing 3% NaCl.

The growth of L-forms of *Serratia* on agar was of interest.[1] Broth cultures consisting of large bodies transferred to agar developed in two different ways. Where the organisms were isolated, the large bodies increased in size, and small granules started to grow at their periphery (Figure 8.1I), embedding themselves in the agar and producing a colony; where the large bodies were crowded, no small granules started to grow. The large bodies grew into irregular shapes (Figure 8.1J), segmented and on the surface of the agar produced a colony consisting of large bodies without growth of granules and the center embedded in the agar.

Inoculated into gelatin media, multiplication of the L-forms, if it occurs, is in the form of large bodies, as in broth. On the surface of gelatin the transferred organisms often grow to very large size and are slightly irregular. After some growth, large bodies developing from *Proteus* bacteria extend on the surface in thin irregular star-like extensions (Figure 8.3B). Occasionally a few colonies of the B type are produced on 30% gelatin by multiplication of the large bodies. This occurs more often with L-forms of staphylococci and streptococci, well adapted to grow on our media, and with L-forms of diphtheroids. The organisms extend on the surface in connected, branching thin sheets, and the colonies consist of large bodies of different sizes (Figure 8.2, A, B).

On the surface of coagulated serum, growth of L-forms occurs also in large bodies. Some L-forms invade the medium, and in these cases they grow in small granules as in agar.

The organisms in all L-forms properly studied with the electron microscope were enclosed in a unit membrane, with the exception of the B type of *Proteus* grown directly from bacteria. Old B type cultures of *Proteus* or the variants obtained from them have not yet been examined, nor have B type L-forms developing in other species. The only structural elements inside the membrane in all L-forms were ribosomes, threads of DNA and discrete granules. The arrangement of the ribosomes and the DNA is often similar to that seen in Gram-negative bacteria. The elementary corpuscles appear to be densely packed with ribosomes but, in somewhat larger forms, areas with DNA threads are apparent.

The very large-sized organisms usually contain multiple large vacuoles and may be transformed into empty blebs. Examination with the light microscope shows occasionally a few small granules in the vacuoles. Sometimes there are masses of granules in the vacuoles, or the full parts of the large body are transformed into granules of different sizes. Small granules of about 0.2 μ have been seen in the large bodies of the L-forms of *Proteus*[20] and of *Staphylococcus*[22] with the electron microscope. Otherwise, the large bodies seem to have a structure similar to that of the smaller organisms. Their structure does not indicate that they are produced by multiplication of granules inside the cell membrane or that granules are preformed in them.

The variable morphology and multiplication of the L-forms on different media suggest certain considerations on the nature of these organisms. After alteration of the cell wall, the ability for growth remains, but the extension of the organisms and the occurrence of division is greatly influenced by the physical properties of the environment. Adherence to a surface, to glass, to membrane filters, to hard agar, or to gelatin makes extension of the organisms possible. Extension in narrow branching strands, observed on the surface of gelatin and membrane filters indicates how the growth invades and extends within agar and on membrane filters. The ability to divide varies in different L-forms and the variability of division probably indicates that division is influenced by the irregularity of the surface to which they adhere. Contact with the gel structure of agar and membrane filters facilitates both extension and division. The small granules within the agar seem to be produced in the same way as the multiplication of large bodies on the surface by irregular growth and irregular segmentation.

Several observations suggest, however, that multiplication of L-forms is a more complex process. When the granules start to grow from the large bodies, condensations appear at their surface first, and growth starts from these condensations. The multiplication of small elongated granules observed with the light microscope is similar: condensations appear at the two ends, and between them the organisms disintegrate. These processes were not apparent in the micrographs but they might be analogous to the development of elementary corpuscles. It does not seem impossible that the development of these corpuscles is in a very irregular way analogous to the usual division of bacteria. In many cases, the segmentation of larger forms appears to be more like disintegration of the organisms in which some parts remain viable, while in other cases it resembles the division of bacteria. Reproduction of viable granules inside the large bodies may give important information on the structure not only of the large bodies but also of bacteria. Our information on these processes is still in a preliminary stage.

A few remarks should be made about the large bodies. They are the connecting link between pleomorphic bacteria and L-forms, and are the only L-form structures which are seen in the natural surroundings of bacteria. They can often be seen in human feces, and I have seen them in large numbers in the nasopharynx of rabbits. They have been seen in scrapings from the urethra in the earliest phase of gonococcal infection. The structure of large bodies developing from bacteria in *Proteus* and in B type L-forms corresponded to the structure of bacteria, including the presence of a double cell wall (Figure 8.4A). Those developing in other L-forms and in PPLO had a similar structure but only a unit membrane (Figure 8.4D). There are no definite indications that the large bodies play a part in the life of bacteria, but there are observations that deserve to be studied. One is that in various cultures of L-forms and bacteria some of the large bodies remain intact in autolyzed cultures. As long as they are present, it is apparent that growth develops in transplants and that it starts from the large bodies. In *Proteus*, large bodies produced from bacteria and in the L-colonies, when transferred to media without penicillin, start to resume bacterial form within an hour, either by elongation or by growth of irregular bacterial forms from the surface of the large bodies. Another observation to which I have repeatedly referred is that bacteria develop by growth not only from the surface of large bodies but sometimes inside the large bodies. In one strain of *S. moniliformis*, this occurred regularly.[8] I have been very much impressed also by the observation that in a strain of *Bacteroides* and in typhoid bacilli the morphological alteration of the bacilli suggested autogamous conjugation. Such observations cannot be made easily and thus far have aroused no interest.[8]

PERMANENT VARIATIONS OF THE L-FORMS

The alteration of the cultures during long cultivation varies considerably in different L-forms. One usual alteration is that the cultures grow more abundantly and their nutritional requirements become simpler. This was marked in the L-forms of beta hemolytic streptococci and staphylococci,[5] while some L-forms of enterococci and of alpha hemolytic streptococci often grow abundantly immediately after isolation. The L-forms of beta hemolytic streptococci at first grow very poorly, especially in broth. After 12 years of transfer from medium to medium they now grow abundantly both on agar and in broth. Their morphology has also changed. The granules growing inside the agar became much smaller and large bodies developed abundantly on the surface of colonies. Similar alterations of the cultures were observed repeatedly in L-forms of *Proteus* and *Salmonella*. In our laboratory one L-form of both species has been carried from medium to medium for over 20 years. These strains originally produced typical colonies with the center embedded in the agar, and small granules grew only inside the agar; growth did not occur in broth. At present the colonies develop on the surface with little or no growth into the agar. The culture consists of a mixture of large bodies decreasing in size to small granules, and the small granules multiply both on the surface of agar and in broth. The organisms have become more refractile and take a deeper staining. The cultures are occasionally extremely pleomorphic. In broth, long thin filaments develop; on agar, tangled filaments can be seen, and thin short filaments radiating from a center ending in knobs which grow to large bodies. These cultures became slowly adapted to grow abundantly in our media and became more like bacteria in many respects, but did not regain the usual bacterial structure.

In addition to this slow adaptation of the culture to the artificial conditions, we observed in the L-forms of the same strain of *Proteus* several sudden variations. One variant developed several times within a few months in two strains of *Proteus* (52 and XK) from B type L-colonies immediately after their growth from bacteria.[3] This variant extended as a thin film floating on the surface of liquid media and produced cultures similar in appearance to those of tubercle bacilli. The medium remained clear and no growth developed in it. The culture consisted preponderantly of small granules from which electron micrographs were made. During the following 14 years, several attempts were made without success to isolate similar cultures from the same two *Proteus* strains and several other freshly isolated strains. Two other variants developed from B type L-cultures of strain 52. During the attempts to obtain the floating cultures, on several occasions cultures were obtained which grew as large dense mucoid masses on the surface and continued to grow submerged in the medium. The other variant was isolated from a freshly isolated B type L-culture of *Proteus* strain 52 when the bacteria started to reproduce in it. At first it reproduced bacteria on penicillin-free media, and almost any organism, small or large, started to grow into bacteria. Not only were the L-forms changed, but also the bacteria reproduced from them. These did not produce spreaders like the bacteria recovered from the A and B type L-cultures and the L-forms obtained from these bacteria were similar to the variant. After about one month's cultivation on media containing penicillin the ability to reproduce bacteria was lost, and during the following year bacteria did not develop in the cultures either on agar or in broth. The culture is extremely pleomorphic. Multiplication of very small granules, thin short filaments or larger ones, sometimes forming star-like arrangements, and large bodies segmenting into several parts were apparent on the surface of the agar. Penetration of the growth into the agar was not frequent and embedded centers rarely developed in the large colonies. Growth was not obtained in liquid media.

The L-forms produced from bacteria by the usual methods on the usual media are well defined in their morphology and requirements for growth. It is necessary to be aware of their variability, especially in studying their possible pathogenicity and in comparing them with PPLO.

Possible Significance of L-Forms

The significance of L-forms in the biology of parasitic and non-parasitic bacteria must be distinguished. Parasitism makes various classes of living organisms well adapted to their special environment but usually makes them unfit to live anywhere else. There is no evidence at present that L-forms are produced and play any role in the life of bacteria in their own world. We have very little information also about the actual role of some of the important biological processes observed in the laboratory, such as conjugation or transduction in their world. It is possible that transformation into L-forms offers protection and helps survival under certain conditions. I have referred to certain processes occurring in the large bodies, especially the development of bacteria inside them, which may indicate the biological significance of the large bodies and deserve thorough study.

There are suggestions that L-forms have a role in the host-parasite interplay. The defensive reactions of the host are directed to a large extent toward the cell wall, and the weakening of the cell wall in the cultures isolated directly from the pathological processes is often apparent. It is an old observation that such cultures are pleomorphic and the bacteria regain their usual forms only after several transplants. In my experience, *Hemophilus influenzae* cultivated from spinal fluid in about one-third of the cases were highly pleomorphic (Figure 8.3G). This was so in all cases of septicemia following tracheobronchitis of young children. After overnight incubation the culture consisted of irregular swollen filaments and large bodies. Meningococci cultivated from spinal fluid are also often pleomorphic. The pleomorphism of *S. moniliformis* and *Bacteroides* cultivated from suppurative processes and septicemia is well known. In many cases, in addition to pleomorphism, L-colonies also develop in these cultures; the first observations on L-forms were made on cultures obtained in this way. In such pleomorphic cultures of *H. influenzae*, meningococci and gonococci, and in pleomorphic cultures of *E. coli*, a slight development of L-forms often occurs (Figure 8.3E), but the cultivation of this slight L-type growth has not been successful. Marked pleomorphism and spontaneous development of L-forms on the usual media, without osmotic protection, have been observed in one case in a strain of alpha hemolytic streptococcus isolated from the bloodstream;[11] the cause of the septi-

cemia was not endocarditis but an old abscess of one kidney. It is of interest that when there was opportunity to examine direct smears from pathological specimens from which pleomorphic cultures were obtained, only regular bacterial forms were seen. We observed only one case of peritonitis in which *Bacteroides* was apparently present in the leucocytes in the L-form. Strains are encountered in various bacteria which, transferred to agar, grow as L-forms without any inducing agent or osmotic protection. Thus, growth of L-forms from a specimen does not give definite evidence that the bacterium was present in the L-form in the lesions. Such evidence can be obtained only by direct observation in microscopic preparations. The development of growth in osmotically protective media only is an important observation, but in itself does not indicate the form in which the bacteria are present in the pathological processes.

Toxin production is retained in L-forms of *Clostridium tetani* and *Vibrio cholerae*,[21] and these L-forms may kill experimental animals. Freshly isolated L-forms of *S. moniliformis*, which easily return to bacteria, kill the experimental animals, but only after reversion to the bacterial form.[9] Otherwise, infection has not been produced by L-forms of highly virulent bacteria. In my opinion, the main reason for the study of L-forms in the infectious processes is their close resemblance to PPLO, several of which are important pathogens. It is also probable that, if L-forms are present in infectious processes, they will be similar in morphology to PPLO.

COMPARISON OF L-FORMS AND PPLO

The physical properties of L-forms, their morphology, and the structure of their colonies on agar are closely similar to those of PPLO. This suggested to Klieneberger that the L-forms were PPLO contaminating the bacterial cultures. After it became apparent that L-forms originate from bacteria, both Klieneberger[13] and Freundt,[10] adhered to the opinion that the similarity between the two groups of organisms is superficial, and, being due to the lack of rigid cell wall, of less importance than the differences between them. My impression is that recent studies have decided the case for close similarity.[6] In comparing such highly variable groups it is necessary to review their entire range of variations and the conditions under which these occur. If we do this, it is apparent that the morphological forms in the cultures, the structure of the organisms and of the colonies and, insofar as it is known, their reproduction, are similar and are influenced in a similar way by the conditions of cultivation. The large bodies play a similar role in multiplication; the influence of the physical environment is similar in both groups, although greater in L-forms than in PPLO.

The close similarity of the colonies on the usual agar media is generally known; this similarity is also present on membrane filters. Both groups stop growing at the same concentration of hard agar and the same pore size of membrane filters, and in both groups the organisms increase in size on these media. Similar also is the behavior of the two groups on gelatin. In young agar colonies the similarity of the extension into the medium and the size of the organism is often close and the colonies are indistinguishable. Electron microscopic studies of young colonies grown inside agar have indicated the essential similarities. The multiplication inside the agar in both groups appears to be irregular growth in several directions, segmentation of the larger organisms and enlargement of the elementary corpuscles. The extension inside the agar does not resemble that of bacteria or actinomyces. The organisms are irregular without determined shape. In the old cultures of L-forms and their variants several properties thought to be characteristic of PPLO, such as growth of small granules in broth and on the surface of agar and the development of short and long filaments, were apparent. The close similarity of the two groups is in contrast to their common dissimilarity in structure and mode of multiplication compared with any other group of microorganisms.

L-forms and PPLO were often compared in broth cultures, in which the L-forms do not multiply as small granules and the similarity of the two groups is not as clearly apparent as in cultures on the surface or inside of agar.

Klieneberger's[12] impression of the separation of L-forms from PPLO is mainly based on the slightly smaller size of PPLO organisms which produce growth on our media as determined by filtration. This is interpreted as the absence of elementary corpuscles in L-forms. Freundt's[10] and Orskov's[16] impression is that PPLO produces a fine undivided mycelium which fragmentates to small granules, the large forms being, in their opinion, products of degeneration. This concept of the structure of PPLO is based on the observation of filaments in the cultures. Filaments are often produced as artifacts. It is apparent in Figure 8.2, I, J, K that filamentous structures take part in multiplication of some L-forms and are not the exclusive property of PPLO.

The usual difference between the cultures of L-forms and PPLO are the smaller size of PPLO colonies together with a much greater ability of the organisms to proliferate and to produce a colony. Multiplication of small granules occurs on the surface of agar and in broth. In transplants from L-forms, very few organisms multiply, preponderantly only the large bodies. The tendency of L-forms to grow into large bodies is also greater. Most strains of PPLO are better adapted than L-forms to grow in our media, and the tendency for autolysis is less. These properties usually permit differentiation of PPLO and L-forms, but in some cases only the knowledge that the culture originated from bacteria indicates that it is an L-form.

Most strains of PPLO intensively studied were isolated from pathological processes and from the mucous membranes of animals and man. Seiffert[18] described their isolation from various other sources, such as soil, well water and decaying wood. This line of study was not followed, and my own efforts to isolate them from such sources gave no results. However, in every sample of soil there were bacteria that produced L-forms, and the L-forms of one were similar in many respects to PPLO. The colonies remained small, and organisms, both inside the agar and at the periphery of the colonies on the surface, were very small. Seiffert and Laidlaw[14] obtained the PPLO-like cultures from filtrates of broth cultures, and it is not impossible that these originated from bacteria. We do not have sufficient information on the occurrence of PPLO in nature. All attempts thus far to prove that accepted PPLO strains descended from bacteria or reproduced bacteria have remained inconclusive. However, regarding the similarity of the two groups, this remains one of the most interesting problems in their study. My impression has remained that the most reasonable supposition about the nature of PPLO is that they are L-forms specialized to live as such. They would be comparable to the *fungi imperfecti*.

Several times I isolated from bacterial cultures organisms which corresponded in morphology to PPLO. They were obtained under conditions in which contamination was not likely. These observations could not be repeated, however, and the serological study of the cultures indicated no resemblance between the bacteria and the PPLO-like strains. Recently, Dr. W. Pachas, working in my laboratory, apparently found a way to isolate regularly cultures from several strains of bacteria corresponding in properties to PPLO and not to the usual L-forms.* These observations need further study.

It is necessary to comment on the identification of L-forms and PPLO because in several publications their identification remains doubtful. According to my experience, definite identification of L-forms and PPLO can be made in most cases only by examination of agar cultures with oil immersion in appropriate stained preparations.[4] It is important to dry the stain on the coverslip because liquid stain disrupts and destroys the growth on the surface, and the connection between the growth on the surface and inside the medium cannot be

* Unpublished data.

observed. The evidence must be clearcut that the colonies suspected of being PPLO or L-forms are produced by growth of organisms, and that the morphology of the organisms corresponds to L-forms or PPLO. Large colonies have to be distinguished from pleomorphic bacterial colonies in which the bacteria are transformed into large bodies. Most characteristic are the small and medium-sized young colonies. Examination in consecutive days indicates their growth, and small granules are clearly visible inside the agar. Staining with methylene blue and azure facilitates the recognition of the cultures. Intact bacteria, L-forms and PPLO are stained with a similar hue. Disintegrating bacteria and L-forms, precipitates and crystal formations, if they are stained at all, present a different pink hue. The arrangement of the granules in the colonies is most characteristic and indicates their growth. Colony-like formations which begin to appear after the first few days have to be examined with special care. Examination with phase contrast is less reliable because of the absence of characteristic staining. Furthermore, phase contrast can be used only with clear and transparent media. The impossibility of identifying PPLO in liquid media inoculated from pathological specimens was pointed out many years ago by Sabin.[17] They must be identified by transferring them to agar media. Attempts to identify L-forms and PPLO in tissues and inside of cells are usually inconclusive.

L-forms and PPLO cannot be identified by the presence of small granules in smears or on the surface of agar, even if they are present in masses, or by the presence of single large forms. The typical arrangement in small or larger colonies and the characteristic staining, together with the penetration of the agar, are necessary for their identification. They must be distinguished from crystal formations and other artifacts that develop during long incubation of the cultures.

The experience of my associates has been that it takes several months to acquire confidence in the identification of PPLO and L-forms, and that it cannot be learned from descriptions and photographs. To avoid gross errors, my advice to those who do not have training in the special techniques needed is to show their cultures and preparations to investigators with experience in this field.

SUMMARY

Bacteria with defective cell wall may grow either as pleomorphic bacterial cultures or as L-forms. Protoplasts, if they multiply, produce L-forms. In pleomorphic cultures, the size and shape of bacteria are altered and large bodies may be produced, but the structure of the colonies and the mode of multiplication are not changed. In the L-forms, regular bacterial forms are not present and the structure of the organisms and the mode of multiplication are altered. The colonies become similar in many respects to those of the pleuropneumonia group of organisms. The large bodies produced in bacterial cultures constitute the transition between the two groups; they may reproduce either bacteria or L-forms. Two types of L-forms are produced in several groups of Gram-negative bacteria. Not only do the L-forms of different bacteria vary from each other, but isolated L-cultures may also change their properties during cultivation. Study of young L-colonies grown within agar media have indicated the close similarity between L-forms and PPLO in morphology, in fine structure, and in the apparent mode of reproduction. The observation of elementary corpuscles in the cultures of L-forms is especially significant. We have no information at present on the possible biological role of pleomorphism and the production of L-forms in the life of bacteria, but various observations indicate that they may play a role in the host-parasite relationship. The study of L-forms in this respect is especially indicated by their similarity to PPLO, an important group of pathogenic organisms.

APPENDIX

DEFINITIONS AND NOMENCLATURE

Pleomorphic Cultures: The size and shape of the bacteria are altered. Filaments with swellings and large irregular bacilli may be present, and the cultures may be transformed *in toto* to large round bodies. The large forms are fragile and are not well preserved in smears. The structure of the colonies is not altered and growth does not invade the medium. Only the regular and slightly altered bacteria multiply.

L-Forms: The morphology of bacteria, the mode of multiplication and the structure of colonies are altered and become similar to those of PPLO (*Mycoplasma*). No bacterial forms are present. The size of multiplying organisms varies from very small to very large. Growth penetrates the agar and elementary corpuscles develop inside the agar. The organisms are easily deformed and destroyed. To identify L-forms and PPLO it is necessary to observe multiplication of small granules embedding themselves in agar media. Two types of L-forms, A and B, are produced in several species of bacteria. They differ in morphology, in ultrastructure, and in the ability to resume bacterial form. As observed in *Proteus*, the main difference between the two types is that in the B type the double cell wall of the bacteria is retained, and organisms are present in the culture which, after elimination of penicillin, immediately resume bacterial form. The A type has only a plasma membrane and bacteria are reproduced in the culture only occasionally. The terms, *stable* and *unstable L-forms*, do not have a definite meaning because almost all L-forms are unstable after isolation from bacteria and lose the ability to reproduce bacteria after long cultivation. In my opinion, these terms should be abandoned; they do not correspond to the A and B types. An L-form which has lost the ability to reproduce bacteria should be designated as *stabilized*, indicating change during cultivation. The L-forms usually change considerably in their properties during long cultivation and permanent variations also occur. These altered strains should be designated individually, like bacterial strains.

Protoplast: This term designates bacteria whose outer cell wall is eliminated by artificial means. They are spherical in liquid media. The plasma membrane is retained, and the inner structure corresponds to that of bacteria with some variation. They usually need high osmotic protection to prevent disintegration, but in some cases 0.5% NaCl is sufficient. Similar structures develop occasionally during autolysis of the cultures. In some cases, they multiply when transferred to agar, and their progeny is indistinguishable from L-forms developing from intact bacteria. However, transformation to protoplasts is not a necessary step in the development of L-forms from bacteria and the morphology of L-forms does not correspond to protoplasts. Osmotic fragility alone is not sufficient to designate a bacterial form as protoplast.

Spheroplasts: This term is used to designate large bodies developing from bacteria in liquid media. They do not differ in any characteristic properties from large bodies studied for a long time both in liquid and solid media. The spherical form is due to physical forces, as in air bubbles and oil droplets. My impression is that this term serves no useful purpose and is an unnecessary complication of the nomenclature.

Large bodies: These are several or many times larger than bacteria, spherical in liquid media, and usually round or polygonal on the surface of solid media. They are mechanically fragile and need a certain amount of osmotic protection to prevent disintegration, usually not more than 0.5% NaCl. They may be vacuolated and transformed to empty blebs. They may multiply in this form or reproduce bacteria or the granules of L-forms. They appear to be the connecting link both in the transformation of bacteria to L-forms and in the retransformation of L-forms to bacteria. The potentialities of these large bodies are variable and little known; they cannot be differentiated at present into different types. A noncommittal name such as large bodies is probably the most appropriate for them.

Elementary corpuscles: They are small, usually spherical bodies increasing in size from 0.05 μ, densely packed with ribosomes and enclosed in unit membranes. They appear to grow from the surface of larger organisms and are connected with transitional forms to the larger organisms. In L-forms, they are seen only in agar cultures; in PPLO, in both agar and liquid medium.

Granules: Spherical, elongated, or irregular organisms usually much smaller than bacteria, increasing in size from that of elementary corpuscles to about 1 μ. In freshly isolated L-forms they multiply only embedded in the agar.

The organisms in cultures of L-forms and PPLO are in continuous transition from the elementary corpuscles to the large bodies; their shape varies according to their environment. These organisms can be identified at present only by cultivation and by observation of their morphology in the cultures. Osmotic fragility is present in higher or lower degree in all of them and does not permit their identification and their differentiation from each other. To extend the meaning of the term "protoplast" to all osmotically fragile bacterial forms would probably be the source of much confusion.

REFERENCES

References to the early literature on the "large bodies" and L-forms are to be found in the review of Dienes & Weinberger,[8] on PPLO and L-forms in the monographs of Freundt[10] and Klieneberger-Nobel.[13] References to the literature on the fine structure of bacteria are to be found in a symposium on this subject published in Bacteriological Reviews, *Vol. 29, pp. 271–358, 1965.*

1. Bandur, B. M., and Dienes, L.: L forms isolated from a strain of *Serratia. J. Bact.* **86:** 829, 1963.
2. Bullivant, S., and Dienes, L.: Electron microscopy of some L forms of bacteria as compared with *Mycoplasma. J. Bact.* (in press).
3. Dienes, L.: Some new observations on L forms of bacteria. *J. Bact.* **66:** 274, 1953.
4. ———: Permanent stained agar preparations of *Mycoplasma* and of L forms of bacteria. *J. Bact.* **93:** 689, 1967.
5. ———: Observations on the morphology and reproduction processes of the L forms of bacteria. I. Streptococci and staphylococci. *J. Bact.* **93:** 693, 1967.
6. Dienes, L., and Bullivant, S.: Comparison of the morphology of PPLO and L-forms of

bacteria with light and electron microscopy. *Ann. N. Y. Acad. Sci.,* 1967 (in press).

7. Dienes, L., and Madoff, S.: Development and growth of L forms of bacteria and PPLO on membrane filters. *Proc. Soc. Exp. Biol. Med.* **121**: 334, 1966.

8. Dienes, L., and Weinberger, H. J.: The L forms of bacteria. *Bact. Rev.* **15**: 245, 1951.

9. Freundt, E. A.: Experimental investigations into the pathogenicity of the L-phase variant of *Streptobacillus moniliformis. Acta Path. Microbiol. Scand.* **38**: 246, 1956.

10. ———: *The Mycoplasmataceae (The Pleuropneumonia Group of Organisms); Morphology, Biology and Taxonomy.* Munksgaard, Copenhagen, 1958.

11. Hijmans, W., and Dienes, L.: Further observations on L forms of *alpha*-hemolytic streptococci. *Proc. Soc. Exp. Biol. Med.* **90**: 672, 1956.

12. Klieneberger, E.: The natural occurrence of pleuropneumonia-like organisms in apparent symbiosis with *Streptobacillus moniliformis* and other bacteria. *J. Path. Bact.* **40**: 93, 1935.

13. Klieneberger-Nobel, E.: *Pleuropneumonia-Like Organisms (PPLO); Mycoplasmataceae.* Academic Press, London, 1962.

14. Laidlaw, P. P., and Elford, W. J.: A new group of filterable organisms. *Proc. Roy. Soc. London B* **120**: 292, 1936.

15. Madoff, S., Burke, M. E., and Dienes, L.: Induction and identification of L-forms of bacteria. *Ann. N. Y. Acad. Sci.,* 1967 (in press).

16. Orskov, J.: Étude sur la morphologie du virus péripneumonique. *Ann. Inst. Pasteur* (Paris) **41**: 473, 1927.

17. Sabin, A. B.: The filtrable microörganisms of the pleuropneumonia group. *Bact. Rev.* **5**: 331, 1941.

18. Seiffert, G.: Ueber das Vorkommen filtrabler Microorganismen in der Natur und ihre Züchtbarkeit. *Zbl. Bakt. Orig.* **139**: 337, 1937.

19. Taubeneck, U.: Untersuchungen über die L-form von *Proteus mirabilis* Häuser. II. Entwicklung und Wesen der L-form. *Zschr. allg. Mikrobiol.* **2**: 132, 1962.

20. Thorsson, K. G., and Weibull, C.: Studies on the structure of bacterial L forms, protoplasts and protoplast-like bodies. *J. Ultrastr. Res.* **1**: 412, 1958.

21. Tulasne, R., and Lavillaureix, J.: Pouvoir pathogène experimental, pour la Souris, d'une souche de forms L des bactéries. *C. R. Soc. Biol.* (Paris) **148**: 2080, 1954.

22. Weibull, C.: Structure of bacterial L forms and their parent bacteria. *J. Bact.* **90**: 1467, 1965.

Figure 8.1. L-colonies and L-forms. All photographs were made from dried stained agar preparations; magnification $\times$ 2250 unless indicated otherwise. *A–G:* Development of L-colonies from enterococcus strain 9790 following exposure to lysozyme. *A:* Protoplasts produced in broth containing 15% sucrose. *B:* Large bodies developing from protoplasts when transferred to agar medium containing 3% NaCl. *C* and *D:* Irregular increase of the large bodies and start of growth of granules (darkly stained) embedding themselves in the medium. *E:* A large body grown to great size; the granules growing from it are also large. *F:* Fully developed L-colonies after 24 hour incubation ($\times$ 250). *G:* After 3 days' incubation, at 6 places in the embedded part of the L-colony, cocci started to grow, forming darkly stained spherical colonies; in wet preparation their position inside the agar was apparent, and also that no cocci were present at the surface; at the periphery of the L-colony there were irregular small secondary colonies of L-forms ($\times$ 250).

H–J: Growth of L-forms of *Serratia* in broth and on agar. *H:* L-forms in broth containing 0.5% NaCl; *I:* transferred to agar medium, in lightly inoculated areas granules start to grow from the periphery of large bodies and produce the usual type of L-colony; *J:* in more heavily inoculated areas, the large bodies increased irregularly in size and segmented.

K–M: Growth of the L-forms of *Staphylococcus* on broth and agar. *K:* A young colony consisting of small granules that extend into the medium; *L:* 24 hour growth of vacuolated very large bodies in broth containing 3% NaCl ($\times$ 250); *M:* transferred from broth to agar, abundant growth of small granules started from the periphery of the large bodies and produced ring-like figures in 6 hours; the vacuolated areas are still visible.

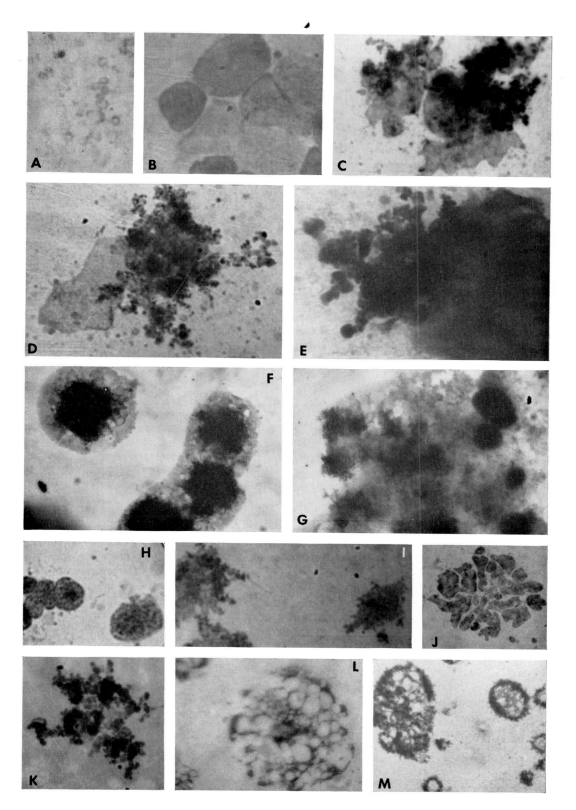

Figure 8.1.

Figure 8.2. L-colonies and L-forms (cont.). All photographs were made from dried stained agar preparations. Magnification $\times$ 2250 unless indicated otherwise. L-forms of *Staphylococcus* on various media. *A–B:* On 30% gelatin containing 3% NaCl, the periphery of large bodies extends on the surface as thin sheets, the edge of which may divide into thin extensions. *C:* On the surface of membrane filters placed on agar medium, the large bodies extend as irregular branching masses; condensations develop at their periphery, and from these, growth penetrates into the pores of the filter. *D:* Early growth inside the filter as elongated branching masses. *E:* Colonies developing in 12 hours on the surface of membrane filters; the large bodies are visible at the periphery of the colonies.

F–I: Growth of L-forms of *Proteus* on various media: *F:* Bacteria inoculated within agar containing penicillin grow to large bodies; within a few hours, small granules start to grow from them, producing B type colonies. *G:* After 16 hours, the colony grows to large size, and the granules to large bodies ($\times$ 250). *H:* Type A L-colony of *Proteus* extending with small granules inside the agar; autolysis is already apparent. *I:* A young colony of a variant of the L-form of *Proteus* on agar surface, showing a large body and thin filaments extending in various directions.

J, K, L: Broth culture of an old A type L-culture of *Salmonella* maintained for 20 years in agar transplants; at present it grows in broth in groups of small or large granules and thin branching filaments ending in swollen knobs.

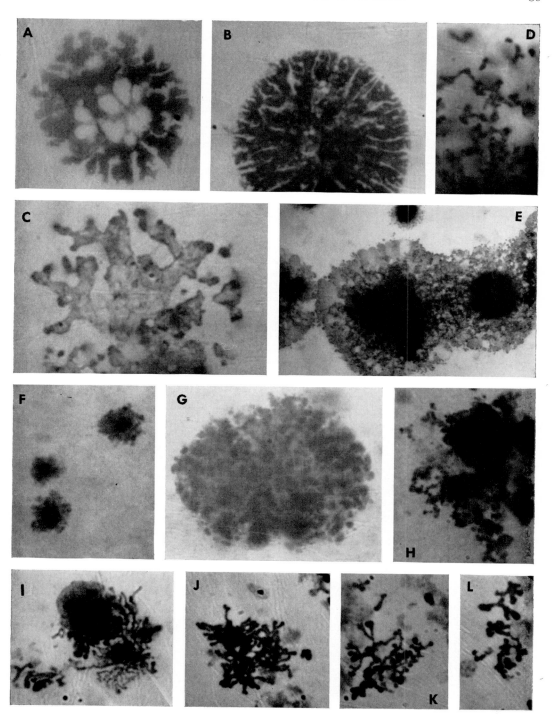

Figure 8.2.

Figure 8.3. Photographs from dried stained agar preparations. *A:* Large bodies of *Proteus* that developed from the bacilli on 30% gelatin containing penicillin ($\times$ 2250). *B:* Large bodies of *Proteus* on 20% gelatin, as in *A,* showing extensions of various shapes ($\times$ 2250). *C:* A colony of PPLO strain K5 grown within agar for 18 hours ($\times$ 2250).

Micrographs *D–L* show pleomorphic cultures of *Escherichia coli, Hemophilus influenzae* and *Streptobacillus moniliformis. D:* The edge of an 18 hour colony of *E. coli* isolated from a case of cystitis; all bacilli in the culture have grown into large bodies; no antibiotics were used ($\times$ 1600). *E:* Same area as in *D,* with the focus adjusted into the agar under the colony; at the edge of the colony a dense growth of granules is visible in the agar ($\times$ 1600). *F:* A young large body of this strain of *E. coli* transferred to ascitic agar produced a dense growth of darkly stained granules extending into the medium ($\times$ 1600). *G:* A colony of *H. influenzae* cultivated from spinal fluid; the bacilli at the edge of the colony have grown to large bodies; the interior of the colony consists of small bacilli ($\times$ 1600). *H* and *I:* Colonies of *S. moniliformis;* the peripheries of two neighboring colonies are shown in *I;* in one colony the bacilli have grown to large bodies ($\times$ 3000). *J, K, L:* Large bodies of *S. moniliformis* which, after a few hours of incubation in transplant, were filled with bacilli (*J,* $\times$ 3000; *K* and *L,* $\times$ 3500).

Figure 8.4. Electron micrographs of several L-forms made from thin sections of young cultures grown within agar media. *A:* The earliest growth of granules from a large body 4 hours after inoculation of *Proteus* bacilli inside agar containing penicillin; the nuclear areas in the large body and the detachment of irregular granules containing nuclear areas are apparent ($\times$ 15,000). *B:* Organisms in a B type L-colony developing from large bodies, as illustrated in *A,* after 18 hours of incubation; the organisms have double cell wall, ribosomes and threads of DNA, like the bacteria ($\times$ 60,000). *C* ($\times$ 15,000) and *D* ($\times$ 60,000) show the edge of an A type colony of *Proteus* embedded in agar; irregular forms, sometimes several microns in length, and elementary corpuscles are visible. With high magnification, the unit membrane and the structure of the organisms are apparent.

Figure 8.5. Electron micrographs of several L-forms and a strain of PPLO made from thin sections of young cultures grown within agar media. *A* ($\times$ 15,000) and *B* ($\times$ 60,000) illustrate a small colony of LX strain isolated from an L-culture of *Staphylococcus* grown within agar for 18 hours; irregular organisms of various sizes and many elementary corpuscles are visible. *C* and *D:* Organisms in PPLO K5 strain after 18 hours of growth within agar; low ($\times$ 15,000) and high ($\times$ 60,000) magnification respectively; the size, shape and structure of the organisms are similar to those of L-forms.

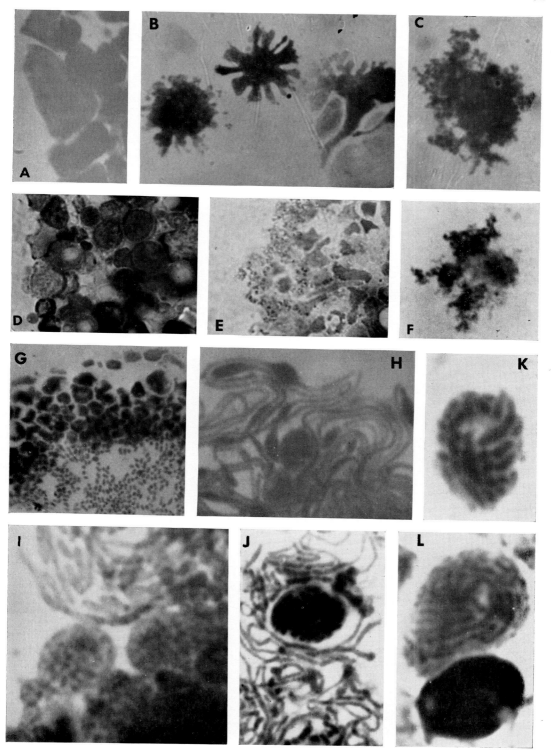

Figure 8.3.

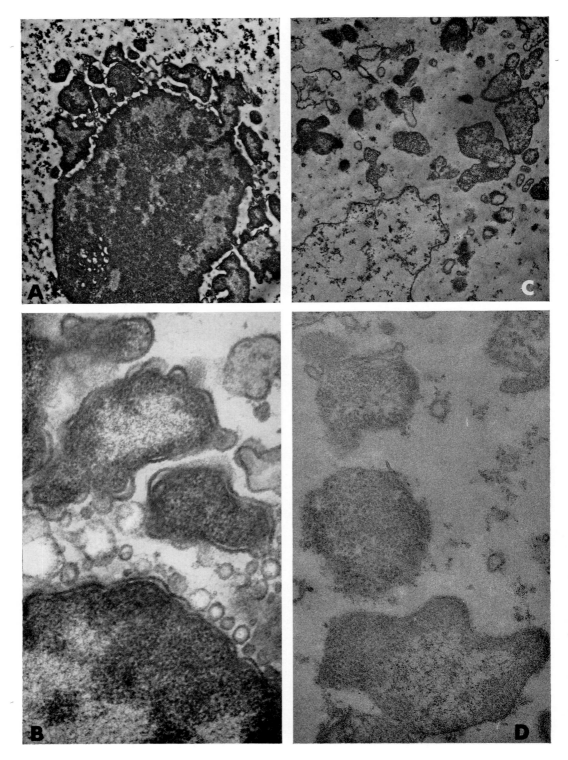

Figure 8.4.

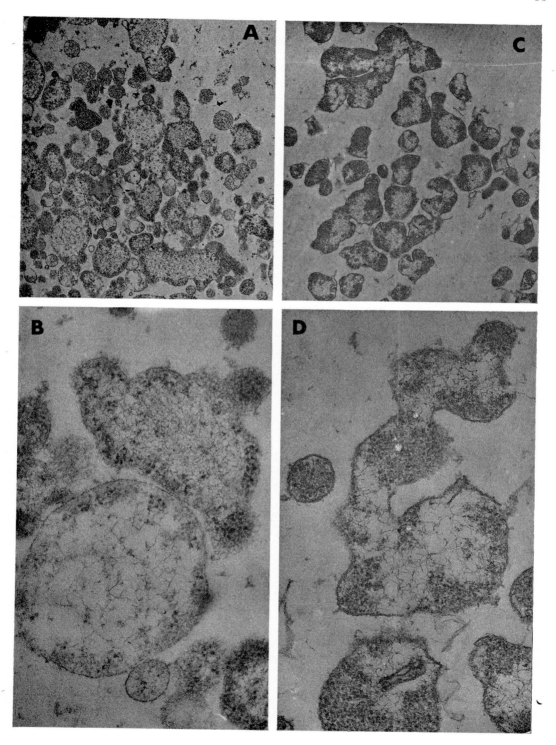

Figure 8.5.

9

Core-Like Structures in Transitional and Protoplast Forms of *Streptococcus faecalis**

Morris Cohen and Ruth G. McCandless

VETERANS ADMINISTRATION CENTER
LOS ANGELES, CALIFORNIA

George M. Kalmanson and Lucien B. Guze

VETERANS ADMINISTRATION CENTER
AND
UCLA SCHOOL OF MEDICINE
LOS ANGELES, CALIFORNIA

During phase contrast light microscopic observations of the effect of different fine structural fixatives on suspensions of stable *Streptococcus faecalis* protoplasts grown in liquid culture, we encountered occasional cells through the center of which there passed a single, barely visible, straight line. An electron microscopic search of sections of such material revealed the presence and organization of a core-like structure corresponding to this line. Literature search disclosed an electron photomicrograph and brief description of a comparable structure, which were included in a paper by Abrams, Nielsen & Thaemert[1] in 1964. Terming it a "tubular structure",

* Research supported in part by U.S. Public Health Service Grant Nos. AI-02257 and AI-03310.

The authors are grateful to Doris M. Harter, Joseph P. Kaslowski and Monica Jacobson for technical assistance, and to Earl G. Hubert for aid in devising different kinds of microbial culture conditions.

they reported its occurrence within membrane ghosts obtained by glucose-metabolic lysis of lysozyme-induced protoplasts of *S. faecalis* (ATCC No. 9790). We found no reports of phase contrast light microscopic observations of this organelle.

The stiff, straight shape of the core-like structure suggests the possibility of its being a polymeric product of residual metabolic and organizational systems which in the original bacterial form of *S. faecalis* participated in synthesis and ordered deposition of some of the cell wall constituents. This organelle may be a unique tool, not only for studies of normal and defective bacterial cell wall, but also with respect to investigational accessibility to certain intracellular morphogenic "organizers". It may be helpful, in formulating an experimental approach to the functional significance of the core-like structure, to consider the present observations of its occurrence and morphology in a penicillin-induced transitional form and in derived unstable and stable protoplast forms of *S. faecalis.*

Terms used in a restricted sense are defined as follows: *Protoplast* refers to any microbe which lacks a cell wall, as determined by electron microscopic examination of sections, and which stemmed originally from a cell wall-bearing form. *Transitional form* refers to a microbe which has responded morphologically to treatment capable of inducing transformation to protoplast form, but which still retains visible cell wall or cell wall residue at the electron microscopic level. The terms *unstable* and *stable*, as applied to protoplasts, refer respectively to reversion or non-reversion to a cell wall-producing form on serial culture in the absence of protoplast-inducing agent. *Core* refers to a narrow linear structure which can occur within cells of the transitional or protoplast forms of *S. faecalis.*

MATERIALS AND METHODS

CULTURE MEDIA AND INCUBATION TEMPERATURES

A solution of 37 g brain heart infusion powder (Difco) in 1 liter distilled water, autoclaved 15 minutes at 10 lbs/in² pressure, was symbolized *BHI*. A solution, symbolized *BHIS*, consisted of the above amount of BHI to which were added, prior to autoclaving, 176 g sucrose and 0.2 ml of 5.1% w/v $MgSO_4 \cdot 7H_2O$. The osmolality of this solution was 950 milliosmolal, as measured by freezing point depression. An autoclaved mixture of 52 g brain heart infusion agar, dehydrated (Difco), 176 g sucrose, 1 liter distilled water, and 0.2 ml of 5.1% w/v $MgSO_4 \cdot 7H_2O$ was symbolized *BHISA*. Bovine serum albumin, fraction V (Armour), in 30% w/v stock solution, filtered through a Seitz filter, was added to all culture media, except to BHI, to give a final concentration of 2% w/v, and this addition was symbolized *BSA*. A sterile water solution of potassium penicillin G (Squibb), 100,000 u/ml, was added to some media prior to use to give a final concentration of 1000 u/ml, and this addition

was symbolized *P*. This penicillin concentration was used to initiate protoplasting or to maintain the unstable protoplast form. Biphasic medium consisted of BHIS + BSA overlying BHISA + BSA. Biphasic medium + P consisted of BHIS + BSA + P overlying BHISA + BSA + P. Flask (125 ml) and tube cultures contained 10–20 ml and 10 ml, respectively, of liquid medium; for biphasic media, this was layered over 10 ml of the agar phase medium. In biphasic tube cultures, the agar phase was formed as a slant. Except for BHI, these nutrient media provided an osmotically stabilizing environment for protoplasts. Incubation temperatures were room temperature (air-conditioned, about 22°C; not air-conditioned, about 25–27°C), 27°C (water bath), and 37°C (incubator).

S. faecalis was grown in BHI or, in preparation for conversion to transitional and protoplast forms, in either BHIS + BSA or biphasic medium. The transitional and unstable protoplast forms were usually cultured in biphasic medium + P, but occasional cultures were in BHIS + BSA + P. The stable protoplast was grown either in BHIS + BSA or in biphasic medium.

ORGANISMS

The strain of *S. faecalis* used in this study was originally isolated from the urine of a patient with pyelonephritis.[2] Stock *S. faecalis*, in the form of stored, frozen, BHI culture aliquots, was thawed to provide inoculum for starting cultures from which inoculum was obtained to initiate protoplasting cultures. At weekly intervals, BHISA + BSA + P plates were inoculated with 0.1 ml of an 18 hour BHIS + BSA culture of this strain. The resultant surface growth (T_0) was used as inoculum one week later to subculture on fresh BHIS + BSA + P plates (T_1), and serial weekly subcultures were prepared. For our use, the unstable protoplast was studied in 1- or 2-day cultures, the inoculum for these being the surface growth on a T_9 subculture. The stable protoplast used in this study was derived originally from a T_{53} subculture on BHISA + BSA + P. This subculture passed

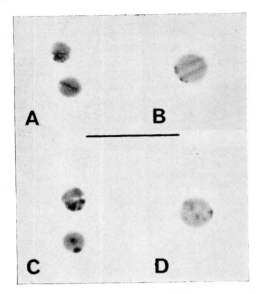

Figure 9.1. Phase contrast light microscopic evidence for linearity of cores in T₅₃ stable protoplast cultured in BHIS + BSA in flasks for 6 days at 22–24°C room temperature. *A:* Lower cell with single core in longitudinal view; *C:* the same cell after rolling over to show core in end-on view; *B:* longitudinal view of two approximately parallel cores in the same cell; *D:* the same two cores in end-on view. Scale line: 10 μ.

successively, by weekly transfer, through eight BHISA + BSA plate subcultures, a single biphasic subculture, and ten BHIS + BSA subcultures without evidence of reversion to a cell wall-bearing form. During our experiments, there were 30 additional, serial, non-reverting, BHIS + BSA subcultures of the T₅₃ isolate. The transitional form was obtained in flask culture as follows: the liquid phase of an overnight, 37°C, test tube culture of *S. faecalis,* in either BHIS + BSA or biphasic medium, was centrifuged, and the sediment then resuspended in an equivalent volume of BHIS + BSA + P for culture in this medium alone or in this medium overlying BHISA + BSA + P (biphasic medium + P).

LIGHT MICROSCOPY

A Carl Zeiss model WL microscope, equipped with the Microflash Device and oil immersion phase contrast optics, was used to photograph microscope slide mounts of liquid cultures at 400X original mag-

nification on 35 mm film. Photomicrography of precisely oriented cells or cell groups under such conditions was time-consuming because of Brownian motion. The degree of up-and-down drift during such motion was sometimes limited by using minimal volumes of culture in the slide mounts. For observation of the small number of large protoplasts present in some cultures, a greater culture fluid volume was required in preparing a slide mount, however, in order to avoid distortion or bursting of these cells.

ELECTRON MICROSCOPY

To 10 volumes of liquid culture was added, with mixing, 1 volume of pH 7.2–7.5

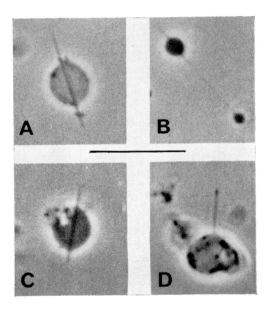

Figure 9.2. Examples of very long cores extending beyond the cell body in T₅₃ stable protoplasts. *A* and *C:* "single cell" colony isolate No. 1 after transfer from 5-day BHISA + BSA 37°C plate culture to tube of BHIS + BSA and incubation at 37°C for 24 hours, then 16 hours more at about 24°C room temperature. *B:* Parent T₅₃ after 24 hour flask culture in BHIS + BSA at about 27°C room temperature; a barely visible, stiff, straight core appears to pass through two cells. *D:* T₅₃ stable protoplast in 2-day BHIS + BSA flask culture incubated at 37°C; a stiff linear structure appears to arise and extend out from the periphery of the cell and may represent a core. Scale line: 10 μ.

fixative, which consisted of 3.9 ml distilled water, 2.0 ml 9.9% w/v KH_2PO_4, 2.2 ml 4.0% w/v KOH pellets, 4.5 ml 60% w/v sucrose, 4.0 ml biological grade glutaraldehyde (Fisher, "50%"), and, dispensed by hypodermic syringe, 1.25 ml polyethylene glycol 200 (Union Carbide Carbowax 200). The mixture was centrifuged for 1 hour at 2200–2700 rpm in a No. 269 rotor in a refrigerated International Centrifuge, model PR-1. After the supernatant fraction was decanted, the sediment was resuspended in residual fluid. To this were added 5.0 ml of a pH 7.2–7.5 mixture consisting of 10.9 ml distilled water, 7.1 ml of stock veronal-acetate solution ($NaC_2H_3O_2 \cdot 3H_2O$ 4.857 g, sodium barbital 7.357 g, NaCl 8.5 g, and distilled water to make 250 ml of solution) 7.9 ml 0.1 N HCl, 12.0 ml polyethylene glycol 200 (dispensed by hypodermic syringe), and 9.6 ml of 5% w/v OsO_4. After 30 minutes in the dark, the suspension was centrifuged 30 minutes, the supernatant fraction was decanted, and the sediment then resuspended in residual fluid. The tubes containing resuspended sediment were warmed momentarily to about 50°C in a water bath. To each tube was added three drops of molten polyethylene glycol 200-agar mixture (9.0 ml polyethlyene glycol 200, 720 mg agar (Difco), 27 ml distilled water, all melted in a boiling water bath and then cooled to about 50°C), the sediment quickly dispersed in this mixture, and the tube chilled in an ice bath. The gel was removed from each centrifuge tube and then cut into small blocks. At about 4°C, the blocks were treated successively for 15 minutes in absolute ethanol, 30 minutes in 1.0% w/v uranyl acetate in absolute ethanol, and 10 minutes in absolute ethanol. At room temperature, the blocks were then passed through successive 10, 20, and 20 minute treatments with absolute ethanol (dried over Linde Molecular Sieves). Subsequently, the blocks were passed through propylene oxide for Epon embedment[3] in No. 5 gelatin capsules.

Sections were cut on a Porter-Blum ultramicrotome with glass or du Pont diamond knives, mounted on Formvar substrates on 100 mesh grids or, for serial sections, on single hole grids, stained with

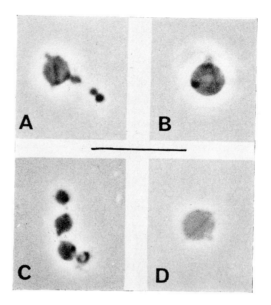

Figure 9.3. Serial, 24 hour, BHIS + BSA, flask subcultures of "single cell" colony isolates of T_{53} stable protoplast. A and D: isolates Nos. 10 and 13, respectively, incubation temperature 37°C, are examples of budding cells, each with a single core. B and C: isolate No. 1, room temperature 26–27°C incubation, showing, respectively, a cell with 5 cores oriented in different directions (photographed at a compromise focus) and an apparent chain of cells, of which the middle two each have a core. Scale line: 10 μ.

alkaline lead citrate,[6] and carbon-coated by vacuum evaporation. Electron photomicrographs, at original magnifications up to 46,000X, were taken with a Hitachi HU-11A electron microscope at 75 kV. A 150 μ condenser aperture and 50 μ objective aperture were employed.

OBSERVATIONS

LIGHT MICROSCOPY

Our first observations of cores were by means of phase contrast microscopy of slide mounts of BHIS + BSA cultures of the T_{53} stable protoplast. Immediately after preparing the slide mount, while the cells drifted across the microscopic field of view, a few of the cells exhibited a fine straight line spanning the cell through its center. Infrequently, more than one line were observed within a cell. As the cell rolled over in the flow of fluid, the line

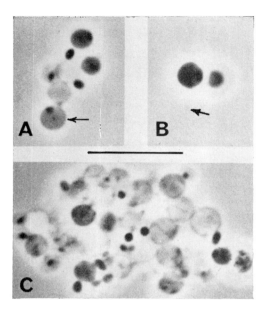

polymorphic cells of different phase contrast optical densities and sizes down to the limits of visibility (Figures 9.2 and 9.3). Some cores extended equally in both directions, rarely in one direction, beyond the cell body, often tapering towards the tip, and attaining overall lengths up to about 10 μ and thicknesses probably extending below the microscope resolving power in visible light. Rarely, a core appeared to be common to two cells and maintained its straightness despite the forces of Brownian motion (Figure 9.2B). Occasionally, a linear structure, perhaps a core, appeared to arise from the periphery of the cell (Figure 9.2D). Multiple cores, occurring in some of the cells about 4 μ or more in diameter, usually did not extend beyond the cell body (Figure 9.3B). The formation of cores was delayed and less

Figure 9.4. Protoplasting cultures of *Streptococcus faecalis:* overnight, 37°C, BHIS + BSA, tube cultures were centrifuged and the sediment then resuspended in equal volume of BHIS + BSA + P for 2-day flask culture at incubator temperature of 37°C (*B*) or water bath temperature of 27°C (*A* and *C*). Some of the smallest cells may still possess cell wall; their great optical density in phase contrast microscopy would prevent detection of a core. *A:* End-on view of core in cell indicated by arrow; the two upper large optically dense cells also have a core in nearly end-on view. *B:* rare instance in a protoplasting culture of a core extending beyond the cell body (distal end indicated by arrow); the extension is obscured by the phase contrast halo and the effect of high contrast photographic paper required to delineate the core within a cell of high optical density. *C:* a group of protoplasting cells of varying optical density with cores in various orientations (compromise focus to maximize the number of cores which could be viewed at a single level of focus). Scale line: 10 μ.

apparently shortened to a dot and then lengthened, indicating the line was a linear structure and not a planar membrane of cell division. Examples are shown in Figure 9.1.

Examination of T_{53} stable protoplast by phase contrast microscopy of liquid cultures of various ages and grown at various temperatures established a range of sizes for the cores. The cores were present in

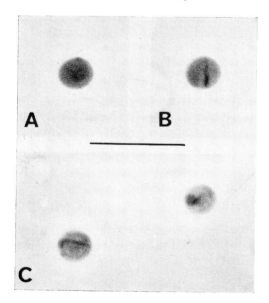

Figure 9.5. Cores in T_9 unstable protoplast exhibiting pronounced tendency towards uneven thickness and phase contrast optical density (*B* and *C*). Some cores also showed slight curvature (*C*). Additional cores visible in *A* and *C* are somewhat oblique from end-on orientation. The cultures were prepared by transferring 1 ml of cell suspension from a T_9 biphasic + P tube culture, incubated at 37°C, to flasks containing 9 ml BHIS + BSA + P for 2-day incubation at 37°C (*A* and *B*) or about 23°C room temperature (*C*). Scale line: 10 μ.

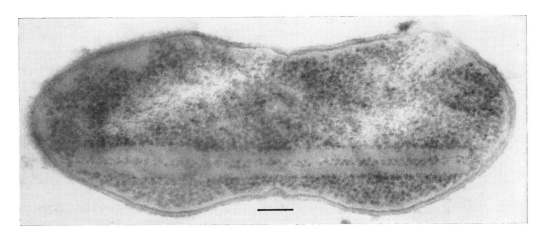

Figure 9.6. Electron microscopic longitudinal view of non-tubular type core, characteristic of thin-walled transitional form of *Streptococcus faecalis*. (Compare with cross-sectioned cores in Figure 9.8.) Thawed frozen stock *S. faecalis* was used as inoculum for an overnight biphasic flask culture at 37°C; the centrifuged sediment of the liquid phase of this culture was dispersed in equal volume BHIS + BSA + P and then layered on BHISA + BSA + P for 24 hours of flask culture at 37°C. Scale line: 0.10 μ.

frequent in cultures incubated at room temperatures below 25°C.

In view of the many subcultures through which T_{53} had passed, its cell polymorphism, its tendency towards chain-like growth in liquid cultures incubated above 25°C, and occurrence of cores in only a small fraction of the cells, it appeared possible the T_{53} population might be heterogenous with respect to ability to form cores. Consequently, the observation that, with incubation overnight at a room temperature of about 23°C, flask cultures of T_{53} stable protoplast in BHIS + BSA yielded a dispersion of single cells, was put to use to obtain "single cell" colony isolates. A second serial overnight 23°C culture provided inoculum for plate culture on BHISA + BSA. Five days later, 20 single colonies were transferred to BHIS + BSA for 24-hour tube culture at 37°C. The 20 tube cultures, brought to about 24°C room temperature, were photographed in numerical order. Cores were only rarely observed until about seven hours at room temperature had elapsed and isolate No. 9 was being photographed. From then on, cores were easily located during photography of succeeding isolates. After the

cultures had been about 16 hours at room temperature, and all the isolates had been photographed, reexamination of isolate No. 1 revealed the presence of numerous cells with cores (Figure 9.2, A and C). Subsequent 24-hour flask subcultures of all 20 isolates and the parent T_{53} stable protoplast culture, incubated at 37°C, showed the same range of polymorphism and the occurrence of cores (Figure 9.3, A and D) in all subcultures. In further serial flask cultures of isolate No. 1 and the parent T_{53} stable protoplast, cores occurred more frequently with incubations at elevated room temperature of 26–27°C (Figures 9.2B, 9.3 B and C) or with 37°C incubation than at room temperature of 22–24°C.

In initial extended examinations of *S. faecalis* and derived T_9 unstable protoplast subcultures grown in biphasic medium + P, only a single core was found, and that was in a cell of T_9. However, if the total growth of *S. faecalis* or T_9 in overnight 37°C tube cultures in BHIS + BSA and in biphasic medium + P, respectively, were centrifuged and each resuspended in equivalent volume fresh BHIS + BSA + P in flasks, and then incubated for two days at 37°C or at about 27°C room tempera-

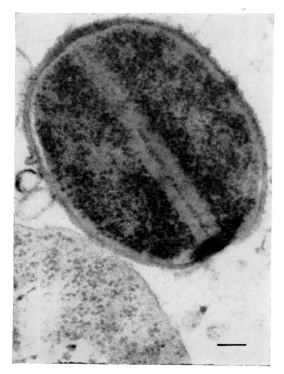

With extended search, sections passing longitudinally through the long cylindrical form of the core were located. In addition, selected presumed cross sections of cores were verified by tracing through serial sections of cumulative depth up to about 1 μ.

Two types of core ultrastructure were observed. Overall, both were cylindrical in shape. One type of core, varying in thickness between 0.08 and 0.11 μ, consisted of an ordered array of ribosome-like particles passing along the axis of the cylinder, the remainder of which appeared nearly structureless and of relatively low electron density. Cores of this type (non-tubular) were usually found in cells with a fairly compact protoplasm (Figures 9.6–9.10), and axially arranged ribosome-like particles appeared to be in continuity with those of the cytoplasm at either end of the core (Figure 9.6). Figure 9.9B possibly represents an early stage of this kind of core. Although cores of this type were found in BHIS + BSA cultures of T$_{53}$ stable protoplast, they were observed in the transitional but not the protoplast forms appearing in cultures of *S. faecalis* grown for the first time in the presence of penicillin.

The other type of core (tubular), occurring only in protoplast forms and often in cells with less compact protoplasm, consisted of an electron-dense tube containing ribosome-like particles in ordered to irregular array (Figures 9.11–9.17). Core thickness was observed to range between 0.08

Figure 9.7. Non-tubular type of core (nearly longitudinal section) in *Streptococcus faecalis* transitional form. Erosion of the thin cell wall is evident. Nearby is a protoplast with less electron-dense protoplasm. The culture was prepared by adding 0.1 ml thawed frozen stock *S. faecalis* to 9.7 ml BHIS + BSA for overnight incubation at 37°C, then resuspending the sediment from the centrifuged culture in equal volume BHIS + BSA + P, then overlaying it on 10 ml BHISA + BSA + P in a flask for 2-day incubation in a 27°C water bath. Scale line: 0.10 μ.

ture, many of the cells developed a core (Figures 9.4 and 9.5). Extension of cores beyond the cell body was rare in both forms; Figure 9.4B is an example.

ELECTRON MICROSCOPY

The fine structure of cores has been observed in penicillin-induced transitional and protoplast forms of *S. faecalis* and in the derived T$_{53}$ stable protoplast form. Observations have yet to be made with T$_9$ unstable protoplasts under the conditions which phase contrast light microscopy revealed to be favorable to core formation.

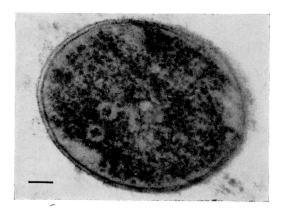

Figure 9.8. Cross section of two cores in *Streptococcus faecalis* transitional form. Culture same as in Figure 9.6. Scale line: 0.10 μ.

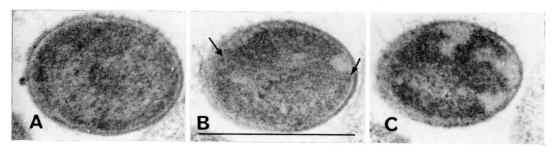

Figure 9.9. Sections Nos. 7, 8, and 9 in a series of 12 serial sections through a proto-plasting culture of *Streptococcus faecalis*; culture same as in Figure 9.6. *B:* Longitudinal view of barely discrete core (arrows point to ends), possibly newly formed, in very thin-walled cell. Scale line: 1.0 μ.

and 0.13 μ, and the overall thickness of the tube wall was between 0.01 and 0.03 μ, depending on the thickness, number, and spacing of electron-dense layers. If the core tube consisted of two electron-dense layers, only the inner one might persist to the tips of the core (Figure 9.14).

Just as was observed by light micros-copy, multiple cores were evident in elec-tron microscopic preparations (Figures 9.8, 9.11, 9.13, 9.16, 9.17). Although both types of core could be found in a single cul-ture, both were never encountered in a single cell.

When a core extended beyond the cell body, the plasma membrane, in favorable sections, followed the contour of the core and its thin layer of surrounding cyto-plasm (Figures 9.13, 9.14).

DISCUSSION

The tubular and non-tubular morpho-logical types of core, which have been ob-served in cultures of *S. faecalis* grown in the presence of a protoplast-inducing con-centration of penicillin, as well as in a de-rived stable protoplast form cultured in the absence of penicillin, have such features in common as (1) a narrow cylindrical shape which, if sufficiently long, projects beyond the cell body in one or both di-rections without piercing the plasma mem-brane, (2) occasional occurrence of sev-eral cores per cell, and (3) a content of ribosome-like particles extending often in regular array along the core axis.

In cultures of *S. faecalis* grown in the presence of penicillin, the non-tubular type

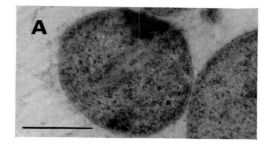

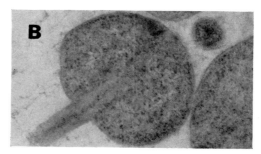

Figure 9.10. T_{53} stable protoplast in 1-day, 37°C, BHIS + BSA, flask culture; oblique sections (probably alternate serial sections) through non-tubular type of core projecting (*B*) beyond the cell body. Scale line: 1.0 μ.

of core occurs in the transitional cell wall-bearing form, whereas the tubular type of core is found in the protoplast forms in these cultures. Both types of core are found in the derived T_{53} stable protoplast form. These observations, coupled with a tendency for the tubular type of core to occur in cells of lesser visible content, might suggest derivation of the tubular type of core from the non-tubular type during cell aging. Conceivably, the electron-dense cy-

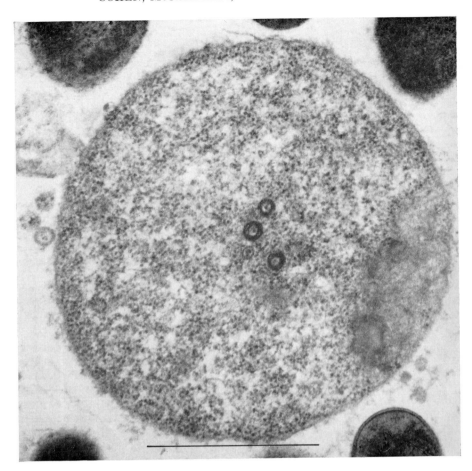

Figure 9.11. Cross section through 3 tubular type cores in a protoplast of a proto-plasting culture of *Streptococcus faecalis;* culture same as in Figure 9.6. This is section No. 9 of 12 serial sections (about 1 μ total depth), in each of which the 3 cores were visible in about the same relative positions, indicating probable parallelism. Two of the electron-dense shells of the cores have a layered appearance. The large fibrous zone at the right margin of the large cell may be a concentration of nuclear substance. Scale line: 1.0 μ.

lindrical shell of the tubular type of core could be the result of condensation accompanying polymerizat:on and/or crosslink-age within the zone of low electron density in the non-tubular type of core. However, if this is the case, it must occur with great rapidity to account for our failure to observe cores suggestive of intermediate morphology, or cores of both morphological types within the same cell.

The initial morphological steps in core formation are unknown. Nielsen & Ab-rams[5] consider that in protoplast mem-brane ghosts of *S. faecalis* "...electron micrographs show a tubular structure ema-nating from the plasma membrane and containing ribosome-like particles..." With neither type of core have we ob-served any confluence with the plasma membrane. Core-membrane contact ob-served by Nielsen & Abrams may have been based on distortions introduced during formation of protoplast membrane ghosts.

Figure 9.9B, as already indicated, may represent, in a transitional form, an early stage in core development, but this is rec-ognizable, perhaps, only by a thin line of low electron density on either side of a

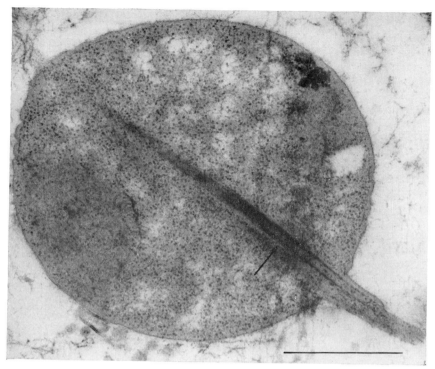

Figure 9.12. Oblique section through tubular type core in protoplast present in protoplasting culture of *Streptococcus faecalis* grown as described in legend to Figure 9.7 except final incubation of 1 day only. Where core projects beyond cell body, it is still surrounded by protoplasm and a plasma membrane. Part of core shell (arrow) may show layering corresponding to that in Figure 9.11. Scale line: 1.0 μ.

linear array of ribosome-like particles which already extends nearly across the cell. Perhaps a linear arrangement of ribosome-like particles, antedating a morphologically distinct core, is not easily discerned because of surrounding closely packed particles. In one other reported instance among microbes (the pleuropneumonia-like organism A5969, *Mycoplasma gallisepticum*) of linear regularity in arrangement of ribosome-like particles, this is recognizable because the particles are in cylindrical, possibly helical array, surrounding a "hollow core", with several such arrays in parallel alignment per cell.[4] In contrast, when the ribosome-like particles in cores appear in most highly ordered array in *S. faecalis* transitional and protoplast forms, the particles, although they may also be helically arranged, are situated in close proximity to the core axis.

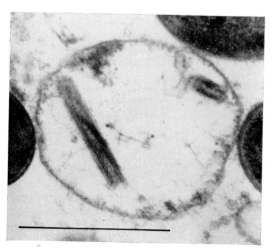

Figure 9.13. Protoplast containing two cores in oblique section but otherwise nearly devoid of protoplasmic structure. To the left and right are thin-walled transitional forms in this protoplasting culture (same as in Figure 9.6). Scale line: 1.0 μ.

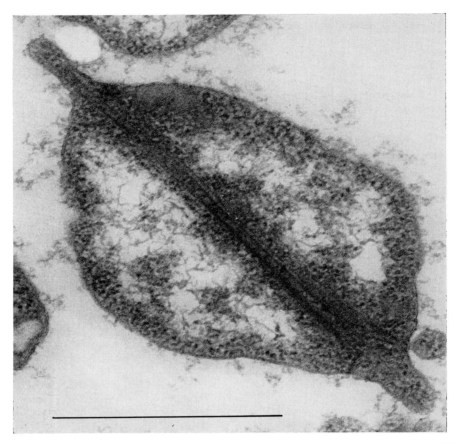

Figure 9.14. Tubular type of core in T₅₃ stable protoplast grown for 2 days at 37°C in BHIS + BSA flask culture. Note zones where the tubular shell may possibly be layered (corresponding to cross section of layered core shells in Figure 9.11) and also continuation of plasma membrane around projecting thin-shelled portion of core. Initial fixation step involved about 4 times the usual glutaraldehyde concentration. Among figures in this paper, this is the only one not based on agar pre-embedment and methacrylate embedding; each step of ethanol dehydration and passage through ethanolic uranyl acetate, ethanolic methacrylate mixture, and methacrylate mixture, was followed by centrifugation and re-suspension of the pellet in residual fluid after decanting the supernatant fraction, with final embedment, prior to 60°C oven polymerization, in very viscous pre-polymerized methacrylate mixture (1:1 ethyl and n-butyl methacrylates, catalyzed with 0.1% w/v 2,2'-azo bis(2-methylpropionitrile)[7]). Scale line: 1.0 μ.

Is a core a linear structure because the ribosome-like particles, which may be involved in synthesis of the surrounding core substance, are in some overall linear arrangement, or is a linear structure imposed by the nature of polymeric orientation within the outer zone of core substance? Whatever the answer may be, the giant cores, which extend beyond the cell body of derived T₅₃ stable protoplasts, suggest

core development involves increase in length and thickness of core substance and an accompanying lengthening of the interior chain of ribosome-like particles.

The structural nature of the core makes it an attractive subject for further investigation. A chain of ribosome-like particles, extending along the axis of such a very special structure, could possibly provide for study a system with specialized

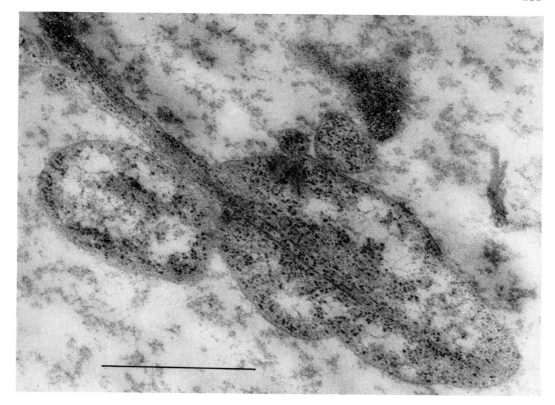

Figure 9.15. Projecting tubular type of core in T_{53} stable protoplast grown 1 day in biphasic medium in flask at 37°C. Note zone of apparent layering in shell of core and continuation of protoplasm and plasma membrane around projecting core. Initial fixation step involved about 4 times the usual glutaraldehyde concentration. Scale line: 1.0 μ.

synthetic capacity in one or more residual metabolic processes involved in cell wall synthesis but unaffected by penicillin or other protoplast-inducing agents. Imagine a giant "polysome" of some 2000 ribosomes!

Chemical analysis of core substance is an essential first step, not only as an indication of the possible function of the axially situated ribosome-like particles, but also as a basis for establishing the kind of relationship which may exist between the two morphological types of core. From the following tests, isolation of cores for those purposes appears feasible.

The straight stiff appearance of the cores in phase contrast microscopy of the protoplasts in liquid culture had suggested the cores may consist, in part, of complexes of linearly arranged polymers, possibly more resistant than the remainder of the cell to disruptive treatments. As an initial test of such resistance, a few microscope slide mounts of cultures were subjected to pressure (either by use of a minimal amount of culture fluid, which caused the larger protoplasts compressed between cover glass and slide to burst, or by careful pressure contact between cover glass and objective lens mount) or to Triton X-100, a nonionic detergent, applied in minute amount at the edge of the cover glass. In both instances, the cores were apparently set free in a clean condition, at the light microscopic resolution level (Figures 9.18–9.20); and, in some instances, apparently single cores were observed to disperse into two or more finer cores, which is in agree-

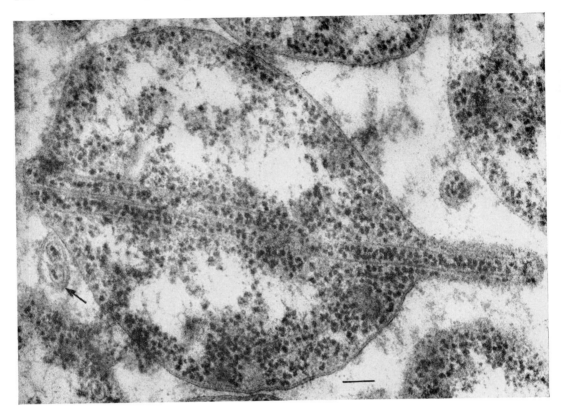

Figure 9.16. Two nearly parallel tubular type cores, in nearly longitudinal section, in T_{53} stable protoplast. An adjacent profile (arrow) may represent a cross section through a narrow protoplast projection containing two cores. Same culture and fixation as in Figure 9.15. Scale line: 0.10 μ.

ment with the electron microscopic observation (Figure 9.17) that multiple cores in protoplasts may sometimes be so closely associated in approximately parallel alignment as to be unresolvable by light microscopy. These microscope slide tests suggest that either passage of a protoplast culture under pressure through a small orifice or treatment with an appropriate concentration of a nonionic detergent might provide suitable starting material from which cores could be fractionated. However, because with excessive Triton X-100 treatment it is possible to cause a core to fade from view without apparent change in size or shape, a physical means of freeing cores might be better from both the isolation and analytical standpoints.

With preparations of free cores, it should be possible, aside from chemical analysis, to test for specific relationship to cell wall substance by, for example, exposure of cores to specifically adsorbing bacteriophage, to lysozyme and other enzymes, and to cell wall antibody complexed with fluorescein for fluorescent microscopy or with ferritin for electron microscopy.

Some cells with cores carry protrusions suggestive of budding, but whether or not cells with cores are capable of reproduction awaits further study. Perhaps the occurrence of multiple cores in larger cells bears on this question because, for example, in the plateau phase of culture growth, those cells incapable, at that time, of further reproduction might continue to produce the synthesizing systems and constituents required for core formation.

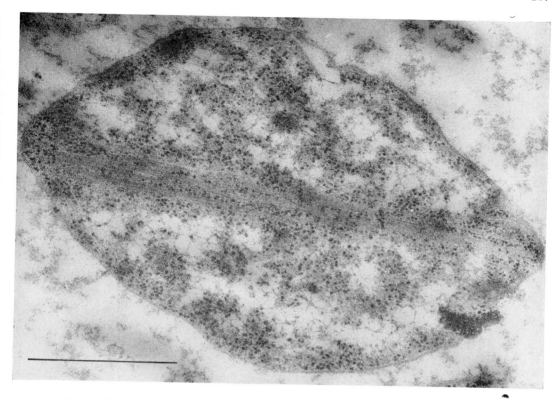

Figure 9.17. Compact group of several, probably parallel, tubular type cores in nearly longitudinal section in T₅₃ stable protoplast. Same culture and fixation as in Figure 9.15. Scale line: 1.0 μ.

What may be said with regard to the immediate cause of core formation? With *S. faecalis,* formation of cores appears to be correlated with the process of protoplast induction and the protoplast state rather than with the specific treatment which may bring this about. Thus, in the work of Abrams and coworkers,[1] the formation of cores was apparently associated with protoplast formation in response to lysozyme treatment of *S. faecalis.* In studies reported in the present paper, cores were not only apparent in protoplasts formed as the result of penicillin treatment, but were also present, perhaps in an earlier morphological stage, in cells with the thin cell walls characteristic of the penicillin-induced transitional form. In addition, cores were formed in both unstable and stable protoplasts derived by serial subculture, the latter in the absence of the

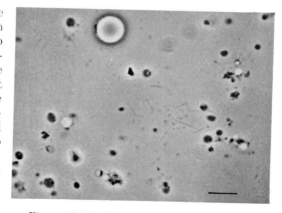

Figure 9.18. Phase contrast light microscopic view of effect of pressure on microscope slide preparation of T₅₃ stable protoplast culture (same culture as in Figure 9.15). A large cell, containing a number of cores, burst, releasing the rod-shaped structures in a visibly intact condition. The small cells exhibited no apparent change with this level of pressure. Scale line: 10 μ.

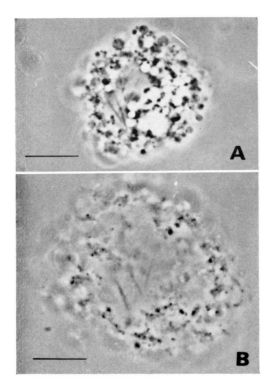

Figure 9.19. Effect of 1% v/v Triton X-100 introduced at the edge of the cover glass in a microscope slide preparation of the T$_{53}$ stable protoplast culture of Figure 9.15. *A*: Condition prior to treatment with Triton X-100: large cell surrounded by many small cells of various sizes and optical densities; the level of focus was displaced from the equator of the large cell in order to show several of the cores which were present in this cell. *B*: Dissolution of cells as Triton X-100 flowed by under the cover glass; some of the cores, in the process of being released, were still visible but blurred as they left the plane of focus. Scale line: 10 μ.

original protoplast-inducing agent. In all of these procedures for obtaining and culturing protoplasts, sucrose was employed in sufficient concentration to provide an osmotically protective environment. We have found transitional and protoplast forms, some with cores, in cultures of *S. faecalis* in BHIS + BSA medium without penicillin.* It appears possible therefore that protoplasting, in this

* Unpublished data.

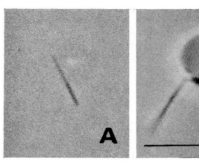

Figure 9.20. Free cores obtained by Triton X-100 treatment as described in the legend to Figure 9.19 (same culture as in Figure 9.15). *A*: The movement of this free core was followed until one end adhered to the cover glass; in a short while, the structure adhered along its entire length, revealing a greater optical density in one half of the core than in the other. *B*: A core in Brownian motion, still attached at one end to the protoplast from which it had just been observed to emerge by extrusion; note the projection on the opposite side of the cell, which may previously have accommodated the end of the core still attached to the cell; extrusion was rare and probably depended on a chance minimal Triton X-100 effect on the plasma membrane in the area covering a projecting core. Scale line: 10 μ.

instance, may have been associated with cell wall-defective mutations, which could be detected only in an osmotically stabilizing medium, which sucrose provided. Similar reasoning may account for isolation of stable protoplast forms after prolonged serial subculture of unstable protoplast forms. Our present working hypothesis concerning core formation is as follows: When, regardless of cause, there is in viable cultures of *S. faecalis* a defective deposition or lack of deposition of continuously synthesized cell wall substituents, the appearance of cores represents a rerouting and redirected deposition of at least some of those cell wall substituents.

SUMMARY

Two types of core-like structure have been distinguished by electron microscopy in *Streptococcus faecalis* grown in a medium containing a protoplast-inducing concentration of penicillin, with the addition of sucrose for osmotic stability of the cells. Each type of core nearly spans the cell, whether the cell still has residual cell wall or has become a protoplast. In the former instance, the core consists, in its most ordered form, of an axial chain of ribosome-like particles surrounded by nearly amorphous substance of low electron density. In the latter, the chain of ribosome-like particles is surrounded by a tubular structure of high electron density, and the particles may not be as closely situated to the core axis. Both types of core have been observed in a derived stable protoplast form of S. faecalis, in which a core can grow to such length as to cause a cell of lesser diameter to protrude around the ends of the core. The possible origin and significance of cores are discussed. Phase contrast light microscopy has not distinguished between the two types of core but has been useful in quickly assessing optimum conditions for core formation and the effects of protoplast-disruptive treatments on core release and morphological stability.*

*Added in proof: After completion of this manuscript, the non-tubular type core was found in S. faecalis cultured in BHI medium. The os-molality of this medium is insufficient for survival of any protoplasts which might arise spontaneously.

REFERENCES

1. Abrams, A., Nielsen, L., and Thaemert, J.: Rapidly synthesized ribonucleic acid in membrane ghosts from *Streptococcus fecalis* protoplasts. *Biochim. Biophys. Acta* **80**: 325, 1964.
2. Guze, L. B., Goldner, B. H., and Kalmanson, G. M.: Pyelonephritis. I. Observations on the course of chronic non-obstructed enterococcal infection in the kidney of the rat. *Yale J. Biol. Med.* **33**: 372, 1961.
3. Luft, J. H.: Improvements in epoxy resin embedding methods. *J. Biophys. Biochem. Cytol.* **9**: 409, 1961.
4. Maniloff, J., Morowitz, H. J., and Barrnett, R. J.: Studies of the ultrastructure and ribosomal arrangements of the pleuropneumonia-like organism A5969. *J. Cell Biol.* **25**: 139, 1965.
5. Nielsen, L., and Abrams, A.: Rapidly labelled ribosomal RNA associated with membrane ghosts of *Streptococcus fecalis*. *Biochem. Biophys. Res. Commun.* **17**: 680, 1964.
6. Reynolds, E. S.: The use of lead citrate at high pH as an electron opaque stain in electron microscopy. *J. Cell Biol.* **17**: 208, 1963.
7. Shipkey, F. H., and Dalton, A. J.: Azodi-isobutyronitrile (ADIB) as a catalyst for embedding tissues in methacrylate for electron microscopy. *J. Appl. Phys.* **30**: 2039, 1959.

10

Morphological Study of the Attachment of Nucleoid to Membrane in Bacilli, Protoplasts and Reverting Protoplasts of *Bacillus subtilis**

Antoinette Ryter

INSTITUT PASTEUR, PARIS, FRANCE

Otto E. Landman

GEORGETOWN UNIVERSITY, WASHINGTON, D.C.

In the first electron microscopic study of thin sections of vegetative Gram-positive bacteria, Chapman & Hillier[2] observed prominent new subcellular organelles near the cell septa—"the peripheral bodies". As electron microscopic techniques improved, similar structures were seen in many species of *Bacillus* and *Streptomyces*, and it became clear that the peripheral bodies consisted largely of tubular and lamellar membrane material.[9, 21] In 1960, Fitz-James[4] showed that such bodies are formed through invagination of the cytoplasmic membrane, and introduced the name *mesosome*. Since then, mesosomes have been demonstrated in many Gram-positive bacteria,[3, 8, 11, 13] and it now seems probable

that they will be found in all Gram-positive and in many Gram-negative strains.

The morphology and localization of mesosomes within the bacteria and their relationship to the plasma membrane and the nucleoid was studied in detail by Ryter & Jacob.[19] Using serial sections of about 20 bacteria to prepare three-dimensionally reconstructed cells, it was shown that all mesosomes retained a connection to the membrane surface from which they had developed, and that each nucleoid was constantly in contact with one and sometimes two mesosomes. These observations suggested that the mesosomes played the role of intermediary between nucleoid and membrane, assuring the link between these two cell constituents which had previously been postulated on the basis of totally unrelated evidence by Jacob and his collaborators.[12] Further evidence for this link was provided by a study of plasmolysis in *Bacillus subtilis*, where a direct attachment

* Dr. Landman's work was supported by grants GB 1836 and GB 4506 from the National Science Foundation. The authors thank Mr. William Webster and Mrs. Claude Fréhel for technical assistance, and Mrs. Enriqueta Bond for help with the manuscript.

of nucleoid to membrane could be discerned following the expulsion of fragmenting mesosomes from the cytoplasm.[19, 22]

During protoplast formation the mesosomes are released[5, 22] and, as of that moment, the protoplasts always appear to be devoid of mesosomes. Even when they are transferred to a medium which permits their multiplication (as L-forms), the multiplying bodies retain the typical protoplast characteristics—namely absence of cell wall and of mesosomes.[22]

The direct attachment between nucleoid and membrane could be demonstrated in freshly formed protoplasts[20] and the statistical study of the number of attachment points visible in thin sections indicates that each nucleoid has probably only one point of attachment. This simple relationship provides some assurance that the observed contact points are not artifacts. Further, these morphological results are in accord with the observations of several authors who have shown that, when protoplasts and spheroplasts are lysed with care, part of the DNA remains associated with the membrane.[7, 10*]

Since protoplasts are capable of multiplying, the absence of mesosomes from protoplasts (and hence the absence of the nucleoid–mesosome attachment point) does not prevent nuclear division or segregation of new viable cells.[14, 22]

What, then, is the function of mesosomes in the nuclear region? Cytochemical studies have shown that the mesosomes, like the membrane, are the sites of oxidation-reduction reactions.[16, 23, 25, 26] Perhaps the regular appearance of mesosomes in the nuclear region of the bacilli indicates that these organelles furnish energy for nuclear functions. Perhaps the mesosomes aid in assuring the orderly and efficient distribution of genomes into daughter cells, following replication.

To obtain further insights concerning the questions of mesosome function and DNA-membrane attachment, it is im-

portant to determine the conditions under which the DNA-membrane attachment is direct, and when it is mediated by a mesosome. By comparing the behavior of cells which exhibit one or the other type of attachment, clues concerning the role of mesosomes may emerge. The present paper reports studies of nucleoid-membrane attachment in *B. subtilis* under various growth conditions, in protoplasts, reverting protoplasts, and in bacilli emerging from reverting protoplasts.

MATERIALS AND METHODS

STRAIN AND CONDITIONS OF CULTURE

B. subtilis strain 168 was employed throughout these studies. The complex medium used in growth and spore germination experiments has been described previously.[17] Similarly, the media and techniques employed in the studies of protoplast formation and L-colony growth have been published.[14, 22] The following procedure was used in protoplast reversion experiments: Bacteria were grown on blood agar base (Difco) plates overnight at 37°C from a spore inoculum, and suspended in SL1 medium to a density of approximately 1.5×10^8/ml as described.[14] After 4 hours of incubation at 37°C the cells were centrifuged, resuspended to the same volume in SL2 medium and incubated 90 minutes more. Sometimes the procedure is interrupted at this point by freezing the cells. After sampling for viable count (usually near 10^9/ml) lysozyme was added to 250 μg/ml and incubation continued for 60–90 minutes more in shallow layers in Erlenmeyer flasks at 33°C without agitation. Using this procedure, survival is usually close to 100 per cent and fewer than 0.01 per cent of the cells give rise to bacillary colonies; the rest form L-colonies. Ten ml of the protoplast suspension are centrifuged at 12,000 G at 10°C and resuspended in SL2 medium. They are then centrifuged, resuspended, and centrifuged once again to remove residual lysozyme. The pellet from this final centrifugation is now taken up in 0.25 ml of R fluid. Samples are plated at

* Also: C. Anagnostopoulos, personal communication, 1966.

low dilutions for assessment of residual bacillary forms, and at high dilutions for viable count. Viability losses in these centrifugation steps are irregular, but sometimes may amount to 90 per cent. Samples (0.001 ml) of the undiluted protoplast slurry are spotted and then spread in a small area onto gelatin reversion medium (GR) in a small petri dish, which is sealed and incubated at 26°C. Approximately 1, 9, 16, 20 and 24 hours after inoculation, three blocks 4 × 4 mm in size and each with a spread spot of inoculum, are cut out of the gelatin plate. One of these is examined in the phase microscope to monitor progress of reversion; the second is dissolved in 5 ml of warm DF fluid[14] for assessment of viable count and reversion on SDM medium. The third block is placed on a 15 × 6 × 1 mm piece of polyethylene in preparation for electron microscopy: a drop of warm AGR agar is now carefully placed on the inoculated surface of this latter block. The agar holds the protoplasts and reverting protoplasts in place at the gelatin surface, so that they remain undisturbed from the time of inoculation through reversion and fixation right to the time of sectioning. Further, the location of the surface is marked for sectioning purposes by the color difference between the two media after fixation. After cooling the agar at 4°C for 15 minutes, cellophane (from dialysis tubing) is wrapped around the block and its plastic support and secured by stapling in order to fasten the composite block to its plastic support and hold it together. Blocks, plastic support and cellophane are then placed in a small tube, covered with glutaraldehyde fixing fluid, stoppered tightly and shipped promptly to the Institut Pasteur for further processing.

MEDIA

AGR agar: a mixture containing 1 part of GR medium and five parts of the following: 18 g/liter Oxoid ⧣2 agar; 1 g/liter KNO_3; 0.3 M sodium succinate; 2 g/liter glucose; 1 g/liter NH_4NO_3; 0.005 M $MgCl_2$.

GR medium: 250 g/liter purified pigskin gelatin (Eastman); 1 g/liter KNO_3; 0.3 M

sodium succinate pH 7.3; 2 g/liter glucose; 1 g/liter NH_4NO_3; 0.005 M $MgCl_2$; 1.25 g/liter acid hydrolized casein (Difco); 0.04 g/liter L-tryptophan. The pH is adjusted to pH 7.3–7.6 with NaOH; pH measurements are made on ten-fold diluted samples. Concentrated sterile stock solutions of the ingredients are added to a concentrated gelatin solution in the order in which they are listed.

R fluid: 1 g/liter KNO_3; 0.5 M sodium succinate pH 7.3; 1 g/liter NH_4NO_3; 0.005 M $MgCl_2$.

SDM medium: 8 g/liter Noble agar (Difco); 1 g/liter NH_4NO_3; 0.005 M $MgCl_2$; 0.5 M sodium succinate pH 7.3; 3.5 g/liter K_2HPO_4; 1.5 g/liter KH_2PO_4; 2 g/liter glucose; 0.02 g/liter L-tryptophan; 0.6 g/liter D-methionine (a reversion inhibitor); 5 ml horse serum.

SL1 medium: a synthetic medium described by Landman & Halle.[14]

SL2 medium: a synthetic medium containing 0.5 M sucrose.[14]

TECHNIQUES FOR ELECTRON MICROSCOPY

Growing bacteria, germinating spores and L-colonies were fixed either in osmium tetroxide, according to Ryter & Kellenberger,[21] or, more recently, by a procedure involving both glutaraldehyde and osmium tetroxide.[20] Protoplasts and reverting protoplasts were always fixed by the latter procedure: samples are placed in a fixing fluid containing 4–6 per cent redistilled glutaraldehyde in 0.1 M cacodylate buffer, pH 6.0. The samples are then sent by air from Washington to Paris. Upon their arrival, four to five days later, they are washed gently, with constant agitation, for five to six hours in veronal buffer, pH 6.0. The cellophane envelopes are then removed and the samples are fixed overnight in osmium tetroxide according to Ryter & Kellenberger.[21] After dehydration and impregnation in Vestopal, the small blocks are oriented in the gelatin capsules in such a way that the boundary between the gelatin and agar media, where the cells are found, is vertical. This boundary serves as a good reference point because gelatin turns black after fixation with osmium tetroxide, while the agar remains light brown.

OBSERVATIONS

B. SUBTILIS DURING GROWTH AND GERMINATION

The cytology of growing *B. subtilis* cells is well known. Three-dimensional reconstructions have shown that the bacteria contain several mesosomes (at least four under the culture conditions used[19]); some of these are found along the membrane, some are in contact with the nucleoid, and others in the vicinity of the septum. The contact between nucleoid and mesosome is occasionally very extensive, so that the nucleoid appears to be enveloping the mesosome (Figure 10.1a); at other times the contact is much less intimate (Figure 10.1, b–e). In any case, it has not yet been possible to identify the true point of attachment with certainty, and it is not known whether this point is at the base of the mesosome or at some other location. Moreover, it may be that attachment of mesosomes to nucleoid is not always present or demonstrable: among 50 three-dimensional reconstructions made by Fuhs,[6] a few nuclei did not show a point of contact with a mesosome. Considering the technical difficulties and the difficulties of interpretation encountered in making such reconstructions, it is not unlikely that an individual failure to find an attachment point is due to an unfavorable plane of sectioning which does not permit distinction of a fine nuclear extension or of a delicate, small mesosome.

A study of spore germination with the technique of three-dimensional reconstruction (about 30 cells were used) has shown that, in a number of recently emerged bacteria, the nucleoid is not linked to a mesosome but appears to be attached to the membrane.[18] More precisely, careful examination of the sections shows that the nuclear material is not in direct contact with the membrane but remains separated from it by a distinctive structure which is difficult to delimit (Figure 10.2 a and b). It appears to consist of several small vesicles which are often veiled by very dense cytoplasm.

PROTOPLASTS AND L-FORMS

Several studies of protoplast formation and of freshly prepared protoplasts have already been published.[5, 22] Protoplasts generally appear as rounded cells, with a centrally located nucleoid which exhibits a fairly loose or open structure. The fixation technique used in the earlier work occasionally caused lysis of the protoplasts and it was not possible at the time to demonstrate with certainty a direct attachment of the nucleus to the membrane. Recently, thanks to the mixed fixation procedure which preserves efficiently the integrity of the protoplasts, direct attachment could be demonstrated beyond a shadow of a doubt. Generally a branch of the nucleoid is seen to extend to the membrane (Figure 10.2c). In certain micrographs, the nuclear material appears as separated from the membrane by small vesicles which resemble the attachment structures observed during germination. In all cases, the small size of this structure renders interpretation difficult and it is not possible at present to be certain that the small vesicles represent a definite structure.

At the point of contact of nucleoid and membrane, one may often observe an appendage attached at the outside of the membrane (Figure 10.2c). This appendage closely resembles the mesosome fragments which are released into the medium during protoplast formation and, quite probably, corresponds to a fragment of the erstwhile nuclear mesosome.

As has been described earlier,[22] sections of L-colonies reveal a great diversity in form, size and appearance of cells. Nevertheless, the absence of wall and of mesosomes is a common characteristic of all the cells. Contact between nucleoid and membrane is observed in quite a number of sections (Figure 10.3a). Although the heterogeneity of the shapes of the L-bodies does not permit a statistical study of the number of such points of contact (similar to the study made with proto-

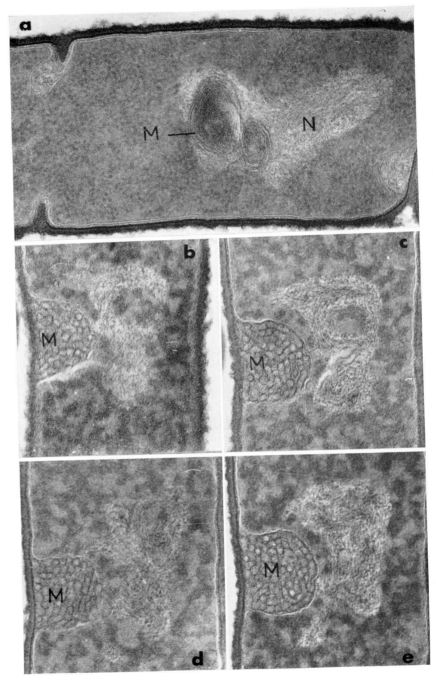

Figure 10.1. *a:* Growing cell of *Bacillus subtilis* containing a large mesosome (M), almost entirely surrounded by nuclear material (N). × 81,000. *b–e:* Four serial sections of the nuclear region of a growing cell: the nucleoid shows only tenuous contact with the mesosome (M). × 63,000.

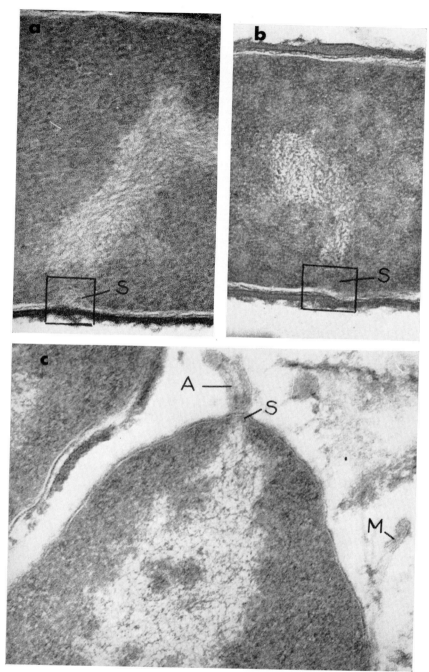

Figure 10.2. *a–b:* Nucleoid of germinating spore, showing direct linkage to the membrane; a small structure (S), consisting of very tiny vesicles, seems to connect the nuclear material with the membrane. *a,* × 82,800; *b,* × 66,600. *c:* Newly formed protoplast of *Bacillus subtilis* showing a direct link of nucleoid to membrane; very tiny vesicles can be seen between the nuclear material and the membrane, resembling the structure (S) shown above. The appendage A, fixed externally to the membrane attachment point, is very probably a fragment of the erstwhile nuclear mesosome, and resembles the mesosome fragments (M) released into the medium during protoplasting. × 117,000.

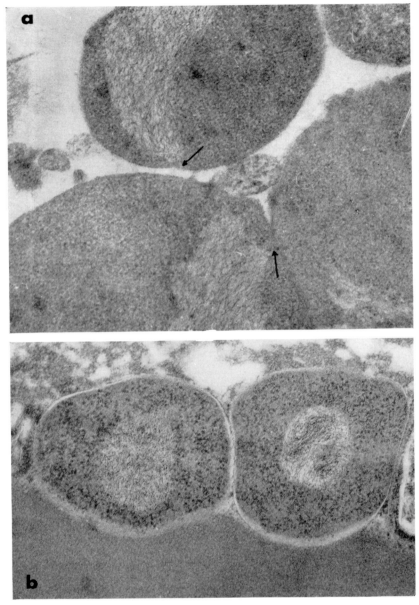

Figure 10.3. *a:* L-forms of *Bacillus subtilis* with nucleoids showing membrane attachment points (arrows). × 55,800. *b:* Protoplasts after one hour of incubation in gelatin reversion medium. The cytoplasm is rather dense and rich in ribosomes and the nucleoids are compact and show a more condensed texture than those of newly formed protoplasts. × 49,500.

plasts), it is reasonable to suppose that these points represent direct nucleoid-membrane attachments.

REVERTING PROTOPLASTS

The examination of protoplasts placed on gelatin reversion media shows they are very similar to freshly formed protoplasts in liquid or agar medium.[22] The nucleoid, however, is less dispersed and its texture is more condensed (Figure 10.3b). Mesosome fragments fixed to the exterior of the membrane have never been detected. It is likely that such fragments are removed by the successive washings to which the protoplasts are subjected before being placed on reversion medium. On the other hand, attachment points of nucleoids to membrane can be seen in a few sections. As in the case of freshly formed protoplasts, one can occasionally distinguish small vesicles between the nuclear material and the membrane (Figure 10.4a).

In samples taken after nine hours of incubation, the protoplasts present a very heterogeneous appearance. Alongside protoplasts which have preserved their original aspect, others may be seen which are no longer bounded by a single membrane but now possess a supplementary layer. In some, this external layer is still very thin (Figures 10.4c and 10.5, a, b), in others it is thick and appears similar to normal wall (Figures 10.4b, 10.5a and 10.6b). All these cells are doubtlessly reverting protoplasts. Whatever the thickness of their wall, the cytoplasm is almost always very dense and the nucleus more condensed than in the protoplasts. Some of these cells are more or less spherical, while others exhibit variable, often branched or bifurcated shapes (Figures 10.4b and 10.5a). The latter undoubtedly correspond to recently reverted cells in the process of division. They are reminiscent of the shapes seen in the phase microscope by Taubeneck & Gumpert[24] during their study of reversion and growth of *Proteus* spheroplasts.

Mesosomes of typical tubular or lamellar structure have never been observed on either non-reverting or reverting proto-plasts. On the other hand, rounded, dense, compartmentalized structures akin to mesosomes can be seen on rare occasions in reverting protoplasts (Figures 10.4c and 10.5a). Such structures have not been observed in other types of *B. subtilis* cells. These structures are always in contact with the membrane but, as far as one can judge, they do not link up to the nucleoid.

The nucleoid of protoplasts in beginning, as well as terminal, stages of reversion may be seen in direct contact with the membrane in an occasional section (Figure 10.5b).

BACILLARY FORMS DERIVED FROM REVERTED PROTOPLASTS

Bacteria formed from reverted protoplasts are bounded by a normal cell wall (Figure 10.6). Their cytoplasm is always very dense, even if relatively poor in ribosomes. The nucleoid is always extraordinarily condensed and presents a cut-off appearance as if it consisted of a filament folded over upon itself. A point of contact of the nuclear filament with the membrane can be observed only in exceptional cases (Figure 10.6b). This is not surprising since the more the nucleoid is drawn out into a slender thread, the less the probability of finding the point of contact. As in reverting protoplasts, normal mesosomes are not found. From time to time, however, the dense compartmentalized structures can again be seen (Figure 10.6a). These never appear to be connected with the nucleus and are most often found near the septum.

In order to ascertain whether these structures are homologous to normal mesosomes, we have inoculated intact *B. subtilis* cells into reversion medium and have examined them in thin sections after different periods of incubation. The sections show that on this hypertonic medium the mesosomes are soon expelled, and lysis of a certain number of bacteria occurs. After 24 hours, no normal mesosomes are visible. However, in a few rare bacteria, the same partitioned structures are found which were

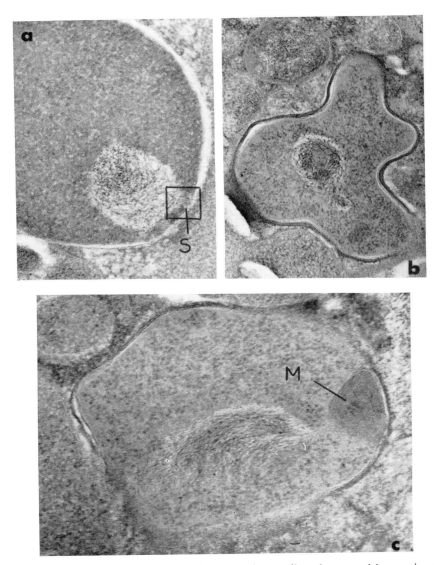

Figure 10.4. *a:* Protoplast incubated in reversion medium for several hours, showing a direct linkage of nucleoid to membrane; as in the case of the young protoplasts, some very small vesicles can be seen between the nuclear material and the membrane (S). × 63,000. *b:* Reverting protoplast surrounded by a fairly thin wall; its shape is multilobed and its nucleus very compact. × 50,400. *c:* Protoplast at an early stage of reversion; the wall is still very thin and a dense structure corresponding to a mesosome can be seen at the membrane (M). × 63,000.

seen in the course of reversion (Figure 10.5*c*). It thus appears likely that these organelles correspond to the mesosomes. Their particular appearance is caused not so much by the hypertonicity of the reversion medium as by the presence of very high concentrations of gelatin. Bacteria in-cubated in hypertonic medium solidified with 2% agar rather than gelatin possess normal mesosomes.[22]

As we have pointed out, the mesosomes observed in reverting and reverted proto-plasts are not only atypical in their ap-pearance but are also very rarely seen. It

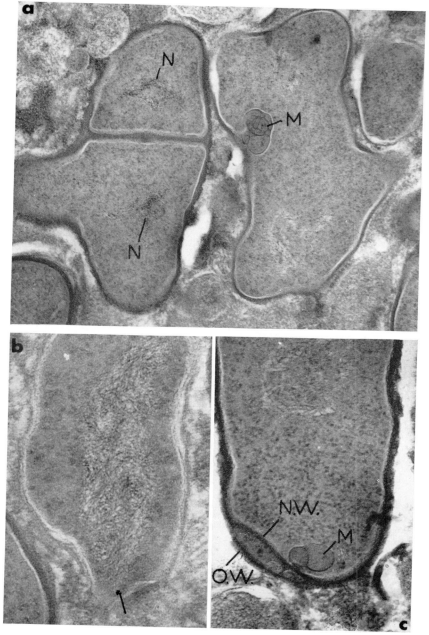

Figure 10.5. *a:* Reverting protoplasts showing various shapes; their nucleoids (N) are very condensed. The cell on the right contains a curious structure which corresponds to a mesosome (M). × 36,000. *b:* Young reverting protoplast surrounded by a very thin wall; its nucleoid shows a direct linkage to the membrane (arrow). × 85,500. *c:* Portion of a *Bacillus subtilis* cell incubated in reversion medium for 24 hours. Its mesosomes have been expelled from the cytoplasm and can still be seen between the old (O.W.) and new (N.W.) parts of the wall. The newly formed mesosome (M) presents the same aspect as the mesosomes appearing in reverting protoplasts. × 58,500.

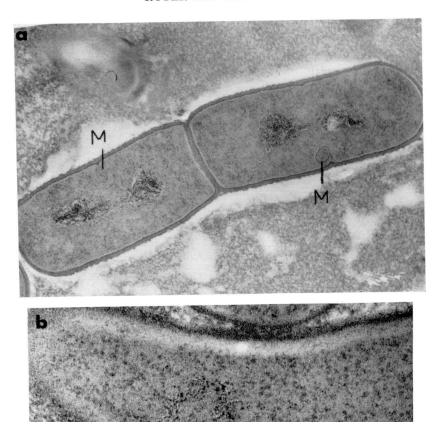

Figure 10.6. *a:* Bacillary form issued from a reverted protoplast; its wall is normal, its nuclei are very condensed, and two mesosomes (M) are located in the vicinity of the newly developing septa. × 32,400. *b:* Reverted forms; in the bacillary form the very condensed nucleoid seems to be directly connected to the membrane at a point (P). × 73,800.

was therefore important to determine whether each cell contained at least one of these structures, or whether some cells were completely devoid of them. Since gelatin medium is very difficult to section, it was not possible to make a sufficient number of serial sections for an adequate study of three-dimensionally reconstructed cells. Instead, we have attempted to answer this question by making quantitative surveys of the number of mesosomes which appear in thin sec-

tions.* As a control, sections of normally growing *B. subtilis* were examined. As we have indicated earlier,[22] *B. subtilis* contains an average of four mesosomes per cell. In our survey of 100 sections of such cells, 102 mesosomes were found. In 100 sections of reverting cells in gelatin medium, only four showed mesosomes. If each reverting cell contained one mesosome, one should find mesosomes in 25

* The details of this quantitative study will be given in a later paper.

per cent of sections. Obviously, the size of reverting cells is not exactly the same as that of normal cells. Making allowance for the size difference, and assuming that reverting cells have twice the volume of normal cells (a maximum estimate) one should still find mesosomes in 18–19 per cent of the sections if each cell had one mesosome. Thus, despite the uncertainties in our assumptions, it is abundantly clear that most of the reverting cells (we estimate 75 per cent) do not contain a mesosome.

DISCUSSION

This morphological study has shown the following:

1. In growing bacteria, the attachment of the nucleoid is generally through the intermediary of a mesosome.

2. Under certain cultural conditions, the attachment of the nucleoid to the membrane is direct. These cultural conditions obtain perhaps at times during growth, often during germination, and always in reversion medium.

3. A distinctive structure appears to be interposed between nucleoid and membrane at their point of contact. This structure can be discerned when the nuclear mesosome is absent.

Reverting protoplasts and bacilli forming from reverting protoplasts are generally completely lacking in mesosomes. The absence of nuclear mesosomes during germination is apparently not accompanied by any disturbance of either DNA replication or nuclear segregation, since these two processes occur in the same fashion and at the same rate as during vegetative growth. It is therefore reasonable to conclude that the nuclear mesosomes are not required for these processes and that at best they play only an accessory role.

The presence of small vesicles, which is often noted in direct attachments in protoplasts and germinating cells, suggests that the attachment of the nuclear material to the membrane is not merely a simple point of contact between DNA and membrane but, rather, consists of a more complex structure. So far, the pictures are still too imprecise to serve as proof for the existence of a special structure of attachment. It goes without saying that a clearcut electron microscopic characterization of such a structure would be of very great interest, since we are presumably dealing with either the swivel[1, 15] or the chromosomal replication site[7, 10, 12] or, perhaps, a combination of the two.

Our study of protoplast reversion has shown that most of the reverting protoplasts and their successor bacillary forms do not have mesosomes. It is likely that the rarity of these organelles can in part be attributed to the special properties of the reversion medium. Nevertheless, it may be concluded that mesosomes are required neither for reversion proper, i.e., for the initiation of cell wall formation,* nor for nuclear or cellular division. Those few mesosomes which are seen in the bacillary forms following reversion always appear at the septum. This suggests that either the presence of mesosomes is relatively important at this location in the cell or that septation is associated with membrane growth which manifests itself by formation of a mesosome.

The condensation of nuclear material which begins at the start of reversion and continues apace as reversion proceeds may also be partly due to the gelatin medium (normal bacteria placed into gelatin medium exhibit a very condensed nucleoid after a few hours). In addition, the presence of some cell wall appears to play a role in this process, since non-reverting protoplasts never show such a condensed nucleus. The condensation of nuclear material does not appear to affect the direct attachment of nucleoid to membrane, since this type of attachment persists all through reversion and in the derived bacillary forms. The rare mesosomes observed are never connected to the nucleoid.

Viewing our results as a whole, it becomes clearly evident that mesosomes are not essential to the functioning of *B. subtilis*. Going further, it may be that these structures do not fulfill any specific role

* To be discussed in a subsequent publication.

beyond that already served by the cytoplasmic membrane. If that were really the situation, the presence of mesosomes in bacteria might mean nothing more than a mere augmentation of membrane functions. We leave it to future biochemical and cytochemical investigations to correct or verify these concepts.

Summary

The mode of attachment of DNA to membrane is examined in *Bacillus subtilis* under various conditions. In bacteria growing on ordinary media, the attachment of nucleoid to membrane is generally through the intermediary of a mesosome. In germinating spores, the DNA is often directly attached to the cytoplasmic membrane; in protoplasts and in protoplasts reverting to the bacillary form in gelatin medium, attachment is always direct. In this case, a distinctive structure appears to be interposed between nucleoid and membrane at their point of contact. Nuclear replication and cell division appear to be normal in cells from germinating spores, in bacteria growing on gelatin reversion medium, and in bacilli forming from reverted protoplasts, yet all three types of cells are often completely devoid of mesosomes. The mesosomes thus do not seem to be required for any essential cellular function and are definitely not necessary for reversion of protoplasts to the bacillary state. Instead, formation of a layer of cell wall appears to be an early step in reversion. Intense nuclear condensation and a peculiar type of mesosome are exhibited by bacilli and reverting protoplasts incubating on gelatin reversion medium.

REFERENCES

1. Cairns, J.: The chromosome of *Escherichia coli. Cold Spring Harbor Symp. Quant. Biol.* **28**: 43, 1963.
2. Chapman, G. B., and Hillier, J.: Electron microscopy of ultra-thin sections of bacteria. I. Cellular division in *Bacillus cereus. J. Bact.* **66**: 362, 1953.
3. Edwards, M. R., and Stevens, R. W.: Fine structure of *Listeria monocytogenes. J. Bact.* **86**: 414, 1963.
4. Fitz-James, P. C.: Participation of the cyto-plasmic membrane in the growth and spore formation of bacilli. *J. Biophys. Biochem. Cytol.* **8**: 507, 1960.
5. ———: Fate of the mesosome of *Bacillus megaterium* during protoplasting. *J. Bact.* **87**: 1483, 1964.
6. Fuhs, G. W.: Symposium on the fine structure and replication of bacteria and their parts. I. Fine structure and replication of bacterial nucleoids. *Bact. Rev.* **29**: 277, 1965.
7. Ganesan, A. T., and Lederberg, J.: A cell-membrane bound fraction of bacterial DNA. *Biochem. Biophys. Res. Commun.* **18**: 824, 1965.
8. Giesbrecht, P.: Über "organisierte" Mitochondrien und andere Feinstrukturen von *Bacillus megaterium. Zbl. Bakt. Paras. Orig.* **179**: 538, 1960.
9. Glauert, A. M., and Hopwood, D. A.: A membranous component of the cytoplasm in *Streptomyces coelicolor. J. Biophys. Biochem. Cytol.* **6**: 515, 1959.
10. Hanawalt, P. C., and Ray, D. S.: Isolation of the growing point in the bacterial chromosome. *Proc. Nat. Acad. Sci. USA.* **52**: 125, 1964.
11. Imaeda, T., and Ogura, M.: Formation of intracytoplasmic membrane system of *Mycobacteria* related to cell division. *J. Bact.* **85**: 150, 1963.
12. Jacob, F., Brenner, S., and Cuzin, F.: On the regulation of DNA replication in bacteria. *Cold Spring Harbor Symp. Quant. Biol.* **28**: 329, 1963.
13. Kellenberger, E., and Ryter, A.: In bacteriology. In: *Modern Developments in Electron Microscopy.* (B. M. Siegel, Ed.). Academic Press, New York, 1964: p. 335.
14. Landman, O. E., and Halle, S.: Enzymically and physically induced inheritance changes in *Bacillus subtilis. J. Mol. Biol.* **7**: 721, 1963.
15. Lark, K. G.: Regulation of chromosome replication and segregation in bacteria. *Bact. Rev.* **30**: 3, 1966.
16. Leene, W., and van Iterson, W.: Tetranitro-blue tetrazolium reduction in *Bacillus subtilis. J. Cell Biol.* **27**: 237, 1965.
17. Ryter, A.: Étude morphologique de la sporulation de *Bacillus subtilis. Ann. Inst. Pasteur* (Paris) **108**: 40, 1965.
18. ———: Relation between membrane synthesis and nuclear division. *Folia Microbiol.* In press.
19. Ryter, A., and Jacob, F.: Étude au microscope électronique de la liaison entre noyau et mésosome chez *Bacillus subtilis. Ann. Inst. Pasteur* (Paris) **107**: 389, 1964.
20. ———: Étude morphologique de la liaison du

noyau a la membrane chez *E. coli* et chez les protoplastes de *B. subtilis. Ann. Inst. Pasteur* (Paris) **110**: 801, 1966.

21. Ryter, A., Kellenberger, E., Birch-Andersen, A., and Maaløe, O.: Étude au microscope électronique de plasmas contenant de l'acide désoxyribonucléique. I. Les nucléoides des bactéries en croissance active. *Z. Naturforsch.* **13b**: 597, 1958.

22. Ryter, A., and Landman, O. E.: Electron microscope study of the relationship between mesosome loss and the stable L state (or protoplast state) in *Bacillus subtilis. J. Bact.* **88**: 457, 1964.

23. Sedar, A. W., and Burde, R. M.: The demonstration of the succinic dehydrogenase system in *Bacillus subtilis* using tetranitro-blue tetrazolium combined with techniques of electron microscopy. *J. Cell Biol.* **27**: 53, 1965.

24. Taubeneck, U., and Gumpert, J.: Some remarks on Gram negative bacteria with experimentally altered surface structures. *Folia Microbiol.* In press.

25. Vanderwinkel, E., and Murray, R. G. E.: Organelles intracytoplasmiques bactériens et site d'activité oxydo-réductrice. *J. Ultrastr. Res.* **7**: 185, 1962.

26. van Iterson, W., and Leene, W.: A cytochemical localization of reductive sites in a Grampositive bacterium; tellurite reduction in *Bacillus subtilis. J. Cell Biol.* **20**: 361, 1964.

11

The Collection of Mesosome Vesicles Extruded During Protoplasting*

Philip C. Fitz-James

UNIVERSITY OF WESTERN ONTARIO MEDICAL SCIENCE CENTER

LONDON, ONTARIO, CANADA

The intracytoplasmic membranous organelles, the mesosomes, are seen in dividing vegetative cells in several structural variations of interconnected vesicles within vesicles. In dividing bacilli, many appear to be associated with the development of the transverse septum at the site of division, maintaining an intimate relation at their apices with the dividing nucleoid. Elsewhere, at or near the cell end, mesosomes can be seen in both thin-sectioned and negatively stained cells to be similarly reaching into the cell from the membrane.

Soon after the existence of these organelles as components of the cytoplasm of growing and sporulating bacilli became known,[6, 21] various attempts at isolation were undertaken in the author's laboratory. Ideally, one would hope to isolate the organelles as intact structures. However, during protoplasting with lysozyme or penicillin, mesosomes are not preserved as such but are extruded from the cell.[7, 16] Likewise, with mechanical disruption extensive displacement of the mesosome occurs through the first rents in the cell wall, and these displaced structures soon break down and become blended with the remnants of the plasma membrane

on further disintegration. Thus, attempts at isolation of intact mesosomes free of plasma membrane have not been successful (cf. Salton & Chapman[17]).

In spite of the concurrent mesosomal extrusion, protoplasting still appeared preferable to disruption for the initial fractionation step. But because mesosomes were extruded, the aim was simply redirected towards the isolation of extruded vesicles rather than the intact organelle. However, it soon became apparent that, although extruded from the cell interior, the mesosomal vesicles are not set free and recoverable in the supernatant, but remain attached as a group or as an interconnected series of everted vesicles on the protoplast surface (Figure 11.1). Small regions of these attached mesosomes are occasionally seen in thin sections of both recently formed protoplasts (Figure 11.2C) and protoplasts induced to grow by aeration in special medium.[5] Because of the thinness of the section, they do not appear as prominent as in the negatively stained whole mounts. Thus, the normal protoplast surface is far from being smooth, as suggested by phase microscopy. Often, the extruded vesicles are grouped at opposite sides of the protoplast, reflecting the original point of membrane invagination before removal of the cell wall. A remarkable similarity in overall architecture

* The author is grateful to Miss Doryth Loewy for her careful and tireless technical assistance throughout this study.

was evident in comparing the extrusion of different protoplasts and, indeed, of protoplasts of different species. Generally, the further out they extended, the smaller the vesicles became. It is not difficult to visualize how such extrusions, shown in Figure 11.1, could arise from the vesicle-within-vesicle profile so commonly seen in thin section.

No such everted structures are seen on the surface of untreated cells in thin sections or in negative-stained smears. Although some parts of the mesosomes are occasionally seen spreading into the wall-membrane space (Figure 11.2A, arrow), intact mesosomes are usually well within the cell, as can be seen in the figure.

The present report outlines a simple procedure that was successful in collecting what appeared to be these extruded vesicles partly free from plasma membrane. The method, when tested on a variety of cultures in various stages of mesosomal size and activity, proved to be effective in its aim. Indeed, the isolated vesicles appeared to be, by isotope labeling, active sites of membrane synthesis and to have a precursor-product relationship to the general plasma membrane of the cell.

Materials and Methods

The methods were largely developed using, as typical mesosome-bearing organisms, *Bacillus megaterium* KM and a *Lactobacillus* which, as a group, have remarkably large mesosomes (Figure 11.2, B and D).[19] *Escherichia coli* K 12 was used as a nonmesosome cell type.

The fractionation procedure was followed by means of electron microscopy. Fixation of pelleted fractions, their dehydration and embedding in polyester (Vestopal, Martin Jaeger, Vésenaz, Geneva), was essentially that described by Kellenberger et al.[12] In negative-stained whole mounts the extruded mesosome, either attached or free, had a characteristic form as well as a different surface texture from that of the plasma membrane of the lysed protoplast. Thus, negative staining proved more useful than thin sec-

tioning in assessing the achievement of a fractionation procedure. Samples for staining were washed free of the buffer or gradient material by mixing with an equal volume of the negative stain solution (1–2% phosphotungstic acid, pH 7.1 with 1 N KOH;[1] 1–2% Na tungstate, pH 6.5[20]) and centrifuged at room temperature. The pellet, resuspended in fresh stain to a suitable density, was mounted by a platinum loop to carbon stabilized Formvar-filmed grids and dried. (Formvar: Shawinigan Products.)

A FRACTIONATION PROCEDURE

Earlier studies of ribosome activity in mechanically disrupted sporulating cells had indicated a tendency of the membranes of bacilli to form lighter and heavier zones on gradient centrifugation. A number of gradient materials were thus tested on whole and lysed protoplast preparations. The most promising results were obtained with gradients of the type used to prepare mammalian microsomes and made with either Ficoll (Pharmacia, Uppsala, Sweden) or sucrose. The latter, being more economical and available, was used more routinely. Ficoll, however, was useful in studying the degree of attachment of extruded mesosomes.

Intact protoplasts subjected to centrifugation down a Ficoll gradient (2–20%) containing sucrose (0.25–0.3 M) and formed on top of a cushion of 40% Ficoll yielded a very small zone at the 20–40 interface considerably richer in vesicles like those of mesosomes when examined by negative staining. The bulk of the material pelleted on the tube bottom. A better yield of what appeared to be mesosomal vesicles was obtained if some form of disruption of the protoplast was used; presumably this partly freed the attached mesosomes. Thus a method found successful in yielding a fraction enriched in mesosomal vesicles was eventually developed, based on osmotic shocking of the protoplasts and sedimenting this lysate down a 5–20% sucrose gradient on a 60% sucrose cushion, all in tris (10^{-2} M), KCl (10^{-2} M), MgCl$_2$ (1.5×10^{-3} M) pH 7.4.[22]

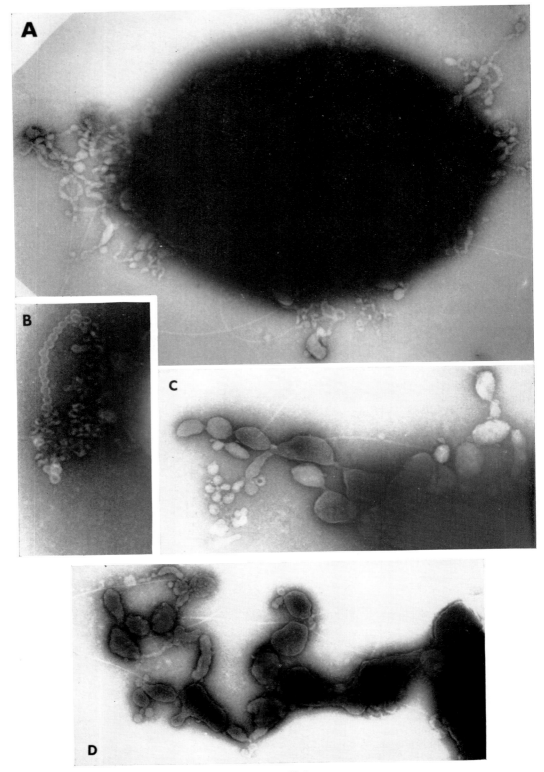

Figure 11.1.

126

Both continuous and discontinuous gradients were compared and found equally suitable, provided the low gradient-cushion interface was sharp. Hence, freshly prepared gradients were better. Protoplast lysates (0.5 ml lysate from 100–500 ml of culture at O.D. 0.3–0.5 at 650 mμ), layered on a gradient in a 5, 15, or 30 ml tube and subjected to 30–60 minutes sedimentation at 25,000 rpm in a swinging-bucket head (Spinco), formed two membrane containing zones—one at the interface (I) and another as a pellet (P) on the tube bottom.

ELECTRON MICROSCOPY OF MEMBRANE FRACTIONS

Examination of these two fractions in the electron microscope by both thin sectioning and negative staining showed that, besides free polysomes in the interface fraction (Figure 11.3A) and ghost occluded or attached polysomes in the pellet (Figure 11.3B), the peculiar interconnected and branched vesicles of the mesosomes recognizable in negative-contrast mounts were in greater numbers in the interface and were no longer attached to plasma membrane (Figure 11.4A and B). Although larger membranes and ghost remnants were limited to the pellet, some smaller pieces of the plasma membrane contaminated the interface, and some mesosomes still attached to the plasma membrane of the ghosts were in the pellet.

Detergent treatment of the protoplast lysates was tried as a means of increasing the yield and relative purity of the mesosomal vesicles in the interface fraction. It was hoped that a certain critical concentration of detergent would be relatively more damaging to the larger plasma membrane ghosts than to the smaller mesosome vesicles. Lubrol W (I.C.I.), a condensate of cetyl alcohol and polyoxyethylene used by Godson & Butler[10] to dissolve bacterial membranes, was found, in concentrations up to 0.03%, both to reduce the recovery of plasma membrane in the pellet and to increase the sharpness and density of the interfacial band. More recently, at the suggestion of Dr. Salton, Nonidet P-40 (Shell Oil Co. of Canada) has been used with similar success.

At low concentrations (0.005–0.015%) of Lubrol W, the pellet fraction was reduced (30–50 per cent) in size and its contained membranes showed some slight damage, particularly along the edges of the sheets (Figure 11.4C). In the interface fraction, the mesosomal membranes also showed slight distortion from the normal with negative staining (Figures 11.4D and 11.5C).

At higher Lubrol concentrations (0.02–0.03%), more severe fragmentation of the plasma membrane of the pellet was seen (Figure 11.5A). Many of the Lubrol-treated pellet membranes were now well endowed with projecting subunits very similar in size and appearance to the knob-like, inner-membrane subunits seen in mitochondria and recently identified with the terminal step of oxidative phosphorylation.[2] The absence of these subunits on the everted mesosomes of B. megaterium and Sporolactobacillus inulinus even after Lubrol treatment assisted recognition of the two membrane types in negative stained smears. The vesicles in the interface fraction, however, did appear expanded and blistered in negatively stained smears (Figure 11.5, B and D), after treatment of the lysate with Lubrol W at 0.02–0.03% final concentration. Again, although the difference between the pellet and interface fractions of Lubrol-treated lysates was striking in negative stains, the difference in appearance of the preparations in thin sections was much less so (Figure 11.3, C and D).

LIPID LABELING OF PROTOPLAST MEMBRANES

The arrangement of mesosomes seen in dividing cells primarily at sites of transverse septa formation, and in sporulating

Figure 11.1. Various arrangements of extruded mesosomes seen on the surface of intact, fixed protoplasts of *Bacillus megaterium* KM. Protoplasts were fixed with 3% glutaraldehyde, washed twice with buffer (0.3 M sucrose, 0.1 M phosphate) and once with potassium phosphotungstate (pH 7.1) solution, then mounted on grids with phosphotungstate. *A:* A whole protoplast ($\times$ 38,000). *B–D:* Edges of protoplasts with attached mesosomes ($\times$ 54,000).

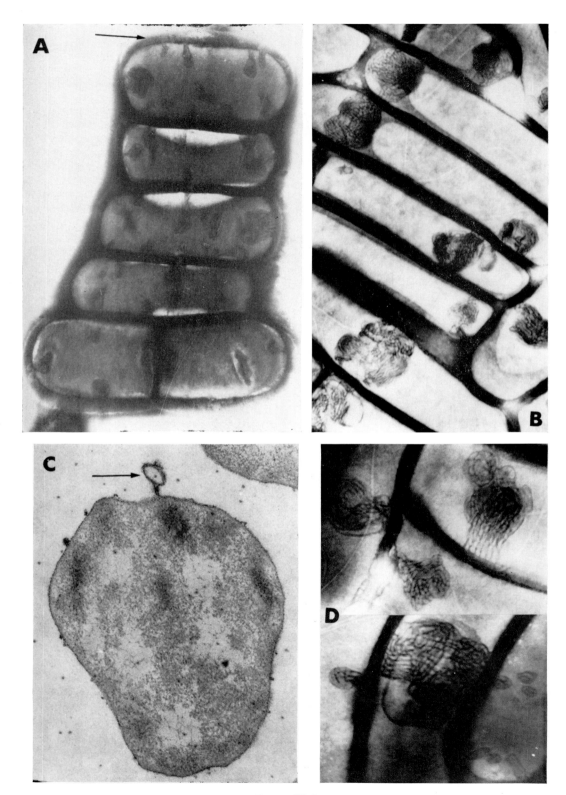

Figure 11.2.

cells continuous with the developing fore-spore membrane, suggested they might, among other functions, be major sites of membrane synthesis. This suspicion was strengthened when recovery of mesosome structure was found to be associated with induced division synchrony and a marked rise in cell phospholipid.[8] If true, then the method of preparing mesosomal vesicles could be tested by comparing the labeling of the lipids of these fractions prepared from cells exposed for short periods to isotopes known to label lipids. Both P^{32} (Atomic Energy of Canada Ltd., Commercial Products, Ottawa) labeled inorganic phosphate and C^{14} labeled acetate (acetate-1-C^{14}, Nenco, Boston), were used to label phospholipids; Fe^{59} (Nenco) was used as a label for membrane cytochromes. For ease of handling and counting, the majority of the studies were done with acetate-1-C^{14}.

The experimental procedure of a typical labeling experiment employing a mild detergent treatment was as follows: Rapidly growing cells of *B. megaterium* KM labeled for 20 minutes prior to harvesting were washed with the corresponding carrier dissolved in 3×10^{-3} M $MgCl_2$ (carrier acetate, 10^{-2} M sodium acetate; carrier phosphate, 0.1 M potassium phosphates at pH 7.2; carrier iron 10^{-4} M $FeCl_2$) then converted to protoplasts by 10–20 minutes exposure to lysozyme (50–200 $\mu g/ml$, Armour Pharmaceutical) at 20–30°C in sucrose (0.5 M), $MgSO_4 \cdot 6H_2O$ (0.016 M), potassium phosphate (0.1 M, pH 7.2). The protoplasts sedimented from the sucrose were worked up at room temperature in 1 to 2 drops of a DNase (Worthington Biologicals) solution (1–5 mg/ml) and just sufficient dilute $MgSO_4$ (0.016 M) added to cause lysis (0.5–1.5 ml), and the preparation put on ice. For detergent treatment before centrifugation, part of the lysate was shaken with a 2% aqueous solution of Lubrol W or Nonidet P-40 added drop by drop from a specially calibrated Pasteur pipette with a drawn-out tip. The preparation was examined by phase contrast after each drop, and the addition ceased when the desired degree of membrane disintegration was observed. Usually two microdrops, or about 0.015 per cent, detergent broke the ghost membranes down to about half their size, while 0.03 per cent left only small pieces of membrane. Fine beaded material, suspected mesosomal remnants and β-hydroxybutyrate granules, did not appear altered at low levels of detergent. A similar final degree of disintegration could also be achieved by directly adding detergent microdrops to the thick whole protoplast suspensions containing DNase.

After gradient centrifugation, the interface zone was removed by either drop collection through a needle pushed into the tube from below or via a hypodermic syringe and bent-tip needle from above. The interface material and the pellet left in the drained tube were suspended up to 1 ml in carrier acetate and shaken with 4 ml of 1:2 methanol:chloroform after the procedure of Folch et al.[9] The lower phase of methanol-chloroform was washed twice by shaking vigorously with equal volumes of "upper phase" (3 vols. chloroform, 44 vols. methanol and 47 vols. carrier wash). One aliquot of the washed lipid-phase was ashed with 60% (w/v) perchloric acid for the estimation of total phosphorus by the method of Ernster et al.[4] Another aliquot was taken to dryness in a glass vial, 10 ml of scintillation mixture (BBOT, Packard) added, and the radioactivity counted on a Scintillation Spectrometer counter (Model 725 Nuclear Chicago Corp., Des Plains, Ill.). C^{14} or Fe^{59} counts, corrected for quenching, were expressed as

Figure 11.2. *A:* Negatively stained whole-cell mount of *Bacillus subtilis* showing the usual arrangement of bacillus mesosomes. Occasionally, part of the mesosomes have become extruded, probably during drying, into the wall-membrane space (arrow) ($\times$ 30,000). *C:* Electron micrograph of a thin section of a recently formed *Bacillus megaterium* protoplast showing part of an extruded mesosome (arrow) at its site of attachment to the plasma membrane; lead and uranyl stained ($\times$ 44,000). *B* ($\times$ 44,000) and *D* ($\times$ 56,000): The extensive mesosomes seen in *Sporolactobacillus inulinus* negatively stained (K-PTA) cells have formed a mat on the grid.

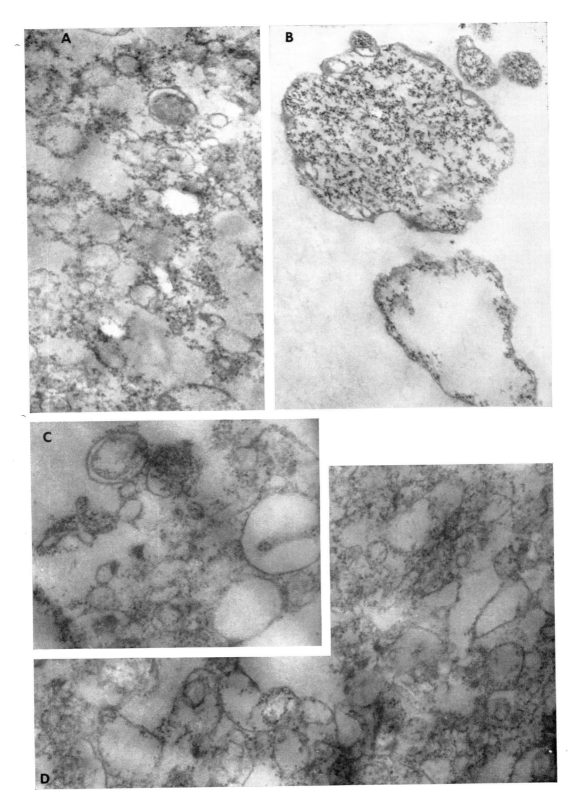

Figure 11.3.

cpm/μg lipid P. Phosphorus radioactivity was measured using a M-6 Geiger-Muller liquid counting tube on the same reduced isobutanol:benzene extract of the Ernster procedure used to measure total lipid-phosphorus.

Results

FRACTIONATION

Acetate-1-C^{14} Labeled Cells

The specific activities of the lipid-soluble material in the total lysate (T) in the interface (I) and pellet (P) fractions of a protoplast lysate and the same lysate treated with detergent (Lubrol W at 0.02%) are shown in Figure 11.6. The cells were labeled with sodium acetate-1-C^{14} (1.3 $\times$ 10^6 cpm/μM; 0.17 μc/ml) for 30 minutes prior to harvesting. With a shorter label period (20 minutes), the interface fraction in the untreated lysate is considerably more active. The distribution of total phospholipid in the two fractions was very similar to that shown in (Figure 11.8b). The enhancement of the specific activity of the interface lipid over that of the pellet was not always as marked as it appears in Figure 11.6. Occasionally, in runs with shorter labeling or possibly because of differences in lysis ghosting procedure, the I fraction on lysis alone, already high, was only slightly improved by detergent action.

The effects of varying concentrations of detergent on the specific activity of the I and P lipids of B. megaterium are shown in Figure 11.7. Usually a maximum effect was seen with from 0.025 to 0.04% Lubrol W. Excess detergent caused a turbidity in the lysates and was avoided. It should also be noted that since lysates of sucrose-stabilized protoplasts aged 1–2 hours at room temperature also became more turbid, the gradient centrifugation at 3–5°C was done right after protoplast rupture. The pellet specific activities for B and C (not shown) in the experiment depicted in the figure were the same or slightly higher than that shown for the "lysis only" pellet. The amounts of pellet were, however, greatly reduced, as indicated in Figure 11.8b. Improvement in the specific activity of the I fraction was usually found on increasing the Lubrol concentration up to 0.03%; with higher Lubrol concentrations the pellet fraction became very small in amount, and was often found to be equally if not more active than the I fraction. Possibly such residual pellets were rich in aggregated mesosomal remnants. Incomplete lysozyme digestion also tended to elevate the pellet activity, presumably due to poor liberation of mesosomal vesicles from within remaining walls.

In most experiments, from 50–60 per cent of the total acetate incorporated in 20 to 30 minutes was recovered as lipid-soluble material, presumably as fatty acids in phospholipid layers. Of the total phospholipid in a crude lysate, 60–80 per cent could be recovered in the two fractions.

In spite of the apparent prevalence of ribosomes in the sections, only 2–3 per cent of the total RNA of the cells was recovered in the interface fraction, and 9–10 per cent in the pellet fraction of lysates of B. megaterium protoplasts. When treated with Lubrol to 0.03%, the total RNA was reduced to 0.8 per cent in the interface fraction and 3.5 per cent in the pellet. So far, no attempts to free the interface fraction of the contaminating ribosomes have been made.

P^{32} Labeling of Cells

Cells labeled with P^{32} prior to harvesting and conversion to protoplasts yielded specific activities in the I and P fractions of lysates very similar to those shown in

Figure 11.3. Thin-section electron micrographs of interface and pellet fractions resulting from cushioned-gradient fractionation of lysates of *Bacillus megaterium* protoplasts ($\times$ 55,000). *A:* Material from an interface fraction showing ribosomes, vesicular profiles; most of the ribosomes are outside the vesicles. *B:* Ghost structures seen in a pellet fraction; most of the ribosomes are within the membrane profiles. *C:* Interface fraction from a protoplast lysate treated with Lubrol W (0.03%). *D:* Pellet fraction from a lysate treated with Lubrol W.

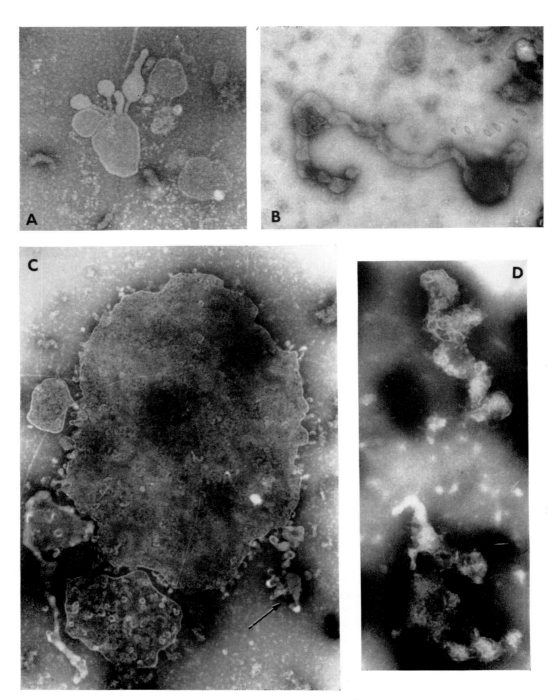

Figure 11.4. Negative-stained fractions of lysed protoplasts. *A:* The free, mesosomal-like vesicles which after gradient centrifugation formed a major part of the interface fraction of protoplast lysates of *Bacillus megaterium;* the negative smears, like the thin sections (Figure 11.3A) contained many ribosomes (× 55,000). *B:* A tubular membranous structure commonly seen in the interface fraction of lysed protoplasts of *Sporolactobacillus inulinus* (× 73,000). *C:* Membrane fractions from the pellet fraction of a lysate of *B. megaterium* treated with Lubrol W at about 0.01%; the edges of the sheet show some fragmentation; the arrow points to a possible mesosome remnant still attached (× 30,000). *D:* Mesosome vesicles in the interface fraction from *S. inulinus* showing slight alteration due to 0.01% Lubrol W (× 77,000); compare with *B.*

Figures 11.6 and 11.7. A detergent enhancement was also observed. However,
prolonged protoplasting (60 minutes) in
phosphate-buffered sucrose reduced the
difference of I/P specific activities.

Iron Labeling of Membrane Fractions

The results of a 20-minute exposure of
B. megaterium KM to Fe^{59} (0.05 μc/ml)
prior to harvesting and protoplasting are
shown in Figure 11.8. Again as with ace-
tate-1-C^{14} and P^{32}, the interface fraction
was considerably enriched with label.
However, unlike the former studies, detergent, even at 0.01% concentration,
markedly reduced the labeled iron bound
to the lipids. As these results indicate, much
of the iron activity, presumably labeled
cytochromes removed from the membrane
by detergent, was recovered largely as soluble material on top of the gradients. Likewise in preliminary enzyme studies of these
fractions, β-hydroxybutyrate reductase, cytochrome oxidase and succinate oxidase
found in "lysed only" membrane fractions
were completely solubilized by quite low
concentrations of Lubrol W (0.03%).

Recentrifugation of Membrane Fractions

The validity of the gradient fractionation procedure was assessed by a variety
of recycling studies. When interface vesicles from protoplast lysates not treated
with detergent were collected, washed
free of sucrose or Ficoll by centrifugation
in buffer, resuspended on and sedimented
again through a density gradient, they reappeared almost entirely at the interface.
If treated with Lubrol W before this recentrifugation, the material was again recovered at the interface, but the amount
was reduced and the specific activity increased (Figure 11.9, A and B). No measurable pellet fraction was recovered from
the second centrifugation cycle of the interface fraction. The pellet fraction of a
protoplast lysate yielded on recycling a
small interfacial layer (one eighth of the
total phospholipid) of slightly higher activity (Figure 11.9C). Lubrol treatment of
the pellet before recentrifugation produced
a small fluffy zone of lower activity above

the cushion interface (Figure 11.9D, A–I)
and a remnant of ghosts at about the same
specific activity as the untreated pellet material (Figure 11.9D, P).

The above results suggest that the mesosome vesicles are being preferentially labeled by C^{14} acetate. Although many of
the extruded mesosomes are sedimented
with the larger ghost membranes, some
are freed, largely by the original osmotic
shocking rather than by subsequent detergent, and can be collected at a gradient-
cushion interface. The results of a number
of recycling runs such as shown in Figure
11.9 supported the EM evidence that the
detergents were improving the specific activity of interface vesicles by dispersing
contaminating plasma membranes.

The studies also indicated that Lubrol
W was not producing a vesicular artifact
with higher activity from the plasma membrane. Thus, a morphological entity very
similar to extruded mesosomes could be
partially separated from the plasma membrane and, when isolated from cells exposed to acetate-1-C^{14} or P^{32} for short
periods, the fraction containing these entities appeared to be more active as site
of phospholipid synthesis.

ANALYSIS OF MESOSOMAL CHANGES

In order to check further the collection
procedure outlined, three biological situations involving, or suspected of involving, mesosomal changes were analysed. It
was also hoped that these studies would
yield some evidence to support the result,
already suggested, that a precursor-product
relationship exists between mesosomes and
plasma membrane.

These types of study were: temperature-
induced synchrony, protoplast and cell
growth with "pulse" and "chase" exposure to lipid labels, and spore germination.

Effect of Temperature Shift Synchrony

When *Bacillus* cells previously chilled to
15°C for 30–40 minutes are rewarmed to
30–32°C, they show a burst of synthesis
and growth leading to a synchronization of
cell division some 40 minutes after rewarming.[11] The marked effect on the mes-

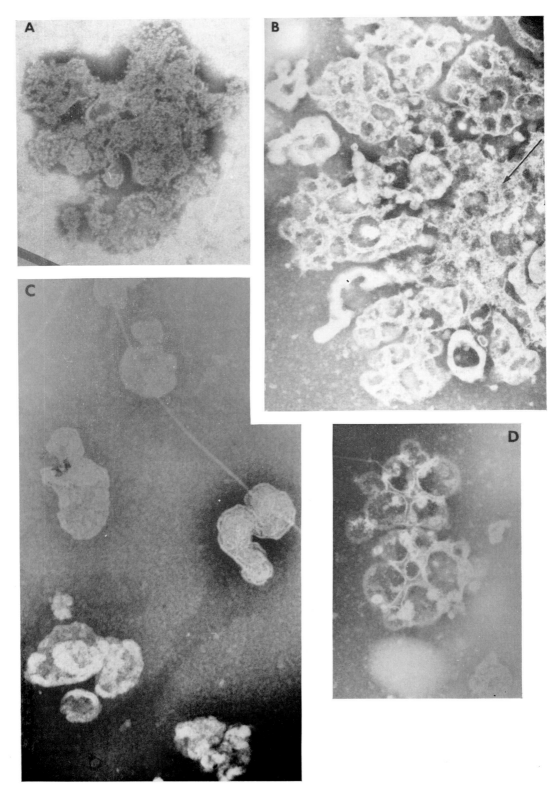

Figure 11.5.

osome during the chilling and the apparent dependence of the subsequent cell division has already been noted.[8]

The sudden chill of the growing cells severely disarranges the mesosome when seen in thin sections (Figure 11.10A). However, a remarkable recovery of the structure was found even after 10 minutes of rewarming (Figure 11.10B). The recovery of the mesosome leading up to synchronous division was also marked by an increase in the rate of phospholipid synthesis (Figure 11.11). By 30 minutes the rewarmed cells were undergoing division (Figure 11.10C). Continued aeration at 15°C led to a slower recovery of the mesosome in a shorter, yet undivided, cell (Figure 11.10D) and a slower rise of phospholipid (Figure 11.11). Such an experiment was repeated on *B. megaterium* KM using acetate-1-C[14] as a lipid label added for 20 minutes prior to protoplasting. The label was added at the times indicated in Figure 11.12 (upper left), and the total uptake of acetate-1-C[14] into trichloroacetic acid precipitated cells of these various times are as shown in the figure. The levels of specific activity of lipid in both the interface and pellet membranes were greatly reduced by the chill (Figure 11.12B), but showed a marked increase when the aerated culture was rewarmed, and only a slight increase if aeration was continued at 15°C. However, in agreement with the thin-section studies which showed marked mesosomal recovery, the increase of the specific activity of the mesosomal vesicle at the interface was more marked than that of the ghost membrane of the pellet (Figure 11.12C). Likewise, the low temperature mesosome recovery, although of a lower order than

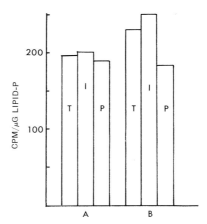

Figure 11.6. Specific activities of the lipids in membranous fractions of *Bacillus megaterium* labeled with acetate-1-C[14] for 30 minutes of Log growth prior to cell harvesting. *T:* Total protoplast lysate; *I:* interface; *P:* pellet fractions after gradient centrifugation. Before (A) and after (B) treatment with Lubrol W at 0.02% final concentration.

that at 32°C, was again accompanied by a more active synthesis of mesosomal vesicles (Figure 11.12D).

Pulse and Chase Experiments

When growing cells exposed to C[14] acetate for 20 minutes are exchanged with a carrier wash to unlabeled medium and aerated for 20–30 minutes, they show, when made into protoplasts, lyzed, and analysed on sucrose gradients, a reverse of the usual labeling ratios. The pellet ghosts are now considerably higher than the interface vesicles. Such a result can also be shown with growing protoplasts. Protoplasts from cells labeled (acetate-1-C[14]) for 20 minutes prior to protoplasting yielded fractions labeled in the usual way

Figure 11.5. Negative-stained fraction of lysed protoplasts. *A:* A remnant of membrane from the pellet fraction of *Bacillus megaterium* protoplast lysate treated with Lubrol W at 0.03%; the knobbed or beaded structures were seen on most of the membrane fragments left in the pellet fraction after exposure to detergent (× 97,000). *C:* A repeat preparation of the fraction shown in Figure 11.4D, but treated with Lubrol W to a final concentration of 0.02% (× 54,000). *B* (× 45,000) and *D* (× 44,000): Vesicular material in the interface fraction of *B. megaterium* protoplast lysates treated with higher concentrations of Lubrol (0.025–0.03%); the vesicles were now blistered and tended to coalesce on the dried smear; what appeared to be small remnants of rougher plasma membrane were occasionally also seen in these fractions (*B,* arrow).

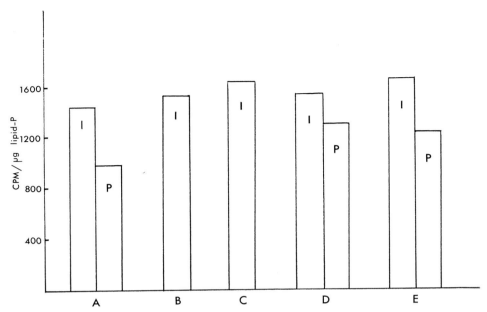

Figure 11.7. The effect of different concentrations of detergent on the specific activity of labeled lipids (acetate-1-C^{14}, 20 minutes exposure before harvesting) in the interface (I) and pellet (P) fractions of protoplast lysates of *Bacillus megaterium* KM. *A:* Osmotic lysis only (no detergent); *B:* Lubrol W, 0.015%; *C:* Lubrol W. 0.03%; *D:* Nonidet P-40, 0.015%; *E:* Nonidet P-40, 0.03%.

—higher in the interface vesicles (Figure 11.13A). A sample of the same labeled protoplasts aerated in a succinate-citrate nutrient medium[5] until all spheres had grown about twice the original diameter (three hours) showed such a greater drop in the interface than in the pellet membrane activity that the normal ratios were reversed (Figure 11.13B). However, a sample of the same growing protoplasts, not previously labeled, when exposed to acetate-1-C^{14} for 20 minutes and then analysed, again showed a much greater activity in the lipid of the mesosomal vesicles (Figure 11.13C). Besides supporting a concept that the mesosome is the initial site of membrane synthesis, these data also indicated that, in spite of its extrusion on the protoplast surface, the everted mesosome can still function in lipid synthesis.

Germination

During germination of *Bacillus* spores massive mesosomal development can be seen in thin sections at the time the spores begin to synthesize DNA (Figure 11.14A) and also later, when they undergo the first division by transverse septation (Figure 11.14, B and C).

To a preparation of *B. megaterium* spores capable of rapidly entering germination, acetate-1-C^{14} was added for 20 minutes at the times indicated in Figure 11.15. The uptakes of label were found to rise markedly about the times the cells were showing great enlargement of their mesosomes. The distribution of label in lipids from the lysed protoplasts of these labeled cells, also shown in the figure, was always higher in the interfacial vesicles (I) than in the pellet (P). Trapping of many of the mesosomes by the lysozyme-resistant spore coats in the pellet fraction may have prevented the I/P differences from being much greater. Certainly the germinating system appears ideal for further studies of mesosomal synthesis.

IN VITRO STUDIES OF ACETATE INCORPORATION

The role of mesosomes as initial sites of membrane synthesis suggested by the above studies was further supported by some preliminary studies of *in vitro* incorporation of acetate-1-C^{14} stimulated by the addition of the two membrane fractions to an incubation mixture developed for the study of yeast protoplast fractions.[15] The incorporation into trichloroacetic acid precipitated samples, expressed as cpm/μg total N, was considerably greater into the interface vesicles of mesosomal origin than into the ghost pellet. Treatment of the lysate before gradient fractionation with Lubrol W reduced the incorporating activity of the mesosome but not the pellet fraction (Figure 11.16a). This might be the result of partial removal of ribosomes from the interface fraction by the detergent. When the incorporation was blocked by shaking with chloroform:methanol and expressed as lipid soluble cpm/μg lipid phosphorus, the mesosomal vesicles were more active than the ghosts in incorporating acetate into lipids, and their activity was not reduced by prior treatment of the lysate with Lubrol W.

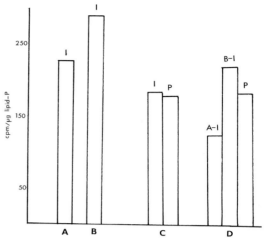

Figure 11.9. Specific activities of acetate-1-C^{14} labeled lipids in protoplast membrane fraction after recentrifugation. The I fraction from a gradient-cushion sedimentation run similar to that shown in Figure 11.6A was collected, divided into halves, washed free of sucrose, and resedimented on a similar gradient without treatment (A) and after the addition of Lubrol W to 0.025% (B). In both tubes, no membranes were recovered as a pellet. The P fraction from a previous sedimentation of lysate (as in Figure 11.6A) when collected, washed and divided into halves, and resedimented down cushioned sucrose gradients, yielded a small I and a larger P fraction when not detergent-treated (C), but two interfacial fractions (A-I and B-I) and a small fraction (D) when Lubrol was added to 0.025% (P).

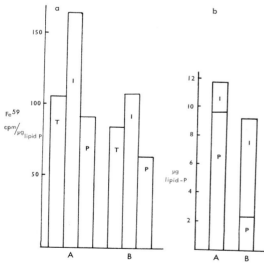

Figure 11.8. *a:* The specific activities in membrane fractions of lipids of *Bacillus megaterium* labeled with Fe^{59} for 20 minutes during Log growth prior to harvesting and protoplasting. Total protoplast lysate (T), interface (I) and pellet (P) fraction after gradient centrifugation; protoplasts lysed with osmotic shocking only (A); lysate treated with 0.02% Lubrol W (B). *b:* Relative distribution of total phospholipid at interface and pellet; before (A) and after (B) treatment of lysate with Lubrol W, 0.02%.

The method for collecting mesosomal vesicles was also tested on lysates of *E. coli* K (penicillin) spheroplasts and found not to yield a distinctive interfacial fraction. Occasionally what appeared to be, by negative staining, vesicles of cell wall lipoprotein material were trapped on top of a gradient cushion, but the majority of the remnant wall and ghost membranes formed a single pellet fraction. The procedure should now be tried on these peculiar variants of *E. coli* which do form intracytoplasmic membrane structures.[18]

Discussion

These results, indicating a precursor-product relationship between mesosomes and membrane, are consistent with Lampen's[13] model for exoenzyme synthesis and liberation. In this model the exoenzyme protein

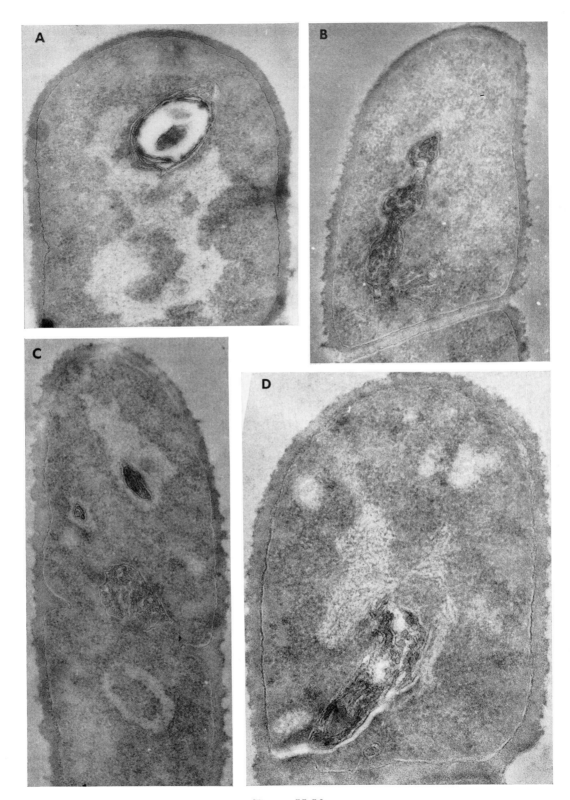

Figure 11.10.

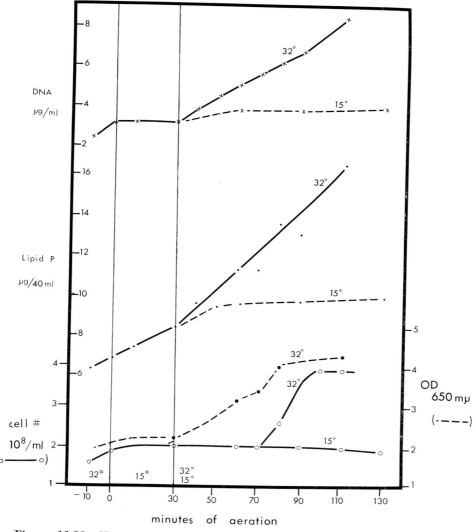

Figure 11.11. Changes in the culture cell-count, optical density (OD), content of DNA,[3] and total lipid phosphorus during temperature-shift synchrony and continued aeration at 15° C.

molecule is synthesized as part of the membrane protein at specialized regions and is later released when the membrane becomes mature. The mesosome is sug-

gested as the site of exoenzyme synthesis and incorporation.

Should mesosomes prove to be the major sites of membrane synthesis, a simple

Figure 11.10. Thin sections of *Bacillus megaterium* KM at various stages of temperature-shift synchronization. *A:* The mesosomal profile seen in practically every cell of an aerated culture 10 minutes after quickly chilling from 32 to 15° C (× 55,000). *B:* The mesosomal arrangement seen in the same culture 10 minutes after returning the temperature to 32° C following 30 minutes at 15° C (× 55,000). *C:* After 30 minutes of rewarming, cell division is underway in nearly all of the elongated cells (× 55,000). *D:* After prolonged aeration at 15° C (50–70 minutes), the cells have hardly grown in length but the mesosomes have largely recovered (× 77,000). (From Fitz-James.[5])

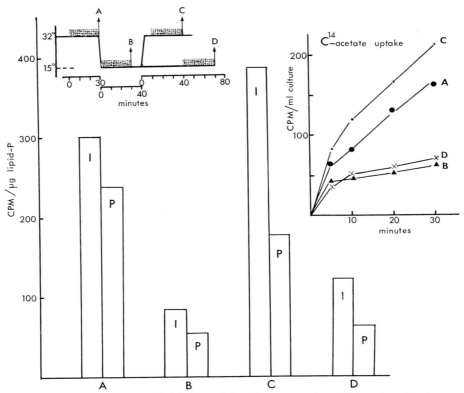

Figure 11.12. Acetate-1-C¹⁴ labeling of *Bacillus megaterium* KM undergoing tempera-ture-shift synchronization. The label was added for 20-minute periods at the times indicated by shaded blocks in upper left, resulting in the total uptakes shown at right for these four periods. The bar graph shows specific activities of the lipids at the interface (I) and pellet (P) fractions, separated by cushioned gradients (sucrose) after treatment of the protoplast lysates with Lubrol W (0.02%).

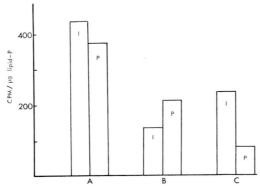

Figure 11.13. Specific activities of acetate-1-C¹⁴ labeled interface (I) and pellet (P) membranes of protoplasts from cells labeled 20 minutes prior to harvesting (A), the same labeled protoplasts grown for 3 hours before lysis and analysis (B), and a sample of not previously labeled growing protoplasts exposed to acetate-1-C¹⁴ for 20 minutes prior to lysis (C).

Figure 11.14. Thin sections of germinating spores showing extensive mesosomal development. *A:* Spore of *Bacillus megaterium* KM at the 40-minute stage of germination; DNA is being repli-cated; the addition of sucrose (0.3 M) to the me-dium has caused the expansion of the region of the cortex where cell wall (arrow) is forming (× 70,000). *B:* Germinating spore of *Bacillus cereus* after 60-minute aeration, cut slightly obliquely; the spore is expanding, the chromatin is separat-ing, but a transverse septum is not yet formed and a mesosome is present at that site (arrow) (× 54,000). *C:* Cell of *B. cereus* after 60–80 minutes germination; the first transverse septum is form-ing and a mesosome is present at that site and at the cell end; serial sections showed both meso-somes were DNA-associated (× 55,000).

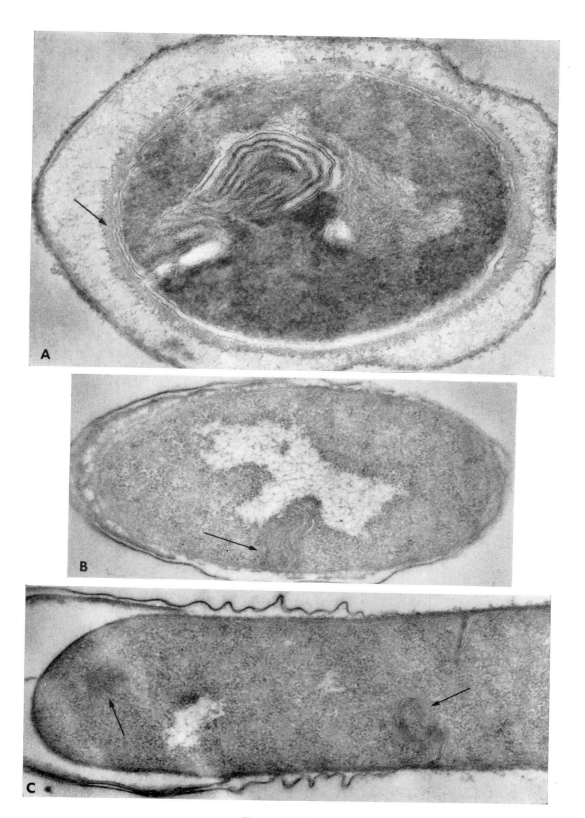

Figure 11.14.

141

mechanism for the membrane-attached DNA to exert control over the balance of growth and differentiation can be visualized. Thus, for example, by a unidirectional synthesis of new membrane, the relative position of the mesosomes within the cell can be shifted, bringing about separation of the replicating DNA. Likewise, the development of a forespore membranous septum and the movement of DNA into this pocket could be engineered by a control of the direction of membrane synthesis from one or more mesosomes. In fact, since mesosomes do appear to play

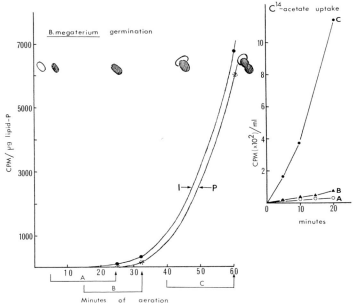

Figure 11.15. *Right:* Uptake of acetate-1-C^{14} into germinating spore of *Bacillus megaterium* added for the 20-minute periods indicated (A, B and C on left). *Left:* the changes in specific activities of the interface vesicles (I) and pellet membrane (P) of cushioned-gradient sedimented lysates of protoplasts made at the times indicated.

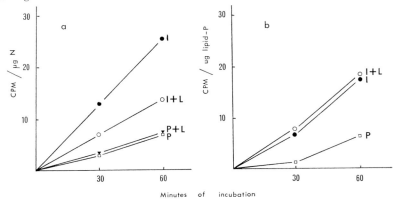

Figure 11.16. *In vitro* incorporation of acetate-1-C^{14} into interfacial (I) and pellet (P) fractions of protoplast lysates, and protoplast lysates treated with Lubrol W (0.015%). *a:* Total incorporation, trichloroacetic acid precipitated. *b:* Incorporation into lipid-soluble fraction; chloroform:methanol extracted. The incubation mixture used,[15] contained (final concentration $\times$ 10^{-3} M): tricine buffer, 42; ATP, 3.2; CoA, 0.2; $KHCO_3$, 6.7; $MgCl_2 \cdot 6H_2O$, 8.0; $MnCl_2$, 0.2; NAD, 0.08; NAD-P, 0.14; glucose, 2.0; C^{14} acetate, 1.6; and bacterial membrane fractions, in 0.016 M $MgSO_4$, 150 μg protein/ml.

an active role in cell differentiation in *Bacillus* species, and since they are probably not contractile, any mechanism of differentiation involving their movement would have to be based on their ability to synthesize new membrane. If the direction in which this new membrane can emerge from the factory is under genetic control, then the role suggested by morphology becomes more plausible. Mazia[14] has already discussed such a role for mesosomes in bacterial cell genome preparation.

SUMMARY

Mesosomes are not extruded free from lysozyme protoplasts but remain attached as everted and apparently still functioning vesicles. They can be partly liberated by osmotic shocking, and when centrifuged through a density interface can be collected reasonably free from plasma membrane. To test this method, a number of situations where mesosomes vary have been studied. The results suggest that mesosomes are chief sites of membrane lipid synthesis. Although polysomes are not noticeably prominent around intact mesosomes, future work should demonstrate whether or not mesosomes are also the main sites of membrane protein synthesis.

REFERENCES

1. Brenner, S., and Horne, R. W.: A negative staining method for high resolution electron microscopy of viruses. *Biophys. Biochem. Acta* **34**: 103, 1959.
2. Chance, B.: Control of energy metabolism in mitochondria: In: *Control of Energy Metabolism* (B. Chance, R. W. Estabrook, and J. R. Williamson, Eds.). Academic Press, New York, 1965: p. 415.
3. Dische, Z.: Color reactions of nucleic acid components. In: *Nucleic Acids: Chemistry and Biology*, Vol. I (E. Chargaff and J. N. Davidson, Eds.). Academic Press, New York, 1955: p. 285.
4. Ernster, L., Zetterström, R., and Linberg, O.: A method for the determination of tracer phosphate in biological material. *Acta Chem. Scand.* **4**: 942, 1950.
5. Fitz-James, P. C.: Cytological and chemical studies of the growth of protoplasts of *Bacillus megaterium. J. Biophys. Biochem. Cytol.* **4**: 257, 1958.
6. ———: Participation of the cytoplasmic membrane in the growth and spore formation of bacilli. *J. Biophys. Biochem. Cytol.* **8**: 507, 1960.
7. ———: Fate of the mesosomes of *Bacillus megaterium* during protoplasting. *J. Bact.* **87**: 1483, 1964.
8. ———: Discussion of: Fuhs, G. W.: Fine structure and replication of bacterial nucleoids. *Bact. Rev.* **29**: 293, 1965.
9. Folch, J., Lees, M., and Sloane Stanley, G. H.: A simple method for the isolation and purification of total lipides from animal tissues. *J. Biol. Chem.* **226**: 497, 1957.
10. Godson, G. N., and Butler, J. A. V.: Preparation of a nuclear fraction from *Bacterium megaterium* and its role in ribonucleic acid biosynthesis. *Biochem. J.* **83**: 3P, 1962.
11. Hunter-Szybalska, M. E., Szybalski, W., and DeLamater, E. D.: Temperature synchronization of nuclear and cellular division in *Bacillus megaterium. J. Bact.* **71**: 17, 1956.
12. Kellenberger, E., Ryter, A., and Séchaud, J.: Electron microscope study of DNA-containing plasms. II. Vegetative and mature phage DNA as compared with normal bacterial nucleoids in different physiological states. *J. Biophys. Biochem. Cytol.* **4**: 671, 1958.
13. Lampen, J. O.: Secretion of enzymes by microorganisms. *Symp. Soc. Gen. Microbiol.* **15**: 115, 1965.
14. Mazia, D.: The partitioning of genomes. *Symp. Soc. Gen. Microbiol.* **15**: 379, 1965.
15. McElroy, F. A.: *Lipid Synthesis in* Lipomyces lipofer. Ph.D. thesis, University of Western Ontario, London, Canada, 1966.
16. Ryter, A., and Jacob, F.: Étude au microscope électronique des relations entre mésosomes et noyaux chez *Bacillus subtilis. C. R. Acad. Sci.* (Paris) **257**: 3060, 1963.
17. Salton, M. R. J., and Chapman, J. A.: Isolation of the membrane-mesosome structures from *Micrococcus lysodeikticus. J. Ultrastr. Res.* **6**: 489, 1962.
18. Schnaitman, C., and Greenawalt, J. W.: Intracytoplasmic membranes in *Escherichia coli. J. Bact.* **92**: 780, 1966.
19. Schötz, F., Abo-Elnaga, I. G., and Kandler, O.: Zur Structur der Mesosomen bei *Lactobacillus corynoides. Zschr. Naturforschg. B.* **20**: 790, 1965.
20. Valentine, R. C.: The shape of protein molecules suggested by electron microscopy. *Nature* **184**: 1838, 1959.
21. van Iterson, W.: Some features of a remarkable organelle in *Bacillus subtilis. J. Biophys. Biochem. Cytol.* **9**: 183, 1961.
22. Warner, J. R., Rich, A., and Hall, C. E.: Electron microscope studies of ribosomal clusters synthesizing haemoglobin. *Science* **138**: 1399, 1962.

12

Isolation and Characterization of Bacterial Membranes*

Milton R. J. Salton

NEW YORK UNIVERSITY SCHOOL OF MEDICINE

NEW YORK, NEW YORK

It has been known for some time that the membranes of Gram-positive bacteria differ from the cell walls in a number of properties, and that these differences can be utilized in following the isolation and characterization of the membrane structures.[13, 24] Our investigations on the characterization of bacterial membranes have had as their principal goal the elucidation of the molecular anatomy of a cell membrane system. As a starting point for these studies, it has obviously been of the utmost importance to isolate the membranes under carefully controlled conditions, where degradation and contamination of the preparations would be reduced to a minimum. The general methods available for membrane isolation by use of cell wall degrading "muralytic" enzyme systems (e.g. lysozyme, phage muralysins, lysostaphin, etc.)[7, 12, 13, 16, 19, 24] are quite familiar and will not be discussed in any detail in this contribution. However, the criteria of assessing the "quality"

* The author is indebted to Dr. Alan W. Bernheimer for gradient electrophoresis data, to Dr. John H. Freer, Mr. Park E. Trefts and Mrs. Margreth D. Schmitt for their participation in various aspects of these studies, and to the National Science Foundation for grant support (GB 2877 and GB 4603) for these investigations.

or homogeneity of the membrane fractions at various stages of the isolation procedure are of considerable importance and relevance to the problems of the specificity of membrane structures and functions.

This paper will report on some of our observations with several lysozyme-sensitive Gram-positive bacteria, including *Micrococcus lysodeikticus*, *Sarcina lutea* and *Bacillus* species. In a previous study we (Salton & Chapman[14]) reported that the total mesosome-plasma membrane system of *M. lysodeikticus* could be isolated by direct lysis in dilute buffer or by osmotic lysis of protoplasts formed in sucrose. The membranes so isolated possessed properties in common with other membrane systems, e.g., "unit membrane" profiles in thin sections, overall thickness of about 75 Å, the tendency to form vesicles. Examination of membrane fractions from these organisms, using negative staining with phosphotungstic acid, showed an appearance similar to that of other membranes (sheets of ring-like structures with central pits or holes). We did not, however, see the stalked sub-structures ("lollipops") which have been observed by several other investigators,[1, 5] and the status of these particles associated with bacterial membranes must await further clarification.

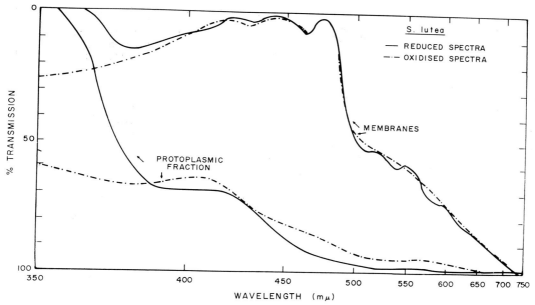

Figure 12.1. Localization of carotenoids and cytochromes in *Sarcina lutea*. Spectra before ('oxidized') and after reduction ('reduced') with Na₂S₂O₄ of the isolated membranes of *S. lutea* (4.4 mg dry weight/ml suspension) and the corresponding protoplasmic fraction.

LOCALIZATION OF CELLULAR COMPONENTS IN MEMBRANES

Since Weibull's characterization of *Bacillus megaterium* membranes,[24] indicating the presence of the cytochrome system in the isolated structures, it has been demonstrated that these components are exclusively localized in the total membrane fractions from *M. lysodeikticus*, *S. lutea* and other *Bacillus* species.[15] Under careful conditions of isolation of the cell membranes, the localization of cytochromes and carotenoids in the membranes can be established as illustrated for *S. lutea* in Figure 12.1. These components are not lost from the membranes subjected to repeated washings and it can be assumed that they are intimately associated with the membrane structures. Although the more conjugated carotenoids form conspicuous "marker molecules" in the bacterial membranes, they do not appear to be indispensable components, since, as shown in Figure 12.2, their formation is markedly inhibited when *S. lutea* is grown in the presence of diphenylamine. The

oxidized and reduced spectra of the membranes isolated from the DPA-grown cells do, however, show the presence of the normal cytochrome system,[15] as can be seen in Figure 12.2.

In addition to cytochromes and carotenoids, it has been shown that cellular phospholipids[23] and menaquinones[6, 18] are largely localized in the bacterial membranes. The menaquinones can constitute up to about 5 per cent of the membrane lipid; they are detectable by ultraviolet spectroscopy of the membrane lipid fractions dissolved in isooctane, and can be determined quantitatively after separation on silica gel G.[18] The characteristic spectra of the membrane menaquinones are illustrated in Figure 12.3.

Thus, the membranes of certain Gram-positive bacteria possess several characteristic "marker" constituents, such as the cytochromes, carotenoids, menaquinones, phospholipids, etc., the fates of which can be followed readily during the isolation and characterization of these structures. Moreover, certain enzymes, such as NADH₂ oxidase,[9, 15] ATPase,[2] and succinic dehydro-

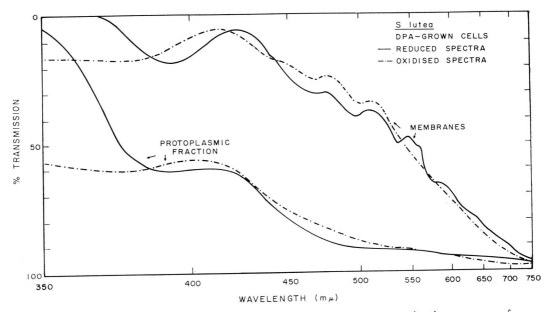

Figure 12.2. Localization of cytochromes in *Sarcina lutea* grown in the presence of diphenylamine to suppress formation of more conjugated carotenoids. Spectra before ('oxidized') and after reduction ('reduced') with Na₂S₂O₄ of the isolated membranes from cells grown in the presence of 25 μg diphenylamine/ml medium, together with spectra of the corresponding protoplasmic fraction.

genase,[5] constitute additional valuable membrane localized components.

As already pointed out by Shockman et al.,[21] defining the homogeneity of membrane preparations presents some problems. The distribution of "markers" such as those discussed above can be established, but the extent of contamination of the membranes with bound protoplasmic constituents is much more difficult to assess. However, there are certain enzymes that appear to be largely "protoplasmic" in origin. One such enzyme which we have investigated is the aliesterase of *B. megaterium* strain KM. Using p-nitrophenyl laurate as a substrate we have followed the course, by spectrophotometric determination of the liberated chromophore, of the activity in intact cells, cell lysates, the protoplasmic fraction, and the unwashed membrane deposit in Veronal buffer at pH 8. The results presented in Figure 12.4 clearly show that the bulk of the activity is present in the intracellular "cell sap" or protoplasmic fraction of

this organism. These observations do not, of course, preclude the possibility that other esterases may be specifically localized in the membranes.

In addition to following the distribution of membrane and cell sap components during isolation of the structures from bacterial lysates, Mr. Park Trefts and I have recently followed the release of protein (determined by the Lowry method) and RNA (estimated by the Orcinol method) on washing the membranes of *M. lysodeikticus* in 0.1 M Tris buffer (pH 7.5) at 0°C. The determinations of the amounts of protein and RNA in the supernatant fluids during consecutive washes are shown in Figure 12.5. These results emphasize the need for an adequate number of washes to reduce the "contaminating" protoplasmic protein and RNA to a minimal level. We have been able to subject washed membranes to two further tests, one involving acrylamide disc electrophoresis of sonicated washed membranes, and the other utilizing the reaction in agar diffusion plates of these preparations against antisera containing protoplasmic antibodies. The sonication released adsorbed proteins that had been retained through inadequate washing, and these proteins could then be detected by separation on gel electrophoresis or by observing lines of identity with cytoplas-mic antigens when tested on agar gel diffusion plates. By the application of these two criteria we have found that the cytoplasmic protein contamination can be reduced to a minimum by six consecutive washes with buffer at 0°C.

Nonetheless, it is worthy of note that membranes from *M. lysodeikticus* and *S.*

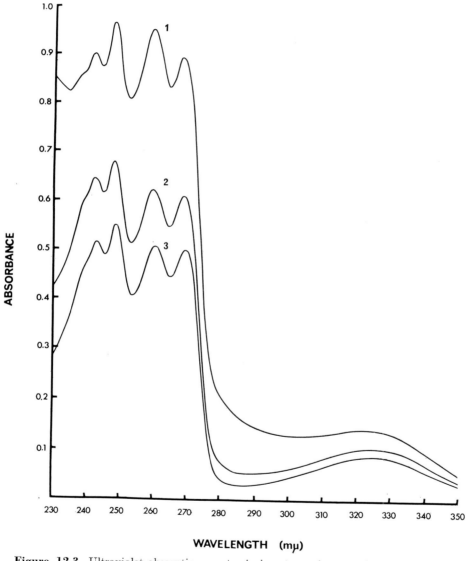

Figure 12.3. Ultraviolet absorption spectra in isooctane of menaquinones separated by thin-layer chromatography of the lipid extracted from isolated membranes, compared with that of authentic menaquinone-7. *Curve 1:* menaquinone-9 from *Sarcina lutea* membranes; *Curve 2:* menaquinone-7 from *Bacillus megaterium* membranes; *Curve 3:* authentic menaquinone-7, 20 μg/ml isooctane. (Data from Salton & Schmitt.[18])

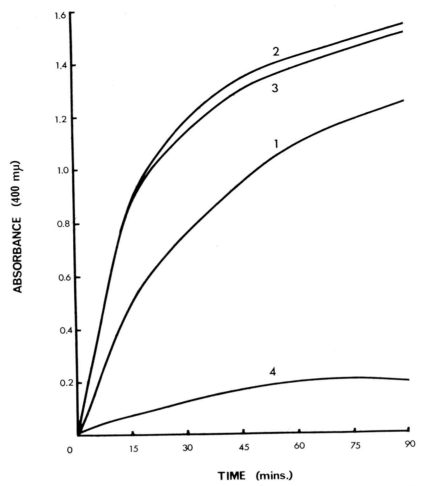

Figure 12.4. Distribution of the aliesterase activity in cell fractions from *Bacillus megaterium* KM, using p-nitrophenyl laurate as substrate in Veronal buffer, pH 8, 37° C, followed spectrophotometrically at 400 mμ after liberation of p-nitrophenol by enzymic hydrolysis. Each cell fraction, derived from washed cell suspensions containing 6.6 mg dry weight original bacterial cells in 0.5 ml, was added to the reactants in a total volume of 5.0 ml. *Curve 1:* intact cells; *Curve 2:* total lysate; *Curve 3:* protoplasmic fraction; *Curve 4:* membrane deposit.

lutea prepared in this way have consistently given two bands when examined by density gradient centrifugation (discontinuous gradients of 50% w/v sucrose at the bottom, 40% sucrose, 30% sucrose and 20% sucrose; centrifugation in SW 25 head for two hours at 24,000 rpm). Apart from the possibility that the membranes in the upper bands are more vesicular, there are no obvious differences with respect to components such as the carotenoids or cytochromes. Further investigation will be needed to elucidate the reasons for these density differences.

FRACTIONATION OF ISOLATED MEMBRANES

The chemical composition of the membranes used in our studies[16] is very similar to that reported for other bacterial membranes.[11] Much is now known about the lipids of microbial membranes[10] but, apart from the presence of cytochromes, $NADH_2$ oxidase, ATPase, etc., there is very little

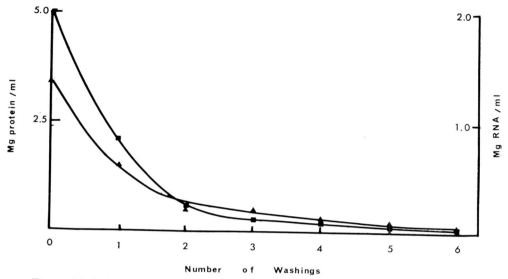

Figure 12.5. Release of protein (determined by the Folin method of Lowry) (*squares*), and RNA (determined by the Orcinol reaction) (*triangles*), on consecutive washing of *Micrococcus lysodeikticus* membranes with 0.1 M Tris buffer, pH 7.5 at 0° C.

information about the variety of proteins or protein subunits in these structures. Resolution of the proteins in cell membranes has been attempted with mitochondrial systems[8, 22] and erythrocyte membranes.[3, 20] Most of these procedures have involved the dissolution of the proteins in suitable detergent-urea mixtures following extraction of the lipids with organic solvents. To avoid the harmful effects of solvents on membrane antigens, we have attempted to devise methods of fractionation which would enable us to resolve the proteins by electrophoresis and, at the same time, retain structural or conformational specificity such as the ability to react with membrane antisera.

In our earlier studies, we found that membranes disaggregated by anionic, cationic or non-ionic detergents, or by exposure to ultrasound, gave products which appeared on examination in the ultracentrifuge to be relatively uniform.[17] It was clear that the apparent physicochemical simplicity of these "subunits" masked the complexity which must exist in a membrane system if indeed it carries out all of the biological functions normally attributed to it. Attempts to resolve the "4.2 S product" from sonicated membranes[17] by

disc electrophoresis on acrylamide gel or by agar gel diffusion against antiserum did not succeed. The material appeared to be excluded from the gels. However, the "subunit" produced by sonication did migrate as a major component containing protein and carotenoid when electrophoresis was carried out in a linear gradient of sucrose ranging from 50% at the bottom to no sucrose at the top, 0.03 M sodium borate buffer at pH 8.4 according to the method of Bernheimer.[4] The results of such an experiment, using 100 mg sonicated membrane of *S. lutea*, are shown in Figure 12.6 and illustrate the separation of a major component from several smaller minor fractions which are apparently devoid of carotenoid.

These observations suggested that it would be necessary to dissociate the lipid from the membrane proteins in order to resolve the products by disc electrophoresis or by agar gel diffusion or immunoelectrophoresis. Accordingly, two fractionation procedures have been developed,* one using deoxycholate treatment (at a final concentration of 1% w/v) of membranes dispersed by sonication in 0.067 M phos-

*M. R. J. Salton and P. E. Trefts, in preparation.

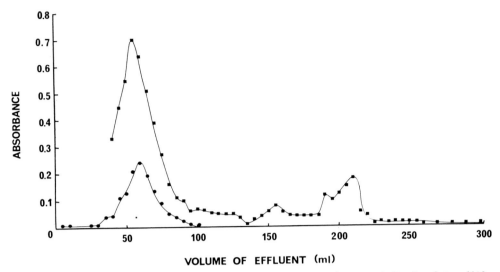

Figure 12.6. Electrophoretic behavior of sonicated membranes of *Sarcina lutea* (100 mg) on a sucrose gradient (0–50%) in 0.03 M sodium borate buffer, pH 8.4; 500 V; 5 ma; 22 hours. *Squares:* absorbance at 280 mμ. *Cirles:* absorbance due to carotenoid at 465 mμ.

phate buffer, pH 7.0, and a second procedure involving disaggregation of the membranes in the phosphate buffer containing 1% v/v Nonidet P-40 (the active constituent is of the polyoxyethylated alkyl phenol type; product of the Shell Company). The initial amounts of lyophilized or freshly prepared membranes present in the membrane-surface-active mixtures were adjusted to approximately 10 mg/ml, w/v. To each of the deoxycholate and Nonidet P-40 disaggregated membrane preparations, 28 g solid ammonium sulfate/100 ml mixture was added, and the fractions were allowed to stand for 1–2 hours at 4°C. On the addition of the ammonium sulfate both preparations became opaque and the deoxycholate-treated product became quite viscous. The gel in the latter fraction was broken by adding Triton X 100 to a level of 1% w/v.

Centrifugation of the fractions for 20 minutes at 3000 G after ammonium sulfate treatment resulted in the separation of a "floating layer" which was readily separated from the slightly turbid "soluble" fraction. The latter (referred to subsequently as Fraction 1) was carefully decanted away from the floating material and dialysed against changes of 0.067 M phosphate buffer (pH 7.0) at 0–2°C. The floating fraction was then rubbed up with distilled water added to give one third of the original volume of the membrane-detergent mixture. On centrifugation of the dispersed floating material (20 minutes at 3000 G) a clear lipid-carotenoid-detergent rich fraction (Fraction 2) and an insoluble residue (Fraction 3) were obtained. The latter fractions were dissolved in the phosphate buffer containing 1% sodium dodecyl sulfate (SDS); very little material insoluble in SDS remained from the Nonidet fractionation procedure, but some insoluble residue persisted in the deoxycholate Fraction 3.

The fractions so obtained from *M. lysodeikticus* membranes were examined for the distribution of carotenoids and cytochromes and the results for the Nonidet procedure are illustrated in Figures 12.7 and 12.8. Disc electrophoresis of the dialysed Fraction 1 from the Nonidet and deoxycholate procedures showed a good separation of components but variation in the intensity of the bands from one experiment to another; the similarity of the patterns to the control protoplasmic fractions led to the conclusion that the proteins in this fraction represented the adsorbed components. By monitoring the washing of the

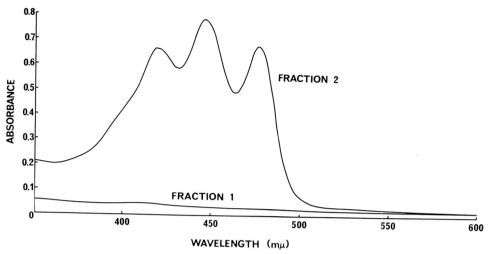

Figure 12.7. Fractionation of *Micrococcus lysodeikticus* cell membranes, 10 mg/ml by disaggregation in 0.067 M phosphate buffer (pH 7), containing 1% v/v Nonidet P-40. Absorption spectra of Fraction 1 (soluble fraction) and Fraction 2 (lipid-carotenoid-detergent rich fraction) obtained as described in text.

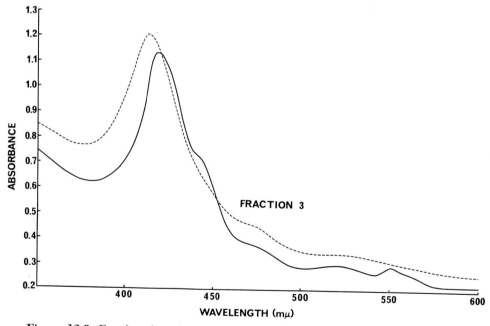

Figure 12.8. Fractionation of *Micrococcus lysodeikticus* cell membranes by disaggregation with 1% Nonidet P-40. Absorption spectra of oxidized (*dashed line*) and reduced (with Na₂S₂O₄) (*solid line*) Fraction 3 solubilized in phosphate buffer containing 1% SDS.

membranes as discussed above, it was possible to reduce Fraction 1 to a minimal level. Thus, the "unique" membrane components were distributed in Fractions 2 and 3. The latter could be resolved by disc electrophoresis with Tris-glycine buffer containing 0.1% SDS. In common with other investigators, we have encountered difficulty in separating the hydrophobic membrane proteins, and this aspect of the problem is being studied further.

Finally, Fraction 2 from both the Nonidet and deoxycholate fractionation procedures contained several antigens reactive with membrane antisera and, moreover, they showed lines of non-identity in gel diffusion plates when tested with the corresponding protoplasmic fractions. Fraction 3, which contained all of the cytochromes (a, b, and c) originally present in the isolated membranes, showed little reaction against membrane antisera. However, we have recently found that, when the solubilized Fraction 3 from *Bacillus subtilis* membranes is injected subcutaneously with Freund's adjuvant, a potent antiserum to the components in this fraction is obtained. This may suggest that some of the potentially antigenic components of the membranes are masked in the intact structures. The fractionation procedures described above have been applied, with very similar results, to membranes from *B. subtilis, S. lutea* and also to erythrocyte membranes, and may therefore be of fairly general use in resolving membrane structures.

Thus, by the development of suitable fractionation procedures which give components retaining antigenic specificity, it is hoped to use these methods as tools for unravelling some of the mysteries of the molecular anatomy of cell membranes and thereby add further to our knowledge of the functions of these biologically important structures.

REFERENCES

1. Abram, D.: Electron microscope observations on intact cells, protoplasts, and the cytoplasmic membrane of *Bacillus stearothermophilus. J. Bact.* **89**: 855, 1965.
2. Abrams, A., McNamara, P., and Johnson, F. B.: Adenosine triphosphatase in isolated bacterial cell membranes. *J. Biol. Chem.* **235**: 3659, 1960.
3. Azen, E. A., Nazhat, R. A., and Smithies, O.: Acidic buffer systems for urea starch-gel electrophoresis. *J. Lab. Clin. Med.* **67**: 650, 1966.
4. Bernheimer, A. W.: Resolution of mixtures of proteins by means of zone electrophoresis in sucrose density gradients. *Arch. Biochem.* **92**: 226, 1962.
5. Biryuzova, V. I., Lukoyanova, M. A., Gel'man, N. S., and Oparin, A. I.: Subunits in cytoplasmic membranes of *Micrococcus lysodeikticus. Dokl. Akad. Nauk SSSR* **156**: 198, 1964.
6. Bishop, D. H. L., and King, H. K.: Ubiquinone and vitamin K in bacteria. 2. Intracellular distribution in *Escherichia coli* and *Micrococcus lysodeikticus. Biochem. J.* **85**: 550, 1962.
7. Browder, H. P., Zygmunt, W. A., Young, J. R., and Tavorima, P. A.: Lysostaphin: enzymatic mode of action. *Biochem. Biophys. Res. Commun.* **19**: 383, 1965.
8. Green, D. E., and Perdue, J. F.: Membranes as expressions of repeating units. *Proc. Nat. Acad. Sci. USA* **55**: 1295, 1966.
9. Hughes, D. E.: The bacterial cytoplasmic membrane. *J. Gen. Microbiol.* **29**: 39, 1962.
10. Kates, M.: Bacterial lipids. *Adv. Lipid Res.* **2**: 17, 1964.
11. Kodicek, E.: Aspects of the constitution of bacterial membranes. In: *Recent Progress in Microbiology; VIII International Congress of Microbiology.* Univ. of Toronto Press, Montreal, 1963: p. 23.
12. Krause, R. M., and McCarty, M.: Variation in the group-specific carbohydrate of group C hemolytic streptococci. *J. Exp. Med.* **116**: 131, 1962.
13. Salton, M. R. J.: *The Bacterial Cell Wall.* Elsevier, Amsterdam, 1964.
14. Salton, M. R. J., and Chapman, J. A.: Isolation of the membrane-mesosome structures from *Micrococcus lysodeikticus. J. Ultrastr. Res.* **6**: 489, 1962.
15. Salton, M. R. J., and Ehtisham-ud-din, A. F. M.: The localization of cytochromes and carotenoids in isolated membranes and envelopes. *Aust. J. Exp. Biol. Med. Sci.* **43**: 255, 1965.
16. Salton, M. R. J., and Freer, J. H.: Composition of the membranes isolated from several Gram-positive bacteria. *Biochim. Biophys. Acta* **107**: 531, 1965.
17. Salton, M. R. J., and Netschey, A.: Physical chemistry of isolated bacterial membranes. *Biochim. Biophys. Acta* **107**: 539, 1965.
18. Salton, M. R. J., and Schmitt, M. D.: Effects of diphenylamine on carotenoids and menaquinones in bacterial membranes. *Biochim. Biophys. Acta*, in press.
19. Schindler, C. A., and Schuhardt, V. T.: Lyso-

staphin: a new bacteriolytic agent for the staphylococcus. *Proc. Nat. Acad. Sci. USA* **51**: 414, 1964.

20. Schneiderman, L. J.: Solubilization and electrophoresis of human red cell stroma. *Biochem. Biophys. Res. Commun.* **20**: 763, 1965.

21. Shockman, G. D., Kolb, J. J., Bakay, B., Conover, M. J., and Toennies, G.: Protoplast membrane of *Streptococcus faecalis*. *J. Bact.* **85**: 168, 1963.

22. Takayama, K., MacLennan, D. H., Tzagoloff, A., and Stoner, C. D.: Studies on the electron transfer system. LXVII. Polyacrylamide gel electrophoresis of the mitochondrial electron transfer complexes. *Arch. Biochem.* **114**: 223, 1964.

23. Vorbeck, M. L., and Marinetti, G. V.: Intracellular distribution and characterization of the lipids of *Streptococcus faecalis* (ATCC-9790). *Biochemistry* (Washington) **4**: 296, 1965.

24. Weibull, C.: Characterization of the protoplasmic constituents of *Bacillus megaterium*. *J. Bact.* **66**: 696, 1953.

13

Comparative Biochemistry of Membranes from *Streptococcus pyogenes* and Derived Stable L-Forms*

Charles Panos

ALBERT EINSTEIN MEDICAL CENTER

PHILADELPHIA, PENNSYLVANIA

Over the years, this laboratory has been concerned with the comparative biochemistry of *Streptococcus pyogenes* and a stable salt-requiring L-form derived from it with the aid of penicillin. More recently, our attention has turned to the study of the membranes isolated from both of these organisms in the belief that biochemical differences in this anatomical component may be related to the L-form's inability to synthesize the rigid cell wall. For brevity and to remain within the space allotted, only biochemical differences will be stressed here. The reader is referred elsewhere for details and for new findings common to both

* Studies supported over the years by research grants (AI-04495 and AI-04543) from the National Institute of Allergy and Infectious Diseases, U.S. Public Health Service, and a contract (NR 103-576) from the Office of Naval Research. The author is a Senior Career Development Awardee (U.S.P.H. 7-K3-GM-15, 531).

These studies could not have been performed without the cooperation of Drs. M. Cohen and L. Doolin, Misses G. Fagan, L. Hynes and D. Bevilacqua. The author would also like to thank the various journals for granting permission for the use of Tables 13.2 and 13.3, and Figures 13.1 and 13.3.

organisms. It should, perhaps, be emphasized that all of these lipid studies were performed with cells obtained at their respective mid logarithmic phases of growth from a complex, lipid pre-extracted growth medium; the total lipid content remaining being no greater than 0.06 per cent of medium dry weight. Suffice it to say, this streptococcus was first converted to the protoplast state by a phage-induced lysin prior to membrane isolation by freeze-thaw procedures.[14] The experimental details and results of these investigations have recently appeared.[3, 11, 12, 14] For clarity, it has been suggested that I define my use of the term 'L-form'. As pertaining to this coccal L-form, it is an osmotically fragile, filterable and reproducing form derived from the parent streptococcus but lacking the characteristic rigid bacterial cell wall.

Our initial studies revealed that isolated L-form membranes contained a significantly higher total fatty acid content (by 56 per cent) than that of streptococcal protoplast membranes, and that their protein content was similar (68 and 59 per cent for protoplast and L-form membranes, respectively).[14] Subsequently, total membrane

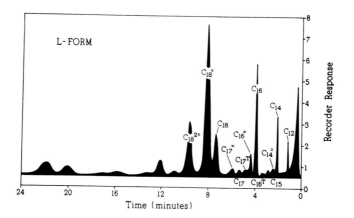

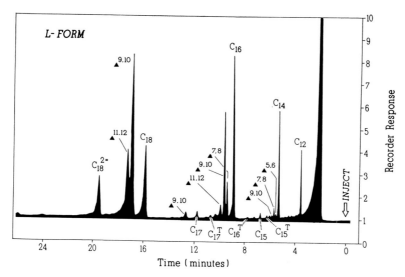

Figure 13.1. Typical (*above*) packed column (butanediol succinate) and (*below*) capillary (Carbowax 1540) gas chromatographic patterns of total fatty acid methyl esters from mid-Log whole cells. Cells from lipid pre-extracted growth media. (Excerpts from data of Panos, Cohen & Fagan.[14])

lipid determinations confirmed these initial fatty acid results by displaying a comparable trend (15.3 and 35.6 per cent for protoplast and L-form membranes, respectively).[3] Thus, although both membranes were predominately lipoprotein in character, the protein-to-lipid ratio was significantly higher in protoplast membranes (4.5:1) than in L-form membranes (1.7:1); these ratios being remarkably similar to those obtained earlier by James et al.[8] with protoplast membranes (4:1) and L-form

envelopes (1.7:1) from tetracycline-resistant *S. pyogenes* strain 416.

Most of our detailed fatty acid studies were performed using capillary gas chromatography, a relatively new dimension capable of resolving positional isomers of long chain monoenoic fatty acids.[11] For illustrative purposes, Figure 13.1 compares a gas chromatogram of a typical packed column to the chromatogram of a capillary column using a methylated fatty acid mixture from this streptococcal L-form. The extremely

TABLE 13.1

Fatty Acid Composition (%)

Membranes from Mid-Log Cells from Lipid Preextracted Growth Media

	Total Content	Palmitic (C_{16}†)	C_{16} Monolefinic				Stearic (C_{18})	C_{18} Monoolefinic		
			Total	7, 8†	9, 10	11, 12		Total	Oleic	cis-Vaccenic
L-form membranes	23.18	26.43	8.74	1.80	6.20	0.74	8.43	31.85	24.91	6.94
		35.17					40.28			
Streptococcus (protoplast) membranes	14.83	31.18	19.39	5.51	12.17	1.71	7.20	26.11	10.65	15.46
		50.57					33.31			

* Carbon atom chain length.
† Position of double bond.
Data from Panos, Cohen & Fagan.[14]

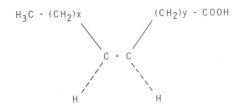

$$x + y = 14$$
Oleic acid (x = 7; y = 7)
cis-Vaccenic acid (x = 5; y = 9)

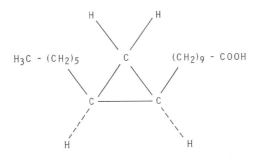

Lactobacillic acid (cyclopropane-ring containing)
cis-11, 12 methyleneoctadecanoic acid

Figure 13.2. *Above:* oleic acid (x = 7; y = 7); *cis*-vaccenic acid (x = 5; y = 9). *Below:* lactobacillic acid (cyclopropane-ring containing); *cis*-11, 12 methyleneoctadecanoic acid.

high resolving power of the capillary column is obvious. The content, composition and type of fatty acids from both whole cell and membrane sources of these organisms have been tabulated and discussed

elsewhere.[14] Pertinent excerpts for this presentation appear in Table 13.1.

Hofmann[7] and coworkers had established the predominating monoethenoid C_{18} fatty acid of bacteria as being *cis*-vaccenic, not oleic, and that both of these isomers were present in a group C streptococcus (Figure 13.2). Thus, the finding that this group A coccus and its membrane contained both of these positional isomers and that *cis*-vaccenic acid prevailed was not unexpected. Of considerable interest and a salient point of these studies, however, was the finding that in L-form whole cell and membrane preparations the prevalence of these two isomers was reversed and oleic acid predominated (Table 13.1). Further, it was quickly established that these isomeric differences persisted over the entire logarithmic growth phase of both organisms and that they were not due to the larger inoculum size necessary for initiation of L-form growth.[12] Suffice it to say that a similar positional isomeric rearrangement was not noted in the hexadecenoic acids from each organism.[14] Also, the percentage of total (i.e., saturated and unsaturated) C_{18} acids was greater than the total C_{16} acids in L-form membranes, whereas the reverse was found in coccal membranes (Table 13.1). Controlled experiments indicated that these changes could not be readily explained as due solely to the increased osmotic environment necessary for this coccal L-form's perpetuation.[18]

The earlier finding of Krembel[9] with a

stable non-salt requiring *Proteus* L-form, in which oleic acid was the only octadecenoic acid found, coupled with our later findings with morphological variants of *Escherichia coli*,[19] and that of others with a *Proteus* and its L-form,[10] in which either cell wall damage or removal was accompanied by significant decreases in cyclopropane-ring containing fatty acids (Figure 13.2), added credance and tempted speculation of a relationship between membrane long chain fatty acid content and composition and cell wall inhibition. This aspect has been discussed in detail elsewhere.[12] It had been established that long chain olefinic acids serve as precursors to cyclopropane-ring formation in certain Gram-negative and -positive organisms,[7] whereas fatty acid synthesis terminates with their monoenoic acid precursors in this coccus and its L-form devoid of such "ring-containing" acids.[14]

Most recently, our laboratory detailed the first comparative study of the complex lipid content and composition of membranes derived from this group A streptococcus and its L-form.[3] Aside from a much greater total lipid content in L-form than in coccal protoplast membranes (see above), the glycolipid content of protoplast membrane lipid (11.3 per cent) was one-half that of the L-form (22.2 per cent), whereas the percentage of phospholipid of the former (1.49 per cent) greatly exceeded that of the latter (0.65 per cent). Figure 13.3 illustrates the separation of membrane lipid mixtures achieved by silicic acid column chromatography. The nonpolar lipid content of the total lipid extract was 23.4 per cent for the protoplast and 34.7 per cent for L-form membranes. Of the five peaks obtained by column chromatography (Figure 13.3), only the two predominating within L-form membranes (peak B, glycolipid; peak D, phospholipid) were characterized in detail from both coccal protoplast and L-form membranes. The chemical characterization of both peaks from each source has been detailed.[3] Figures 13.4 and 13.5 are proposed structures[12] for the glycolipid and phospholipid, respectively, that are consistent with the analytical data obtained.[3] The major glycolipid was identified as diglucosyldiglyceride. The phospholipid was of the cardiolipin type, being a polyglycerol phosphatide.

The polyglycerolphosphatide (Figure 13.5) from both membranes was of the G-P-G-P-G type (G = glycerol, P = phosphorus). The finding of an ester:phosphorus molar ratio of 5:2 for protoplast lipid pointed to the fact that all of the hydroxyl groups were esterified by fatty acids. A ratio of 1.9:1 from that of the L-form, on the other hand, indicated that one hydroxyl group might not be esterified, implying a structural difference between these two membranes. Absolute verification of this most interesting aspect and its significance, however, must await the accumulation of sufficient quantities for further study.[3] Although phosphatidylcholine had been reported as a major component in membrane lipids of two strains of a group A streptococcus harvested (after 18 hours) from a crude medium,[5] choline was not detected in this major phospholipid from each membrane source when obtained from organisms grown at their respective mid Log growth phases from a lipid pre-extracted growth medium.

Earlier in this presentation it was mentioned that oleic acid prevailed in L-form membranes, whereas its positional isomer *cis*-vaccenic acid predominated in protoplast membranes (Table 13.1). The distribution of the major fatty acids in glycolipid (peak B) and phospholipid (peak D) from both sources (see Figure 13.3) is tabulated in Table 13.2. The finding of the altered but consistent prevalence of each of these acids in these glycolipid and phospholipid fractions confirmed our earlier report that conversion to the L-form results in a change in its C_{18} monoolefinic acid content.[3, 14]

In order to interpret these lipid findings in a more meaningful manner, and because of accumulating streptococcal cell wall biosynthesis data,[6, 16, 20] it seemed feasible to attempt an antithetical approach to the problem of "wall" formation by employing cell-free extracts and membranes from this coccal L-form. As is known, a basic structure of group A coccal cell walls is the group-specific C polysaccharide. Heymann et al.[6] had established that such purified cell walls and their C polysaccharide are

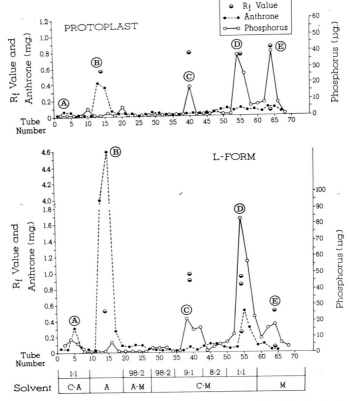

Figure 13.3. Silicic acid column chromatography of total lipid extracts from *Streptococcus pyogenes* protoplast and L-form membranes. Ordinate indicates anthrone content per tube and R_f values of fractions on silicic acid impregnated paper (diisobutyl ketone, acetic acid, water; 40:20:3); phosphorus per tube on right. Total lipid on columns, 34.4. and 142.9 mg from protoplast and L-form membranes, respectively. Peak *B* identified as glucosylglucosyl diglyceride; peak *D*, major spots of higher R_f contain polyglycerol phosphatide with a possible trace of phosphatidyl glycerol. Smaller peaks not characterized further. C: chloroform. A: acetone, M: methanol. (From Cohen & Panos.[3])

largely composed of two carbohydrates, L-rhamnose and N-acetyl-D-glucosamine, and that the former predominates. When associated with the rigid cell wall, this methylpentose is almost entirely present as a polymer. Thus, cell wall formation is apparently closely related to polymeric rhamnose biosynthesis in the group A streptococci. Therefore, it was important to attempt to relate inhibition of cell wall formation in this L-form with an inability to transfer rhamnosyl units from TDP-rhamnose (a proposed cell wall polysaccharide precursor in group A streptococci) to a preexisting membrane acceptor site, or with

an intracellular rhamnose-containing nucleotide malfunction.[13]

These studies also afforded an opportunity to determine and compare the monomeric and polymeric rhamnose contents of the intact *S. pyogenes* and a protoplast and L-form derived from it (Table 13.3). The significant decrease in total and polymeric rhamnose contents in this coccus upon cell wall removal (i.e., resulting protoplast) supports an implication of polymeric rhamnose in cell wall biosynthesis. Also, the difference observed in the rhamnose-type distribution within the L-form and protoplast suggests that they are not identical, since the former possessed only 1/17th as much polymeric rhamnose as found within the latter.[13]

Next, employing protoplast and L-form membrane particles and *preformed* TDP-^{14}C-rhamnose, incorporation of radioactivity into membrane polysaccharide was investigated. As was known, earlier studies by others[16, 20] with a similar coccal membrane transfer system had demonstrated the addition of this methylpentose to a preexisting rhamnose polymer in membranes. Also, the specificity of this addition was apparent by the inability of this polymer to accept acetylglucosamine from UDP-N-acetylglucosamine.[20] The presence of this bound rhamnose polymer in membranes capable of enlarging it led to the conclusion of a precursor relationship to cell wall C poly-

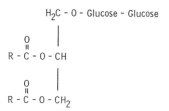

Figure 13.4. Proposed structure of glycolipid from isolated streptococcal protoplast and L-form membranes.

CH₂ - O - CO - R₁
CHO - CO - R₂
CH₂ - O - P - O - CH₂ - CH - CH₂ - O - P - O - CH₂
OH   O(-H)*   OH

CH₂ - O - CO - R₄
CHO - CO - R₃

R = long chain fatty acids

Membrane Source		Ester:Phosphorus Molar Ratio
L-form	above structure	1.9:1
Strep. (protoplast)	*(- CO - R₅)	5:2

Figure 13.5. Proposed structure of phosphatide from isolated streptococcal protoplast and L-form membranes. (From Panos.[12])

TABLE 13.2

*Major Fatty Acid Components of Polar Lipids of Protoplast and L-Form Membranes**

Fatty Acid	Fraction B†		Fraction D†	
	Protoplast	L-Form	Protoplast	L-Form
Palmitic	42.2	38.4	35.8	31.8
C₁₆ Monoolefinic‡	23.5	6.2	23.7	7.4
Stearic	7.5	8.5	6.9	12.6
Oleic	9.1	27.2	10.4	25.1
cis-Vaccenic	14.5	9.1	13.6	12.6

* Per cent of total fatty acids. Determined by capillary gas chromatography (Golay), Carbowax 1540, 150 ft, at 185° C. Fatty acids obtained by mild alkaline hydrolysis.

† From silicic acid column chromatography, B = glucosyl diglyceride; D = phosphatide.

‡ Mixture of three positional isomers (see Table 13.1).

Data from Cohen & Panos.[3]

TABLE 13.3

Rhamnose-Type Distribution in Whole Cells (%)

	Monomeric	Polymeric	Total rhamnose content*
Streptococcus	4.3	95.7	5.6
Protoplast	68.3	31.7	0.5
L-form	95.3	4.7	0.2

* % dry weight of whole, mid-Log grown cells. Data from Panos & Cohen.[13]

saccharide in a group A coccus.[20] Thus, the ability of coccal protoplast membranes from this *S. pyogenes* to transfer rhamnose was expected, and was in accord with the comparatively high polymeric rhamnose content of the intact protoplast (Table 13.3). The complete inability of L-form membranes, however, to incorporate labeled rhamnose, together with the almost complete lack of polymeric rhamnose within the intact L-form, served to confirm the plausible involvement of this polymeric methylpentose precursor in cell wall polysaccharide synthesis.[13]

Finally, it was demonstrated that L-form and protoplast *cell-free extracts* could form TDP-rhamnose from glucose-1-phosphate[13] or from glucose and various disac-

TABLE 13.4

*Antibiotic Inhibition of Growth**

	Strepto- coccus pyogenes[†]	L-form[†]	Strepto- coccus faecalis[‡]	Proto- plast[‡]
Penicillin G.......	0.06	>300	20	>400
Bacitracin.........	5	>300	5	5
Puromycin........	30	2.5–25§	25	25
Ristocetin........	1	>300	5	1

* Minimal inhibitory concentration (μg/ml medium) decreasing growth to 50 per cent of that in control cultures.

† Excerpts of data from Panos, Cohen & Fagan.[15] Growth = increase in numbers and turbidity.

‡ Excerpts of data from Shockman and Lampen.[18] Growth = increase in both volume of individual protoplasts and in turbidity.

§ Growth inhibition or lysis (see text).

charides.* This only served to strengthen the belief of a possible involvement of the membrane in cell wall biosynthesis and led to the conclusion that inhibition of cell wall formation in the L-form may be the result of deficient membrane acceptor sites, or of the membrane enzymes necessary to effect such a transfer, or of both. Thus, although unable to synthesize a cell wall, the L-form continues to retain the ability to form the implicated cell wall precursor, TDP-rhamnose.

As a sequel to these studies and continuing our pursuit of membrane differences, antibiotic inhibition and binding studies with this group A coccal L-form were performed,[15] and the results compared with similar studies performed by others[18] with *Streptococcus faecalis* protoplasts (Table 13.4). A compilation of the results from these two serologically distinct streptococci (*S. faecalis* and *S. pyogenes*) revealed that they respond similarly to equal concentrations of puromycin, bacitracin and ristocetin. However, the fact that their wall-less derivatives required great quantitative differences for obtention of comparable results indicated possible membrane differences between protoplasts and L-forms after conversion from their respective parental cocci. It also should be mentioned

* L. Doolin and C. Panos, unpublished results.

that puromycin, an inhibitor of protein synthesis, lysed the intact L-form.[15] A similar response was not observed with *S. faecalis* protoplasts.* Finally, binding studies with tritium-labeled penicillin demonstrated that the intact L-form and parent *S. pyogenes* bind this antibiotic to the same extent (0.70 and 0.69 μg/g dry weight cells, respectively), (a) indicating that binding capacity is not apparently influenced by the inability of L-form membranes to incorporate rhamnose, and (b) suggesting that the penicillin-binding sites are probably distinct from those concerned with group A streptococcal cell wall formation. Details of these studies have appeared recently.[15]

Thus, the biochemical data accumulating with this coccal L-form point to membrane structural and enzymatic alterations after or during cell wall removal, and substantiate past beliefs that conversion to the L-form results in more than merely the removal of the rigid cell wall. Since recent work has implicated lipid involvement in Gram-positive and -negative bacterial cell wall biosynthesis,[1, 17] I would like to conclude by speculating or attempting to coordinate and relate the membrane differences already mentioned to this coccal L-form's inability to synthesize a cell wall.

Perhaps of greater importance, since it may be related to the L-form's inability to utilize TDP-rhamnose for membrane polymeric rhamnose formation, is glycolipid accumulation (diglucosyldiglyceride) in L-form membranes. Since this aspect has been discussed elsewhere,[12] only a brief synopsis will be given here. That the loss of the L-form's ability to transfer rhamnosyl units to a polymeric rhamnose-membrane acceptor is responsible for the accumulation of this glycolipid is obvious and tempting. Added impetus and importance is given to this possibility because of (a) the established fact that labeled glucose serves as a source for coccal cell wall rhamnose biosynthesis, and (b) recent findings indicating that glycolipids are probably more widely distributed in bacteria than hitherto suspected and that they may be instrumental

* G. D. Shockman, personal communication.

in microbial polysaccharide biosynthesis.[2] It is conceivable, on the other hand, that glycolipid accumulation might be the result of elevated quantities of the cell wall precursor, UDP-muramic acid peptide, present in this L-form even when grown in the absence of penicillin.[4]

Anderson & Strominger[1] had reported on the involvement of a cardiolipin-related phospholipid intermediate in cell wall glycopeptide synthesis. However, although an appreciably decreased polyglycerol phospholipid content in membrane lipids was observed in the L-form (see above), the amount still remaining made it appear unlikely that it could be a primary reason of the L-form's cell wall inhibition defect.[3] In this respect, the importance of the possible ester:phosphorus molar ratio difference for each membrane source (Figure 13.5), as mentioned above, must await further study.

These collective membrane differences between S. pyogenes (protoplasts) and resulting stable L-form may be either the result of cell wall inhibition and/or an attempt by this reproducing L-form to compensate for this defect by strengthening or altering its membrane. Membrane alterations in the L-form have been reflected, biochemically, in its (a) elevated total membrane fatty acid and complex lipid content, (b) increased but reversed positional isomeric octadecenoic acid composition, (c) glycolipid and phospholipid redistribution, (d) rhamnose whole cell, membrane and enzymatic studies, and (e) antibiotic investigations. Physically, these lipid differences probably account for the increased fragility and susceptibility to osmotic or vibrational stress of newly formed protoplasts, as compared with the L-form, so apparent during the preparation of membranes for these studies. Morphologically, they may be reflected by the apparent lack of an orderly cellular division process so characteristic of bacterial L-form growth.

Currently, confusion and ambiguity exist concerning the relation or distinction between bacterial L-forms and protoplasts. Although, in the opinion of this author, a relationship probably exists between each of these biological derivatives, sufficient data are presently unavailable for an accurate delineation of each to be made at this time. It is hoped that these biochemical data, only cursorily treated here, will eventually aid in solving this microbial enigma.

SUMMARY

This biochemical synopsis has dealt with major differences at the cellular and subcellular levels between Streptococcus pyogenes and an L-form derived from it. It is felt that a foundation for characterizing this L-form in terms of its parent streptococcus and in terms of its own unique biochemical characteristics has begun to be realized.

REFERENCES

1. Anderson, J. S., and Strominger, J. L.: Isolation and utilization of phospholipid intermediates in cell wall glycopeptide synthesis. Biochem. Biophys. Res. Commun. 21: 516, 1965.
2. Brundish, D. E., Shaw, N., and Baddiley, J.: The occurrence of glycolipids in Gram-positive bacteria. Biochem. J. 95: 21c, 1965.
3. Cohen, M., and Panos, C.: Membrane lipid composition of Streptococcus pyogenes and derived L form. Biochemistry (Washington) 5: 2385, 1966.
4. Edwards, J., and Panos, C.: Streptococcal L forms. V. Acid-soluble nucleotides of a group A Streptococcus and derived L form. J. Bact. 84: 1202, 1962.
5. Freimer, E. H.: Studies of L forms and protoplasts of group A streptococci. II. Chemical and immunological properties of the cell membrane. J. Exp. Med. 117: 377, 1963.
6. Heymann, H., Manniello, J. M., and Barkulis, S. S.: Structure of streptococcal cell walls. I. Methylation study of C-polysaccharide. J. Biol. Chem. 238: 502, 1963.
7. Hofmann, K. Fatty Acid Metabolism in Microorganisms. Wiley, New York, 1963.
8. James, A. M., Hill, M. J., and Maxted, W. R.: A comparative study of the bacterial cell wall, protoplast membrane and L-form envelope of Streptococcus pyogenes. Antonie Leeuwenhoek 31: 423, 1965.
9. Krembel, J.: Étude des lipides de la forme L stable de Protéus P 18: identification des acides gras de la fraction acétonosoluble. Path. et Microbiol. 26: 592, 1963.
10. Nesbitt, J. A., III, and Lennarz, W. J.: Comparison of lipids and lipopolysaccharide from the bacillary and L forms of Proteus P18. J. Bact. 89: 1020, 1965.
11. Panos, C.: Separation and identification of

positional isomers of bacterial long chain monoethenoid fatty acids by Golay column chromatography. *J. Gas Chrom.* **3**: 278, 1965.

12. ———: L-forms, lipid alterations and inhibition of cell wall biosynthesis. *Ann. N. Y. Acad. Sci.,* 1967, in press.

13. Panos, C., and Cohen, M.: Cell wall inhibition in a stable streptococcal L-form. *Biochim. Biophys. Acta* **117**: 98, 1966.

14. Panos, C., Cohen, M., and Fagan, G.: Lipid alterations after cell wall inhibition; fatty acid content of *Streptococcus pyogenes* and derived L-form. *Biochemistry* (Washington) **5**: 1461, 1966.

15. ———: Antibiotic inhibition and binding studies with a group A streptococcal L-form. *J. Gen. Microbiol.* **46**: 299, 1967.

16. Pazur, J. H., and Anderson, J. S.: Enzymic transfer of rhamnosyl units from thymidine diphosphate rhamnose to bacterial cell-wall fragments. *Biochim. Biophys. Acta* **74**: 788, 1963.

17. Rothfield, L., and Pearlman, M.: The role of cell envelope phospholipid in the enzymatic synthesis of bacterial lipopolysaccharide. *J. Biol. Chem.* **241**: 1386, 1966.

18. Shockman, G. D. and Lampen, J. O.: Inhibition by antibiotics of the growth of bacterial and yeast protoplasts. *J. Bact.* **84**: 508, 1962.

19. Weinbaum, G., and Panos, C.: Fatty acid distribution in normal and filamentous *Escherichia coli. J. Bact.* **92**: 1576, 1966.

20. Zeleznick, L. D., Boltralik, J. J., Barkulis, S. S., Smith, C., and Heymann, H.: Biosynthesis of streptococcal cell walls: a rhamnose polysaccharide. *Science* **140**: 400, 1963.

14

Purification and Characterization of Protoplast Membrane ATPase*

Adolph Abrams and Carl Baron

UNIVERSITY OF COLORADO SCHOOL OF MEDICINE
DENVER, COLORADO

In 1959 an investigation of ATPase* in *Streptococcus faecalis* was initiated after it was observed that protoplasts of this organism exhibited remarkable swelling and contraction phenomena dependent on energy metabolism, i.e., glycolysis[2, 3] (see Discussion). In an attempt to explain these observations, it was postulated that the metabolically dependent swelling and contraction might be due to an interaction of ATP with a membrane-bound ATPase. On examination of the membrane ghosts derived by lysis of the protoplasts, it was found that they contain a highly active, firmly bound ATPase.[7] Subsequently it was shown that the enzyme was maintained in a bound form in the presence of multivalent cations (Figure 14.1) and that many washings of the membrane in the absence of such cations led eventually to the release of the enzyme in a soluble form.[5] The enzyme has now been isolated in a practically pure form, and it is the principal purpose

of this presentation to describe some of its molecular properties.

The membrane ghost preparations used in the experiments to be described here have been examined by electron microscopy[8] (Figure 14.2). They consist mainly of spheres of plasma membranes, but some vacuoles, tubular structures and very thin filaments are also observed. The principal lipid of the membrane appears to be a diphosphatidylglyceride ("cardiolipin");[11, 19] its constituent fatty acids have been characterized.[11] The membrane ghosts also contain some bound ribosomes, and there is evidence that these are not identical to cytoplasmic ribosomes.[8, 14]

MATERIALS AND METHODS

PREPARATION OF PROTOPLASTS AND SOLUBILIZED MEMBRANE ATPase

Lysozome can digest the isolated cell walls of *S. faecalis* (ATCC 9790) practically completely,[1] and it is used to convert these cells to protoplasts in the presence of an appropriate osmotic stabilizer. The preparation of protoplasts and membrane ghosts from *S. faecalis* (ATCC 9790) and the procedure for releasing the membrane ATPase in a soluble form have been described previously.[5] For a typical prepara-

* Study supported in part by Grant No. GM 05810 from the National Institutes of Health, U.S. Public Health Service.

Abbreviations: ATPase, adenosine triphosphatase; GTPase, guanosine triphosphatase; ITPase, inosine triphosphatase; 2-ME, 2 mercaptoethanol; DTT, dithiothreitol; Pi, inorganic phosphate.

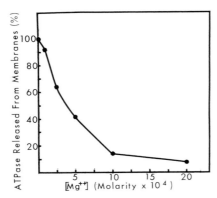

Figure 14.1. Effect of Mg⁺⁺ on the release of ATPase from *Streptococcus faecalis* membrane ghosts.[5]

tion of solubilized ATPase in the amounts needed for the subsequent purification procedure, described here, we started with cells harvested in the stationary phase of growth from four liters of growth medium. After the exhaustive washing of membrane ghosts as described previously, 72 per cent of the membrane ATPase was released into the 8th, 9th and 10th wash of 100 ml each. These wash fluids were pooled and constitute the starting material for the isolation of the pure enzyme described in this paper.

GEL ELECTROPHORESIS

Electrophoresis was carried out in the vertical direction in 3 mm thick 5% polyacrylamide gel slabs with running tap water as the coolant using the apparatus described by Raymond[17] (E. C. Corp., Philadelphia, Pa.). The gels were prepared with Tris glycine buffer pH 8.5 (0.015 M Tris, 0.07 M glycine) with or without urea as indicated, and they were prerun for 30 minutes. The electrode compartments contained the same buffer as the gel, except that in the case of 8 M and 10 M urea gels the compartment buffer contained 3 M urea. All samples were diluted with the solvent used in the gels and 20 μl containing about 5–20 μg protein were introduced into the gel. Bovine serum albumin was always run as a reference protein for the purpose of comparing mobilities in the gels;

300 V (17 V/cm) were applied to the gel and the direction of migration of the proteins was towards the positive electrode.

DETECTION OF PROTEIN AND ENZYME ACTIVITY ON THE GELS

Proteins were detected by staining with 1% amido black in methanol-H_2O-acetic acid 5:5:1 for about 30 minutes, followed by electrolytic destaining of the background. To locate directly the position of ATPase activity, the gel was incubated with a solution of 0.005 M ATP and 0.005 M $MgCl_2$ in 0.1 M Tris Cl pH 7.5 at 38°C. usually for about 30 minutes. The excess ATP solution was then withdrawn, and the Pi liberated by the enzyme reaction was detected by immersing the gel in a solution, at room temperature, containing 9.4% perchloric acid, 1% ammonium molybdate, 0.25% reducing mixture (6 parts sodium sulfite, 6 parts sodium bisulfite, and 1 part 1-amino-2-napthol-4 sulfonic acid). In a few minutes a blue band appears against an almost colorless background, denoting the position of the enzyme; eventually the entire background becomes blue. In order to detect GTPase and ITPase activity on the gel, GTP or ITP was used as the substrate.

OTHER METHODS

Quantitative assays of ATPase activity were performed as previously described.[5] A unit of activity is defined as that amount of enzyme which splits 1 μmol of ATP per minute at 38°C. Protein was determined by the method of Lowry et al.,[13] or by absorbency at 230 mμ when indicated, using bovine serum albumin as a standard. The absorbency method was employed particularly for measuring the small amounts of purified ATPase protein in the fractions collected after zone sedimentation.

EXPERIMENTAL PROCEDURES AND RESULTS

ISOLATION OF THE ATPase

The starting material for the isolation procedure to be described was the highly dilute semipurified soluble ATPase extracted from the membrane ghosts as previously described[5] (see Methods). The

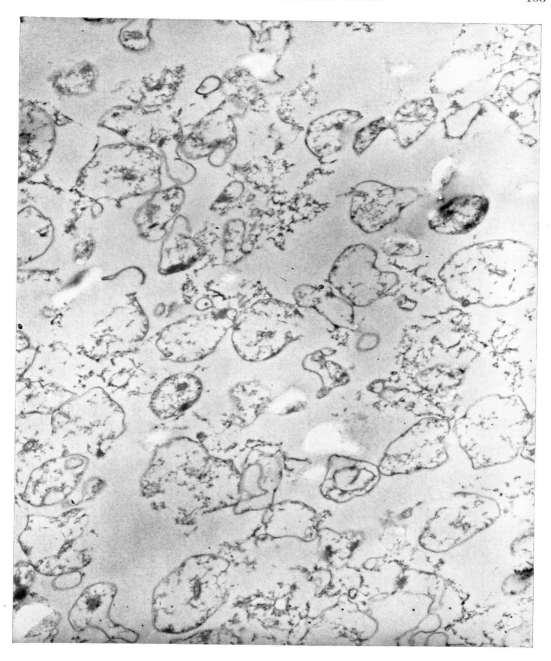

Figure 14.2. Electron micrograph of a section through a pellet of washed membrane ghosts obtained by metabolic lysis of *Streptococcus faecalis* protoplasts. Fixation in osmium tetroxide. × 16,800. (Courtesy of Dr. J. Thaemert.)

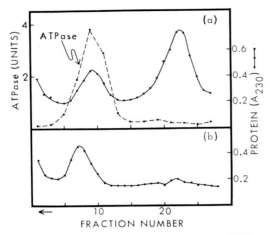

Figure 14.3. Purification of membrane ATPase by zone sedimentation. *a:* Several portions of the (NH$_4$)$_2$SO$_4$ precipitated ATPase, each containing about 3 mg protein, were layered onto 5 ml of 4–16% sucrose gradients in 0.033 M Tris Cl buffer, pH 7.5; centrifugation was carried out for 16 hours at 5°C at 34,000 rpm in the Spinco Model L2 centrifuge; fractions of 0.2 ml were collected from the bottom of the tube and diluted with 0.8 ml Tris Cl buffer; the absorbency of each fraction was measured at 230 mμ, and 25 μl from every odd fraction was assayed for ATPase activity. The ATPase was recovered from pooled fractions 5–12 by (NH$_4$)$_2$SO$_4$ precipitation; electrophoretic analysis is shown in Figure 14.4. *b:* Repeated zone sedimentation of ATPase isolated as in *a* above; electrophoretic analysis is shown in Figure 14.5.

procedure for isolating the enzyme from the extract was carried out in essentially three steps.

Treatment with RNase and Precipitation with (NH$_4$)$_2$SO$_4$

RNase (1 μg/ml) was added to the membrane extract, the mixture was placed in a dialysis bag and immersed in four times its volume of saturated (NH$_4$)$_2$SO$_4$ (4°C.) adjusted previously to pH 7.5–8.0. After equilibration overnight at 4°C., the precipitate which formed was removed by centrifugation at 4°C. and then taken up in about 1 ml of water. The concentrated enzyme solution was dialyzed a few hours against water to remove most of the (NH$_4$)$_2$SO$_4$. This was necessary in order to layer the solution onto sucrose gradients.

Purification of the Enzyme by Zone Sedimentation

Portions of the concentrated enzyme solution, usually 0.25 ml, were layered onto 5 ml sucrose gradients and then centrifuged in a swinging bucket rotor. Figure 14.3*a* gives the conditions of centrifugation and illustrates a typical sedimentation profile of protein and ATPase activity. It is clear that after centrifugation there is a symmetrical peak of protein in the lower portion of the tube which coincides closely with a single peak of ATPase activity. The specific enzyme activity (units/mg) determined at three different points in the peak for three different enzyme preparations was very nearly the same (59 ± 6 units/mg) (Table 14.1). This constancy of specific activity indicates that the enzyme separated by zone sedimentation is homogeneous or very nearly so. It should also be noted in Figure 14.3*a* that the ATPase zone is well resolved from the bulk of non-active protein, which sediments much more slowly.

For the determination of protein in the fractions collected after zone sedimentation we used A$_{230}$ rather than A$_{280}$ readings, since the latter were very low. The A$_{260}$ values were even lower than the A$_{280}$ and it may therefore be concluded that the ATPase separated on the gradient was free of contaminating nucleotide material. It is worth pointing out that the prior treatment of the crude membrane extract with RNase is essential to achieve this result, for without it there is a severe overlap of the enzyme

TABLE 14.1

Recovery and Specific Activity of Purified ATPase Isolated from Streptococcal Membranes

	Total Protein	Total Activity	Specific Activity
	mg	*units*	*units/mg*
Membrane ghosts, washed IX	786	570	0.7
Purified enzyme	1.5	86	59 ± 6*

* Average of 9 determinations from 3 different points in a zone of sedimentation of 3 different enzyme preparations. (See text and Figure 14.3a.)

peak with slower sedimenting RNA containing impurities.

Precipitation of the Purified Enzyme

For the third and final step in the isolation, the fractions which contained the ATPase (Nos. 5 to 12, Figure 14.3*a*) were pooled and the enzyme was precipitated once again with 80% saturated $(NH_4)_2SO_4$ by dialysis as described above. After dissolving the precipitate in about 1 ml of water, the solution was dialyzed against H_2O. A slight cloudiness in some preparations was removed by centrifugation. The yield and the specific activity of a typical purified enzyme preparation is shown in Table 14.1.

Analysis of the purified enzyme by acrylamide gel electrophoresis shows one protein band (Figure 14.4, sample 2). Three additional samples of the purified enzyme were also run on the same gel (Figure 14.4,

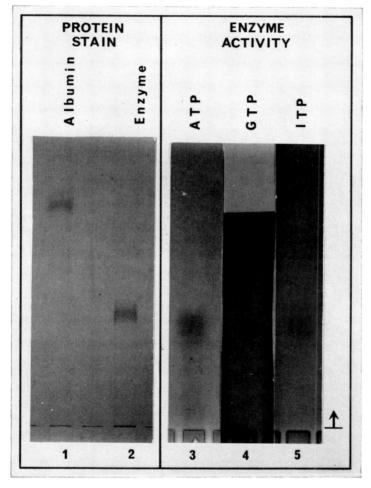

Figure 14.4. Electrophoretic analysis of purified ATPase and the specificity of the enzyme. Sample 1, Bovine serum albumin (10 μg); samples 2–5, ATPase (4.4 μg protein, 0.25 units). Samples 1 and 2 were stained with amido black. The gel was run for 100 minutes at 300 V. Samples 3, 4 and 5 were stained for nucleotide triphosphatase activity (see Methods), run for 100 minutes at 300 V. Samples 3, 4 and 5 were stained for nucleotide triphosphatase activity (see Methods), using different substrates as indicated.

samples 3, 4, 5), and each was tested for enzyme activity by direct reaction on the gel with ATP, GTP, and ITP respectively. The results show a single zone of liberated Pi for each substrate, and these zones coincide with the position of the enzyme when it is stained for protein with amido black. Thus, there can be little doubt that the same enzyme splits all three substrates. This result confirms earlier work which indicated that ATPase and GTPase activities reside in a protein of the same molecular weight, as judged by zone sedimentation analysis.[5]

We have observed that the purified enzyme may contain very small amounts of enzymatically active aggregates which migrate into the gel only a short distance. It should be emphasized that this slow migrating enzyme activity was observed only after prolonged incubation of the gel with ATP and that no protein was detected in that region.

THE SUBUNIT STRUCTURE OF THE MEMBRANE ATPASE

The fairly high sedimentation constant of the streptococcal membrane ATPase, about 13S,[5] suggested that it was probably composed of subunits. In order to demonstrate subunits associated by means of noncovalent forces, the purified enzyme was electrophoresed in gels containing 8 M urea. As a result, five protein bands appeared instead of the single band observed in gels without urea. To satisfy ourselves that this finding was not due to contaminations, however unlikely this seemed, the purified enzyme was recycled once more through the purification procedure by means of another zone sedimentation and $(NH_4)_2SO_4$ precipitation as described in the previous section. As expected, the result of the repeated zone sedimentation, illustrated in Figure 14.3b, shows only one protein band; gel electrophoresis of the protein precipitated from the zone sedimentation band also shows only one protein band (Figure 14.5, sample 1). When this recycled purified enzyme was electrophoresed in 8 M urea, five protein bands were observed, as shown in Figure 14.5, sample 2, thus corroborating the results obtained with the enzyme that

was carried through the purification procedure only once. It is evident then that the five protein bands appearing after electrophoresis in gels with 8 M urea are derived from the ATPase molecule and no other protein. They are designated x, y, α, β and γ in the order of increasing mobility. Further confirmation comes from quantitative densitometry of the gel, which shows that the sum of the protein in the five bands was reasonably accounted for by the protein in the intact enzyme (Figure 14.6).

The recycled purified ATPase was examined next in gels containing 10 M rather than 8 M urea and, as can be seen in Figure 14.5, sample 3, the same five bands appeared, with no apparent change in their relative quantities. Since increasing the urea concentration caused no further change, it seems that the maximum degree of dissociation of the protein into subunits attainable with urea was achieved. There was the possibility, however, that one or more of the bands was composed of polypeptide chains linked covalently through disulfide bonds. In order to test this possibility, samples of the recycled purified enzyme were treated with two different concentrations of mercaptoethanol, and also with dithiothreitol, and then examined again by gel electrophoresis in 10 M urea. The results are shown in Figure 14.5, samples 4, 5 and 6. It can be easily seen, first of all, that, after treatment with the thiol reagents, the x and y bands disappeared and the intensity of the α band increased markedly, while no apparent quantitative change was evident in the β and γ bands. Second, quantitative densitometry of the gel (Figure 14.6 and Table 14.2) shows that the increase in the α band is accounted for by the loss of the x and y bands. Finally, it should be noted that after treatment with thiol reagents the relative amounts of α, β and γ proteins are very nearly in the ratio of 2:2:1 (Figure 14.6, Table 14.2), and the same result was obtained with both mercaptoethanol and dithiothreitol over a tenfold concentration range of these reducing agents. These results suggest that the x and y proteins are disulfide polymers of the α subunit, and therefore it may be con-

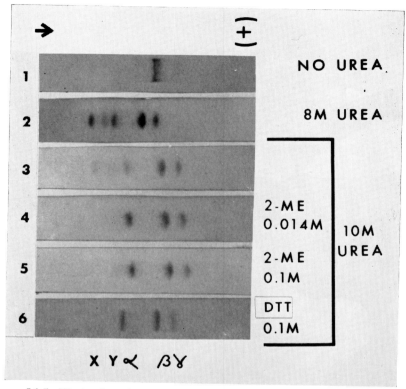

Figure 14.5. Electrophoresis of membrane ATPase in acrylamide gels containing urea, and the effect of thiol reagents. The ATPase preparation was purified twice through zone sedimentation (Figure 14.3b; see text). Sample 1, no urea, run for 100 minutes at 300 V; Samples 2–6, with urea as indicated, run for 240 minutes at 300 V. Some samples were treated with thiol reagents as indicated, prior to application to the gel. 2-ME: Mercaptoethanol; DTT: dithiothreitol. Samples 2–6 contained about twice as much protein as Sample 1.

cluded that the ATPase is actually composed of three different types of subunits, the ones designated α, β and γ, in a noncovalent type of association.

HEAVY COMPLEXES OF THE ATPase IN THE MEMBRANE

When the membrane ghosts are extracted with the Na deoxycholate (0.2%), heavy complexes of ATPases, ranging from about 25S to 100S can be detected by density gradient sedimentation analysis (Figure 14.7). These heavy complexes could very well be more representative of the actual state of the enzyme in the membranes of the intact cell than the 13S form of the enzyme. In this regard it is interesting that

the heavy complexes are converted to the 13S form by dialysis. Therefore, it would appear that a dialyzable substance, possibly a multivalent cation, is responsible for holding the heavy complexes together.

DISCUSSION

The ATPase which we have isolated from streptococcal membranes appears to be homogeneous, as judged by zone sedimentation analysis and by zone electrophoresis in acrylamide gels. After electrophoresis of the enzyme in gels containing urea, five protein bands appear, designated x, y, α, β and γ in the order of increasing electrophoretic mobility. However, the two slower-moving proteins, x and y, are completely eliminated

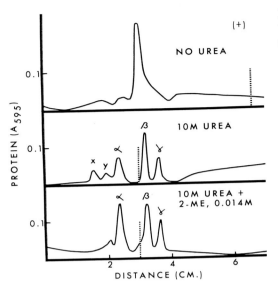

Figure 14.6. Densitometry of gel electrophoretic patterns of membrane ATPase. The patterns are, from top to bottom, Samples 1, 3, and 4 of Figure 14.5. The gel was scanned with a Photovolt densitometer using a 595 mμ filter, and the optical density was recorded continuously. Samples 3 and 4 contained about twice as much protein as Sample 1. The vertical dotted line in each pattern represents the position of bovine serum albumin run in the gel at the same time as the ATPase sample.

by thiol reagents and are apparently converted to the α protein. Thus, when thiol reducing agents are present, urea splits the ATPase into only three proteins, α, β and γ. Furthermore, the three proteins are always found in an apparent ratio of 2:2:1 despite attempts to change this pattern by increasing the urea concentration in the gel or by increasing the concentration of thiol reagents (Figures 14.5 and 14.6; Table 14.2). On the basis of the evidence obtained thus far we conclude, first of all, that the native streptococcal membrane ATPase is made up of three different types of subunits, α, β and γ, in a non-covalent type of association, and, second, that the α subunit is a sulfhydryl protein which oxidizes easily, but only partially, to disulfide polymers (proteins x and y) under the conditions used. Consistent with this view is the fact that the α, β and γ proteins migrate faster than the intact enzyme, and that the x and

γ proteins migrate slower than the α protein, as expected, in gels with molecular sieving properties such as polyacrylamide (Table 14.2). It also seems likely from the

TABLE 14.2

Analysis of Electrophoretic Pattern of Purified ATPase

Electrophoretic Component	Relative Mobility (Albumin = 1)	Total Protein (%)	
		−mercaptoethanol	+mercaptoethanol
Intact enzyme	0.45	100	
x	0.52	12	0
y	0.65	5	0
α	0.75	22	43
β	1.07	41	37
γ	1.20	20	19

The relative amounts of protein were calculated from the areas under the peaks, measured with a planimeter, in the densitometric tracings shown in Figure 14.6. The total area in one pattern is taken at 100; x, y, α, β and γ are the protein bands observed in gels containing urea (Figure 14.5).

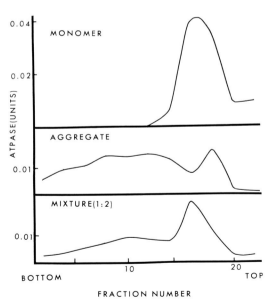

Figure 14.7. Sedimentation of monomer and "Aggregated" forms of membrane ATPase. Sedimentation for 3 hours in a 5–20% sucrose gradient containing 0.01 M Tris Cl pH 7.5, 0.001 M MgCl₂ and 0.01 M KCl. The monomer form is about 13S. (See text.)

results obtained with thiol reagents that α, β and γ are single polypeptide chains.

An evaluation of the number of each type of subunit in a molecule of ATPase must await a determination of their molecular weights. However, if we assume that the three types of subunits have about the same molecular weight, and in view of the observed proportions of 2:2:1, then a tentative subunit composition may be formulated as $\alpha_{2n}\beta_{2n}\gamma_n$. A minimal molecular weight of the intact ATPase of approximately 350,000 has been reported on the basis of zone sedimentation.[5] Since the molecular weights of single polypeptide chains are usually somewhere between 10,000 and 100,000, it is reasonable to expect that the value of n lies between 1 and 5.

It is of interest to compare the streptococcal membrane enzyme with other ATPases whose subunit structures have been studied. The ATPases of protozoan cilia,[10] animal muscle myosin,[18] and animal mitochondria,[15, 16] like the one from streptococcus, have high molecular weights and are composed of many subunits. However, in contrast to the bacterial enzyme, they all appear to contain only one type of subunit.

Although without evidence, we may surmise that one of the subunits in the ATPase contains the active site, while another has some other function, such as a regulatory one, as in the case of aspartate transcarbamylase,[9] which has two non-identical subunits. Since the streptococcal membrane ATPase contains a third type of subunit, an interesting possibility to consider for its function is that it contains the site for attachment to membranes.

In concluding this discussion we shall review the principal features of metabolic swelling and metabolic contraction of intact protoplasts, which prompted these investigations of ATPase in the first place. In the initial observation,[2] shown in Figure 14.8, it was found that S. faecalis protoplasts osmotically stabilized with sucrose undergo a cycle of iso-osmotic swelling and contraction when glucose is added. The swelling phase was correlated with glycolysis and an increased permeability to sucrose, while the contraction phase began immediately after cessation of glycolysis and was correlated with a decreased permeability to sucrose.[3] Intracellular K^+ ions were also required for the glycolysis-linked swelling

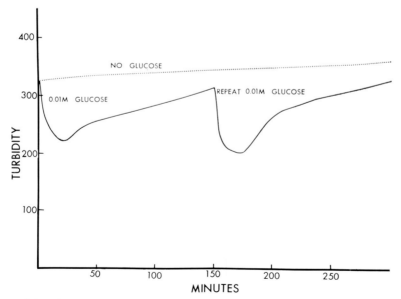

Figure 14.8. Reversible metabolic swelling of protoplasts osmotically stabilized in 0.4 M sucrose—0.075 M K phosphate, pH 7.2. *Lower curve:* 0.01 M glucose added at zero time and again at 150 minutes; *upper curve:* control with no glucose. (From Abrams.[2])

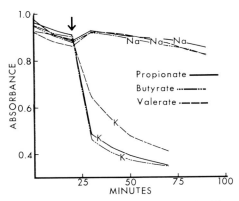

Figure 14.9. The effect of glycolysis, K⁺ and Na⁺ on protoplasts stabilized with propionate, butyrate and valerate. Protoplasts of *Streptococcus faecalis* previously depleted of K⁺ were osmotically stabilized in solutions containing salts of monocarboxylic acids (0.4 M) and phosphate (0.075 M, pH 7.2). The cations were either all K⁺ or all Na⁺ as indicated on the curves. Glucose (0.01 M) was added at the time shown by the arrow. The rate of swelling during glycolysis, observed photometrically, indicates that the rate of penetration of the K salts during glycolysis becomes very rapid, while the penetration rate of the Na salt remains unchanged. The substitution of Na⁺ for K⁺ does not alter the initial rate of glycolysis as measured by continuous titration of acid production at constant pH (pH stat). (From Abrams.[4])

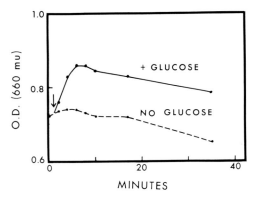

Figure 14.10. Metabolic contraction of protoplasts osmotically stabilized with 0.4 M NH₄Cl − 0.075 M K phosphate, pH 7.2. Glucose (0.01 M) was added at time indicated by arrow. Temperature: 25°C.

in sucrose, and the activity of the K⁺ ions was competitively inhibited by Na⁺ ions without inhibiting glycolysis.[2, 3] On the

basis of these observations, it was postulated that K⁺ ions and the ATP generated during glycolysis interacted with membrane ATPase, thus inducing conformational changes in the membrane, with a consequent increased downhill penetration of the external osmotic stabilizer, namely sucrose. The breakdown of the ATP by the membrane ATPase would then be expected to result in a return of the membrane to its initial impermeable state. This interpretation of "reversible metabolic swelling" in sucrose suggested that protoplasts suspended in other types of osmotic stabilizers might behave differently during glycolysis. This turned out to be the case. Two examples are given in Figures 14.9 and 14.10, which illustrate the response of protoplasts to glucose addition when they are osmotically stabilized in K⁺ and Na⁺ salts of simple fatty acids[4] (Figure 14.9) and in NH₄Cl (Figure 14.10). In the K⁺ salts of fatty acids, glycolysis causes extremely rapid irreversible swelling with complete lysis (metabolic lysis), while no swelling is obtained with the Na⁺ salts, although the glycolysis rate is unimpaired. Metabolic lysis of protoplasts in glycylglycine[6] and in D and L isomers of amino acids[4] has also been observed. By contrast, the protoplasts in NH₄Cl *contracted* during glycolysis (Figure 14.10), and there was no metabolic swelling at all. This energy-dependent contraction appears to be quite analogous to the ATP-dependent contraction of mitochondria described by Lehninger.[12] Nevertheless, it still remains to be shown whether or not ATP and membrane ATPase in protoplasts are involved in metabolic swelling and contraction of these bodies.

SUMMARY

The adenosine triphosphatase (ATPase) released in a soluble form from streptococcal membrane ghosts was isolated in pure form using a combination of (NH₄)₂-SO₄ precipitation and zone sedimentation. Analysis of the purified enzyme by acrylamide gel electrophoresis showed a single protein band. This protein band exhibited ATPase, GTPase and ITPase activity when tested by direct application of ATP, GTP and ITP solutions, respectively, to the gel.

In gels containing 8 M or 10 M urea, five protein bands, designated x, y, α, β and γ in the order of increasing mobilities, were observed. Their mobilities were all greater than that for the intact enzyme. The x and y proteins were completely converted to the α protein by mercaptoethanol or dithiothreitol and the amounts of α, β and γ were then found by densitometry to be in a ratio close to 2:2:1. This pattern was not changed by increasing the concentration of thiol reagent. It is concluded that the streptococcal membrane ATPase is made up of three different types of subunits α, β and γ, in non-covalent association, and that the α subunit is a sulfhydryl protein which oxidizes readily to disulfide polymers.

Large aggregates of the enzyme (approximately 25S–100S) were obtained when the membranes were extracted with deoxycholate.

A possible physiological role of the enzyme is discussed in connection with glycolysis-dependent swelling and contraction of intact protoplasts.

REFERENCES

1. Abrams, A.: O-acetyl groups on the cell wall of Streptococcus faecalis. J. Biol. Chem. 230: 949, 1958.
2. ———: Reversible metabolic swelling of bacterial protoplasts. J. Biol. Chem. 234: 383, 1959.
3. ———: Metabolically dependent penetration of oligosaccharides into bacterial cells and protoplasts. J. Biol. Chem. 235: 1281, 1960.
4. ———: Discussion on: State of the intracellular amino acids. In: Amino Acid Pools; Distribution, Formation and Function of Free Amino Acids (J. Holden, Ed.). Elsevier, Amsterdam, 1962: p. 762.
5. ———: The release of bound adenosine triphosphatase from isolated bacterial membranes and the properties of the solubilized enzyme. J. Biol. Chem. 240: 3675, 1965.
6. Abrams, A., and McNamara, P.: Polynucleotide phosphorylase in isolated bacterial cell membranes. J. Biol. Chem. 237: 170, 1962.
7. Abrams, A., McNamara, P., and Johnson, F. B.: Adenosine triphosphatase in isolated bacterial cell membranes. J. Biol. Chem. 235: 3659, 1960.
8. Abrams, A., Nielsen, L., and Thaemert, J.: Rapidly synthesized ribonucleic acid in membrane ghosts from Streptococcus faecalis protoplasts. Biochim. Biophys. Acta 80: 325, 1964.
9. Gerhart, J. C., and Schachman, H. K.: Distinct subunits for the regulation and catalytic activity of asparate transcarbamylase. Biochemistry (Washington) 4: 1054, 1965.
10. Gibbons, I. R., and Rowe, A. J.: Dynein: a protein with adenosine triphosphatase activity from cilia. Science 149: 424, 1965.
11. Ibbott, F. A., and Abrams, A.: The phospholipids in membrane ghosts from Streptococcus faecalis protoplasts. Biochemistry (Washington) 3: 2008, 1964.
12. Lehninger, A. L.: Water uptake and extrusion by mitochondria in relation to oxidative phosphorylation. Physiol. Rev. 42: 467, 1962.
13. Lowry, O. H., Rosebrough, N. J., Farr, A. L., and Randall, R. J.: Protein measurement with the folin phenol reagent. J. Biol. Chem. 193: 265, 1951.
14. Nielsen, L., and Abrams, A.: Rapidly labelled ribosomal RNA associated with membrane ghosts of Streptococcus fecalis. Biochem. Biophys. Res. Commun. 17: 680, 1964.
15. Penefsky, H. S., and Warner, R. C.: Partial resolution of the enzymes catalyzing oxidative phosphorylation. VI. Studies on the mechanism of cold inactivation of mitochondrial adenosine triphosphatase. J. Biol. Chem. 240: 4694, 1965.
16. Pullman, M. E., Penefsky, H. S., Datta, A., and Racker, E.: Partial resolution of the enzymes catalyzing oxidative phosphorylation. I. Purification and properties of soluble, dinitrophenol-stimulated adenosine triphosphatase. J. Biol. Chem. 235: 3322, 1960.
17. Raymond, S.: A convenient apparatus for vertical gel electrophoresis. Clin. Chem. 8: 455, 1962.
18. Small, P. A., Harrington, W. F., and Kielley, W. W.: The electrophoretic homogeneity of myosin subunits. Biochim. Biophys. Acta 49: 462, 1961.
19. Vorbeck, M. L., and Marinetti, G. V.: Intracellular distribution and characterization of the lipids of Streptococcus faecalis (ATCC 9790). Biochemistry (Washington) 4: 296, 1965.

15

The Relationship of the Cell Wall to Electrolyte and Volume Regulation in Microorganisms*

Aser Rothstein

UNIVERSITY OF ROCHESTER SCHOOL OF MEDICINE AND DENTISTRY

ROCHESTER, NEW YORK

In the walled cell, the volume of the protoplast is determined by the space enclosed within the wall. Under most circumstances, the osmotic pressure within the protoplast is greater than that of the medium, resulting in a swelling pressure (turgor) against the wall that is resisted by its mechanical strength.[2, 17, 18, 31] The size of the protoplast is therefore determined by the mechanical properties of the wall, the amount of stretch that occurs with a given osmotic pressure difference. The volume of the cells responds to changes in external or internal osmotic pressure only to the small degree allowed by the elasticity of the wall.

While the volume of the walled cell is maintained within narrow limits despite differences in osmotic pressure between the protoplast and the environment, essential mechanisms have been evolved that allow controlled changes in volume to occur during growth. The osmotic pressure within the protoplast becomes considerably greater than that of the medium, largely because of accumulation of electrolytes and, under certain circumstances, of amino acids or

sugar.[3, 7, 43] The wall undergoes temporary softening and it consequently is stretched by the turgor pressure.[19] As the new volume is attained, additional wall material is synthesized and the wall "hardens". Under these circumstances cell division usually occurs, so that the end result is a doubling of the total protoplast volume, with each daughter protoplast assuming the same volume as the original parent cell.

Perhaps the primary physiological problem imposed upon the protoplast by the removal of its wall is that associated with volume regulation. Most non-walled forms of microorganisms such as protoplasts of *Micrococcus lysodeikticus*,[8, 17, 26] *Escherichia coli*,[26, 35, 39] *Sarcina lutea*,[17] *Bacillus megaterium*,[42] and *Bacillus subtilis*,[36] behave approximately as osmometers as the tonicity of the external medium is changed. Such behavior implies that the cells are approximately in osmotic equilibrium with the medium, and that mechanical resistance to changes in volume is minimal. At the limit of swelling reached by dilution of the medium, the protoplasts undergo osmotic lysis.[16, 43] Other wall-less forms, such as the L-form and *Mycoplasma*[24, 25, 26, 29, 44] show varying degrees of resistance to osmotic lysis, with the resistance influenced by bivalent cations and substances such as

* This study is based on work performed under contract with the United States Atomic Energy Commission at The University of Rochester Atomic Energy Project.

spermine.[15] The nature of the resistance has not been definitively elucidated. It may be due to mechanical strength of the protoplast membrane. or to the fact that the protoplast can swell without breaking the membrane, or to leakage of osmotic content out of the protoplasts when they are exposed to hypotonic media. For example, a transient release of cellular materials on "osmotic shock" has been demonstrated in microorganisms.[9]

Naked protoplasts must be protected from lysis by media of high osmotic pressure using non-penetrating solutes such as sucrose or salts.[43] But even if so protected, the entire mechanism of the controlled increase in size during the cell division cycle is likely to be seriously disturbed. In the walled cell, during growth, the size is determined by the balance between the increasing osmotic pressure on the protoplast, the constant osmotic pressure of the medium, and the mechanical strength of the wall. In the naked protoplast the accumulation of cellular materials and consequent increase in protoplast osmotic pressure is not balanced by the wall strength and considerable swelling and even lysis can result.

Because electrolytes constitute a major osmotic component, the cell volume is to a large degree determined by the electrolyte content, and in turn the regulation of volume is largely a matter of the regulation of electrolytes.[31] For this reason the present paper will be concerned with a comparison of electrolyte and volume regulation in naked and in walled cells, with special reference to the events during the growth and cell division cycles. The problem of volume regulation has not, to my knowledge, been studied in any detail in bacterial protoplasts. Nevertheless, the factors involved must be similar to those that have been described in some detail for naked cells from animals. A review of volume regulation in naked animal cells may, therefore, be helpful in understanding some of the problems faced by naked bacterial cells.

VOLUME REGULATION IN NON-GROWING NAKED CELLS

The naked cell is surrounded by a thin membrane (of the order of 100 Å) composed of a bilayer of lipid with protein together with other substances, especially carbohydrates, overlaying the lipids.[27] The mechanical strength or elasticity of this membrane plays probably only a minor role in determining cell volume. For example, in the red blood cell, the inward pressure exerted by the membrane is about 2 mm of water, equal to a concentration difference of only 1×10^{-5} mols/liter.[23] It must be concluded that the volume of the cell is determined by internal factors, such as the total osmotic content. It cannot be excluded that mechanical factors play no role in cells with a great deal of internal structure, such as muscle, but this would not apply to most cells, and certainly not to bacterial protoplasts, which have a minimum of structure.

Most naked cells are considerably more permeable to water than to physiological solutes, usually by orders of magnitude,[28] so that the water should tend to reach equilibrium distribution. Indeed, careful measurements indicate the virtual equality of osmotic pressure of the cell "sap" and of the medium, with no conclusive evidence of any "water pump" that would disturb the equilibrium.[28] Assuming, then, that water is in equilibrium distribution and that mechanical restraints are minimal, the volume of the cell will be determined by its total osmotic content, and regulation of volume will have to be accomplished by the regulation of osmotic content. The total osmotic content is made up of two fractions, the non-diffusible materials of the cell, primarily the biopolymers, such as proteins and nucleic acids, and the diffusible substances, largely electrolytes. The contribution of the non-diffusible component (colloid osmotic component) in terms of mols is relatively small because of the high molecular weight. This is compensated to some degree, however, by the anomalous behavior of the osmotic coefficient of proteins (and of large molecules in general) or condensed systems.[6] For example, hemoglobin at a low concentration has an osmotic coefficient of unity, but at the concentration found in the red blood cell (5 mM), the osmotic coefficient is 3.3. Thus, in the red blood cell, the hemoglobin contributes only 1.7 per cent of the solute particles, while it contributes 5.8

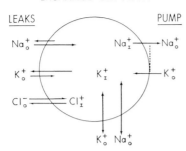

EXCHANGE DIFFUSION

Figure 15.1. The balance of ion fluxes in the red blood cell. (From Tosteson & Hoffman.[41])

per cent of the cellular osmotic pressure,[6] equivalent to 4.4 mm of mercury.

The colloid component of the cellular osmotic pressure represents an important factor in the volume regulation of the cell because it can never be completely compensated by inflow of water, but only by some force working in the opposite direction. If no such compensating force exists, the cell will rapidly swell and burst, a phenomenon called colloid osmotic lysis.[5] In walled cells, the compensating force is a pressure exerted by the cell wall, but in naked cells the primary compensating mechanism usually consists of a non-equilibrium distribution of electrolytes, especially Na^+ and K^+. The electrolyte distribution is maintained by a steady state that depends on the balance between the transport systems that move the ions in the "uphill" direction, away from equilibrium distribution, and the "downhill" leakage of ions in the direction of equilibrium distribution.[41] If the ions are allowed to approach equilibrium distribution by reducing the transport or by increasing the ion leaks, then the colloid osmotic effect becomes uncompensated, the cells swell and may undergo osmotic lysis.

The naked cell in which the factors involved in volume regulation have been most intensively studied is the erythrocyte.[40, 41] It can serve as a useful prototype system. Its only structure is the cell membrane, which is responsible for its disc shape and for its permeability properties. Almost the entire colloid osmotic pressure is contributed by hemoglobin, and the bulk of the diffusible components are simple ions, Na^+, K^+, Cl^- and HCO_3^-. Its metabolism is low and relatively uncomplicated. Yet this simple cell is capable of maintaining large electrolyte gradients of Na^+ and K^+ and of regulating its volume within very narrow limits. The K^+ in the cell is 100 mM compared to 5 mM in plasma, whereas the Na^+ in the cell is only 20 mM compared to 144 mM in plasma.[10] It should be noted that the total osmolarities inside and outside the cell are equal. Because the cell is relatively permeable to water, water inside the cell is in equilibrium with water outside the cell. Because the red blood cell is also relatively permeable to anions, the Cl^-, OH^-, and HCO_3^- are also at equilibrium distribution. At the pH of the cell, the hemoglobin has a net negative charge of 50 mM. Thus, the anion equilibrium is that predictable from the Donnan equation, but the inside concentration less than that outside. The Donnan ratio ($Cl_i : Cl_0$) is in this case about 0.7. From this value, the potential across the cell membrane can be calculated from the Nernst equation to be 5 mV. In contrast to the anions, the cations, Na^+ and K^+, are not at equilibrium distribution. The ratios $Cl_i : Cl_0$, $Na_0 : Na_i$ $K_0 : K_i$, are not equal, being 0.7, 7, and 0.004. Also, the total osmolarity of the diffusible ions within the cells *is less than that in the medium* by an amount equal to the osmolarity of hemoglobin.

The non-equilibrium distribution of the cations is maintained by the active transport systems (pumps) that compensate for the downhill leakage by the expenditure of metabolic energy in the form of ATP.[11] The exact nature of the cation pumps is not known, but they reside in the cell membrane and are associated with a specific ATPase activity.[22] The energy requirement is minimized by the low cation permeability of the cell membrane, lower by a factor of 10^6 than that of Cl^-. The exact balance of cell volume, colloidal osmotic pressure, ion contents, pump fluxes and leak fluxes has been worked out by Tosteson & Hoffman[41] using the model depicted in Figure 15.1.

The relationship of electrolyte regulation

to volume regulation can be readily observed under conditions where the electrolyte regulation is disturbed. For example, if the cells are treated with low concentrations of lead,[20, 21] they become more permeable to K$^+$ (but not to Na$^+$). The leakage of K$^+$ down its electrochemical gradient increases. Because electroneutrality is maintained, an equivalent loss of Cl$^-$ also occurs, and the loss of osmotic content leads to a loss of water and to a shrinkage of the cells, the shrinkage being determined by the permeability to K$^+$. If, on the other hand, the agent increases the permeability both to K$^+$ and to Na$^+$, as is the case with organic mercurials,[38] the cells gain Na$^+$ and lose K$^+$. Depending on the relative permeabilities, they may initially shrink or swell. Ultimately, however, the higher permeabilities will lead to a dissipation of the Na$^+$ and K$^+$ gradients (because the cation pumps cannot keep up with the leaks). The colloidal osmotic pressure will be less well compensated and a new steady state will be established at a larger volume. If the permeability is sufficiently increased, the ion gradient will be entirely dissipated and the colloidal osmotic pressure cannot be compensated. The cells will then swell until they burst, unless they are protected by a non-penetrating solute of osmotic pressure at least equal to the colloidal osmotic pressure. A good example is found in cells treated with antibody, in which a relatively large hole (15–20 Å) is dissolved in the membrane.[34] An explosive bursting of the cells occurs unless they are protected by addition of a non-diffusible solute, in this particular case dextran of a molecular size larger than the hole in the membrane.

The important role of the inflow of the external cation in swelling is illustrated by the following experiments. Cells were treated with sulfhydryl agent, p-chloromercuribenzoate (PCMBS), which increases the permeability both to Na$^+$ and to K$^+$.[38] If the cells were suspended in isotonic NaCl, they lost K$^+$ and gained Na$^+$, but the gain of Na$^+$ was somewhat more rapid, so that they slowly increased in volume and ultimately underwent hemolysis. If the same cells were suspended in choline

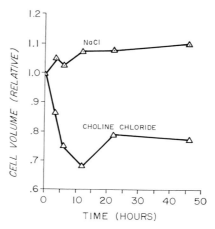

Figure 15.2. Effect of p-chloromercuribenzoate (PCMBS) on erythrocyte volume (hematocrit method); choline chloride vs. NaCl as suspending medium. The cell volumes are expressed relative to the controls in NaCl or choline chloride without PCMBS. In this experiment the concentrations of cells and agent were increased threefold to 15% and 6 × 10^{-5} M/liter in order to obtain measurable volume differences.

chloride, they lost K$^+$, but the defect produced in the membrane did not render them permeable to choline; instead of swelling, the cells decreased considerably in volume with no hemolysis (Figure 15.2).

Volume changes can also be produced by inhibiting the cation transport system. The most specific inhibitors in animal cells are the cardiac glycosides. With the pump inhibited, the ion gradients are dissipated and swelling occurs at a rate that is determined by the permeability to the cations.[40] Another common method of reducing the activity of the transport systems is to reduce the temperature. At low temperature the cation permeability is also reduced, but the transport systems, being metabolically dependent, are reduced even more. The cells lose K$^+$ but gain more Na$^+$ and swell in size, leading ultimately to lysis. On rewarming, the transport systems are reactivated, the ion gradients are re-established, and the cells shrink to normal size.[10]

Some studies of volume changes have been made with other naked cells, such as muscle, nerve, kidney, and liver. In these cells the exact parameters in terms of trans-

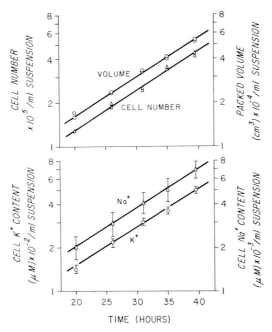

Figure 15.3. The increase in cell number, total packed volume (before inulin space correction) and total Na^+ and K^+ content in randomly growing cells. Bars indicate standard errors.

port fluxes, leak fluxes, relative cation and anion permeabilities, and colloid osmotic content are quite different from those of red blood cells. Also, the cells may have considerable internal structure. Nevertheless, the same general pattern of volume regulations can be seen. The colloidal osmotic pressure tends toward swelling, with this tendency largely compensated by an appropriate non-equilibrium distribution of electrolytes. Mechanical factors due to the internal cellular structure substitutes may play a role, but it has not been carefully evaluated.[14, 28, 37]

THE GROWING NAKED CELL

In the non-growing cell a steady state distribution of electrolytes is maintained, such that the internal and external osmotic pressures are approximately equal and the size of the cell is constant. In growing cells, on the other hand, a continuous increase in volume must occur. A detailed study of this process has been made with tissue culture cells (mouse leukemic lymphoblast L 5178

Y) that can be grown in suspension culture.[13] The cells increase in numbers in an exponential fashion with a doubling time of 11.3 hours. In a randomly growing population the number of cells, the total volume of the population, and the total Na^+ and K^+ content also increase exponentially with the same half-time (Figure 15.3). The volume of the "average" cell in the population is 1200 μ^3. The cellular K^+ and Na^+ concentrations are 136 and 19 mM/liter of cell water (a ratio of 7:1), whereas those of the medium are 5.4 and 136 mM (a ratio of 1:26). Thus the cells constantly maintain an outward gradient of K^+ and an inward gradient of Na^+. The total discrimination in favor of K^+ is of the order of 180:1.

The cellular content of Na^+ and K^+ is determined by the influx and efflux of each cation. It is obvious that in growing cells, with an exponentially increasing cation content, the influx must always exceed the outflux. Indeed, the net flux must lead to a doubling of the cation content each generation time (11.3 hours). The net fluxes, however, are small compared to the unidirectional fluxes, five per cent for K^+ and one per cent for Na^+. In other words, the accumulation of K^+ and Na^+ occurs because the influxes are five per cent and one per cent larger than the outfluxes. The large difference between net fluxes and unidirectional fluxes can also be seen from the isotopic exchange time. Half the K^+ exchanges in 33 minutes, and half the Na^+ in 5 minutes, compared to a doubling of Na^+ and K^+ content in 11.3 hours. Only a small fraction of the total cation inflow represents net gain and the rest represents either a one-for-one exchange of like cations (exchange diffusion) or the balance of pumps against leaks involved in the maintenance of the large cation gradients responsible for the volume regulation.

The data on randomly growing populations represent the behavior of the "average" cell. In order to determine the behavior of an individual cell during its division cycle, it is necessary to study synchronously dividing cells. It is found that the volume of each individual cell increases along the same exponential curve as the whole population, and that after cell division the volume of each daughter cell increases along the same exponential. It must be concluded therefore that the total osmotic content of each cell must also increase in the same exponential fashion. An examination of the individual cation content and fluxes, however, reveals that the control of osmotic content involves discontinuities for particular cations. The Na^+ and K^+ content does not follow the exponential for growth, but fluctuates considerably (Figure 15.4). During the period when the cells are actually dividing with a consequent doubling of the surface area, the K^+ content increases along the exponential line that describes the increase in volume. Thus the net flux of K^+ does not change as a function of volume. The Na^+ content, on the other hand, falls rapidly, indicating a net efflux at the time of cell division. Starting about two hours post-division, the K^+ content falls for the next three or four hours, and thereafter increases rapidly to make up the deficit. Although the Na^+ content increases during this period, it does not compensate completely for the K^+ deficit. Some other substances, perhaps amino acids, must contribute significantly to the osmotic pressure during this period.

An examination of the unidirectional fluxes of K^+ during the division cycle indicates that the influx, efflux and net flux for each daughter cell immediately after division is one-half of those for parent cell. In other words, the splitting of the cell and the doubling of the surface does not change the K^+ fluxes. Two hours after division, however, at the start of the S period of the cycle (the synthetic period), the unidirectional fluxes increase by about a factor of two (Figure 15.5). Thus the doubling of the unidirectional flux that must occur during each division cycle takes place suddenly at a particular point in the cycle. The net flux of K^+ has two discontinuities: on the average the influx is five per cent higher than the efflux; two hours after the cell division, however, the efflux is slightly greater than the influx and a transient net loss of K^+ occurs; from five to seven hours after division the influx is more than five per cent higher than the efflux and the deficit of K^+ content is eliminated.

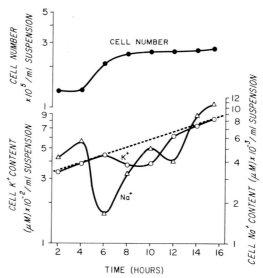

Figure 15.4. Changes in cell count and total cellular Na^+ and K^+ contents in a synchronously growing population. Synchronization was induced by methotrexate-hypoxanthine-TdR treatment; t = 0 on abscissa is the time the cells were transferred into TdR-containing growth media. The dashed line represents total packed volume.

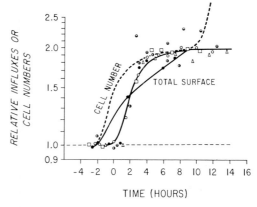

Figure 15.5. Relative changes in K^+ influx, cell counts, and total cell surface in a synchronously growing population. The line for influx was drawn by eye.

It is not yet possible, with the limitations of the existing information, to describe the regulation of volume changes in a growing cell in a quantitative manner. It is obvious, however, that the regulation in a naked cell must be a precise one because any change in total osmotic content is immediately reflected in a change in volume. Yet during the cell division cycle, despite the sudden changes in cell surface, the uptake of large quantities of amino acids and carbohydrates and the synthesis of cellular colloids, the volume must increase in a uniform and controlled manner. Because K^+ and Na^+ are the major osmotic components, the control is probably exerted on the mechanisms of influx and efflux of these cations.

ELECTROLYTE AND VOLUME REGULATION IN WALLED CELLS

The walled cells constitute thousands of species living in every conceivable environment. Electrolyte metabolism and volume regulation, however, have been examined in only a handful of organisms, and extensively only in yeast,[31] E. coli,[32, 33]* and plant roots.[2] Nevertheless, a pattern is evident, which can be summarized in four statements:

1. The volume of the cell is fixed primarily by the volume enclosed by the wall, a structure of mechanical strength sufficient to allow only a small degree of stretching or shrinking under osmotic gradients. Thus, in contrast with the naked cell, volume regulation is largely divorced from electrolyte regulation. Conversely, electrolytes are to a large degree relatively unregulated in terms of maintenance of a constant cellular ionic composition and ionic content.

2. In contrast to the naked cell, the walled cell is not in osmotic equilibrium with the environment. In fact, the osmotic pressure within the cell is always higher than that of its environment (unless experimentally altered), so that the protoplast always tends to swell against the wall, creating a "turgor" pressure. This situation exists regardless of the osmotic pressure of the environment—fresh water, physiological saline, or brine. For example, Staphylococcus aureus, M. lysodeikticus and Aerobacter chromobacter may have an internal osmotic pressure of 25–30 atmospheres; the first two can live in normal saline (8 atmospheres), and the third organism lives in brine (22 atmospheres). For this reason, removal of the wall by enzymatic action results in an explosive swelling, unless the protoplast is protected by a medium of higher osmotic pressure than the normal environment's.[17, 43]

3. In maintaining or developing high osmotic pressures, the cells, whether living in fresh water, body fluids, sea water, or brine, accumulate high concentrations of cations by mechanisms that involve a high degree of discrimination in favor of K^+.

4. During the cell division cycle, the osmotic pressure is markedly increased, largely by the specific accumulation of K^+. In fact, the osmotic content must be approximately doubled before or during each cell division cycle. The growth cycle is triggered by a softening of the wall, so that it is stretched by the turgor pressure. As stretching occurs, new wall material is synthesized, and after division the wall becomes rigid again until the start of the next cycle.

The specific details of electrolyte metabolism differ considerably from organism to organism, and also with the nature of the environment. Certain essential features, however, are common to all organisms. Some details of the systems in the two organisms for which most information is available, E. coli and yeast, will therefore be reviewed briefly. Each faces different osmotic and electrolyte problems, one having a normal habitat in animal fluids (essentially "normal saline"), and the other in fresh water.

In E. coli, the alkali metal cations pass through the membrane by both downhill (passive) transport and "uphill" (active) transport.[32, 33] † The latter involves an inward movement of K^+ and outward movement of Na^+. The membrane is also permeable to anions, such as Cl^-. During the stationary phase of cells suspended in a saline solution, the active cation transport is minimal, the ion gradients are largely dissipated, and the osmotic pressure approaches that of the medium. The cell comes to virtual equilibrium with its environment, with Na^+ and Cl^- distributions approaching those expected in a simple Donnan system. During log phase of growth, on the other hand, the Na^+ content of the cell is

---

* See also Epstein & Schultz, p. 186.

† See also Epstein & Schultz, p. 186.

reduced to the level of 50 mM (compared to 120 mM in the medium) and the K^+ is increased to 211 mM (compared to 5 mM in the medium). The osmotic pressure of the cellular contents is increased considerably above that of the medium, to a level of 500 to 600 mOsm, compared to 265 mOsm in the medium. K^+, is not, of course, the only contribution to the increased osmotic content of cells. For example, the amino acid pools may also increase to a marked degree.[9]

On changing from the stationary phase to the log phase, the active transport system for Na^+ and K^+ is stimulated. It extrudes Na^+ and takes up K^+, resembling the forced exchange of Na^+ and K^+ in animal cells, and is primarily responsible for changes in cation composition. A second kind of exchange, cellular H^+ from metabolic reactions for K^+ from the medium, is probably responsible in large part for the increased osmotic content of the cell.

In yeast, and probably in all fresh water forms, the pattern is somewhat different. Because the salt concentration of the medium is low, the cells have exceedingly small leakages of ions, either of cations or of anions, presumably to prevent the extreme salt dilution that would otherwise occur in the cytoplasm.[30] In the stationary phase, unlike *E. coli,* the active transport systems are still operative, especially in the presence of substrates. Because of the relatively small leakage of ions and the very high activity of the transport systems, the cell is able to maintain very high gradients of K^+ and of osmotic pressure or, in the presence of substrate, to increase them. For example, in cake yeast, the K^+ concentration in the cell is about 150 mM. If the cells stand at room temperature, the K^+ content will slowly fall. If given glucose plus potassium phosphate, however, the K^+ level can increase to 300 mM within 15 minutes.

The electrolyte level in the cell is not regulated. Rather, the cell is geared to accumulate electrolytes, particularly K^+, Mg^{++} and HPO_4^-. The factors which determine the final level are not concerned with regulation but with physiological limits, such as the supply of substrate, the concentrations of electrolytes in the medium,

the pH of the medium and of the cell. If the supply of substrate and electrolyte is adequate, a major limitation on accumulation is the acid-base balance of the cell. Because the membrane is relatively impermeable to anions, accumulation of K^+ must be balanced by excretion of another cation in order that electroneutrality be maintained. Normally the cation used for exchange is H^+ derived from metabolism. The net result of K^+ accumulation is therefore an acidification of the medium and alkalinization of the cell, with K^+ being balanced by organic anions such as succinate, citrate and acetate. The limiting factor in uptake may be the low pH of the medium or the high pH of the cytoplasm. The accumulation of phosphate results in pH changes in the opposite direction, because the phosphate is exchanged for OH^-. If K^+ and phosphate are present together, the changes in pH tend to cancel out. Consequently, much larger amounts of both K^+ and phosphate can be accumulated. The phosphate does not contribute much to the osmotic pressure because it is largely converted in the cell to insoluble granules of highly polymerized polyphosphate. The K^+, however, is mostly in the form of free ion and is a major factor in the osmotic pressure.

The mechanism for transporting cations is highly specific for K^+. The actual array of specificities and relative affinities for the transport systems are as follows: K^+, Rb^+, Cs^+, Na^+, Li^+, Mg^{++}.[1, 4] Furthermore, the specificity for K^+ may be amplified at low pH or in the presence of Ca^{++} because the transport rate for the other ions is specifically reduced.

During growth of a yeast population, two related phenomena are observed. During the stationary phase, the capacity of the active transport system decreases gradually, so that it is only 50 per cent as high after 16 hours and 30 per cent of normal after 48 hours. On reinoculation into fresh growth medium, during the lag period before growth commences, the capacity of the transport system increases, reaching a maximum value during the log phase of growth.* The

* L. Wotring and A. Rothstein, unpublished observations.

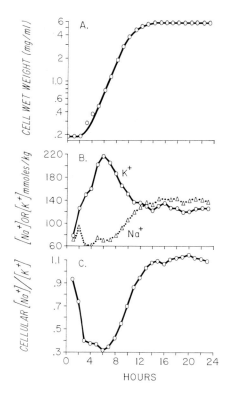

Figure 15.6. Time course of cell growth (*A*), K⁺ and Na⁺ content (*B*) and Na⁺:K⁺ ratio (*C*) in yeast grown at 29°C in Bacto-yeast nitrogen base enriched with NaCl. Cell wet weight was obtained by multiplying the cytocrit by 0.76 in order to correct for intercellular water (From Jones, Rothstein, Sherman & Stannard.[12])

cation concentration of the cell increases in parallel, almost doubling in value. During the accumulation of electrolyte, the discrimination in favor of K⁺ increases dramatically.[12] For example, in cells grown in a medium containing a 20:1 ratio of Na⁺:K⁺, the level of the two cations during the stationary phase was about equal. During the log phase of growth, the Na⁺ decreased and the K⁺ increased fourfold, so that the ratio of Na⁺:K⁺ decreased to 0.3:1. At the end of log phase, the K⁺ concentration fell, while the Na⁺ rose, bringing the ratio once again to 1:1 (Figure 15.6).

The increase in tonicity, and the increased discrimination observed in growing *E. coli* and yeast represent the behavior of the "average" cell during the population cycle.

The changes in electrolyte balance of individual cells during the division cycle have not been described.

DISCUSSION

The sizes of cells are probably related in some manner to the surface-to-volume ratio, which is in turn related to the necessity for rapid exchanges of materials between the cell and its environment. In the course of evolution two basic patterns of volume control have developed. In the naked cells, the cytoplasm is in osmotic equilibrium with the medium; the tendency to swell because of the osmotic pressure of the non-diffusible components of the cell is compensated by the regulation of the content of the cations Na⁺ and K⁺ using a balanced system of ion pumps and leaks. In non-growing cells, the volume can be maintained within fairly narrow limits if the cells are provided with a stable electrolyte environment and with the substrates that supply the energy for the transport systems; during the cell division cycle, a regulated continuous exponential increase in osmotic content results in continuous osmotic swelling of the mother and daughter cells.

In the walled cells, the size is to a large degree independent of the osmotic content. In forms that live in saline, such as *E. coli*, the cells almost reach electrolyte equilibrium during nongrowing periods because the activity of the ion pumps is reduced to a low level, the colloidal osmotic pressure being compensated by the strength of the wall. In fresh water forms such as yeast, the cytoplasm cannot be allowed to come to equilibrium because the dilution of electrolytes of the cytoplasm would be intolerable. Thus, in yeast, the leaks are minimal and pumps do not shut off. During the cell division cycle the internal osmotic pressure must be increased sufficiently above that of the medium to stretch the wall to its new size. In contrast to the naked cell, however, the accumulation of electrolyte is not coincident with, but precedes the increase in volume. Once the turgor pressure exists, the triggering of growth resides in the cell wall mechanisms for softening, stretching and synthesis. In common with the naked cells, however, the mechanism of electrolyte accumulation involves systems discriminatory against Na^+ and in favor of K^+, probably reflecting a common evolutionary origin.

In naked protoplasts that have arisen spontaneously or because of man-made interference with cell wall synthesis, the ability to survive and grow depends largely on the ability of the organism to handle its osmotic size regulation without the supporting wall. Unfortunately, little in the way of specific information on electrolyte and volume regulation has been published concerning protoplasts and wall-less forms. The *Mycoplasmas* and perhaps some L-forms are resistant to osmotic lysis, whereas protoplasts of other forms, prepared experimentally, behave as osmometers and have little resistance to osmotic lysis.[26] The nature of these differences has not been analysed in any detail. That success of the *Mycoplasma* and L-forms in their ability to grow might be due to mechanical factors in the cell membrane is strongly suggested by the influence of bivalent cations and pH on osmotic resistance. Or they may have a very low permeability to water. Or they may have a tolerance to large changes in cell size that would accompany the changes in electrolyte content. The other forms, the protoplasts, can be protected against immediate lysis on removal of the cell wall by use of high osmotic media. For successful growth, however, the protoplast must maintain a controlled increasing osmotic content and size geared to the division cycle. Unfortunately, most microorganisms tend to accumulate very large amounts of sugars, amino acids and electrolytes in an unregulated fashion. In the absence of the wall, the organisms cannot tolerate such a large increase in osmotic content. Their large, unregulated appetite for substrates leads to "overeating", to excessive swelling, and to lysis. The growth of protoplasts might be more successful if the experimenter compensated for the lack of osmotic regulation by placing the organisms on a starvation or bare subsistence diet with respect to K^+ and nutrients (particularly sugars and amino acids). Some adjustment of the external osmotic pressure and salt content during growth stages may also be helpful.

SUMMARY

The removal of the cell wall from microorganisms imposes serious problems of volume regulation on the liberated protoplast. Unfortunately, little is known concerning the capacity for volume regulation in the wall-less forms. The factors involved are, however, similar to those that operate in naked animal cells in which detailed studies of volume regulation have been made. A comparison of volume regulating systems in naked animal cells and in walled microorganisms can, therefore, be expected to throw some light on the problems faced by the naked protoplast. The volume of the walled cell is a function of the turgor pressure of the protoplast balanced against the elasticity of the cell wall, with changes in volume during growth brought about by an increased internal osmotic pressure (largely K^+), and by a softening and stretching of the wall. In contrast, the naked cell is in virtual osmotic equilibrium. The volume is determined almost entirely by the osmotic content, that is in turn determined to a large degree by the steady state distribution of Na^+ and K^+ with active transport of the cations balanced against leaks. During growth of an animal cell a closely regulated increase in osmotic content and volume occurs. When the wall is removed from a normally walled cell, the naked protoplast must not only be protected from immediate osmotic lysis but in addition, if it is to grow, it must increase its osmotic content and thereby its size in a controlled and orderly manner, a task for which it is poorly prepared because it has heretofore relied on the wall to compensate for excessive accumulation of solutes. Organisms such as the L-forms and *Mycoplasmas* have been able to adapt themselves to the new situation, but some protoplasts may need the cooperation of the experimenter in order to cope with their inability to regulate their osmotic content.

REFERENCES

1. Armstrong, W. M., and Rothstein, A.: Discrimination between alkali metal cations by

yeast. I. Effect of pH on uptake. *J. Gen. Physiol.* **48:** 61, 1964.

2. Bennet-Clark, T. A.: Water relations of cells. In: *Plant Physiology, Vol. 2: Plants in Relation to Water and Solutes* (F. C. Stewart, Ed.). Academic Press, New York, 1959: p. 105.

3. Cohen, G. N., and Monod, J.: Bacterial permeases. *Bact. Rev.* **21:** 169, 1957.

4. Conway, E. J., and Duggan, F.: A cation carrier in the yeast cell wall. *Biochem. J.* **69:** 265, 1958.

5. Davson, H.: *A Textbook of General Physiology* (3rd ed.). Little, Brown; Boston, 1964.

6. Dick, D. A. T.: *Cell Water.* Butterworth, London, 1966.

7. Gale, E. F.: Assimilation of amino acids by Gram-positive bacteria and some actions of antibiotics thereon. *Adv. Protein Chem.* **8:** 285, 1953.

8. Gilby, A. R., and Few, A. V.: Osmotic properties of protoplasts of *Micrococcus lysodeikticus. J. Gen. Microbiol.* **20:** 321, 1959.

9. Halvorson, H. O., and Cowie, D. B.: Metabolic pools of amino acids and protein synthesis in yeast. In: *Membrane Transport and Metabolism* (A. Kleinzeller and A. Kotyk, Eds.). Academic Press, New York, 1961: p. 479.

10. Harris, J.: The reversible nature of the potassium loss from erythrocytes during storage of blood at 2-5° C. *Biol. Bull.* **79:** 373, 1940.

11. Hoffman, J. F.: Discussion in: *Regulation of the Inorganic Ion Content of Cells* (CIBA Foundation Study Group No. 5) (G. E. W. Wolstenholme, and C. M. O'Connor, Eds.). Churchill, London, 1960: p. 88.

12. Jones, W. B. G., Rothstein, A., Sherman, F., and Stannard, J. N.: Variation of K⁺ and Na⁺ content during the growth cycle of yeast. *Biochim. Biophys. Acta* **104:** 310, 1965.

13. Jung, C., and Rothstein, A.: Cation metabolism in relation to cell size in synchronously grown tissue culture cells. *J. Gen. Physiol.,* in press.

14. Kleinzeller, A.: The volume regulation in some animal cells. *Arch. Biol.* (Liege) **76:** 217, 1965.

15. Mager, J. Spermine as a protective agent against osmotic lysis. *Nature* **183:** 1827, 1959.

16. McQuillen, K.: Bacterial protoplasts. In: *The Bacteria, Vol. I: Structure* (I. C. Gunsalus and R. Y. Stanier, Eds.). Academic Press, New York, 1960: p. 249.

17. Mitchell, P., and Moyle, J.: Liberation and osmotic properties of the protoplasts of *Micrococcus lysodeikticus* and *Sarcina lutea. J. Gen. Microbiol.* **15:** 512, 1956.

18. ———: Osmotic function and structure in bacteria. *Symp. Soc. Gen. Microbiol.* **6:** 150, 1956.

19. Nickerson, W. J., Falcone, G., and Kessler, G.: Polysaccharide-protein complexes of yeast cell walls. In: *Macromolecular Complexes* (M. V. Edds, Jr., Ed.). Ronald, New York, 1961: p. 205.

20. Passow, H.: Ion and water permeability of the red blood cell. In: *The Red Blood Cell* (C. Bishop and D. M. Surgenor, Eds.). Academic Press, New York, 1964: p. 71.

21. Passow, H., Rothstein, A., and Clarkson, T. W.: The general pharmacology of the heavy metals. *Pharmac. Rev.* **13:** 185, 1961.

22. Post, R. L., Merritt, C. R., Kinsolving, C. R., and Albright, C. D.: Membrane adenosine triphosphatase as a participant in the active transport of sodium and potassium in the human erythrocyte. *J. Biol. Chem.* **235:** 1796, 1960.

23. Rand, R. P., and Burton, A. C.: The pressure inside red cells and the "metabolic pump". *Biophys. J.* **4:** 491, 1964.

24. Razin, S.: Osmotic lysis of Mycoplasma. *J. Gen. Microbiol.* **33:** 471, 1963.

25. ———: Factors influencing osmotic fragility of Mycoplasma. *J. Gen. Microbiol.* **36:** 451, 1964.

26. Razin, S., and Argaman, M.: Lysis of Mycoplasma, bacterial protoplasts, spheroplasts and L-forms by various agents. *J. Gen. Microbiol.* **30:** 158, 1963.

27. Robertson, J. D.: The ultrastructure of cell membranes and their derivatives. *Biochem. Soc. Symp.* **16:** 3, 1959.

28. Robinson, J. R.: Water regulation in mammalian cells. *Symp. Soc. Exp. Biol.* **19:** 237, 1965.

29. Rodwell, A. W.: The stability of *Mycoplasma mycoides. J. Gen. Microbiol.* **40:** 227, 1965.

30. Rothstein, A.: Relationship of the cell surface to electrolyte metabolism in yeast. In: *Electrolytes in Biological Systems* (A. M. Shanes, Ed.). American Physiological Society, Washington, D.C., 1955: p. 65.

31. ———: Membrane function and physiological activity in microorganisms. In: *The Cellular Functions of Membrane Transport* (J. F. Hoffman, Ed.). Prentice-Hall, Englewood Cliffs, 1963: p. 23.

32. Schultz, S. G., Epstein, W., and Solomon, A. K.: Cation transport in *Escherichia coli.* IV. Kinetics of net K uptake. *J. Gen. Physiol.* **47:** 329, 1963.

33. Schultz, S. G., Wilson, N. L., and Epstein, W.: Cation transport in *Escherichia coli*. II. Intracellular chloride concentration. *J. Gen. Physiol.* **46**: 159, 1962.

34. Sears, D. A., Weed, R. I., and Swisher, S. N.: Differences in the mechanism of *in vitro* immune hemolysis related to antibody specificity. *J. Clin. Invest.* **43**: 975, 1964.

35. Sistrom, W. R.: On the physical state of the intracellularly accumulated substrates of β-galactoside-permease in *Escherichia coli*. *Biochim. Biophys. Acta* **29**: 579, 1959.

36. Smith, L.: Structure of the bacterial respiratory-chain system; respiration of *Bacillus subtilis* spheroplasts as a function of the osmotic pressure of the medium. *Biochim. Biophys. Acta* **62**: 145, 1962.

37. Swan, A. G., and Miller, A. T., Jr.: Osmotic regulation in isolated liver and kidney slices. *Amer. J. Physiol.* **199**: 1227, 1960.

38. Sutherland, R., Rothstein, A., and Weed, R. I.: Localization of erythrocyte membrane sulfhydryl groups essential for normal cation permeability. *J. Cell. Physiol.*, 1967, in press.

39. Tabor, C. W.: Stabilization of protoplasts and spheroplasts by spermine and other polyamines. *J. Bact.* **83**: 1101, 1962.

40. Tosteson, D. C.: Regulation of cell volume by sodium and potassium transport. In: *The Cellular Functions of Membrane Transport* (J. F. Hoffman, Ed.). Prentice-Hall, Englewood Cliffs, 1964: p. 3.

41. Tosteson, D. C., and Hoffman, J. F.: Regulation of the cell volume by active cation transport in high and low potassium sheep red cells. *J. Gen. Physiol.* **44**: 169, 1960.

42. Weibull, C.: Osmotic properties of protoplasts of *Bacillus megaterium*. *Exp. Cell Res.* **9**: 294, 1955.

43. ———: Bacterial protoplasts; their formation and characteristics. *Symp. Soc. Gen. Microbiol.* **6**: 111, 1956.

44. Williams, R. E. O.: L forms of *Staphylococcus aureus*. *J. Gen. Microbiol.* **33**: 325, 1963.

16

Ion Transport and Osmoregulation in Bacteria*

Wolfgang Epstein† and Stanley G. Schultz‡

HARVARD MEDICAL SCHOOL

BOSTON, MASSACHUSETTS

Osmoregulation at the cellular level must satisfy both the physiological demands made on the cell and the restrictions imposed by its structure. Most animal cells do not have to adjust to changes in the osmolality of the medium surrounding them, since constancy of the internal milieu is achieved by special organs which control the osmolality of the whole organism within narrow limits. Nevertheless, animal cells must osmoregulate, since they contain high concentrations of nondiffusible osmotically active solutes and their mechanically weak plasma membranes do not withstand more than minute differences in osmotic pressure. Thus, to avoid rupture, these cells must extrude solutes. Considerable evidence suggests that this type of regulation is mediated by an active extrusion of Na^+ by the cell.[23] Bacterial cells, on the other hand (with the exception of those living exclusively in controlled environments such as the ocean), must adapt to growth in media of widely varying osmolality. However, they have no physical need for precise osmoregulation, since the presence of a mechanically protective cell wall allows them to withstand sizeable osmotic pressure differences without rupture. The evidence to be discussed below indicates that growing bacteria regulate their osmolality well above that of the medium. The mechanisms underlying osmoregulation will be examined and a model for such regulation, encompassing an osmotically sensitive ion pump, will be presented.

The focus of this article is on bacteria as osmotic systems, so terms such as *plasma membrane* and *wall* will refer to their osmotic function, the former as the permeability barrier of the cell to small molecules and the latter as the structure responsible for virtually all of the mechanical strength of the cell envelope. *Turgor pressure*[14, 22] is the stress produced in the cell envelope by the difference in osmotic pressure across the plasma membrane. Using terms introduced by Britten & McClure,[3] *downshock* will refer to a sudden decrease, and *upshock* to a sudden increase in medium osmolality. The water activity of solutions will be expressed in *osmolal* units, a 1 osmolal solution being defined as a solution whose water activity is equal to that of a 1 molal solution of a hypothetical non-dissociating solute whose molal osmotic coefficient[29] is unity at all concentrations.

* Work supported by grants from the National Science Foundation and the Atomic Energy Commission.

† Training Fellow of the Basic Science Research Training Program, U.S. Public Health Service (2G-466) of the Department of Medicine, New York University Medical Center, presently on leave.

‡ Established Investigator, American Heart Association.

Osmotic Properties of Bacteria

More than 60 years ago Fischer[14] described the osmotic properties of bacteria, and with but few changes his views still stand. He demonstrated that most Gram-negative organisms have a plasma membrane with permeability properties very similar to those of plant and animal cells. The surrounding wall was recognized as a mechanical support which hindered the movement of sufficiently large macromolecules but allowed small molecules to pass freely. Fischer measured the osmolality of bacteria by suspending cells in test solutions containing varying concentrations of an impermeant solute. The lowest concentration causing *plasmolysis*, the visible retraction of the plasma membrane and its contents from the wall, was taken as a measure of cell osmolality. Fischer found that the minimum osmolality producing plasmolysis was always somewhat higher than that of the medium in which the cells were grown, and concluded that a turgor pressure of the order of several atmospheres was characteristic of these cells. Fischer was unable to plasmolyze Gram-positive bacteria, an observation that is still not entirely explained. Mitchell & Moyle[25] have shown that at least one Gram-positive organism, *Staphyloccocus aureus*, is markedly hyperosmolal to its growth medium; its turgor pressure is 20 to 30 atmospheres. The inability to plasmolyze Gram-positive bacteria is presumably related in part to their high osmolality, and to tight adhesion of the plasma membrane to the wall, so that osmotic forces tending to separate the membrane from the wall cause shrinkage of the whole organism, and in some cases collapse of wall and membrane together, rather than plasmolysis.[25]

The physiological importance of the maintenance of a positive turgor pressure and of regulating this turgor pressure are suggested by a variety of observations. Fischer[14] noted that plasmolyzed cells do not grow. Knaysi[22] found that the turgor pressure of rapidly growing *Escherichia coli* is several times that of the stationary phase cells. A requirement of a positive turgor pressure for macromolecular synthesis in *E. coli* is shown by the fact that decreasing the turgor pressure by upshock causes a temporary cessation of nucleic acid and protein synthesis, these processes resuming again as the turgor pressure increases.[2, *] Bacteria appear to regulate their osmolality to maintain a constant turgor pressure in the face of varying medium osmolality. Plasmolysis measurements on growing *E. coli* showed that the turgor pressure of these cells changed by only 20 per cent when medium osmolality varied over a tenfold range.[22] In measurements on the freezing points of heat-killed cell concentrates Christian & Ingram[7] reported that the cell osmolality of a variety of bacterial species was close to, and in general slightly higher than that of the solid medium on which they were grown. Maintenance of a constant turgor pressure in media of different osmolality is also supported by indirect evidence, to be presented below.

Cell Osmotic Solutes

Bacteria contain high concentrations of a number of low-molecular weight substances, and most of these appear to contribute to the cell osmolality. Theories attributing the accumulation of amino acids [3, 16, 24] and ions[12] to binding by specific sites in the cell have lost favor as more and more work indicates that most of these substances are osmotically active. The arguments for this point of view have been reviewed by Mitchell[25] and by Kepes & Cohen,[20] and rest largely on the following evidence: (a) gentle treatments that impair the integrity of the plasma membrane lead to rapid loss of much of the accumulated solutes;[3, 6, 25] (b) studies with broken cell systems have failed to show the massive and highly specific binding required to explain retention of the solutes on this basis;[20] (c) the ability to take up and accumulate sugars and other compounds depends on the induced synthesis of a macromolecule located in the plasma membrane;[15, 20] (d) metabolic poisons rapidly block the ability of the cell to ac-

* Also: W. Epstein, unpublished observations.

TABLE 16.1

*Solute Concentrations in Four Bacterial Species**

Bacteria	Medium		Cells				
	Na$^+$	K$^+$	Na$^+$	K$^+$	Amino acids	Cl$^-$	PO$_4^{\equiv}$
	mM				*mM*		
Salmonella oranienburg	150	25	130	240	110	<5	50
Staphylococcus aureus	150	25	100	680	440	8	80
Vibrio costicolus	1000	4	680	220	330	140	70
Halobacterium salinarium	4000	32	1370	4600	210	3600	90

* Data from Christian & Waltho;[10] some of the values have been rounded off. *V. costicolus* and *H. salinarium* are halophilic, the former requiring moderate and the latter high salt concentrations for growth.

cumulate or maintain large solute pools;[19, 31] (*e*) downshock with distilled water leads to rapid loss of large fractions of cell solutes;[3, 5, 6, 13] and (*f*) the low freezing points of cell contents can only be explained if most of the cell solutes are osmotically active.[25] An elegant demonstration of the osmotic activity of accumulated β-galactosides was provided by Sistrom,[32] who showed that the accumulation of these compounds by *E. coli* spheroplasts produced cell swelling, as evidenced by a decrease in turbidity of cell suspensions. Direct measurements of the state of solutes in bacterial cells have not been possible due to the small size of these cells, but direct measurements of the mobility and activity of K$^+$ have been made in some animal cells and have shown that this ion is not bound to any great extent.[17, 18] Complex theories based on metabolically dependent binding of various solutes can account for most of the above observations, but certainly the simplest and most direct interpretation is that the solutes are not bound but are maintained at high concentrations by active transport mechanisms which reside in the plasma membrane.

Some of the low-molecular weight ions in the cell must have quite low osmotic activity coefficients. The presence of anionic polyelectrolytes in the cell leads to an interaction with cations resulting in a reduction in the osmotic activity of the latter.[1] Mg^{++}, polyvalent cations in general, and some phosphate compounds, show significant binding to nucleic acid and/or protein *in vitro,* and therefore are probably bound *in vivo* to a considerable extent. But, except for these cases, most of the ions, amino acids, and metabolic intermediates in the cell must be presumed to be free and to contribute to the internal osmolality. Regulation of the cell osmolality thus entails control of the concentration of one or more of these small molecules.

CELL K$^+$

For a knowledge of the cell solutes and their behavior one is indebted largely to the work of J. H. B. Christian. Data[10] on the concentrations of major cell solutes in a number of representative bacterial species are presented in Table 16.1. The pools of amino acids, Na$^+$ and K$^+$ are high in all of the species, but the behavior of K$^+$ is especially noteworthy, since in all species this cation is much more concentrated in the cell than in the medium. In the extreme halophile, cell K$^+$ attains the impressive concentration of 4.6 molal. The importance of K$^+$ in osmoregulation is further supported by other data of Christian & Waltho[9] showing a good correlation between the highest medium osmolality permitting growth of a variety of bacterial species and the K$^+$ content of the cells when they are grown in a standard broth medium (Figure 16.1). Many factors, such as the tolerance of cell enzymes to low water activity or high ionic strength, should affect osmotic tolerance, but if a positive turgor pressure is required for growth, then a *sine qua non* of osmotic adaptation is the ability of the cells to increase their osmolality above that of the medium. The data in Figure 16.1 suggest that the ability to accumulate K$^+$ is of paramount importance for such osmoregulation.

To approach the mechanism of osmoregulation, the dynamic behavior of solutes in growing cells must be examined. Stationary phase cells, used in the studies of Christian and associates,[5, 7, 9, 10, 11] change their composition with time[31] and may have quite different solute composition than do growing cells.[31, 34] Figure 16.2 shows the relationship of K^+ content in growing *E. coli* to medium osmolality. Over the lower range of osmolalities an increase of 180 mOsm in the medium results in a 100 mM increase in cell K^+. The maintenance of electroneutrality requires that each equivalent of K^+ accumulated be exchanged for an equivalent of another cation, or be accompanied by an equivalent of anion. If there is concomitant monovalent anion accumulation, and if both K^+ and the accompanying anion have the same osmotic activity that K salts have in free solution, then cell osmolality would increase exactly as much as medium osmolality. Since, as will be seen below, there is evi-

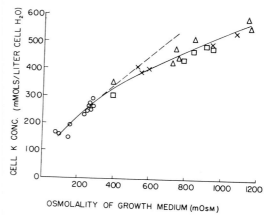

Figure 16.2. Effect of the osmolality of the growth medium on the $[K^+]_i$ of growing *Escherichia coli*. Each point represents the average of 3 to 10 replicate determinations on cells grown with glucose as substrate. The symbols indicate the agent used to adjust the osmolality: $\times$: glucose; $\square$: NaCl; $\triangle$: sucrose; $\bigcirc$: no agent added, standard or dilute medium used. The pH ranged from 6.7 to 7.1. The dashed line is the tangent to the curve over the range of 100 to 400 mOsm. (From Epstein & Schultz.[13])

dence to indicate that anion accumulation does occur, these observations show that accumulation of K^+ and an accompanying monovalent anion can explain osmoregulation in *E. coli* over a considerable range of osmolalities. At high osmolalities this relationship no longer holds; other solutes probably make increasing contributions to cell osmolality in concentrated media.

The only other cell solute whose concentration has been reported to be dependent on medium osmolality is proline;[3] no other amino acids appear to behave in a similar fashion.* These high cell proline concentrations depend on a high concentration of proline in the medium; *E. coli* growing in proline-free media have very small proline pools even in media of high osmolality.[3, †] By contrast, the osmotic dependence of cell K^+ concentration in *E. coli* is independent of medium K^+ concentration and holds for all growth conditions that have been investigated.[13, 33] Pro-

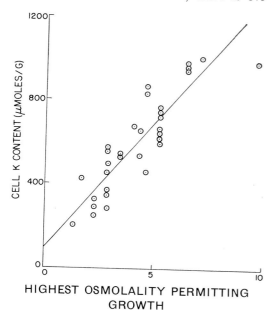

HIGHEST OSMOLALITY PERMITTING
GROWTH

Figure 16.1. Correlation between the K^+ content of 32 strains of bacteria and their ability to grow at low osmolality. The K^+ content was measured in stationary phase organisms grown in a broth medium of 0.39 osmolality. The osmolality was increased by the addition of NaCl to the broth medium. The line is the least-squares line for all of the points. (Redrawn from data of Christian & Waltho.[9])

* J. H. B. Christian, personal communication, 1966.

† W. Epstein, unpublished observations.

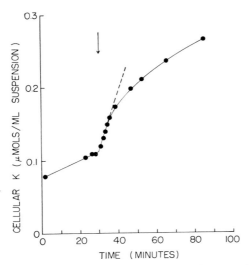

Figure 16.3. Effect of a sudden increase in osmolality on K^+ content of *Escherichia coli* growing in 1.2 mM K^+ medium. At the arrow the osmolality was increased from 202 to 635 mOsm by adding a concentrated solution of glucose in growth medium. The K^+ content of the pre-upshock samples has been multiplied by 0.8 to correct for the dilution produced by upshock. (From Epstein & Schultz.[13])

line may contribute to osmoregulation under some conditions, but it can hardly be part of a common basic mechanism of osmoregulation.

DOWNSHOCK

The mechanisms that the cell uses to control osmolality are revealed in the response of the cells to osmotic stress. Downshock results in a rapid fall in the osmolality of the cell. This effect is undoubtedly due to the development of an osmotic pressure difference too great to be sustained by the cell wall, with the result that the cell membrane is deformed and becomes very permeable to small solutes for a brief period. Amino acids,[3] nucleotides and other phosphate compounds,[3, 5, 6] K^+ [5, 6, 13] and sugars* are all lost rapidly in downshock. When the degree of downshock is moderate no permanent damage to the cell occurs, but more severe osmotic stresses cause extrusion of the protoplast through defects

* W. Epstein, unpublished observations.

in the wall (plasmoptysis) and death of the cell.[8, 22]

The role of the cell wall in resisting osmotic stress is illustrated by the response of different bacteria to downshock. In *E. coli*, exposure to a solution only slightly hypotonic to the growth medium causes loss of solutes,[13] while in *S. aureus*, with its thick wall, a much larger difference in osmotic pressure is required before the cell will leak K^+ and other solutes.[6] In *E. coli* the osmotic stress that the cell can withstand is dependent on temperature, the cell showing leakage of K^+ at 2°C under a degree of osmotic stress insufficient to cause leakage at 37°C.[13] Similar effects of temperature have been observed for retention of proline[21] and arabinose[26] pools in *E. coli*.

UPSHOCK

The response of the cells to upshock reveals the participation of active transport in increasing cell solute concentration. Ørskov[27] was the first to note that plasmolysis of non-growing *E. coli*, produced by upshock, is rapidly reversed when the medium contained both K^+ and substrate, that this reversal of plasmolysis is accompanied by the uptake of K^+, and that the uptake of K^+ is blocked by metabolic inhibitors. He concluded that an active K^+ uptake mechanism was responsible, and suggested a model for K^+ uptake similar to that proposed below. A quantitative determination of the accumulation of K^+ by *Salmonella oranienburg* was reported by Christian,[4] who found that within 60 minutes after resuspension the bacteria had reached a K^+ content very close to that seen in *E. coli* growing in media of comparable osmolality. Upshock in *E. coli* results in a rapid uptake of K^+ (Figure 16.3). This K^+ uptake is not accompanied by the uptake of any of the anions present in the medium.[13] Thus, K^+ must be exchanged for another cation. That this cation is H^+ was deduced from the facts that cell Na^+ concentration does not change, and that the properties of this K^+ uptake mechanism are very similar to those found for a K^+ uptake mechanism coupled to H^+ secretion in this organism.[30] *E. coli* produces considerable acid when using substrates that enter the glycolytic pathway, so the source and availability of the H^+ ions present no problem. Since each mole of H^+ requires the production of an equivalent of anion, this uptake of K^+ in exchange for H^+ results in the net uptake of one mole of K^+ with one equivalent of anion, anion that normally would be excreted accompanied by H^+. Most of the acids secreted by *E. coli* are univalent,[28] so this mechanism can account for the observed relationship between cell K^+ concentration and medium osmolality found in the growing cells (Figure 16.2).

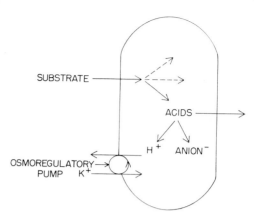

Figure 16.4. A schematic representation of the model of osmoregulation discussed in the text.

A MODEL OF OSMOREGULATION

The mechanism described in the preceding section is presented schematically in Figure 16.4. The essential element of this model is the osmotically sensitive transport system, the K^+-H^+ pump, that takes up K^+ in exchange for H^+ produced in the cell. To effect feedback-controlled osmoregulation, this uptake process should be active when turgor pressure is low and inhibited when turgor pressure is high. Sensitivity of a transport process to the mechanical effects of a difference in osmotic pressure is not an unreasonable postulate, since it is the membrane that is both the site of transport processes and the boundary between two regions of different osmolality. Such an osmotically sensitive pump can account for the rapid adaptation to a change in medium osmolality and carry out osmoregulation during growth in a medium of constant composition. To carry out regulation in growing cells the K^+-H^+ pump would have to be only partially inhibited by the turgor pressure found in growing cells; it should continue to function at just the proper rate to maintain cell K^+ and osmolality constant as cell volume increases.

This model is based on work carried out in *E. coli*, but the evidence (Table 16.1 and Figure 16.1) linking K^+ accumulation to osmoregulation indicates that it may apply to all bacteria. The mechanism of K^+ uptake in bacteria has been subjected

to detailed examination in only two species, but in each of these good evidence for a K^+-H^+ exchange mechanism has been obtained.[30, 34] A K^+-H^+ pump could well be common to all bacteria. The fact that many bacteria do not secrete acid does not constitute evidence against the existence of a K^+-H^+ pump in such bacteria, since the small amount of H^+ secreted by such a mechanism would be masked by the shifts in pH dictated by the catabolic pathways being used by the cell.

Plausible though this model of osmoregulation may be, it has not yet been tested in sufficient detail. One important postulate, that K^+ is accumulated with equimolar amounts of low-molecular weight anions, remains to be confirmed by identification of the postulated anions and measurement of their concentration in the cell. Cell solutes such as amino acids and metabolic intermediates do not appear to play a primary role in osmoregulation, but no comprehensive study of the behavior of these solutes in growing cells has been carried out. Clearly, more work is needed to test the above model for *E. coli* and to examine its applicability as a mechanism of osmoregulation for other bacterial species.

SUMMARY

Bacteria maintain an internal osmolality well above that of the medium in which they grow. This elevated osmolality is due to the accumulation of a number of substances of low molecular weight. Internal osmolality appears to be regulated to maintain a rather constant difference in osmotic pressure between cell contents and the medium. From a consideration of the behavior of cell solutes in different species and under different conditions, one is led to conclude that K$^+$ accumulation probably plays an important role in bacterial osmoregulation. A model for osmoregulation whose central feature is an osmotically sensitive K$^+$ uptake mechanism is proposed. This model fits the known facts of osmoregulation in *Escherichia coli* and may be applicable as a general model of bacterial osmoregulation.

REFERENCES

1. Alexandrowicz, Z.: Osmotic and Donnan equilibriums in poly(acrylic acid)-sodium bromide solutions. *J. Polymer Sci.* **56:** 115, 1962.

2. Bolton, E. T., Britten, R. J., Cowie, D. B., Leahy, J. J., McClure, F. T., and Roberts, R. B.: in *Yearbook 56,* p. 124. Carnegie Institution of Washington, Washington, 1957.

3. Britten, R. J., and McClure, F. T.: The amino acid pool in *Escherichia coli. Bact. Rev.* **26:** 292, 1962.

4. Christian, J. H. B.: The water relations of growth and respiration of *Salmonella oranienburg* at 30°. *Aust. J. Biol. Sci.* **8:** 490, 1955.

5. ———: The effects of washing treatments on the composition of *Salmonella oranienburg. Aust. J. Biol. Sci.* **11:** 538, 1958.

6. ———: The effects of washing treatments on the composition of *Staphylococcus aureus. Aust. J. Biol. Sci.* **15:** 324, 1962.

7. Christian, J. H. B., and Ingram, M.: The freezing points of bacterial cells in relation to halophilism. *J. Gen. Microbiol.* **20:** 27, 1959.

8. ———: Lysis of *Vibrio costicolus* by osmotic shock. *J. Gen. Microbiol.* **20:** 32, 1959.

9. Christian, J. H. B., and Waltho, J. A.: The sodium and potassium content of non-halophilic bacteria in relation to salt tolerance. *J. Gen. Microbiol.* **25:** 97, 1961.

10. ———: Solute concentrations within cells of halophilic and non-halophilic cells. *Biochim. Biophys. Acta* **65:** 506, 1962.

11. ———: The composition of *Staphylococcus aureus* in relation to the water activity of the growth medium. *J. Gen. Microbiol.* **35:** 205, 1964.

12. Cowie, D. B., Roberts, R. B., and Roberts, I. Z.: Potassium metabolism in *Escherichia coli.* I. Permeability to sodium and potassium ions. *J. Cell Physiol.* **34:** 243, 1949.

13. Epstein, W., and Schultz, S. G.: Cation transport in *Escherichia coli.* V. Regulation of cation content. *J. Gen. Physiol.* **49:** 221, 1965.

14. Fischer, A.: *Vorlesungen über Bakterien* (2nd ed.). Fischer Verlag, Jena, 1903: p. 20.

15. Fox, C. F., and Kennedy, E. P.: Specific labeling and partial purification of the M protein, a component of the β-galactoside transport system of *Escherichia coli. Proc. Nat. Acad. Sci. USA* **54:** 891, 1965.

16. Gale, E. F.: Assimilation of amino acids by Gram-positive bacteria and some actions of antibiotics thereon. *Adv. Protein Chem.* **8:** 285, 1953.

17. Hinke, J. A. M.: The measurement of sodium and potassium activities in the squid axon by means of cation-selective micro-electrodes. *J. Physiol.* (London) **156:** 314, 1961.

18. Hodgkin, A. L., and Keynes, R. D.: The mobility and diffusion coefficient of potassium in giant axons from *Sepia. J. Physiol.* (London) **119:** 513, 1953.

19. Horecker, B. L., Osborn, M. J., McLellan, W. L., Avigad, G., and Asensio, C.: The role of bacterial permeases in metabolism. In: *Membrane Transport and Metabolism* (A. Kleinzeller and A. Kotyk, Eds.). Academic Press, London, 1961: p. 378.

20. Kepes, A., and Cohen, G. N.: Permeation. In: *The Bacteria, Vol. 4: The Physiology of Growth* (I. C. Gunsalus and R. Y. Stanier, Eds.). Academic Press, New York, 1962: p. 179.

21. Kessel, D., and Lubin, M.: Transport of proline in *Escherichia coli. Biochim. Biophys. Acta* **57:** 32, 1962.

22. Knaysi, G.: *Elements of Bacterial Cytology* (2nd ed.). Comstock, Ithaca, 1951: p. 155.

23. Leaf, A.: On the mechanism of fluid exchange of tissues *in vitro. Biochem. J.* **62:** 241, 1956.

24. Mandelstam, J.: The free amino acids in growing and non-growing populations of *Escherichia coli. Biochem. J.* **69:** 103, 1958.

25. Mitchell, P. D., and Moyle, J.: Osmotic function and structure in bacteria. *Symp. Soc. Gen. Microbiol.* **6:** 150, 1956.

26. Novotny, C. P., and Englesberg, E.: The L-arabinose permease system in *Escherichia coli* B/r. *Biochim. Biophys. Acta* **117:** 217, 1966.

27. Ørskov, S. L.: Experiments on active and passive permeability of *Bacillus coli communis*. *Acta Path. Microbiol. Scand.* **25**: 277, 1948.

28. Roberts, R. B., Abelson, P. H., Cowie, D. B., Bolton, E. T., and Britten, R. J.: *Studies of Biosynthesis in* Escherichia coli. Carnegie Institute of Washington, Washington, D.C., 1957.

29. Robinson, R. A., and Stokes, R. H.: *Electrolyte Solutions* (2nd ed.). Academic Press, New York, 1959.

30. Schultz, S. G., Epstein, W., and Solomon, A. K.: Cation transport in *Escherichia coli*. IV. Kinetics of net K uptake. *J. Gen. Physiol.* **47**: 329, 1963.

31. Schultz, S. G., and Solomon, A. K.: Cation transport in *Escherichia coli*. I. Intracellular Na and K concentrations and net cation movements. *J. Gen. Physiol.* **45**: 355, 1961.

32. Sistrom, W. R.: On the physical state of the intracellularly accumulated substrates of β-galactoside-permease in *Escherichia coli*. *Biochim. Biophys. Acta* **29**: 579, 1958.

33. Weiden, P. L., Epstein, W., and Schultz, S. G.: Cation transport in *Escherichia coli*. VII. Potassium requirement for phosphate uptake. *J. Gen. Physiol.*, in press.

34. Zarlengo, M. H., and Schultz, S. G.: Cation transport and metabolism in *Streptococcus fecalis*. *Biochim. Biophys. Acta* **126**: 308, 1966.

17

Penicillin Effect on Sodium and Potassium Transport in Bacterial and Protoplast Forms of *Streptococcus faecalis**

Clarence S. Potter

VETERANS ADMINISTRATION CENTER, LOS ANGELES,
CALIFORNIA

*John Z. Montgomerie, George M. Kalmanson and
Lucien B. Guze*

VETERANS ADMINISTRATION CENTER
AND UCLA SCHOOL OF MEDICINE
LOS ANGELES, CALIFORNIA

The experiments of Strominger, Park, Tipper and their colleagues have provided convincing evidence that the target enzyme through which penicillin produces a lesion in bacterial cell wall synthesis is the transpeptidase which crosslinks the mucopeptide polymers.[10, 11, 13] Penicillin is thought to affect the transpeptidation step by its structural resemblance to D-alanyl-D-alanine, a part of one of the substrates.[11] The lack of crosslinkage of the mucopeptide polymers into the sacculus[12] results in a defective cell wall, unable to keep its shape and lend support to the cytoplasmic membrane beneath, leading under ordinary conditions to irreversible damage to the membrane, followed by death of the cell.

While the explanation of the sequence of events is quite satisfactory for the action of penicillin on bacteria in ordinary medium, unanswered questions remain about the survival of penicillin-produced protoplasts† in an osmotically buffered medium. In this case, the osmotic pressure of the medium is designed to oppose that of the cell contents to keep the cytoplasmic membrane undamaged during removal of its structural support, the cell wall, by penicillin.

One of the factors in protoplast survival might be major shifts of cations into and out of the cell. The present studies were designed to examine the cation shifts in *Streptococcus faecalis* in the presence of penicillin.

MATERIALS AND METHODS

ORGANISM

A strain of *S. faecalis*, previously described,[3] was used.

---

* Supported by U.S. Public Health Service Grants AI 02257 and AI 03310.

† As used in this paper, a *protoplast* is an osmotically fragile microbial form with an unknown amount of residual cell wall.

MEDIA

Basic media were brain heart infusion broth and brain heart infusion agar (Difco). Osmotically stabilized media contained, in addition, 0.5 M sucrose, 40 μM magnesium sulfate, and 2% bovine serum albumin (Armour). One thousand units of penicillin per ml (buffered potassium penicillin G, Squibb) were incorporated into the media where indicated. Two thousand units of penicillinase per ml (Baltimore Biological Laboratories) were incorporated into agar of plates used for assays of penicillin-containing cultures.

EXPERIMENTAL DESIGN

The cells, obtained by centrifugation from an 18-hour stationary culture of *S. faecalis* in one liter of broth, were resuspended in about 30 ml of the same broth. One 10 ml aliquot was used to determine the zero time cellular sodium and potassium levels. The remaining two 10 ml aliquots were used to inoculate two prewarmed flasks, each containing one liter of osmotically stabilized broth, and one of which also contained penicillin. The flasks were incubated at 37°C, and samples were taken at one and four hours to determine cellular sodium and potassium and to assay numbers of bacteria and protoplasts present.

ASSAYS FOR NUMBERS OF BACTERIA AND PROTOPLASTS

In order to determine the numbers of bacteria and protoplasts present in a specimen, aliquots were simultaneously cultured by two techniques and the differences calculated. One aliquot was plated on basic agar without osmotic stabilizer. Dilutions for these platings were made through distilled water, and the results were referred to as "non-stabilized" counts. Organisms were also plated on osmotically stabilized agar. Dilutions for these platings were made through osmotically stabilized broth, and the results were referred to as "osmotically stabilized" counts. The difference in the numbers of colony-forming units detected on the non-stabilized compared to stabilized agar represents an osmotically fragile microbial population (protoplasts).

INTRACELLULAR SODIUM AND POTASSIUM DETERMINATION

A slight modification of the method of Schultz & Solomon[6] was used. A concentrated cell suspension obtained from the samples by centrifugation was used to fill cytocrit tubes,[6] which were then further centrifuged in plastic padded tubes (Flexible Mold Material, Fry Plastics Co., Los Angeles, California) for the SW 25.2 rotor of the Spinco Model L-2 ultracentrifuge. After 30 minutes at 20,000 G, wet and dry weights of the resulting pellets were determined, the pellets were digested with 0.4 ml concentrated nitric acid and heated to dryness. The resulting ash was extracted with 2 ml of 0.02% Acationex (Scientific Products). Sodium and potassium were determined flame-photometrically. The amount of sodium and potassium contributed by the medium trapped in the pellet was calculated from the medium concentrations of the ions and from the amount of medium present in each pellet, as determined with ^{131}I-labeled serum albumin (Abbott Laboratories). The intracellular concentrations of sodium and potassium were calculated by the formulation of Schultz & Solomon,[6] and expressed as mEq/liter of intracellular water.

RESULTS

The results of a typical experiment are given in Table 17.1. High concentration gradients for both sodium and potassium, cellular to medium ratio, were maintained by the cells of the 18-hour stationary culture. For sodium the cellular to medium ratio was nearly 3, while the gradient for potassium was slightly larger with a cell-to-medium ratio of more than 4. Upon transfer to fresh medium and incubation in the absence of penicillin, growth occurred, and there was a rapid loss of cellular sodium during the first hour. At the same time, a large amount of potassium was accumulated by these cells to a level more than 30 times that of the medium. By four hours these cells had lost potassium and gained sodium.

TABLE 17.1

Intracellular Sodium and Potassium Concentrations of Streptococcus faecalis *Incubated in the Presence and Absence of Penicillin*

Time (hrs.)	Cation concentrations* (mEq/liter intracellular water)			
	Plus penicillin		Control	
	Na$^+$	K$^+$	Na$^+$	K$^+$
0	444†	52	444	52
1	660	155	150	457
4	562	81	334	189

* Medium concentrations: Sodium, 166 mEq/liter; potassium, 12.4 mEq/liter.

† Zero time intracellular Na and K concentrations were determined on cells of the 18-hour stationary culture used as inoculum for each flask. Data from Potter, Montgomerie, et al.[5a]

TABLE 17.2

Numbers of Bacteria and Protoplasts in Cultures of Streptococcus faecalis *Incubated in the Presence and Absence of Penicillin*

Time (hrs.)	Colony forming units × 10^{-7}		
	Plus penicillin		Control
	Non-stabilized	Staibilzed*	Non-stabilized
0	28	—	28
1	7.8†	11	70
4	4.2	12	200

* "Stabilized" indicates presence of osmotic stabilizer (see text).

† Protoplast population represented by difference between stabilized and non-stabilized count. Data from Potter, Montgomerie, et al.[5a]

When cells of 18-hour stationary culture were transferred to fresh medium containing penicillin, a different sequence of events was seen. Rather than sodium being extruded as in the control cells, a large amount of sodium was gained during the first hour to a level four times that of the medium. At the same time, potassium was accumulated, but to a level only one-third that of the control cells.

The data of Table **17.2** demonstrate that in the absence of penicillin growth occurred, and that in the presence of peni-

cillin protoplasts were produced in increasing numbers as the experiment progressed.

DISCUSSION

In light of present-day concepts of ion transport, three factors were considered which might contribute to the ion distributions found in these experiments: (1) An active pump leading to extrusion of sodium from the cell, (2) an active pump leading to intracellular potassium accumulation, and (3) a transmembrane potential. Neither the intracellular binding of large amounts of ions[8] nor an active pump leading to intracellular accumulation of sodium have been established, and hence will not be considered here.

The 18-hour stationary culture of *S. faecalis* contained an intracellular sodium concentration nearly three times that of the medium. Although unusual, a high intracellular sodium has also been reported for *Leuconostoc citrovorum* by Christian & Waltho.[1] The means by which *S. faecalis* maintains a high intracellular concentration of sodium is not known. However, in preliminary experiments, chloride and sodium levels of stationary cells have been compared. The two oppositely charged ions showed cell-to-medium concentration ratios which were reciprocals, as would be expected if both ions were passively distributed in response to a transmembrane potential.[2] This suggests that a transmembrane potential, cellular contents negative, maintains the sodium gradient. Such a transmembrane potential represents a different situation from that of *Escherichia coli*,[7] in which essentially no transmembrane potential was found in the stationary cells. However, *E. coli* had essentially no concentration gradients for sodium and potassium under these conditions.[6]

During growth in the absence of penicillin, cellular sodium fell, and a large amount of potassium was accumulated during the first hour. This is an expected result for actively metabolizing cells[8] and was also found for *E. coli*.[6] Since the concentration ratios for the two like-charged ions are quite different, one or both must be actively transported against its electro-chemical gradient. With a cell-to-medium concentration ratio of more than 30, an active pump leading to potassium accumulation is likely.

When *S. faecalis* was incubated with penicillin, the cellular sodium concentration increased to four times that of the medium, while cellular potassium rose to only one-third that of controls. The mechanism of the penicillin effect on ion fluxes is not known. However, an alteration of transmembrane potential toward a more negative intracellular environment could account for the sodium gradient observed. The cell-to-medium ratio for potassium was considerably higher than that for sodium, though less than the potassium cell-to-medium ratio for controls. These observations could be explained if penicillin partially inhibited an active pump leading to potassium accumulation. This conclusion is reinforced by the results of Hancock & Fitz-James,[4] who earlier examined the rate of potassium efflux from *Bacillus megaterium* in the presence of penicillin. They found this rate to be increased by penicillin in "isotonic" medium, but not when 0.3 M sucrose was used as an osmotic stabilizer. If penicillin does not cause increased efflux in osmotically stabilized media, the decrease in potassium accumulation compared to the controls must be inhibition of an inward directed active pump.

That the penicillin effect on ion fluxes was linked to production of a cell wall lesion was indicated by two additional experiments. In the first, penicillin was added to an 18-hour stationary culture which was further incubated without change of medium. Under these conditions, no bacteria were killed, no protoplasts were formed, and no alterations of intercellular sodium and potassium levels were found. In the second experiment, use was made of a stable protoplast originally produced from *S. faecalis* by penicillin. This organism was considered stable since, during more than 30 transfers in the absence of penicillin on osmotically stabilized medium, no reversion to the bacterial form was found. In-cubation of this stable protoplast with penicillin resulted in no detectable changes in cellular levels of either sodium or potassium.

Concerning the relationship between the effect of penicillin on ion fluxes and its effect on cell wall synthesis, three possibilities must be examined: First, through the inhibition of cell wall synthesis, ion fluxes are disturbed in some secondary manner. Second, through interference with ion fluxes, penicillin institutes, as a secondary effect, a lesion in cell wall synthesis. And last, that the penicillin effects on cell wall synthesis and on ion fluxes are independent—a second action of penicillin.

The lack of penicillin effect on fluxes of non-growing bacteria and on growing stable protoplasts is evidence against independence of the two effects. With respect to the second possibility, a change in ion fluxes across the cell membrane might interfere with the production of the transpeptidase enzyme whose inaction is thought to cause the lesion in cell wall synthesis.[10, 11, 13] However, the structural similarity pointed out by Tipper & Strom-inger[11] between penicillin and part of the substrate for the enzyme makes it more likely that the action of penicillin is direct inhibition of transpeptidase action rather than inhibition of transpeptidase production. With respect to the first possibility, Strom-inger[9] has observed that the time for half-maximum accumulation of cell wall precursors is about 15 minutes after penicillin treatment of *Staphylococcus aureus*. Such an accumulation of precursor could conceivably alter transmembrane potentials and inhibit active pumps to bring about changes in ion fluxes. On the other hand, it is possible that the cell membrane and the cell wall are not nearly the independent entities, from a functional standpoint, that have been assumed. In addition to its role of structural support for the cell membrane, the cell wall may play an intimate role in the biochemical functioning of the membrane, including ion transport.

The cation shifts observed in these experiments might explain the limited survival of protoplasts following exposure of bacterial cells to penicillin. For example, only one cell in 10,000 was capable of survival and growth as a protoplast when *S. faecalis* was exposed to penicillin in an osmotically buffered medium.[5] It is possible that only a few cells of the penicillin-treated population were able to make the cation transitions rapidly enough to survive.

SUMMARY

Net fluxes of sodium and potassium were measured in *Streptococcus faecalis,* incubated in a medium osmotically stabilized with 0.5 M sucrose in the presence of 1000 units/ml of penicillin. During formation of protoplasts, sodium net flux in these cells was reversed as compared with controls, resulting in intracellular sodium levels higher than those in stationary cells and four times that of the medium. Although the penicillin-treated cells accumulated potassium, they did so to a lesser extent than controls. The lack of penicillin effect on net ion fluxes of non-growing bacteria and of growing stable protoplasts is evidence that the two effects (production of a lesion in cell wall synthesis and alteration of net ion fluxes) are related.

REFERENCES

1. Christian, J. H. B., and Waltho, J. A.: The sodium and potassium content of non-halophilic bacteria in relation to salt tolerance. *J. Gen. Microbiol.* **25:** 97, 1961.
2. Cirillo, V. P.: Symposium on bioelectrochemistry of microorganisms. I. Membrane potentials and permeability. *Bact. Rev.* **30:** 68, 1966.
3. Guze, L. B., Goldner, B. H., and Kalmanson, G. M.: Pyelonephritis. I. Observations on the course of chronic non-obstructed entero-coccal infection in the kidney of the rat. *Yale J. Biol. Med.* **33:** 372, 1961.
4. Hancock, R., and Fitz-James, P. C.: Some differences in the action of penicillin, bacitracin, and vancomycin on *Bacillus megaterium. J. Bact.* **87:** 1044, 1964.
5. Kubota, M. Y., Montgomerie, J. Z., Potter, C. S., Kalmanson, G. M., and Guze, L. B.: Effect of penicillin concentration on protoplast production with *Streptococcus faecalis. Antimicrob. Agents Chemother.* 1966: p. 300.
5a. Potter, C. S., Montgomerie, J. Z., Kalmanson, G. M., and Guze, L. B.: Penicillin effect on intracellular sodium and potassium concentrations of bacterial and protoplast forms of *Streptococcus faecalis. Ibid.,* p. 297.
6. Schultz, S. G., and Solomon, A. K.: Cation transport in *Escherichia coli.* I. Intracellular Na and K concentrations and net cation movement. *J. Gen. Physiol.* **45:** 355, 1961.
7. Schultz, S. G., Wilson, N. L., and Epstein, W.: Cation transport in *Escherichia coli.* II. Intracellular chloride concentration. *J. Gen. Physiol.* **46:** 159, 1962.
8. Solomon, A. K.: Ion transport in single cell populations. *Biophys. J.* **2:** 79, 1962.
9. Strominger, J. L.: Microbial uridine-5'-pyrophosphate N-acetylamino sugar compounds. I. Biology of the penicillin-induced accumulation. *J. Biol. Chem.* **224:** 509, 1957.
10. Tipper, D. J.: An uncross-linked intermediate in bacterial cell wall synthesis and the inhibition of its cross-linking by penicillin. *Fed. Proc.* **25:** 344, 1966.
11. Tipper, D. J., and Strominger, J. L.: Mechanism of action of penicillins: a proposal based on their structural similarity to acyl-D-alanyl-D-alanine. *Proc. Nat. Acad. Sci. USA* **54:** 1133, 1965.
12. Weidel, W., and Pelzer, H. Bagshaped macromolecules—a new outlook on bacterial cell walls. *Adv. Enzym.* **26:** 193, 1964.
13. Wise, E. M., Jr., and Park, J. T.: Penicillin: its basic site of action as an inhibitor of a peptide cross-linking reaction in cell wall mucopeptide synthesis. *Proc. Nat. Acad. Sci. USA* **54:** 75, 1965.

18

Discussion

Dr. Claes Weibull, Chairman

Drs. Roger Cole, Philip C. Fitz-James, Otto E. Landman

CHAIRMAN WEIBULL: I would like to ask a question of Dr. Fitz-James about his collected mesosomes. Did you look for some enzymes in the isolated mesosomes?

DR. FITZ-JAMES: We did look for some succinic dehydrogenase, and all I can say is that at the high Lubrol concentration both the interface and the pellet fractions were completely inactive, the activity being located in the supernatant fraction. It was stripped off.

DR. COLE: I would like to refer briefly to the morphology of these organisms as seen by electron microscopy. We have been working with group A streptococcal L-forms and some other streptococci, which show in the media we use a form of growth that no one has described in terms of electron microscopy: there is tremendous accumulation, at about three days—the peak of logarithmic growth—of very large multiloculated bodies. These, in turn, contain myriads of very small bodies which we call elementary bodies; some of these are filamentous; some are as small as 500 Å in diameter (although other evidence from filtration experiments indicates that bodies this small are incapable of forming colonies

when replated). I wonder if any of the other electron microscopists, or anybody else, has any similar observations.

I also have a question regarding the organisms which revert to *Bacillus subtilis* and have cell walls but do not contain mesosomes (which apparently are the majority): can cells without mesosomes go on to form the new population of presumably normal *B. subtilis* cells, which can then behave in cellular division and replication in a normal fashion?

DR. LANDMAN: Examination of thick sections shows that only a quarter of the cells that have reverted and are already dividing contain mesosomes; three quarters are devoid of mesosomes. So, the idea is that division can in fact occur in the complete absence of mesosomes.

DR. COLE: If you keep going on, is the end result a population without mesosomes?

DR. LANDMAN: The particular medium we use produces that sort of effect. It would be necessary to continue using that medium, which is something we have not tried. As far as we can tell, the cells keep going on the same way.

III.
GENERAL CONSIDERATIONS OF PROTOPLASTS, SPHEROPLASTS AND L-FORMS

Morton Hamburger
Frederick A. Rasmussen, Jr.
CO-CHAIRMEN

19

L-Forms, Protoplasts, Spheroplasts:
A Survey of *in Vitro* and *in Vivo* Studies

Ruth G. Wittler

WALTER REED ARMY INSTITUTE OF RESEARCH
WASHINGTON, D.C.

As subjects of interest and study, L-forms, protoplasts and spheroplasts are relatively new. L-forms of bacteria were first described only a little over 30 years ago, and protoplasts of bacteria less than 15 years ago. As phenomena of microbial growth, however, these morphologic variants must be about as old as are the bacteria themselves. Whereas interest in L-forms and protoplasts was, at first, purely academic and restricted to relatively few laboratories, interest now, as the calling of this conference demonstrates, is widespread among physicians and scientists engaged in diverse disciplines.

A historical survey of the complete field of microbial protoplasts, spheroplasts and L-forms would have to be either extremely superficial or prohibitively long. Moreover, the literature dealing with many areas of the field has already been discussed in a number of excellent reviews, so that here these reviews need only to be indicated.

One aspect of the subject that has not been treated comprehensively in any of the earlier reviews and which, in fact, has only lately evoked general interest, is that of occurrence, behavior and role of L-forms, protoplasts, spheroplasts and transitional forms of bacteria *in vivo*. The literature on this aspect I will, therefore, discuss in greater detail.

LITERATURE ON PRODUCTION, MORPHOLOGY, BIOLOGY AND BIOCHEMISTRY OF BACTERIAL VARIANTS

The concept of bacteria capable of reproduction in a morphologic form completely different from the classical bacterial form has its origins in some of the very early studies on filterable and "gonidial" or granule-like forms of bacteria, a subject reviewed by Hadley[28] and by Klieneberger-Nobel.[40] The discovery of the first L-form, that of *Streptobacillus moniliformis*, by Klieneberger in 1935, and the production of L-forms from many other genera of bacteria by Dienes from 1939 onward have been described in reviews by Dienes & Weinberger,[14] Tulasne,[71] and Klieneberger-Nobel.[41] These publications also cover a wealth of information on morphology, cultivation, life cycles, and biological and biochemical properties of stable and unstable L-forms. A partial list of other reviews and texts which lead the reader to still further literature on L-forms are those by Tulasne,[72] Minck,[56] Minck & Lavillaureix,[58] Freundt,[18] Terranova,[68] Timakov & Kagan,[69] and Klieneberger-Nobel.[42] Many of these reviews include discussions on the similarities and distinctions between L-forms and mycoplasmas, while others examine the similarities and distinctions between L-forms and other more or less related variants. The physiology and chemistry of L-forms have been reviewed by Smith[66] and compared with the physiology and chemistry of the pleuropneumonia-like organisms. A precise definition for at least one morphologic variant, the L-form, was agreed upon and published by a group of investigators[4] who met in Lausanne in 1956.

The concept of protoplast is actually derived from botany, where the term is used to designate that part of the plant cell which is the inner, metabolically active portion surrounded by a semipermeable cytoplasmic membrane distinct from the outer, rigid cell wall. Bacterial protoplasts were experimentally produced by Tomcsik & Guex-Holzer[70] in 1952 and independently by Weibull[76] in 1953. The organism used for these studies was *Bacillus megaterium*, and the inducing agent employed was lysozyme. It was Weibull who named the spherical, cell wall-free bodies *protoplasts*. Agreement on the definition of the term protoplast when applied to bacteria was reached by Brenner and others.[6]

In 1956 Lederberg[48] and several other investigators,[2, 60, 83] using different inducing techniques, produced protoplast-like bodies from *Escherichia coli*. The term *spheroplast* has come into use to distinguish those forms derived from Gram-negative organisms (and from certain Gram-positive organisms) which, though osmotically sensitive spheres, yet retain parts of the cell wall structure and may reproduce or revert to classical bacterial form.

Extensive reviews dealing with the production, morphology, physical, chemical, and biological properties and behavior of protoplasts and spheroplasts have been published by Weibull[77, 78] and McQuillen.[52, 53] Spizizen[67] has published detailed methodology for the preparation and use of protoplasts. A comprehensive and recent review by Martin[49] includes a discussion of the interaction of bacteriophages and phage fragments with protoplasts and spheroplasts, as well as a brief discussion of yeast protoplasts.

IN VIVO STUDIES

BACTERIAL VARIANTS IN EXPERIMENTAL HOSTS

The first investigator to isolate an L-form directly from an animal host was Klieneberger,[39] who in 1938 reported the cultivation of the L-form of *S. moniliformis* from the lungs of a laboratory rat. The L-form occurred "as an independent organism (not associated with the bacillus) in the lung lesions". This finding was the starting point for the many subsequent investigations on the occurrence and behavior of L-forms and related variants *in vivo*, and on their possible role in pathogenicity.

Klieneberger[39] examined the question of pathogenicity of L-forms and reported "that mice could not be infected by any of the conventional routes by the L-form of a *S. moniliformis* strain which itself was pathogenic."[41] Dienes, on the basis of his own investigations on injection of animals with L-forms, came to the same conclusion as Klieneberger, i.e., that "when bacteria were transformed into L-forms, their pathogenicity had disappeared in all cases."[14] Both of these investigators had, nevertheless, noted that when unstable L-forms reverted in the experimental animal to bacterial forms, the bacteria were again pathogenic, and the animal succumbed to the bacterial infection.

In the middle 1950's Freundt[17] carried out one of the classical studies confirming earlier investigations[39, 63, 65] on the nonpathogenicity of L-forms *per se*, and again demonstrated that pathogenicity became evident only after reversion to the bacterial form had occurred *in vivo*. In mice inoculated with a partially stabilized L-form of *S. moniliformis*, infection remained latent until reversion from L- to bacillary form occurred; then the mice succumbed to streptobacillary infection. Furthermore, he showed that vaccination with the L-form of this organism was relatively effective in protecting mice challenged with the L-form, but completely ineffective in protecting against challenge with the bacillary form.

A study by Wittler[79] accorded with and extended these observations. Mice were inoculated intranasally with unstable L-forms of *Hemophilus pertussis* (today these variants would be termed "glycine induced spheroplasts"). Reversion *in vivo* of the variant form to classical bacillary form was followed in stained impression preparations made from the lungs of mice sacrificed from the second to the twenty-fourth post-inoculation day. There was generally rapid conversion *in vivo* to the bacillary form, accompanied by morbidity or death of the mice. One mouse, however, which had been inoculated intranasally and which showed a mild illness, was sacrificed 14 days after inoculation; its lungs were found to contain no bacilli but only small granule-like forms which in culture reverted slowly through various transitional stages to *H. pertussis*. This finding seemed to indicate that in an appropriate *in vivo* environment the variant form, in the absence of revertant bacteria, might exert a slight pathogenic effect.

Recent investigations have also suggested that variant forms, inoculated into a site that allows their persistence, may retain a low degree of pathogenicity. Koptelova and associates[44, 45] studied experimental meningitis and meningoencephalitis in rabbits inoculated with stable L-forms of streptococci and staphylococci. The normal coccal forms were inoculated into other rabbits for comparison. The suboccipital route of infection was employed. Whereas infection with normal bacteria produced an acute meningitis with a frequently lethal outcome in 40 to 80 per cent of the animals in two to five days, L-form infection produced a somewhat similar clinical picture but ran a longer and more torpid course, killing about 12 per cent of some 30 animals, usually between the seventh and fifteenth day. Cerebrospinal fluid, drawn at various times during the course of the infection, yielded cultures positive for L-forms on the second to fifth day from 50 per cent of the animals injected; these L-form cultures could not be maintained in further serial subculture. The authors did not state whether L-forms or bacterial forms were isolated from rabbits dying between the seventh and fifteenth day. However, histologic examination showed marked pathologic changes in the brain both early and late in L-injected animals.

The effect of the the site of injection on the survival and persistence of bacterial variants *in vivo* was also illustrated by Alderman & Freedman.[1] They injected penicillin produced protoplasts of *E. coli* into the renal medulla of rabbits and demonstrated the ability of these protoplasts, even when given in relatively small numbers, to survive and multiply in the hypertonic environment of the renal medulla. Infection was initiated, and *E. coli* revertants were isolated from the kidneys at autopsy. Far greater numbers of bacilli were required to infect the renal cortex.

Although L-forms *per se* have only rarely been shown to initiate infection apparent at a clinical level, their toxicity was early attested. Minck[54, 55] in 1950 was the first to demonstrate experimentally the toxigenicity of L-forms. He injected mice intraperitoneally with the stable L-form of *Vibrio cholerae*; the organism produced peritonitis and killed many of the mice within three days. Death was apparently caused by the vibrio endotoxin which was retained by the L-form.

In the same laboratory, Lavillaureix and Tulasne[46, 73, 74] continued with studies on vibrios using the L-form of a vibrio isolated from water in Egypt. This organism was pathogenic when injected intraperitoneally into mice and could be reisolated several days later from the peritoneum of animals that succumbed. Heat-killed L-forms and L-form extracts were also lethal. Thus the L-form retained the endotoxic properties of the parent vibrio which also, whether alive or heat-killed, was lethal for mice.

A demonstration of the retention of an exotoxin by L-forms was reported by Scheibel & Assandri.[62] The stabilized L-forms of *Clostridium tetani* injected intramuscularly were shown to retain the capacity to produce tetanus toxin, and the amount of toxin produced by the L-form was of the same order of magnitude as that produced by the parent bacillus.

Using unstable L-forms (glycine-induced spheroplasts) of *H. pertussis*, Wittler* found that inoculation of relatively large doses intraperitoneally into mice produced a rapidly fatal toxemia just as did the bacillary form of the organism. The L-form was, however, somewhat more toxic than the bacillus when equivalent amounts of organisms, based on nitrogen content, were injected.

Other investigators using the intravenous route of inoculation have found L-forms less toxic than the parent bacterial forms. Dasinger & Suter[12] compared the toxicity of stabilized, penicillin-produced L-forms of *Salmonella paratyphi* B with that of the parent bacterium. Intravenous inoculation into mice made highly sensitive to endotoxic shock showed that the L-form was 5.5–9 times less toxic than the bacterial form.

Recently, Kagan and associates[37] studied the toxigenic and immunogenic properties of penicillin-produced L-forms of *Salmonella typhimurium*. The L-forms did not kill sensitive animals when injected intravenously or intraperitoneally, but instead were highly dermatotoxic when injected intracutaneously into rabbits. The L-forms were immunogenic, but some immunized animals developed marked reactions, including severe abscesses, while others developed a high degree of reactivity which resulted in death.

The production of abscesses by L-forms, just mentioned above, was a subject that had been investigated a decade earlier by Minck & Fruhling.[57] They found that intradermal or subcutaneous inoculation of "nonpathogenic" L-forms into guinea pigs or rabbits produced abscesses which evolved slowly through various stages toward final healing. These abscesses were of a type quite different from those provoked by the parent bacterial forms. Although Giemsa stains of pus from the lesions revealed great numbers of small granules located both intra- and extracellularly, all cultures in a variety of media remained

* Unpublished data.

sterile. The authors speculated on the possibility that these sterile abscesses might have been provoked by chemical constituents of the L-forms, especially lipids, since ether and chloroform extracts produced similar abscesses.[56]

Embryonated eggs have been employed from time to time to test for pathogenicity of L-forms, and diverse experimental results have been obtained.[9, 32] Hannoun and colleagues[29] studied the effect of the "granular" form of *Streptococcus viridans sanguis* in embryonated eggs; after inoculation into the yolk sac, there was a period of delay before the appearance of lesions, which were found to contain the normal streptococcal form.

Brier and associates[7] used unstable antibiotic-induced L-phase cultures of *Staphylococcus*, *Proteus*, *Salmonella* and *Escherichia* for injection into the allantoic sac. When the infected eggs were treated with appropriate antibiotics, the organisms remained in the L-phase, and the embryos survived. When antibiotic treatment ceased, or when no antibiotic treatment was given, the organisms reverted rapidly to classic bacterial form and killed the embryos.

In contrast to these reports, Minck[56] found that serial passage of a stable *Proteus* L-form in the yolk sac of embryonated eggs resulted in lesions and death of the embryos. The L-form could regularly be recovered in culture from the yolk sac.

There would seem to be a need for further studies comparing routes of inoculation, ages of embryos, species of bacterial L-forms and degrees of stability of the L-forms before the conflicting observations on pathogenicity for eggs can be resolved.

At the borderline, between *in vivo* and *in vitro* studies, there are a few recent publications dealing with the effect of bacterial variants on animal cells or tissue cultures. Lavillaureix[47] had previously examined this subject. Freeman & Rumack[16] in 1964 reported on the cytopathogenic effect of glycine- and penicillin-produced spheroplasts of *Brucella suis* on monocytes from guinea pig peritoneal exudates. Spheroplasts prepared from smooth *B. suis* were phagocytized faster than the normal smooth bacilli, whereas spheroplasts from rough *B. suis* were phagocytized to a lesser extent than normal rough bacilli. Microscopic observation showed that spheroplasts from both smooth and rough bacilli had destroyed a major portion of the phagocytes within four hours.

Kagan and associates[35, 36] studied the cytopathogenic effect of stable L-forms of typhoid bacilli and group A beta-hemolytic streptococci in tissue cultures. The tissues used were chick embryo fibroblasts, monkey kidney, human embryonic kidney, Hep₂ and CMH. The L-forms all showed a high degree of cytopathogenicity for chick embryo fibroblasts but varied from strain to strain in their effects on other cell cultures. The authors noted a relatively greater cytopathogenic effect by L-strains which had been isolated from patients.

In this area there is both need and scope for investigations on the interactions between L-forms and isolated tissue cells, where pathogenicity and toxicity can be described in terms of events that can be followed at a cellular level.

CONVERSION OF BACTERIA TO VARIANT FORMS IN EXPERIMENTAL HOSTS

The conversion *in vitro* of classical bacteria to L-forms and large bodies had been charted in considerable detail by the 1950's. Investigators next sought to demonstrate a similar conversion of bacterium-to-variant form *in vivo* and to interpret its significance both for the host and for the microbe. These workers injected animals with normal bacteria and at autopsy cultured for L-forms or other variants.

Wittler[79] in 1952 inoculated normal and immunized mice intraperitoneally and intranasally with the bacillary form of *H. pertussis*. In serial, stained preparations made at autopsy, it was apparent that the bacilli underwent a change in the lungs and peritoneal cavity to the L-form, and that the rate and extent of this transformation increased with the duration of the infection and with the degree of im-

munity in the mice. Furthermore, the *in vivo* survival of the L-form was influenced by the site of the infection, persistence of L-forms being considerably longer in the lungs than in the peritoneum. From some of the immunized and challenged mice no bacilli were cultivated, only large and small round or pleomorphic bodies and small granules frequently embedded in a matrix of amorphous material. On agar these variant forms reverted slowly through various transitional stages to *H. pertussis*.

A few years later Grasset and associates[20-23] studied the morphologic transformation of *Proteus*, *Klebsiella*, *Escherichia* and *Pasteurella* bacilli in the peritoneum of mice. Immediately after inoculation of the bacilli, the mice were treated with penicillin or with specific immune serum. Examination by phase contast microscopy of the peritoneal fluid of sacrificed animals revealed the change from normal bacillary forms to filamentous forms, globular bodies and L-forms.

Comparable observations on the association of immunity and *in vivo* conversion to variant form were made in 1960 by Carey and associates.[8] They injected mice intraperitoneally with various bacterial species, *Salmonella*, *Shigella*, *Proteus* and *Escherichia*, and noted that the rod shaped organisms changed *in vivo* to protoplast-like forms. Specific immunity or increased nonspecific resistance in the mice increased the rate and the percentage of change to protoplast form.

The association of antibiotic therapy and *in vivo* conversion to variant form demonstrated earlier by Grasset was also followed up in later investigations. Guze and Kalmanson[25, 26, 27, 38] produced experimental enterococcal pyelonephritis in rats by intravenous injection of *Streptococcus faecalis*. Treatment with penicillin effected an apparent cure as judged by standard bacteriologic cultures of kidney homogenates. However, when the homogenates were cultured on osmotically stabilized media, it was found that the protoplast form of the enterococcus persisted in the kidney for at least 13 weeks after therapy.

There was no significant protoplast formation in the kidneys of infected but untreated rats. Furthermore, it was found that erythromycin, which was ineffective against the bacterial form of the infection, was able to kill the protoplast form *in vivo*.

Conversion of a bacterium to L-form *in vivo* appears to be associated not only with suitability of infection site, enhanced immunity or antibiotic therapy of the experimental host, but also with the relative virulence of the initial bacterial inoculum. This was demonstrated by Mortimer[59] in a carefully controlled study on the conversion of group A streptococci to typical L-forms in mice. The mice were inoculated intraperitoneally with lethal doses of streptococcal strains of lower or higher virulence. At death the animals were autopsied, and peritoneal exudate and heart blood were cultured on L-form medium and blood agar plates. Fifteen of 36 mice inoculated with the less virulent strains yielded typical L-type colonies on L-form medium containing penicillin, whereas only two of 58 mice inoculated with the more virulent strains yielded L-colonies. When blood and peritoneal exudate were cultured on L-form medium containing no penicillin, confluent streptococcal growth was obtained. Mortimer went on to show that the L-forms originated *in vivo*, not simply on the penicillin agar. He suspended, in osmotically stabilized broth, blood or peritoneal exudate from mice that had succumbed to infection, and passed the suspensions through millipore membrane filters which retained the normal bacterial form. The filtrates were cultured on media with and without penicillin. No bacterial colonies appeared on any of the media, but typical L-form colonies grew out even on media without penicillin. The L-forms isolated from these mice could be propagated in series on penicillin-containing medium as typical L-form colonies and reverted to streptococci on penicillin-free medium. Serologic typing proved that both the L-forms isolated from mice and the revertant streptococci were of the same specific type as the respective parent organism originally inoculated. Mortimer thus demonstrated that mice inoculated with streptococci of relatively low virulence yielded a higher proportion of L-forms than mice inoculated with more highly virulent streptococci, and that conversion to the L-form took place *in vivo*.

I should mention yet one recent tissue culture study in which Hatten & Sulkin[30, 31] inoculated a virulent strain of *Brucella abortus* into hamster kidney tissue cultures and recovered various colonial types of unstable L-forms of *B. abortus*. These authors showed that treatment with tetracycline or a combination of penicillin and streptomycin reduced the number of positive L-form cultures obtained from the infected tissue cells.

ISOLATION OF BACTERIAL VARIANTS FROM HUMAN INFECTIONS

The first report on the isolation of an L-form from a human being was that of Dienes & Smith[13] in 1944. They cultivated the L-form of a *Bacteroides* sp. from a clinical specimen of "pus accumulated in the peritoneal cavity following infection of the fallopian tubes". Since the primary isolate of pure L-colonies could not be maintained in subculture, and reinoculation of the pus into other media yielded a mixture of L-forms and bacilli, the authors themselves expressed certain doubts as to whether the organism existed in the L-phase in the host.

Another seven years passed before Dolman and associates[15] described the isolation of the L-form of *S. moniliformis* from the blood of two Indian children with rat-bite fever. During the first eight weeks of their illness, only the streptobacillary form of the organism was isolated from repeated blood cultures. However, after large doses of penicillin were administered to the patients, their blood cultures became negative for streptobacilli but positive for the L-form of the organism. Since penicillin did not eradicate the L-form bacteremia, successive courses of aureomycin, streptomycin and organic arsenicals were administered, after which the blood cultures became negative for all organisms, and the patients presented no further symptoms of infection.

In its major aspects the Dolman study was a forerunner of that reported by Wittler and colleagues[81] in 1960. The latter was a long-term bacteriologic investigation of a patient with an interventricular septal defect and subacute bacterial endocarditis. Blood and bone marrow cultures taken from the patient before the start of antibiotic treatment yielded a microaerophilic *Corynebacterium* sp. During penicillin therapy (at times in combination with other antibiotics) the clinical symptoms subsided, and bacilli disappeared from the blood, but transitional forms, including unstable L-forms, appeared and persisted in the host. Each time penicillin treatment was interrupted, the patient suffered a recurrence of fever and illness, and the bacillary form of the organism reappeared in her blood. Thus it appeared that the antibiotic sensitive *Corynebacterium* was associated with active stages of the infection, whereas the persistent and antibiotic resistant transitional form of the organism was associated with latent stages of the infection.

During four years of daily penicillin treatment, while the patient remained symptom-free, the transitional form of the organism could regularly be isolated from her blood and reverted to the parent *Corynebacterium* in appropriate culture media. The need for surgical repair of the septal defect was clearly indicated, but posed a grave risk as long as the bacteremia persisted. Therefore a heat-killed vaccine was prepared from one of the patient's *Corynebacterium* strains which had been isolated in its transitional form and then reverted to the bacillus. It was hoped that the autogenous vaccine would stimulate the host's antibacterial defenses, specific and nonspecific, and, in conjunction with antibiotics, prevent reversion to the bacillus during surgery. The vaccine was given subcutaneously in small increasing doses for nearly a year. It was soon found that penicillin could be discontinued without the former concomitant reappearance of the bacillus. After six months of vaccine therapy alone, although the transi-

tional form could still be isolated from the blood, reversion could no longer be obtained in culture media. After another half year during which no revertable isolates were obtained, open heart surgery to repair the septal defect was successfully accomplished, and the patient recovered.[80]

The isolation of microbial variants from the blood of endocarditis cases has since been reported by a number of other laboratories. Kagan & Mikhailova[34] described the isolation of L-forms of streptococci from the blood of patients with septic endocarditis or "rheumatism" (this term was not defined). Primary blood cultures as well as subsequent passages were made on media with and without penicillin and osmotic stabilizer. From 13 out of a total of 20 patients with rheumatism, L-forms were isolated upon primary culture: from three using media without penicillin, from six using media both with and without penicillin, and from four using penicillin media only. Streptococci were not isolated upon primary culture, and only L-colonies grew in the first and second passages. Reversion to streptococci took place on media without penicillin in three to four months after four to six passages, and was preceded by development of transitional and heteromorphic forms. From 14 septic endocarditis cases, six L-cultures were isolated, one of which grew in primary culture on media without penicillin, two on media both with and without penicillin, and three on penicillin media only. Of the seven primary L-isolates from rheumatism and septic endocarditis obtained on penicillin media only, three eventually reverted to streptococci. There were three septic endocarditis cases in which both L-forms and streptococci appeared in the primary cultures, the L-colonies on media with penicillin, the streptococci on media without penicillin. Here it was impossible to determine which the *in vivo* form of the organism had been. From five other cases of rheumatism or septic endocarditis, streptococci only were recovered on primary culture in the absence of penicillin. None of these strains gave rise to L-forms when passed serially on penicillin media. These results led the authors to conclude that in rheumatism and septic endocarditis the pathogen could exist in the host in the L-form.

L-forms of *S. faecalis* were cultivated by Tunstall & Mattman[75] and Mattman & Mattman[50] from patients with subacute bacterial endocarditis and septicemia. These patients had not responded to antibiotic treatment, although on routine diagnostic media their blood cultures were negative for organisms. Cultivation of blood and spinal fluid of the patients in a special L-form medium yielded spheroplasts, L-forms and transitional forms which on further subculture reverted to *S. faecalis*.

The first case of endocarditis from which protoplasts of a yeast were isolated appeared just this year. Rosner[61] described a fatal case of endocarditis caused by *Candida tropicalis*. Although the patient was given adequate antibiotic therapy, and routine blood cultures were negative for growth, there was clinical evidence of active endocarditis. Osmotically stabilized medium was then employed for another series of blood cultures. Eight out of nine successive blood cultures in this series yielded osmotically sensitive protoplasts of *C. tropicalis*. The protoplasts required 103 days in culture to revert to the yeast form. Post-mortem tissue sections from mitral valve lesions and embolus revealed yeast cells with and without visible cell walls.

Infections other than endocarditis have also yielded variant growth forms. In 1962 there was a publication by Klodnitskaia[43] concerning the isolation on culture media and in embryonated eggs of L-forms of streptococci from 28 of 42 scarlet fever patients treated with penicillin.

In the same year Wittler and associates[82] reported the finding of transitional forms and unstable L-forms in cultures of the blood of rheumatic fever patients. These forms could not be maintained in subculture, and their reversion and identification was never obtained. At a later time Wittler and Mortimer* collaborated in an effort to confirm the above observations. They cultured numerous blood specimens from

* Unpublished studies.

untreated and treated rheumatic fever cases, using a variety of media suitable for L-forms, and never obtained any growth at all in their cultures.

Shchegolev & Starshinova[64] cultured the blood of typhoid patients and carriers on media with and without penicillin. The bacterial form of *Salmonella typhi* was isolated at the onset of the disease, but "granular L-form elements" were isolated later on during the convalescent period.

Eleven patients with a history of recurring boils and staphylococcal infections were studied by Godzeski and associates.[19] Blood from these patients cultured in L-form medium yielded L-phase cells but no classical bacterial forms. Continued daily transfer on brain heart infusion medium resulted in reversion to classical staphylococci.

A comprehensive study on the isolation of stable and unstable L-forms and transitional (heteromorphic) forms from the cerebrospinal fluid of patients with purulent meningitis was carried out by Kagan and her colleagues[33] in 1965. Cultures were made on beef heart-horse serum-yeast media with or without penicillin and osmotic stabilizer (magnesium ions and sucrose). Of 144 patients with meningitis, including eight with brain abscesses, bacterial forms were isolated from 14 per cent, mixed cultures of bacterial and L-forms from 3.4 per cent, unstable L- and transitional forms from 2.8 per cent, and stable L-forms from 15 per cent. The bacterial species to which unstable forms reverted included streptococci, staphylococci, pneumococci and *Hemophilus influenzae*. The authors did not attempt to distinguish the stable L-forms from possible *Mycoplasma* species. They noted that there was a high incidence of stable and unstable L-forms in patients with severe and protracted meningitis, whereas cultures negative for organisms were obtained from the patients after they reached the phase of complete recovery.

Still other instances of variant forms in human case material can be found in publications by Mattman and associates,[51] Barile and others,[3] Charache & Kaslick,[10] and Chatterjee.[11]

Not only have blood, spinal fluid and tissues of patients come under minute examination for microbial variants, but urine from patients presenting various urinary tract infections has become a subject for intensive investigation. One of the first reports of protoplasts in the urine of a patient was by Braude, Siemienski & Jacobs.[5] These investigators, in preliminary laboratory studies, first verified that pathogenic urinary bacteria could be converted *in vitro* to protoplasts by incubation in hypertonic (but not hypotonic) human urine to which penicillin was added. They then treated a patient who had a mixed *Proteus mirabilis* and enterococcus infection with penicillin, and four hours later found that the catheterized urine samples contained conversion forms of *Proteus*. The 17 hour urine specimen contained fully developed protoplasts and various intermediate forms. Ability of the protoplasts to revert *in vivo* and cause pyelonephritis was experimentally confirmed by injection of these variants into the bladders of rats.

Carrying this line of investigation still further, Gutman and colleagues[24] published a well planned and controlled study on the isolation of bacterial variants from the urine of patients with chronic bacteriuria. Urine specimens were osmotically stabilized with sucrose, filtered through 0.45 μ millipore filter membranes, and cultured in serum-yeast-sucrose medium. Isolation of L-forms or protoplasts was obtained from 11 of 57 patients with chronic urinary tract infection and pyelonephritis. Cultures were generally positive for variant forms of enteric bacteria when the patients were receiving antibiotic therapy, although five of these patients who had received no antibiotics for at least six weeks also yielded cultures positive for variant forms. Patients from whom variant forms were isolated during treatment with antibiotics were found to relapse upon completion of the course of therapy, and the parent form of the original infecting bacterium was again found in the urine. The authors conclude that their findings "suggest that L-forms and protoplasts may play a role in microbial persistence of chronic renal infection".

SUMMARY

In conclusion, the findings brought to light by a quarter of a century of experimental investigations on microbial variants *in vivo* may be summarized as follows:

Microbial variants *per se* have either greatly reduced or no apparent infectivity when injected into an experimental host.

They may, however, revert *in vivo*, and the reverted bacterial form may then display all or most of the pathogenic properties of the original bacterium.

Microbial variants may retain the endotoxin or the exotoxin of the parent bacterium and may exhibit a toxigenicity approximately equal to that of the parent form.

Microbial variants may form spontaneously *in vivo*.

Factors which, on the basis of experimental evidence, appear to encourage the formation of microbial variants *in vivo* include: (*a*) antibiotic treatment of the host, (*b*) specific or nonspecific resistance of the host, (*c*) suitability of the *in vivo* site for establishment of an infective locus, and (*d*) relatively low to moderate virulence of the infecting bacterium.

Microbial variants may persist *in vivo* under environmental conditions that would be inimical to the persistence of the normal bacterial form and may contribute to the establishment of subclinical or chronic infection in the host.

This body of observations on microbial variants, *in vitro* as well as *in vivo*, acquired through the labor of hundreds of individual investigators, represents one of the most significant contributions of modern bacteriology, a contribution with far-reaching implications for medical and other scientific fields.

REFERENCES

1. Alderman, M. H., and Freedman, L. R.: Experimental pyelonephritis. X. The direct injection of *E. coli* protoplasts into the medulla of the rabbit kidney. *Yale J. Biol. Med.* **36:** 157, 1963.
2. Amano, T., Seki, Y., Fujikawa, K., Kashiba, S., Morioka, T., and Ichikawa, S.: The isolation and characterization of protoplasts from *Escherichia coli* B with the treatment

of leucocytes extract. *Med. J. Osaka Univ.* **7**: 245, 1956.

3. Barile, M. F., Graykowski, E. A., Driscoll, E. J., and Riggs, D. B.: L form of bacteria isolated from recurrent aphthous stomatitis lesions. *Oral Surg.* **16**: 1395, 1963.

4. Bassermann, J., Carrère, L., Fasquelle, R., Hauduroy, P., Klieneberger-Nobel, E., Penso, G., Roux, J., and Tunçman, Z. M.: 'L forms' of bacteria. *Nature* **179**: 461, 1957.

5. Braude, A. I., Siemienski, J., and Jacobs, I.: Protoplast formation in human urine. *Trans. Ass. Amer. Physicians* **74**: 234, 1961.

6. Brenner, S., Dark, F. A., Gerhardt, P., Jeynes, M. H., Kandler, O., Kellenberger, E., Klieneberger-Nobel, E., McQuillen, K., Rubio-Huertos, M., Salton, M. R. J., Strange, R. E., Tomcsik, J., and Weibull, C.: Bacterial protoplasts. *Nature* (London) **181**: 1713, 1958.

7. Brier, G., Ellis, L., and Godzeski, C. W.: Survival in vivo (in ovo) of L-phase bacteria. *Antimicrob. Agents Chemother.* 1962: p. 854.

8. Carey, W. F., Muschel, L. H., and Baron, L. S.: The formation of bacterial protoplasts *in vivo. J. Immun.* **84**: 183, 1960.

9. Carrère, L., Roux, J., and Mandin, J.: Culture des organismes L sur membrane chorio-allantoide d'embryon de poulet. *Montpellier Méd.* **47**: 438, 1955.

10. Charache, P., and Kaslick, D.: Isolation of protoplasts in human infection. *Clin. Res.* **13**: 293, 1965.

11. Chatterjee, B. R.: Growth habits of *Mycobacterium leprae*: their implications. *Int. J. Leprosy* **33**: 551, 1965.

12. Dasinger, B. L., and Suter, E.: Endotoxic activity of L-forms derived from *Salmonella paratyphi* B. *Proc. Soc. Exp. Biol. Med.* **111**: 399, 1962.

13. Dienes, L., and Smith, W. E.: The significance of pleomorphism in Bacteroides strains. *J. Bact.* **48**: 125, 1944.

14. Dienes, L., and Weinberger, H. J.: The L forms of bacteria. *Bact. Rev.* **15**: 245, 1951.

15. Dolman, C. E., Kerr, D. E., Chang, H., and Shearer, A. R.: Two cases of rat-bite fever due to *Streptobacillus moniliformis*. *Canad. J. Public Health* **42**: 228, 1951.

16. Freeman, B. A., and Rumack, B. H.: Cytopathogenic effect of *Brucella* spheroplasts on monocytes in tissue culture. *J. Bact.* **88**: 1310, 1964.

17. Freundt, E. A.: Experimental investigations into the pathogenicity of the L-phase variant of Streptobacillus moniliformis. *Acta Path. Microbiol. Scand.* **38**: 246, 1956.

18. ———: Taxonomic problems. A. Relation to bacterial L-phase variants. In: *The Mycoplasmataceae (The Pleuropneumonia Group of Organisms): Morphology, Biology and Taxonomy.* Munksgaard, Copenhagen, 1958: p. 90.

19. Godzeski, C. W., Brier, G., Griffith, R. S., and Black, H. R.: Association of bacterial L-phase organisms in chronic infections. *Nature* **205**: 1340, 1965.

20. Grasset, E.: Observations comparées sur la production *in vivo* et *in vitro* de formes L de *Proteus vulgaris* et *Klebsiella pneumoniae* sous l'influence d'anticorps spécifiques. *Ann. Inst. Pasteur* (Paris) **89**: 111, 1955.

21. Grasset, E., and Blondel, B.: Les formes L des pasteurella: facteurs engendrant leurs transformations. *Schweiz. Z. allg. Path.* **19**: 598, 1956.

22. Grasset, E., and Bonifas, V.: Modalités de transformation en formes L *in vivo* de *Proteus vulgaris* et d'autres *Enterobacteriaceae* sous l'action de la pénicilline. *Ann. Inst. Pasteur* (Paris) **88**: 651, 1955.

23. ———: Sur l'obtention de formes L de Klebsiella pneumoniae en milieu liquide et chez la Souris sous l'action de la pénicilline. *Schweiz. Z. allg. Path.* **18**: 1074, 1955.

24. Gutman, L. T., Turck, M., Petersdorf, R. G., and Wedgwood, R. J.: Significance of bacterial variants in urine of patients with chronic bacteriuria. *J. Clin. Invest.* **44**: 1945, 1965.

25. Guze, L. B., and Kalmanson, G. M.: Action of erythromycin on "protoplasts" in vivo. *Science* **146**: 1299, 1964.

26. ———: Effect of erythromycin on in vivo "protoplast" infection. *Antimicrob. Agents Chemother.* **4**: 730, 1964.

27. ———: Persistence of bacteria in "protoplast" form after apparent cure of pyelonephritis in rats. *Science* **143**: 1340, 1964.

28. Hadley, P., Delves, E., and Klimek, J.: The filtrable forms of bacteria: I. A filtrable stage in the life history of the Shiga dysentery bacillus. *J. Infect. Dis.* **48**: 1, 1931.

29. Hannoun, C., Vigouroux, J., Levaditi, J., and Nazimoff, O.: Étude des formes L des bactéries apparues spontanément *in vivo*. III. Histopathologie comparée des lésions provoquées par la bactérie normale et par ses formes modifiées. *Ann. Inst. Pasteur* (Paris) **92**: 231, 1957.

30. Hatten, B. A., and Sulkin, S. E.: Intracellular production of *Brucella* L forms. I. Recovery of L forms from tissue culture cells infected with *Brucella abortus. J. Bact.* **91**: 285, 1966.

31. ———: Intracellular production of *Brucella* L

forms. II. Induction and survival of *Brucella abortus* L forms in tissue culture. *J. Bact.* **91**: 14, 1966.

32. Heilman, F. R.: A study of Asterococcus muris (Streptobacillus moniliformis). II. Cultivation and biochemical activities. *J. Infect. Dis.* **69**: 45, 1941.

33. Kagan, G. Y., Koptelova, E. I., and Pokrovsky, B. M.: Isolation of pleuropneumonia-like organisms, L-forms and heteromorphous growth of bacteria from the cerebrospinal fluid of patients with septic meningitis. *J. Hyg. Epidem.* (Praha) **9**: 310, 1965.

34. Kagan, G. Y., and Mikhailova, V. S.: Isolation of L-forms of streptococci from the blood of patients with rheumatism and endocarditis. *J. Hyg. Epidem.* (Praha) **7**: 327, 1963.

35. Kagan, G. Y., and Rakovskaya, I. V.: The cytopathogenic action of the L-forms of certain pathogenic bacterial species in tissue cultures. *Biull. Eksp. Biol. Med.* **57**(6): 69, 1964 (in Russian).

36. Kagan, G. Y., Rakovskaya, I. V., Koptelova, E. I., Prozorovsky, S. V., Zhiv, B. V., and Komm, S. G.: Comparative characteristics of the cytopathogenic effect produced by diverse types of the L-form bacteria and mycoplasms types in tissue cultures. *Vestn. Akad. Med. Nauk. SSSR* **20**(8): 66, 1965 (in Russian).

37. Kagan, G. Y., Shchegolev, A. G., and Prozorovsky, S. V.: Pathogenic and immunogenic properties of S. typhimurium L-forms obtained under the action of penicillin. *Antibiotiki* **9**(8): 722, 1964 (in Russian).

38. Kalmanson, G. M., and Guze, L. B.: Role of protoplasts in pathogenesis of pyelonephritis. *JAMA* **190**: 1107, 1964.

39. Klieneberger, E.: Pleuropneumonia-like organisms of diverse provenance: some results of an enquiry into methods of differentiation. *J. Hyg.* (Camb.) **38**: 458, 1938.

40. Klieneberger-Nobel, E.: Filterable forms of bacteria. *Bact. Rev.* **15**: 77, 1951.

41. ———: L-forms of bacteria. In: *The Bacteria, Vol. I: Structure* (I. C. Gunsalus and R. Y. Stanier, Eds.). Academic Press, New York, 1960: p. 361.

42. ———: Similarities and differences between pleuropneumonia-like organisms and L-forms of bacteria. In: *Pleuropneumonia-Like Organisms (PPLO) Mycoplasmataceae*. Academic Press, London, 1962: p. 75.

43. Klodnitskaia, N. S.: On the problem of the etiology of scarlet fever. IV. Isolation of the L-form of streptococcus from penicillin-treated patients with scarlet fever and experience in the production of ovohemocultures. *Zh. Mikrobiol.* **33**(5): 31, 1962 (in Russian).

44. Koptelova, E. I., and Pokrovsky, V. I.: Experimental meningitis of rabbits caused by the L-form streptococci. *Zh. Mikrobiol.* **41**(10): 90, 1964 (in Russian).

45. Koptelova, E. I., Pokrovsky, V. I., and Gorshkova, E. P.: A model of experimental meningitis in rabbits caused by L-forms of streptococci and staphylococci. *Vestn. Akad. Med. Nauk. SSSR* **20**(8): 60, 1965 (in Russian).

46. Lavillaureix, J.: Première étude sur les propriétés pathogènes d'une souche de formes naines (formes L) fixée, obtenue à partir d'un vibrion. *C. R. Acad. Sci.* (Paris) **239**: 1155, 1954.

47. ———: Action de formes L pathogènes sur des cultures de cellules cancéreuses. *C. R. Acad. Sci.* (Paris) **244**: 1098, 1957.

48. Lederberg, J.: Bacterial protoplasts induced by penicillin. *Proc. Nat. Acad. Sci. USA* **42**: 574, 1956.

49. Martin, H. H.: Bacterial protoplasts—a review. *J. Theor. Biol.* **5**: 1, 1963.

50. Mattman, L. H., and Mattman, P. E.: L forms of *Streptococcus fecalis* in septicemia. *Arch. Intern. Med.* (Chicago) **115**: 315, 1965.

51. Mattman, L. H., Tunstall, L. H., Mathews. W. W., and Gordon, D. L.: L variation in mycobacteria. *Amer. Rev. Resp. Dis.* **82**: 202, 1960.

52. McQuillen, K.: Capabilities of bacterial protoplasts. *Symp. Soc. Gen. Microbiol.* **6**: 127, 1956.

53. ———: Bacterial protoplasts. In: *The Bacteria, Vol. I: Structure* (I. C. Gunsalus and R. Y. Stanier, Eds.). Academic Press, New York, 1960: p. 249.

54. Minck, R.: Obtention de formes L à partir des vibrions cholériques. Propriétés pathogènes. Application à la protection des souris contre la maladie expérimentale. *C. R. Acad. Sci.* (Paris) **231**: 386, 1950.

55. ———: Les formes L du vibrion cholérique. Étude de quelques-unes de leurs propriétés. *Schweiz. Z. allg. Path.* **14**: 595, 1951.

56. ———: Organismes du type de la péripneumonie des bovidés et formes L des bactéries. *Rev. Immun.* (Paris) **19**: 86, 1955.

57. Minck, R., and Fruhling, L.: Obtention chez le Lapin de lésions dermiques après inoculation de formes L. *C. R. Soc. Biol.* (Paris) **148**: 2091, 1954.

58. Minck, R., and Lavillaureix, J.: La transformation L des bactéries. *Ann. Biol. Clin.* (Paris) **32**: 153, 1956.

59. Mortimer, E. A., Jr.: Production of L forms of group A streptococci in mice. *Proc. Soc. Exp. Biol. Med.* **119:** 159, 1965.

60. Repaske, R.: Lysis of Gram-negative bacteria by lysozyme. *Biochim. Biophys. Acta* **22:** 189, 1956.

61. Rosner, R.: Isolation of *Candida* protoplasts from a case of *Candida* endocarditis. *J. Bact.* **91:** 1320, 1966.

62. Scheibel, I., and Assandri, J.: Isolation of toxigenic L-phase variants from Cl. tetani. *Acta Path. Microbiol. Scand.* **46:** 333, 1959.

63. Schnauder, G.: Tierexperimente zur Frage der epidemiologischen Bedeutung der L-formen. *Zschr. Hyg. Infektionskr.* **141:** 404, 1955.

64. Shchegolev, A. G., and Starshinova, V. S.: Isolation of L-form bacteria from typhoid patients and carriers. *Zh. Mikrobiol.* **41(7):** 15, 1964 (in Russian).

65. Silberstein, J. K.: Observations on the L forms of Proteus and Salmonella. *Schweiz. Z. allg. Path.* **16:** 739, 1953.

66. Smith, P. F.: Comparative physiology of pleuropneumonia-like and L-type organisms. *Bact. Rev.* **28:** 97, 1964.

67. Spizizen, J.: Preparation and use of protoplasts. In: *Methods in Enzymology*, Vol. V (S. P. Colowick and N. O. Kaplan, Eds.). Academic Press, New York, 1962: p. 122.

68. Terranova, T.: Aspetti biologici delle forme L dei batteri. *Riv. Biol.* **50:** 215, 1958.

69. Timakov, V. D., and Kagan, G. Y.: L-forms of bacteria. *Vestn. Akad. Med. Nauk. SSSR* **15(11):** 25, 1960 (in Russian).

70. Tomcsik, J., and Guex-Holzer, S.: Änderung der Struktur der Bakterienzelle im Verlauf der Lysozym-Einwirkung. *Schweiz. Z. allg. Path.* **15:** 517, 1952.

71. Tulasne, R.: Les formes L des bactéries. *Rev. Immun.* (Paris) **15:** 223, 1951.

72. ————: Bilan de nos connaissances sur les cycles bactériens du type L et sur les formes L des bactéries. *Biol. Méd.* (Paris) **45:** 391, 1955.

73. Tulasne, R., and Lavillaureix, J.: Pouvoir pathogène expérimental, pour la Souris d'une souche de formes L des bactéries. *C. R. Soc. Biol.* (Paris) **148:** 2080, 1954.

74. ————: Mécanisme de l'action pathogène d'une forme L des bactéries d'origine vibrionnienne. *C. R. Soc. Biol.* (Paris) **149:** 178, 1955.

75. Tunstall, L. H., and Mattman, L. H.: Growth of hemolytic streptococci in vitamin free medium. *Experientia* **17:** 190, 1961.

76. Weibull, C.: The isolation of protoplasts from *Bacillus megaterium* by controlled treatment with lysozyme. *J. Bact.* **66:** 688, 1953.

77. ————: Bacterial protoplasts; their formation and characteristics. *Symp. Soc. Gen. Microbiol.* **6:** 111, 1956.

78. ————: Bacterial protoplasts. *Ann. Rev. Microbiol.* **12:** 1, 1958.

79. Wittler, R. G.: The L-form of *Haemophilus pertussis* in the mouse. *J. Gen. Microbiol.* **6:** 311, 1952.

80. ————: Discussion of: Chatterjee, B. R.: Growth habits of *Mycobacterium leprae*: their implications. *Int. J. Leprosy* **33:** 555, 1965.

81. Wittler, R. G., Malizia, W. F., Kramer, P. E., Tuckett, J. D., Pritchard, H. N., and Baker, H. J.: Isolation of a corynebacterium and its transitional forms from a case of subacute bacterial endocarditis treated with antibiotics. *J. Gen. Microbiol.* **23:** 315, 1960.

82. Wittler, R. G., Tuckett, J. D., Muccione, V. J., Gangarosa, E. J., and O'Connell, R. C.: Transitional forms and L forms from the blood of rheumatic fever patients. In: *Eighth International Congress of Microbiology* (Abstracts). Montreal, 1962: p. 125.

83. Zinder, N. D., and Arndt, W. F.: Production of protoplasts of *Escherichia coli* by lysozyme treatment. *Proc. Nat. Acad. Sci. USA* **42:** 586, 1956.

20

Production and Cultivation of Staphylococcal L-Forms

Judith H. Marston

BAYLOR UNIVERSITY COLLEGE OF MEDICINE

HOUSTON, TEXAS

Morphological variants of bacteria have intrigued microbiologists for years. Areas of investigation have included the relationship of the variants to their "parent" cells and to each other, their role in disease production and, since 1958, their possible role as microbial persisters. McDermott[9] suggested that bacterial L-forms might be variants that could survive *in vivo* under the influence of antibiotics on the basis of an "adaptive plasticity".

Within this broad framework investigations began on the L-forms of *Staphylococcus aureus*.

The term *L-forms*, as it is used here, designates cells without rigid form, derived from bacteria, but which do not revert to bacteria. These cells can be propagated indefinitely and have a characteristic colony on solid media. The *L-colony* of staphylococci is unlike the bacterial colony in that the center portion is embedded in the agar and the peripheral growth on the agar surface is thin and vacuolated, giving the familiar "fried egg" appearance; developing or "immature" L-colonies are not distinctive in their gross appearance, but phase contrast microscopic studies show them to be composed of aggregates of large bodies. The term *large body* denotes a transitional stage in the development of the L-forms from the parent bacterium; individual large bodies may be five to ten times larger than the bacterial cell and frequently contain granular elements. Representative illustrations are shown in Figures 20.1, 20.2 and 20.4

MATERIALS AND METHODS

ORGANISMS

Eight penicillin-sensitive strains of *S. aureus* have been studied and described previously.[6] Penicillin-resistant and methicillin-resistant strains of *S. aureus* have been obtained through the courtesy of Dr. Ellard M. Yow and Dr. B. M. Kagan. Recently most of our studies have utilized a strain of *S. aureus* isolated from a patient with a staphylococcal septicemia and designated as strain 160 (Read). This strain is sensitive to 0.1 μg of penicillin G, coagulase and mannitol positive, and of phage type 52A/79.

MEDIA

The basal medium used for induction of staphylococcal L-forms is Bacto brain heart infusion agar (Difco) with sodium chloride added to give a final concentration of 5%. Heat inactivated, filtered horse serum (20%) is added just prior to pouring plates.

When inducing penicillin-sensitive staphylococci to the L-form, buffered crystalline penicillin G is used in the agar at a concentration of 1000 units/ml. Penicillin-resistant and methicillin-resistant strains of staphylococci are induced by a number of the semisynthetic penicillins, e.g., methicillin, sodium nafcillin, and cephalosporin, all at a concentration of 1000 μg/ml of medium. All strains of staphylococci that we have investigated may be induced with lysostaphin[11, 12] in concentrations of 0.1 unit/ml to 1.0 unit/ml in the basal medium.

Broth cultures of staphylococcal L-forms are initiated in Penassay broth (Antibiotic medium No. 3, Difco) containing 5% NaCl, 20% inactivated horse serum, and 1000 units or μg of the appropriate antibiotic per ml of broth.

INDUCTION OF L-FORMS

The staphylococci are routinely grown on agar slants for 8–12 hours at 35°C and a standard loop is used to transfer the inoculum to the surface of L-form agar plates containing the antibiotic. The plates are streaked for isolation if the inoculum is heavy; however, dilutions of the inoculum may be made in broth or saline and, if approximately 10^5 cells/ml are used, the inoculum may be spread over the entire surface of the plate by a sterile glass rod. Plates are sealed with large rubber bands to prevent loss of moisture, incubated at 35°C and examined daily.

Colonies appearing on these plates are transferred to fresh agar by the agar-block technique. Squares of agar containing heavy concentrations of colonies are cut out and placed face down on the fresh surface. A slight pressure is exerted on the transferred block and it is moved slowly over the surface; the block is allowed to remain in contact with the medium, since growth of newly isolated L-colonies often occurs only at this interface.

Agar blocks are also used to initiate growth of staphylococcal L-forms in broth. Several blocks are cut from an area of heavy growth of L-colonies, and are transferred to the broth medium. Broth cultures are routinely prepared in our laboratory in Roux bottles containing 200 ml of me-dium. The bottles are incubated at 35°C with the offset side down to provide a large surface area.

Anaerobic conditions are not required for induction or cultivation of staphylococcal L-forms.

MICROSCOPIC METHODS

Examination of growth on L-form agar is made by low power light microscopy of the colonies or by using methylene blue-azure II stained coverslips overlayed on colonies after the method of Dienes & Weinberger.[4] Phase contrast microscopic examinations are made using unstained agar block preparations and on wet mounts from broth cultures. Techniques for electron microscopy of staphylococcal L-forms have been published previously.[1]

RESULTS

It should be noted that the results reported herein for induction and growth of L-forms from penicillin-sensitive staphylococci also apply to penicillin-resistant and methicillin strains, the only exception being the substitution of semisynthetic penicillins or lysostaphin in the induction or cultivation medium (see Materials and Methods). No gross differences are apparent among the L-forms of various strains induced by any of the antibiotics.

GROWTH OF L-FORMS ON AGAR

Direct streaking of strains of staphylococci onto L-form agar containing the appropriate antibiotic results in the appearance of immature colonies in 24–48 hours, and mature colonies within three to five days. A sequence in the development of L-form colonies has been established by phase contrast microscopy and is presented in Figure 20.1.

Under the influence of penicillin G or other antibiotics, in a hypertonic environment, bacterial cells become enlarged and somewhat pleomorphic. Staphylococci enlarge at this stage to approximately five to ten times their original diameter and are described as large bodies. In the development of L-colonies the large bodies appear to coalesce or aggregate with an

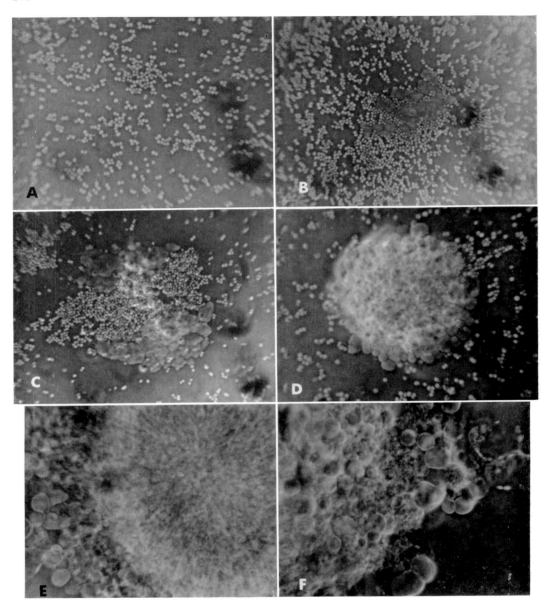

Figure 20.1. *a–e:* Development of an L-colony of *Staphylococcus aureus*. Photographic sequences taken at 12-hour intervals show formation and aggregation of "large bodies" with development of a dense central area. *f:* Appearance of peripheral area. Unstained agar block preparation; phase micrographs. × 740.

increase in number during a 24-hour period. Between 24 and 36 hours the center of the aggregation becomes ill-defined and presents a granular, amorphous appearance by phase contrast microscopy. Large bodies are clearly seen at the edge of the developing colony.

Time-lapse cinematography using an interference microscope* has defined this

* J. H. Marston, unpublished observations.

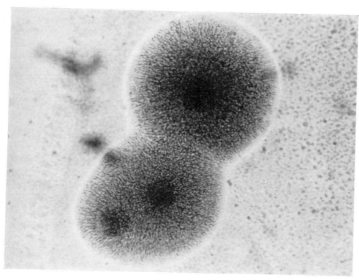

Figure 20.2. Mature L-colonies of staphylococci. Dark central areas represent areas of growth into agar of three adjacent colonies. Unstained preparation; light micrograph. × **100.**

stage as a time of intense activity at the site of colony formation with lysis of large bodies, changes in density at the center of the colony, and the appearance of large bodies at the periphery, which also lyse and reappear as the colony increases in size.

At 48–72 hours, and sometimes longer with newly induced L-cultures, the mature and typical L-colony is apparent. Grossly, the colony is small (0.5–1.0 mm) and translucent; it is not highly pigmented and thus is recognizable when it occurs among colonies of the "parent" staphylococci. Microscopically the distinction is even more striking; a micrograph of an L-colony is presented in Figure 20.2.

The dense center of the colony is apparently an area that represents growth of the L-form units into the agar medium, while peripheral growth is surface growth. Electron microscopic studies of staphylococcal L-form colonies fixed *in situ* in agar confirm this statement. Similar observations have been made on other L-form colonies and of *Mycoplasma* colonies by Razin & Oliver.[10]

TRANSFER OF L-FORMS

Agar-to-agar transfer of L-forms is accomplished most readily by the agar block technique (see Materials and Methods). Colonies are rubbed off and deposited on the fresh agar surface as the block is moved across the plate. This is advantageous with recently induced cultures, in which the colonies are quite small and closely adherent to the agar surface. Often new colonies form only at the edge or underneath the agar block. With older, and perhaps better adapted, colonies of staphylococcal L-forms, growth is more luxuriant; colonies are much larger (4–5 mm in diameter) and organisms may be transferred by an inoculating loop as one would transfer bacterial cells.

Incubation time is appreciably shortened as L-form cultures are carried through successive transfers, typical L-colonies appearing in 24 hours.

Cultures of staphylococcal L-forms in broth are initiated by inoculating the medium with several blocks containing L-colonies. Each Roux bottle is inoculated with five or six agar blocks, each approximately 1 cm². Such culture bottles may be incubated flat to provide a large surface area; growth is profuse in bottles handled in this manner. Strands of slime-like growth arise from the inoculum blocks

Figure 20.3. Slime-like sediment in broth culture of L-forms of strain 160 (*Staphylococcus aureus*).

after 3–5 days incubation, and this slime is transferred to fresh broth medium.

GROWTH OF L-FORMS IN BROTH

Serial transfers of broth cultures of staphylococcal L-forms are accomplished most frequently by transfer of the culture slime. While the slime is characteristic of growth of all strains of staphylococcal L-forms in the medium given here, investigation has shown that viable L-forms also exist in the turbid broth exclusive of the slime matrix. Figure 20.3 shows slime in the turbid culture.

In the long-term cultivation of the L-forms in broth several modifications may be made. The serum concentration in the medium may be reduced to 5%, and the NaCl may be reduced to 2.0% final concentration, but no lower for good growth. The antibiotic may be omitted when subcultures indicate that there is no reversion of the parent bacterial cells in the absence of the antibiotic.

Growth of staphylococcal L-forms in a serum-free medium has been reported by Weibull & Gyllang[14] and Mattman and associates.[8] Experiments in our laboratory have shown that serum can be omitted entirely from broth and agar media used in serial transfer of L-form cultures, but yield of organisms are very low and the cultures die out rapidly. Only two of nine

L-form cultures were able to grow for more than three transfers in serum-free medium, indicating that perhaps the requirement for serum is strain-specific.

We have been unsuccessful in adapting staphylococcal L-forms to prolonged cultivation in broth media containing 0.3–1.2 M sucrose. Although these concentrations of sucrose will maintain an osmotically favorable environment for developing L-forms, it has been our experience that sucrose is inhibitory to continuing growth in Penassay broth. The reasons for this have not yet been determined.

MORPHOLOGY OF L-FORMS

The typical L-form colony has been described above. Limited information on the morphology of the cellular units within the colony may be obtained by phase contrast microscopy and/or by the stained coverslip method. No distinct morphology can be discerned by conventional staining techniques of smears made from growth on agar.

Broth cultures are more suitable for studies on cellular morphology. Wet-mount preparations examined by phase-contrast microscopy show morphological units of varying sizes; most striking are the large bodies which are present in large numbers (Figure 20.4*a*). These transitional forms often appear as empty spheres, but granules and small units are seen in others. Small cellular units are apparently bound by a limiting membranous structure, the details of which are beyond the limit of resolution of the light or phase microscope (Figure 20.4, *b* and *c*).

Electron microscopy proved to be a valuable tool for defining ultrastructure of staphylococcal L-forms. Figures 20.5 and 20.6 are representative of thin sections of L-form units from broth cultures. Negatively stained preparations offer further evidence of the variation in size, shape and structure of the cellular elements of L-forms of *S. aureus* (Figure 20.7).

DISCUSSION

Many bacterial species produce L-forms and L-colonies in response to appropriate cultural conditions.[3, 4] It is well established that cultural requirements will vary with different species and no single medium nor set of physical conditions is applicable to production and cultivation of all L-forms.

A variety of inducing agents have been used in the past.[5] With both antibiotic-sensitive and resistant strains of staphylococci it has been shown that penicillin G, methicillin, sodium nafcillin and cephalosporin are effective inducers of L-forms.[7] We have recently studied the efficiency of lysostaphin as an inducing agent in our basic medium and have successfully obtained typical L-colonies in response to concentrations ranging from 0.1 unit to 1.0 unit of lysostaphin per ml of medium.

L-forms of *S. aureus* are readily produced on an agar medium with a high sodium chloride concentration and added inactivated horse serum, under the influence of the antibiotics mentioned above. These cultural conditions are not unique for staphylococcal L-forms; streptococcal and diphtheroid L-forms have been produced on such a medium.[3] However, L-forms of some other organisms, e.g., pigmented and non-pigmented *Serratia marcescens*, are not induced with ease on media that have a high salt concentration.*

The exact roles of the media components in the production and cultivation of L-forms have not yet been adequately established. The role of the agar in development of the characteristic L-form colony has been discussed,[2] and the high salt requirement of some L-forms has been related to maintenance of a satisfactory physical environment.[3] The further role of salt in the stabilization of the lipid membrane was recently mentioned by Smith.[13] Differences in the nature of the lipid and the amount present in L-form membranes were suggested as factors that might account for differences in the requirement for salt among various species. This intriguing possibility is certainly an area for investigation.

In the cultivation of staphylococcal L-forms certain media components can be altered, at least quantitatively. Stock laboratory cultures may be cultivated on agar

* J. H. Marston, unpublished results

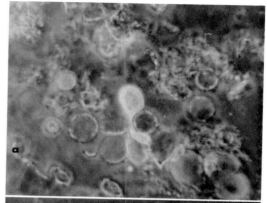

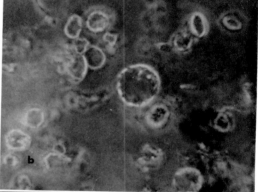

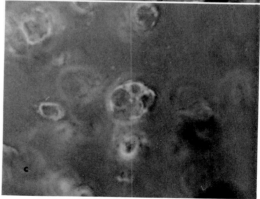

Figure 20.4. Large bodies in L-form broth culture. *a:* Large bodies of various sizes and densities; *b:* granular large bodies with intensely refractile limiting membranes; *c:* large body showing inclusion of small units. Wet-mount preparations, unstained; phase micrographs. × 740.

or in broth in which the concentration of sodium chloride is reduced to 2.0% and that of horse serum to 5.0%. At no time in our experience has it been pos-

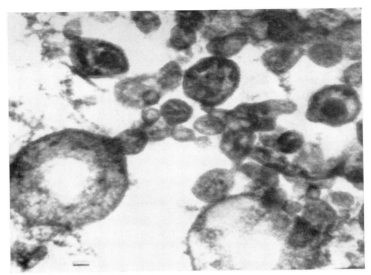

Figure 20.5. Ultra thin section of L-forms from broth culture (strain 160). × 25,000; bar = 0.1 μ.

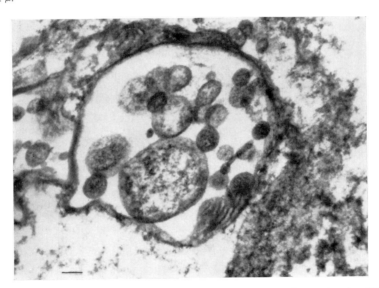

Figure 20.6. Ultra thin section of L-forms from broth culture (strain 160). Note definitive membranes limiting small elements. × 40,000; bar = 0.1 μ.

sible to eliminate these two components from the basal media and maintain prolonged growth or viability. With different basal nutrient media the requirement for both salt and serum may perhaps not be critical. Weibull & Gyllang[14] reported growth of staphylococcal L-forms without high concentrations of salt and without serum; Mattman and associates,[8] using a semi-defined medium, grew L-forms of staphylococci without these two components, although sucrose was used in some studies to provide an osmotically favorable environment.

Growth of staphylococcal L-forms in Penassay broth with 2–5% sodium

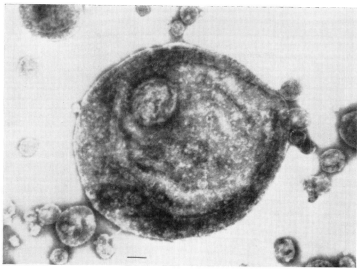

Figure 20.7. Negative-stained preparation of strain 160 L-forms. × 40,000; bar = 0.1 μ.

chloride and 5–10% horse serum is in the form of aggregates of cellular units ("microcolonies"[15]) in a slime-like material. Treatment of the culture slime with magnesium-activated deoxyribonuclease drastically reduces its viscosity, presumably without destroying the viability of the L-forms. Quantitative counts of L-forms may be made on DNase-treated cultures. Similarly, the slime material can be dispersed by sonic disintegration and viable forms recovered. Growth occurs without the slime accumulation in broth supplemented only with 1.2 M sucrose,[1] but cultures die out after one or two transfers. While a high sodium chloride concentration seems requisite for induction and continued cultivation of staphylococcal L-forms, these L-forms can survive in 0.85% sodium chloride, cesium chloride (20% w/v) or potassium tartrate (20% w/v) for several days. Distilled water causes rapid lysis of staphylococcal L-forms.[15]

The ability of L-forms of *S. aureus* to grow profusely in a liquid medium has facilitated studies on morphology and metabolic activities. The relative resistance of L-forms to sonic disintegration has allowed the use of this method to obtain homogeneous suspensions for electron microscopic observations, and washing of such suspensions in normal saline has provided material presumably free of contaminating medium components for antigenic analysis.

Continuing studies of staphylococcal L-forms are necessary to delineate better their relationship to the parent bacterial forms. Even more important will be investigation of the relation of L-forms of staphylococci to other L-forms, especially by utilization of biochemical and immunological techniques. Additional knowledge of L-forms as biological entities will enhance future work on their role in disease processes and, in particular, as they may relate to microbial persistence.

SUMMARY

Strains of *Staphylococcus aureus* may be induced to L-forms by the action of antibiotics on an appropriate culture medium. L-colonies appear in 24–48 hours as aggregations of large spherical cellular elements with subsequent development of a dense granular area in the center of the colony. Within three to five days a typical L-colony is visible by low power light microscopy.

L-forms may be transferred to a fresh agar surface by the agar block technique, and to broth by inoculating the medium with several blocks of agar containing L-colonies. Broth-to-broth transfer may then be made.

Staphylococcal L-forms require a high concentration of sodium chloride and horse serum for induction and growth when a basal medium of meat infusion is used.

Growth in broth cultures most frequently occurs as a slime-like material. Enzymatic treatment or sonic disintegration provides a homogeneous suspension of viable staphylococcal L-forms for further study.

REFERENCES

1. Dannis, D. C., and Marston, J. H.: Fine structure of staphylococcal L-forms. *Texas Rep. Biol. Med.* **23**: 729, 1965.

2. Dienes, L.: Comparative morphology of L forms and PPLO. In: *Recent Progress in Microbiology* (N. E. Gibbons, Ed.). Univ. of Toronto Press, Toronto, 1963: p. 511.

3. Dienes, L., and Sharp, J. T.: The role of high electrolyte concentration in the production and growth of L forms of bacteria. *J. Bact.* **71**: 208, 1956.

4. Dienes, L., and Weinberger, H. J.: The L forms of bacteria. *Bact. Rev.* **15**: 245, 1951.

5. Klieneberger-Nobel, E.: L forms of bacteria. In: *The Bacteria, Vol. 1: Structure* (I. C. Gunsalus and R. Y. Stanier, Eds.). Academic Press, New York, 1960: p. 365.

6. Marston, J.: Observations on L forms of staphylococci. *J. Infect. Dis.* **108**: 75, 1961.

7. Marston, J. H., Bartlett, D., and Yow, E. M.: L form induction of antibiotic-resistant staphylococci. *Texas Rep. Biol. Med.* **21**: 445, 1963.

8. Mattman, L. H., Tunstall, L. H., and Rossmoore, H. W.: Induction and characteristics of staphylococcal L forms. *Canad. J. Microbiol.* **7**: 705, 1961.

9. McDermott, W.: Microbial persistence. *Yale J. Biol. Med.* **30**: 257, 1958.

10. Razin, S., and Oliver, O.: Morphogenesis of mycoplasma and bacterial L-form colonies. *J. Gen. Microbiol.* **24**: 225, 1961.

11. Schindler, C. A., and Schuhardt, V. T.: Lysostaphin: a new bacteriolytic agent for the staphylococcus. *Proc. Nat. Acad. Sci. USA* **51**: 414, 1964.

12. ———: Purification and properties of lysostaphin—a lytic agent for *Staphylococcus aureus. Biochem. Biophys. Acta.* **97**: 242, 1965.

13. Smith, P. F.: Comparative physiology of pleuropneumonia-like and L-type organisms. *Bact. Rev.* **28**: 97, 1964.

14. Weibull, C., and Gyllang, H.: Metabolic properties of some L forms derived from Grampositive and Gram-negative bacteria. *J. Bact.* **89**: 1443, 1965.

15. Williams, R. E. O.: L forms of *Staphylococcus aureus. J. Gen. Microbiol.* **33**: 325, 1963

21

Staphylococcal Spheroplasts as Persisters

Long-term Population Curves of L- and Vegetative Colonies in Presence of Methicillin, with Observations on Reversion*

Morton Hamburger and Judith Carleton

UNIVERSITY OF CINCINNATI COLLEGE OF MEDICINE
AND CINCINNATI GENERAL HOSPITAL
CINCINNATI, OHIO

The persistence of bacterial cells in culture media or in the mammalian body after the initial powerful bactericidal action of penicillin has intrigued microbiologists and clinical investigators alike, ever since Bigger[2] called attention to the phenomenon more than 20 years ago. In 1958, McDermott's suggestion that persisters might be protoplasts[17] stimulated the interest of clinical people in the possible role of these naked cells, of whose existence microbiologists were already fully aware.

The term *spheroplast,* as employed in this paper, designates a cell deprived of the greater part of its cell wall as a result of growth in the presence of penicillin or one of its derivatives. The term carries no implication of the presence or absence of small amounts of cell wall or of the capacity or lack of capacity of the spheroplast to revert to the vegetative form of staphylococcus.†

At the time we initiated our experiments, Marston[15] had succeeded in growing and propagating staphylococcal spheroplasts in broth by inoculating the broth with staphylococcal L-colonies. She, as well as Kagan and his associates,[10] had also shown that L-colonies could be serially transferred, apparently indefinitely, on appropriate agar in the presence or absence of the inducing agent. In the absence of the inducing antibiotic, reversion to the vegetative form would sometimes occur.

In order to learn whether, under appropriate conditions, persisters might be spheroplasts, it seemed worthwhile to investigate a system where developing spheroplasts could be protected over long

* This investigation was supported by Research Grant AI 03523 from the National Institute of Allergy and Infectious Diseases, U.S. Public Health Service.

† The term *L-form* has been endowed with several different shades of meaning since its original introduction into the microbiological literature by Klieneberger-Nobel. In this paper we shall not use the term L-form except in reference to the writings of other investigators. We shall instead refer to *L-colonies,* the typical "fried egg" colonies generally recognized as originating from spheroplasts.

periods of time by additional NaCl in the broth.[6]

MATERIALS AND METHODS

MEDIA EMPLOYED

Broth. Brain heart infusion (BHI) broth (Difco) was the basal medium employed in all these experiments. The concentration of NaCl in BHI is 0.5%. In some experiments enough NaCl was added to increase this concentration to 5%; in others, 5% NaCl and 10% human serum were added to the BHI broth. The latter will henceforth be referred to as S-S (serum-salt) broth.

Agar plates. At appropriate intervals the following subcultures were made from the flasks of broth: (1) Pour plates were prepared in 1.5% ordinary BHI agar with appropriate amounts of beta lactamase (*Bacillus cereus* penicillinase, Neutrapen, Riker)[3] for demonstration of vegetative colonies. (2) Samples were flooded on the surface of BHI with 1.05% Noble agar plus S-S (hereafter referred to as S-S plates) for demonstration of L-colonies; after flooding, the sample was spread with an L shaped glass rod. (3) In some of the experiments, samples were flooded on S-S plates plus 100, 10 or 5 mcg/ml methicillin [sodium 6-(2,6-dimethoxybenz-amido) penicillinate]. The agar in (2) and (3) was poured in plastic petri dishes and the tops sealed with tape after inoculation.

Serum. Blood was drawn from a normal subject into a 500 ml sterile vacuum bottle and allowed to clot at room temperature. Serum was removed from the clot after 24 hours, centrifuged, and heated at 56°C for 30 minutes. It was then passed through a series of Millipore filters of pore size 1.2 mμ, 0.45 mμ, and 0.22 mμ. The serum was stored at 4°C until used.

STRAINS OF STAPHYLOCOCCI

Penicillinase-producing strains included a group III staphylococcus known as the August Harmon,[8] recovered from a human case of endocarditis, and the Heisler strain, an 80/81 staphylococcus recovered from the blood of a human patient. With an inoculum of 10^6 cells/ml, the minimal inhibiting concentration (MIC) of penicillin G for the August Harmon and Heisler strains is 1500 mcg/ml. The MIC of methicillin is 3.12 mcg/ml.

MAINTENANCE OF METHICILLIN CONCENTRATION

The concentration of methicillin in each flask was measured frequently by a twofold tube dilution test. A concentrated solution of methicillin in S-S broth (1 ml or less) was added every day to compensate for deterioration of antibiotic at incubator temperature. This amount was approximately 30 per cent of the total methicillin in the flask.

RESULTS

Figure 21.1 shows the relative numbers of L-colonies and classical vegetative colonies subcultured from three flasks of BHI broth containing 100 mcg/ml methicillin, but differing from one another in their salt and serum contents. Curve A shows an experiment performed with normal BHI, which contains 0.5% NaCl; L-colonies did not develop on S-S plates, nor were spheroplasts identifiable by phase contrast or Gram stain. Curve B was constructed from subcultures of an identical flask to which had been added 10% serum and 5% NaCl. Here the rate of disappearance of vegetative staphylococci was slower than in normal BHI broth, as it always is; L-colonies appeared on the 5th day and rapidly increased in numbers, as vegetative colonies decreased; the experiment was terminated at the end of 20 days.

Periodic examination of the broth in such flasks by phase contrast has been interesting but, because of the spherical shape of the staphylococcal cell, more difficult to interpret than similar studies with rods. In contrast with phase observations on *Escherichia coli* incubated with penicillin,[14] where conversion of rods to spheres is so obvious, half-hourly observations of staphylococci have not revealed discernible significant changes in the morphology of the individual cells. Many of them assume what we call in our labora-

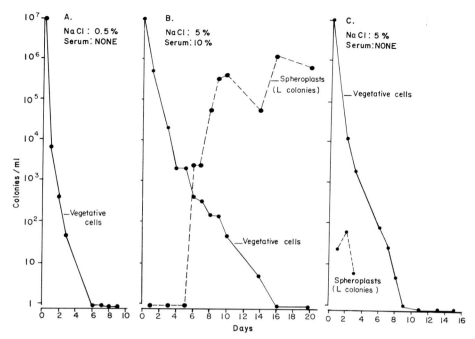

Figure 21.1. Bactericidal action of methicillin (100 γ/ml) against *Staphylococcus aureus* and development of spheroplasts in brain heart infusion broth. Growth of vegetative and L-colonies in subcultures in agar. (From Hamburger & Carleton.[6])

tory jargon a "mothy" appearance and many seem a little larger than cells in broth free of penicillin, but these differences are debatable. By the end of 24 hours, however, we usually find rare large unquestionable spheroplasts whose numbers slowly increase. Large Gram-negative spheres begin to appear during this time, and can be found for many weeks. Further evidence of persistence of vegetative staphylococci during the first week is provided by the finding of Gram-positive cocci in diminishing numbers.

The role of serum, as either a protector of spheroplasts or a promoter of growth of L-colonies, is well known. Curve C in Figure 21.1 shows what happens when the broth is rendered hypertonic but serum omitted from the system. Despite the hypertonic environment, only a few L-colonies developed, following which no more appeared. Spheroplasts were not seen by phase microscopy, nor were large Gram-negative spheres found.

In the interest of economy, another experiment was performed to discover if smaller amounts of serum might suffice. Figure 21.2 demonstrates that the growth curve of L-colonies was identical whether the serum concentration was 1%, 5% or 10%. However, the substitution of 0.1% agar for serum in the flasks effectively promoted spheroplasts and the growth of L-colonies, as reported by Marston.[16] A three-week experiment is shown in Figure 21.3.

The persistence in the flask of spheroplasts capable of forming L-colonies for periods up to at least three weeks raised the question as to just how long they might remain viable. Without having yet reached the limit, we have learned that they may survive and form L-colonies for as long as 24 weeks, as shown in Figure 21.4. In this experiment, vegetative cells persisted in small numbers up to the 20th week of incubation. The experiment also taught us that the time when vegetative staphylococci finally disappear is not as predictable as we had first believed. In

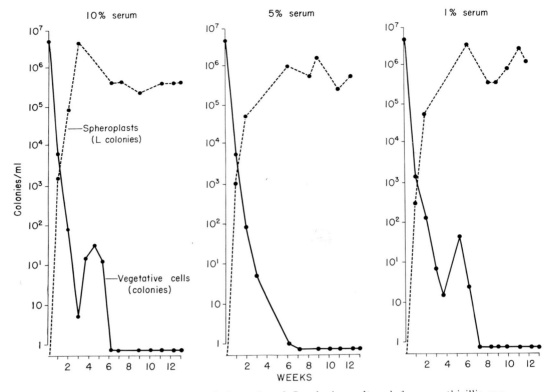

Figure 21.2. Vegetative staphylococci and L-colonies cultured from methicillin-containing flasks of hypertonic broth with 1%, 5% and 10% serum.

no instance, however, have we seen vegetative colonies approach the number of L-colonies.

When the spheroplasts are removed from the flask, they can be propagated on agar or in broth, with or without methicillin. We have now serially transferred stable spheroplasts in S-S broth for more than two years, either directly from flasks or started from L-colonies. The same strains have been adapted to grow in 2%, and some in 1.25% salt broth with serum. Some strains have also been adapted to grow in 5% NaCl broth in the absence of serum, without reverting to the vegetative form.

REVERSION OF SPHEROPLASTS TO VEGETATIVE
    STAPHYLOCOCCI

Both theoretical and practical considerations demand explanations of when, why, and how spheroplasts will resume manufacture of cell wall and revert to vegetative staphylococci. Schönfeld[18] reported that L-colonies induced on agar plates containing penicillin reverted to classical staphylococci when the plates were flooded with penicillinase. Marston[16] found that addition of yeast extract to serum-free agar containing 2.5% NaCl promoted reversion of staphylococcal L-colonies.

At a conference on the staphylococcus in New York, Dr. Stephen Morse asked Dr. Ben Kagan: "I wonder if you have tried any tricks to induce reversion?" Dr Kagan replied, "They seem to do it when they want to".[9] We too have been unable to define nicely predictable situations where reversion will take place. We have learned, however, that the opposites of two factors conducive to formation of L-colonies from spheroplasts seem to promote reversion of spheroplasts to classic vegetative staphylococci.[7] The factors favoring reversion are the omission of serum from agar plates and an increase in the concentration of the agar. Furthermore, the farther removed in time from the inducing antibiotic, the less likely is reversion to occur, even though these two conditions be met. Thus, we have not been able to induce reversion of several strains of spheroplasts which have been serially passed in broth beyond about the 15th passage, nor of L-colonies passed similarly on methicillin-free agar.

The effect of agar concentration and of omission of serum was demonstrated in subcultures from a flask in its 44th day of incubation. No vegetative colonies had grown in normal BHI agar plates during the previous eight days, nor during a subsequent 88 days. The relative numbers of vegetative and L-colonies which grew in subcultures on 1.5% and 0.7% agar, with and without serum, in plates containing 4, 3, 2 and 1% NaCl respectively, are shown in Table 21.1.

The table demonstrates the following points:

1. Serum promotes growth of L-colonies.

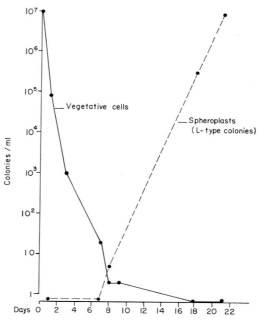

Figure 21.3. Effect of 0.1% agar as substitute for serum in promoting growth of staphylococcal spheroplasts. Brain heart infusion broth with 100 mcg/ml methicillin and 5% NaCl.

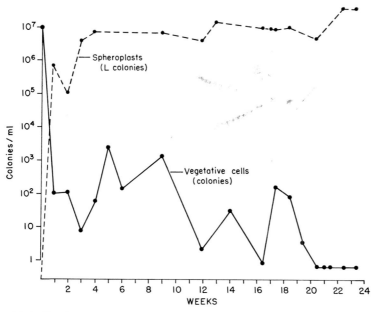

Figure 21.4. Persistence of large numbers of spheroplasts and ultimate disappearance of vegetative staphylococci, 20 weeks (methicillin-serum-hypertonic salt broth).

Table 21.1

Effect of Omission of Serum and Increase in Agar Concentration
on Reversion of Staphylococcal Spheroplasts*

NaCl %	Vegetative Colonies/L-Colonies							
	1.5 % agar				0.7 % agar			
	4	3	2	1	4	3	2	1
10% serum	1/TNC	0/TNC	25/TNC	0/TNC	0/TNC	0/TNC	15/TNC	1/TNC
No serum	81/280	92/200	34/82	3/0	0/TNC	8/TNC	71/600	10/35

TNC = greater than 3000 L-colonies.
* Adapted from Hamburger & Carleton.[7]

The number of countable L-colonies in each serum-containing plate exceeded that in the corresponding serum-free plate.

2. The omission of serum led not only to a diminution in the number of L-colonies, but also to an increase in the number and proportion of vegetative colonies. It would appear that a factor inhibiting reversion was removed.

3. The effect of hard agar in inducing reversion is best seen in the serum-free plates. The proportion of vegetative colonies was substantially higher on hard than on soft agar.

An interesting but unexplained observation is the higher proportion of vegetative colonies on the plates with 2% NaCl. This is reminiscent of Marston's production of reversion on plates containing 2.5% NaCl plus yeast extract.[16] We have not found reversion under the latter conditions, however.

FATE OF HALVES OF L-COLONIES TRANSFERRED TO SERUM-FREE ISOTONIC OR HYPERTONIC BROTH

Spheroplasts which may have been induced by methicillin in hypertonic but serum-free broth did not survive and lacked the capacity to form L-colonies.[6] Whether or not the spheroplasts which comprise an already formed L-colony can survive in serum-free broth seemed worth investigating.

L-colonies were cut in half with a sharp scalpel. One half, with a little adhering agar, was placed in a tube of normal isotonic BHI broth. Spheroplasts will not survive in this environment, but even very small numbers of vegetative staphylococci will multiply rapidly. The other half of the L-colony was placed in hypertonic (5% NaCl) BHI. The tubes were incubated at 37°C.

Figure 21.5 is a flow diagram of such an experiment. Of five half colonies placed in isotonic broth, two failed to grow, but three reverted to vegetative staphylococci in three to eight days. The spheroplasts seem to have been protected by agar during the process of reversion. By contrast, four of the halves incubated in hypertonic agar reverted within 24 hours. The fifth gave pure spheroplast growth. This culture, designated ⚹5, was then plated on S-S agar, giving a pure growth of L-colonies. Three of these L-colonies were then divided and cultured as described: no growth occurred in isotonic broth; in hypertonic broth, one half reverted promptly, but two grew as typical spheroplasts. One of these (⚹17) survived five passages in serum-free hypertonic broth, each broth passage giving rise only to L-colonies. On the sixth passage, reversion occurred. All the reverted strains possessed the phage typing pattern of the original Harmon strain. Because of the possibility that inhibited, invisible, but viable staphylococci might have survived on the agar between colonies, pieces of such agar were removed and incubated in S-S broth. No growth ever occurred.

DISCUSSION

These experiments demonstrate that the initial bactericidal action of methicillin upon staphylococci in broth may be fol-

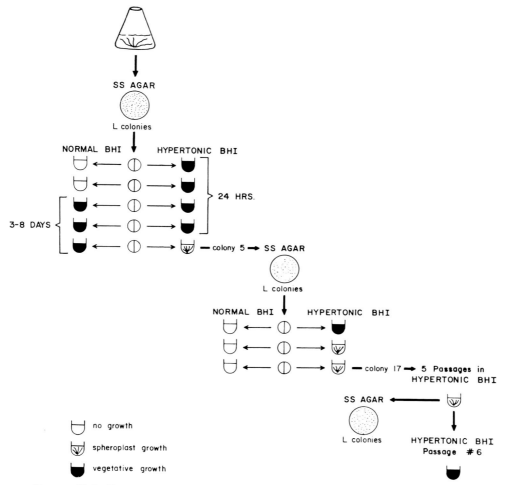

Figure 21.5. Pattern of reversion of methicillin-induced staphylococcal spheroplasts. (From Hamburger & Carleton.[7])

lowed by two types of persisters. In isotonic serum-free broth, persisters are vegetative staphylococci, presumably in a lag phase of growth.[5] In broth rendered hypertonic with NaCl and fortified with serum or 0.1% agar, vegetative staphylococci persist in diminishing numbers for varying periods of time. Late in the first week's incubation, however, spheroplasts capable of forming L-colonies appear and greatly outnumber vegetative staphylococci. They may persist for many weeks after vegetative staphylococci have disappeared.

A great deal of discussion has been generated in attempts to define the factors

which determine whether an antibiotic-produced spheroplast will become "stable" or will revert to the classic vegetative form. Reversion, when it occurs, is more apt to take place fairly soon after removal of the inducing antibiotic than after the culture has established an independent life in antibiotic-free media. Furthermore, certain environmental conditions favor reversion of staphylococcal[7, 16] and other spheroplasts.[4, 11, 12, 13] Increase in concentration of agar and omission of serum are two important situations favoring reversion. These conditions, however, are ineffective in promoting reversion of strains of staphylococcal spheroplasts which have been propagated in antibiotic-free medium for long periods.[7] Whether "stable" spheroplasts, after years of serial culture in the spheroplast state, can revert by means of some hitherto undiscovered stimulus, or whether they have become genetically incapable of rebuilding cell wall, is not known at present.

What is the role of spheroplasts in infection, either as spontaneous variants or as persisters during and after antibiotic therapy? Our experiments have demonstrated that, under favorable environmental conditions, spheroplasts may persist for many months *in vitro*. Critical questions which must be answered before their role in disease can be firmly established are:

1. Under what conditions, if any, are spheroplasts, without cell walls, pathogenic?

2. Under what conditions will spheroplasts rebuild cell wall and resume the known pathogenic vegetative state?

3. What tissues provide sufficient hypertonicity to permit survival and growth of spheroplasts?

4. Are spheroplasts, which at first survive only in hypertonic environments, capable of adapting to environments of lower tonicity?

SUMMARY

The persistence of vegetative staphylococci and of spheroplasts capable of forming L-colonies following inoculation of vegetative staphylococci into brain heart infusion broth containing methicillin has been followed over days or weeks. In isotonic broth, vegetative staphylococci persisted in small numbers for about a week after the initial sharp drop in numbers caused by methicillin. No spheroplasts were seen by phase microscopy nor did L-colonies grow on appropriate medium.

In broth rendered hypertonic by 5% NaCl and fortified by serum or 0.1% agar, spheroplasts were seen microscopically on the second day of incubation and increased in numbers speedily. L-colonies began to appear on the 5th day and rapidly increased as vegetative colonies decreased or disappeared. L-colonies were cultured in large numbers from the broth for as long as 24 weeks. Vegetative colonies persisted in small numbers for variable periods of time (3 to 20 weeks).

In broth rendered hypertonic but free of serum, very few L-colonies developed, and these were recovered only for a few days.

Population curves of vegetative staphylococci and L-colonies were virtually the same, whether the concentration of serum in the broth was 1%, 5% or 10%.

Reversion of spheroplasts to vegetative staphylococci was more likely to occur when the spheroplasts were not too far removed in time from the inducing agent, methicillin. Two environmental conditions conducive to reversion were omission of serum and, in plates, increase in concentration of agar. None of these conditions, however, could bring about uniformly predictable reversion.

REFERENCES

1. Banville, R. R.: Factors affecting growth of *Staphylococcus aureus* L forms on semidefined medium. *J. Bact.* **87:** 1192, 1964.

2. Bigger, J. W.: Treatment of staphylococcal infections with penicillin by intermittent sterilisation. *Lancet* **2:** 497, 1944.

3. Carleton, J., and Hamburger, M.: Unmasking of false-negative blood cultures in patients receiving new penicillins. *JAMA* **186:** 157, 1963.

4. Godzeski, C. W., Brier, G., and Pavey, D. E.: L-phase growth induction as a general characteristic of antibiotic-bacterial interaction in the presence of serum. In: *Antimicrobial Agents and Chemotherapy—1962* (J. C. Sylvester, Ed.). American Society for Microbiology, Ann Arbor, 1963: p. 843.

5. Gunnison, J. B., Fraher, M. A., and Jawetz, E.: Persistence of *Staphylococcus aureus* in penicillin *in vitro*. *J. Gen. Microbiol.* **35:** 335, 1964.

6. Hamburger, M., and Carleton, J.: Staphylococcal spheroplasts and L colonies. I. Population curves of vegetative staphylococci and spheroplasts in methicillin-containing broth over long periods. *J. Infect. Dis.* **116:** 221, 1966.

7. ———: Staphylococcal spheroplasts and L colonies. II. Conditions conducive to rever-

sion of spheroplasts to vegetative staphylococci. *J. Infect. Dis.* **116:** 544, 1966.

8. Hamburger, M., Carleton, J., Walker, W. F., and Clark, K. L.: A study of experimental staphylococcal endocarditis in dogs. II. Penicillin-sensitive mutants arising from penicillin-resistant Staphylococcus aureus during the course of experimental canine endocarditis. *Arch. Intern. Med.* (Chicago) **105:** 668, 1960.

9. Kagan, B. M.: Staphylococcal L-forms—ecologic perspectives. *Ann. N. Y. Acad. Sci.* **128:** 81, 1965.

10. Kagan, B. M., Molander, C. W., and Weinberger, H. J.: Induction and cultivation of staphylococcal L forms in the presence of methicillin. *J. Bact.* **83:** 1162, 1962.

11. Kagan, G. Y., and Levashov, V. S.: Methods for obtaining L-forms of the group A hemolytic streptococci and their reversion into bacterial cultures. *Zh. Mikrobiol. Epidemiol. Immunobiol.* **30**(12): 68, 1959.

12. Landman, O. E., and Ginoza, H. S.: Genetic nature of stable L forms of Salmonella paratyphi. *J. Bact.* **81:** 875, 1961.

13. Landman, O. E., and Halle, S.: Enzymically and physically induced inheritance changes in *Bacillus subtilis. J. Mol. Biol.* **7:** 721, 1963.

14. Lederberg, J.: Bacterial protoplasts induced by penicillin. *Proc. Nat. Acad. Sci. USA* **42:** 574, 1956.

15. Marston, J.: Cultivation of staphylococcal L forms in a liquid medium. *J. Bact.* **81:** 832, 1961.

16. ———: Observations on L forms of staphylococci. *J. Infect. Dis.* **108:** 75, 1961.

17. McDermott, W.: Microbial persistence. *Yale J. Biol. Med.* **30:** 257, 1958.

18. Schönfeld, J. K.: "L" forms of staphylococci; their reversibility; changes in the sensitivity pattern after several intermediary passages in the "L" phase. *Antonie Leeuwenhoek* **25:** 325, 1959.

22

The *In Vitro* Production, Cultivation and Properties of L-Forms of Pathogenic *Neisseriae*

Richard B. Roberts

THE ROCKEFELLER UNIVERSITY
NEW YORK, NEW YORK

The persistence and recurrence of bacterial infections despite "adequate" antibiotic therapy have been theoretically explained in part by the *in vivo* production of bacterial L-forms. The production of L-forms in an experimental animal[8] and the recovery of L-forms from human clinical specimens[4] have been supportive evidence for this hypothesis.

Because L-forms of *Neisseria meningitidis* and *Neisseria gonorrhoeae* may persist both during prophylaxis and in certain clinical disease states, initial *in vitro* investigations of these bacterial variants were undertaken.[12, 13, 14] This review summarizes these findings to date.

In this report, *L-forms* are defined as bacterial variants which may be produced by substances that inhibit bacterial cell wall synthesis and are, in turn, serially propagated on artificial medium.

MATERIALS AND METHODS

ORGANISMS

The group B meningococcal strains used in these studies have been described previously.[14] Group A and C strains are summarized in Table 22.1. These strains, obtained from the Department of Bacteriology, Walter Reed Army Institute of Research, Washington, D.C., and hereafter designated 45, 98, 47 and 95, were sensitive to sulfadiazine; three of the four were recent isolates from the spinal fluid or blood of patients with meningitis; the source of strain 95 was not known. All strains of *N. meningitidis* had identical fermentative reactions.

N. gonorrhoeae strain 424 was a recent isolate from a patient with acute Bartholin's abscess.[12]

MEDIA AND GROWTH CONDITIONS

Meningococci and gonococci were subcultured either in BBL Eugon broth or on Difco Mueller-Hinton chocolate agar (4% defibrinated sheep blood). Broth cultures were placed on a reciprocating shaker and incubated aerobically at 37°C for 8–12 hours. Cultures on agar were incubated at 37°C in the presence of moisture and CO_2 (candle jar) for 18–24 hours.

The medium for the production of meningococcal L-forms was brain heart infusion (Difco) of pH 7.2–7.4, containing 1.2% agar, 10% sucrose, 0.5% yeast extract and 10% inactivated (60°C for 30 minutes) horse serum; this medium is hereafter designated BRHIA. L-forms were serially propagated on BRHIA con-

TABLE 22.1

Meningococci Employed for
L-Form Production

Organism No.	Group	Sulfadi-azine Sensi-tivity (M.I.C.-mg%)	Source of Isolates	Place and Time of Isolation
45-Eur.	A	0.05	Spinal Fluid	Germany, October, 1964
98-Eur.	A	0.05	Spinal Fluid	Germany, October, 1965
47-VI	C	0.05	Blood	United States, September, 1964
95-Eur.	C	0.05	—	Germany, October, 1965

taining benzylpenicillin (1000 units/ml). Plate cultures were incubated at 37°C in the presence of moisture and CO_2 (candle jar).

L-forms of *N. gonorrhoeae* were produced and cultivated under identical conditions, except that (*a*) 100 units/ml benzylpenicillin were added to the medium and (*b*) plate cultures were incubated at 36°C.

PRODUCTION AND PROPAGATION OF L-FORMS

The method for production of L-forms was the gradient plate technique.[14] The antibiotics tested were benzylpenicillin, methicillin, ampicillin, cycloserine, cephalothin, vancomycin, ristocetin, erythromycin, novobiocin, tetracycline, bacitracin and sulfisoxazole.[13] Meningococcal L-form cultures were serially transferred every 2–4 days, whereas gonococcal L-forms were subcultured every 4–6 days.

Group B meningococcal L-forms were also adapted for growth in a broth medium.[14] After three serial passages on BRHIA with penicillin and 10% rabbit serum, large agar blocks with L-form growth were transferred to 125 ml flasks containing 25 ml of BRHIA with penicillin. The inoculated agar was then overlaid with 10 ml of brain heart infusion containing 0.01% agar, 10% sucrose, 0.5% yeast extract and 1000 units/ml benzylpenicillin (BRHIB). Both the agar and broth contained 10% rabbit serum in place

of horse serum. On the third and sixth day after inoculation, 0.2 ml of broth was subcultured on BRHIA with penicillin. Following incubation for 48–72 hours, these subcultures on agar were in turn transferred to other flasks with diphasic media. This procedure was repeated until a heavy growth of L-form colonies appeared in the broth. One ml of the broth culture was then serially transferred to 25 ml of BRHIB. All L-form broth cultures were incubated at 37°C in the presence of CO_2 (candle jar) for 4–6 days.

MORPHOLOGY OF L-FORMS

Colony morphology of meningococcal and gonococcal L-forms was examined by light microscopy and by the Dienes stained agar technique[6] with phase contrast microscopy.

Electron microscopy of meningococcal L-forms was performed by Dr. H. Goldstein.* L-form colonies produced by penicillin and transferred for 15 serial passages on BRHIA containing penicillin were removed from the agar medium in blocks not greater than 1 mm². These colonies were fixed in 2% glutaraldehyde (sodium citrate buffer, pH 7.0) for 24 hours at 4°C and were then post-fixed in 1% osmium tetroxide (potassium phosphate, pH 7.0) for one hour. Following fixation, the material was dehydrated in graded dilutions of ethyl alcohol and was embedded in Epon 812. Sections were stained with 1% alcoholic uranyl acetate and lead citrate[11] and were examined with an RCA-EMU electron microscope.

BIOCHEMICAL PROPERTIES OF L-FORMS

Carbohydrate fermentations were tested on Difco heart infusion agar.[1] The indophenol oxidase test was performed by adding a solution of tetramethyl-p-phenylenediamine to a two-day growth of L-form colonies on agar.

MEMBRANE FILTRATION OF L-FORMS

Parent meningococci and their L-forms were filtered through Millipore membrane

* Department of Experimental Pathology, Walter Reed Army Institute of Research.

filters of six different pore sizes. An 18 hour growth of parent meningococci on chocolate agar was transferred to 15 ml of Eugon broth. Two ml aliquots of the broth suspension were filtered from hypodermic syringes through 13 mm diameter filters (placed in Swinney adapters). Serial dilutions of the broth suspensions in Eugon broth and subsequent colony plating were done before and after each filtration experiment. Meningococcal L-forms were harvested from BRHIA, suspended in Eugon broth and processed in a similar manner. The following are the Millipore filters and pore sizes (in μ) used: AA, 0.80; DA, 0.65; HA, 0.45; PH, 0.30; GS, 0.22; and VC, 0.10.

PRESERVATION OF L-FORMS

The viability of meningococcal L-forms was examined following (a) incubation of broth cultures over a wide range of temperatures, and (b) storage of frozen agar and broth cultures. Five ml of L-form broth cultures in 18 standard 15 × 120 mm test tubes were placed in a "Poly-Temp" thermostat temperature gradient bar (Lab-Line Instruments, Inc., Chicago, Ill.). The temperature gradient was adjusted to 18–43°C. Aliquots of 0.1 ml were removed from each tube before incubation and at weekly intervals thereafter, serially diluted in Eugon broth, and plated onto BRHIA containing penicillin. These plates were incubated at 37°C in the presence of moisture and CO_2 (candle jar) and the number of viable colony-forming units determined.

Broth and agar cultures of L-form colonies were placed in 45 × 15 mm screwcap vials, frozen with acetone and dry ice and immediately stored at temperatures of −24°C, −60°C and −196°C (liquid nitrogen). At intervals of 6–12 months, samples were removed and cultured on fresh BRHIA. All viable samples were subcultured three times before being discarded.

REVERSION OF L-FORMS AND PROPERTIES OF REVERTANTS

To allow reversion to the bacterial form, L-form colonies from every tenth serial passage on media containing an antibiotic were transferred to antibiotic-free BRHIA and subcultured until bacterial colonies appeared.[12, 13, 14] These revertant organisms were subsequently transferred to Mueller-Hinton chocolate agar, examined by Gram stain and identified by serologic agglutination (macroscopic slide technique) and/ or by carbohydrate fermentations.[2]

RESULTS

PRODUCTION AND PROPAGATION OF L-FORMS

L-forms were produced by penicillin from meningococci of groups A, B and C. Growth of L-forms appeared on gradient plates between the trough and bacterial growth (Figure 22.1A). To date, all strains (two group A, four group B, and two group C) have had at least 100 serial passages on BRHIA containing penicillin. Selected stabilized variants of L-forms from group B meningococci (strains 78, 79, Ne-15, and 55) were recovered on penicillin-free BRHIA and have had over 50 serial transfers on this medium.[14]

L-forms from parent or revertant group B meningococci also have been produced by methicillin, ampicillin, cycloserine, cephalothin, ristocetin, bacitracin and vancomycin.[13] For comparative studies, only the antibiotic-induced L-forms from meningococcal parent strain 79 or revertant strain 79R were subcultured for ten serial passages on BRHIA containing the antibiotic responsible for their production. All L-forms propagated well on these media. Meningococcal L-forms have not been produced by novobiocin, tetracycline, erythromycin, or sulfisoxazole.

L-forms of *N. gonorrhoeae* have also been produced by the penicillin gradient plate technique.[12] Because L-form growth was minimal and longer periods of incubation were required, production of these L-forms from parent gonococci was more difficult than production of meningococcal L-forms. To date, gonococcal L-forms have had over 50 serial passages on BRHIA containing penicillin, and selected stabilized variants have been recovered and transferred on penicillin-free medium. The production of L-forms from parent gono-

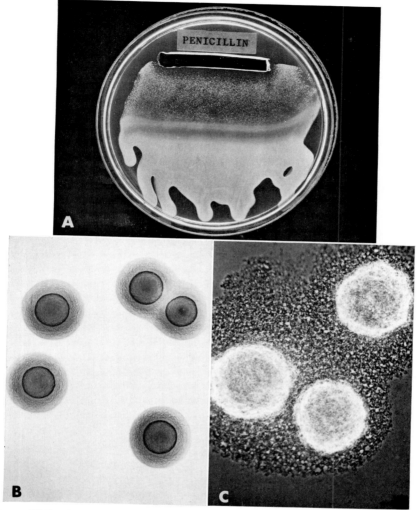

Figure 22.1. *A:* Gradient plate containing penicillin; meningococcal L-form colonies appear between the trough and bacterial growth. × 0.75. *B:* A three-day growth of meningococcal L-forms; colonies have a central area and well-defined peripheries. × 28.5. *C:* Three meningococcal L-form colonies with central cores and peripheral vacuoles; Dienes' stain with light microscopy. × 240.

cocci by other antibiotics has not been tested.

L-forms from revertant gonococci were produced on BRHIA without antibiotics.[12] Subsequent studies demonstrated that sucrose and serum were the operative medium constituents for L-form production.

OPTIMAL GROWTH CONDITIONS FOR L-FORMS

The conditions necessary for optimal growth of meningococcal and gonococcal L-forms on agar medium are shown in

Table 22.2. Although maximal growth of gonococcal L-forms was achieved by adding 100 units/ml benzylpenicillin to the medium and incubating culture plates at 36°C for 4–6 days, the degree of growth was less than that of meningococcal L-forms.

MORPHOLOGY OF L-FORMS

Colonies of L-forms from all serological groups of meningococci, as well as of L-forms produced by each antibiotic were

TABLE 22.2

Optimal Growth Conditions for Meningococcal and Gonococcal L Forms

	Meningococcal L-Forms	Gonococcal L-Forms
Medium	Brain heart infusion	Brain heart infusion
Agar %	1.1–1.3	1.1–1.3
Osmotic stabilization	Sucrose (10% or >)	Sucrose (10% or >)
Serum	Horse (5% or >)*	Horse (10% or >)
pH	7.0–7.8	7.2–7.4
Environment	CO_2 (candle jar)	CO_2 (candle jar)
Temperature (°C)	34–38	35–36

* Meningococcal L-forms grew equally well on horse, rabbit or human serum.

morphologically similar. All L-form colonies had well-demarcated cores which penetrated into the agar, and sharply defined peripheries (Figure 22.1B). Colony size was variable and was determined by the duration of growth and colony crowding.

The morphology of gonococcal L-form colonies was similar (Figure 22.2A). Central cores and well-defined, lighter peripheries were seen, though, in general, the central areas were darker than those observed in L-form colonies of meningococci.

Structural elements in colonies of both organisms were identical when stained and examined by light and phase contrast microscopy. Figure 22.1C shows three meningococcal L-form colonies; intermediate-sized phase–dense bodies, peripheral vacuoles and small granules are seen; these structures can be seen more clearly in Figure 22.2B, which shows a section of a gonococcal L-form colony. In some areas, small granules line the border of the peripheral vacuoles.

Electron micrographs of L-forms cultured on agar exhibit two major struc-

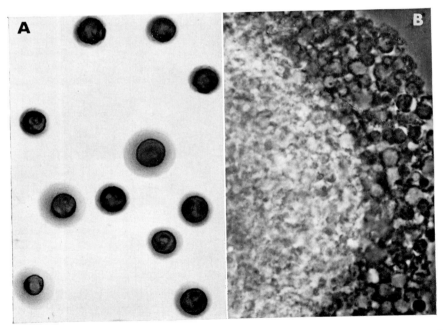

Figure 22.2. *A:* An eight-day growth of gonococcal L-forms; colonies have a dark central area and peripheries which vary in width. × 30.4. *B:* A five-day growth of a gonococcal L-form colony; periphery in focus, demonstrating intermediate-sized phase-dense bodies and peripheral vacuoles; small granular bodies line the border of the vacuoles; Dienes' stain with phase contrast microscopy. × 1280.

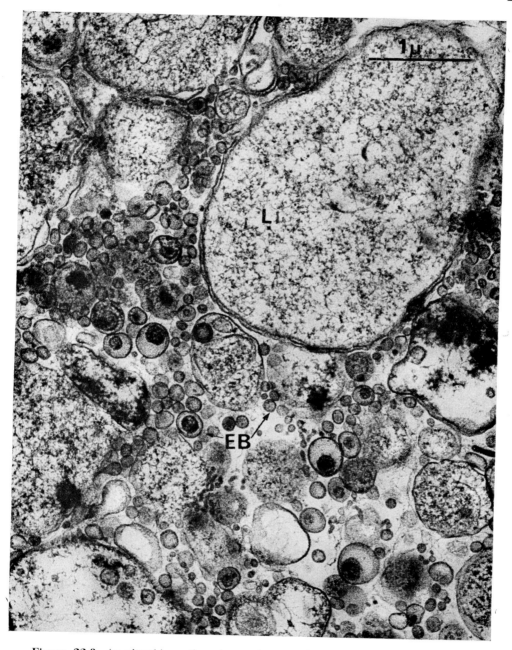

Figure 22.3. An ultrathin section of a meningococcal L-form colony. Large bodies (L) are surrounded by two electron-dense membranes and are partially devoid of cytoplasmic material. Numerous smaller elementary bodies (EB) are seen. × 28,100.

tures, the small elementary body and the large body (Figure 22.3). Elementary bodies were round or oval and varied in diameter (400–3000Å); they commonly were found between the large bodies. The smaller elementary bodies were often aligned in a linear bead-like arrangement. The large bodies also varied in diameter,

TABLE 22.3

Membrane Filtration of Parent Meningococci and Their L-Forms

Membrane Pore Size	Colonies per ml	
	Parent	L-Form
Prefiltration	2.4×10^{10}	1.6×10^7
0.80μ	1.0×10^6	1.4×10^5
0.65μ	3.0×10^1	1.2×10^5
0.45μ	0	1.0×10^4
0.30μ	0	1.6×10^2
0.22μ	0	0
0.10μ	0	0

contained less electron-dense material and occasional strands of filamentous material; these larger structures were surrounded by two electron-dense membranes.

BIOCHEMICAL PROPERTIES OF L-FORMS

All meningococcal L-forms produced acid from dextrose and maltose, but not from sucrose.[13, 14] The fermentation of carbohydrates by gonococcal L-forms was unsuccessful because the growth of these L-forms was inhibited by 2% NaCl in the medium.[12] The indophenol oxidase test by L-forms of both pathogenic *Neisseriae* was positive.

MEMBRANE FILTRATION OF L-FORMS

Results of the filtration of meningococcal L-forms and their parent strains are shown in Table 22.3. Parent meningococci did not pass through a pore size of 0.45 μ or less. After filtration through 0.45 μ and 0.30 μ pore size filters, L-forms were recovered, though a significant number of these organisms were removed from the suspension. L-forms did not pass through a 0.22 μ or a 0.10 μ pore size filter.

ANTIBIOTIC SENSITIVITIES OF L-FORMS

The relative sensitivities of L-forms of pathogenic *Neisseriae* and their parent strains to 12 antibiotics has recently been reviewed.[12, 13] Meningococcal L-forms were more resistant than the parent strain to seven of eight antibiotics that inhibit bacterial cell wall synthesis; ristocetin was

the exception. Each organism had similar sensitivities to novobiocin, tetracycline, erythromycin, and sulfadiazine.

Gonococcal L-forms were more resistant than the parent strain to penicillin, ampicillin, methicillin, cycloserine, and cephalothin, whereas both organisms had similar sensitivities to all other antibiotics tested.

PRESERVATION OF L-FORMS

Results of incubation of meningococcal L-forms for eight weeks at different temperatures are shown in Figure 22.4. Growth of L-forms did not occur at temperatures below 27°C or above 39°C: L-forms were not recovered from cultures incubated at these two temperatures after two and three weeks, respectively. At temperatures between 29–33°C, one per cent of L-forms remained viable for seven to eight weeks.

Frozen agar and broth L-form cultures were not viable after storage at −26°C. When frozen cultures were stored at −60°C or −196°C, they each remained viable for at least six months to one year. Other studies indicate that lyophilization of L-form cultures suspended in skim milk, BRHIB, or horse serum kills over 99 per cent of meningococcal L-forms.

REVERSION OF L-FORMS AND PROPERTIES OF REVERTANTS

Revertant strains were obtained from L-forms produced by each antibiotic.[12, 13, 14] All revertant organisms were Gram-negative diplococci. Revertant meningococci produced acid from dextrose and maltose, but not from sucrose, whereas revertant gonococci produced acid only from dextrose. In addition, serologic agglutination of each revertant meningococcus was identical to that of its respective parent strain. Parent and revertant organisms had similar sensitivities to all antibiotics tested.

DISCUSSION

L-forms of *N. meningitidis* were produced only by those antibiotics that inhibit bacterial cell wall synthesis. Previous studies[13] have shown that L-form produc-

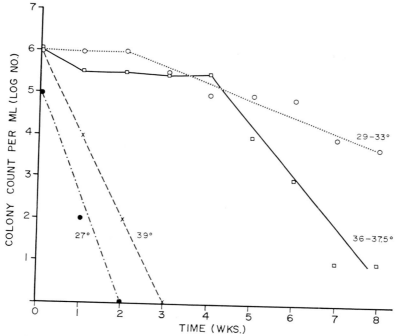

Figure 22.4. Temperature effect on viability of meningococcal L-forms; in broth cultures incubated at 27–39°C temperatures, 1% of organisms remained viable at 29–33°C for 7–8 weeks.

tion occurs over a variable range of antibiotic concentrations.

L-forms of revertant *N. gonorrhoeae* however, were produced on BRHIA without antibiotics. Previous studies have shown that complement and specific antibody are essential for the production of protoplasts and spheroplasts of certain bacteria.[3, 7, 10] Our studies demonstrate that serum is necessary for gonococcal L-form production and propagation. Because commerical horse serum, inactivated and stored at 4°C, was used in these studies, neither adequate complement nor specific antibody was present. Other serum factors must be responsible for the production of gonococcal L-forms by this method.

L-forms of pathogenic *Neisseriae* were serially propagated on similar medium (BRHIA). Optimal growth of L-forms was observed, although these findings may well be modified when specific chemical growth requirements of these organisms are defined.

The size and structure of elementary bodies seen in ultrathin sections of meningococcal L-form colonies closely resemble those described for other bacterial L-forms.[16, 17] The vesicular appearance of large bodies has also been reported.[15, 16] These findings suggest that L-forms from different bacteria have a similar ultrastructure, and that electron microscopy may not be useful in the specific identification of these organisms.

Filtration methods have previously been used to separate L-forms from bacteria in animal and human material.[4, 8] The *in vitro* studies described in this report suggest that this method may also be applicable to the *in vivo* study of meningococcal L-forms, though significant numbers of organisms may be lost during filtration (pore size 0.45 μ).

Methods of storing *Mycoplasma* strains have been reported,[5, 9] but we are not aware of previous reports describing the preservation of L-forms. The present studies indicate that only one per cent of L-forms adapted to a broth medium remained viable at 29–33°C for seven to eight weeks. For adequate preservation, freezing of either broth or agar cultures and storage at −60 to −196°C is recommended.

SUMMARY

L-forms of pathogenic *Neisseriae* were produced by the penicillin gradient plate technique. L-forms of group B *Neisseria meningitidis* were also produced by methicillin, ampicillin, cephalothin, cycloserine, ristocetin, bacitracin, and vancomycin. Meningococcal L-forms were propagated on medium containing the antibiotic responsible for their production, and all L-forms had similar growth, morphologic, and biochemical properties. Stabilized L-form variants of both *Neisseriae* were obtained on antibiotic-free medium. Sensitivities of L-forms and parent organisms to 12 antibiotics were determined. Meningococcal L-forms, unlike parent strains, passed through membrane filters with a 0.45 μ pore size. One per cent of broth cultures of meningococcal L-forms remained viable at 29–33°C for seven to eight weeks, whereas frozen broth or agar cultures stored at −60 or −196°C were viable for at least six months to one year.

Revertant organisms were obtained from both meningococcal and gonococcal L-forms. All revertant bacteria had the same morphologic appearance, serologic agglutination, fermentative properties, and antibiotic sensitivities as their respective parent strains. The only difference observed between these two organisms was the property of revertant strains to produce L-forms more readily than the parent bacterium. In fact, L-forms from revertant gonococci were produced on a suitable medium containing only sucrose and serum. Further studies are necessary to determine specific procedures for the identification of L-forms of pathogenic *Neisseriae* before their possible role in human disease can be defined.

REFERENCES

1. Edward, D. G. ff.: An investigation of the biological properties of organisms of the pleuropneumonia group, with suggestions regarding the identification of strains. *J. Gen. Microbiol.* **4**: 311, 1950.

2. Evans, J. R., Hunter, D. H., Cary, S. G., and Rust, J. H., Jr.: Simplified method for determination of sulfadiazine sensitivity and fermentation reactions of *Neisseria meningitidis*. *Bact. Proc.* 1964: p. 56.

3. Freeman, B. A., Musteikis, G. M., and Burrows, W.: Protoplast formation as the mechanism of immune lysis of *Vibrio cholerae*. *Proc. Soc. Exp. Biol. Med.* **113**: 675, 1963.

4. Gutman, L. T., Turck, M., Petersdorf, R. G., and Wedgwood, R. J.: Significance of bacterial variants in urine of patients with chronic bacteriuria. *J. Clin. Invest.* **44**: 1945, 1965.

5. Kelton, W. H.: Storage of *Mycoplasma* strains. *J. Bact.* **87**: 588, 1964.

6. Madoff, S.: Isolation and identification of PPLO. *Ann. N. Y. Acad. Sci.* **79**: 383, 1960.

7. Michael, J. G., and Braun, W.: Serum spheroplasts of *Shigella dysenteriae*. *Proc. Soc. Exp. Biol. Med.* **100**: 422, 1959.

8. Mortimer, E. A., Jr.: Production of L forms of group A streptococci in mice. *Proc. Soc. Exp. Biol. Med.* **119**: 159, 1965.

9. Morton, H. E. The preservation of pleuropneumonialike organisms (PPLO) by lyophilization. *Bact. Proc.* 1963: p. 51.

10. Muschel, L. H., Carey, W. F., and Baron, L. S.: Formation of bacterial protoplasts by serum components. *J. Immun.* **82**: 38, 1959.

11. Reynolds, E. S.: The use of lead citrate at high pH as an electron-opaque stain in electron microscopy. *J. Cell Biol.* **17**: 208, 1963.

12. Roberts, R. B.: L form of *Neisseria gonorrhoeae*. *J. Bact.* **92**: 1609, 1966.

13. ———: Production of L forms of *Neisseria meningitidis* by antibiotics. *Proc. Soc. Exp. Biol. Med.* **124**: 611, 1967.

14. Roberts, R. B., and Wittler, R. G.: The L form of *Neisseria meningitidis*. *J. Gen. Microbiol.* **44**: 139, 1966.

15. Thorsson, K. G. and Weibull, C.: Studies on the structure of bacterial L forms, protoplasts and protoplast-like bodies. *J. Ultrastr. Res.* **1**: 412, 1958.

16. Van Den Hooff, A., and Hijmans, W.: An electron microscope study of L forms of group A streptococci. *Antonie Leeuwenhoek* **25**: 88, 1959.

17. Weibull, C., Mohri, T., and Afzelius, B. A.: The morphology and fine structure of small particles present in cultures of a Proteus L form. *J. Ultrastr. Res.* **12**: 81, 1965.

23

The Response of Growing Protoplasts to Various Doses of Vitamins A and E

Philip C. Fitz-James

UNIVERSITY OF WESTERN ONTARIO MEDICAL SCIENCE CENTER
LONDON, ONTARIO, CANADA

The damaging effects of vitamin A alcohol* in excess of a critical concentration have been extensively studied by Lucy, Dingle and their associates on mammalian membranes.[2, 3, 10, 11, 12] Similarly, the protective effect of vitamin E against the damage due to excess vitamin A penetration of membranes has also been shown by Lucy and Dingle.[4, 11]

Since growing protoplasts of *Bacillus megaterium* are useful for studying the mode of action of wall and membrane antibiotics,[7] their sensitivity to a number of membrane-active agents was also studied. It was found that the actively growing membrane system of enlarging but non-dividing *B. megaterium* protoplasts offered a system more sensitive than non-growing protoplasts[9] for the study of the effects of adding small doses of vitamins A and E.

This paper reports the changes in optical density brought about by the additions of vitamin A, vitamin E, and the two together on protoplasts growing in osmotically supported media. The structure of the membranes following these treatments was compared by both thin section and negative staining techniques, and differences were found. It was also noted, incidentally, that vitamin E-stabilized protoplasts reverted more readily to the vegetative form than untreated ones.

METHODS

Sucrose-stabilized protoplasts were made from rapidly dividing cells of *B. megaterium* KM by a method already described.[5] They were grown in either a succinate growth medium,[6] or a medium made by mixing equal parts of double strength heart infusion broth (Difco) and 0.6 M sucrose containing 0.032 M $MgSO_4$; the mixture was buffered by the addition of sterile M potassium phosphate pH 6.8 or 7.2 to a final concentration of 0.05 M.

Stock solutions of vitamin A alcohol (20 mg/ml) and vitamin E (100 mg/ml) DL as alpha tocopheryl acetate (Nutritional Biochemicals) were prepared in 70% ethanol and added in μl quantities, for the final concentration required, to 20 ml of protoplast culture aerated by gentle shaking in 300 ml nephalo culture flasks (Bellco). Control flasks received an equal amount of 70% alcohol. The optical densities of the control and treated flasks were followed with a Coleman spectrophotometer (Model 14) at a wavelength of 650 mμ. Cultures were observed by phase microscopy of coverslip smears and by electron microscopy of the protoplast membranes by thin sectioning and negative staining. For thin sectioning, a 5–10 ml

---

* Unless otherwise noted, the term *vitamin A* indicates the alcohol form.

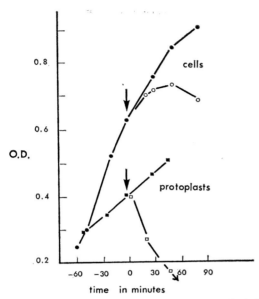

Figure 23.1. The effect of vitamin A alcohol (20 μg/ml), added at time 0, on the growth of cells and protoplasts of *Bacillus megaterium* KM in heart infusion broth containing 0.3 M sucrose. Solid markers: control; open markers: vitamin A.

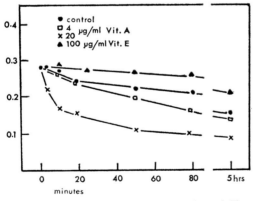

Figure 23.2. Effect of vitamins A and E on the stability of non-growing protoplasts suspended in sucrose (0.3 M), MgSO₄ (0.016 M), K phosphate 0.05 M, pH 7.2). Ordinate: optical density.

sample of the culture was prefixed by the addition of a tenth the volume of 1% OsO₄, then mixed and centrifuged. This prefixation formed ghosts if protoplasts were not already lysed. The membrane pellet was then embedded in 0.25% agar, and the fixation and embedding procedure

continued according to the method of Kellenberger, Ryter & Séchaud.[8] For negative staining, an aliquot of culture was first lysed by adding it to an equal volume of distilled water followed by centrifugation; the resulting pellet, suspended in a small amount of 2% sodium tungstate pH 6.5,[14] was immediately mounted on carbon-stabilized Formvar-coated grids. (Formvar: Shawinigan Products.)

RESULTS

A comparison of the effects of vitamin A on cells and protoplasts growing in heart infusion-sucrose is shown in Figure 23.1. At 5 μg/ml (17 μM) the effect on the growing protoplasts was almost as dramatic as that shown in the figure. Cells, however, when aerated with 20 μg/ml vitamin A in the same medium, with or without added sucrose, responded much less dramatically (Figure 23.1). After aeration for an hour with 20 μg/ml, a plating of the cell culture with sucrose showed approximately one per cent survival, while a plating of a culture without sucrose was sterile.

As Kinsky[9] has already reported, vitamin A was found to have a lytic effect on freshly formed non-growing protoplasts. However, the static protoplasts stabilized in sucrose-Mg phosphate were here considerably less sensitive than the growing ones (Figure 23.2). Different batches of protoplasts were found to have different responses to the same concentration of vitamin A; generally, the older the protoplast preparation, the less responsive they were.

The action of the two fat soluble vitamins alone and in combination on protoplasts growing in the cationic succinate growth medium[6] are shown in Figure 23.3. Vitamin A at 20 μg/ml caused a severe and sudden lysis, and at 4 μg/ml a less severe fall in optical density. The addition of α-tocopherol at 100 μg/ml produced a better growth response than the control with or without the addition of ethanol. Vitamin E at a concentration of 100 μg/ml was insufficient to protect the growing protoplast structures from lysis by 10 μg/ml of vitamin A. This concentration of vitamin E was, however, sufficient to protect the protoplasts against a dose of 5 μg/ml (17 μM) of vitamin A (Figure 23.4). Again, the vitamin E alone permits a greater growth of the protoplast spheres than the control.

Attempts to find an effect partway between that shown by the control and the 4 μg/ml concentration of vitamin A were unsuccessful. At 2 and 3 μg/ml of vitamin A the response was as good as, if not better than, the control, and like that of vitamin E at 100 μg/ml. In separate experiments, vitamin A aldehyde was found to be ineffective in causing lysis of the growing protoplasts.

In the phase contrast microscope, shortly after the addition of vitamin A to protoplasts not stabilized by sufficient vitamin E, a remarkable blebbing of the profile was seen in those protoplasts not yet fully lysed. One, two, and sometimes three, large blisters could be seen on the surface of the protoplasts before lysis, and even in some of the ghosts when lysis

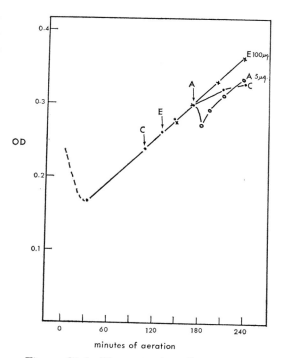

Figure 23.4. The protective effect of vitamin E at 100 μg/ml from the effect of vitamin A at 5 μg/ml on growing protoplasts. At *C* the control flask received an equivalent amount of solvent (70% alcohol).

was complete. No such blebs were ever seen on the control or the vitamin E-treated protoplasts. However, those protoplasts treated with vitamin A but well stabilized with sufficient vitamin E did show localized blebs on the outline, in spite of their not undergoing lysis. The drop in optical density on adding vitamin A to vitamin E-protected cultures (Figure 23.4) can be associated with the onset of these surface distensions. Similar local distensions in the cell membrane of fibroblasts and surface indentations and vacuoles in rabbit erythrocytes after vitamin A treatment have also been described.[12]

The differences seen in the membrane profiles of these growing protoplasts treated with vitamin A and E were difficult to interpret. However, vitamin E profiles did appear to be slightly more prominent than the control, and much more prominent

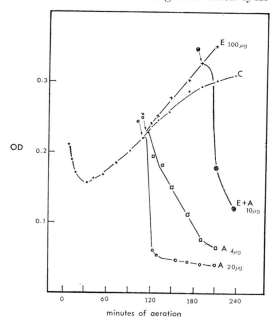

Figure 23.3. The effect of adding various doses (in μg/ml) of vitamin A to growing protoplasts of *Bacillus megaterium* KM. Vitamin E at 100 μg/ml did not protect against the effect of 10 μg/ml vitamin A.

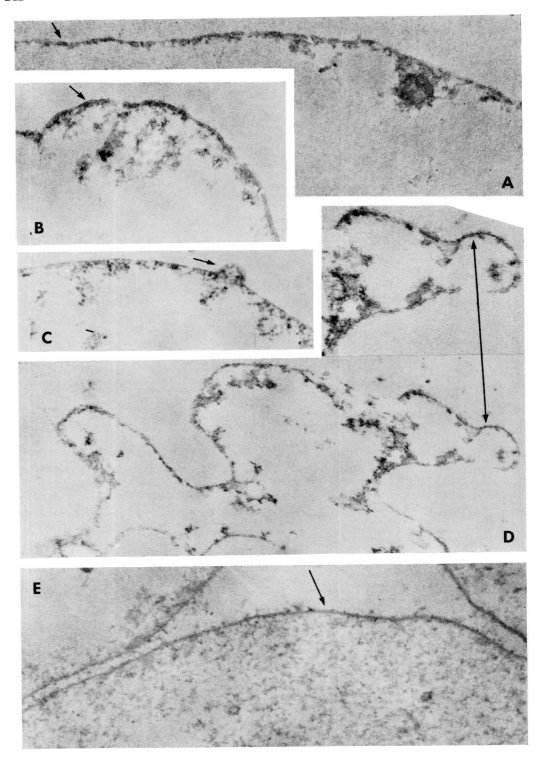

Figure 23.5.

than the vitamin A-treated ones; some of this difference might be the result of greater adherence of cytoplasmic material to the membrane (Figure 23.5, A, B, C). The membranes of the vitamin A-treated protoplasts, however, were always thinner and the profiles much less circular. In places the membrane appeared to be completely destroyed, and the usual typical double-tract lamellar appearance of plasma membrane was difficult to find (Figure 23.5, D and insert). This absence of the usual unit-membrane structure appeared to be more striking in ghost remnants treated with higher doses of vitamin A (Figure 23.5C). Small blebs on the membrane profile were often seen on the membranes of treated protoplasts and are possibly smaller versions of the blisters seen by phase microscopy. The membrane was remarkably thin in such regions (Figure 23.5C, arrow). The profile of the membranes of those protoplasts treated with 5 μg/ml vitamin A, following stabilization with sufficient vitamin E to prevent lysis, were, like the control, more spherical, suggesting greater rigidity, and more continuous in their outline (Figure 23.5E).

Negative staining was equally effective, if not more striking, in demonstrating the differences in these membrane structures. In general appearance, the profiles of vitamin E-treated protoplasts were quite similar to those of the membranes of control protoplasts (Figure 23.6, A and C). However, the membranes from the vitamin A-treated protoplasts generally appeared much less dense and more shredded than those of either the control or the vitamin E protoplasts (Figure 23.6B).

Many peculiar stalked bodies could be seen attached to the membranes of the growing protoplasts. These have occasionally been seen before on the membranes of the non-growing protoplasts of this same species but were more prominent on those of the growing protoplasts; they do not show particularly well in Figure 23.6 A. They were even more prominent than the control, however, on those membranes from protoplasts that had been stabilized with vitamin E (Figure 23.6 C, arrows). They were also seen on the membranes of vitamin A-treated protoplasts, but only on localized, more dense parts of the residual membrane. The nature of these structures is unknown. Dr. Dina Abrahms has also seen similar structures on protoplast membranes.* Their preservation by tocopherol and their relative absence on membranes from vitamin A-treated protoplasts suggest they are somewhat unstable components of the membrane. They were of variable length, up to 650 Å, with six tiers of 50 × 120 Å each, spaced about 100 Å apart. In some regions, three to six globular subunits 30–50 Å in diameter could be seen making up a tier. Conceivably, these structures might represent a helical extrusion of globular micelles of the type depicted by Lucy & Glauert[13] in artificial assemblies of phospholipids and cholesterol and saponin; they were often seen lying free in the tungstate background of these preparations.

VITAMIN E ENHANCEMENT OF REVERSION

When flasks of growing protoplasts are left standing overnight, a few reverting

* Personal communication.

Figure 23.5. Electron micrographs of thin sections of "ghost" membranes from control and treated protoplasts. All except C from protoplasts grown in succinate growth medium. A: Segment of a ghost membrane from a control culture showing some adherence of cytoplasmic material and the double-track membrane profile (arrow); × 76,000. B: Vitamin E-treated membranes from lysed cultures showed a better preservation of the usual membrane profile (arrow); × 76,000. C: Membrane profile from a protoplast lysed with 20 μg/ml vitamin A while growing in HIB-sucrose; the membrane is very thin and the typical unit membrane cannot be seen; blebs where the membrane seemed deficient were common (arrow); × 76,000. D: Membrane profile of protoplasts lysed with 4 μg/ml vitamin A while growing in succinate-growth medium; in some areas, typical membrane lamellae are found at this critical dose level (arrows and insert, upper D); × 70,000; insert × 110,000. E: Profile of a ghost from a growing protoplast treated first with 100 μg/ml vitamin E and then with 5 μg/ml vitamin A; the overall membrane structure and the lamellar structure, where seen, are more delicate (arrow); × 76,000.

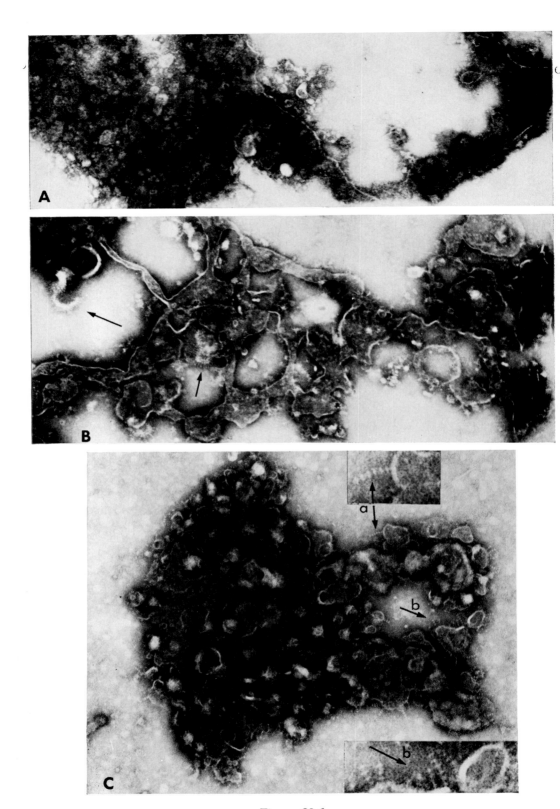

Figure 23.6.

forms are often found lying in the slimy sediment at the bottom of the flask (Figure 23.7 A). Typical dividing bacilli of *B. megaterium* KM can be recovered by either continuous observation or plating out these sediments. Protoplasts which have not begun to grow do not give rise to bacilli when plated on ordinary medium. In the flasks of vitamin E-treated growing protoplasts that had been stabilized with sufficient concentrations of vitamin E, a considerably higher proportion of reverting forms was encountered. The reversion of these growing protoplasts could be observed by mounting them on microscope slides between cover-slip and thin blocks of agar (0.2–0.5%) containing protoplast growth medium (Figure 23.7 B). When protoplasts treated with vitamin E were mounted in agar plus vitamin E-containing growth medium they showed a higher proportion of reverting forms than did protoplasts not treated with vitamin E.

DISCUSSION

Although *B. megaterium* KM has no requirement for vitamins A or E, the effects of these vitamins on the membrane of growing protoplasts are very similar to those already described on the membrane of mammalian erythrocytes, fibroblasts,[12] and isolated lysosomes.[1] As with the mammalian membrane systems, a critical concentration of vitamin A is required before the protoplast membrane breaks down. However, while the erythrocyte releases its hemoglobin above a concentration of 20 μM,[3] and the isolated rat liver lysosome begins to lyse and liberate acid phosphatase only above 31–36 μM,[1] the growing protoplasts were rapidly lysed by vitamin A at a critical concentration of

12–14 μM. This sensitivity is even more remarkable if one takes into account the fact that the mammalian critical concentrations were determined at 37°C, while 30°C was the temperature used for *B. megaterium*.

Although one should not expect thin-section electron micrographs of membranes to reflect the vitamin A-induced changes in molecular architecture, considerable differences were found in the profiles of the membranes from control and treated growing protoplasts. The profile usually associated with a bimolecular lamellar structure was rare in the sections of membranes of protoplasts lysed with the critical concentration (14 μM) of vitamin A, and completely absent when a higher dose (70 μM) was used for lysis. Moreover, in areas where the membrane was distended the profile was so thin that it appeared the vitamin A treatment might have removed part of the structure. Even the membranes from growing protoplasts treated with vitamin A in excess yet protected with vitamin E did not present the same dense lamellar profile seen in the control or in those treated with vitamin E only. Instead, where a double profile was seen, it was much more delicate in outline. It is thus, tempting to interpret these electron micrographic changes in the light of the proposals that vitamin A promotes the transformation of the membrane molecular architecture from the leaflet to the globular micellar form,[13] and that vitamin E enables the micellar architecture to persist, when an excess of vitamin A has entered the membrane, by preventing the damage associated with its oxidation.[4]

It will be of interest to see if future work will show that the tightly wound and presumably more flexible mesosomal membrane contains a higher proportion of globular micelle structure and has a dif-

Figure 23.6. Negative-stained smears of membranes from growing protoplasts; × 54,000; inserts, × 150,000. *A:* Control protoplast membrane lysed by tungstate washing. *B:* Membrane from protoplast lysed with vitamin A (20 μg/ml); the membrane sheets were much less dense, more free of adhering cytoplasm, and rather shredded; small regions or vesicles of membrane were endowed with beaded stalks (arrows). *C:* Membrane from a protoplast grown in the presence of vitamin E (100 μg/ml) and lysed by tungstate washing; much of the crumpled and distorted material is endowed with beaded stalks (insert and arrows, *a* and *b*).

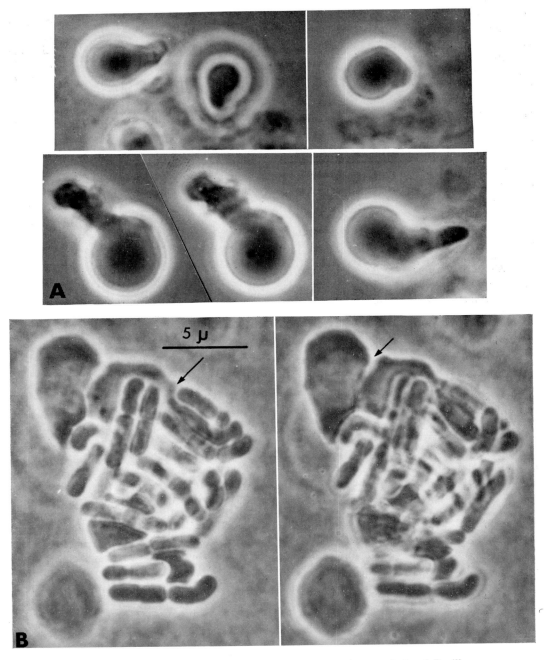

Figure 23.7. *A:* Phase contrast micrograph of untreated protoplasts of *Bacillus megaterium* KM after 6 hours aeration at 30°C in succinate-growth medium and overnight incubation without shaking; a few of the protoplasts in the thin layer of partly lysed and viscous sediment are beginning to revert to cells (magnification as for B). *B:* Phase contrast photomicrographs at two levels of focus of protoplasts of *B. megaterium* KM which, after six hours growth in the presence of vitamin E (100 μg/ml), were mounted between soft agar and coverslip and incubated overnight; the microcolony of typical bacilli can be traced back (arrows) to the original compressed protoplast.

ferent sensitivity to vitamin A alcohol than the less flexible plasma membrane, presumably the site of the more typical leaflet structure. This interest is now accentuated in view of the apparent precursor-product relationship between mesosome and ghost membrane reported elsewhere in this volume.* Indeed, it has already been suggested that, since the micellar arrangement would more easily permit the insertion of additional lipid micelles, this structure should be found at the site of new membrane synthesis.[10]

SUMMARY

These studies have shown that the growing protoplast system can be used for demonstrating the actions of fat-soluble vitamins A and E and suggest a useful system for further studies. These observations on bacterial membrane sensitivity to the fat-soluble vitamins might possibly be of assistance to those studying the reversion of protoplasts and L-forms to bacilli.

REFERENCES

1. Bassett, B. E., and Packer, L.: Response of isolated lysosomes to vitamin A. *J. Cell Biol.* **27:** 448, 1965.
2. Dingle, J. T., Glauert, A. M., Daniel, M., and Lucy, J. A.: Vitamin A and membrane systems. I. The action of the vitamin on the membranes of cells and intracellular particles. *Biochem. J.* **84:** 76P, 1962.
3. Dingle, J. T., and Lucy, J. A.: Studies on the mode of action of excess of vitamin A. 5. The effect of vitamin A on the stability of the erythrocyte membrane. *Biochem. J.* **84:** 611, 1962.
4. ———: Vitamin A and membrane systems: interactions of vitamin A and vitamin E. *Biochem. J.* **86:** 15P, 1963.
5. Fitz-James, P. C.: Studies on the morphology and nucleic acid content of protoplasts of *Bacillus megaterium. J. Bact.* **75:** 369, 1957.
6. ———: Cytological and chemical studies of the growth of protoplasts of *Bacillus megaterium. J. Biophys. Biochem. Cytol.* **4:** 257, 1958.
7. Hancock, R., and Fitz-James, P. C.: Some differences in the action of penicillin, bacitracin, and vancomycin on *Bacillus megaterium. J. Bact.* **87:** 1044, 1964.
8. Kellenberger, E., Ryter, A., and Séchaud, J.: Electron microscope study of DNA-containing plasms. II. Vegetative and mature phage DNA as compared with normal bacterial nucleoids in different physiological states. *J. Biophys. Biochem. Cytol.* **4:** 671, 1958.
9. Kinsky, S. C.: Comparative responses of mammalian erythrocytes and microbial protoplasts to polyene antibiotics and vitamin A. *Arch. Biochem. Biophys.* **102:** 180, 1963.
10. Lucy, J. A.: Globular lipid micelles and cell membranes. *J. Theor. Biol.* **7:** 360, 1964.
11. ———: Vitamin A and oxygen: studies relevant to the actions of vitamin E in membranes. *Biochem. J.* **99:** 57P, 1966.
12. Lucy, J. A., and Dingle, J. T.: Fat-soluble vitamins and biological membranes. *Nature* **204:** 156, 1964.
13. Lucy, J. A., and Glauert, A. M.: Structure and assembly of macromolecular lipid complexes composed of globular micelles. *J. Mol. Biol.* **8:** 727, 1964.
14. Valentine, R. C.: The shape of protein molecules suggested by electron microscopy. *Nature* **184:** 1838, 1959.

* See pp. 124–143.

24

The Relationship of Autolysin to Lysozyme Sensitivity of *Streptococcus faecalis* 9790*

Gerald D. Shockman, J. Stuart Thompson and Margaret J. Conover

TEMPLE UNIVERSITY SCHOOL OF MEDICINE
PHILADELPHIA, PENNSYLVANIA

The conversion of bacteria to protoplasts, spheroplasts or L-forms involves the removal of all or part of the external rigid cell wall. The chemical components of the wall peptidoglycan (mucopeptide, murein) have been found in all bacteria thus far examined (see reviews[38, 55]). This polymer, when highly crosslinked, is responsible for the rigidity and shape of the cell wall of at least Gram-positive bacteria.[10, 38] In several bacterial species, it has now been clearly established that this polymer consists of alternating units of N-acetylglucosamine and N-acetylmuramic acid in β, 1–4 linkages with peptide substitutions on the N-acetylmuramic acid moiety. These peptides are crosslinked either by peptide cross bridges or, in some cases, directly from the ϵ-amino group on one peptide to a terminal carboxyl on another.[10, 26, 27, 31, 38, 55] Enzymatic rupture of either the hexosamine backbone or the

peptide crosslinks results in dissolution of the otherwise insoluble peptidoglycan polymer and/or the wall containing this polymer.[10, 38] This indicates that the three-dimensional crosslinked structure is required to maintain the insolubility and rigidity of the polymer. Such a requirement is supported by Martin's[20] finding that *Proteus* L-forms may contain a full complement of peptidoglycan components, but that this peptidoglycan contains a higher percentage of terminal amino and carboxyl groups than does the parent organism. *Proteus* L-form peptidoglycan is therefore no longer highly crosslinked, and the cell is no longer a rigid rod.

Lysozyme hydrolyzes the β, 1–4 N-acetylmuramyl-N-acetylglucosamine linkage in the polysaccharide "backbone" of the peptidoglycan.[10, 38] Although walls of probably all bacteria contain peptidoglycan, lysozyme does not dissolve cells or walls of all bacteria, not even of all Gram-positive bacteria, especially without further or additional treatments. Many reasons have been proposed for resistance to lysozyme lysis, but in only a few instances have investigations led to satisfactory conclusions. The presence of O-acetyl groups decreases lysozyme sensitivity,[1, 4, 5, 29, 30, 32] but this does not appear to be the sole

* Investigations supported by U.S. Public Health Services Research Career Award 1-K3-AI 4792 to G. D. Shockman, a research grant (AI 5044) from the National Institute of Allergy and Infectious Diseases, and a research grant from the National Science Foundation (GB 4466).

The authors thank Mr. F. Carfagno for his assistance with the experiments described in Table 24.1 and Figure 24.3.

cause for lysozyme resistance. For example, Gram-negative bacteria, such as *Escherichia coli,* cannot be lysed by lysozyme alone, but (1) the isolated peptidoglycan from *E. coli* has been shown to be hydrolyzed by lysozyme;[19] (2) lysozyme plus EDTA[34] or lysozyme at pH 9[57] have been used to prepare spheroplasts and to lyse certain Gram-negative bacteria; and (3) in a number of instances it has been shown that, while lysozyme treatment did not result in cellular lysis, exposure of the treated cells to pH 10.5 or higher (Nakamura effect) resulted in rapid cellular lysis.[12, 13, 14] Such results indicate that lysozyme-sensitive bonds are present in the peptidoglycan of many lysozyme-resistant bacteria.

Lysozyme has been known for many years to be present in body tissues and fluids[8]. The idea that lysozyme protects against bacterial invaders has not received wide support, primarily because only a relatively few Gram-positive saphrophytic species are dissolved, and most pathogens, especially Gram-negative bacteria, are resistant to dissolution. Also, there is a paucity of substantial (and difficult to obtain) evidence for a role for lysozyme *in vivo.*

Our recent investigations of the autolysin of *Streptococcus faecalis* 9790 necessitated a comparison of the autolysin with egg white lysozyme.[45] Some of the results of these studies, summarized below, indicate that the presence of an autolysin and its activators can contribute significantly to apparent lysozyme sensitivity. Extension of these observations leads us to a renewed interest in tissue lysozyme as a contributor to body defenses and as a factor in the *in vivo* formation of protoplasts, spheroplasts and L-forms. We would like to propose the hypothesis that, in the body, lysozyme, together with autolysins, other enzymes, activators and environmental factors, can at least enhance the lysis of cells that have been recently multiplying.

MATERIALS AND METHODS

All of the materials and methods used have been previously described.[7, 41, 42, 44, 45] The legends for the figures and the tables

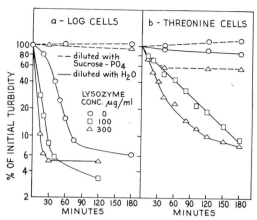

Figure 24.1. Development of osmotic sensitivity of Log and threonine-deprived cells during incubation at 38°C in sucrose phosphate solutions with and without lysozyme. Suspensions of Log cells (7000 μg cells/ml) and threonine-deprived cells (5000 μg cells/ml) were incubated in 0.5 M sucrose containing 0.05 M, pH 6.5 sodium phosphate buffer and the lysozyme concentrations indicated in the figure. Samples were taken at the indicated time intervals and diluted 1:15 with either the same sucrose phosphate solution, or 1:20 with water, and the turbidities of the diluted samples were read. Results are expressed as percentages of the turbidity of the cell suspension diluted at 0 time in a comparable manner. (From Shockman, Conover et al.[41])

include the methods used for the experiments described.

RESULTS AND DISCUSSION

Several years ago[41] we observed that cells from stationary phase, threonine-deprived cultures of *S. faecalis* appeared to be more resistant to lysozyme than were cells taken from the exponential (Log) phase of growth (Figure 24.1). Relatively high concentrations of lysozyme (300 μg/5.6 mg dry weight of cells) and prolonged incubations were needed to obtain osmotically fragile bodies free of wall components (protoplasts) from stationary phase cultures (Figure 24.1*b*), while we could prepare protoplasts in the absence of lysozyme from Log phase cells (Figure 24.1*a*). The autolytic enzyme system present in Log phase *S. faecalis* cultures was contributing to their apparent lysozyme sensitivity.

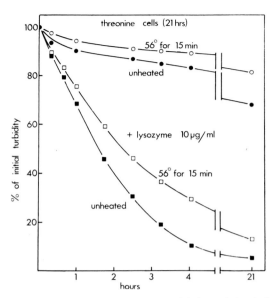

Figure 24.2. Lysozyme sensitivity of heated (56°C for 15 minutes) and unheated cells from threonine-deprived stationary phase *Streptococcus faecalis* 9790 cultures. Cells were grown on threonine-limited growth medium (4.5 μg/ml threonine). Growth was stopped after 21 hours by rapidly chilling the cultures, and cells were harvested and washed on the centrifuge in the cold. The cells were suspended in sterile water and added to tubes containing phosphate buffer, some of which were exposed to 56°C for 15 minutes (*open symbols*), while the others remained on ice. The heated tubes were chilled and lysozyme (*squares*) or water (*circles*) was added. The tubes were incubated in a 37°C water bath, and at appropriate intervals their turbidities were read at 675 mμ. The final phosphate buffer concentration was 0.05 M (pH 6.8) and the cell concentration was 300 μg/ml dry weight.

Sensitivity to lysozyme can be examined in cells that have been heated (56°C for 15 minutes) to at least partially inactivate their autolytic enzyme system. As shown in Figure 24.2, such mild heating decreased autolysis and disproportionately decreased apparent lysozyme sensitivity, even when cells autolyzed extremely slowly in the absence of lysozyme. When dealing with whole cells, it is important not to heat them so extensively that the protoplast coagulates or becomes "fixed", so that complete wall dissolution does not produce visible lysis.[35] With cells, it is difficult to heat-in-

activate autolysis completely and still retain a dissolvable substrate.

At first it was thought that heating changed the wall substrate in some way to decrease its lysozyme sensitivity. The bulk of the evidence, however, indicates that the presence of even a small amount of autolysin in cells or walls can contribute significantly and perhaps disproportionately to the observed lysozyme sensitivity. When various types of heat-inactivated cells were compared as substrates, what seemed to be a difference in lysozyme sensitivity often disappeared, as in the report that hydroxylysine incorporation decreased lysozyme sensitivity of *S. faecalis*.[46] When lysozyme sensitivities of heat-inactivated lysine and lysine-plus-hydroxylysine grown *S. faecalis* 9790 cultures were compared[44] (Table 24.1), it became clear that hydroxylysine grown cultures (Samples H1 to H6) were at least as susceptible to lysozyme as were exponential phase lysine-grown cultures (Samples L1 and L2). This includes cells that had incorporated hydroxylysine for as long as 21 hours (Sample H6). Post-exponential lysine-grown cells (Samples L3 and L4) were more rapidly digested by lysozyme, but had almost begun to autolyze from lysine exhaustion when harvested[41, 43] and probably had suffered some autolytic damage. Samples H8, H10, H12 and T2 were not heated before lysozyme addition and indicate again that autolysis can supplement lysozyme action even in cells that have been incubated for 18 to 20.5 hours after the termination of exponential growth. In the absence of lysozyme, these unheated post-exponential phase cells autolyzed very slowly, at rates comparable with that shown in Figure 24.2 for unheated threonine-deprived cells. Sample T1 (heat-inactivated threonine-deprived stationary phase cells) was somewhat more resistant to lysozyme, indicating that resistance to lysozyme may develop under appropriate conditions.

Lysozyme sensitivities can be more directly compared using isolated walls as substrate. A more direct relationship between bonds hydrolyzed and dissolution should be obtained. Figure 24.3A shows that (a) walls from Log phase cells (Log)

TABLE 24.1

Lysozyme Digestion of Heat-Inactivated Exponential and Post-Exponential Streptococcus faecalis *Cells*

1 Expt. No.	2 Sample No.	3	4	5	6 Lysine μg/ml	7 Hydroxyly-sine μg/ml	8 Incubation[a] time (hrs.)	9 AOD at harvest	10 Growth phase[b]
		\% of initial turbidity							
		30 min	60 min	120 min					
1	L 1	74	59	42	14.8	—	2.7	420	E
	L 2	72	58	40	14.8	—	2.9	560	E
	L 3	64	43	29	14.8	—	3.7	740	PE 0.7
	L 4	56	40	30	14.8	—	4.6	710	PE 1.6
	H 1	70	55	36	14.8	20	2.6	410	E
	H 2	68	52	34	14.8	20	2.9	540	E
	H 3	69	54	36	14.8	20	3.6	850	PE 0.6
	H 4	71	55	37	14.8	20	4.5	1,000	PE 1.5
2	H 5	71	55	35	14.8	20	5.9	1,100	PE 2.9
	H 6	71	56	38	14.8	20	24	1,225	PE 21
3	H 7	68	47	27	8.0	20	23.5	1,300	PE 20.5
	H 8[c]	61	34	12	8.0	20	23.5	1,300	PE 20.5
	H 9	72	53	31	8.0	80	23.5	2,000	PE 20.5
	H 10[c]	66	43	17	8.0	80	23.5	2,000	PE 20.5
4	H 11	67	49	29	14.0	20	21.5	1,330	PE 18
	H 12[c]	55	30	9	14.0	20	21.5	1,330	PE 18
	T 1	86	75	54	Growth limited by 4.5 μg threonine/ ml		21.5	800	PE 18
	T 2[c]	84	68	40			21.5	800	PE 18

Corresponding heated controls without lysozyme were carried out in all cases. The average of all of these (14) at 120 min was 94.4 ± 1.0% of their initial turbidities.

[a] From AOD 10.

[b] E = exponential; PE = post exponential. (Time in hours after end of exponential growth.)

[c] Samples H8, H10, H12 and T2 were not heat-inactivated.

The experiments summarized above were carried out as follows. Cells were grown in medium containing growth-limiting amounts of lysine or lysine plus hydroxylysine (Columns 6 and 7). Samples were removed at the times and turbidities indicated in Columns 8 and 9. Each sample was chilled rapidly to 0°C in an ice bath, aseptically washed 3 times with ice-cold sterile distilled water, and resuspended in cold water so that 1.0 ml would give a turbidity equivalent to 370 μg (dry weight) per ml after final dilution to 6.0 ml with buffer and lysozyme. Duplicate 1.0 ml cell samples were added to 3.0 ml of cold sterile 0.1 M sodium phosphate buffer (pH 6.5), mixed thoroughly, and put in a 56°C water bath. This temperature was maintained for 15 min to inactivate the autolytic system. After rapid cooling to 2°C in an ice bath, 2.0 ml of lysozyme (30 μg/ml) or water were added, and contents of the tubes were mixed. To obtain the initial turbidity readings (time zero) individual tubes were placed in a 37.8°C water bath for a few seconds and then immediately read in the spectrophotometer. This procedure avoids fogging of the cold tubes in the spectrophotometer. Readings were taken at 20- to 40-min intervals for 5 hours and the next day. (From Shockman, Thompson & Conover.[44])

autolyzed slowly in 0.01 M phosphate buffer (curve 1), and more slowly in 0.05 M phosphate (curve 2); (*b*) walls from valine-deprived stationary phase cells (Val walls) barely autolyzed in either 0.01 M or 0.05 M phosphate (curve 3); (*c*) the addition of lysozyme (12 μg/0.7 mg wall in 0.05 M phosphate) increased the rate of lysis of both wall types (curves 4 and 5) but the Log walls were more rapidly dissolved. When autolysis of walls was nearly completely heat-inactivated (Figure 24.3 B) both types of walls were dissolved by lysozyme at the same much reduced rate

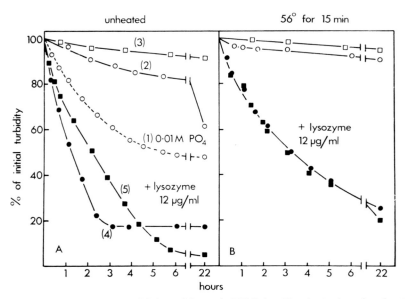

Figure 24.3. Lysozyme sensitivity of heated (56°C for 15 minutes) and unheated cell walls from exponential phase (*circles*) and valine-deprived (*squares*) *Streptococcus faecalis* 9790 cultures. Cell walls were isolated, washed, and stored frozen in 0.15 M maleate as previously described.[45] Walls were removed from the maleate by centrifugation and, in the cold, suspended in the appropriate concentration of phosphate buffer to give a final density of about 700 μg/ml. For *B*, the samples of walls were heated as described for cells in Figure 24.2. Lysozyme was added to the appropriate tubes (*solid symbols*) to give the final concentration indicated. The phosphate buffer concentration for the tubes containing lysozyme and their controls was 0.05 M phosphate buffer, pH 6.8, while that for autolysis was 0.01 M, pH 6.7. Except for unheated Log walls (*dashed line*) in the absence of lysozyme (*open symbols*), virtually the same autolysis curves were obtained in both buffer concentrations, so that only the curve at 0.05 M is shown. Turbidity was measured spectrophotometrically (450 mμ) at appropriate time intervals.

(about 190 minutes to reach 50 per cent of the initial turbidity, compared with about 130 minutes for unheated Val walls and about 75 minutes for unheated Log walls). Thus, walls behaved similarly to whole cells; heat-inactivation resulted in an unexpectedly large decrease in lysozyme sensitivity, even with the Val walls which autolyzed extremely slowly. It seems that although autolysis alone may cause little or no wall dissolution (e.g., unheated Val walls), it may disproportionately contribute to the rate, and perhaps extent, of wall dissolution upon lysozyme treatment.

The effect of proteolytic enzymes is a second factor in wall dissolution. The peptide portion of the wall peptidoglycan is not hydrolyzed by the common proteolytic enzymes of animal, plant and bacterial

origin.[38] Specific peptidases that attack linkages in the peptide portion of peptidoglycan have been obtained from broths of *Streptomyces* by Ghuysen and collaborators.[10, 26, 27, 31] Proteolytic enzymes have frequently been used in the isolation and purification of cell walls to free them of cytoplasmic contamination.[38] The resistance of these peptides to the usual proteolytic enzymes is understandable since they contain D-isomers of certain amino acids (D-alanine, D-glutamic and, occasionally, D-aspartic acid). However, Montague[25] reported that while trypsin alone had little or no effect on isolated walls of *S. faecalis* NCTC 6782, it did cause a further release of rhamnose and phosphorus from autolyzed and partially lysozyme-degraded walls. When the walls of this organism were heated at 100°C for 10 minutes and then partially degraded with lysozyme, trypsin had little or no effect. Also, Bleiweis & Krause[3] found that trypsin treatment activated autolysis of cell walls of a group D, strain 76, streptococcus. As shown in Table 24.2, trypsin greatly increased the rate of lysis of walls from Log phase *S. faecalis* 9790, but had little or no effect on walls from stationary phase valine- or threonine-deprived cells, or on sodium decylsulfate (SDS) treated walls from Log phase cells. Extremely low concentrations of trypsin (0.02 μg/ml) were effective in increasing the rate of lysis of Log walls.[45] SDS treatment can completely inactivate autolysis of *S. faecalis* walls, probably by denaturation or removal of the autolytic enzyme.[45] Except for carboxypeptidase, treatment with any of a number of proteolytic enzymes, such as papain, ficin, pronase, subtilisin BPN′ (Nagarse), and pepsin, increased the rate of lysis of Log walls. Since proteolytic enzymes had virtually no effect on detergent-inactivated walls or on walls of stationary phase cells, it seemed unlikely that proteolytic digestion of peptidoglycan was a factor in itself, but that via proteolytic or esterase activity an endogenous wall lytic enzyme was being released or activated *in situ*. The absence of an increase in N-terminal groups during wall autolysis or trypsin-catalyzed wall autolysis[45] supports the idea that the cleavage of peptide bonds is not a major factor.

The catalytic effect of trypsin on autolysis of Log walls has aided us in isolating a soluble autolytic enzyme (autolysin) from lysates of Log walls. Although the autolysin cleaves the lysozyme-sensitive bond in the wall peptidoglycan substrate (the β, 1–4 N-acetylmuramyl-N-acetylglucosamine linkage), it differs from egg white lysozyme in a number of respects which can be summarized as follows:[45] (1) The autolysin is excluded from Biogel P-60 while lysozyme is eluted at over three times the void volume, indicating that the autolysin has an apparent molecular weight in excess of 50,000, if it is not still attached to wall fragments. (2) While the

TABLE 24.2

Effect of Trypsin on Autolysis of Cell Walls

Cell Walls from	Trypsin mg/ml	Lysis	
		Rate* units	Extent† %
Log phase cells	—	34	15
	0.1	200	14
SDS treated‡	—	6	87
	0.1	7	87
Stationary phase Valine-deprived cells	—	6	78
	0.1	9	75
Threonine-deprived cells	—	3	92
	0.1	4	90

* Lysis rate: one unit equals a decrease of 0.001 O.D./hour at 37° C of 0.7 mg/ml walls in 0.02 M phosphate buffer, pH 7.0, read at 450 mμ in 12 mm diameter tubes in a Spectronic 20 equipped with an A. H. Thomas Co. absorbency digital readout.

† Extent of lysis: percentage of initial turbidity remaining after 22 hours at 37° C.

‡ Walls extracted twice with 2% sodium decylsulfate (SDS) in the cold and washed 4 times to remove the SDS. The SDS-treated walls used in this experiment were not completely inactivated.

Conditions of culture growth and of cell wall isolation were essentially as previously described.[45] (From Conover, Thompson & Shockman.[7])

autolysin is more active on walls from Log phase *S. faecalis* than it is on walls of *Micrococcus lysodeikticus*, lysozyme is more active on walls of *M. lysodeikticus*. (3) Lysozyme dissolves the "mucopeptide residue" remaining after trichloroacetic acid (TCA) extraction of both *S. faecalis* and *M. lysodeikticus* walls more rapidly than it acts on untreated walls, while the autolysin dissolved such extracted walls more slowly; although TCA might not remove completely wall teichoic acid and rhamnose polysaccharide, these observations suggest that the presence of either or both of these polymers inhibits lysozyme, but favorably affects the activity of the autolysin. (4) The *S. faecalis* autolysin exhibits zero order kinetics on walls of *S. faecalis*, which differs from egg white lysozyme digestion of walls of either *S. faecalis* or *M. lysodeikticus*. (5) The presence of O-acyl groups inhibits lysozyme

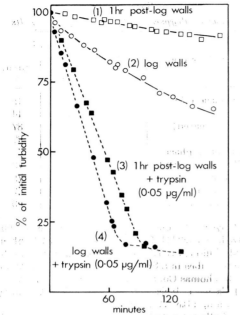

Figure 24.4. Autolysis of Log and 1 hour post-Log walls in the absence (*solid lines*) and presence (*dashed lines*) of trypsin (0.05 μg/ml). Walls were isolated as previously described from Log phase cultures (*circles*) and from threonine-deprived cultures approximately 1 hour after the end of the exponential growth phase and threonine exhaustion (*squares*). Walls were suspended, and incubated, in 0.01 M phosphate buffer, pH 6.7, as described for Figure 24.3.

action, but does not drastically affect autolysin sensitivity of *S. faecalis* or *M. lysodeikticus* walls. N acylation, on the other hand, increased sensitivity of both substrates to lysozyme, but had somewhat different effects on the sensitivity of the two substrates for autolysin. N-acylation had only relatively small effect on walls of *S. faecalis*, but greatly decreased the sensitivity of *M. lysodeikticus* walls to autolysin. Acylation with acetic anhydride also blocks free amino groups,[30] and free ε amino groups of lysine are relatively frequent in walls of *M. lysodeikticus*.[37] It is therefore possible that the nature and degree of crosslinking or substitution of the peptide portion of the mucopeptide could affect autolysin sensitivity. (6) Although we have not made a direct comparison with the products of lysozyme digestion,

the products of autolysis of Log walls of *S. faecalis* are not dialyzable. (7) The buffer concentrations for optimum activity differ. The maximum rate for autolysin activity occurs in 0.005 to 0.01 M phosphate, while lysozyme is more active at higher buffer concentration (0.05 M phosphate).

Autolysis is not unique to *S. faecalis* 9790. Evidence for autolysins in other closely related species has already been mentioned.[3, 25] *E. coli*,[24, 55] *Bacillus cereus*,[24] *Bacillus licheniformis*,[15] a transformable strain of *Bacillus subtilis*,[56] *Staphylococcus aureus*,[23] and *M. lysodeikticus*[23] are among those bacteria which have been observed to autolyze or to have an autolytic system. If, in addition, activation of an autolysin with a proteolytic or other type of enzyme is a factor, perhaps there are other examples of autolysins which are not detectable except after activation. The data presented in Figures 24.2 and 24.3 suggest that there may be small amounts of autolysin present in walls from stationary phase cells of *S. faecalis* that contribute to the rate of lysozyme digestion of these cells or walls. To this data we can add the preliminary results of some recent experiments. Walls were isolated from Log phase cells and from cells which had grown for about one hour after threonine exhaustion. These walls were allowed to autolyze in 0.01 M phosphate buffer, pH 6.7, with and without trypsin (0.05 μg/ml). As shown in Figure 24.4, in the absence of trypsin, walls isolated from cells grown for one hour after the end of the exponential growth phase (curve 1) autolyzed much more slowly than walls from Log phase cells (curve 2). This is consistent with the previously observed decreased autolysis of cells harvested after the end of the exponential growth phase.[40] However, in the presence of trypsin (Figure 24.4, curves 3 and 4), walls from both types of cells autolyzed much more rapidly and at nearly the same rate.

These results suggest that: (1) these post-exponential phase cells and walls may contain more autolysin than the autolysis of these walls in the absence of trypsin suggests; (2) the apparent rapid increase in resistance to cellular autolysis after the end of the exponential growth phase[40] may be due merely to lack of proper autolysin activation; and (3) the autolysin present in the walls can not only contribute to apparent lysozyme sensitivity, but can result in what appears to be proteolytic digestion of the wall. It should be recalled that walls from older stationary phase cultures (e.g., 20 to 42 hours) did not autolyze at a significant rate, even in the presence of trypsin (Table 24.2). Therefore, activation of the wall autolysin may be only one of several factors in the increased autolysis resistance of stationary phase *S. faecalis* cultures. A change in the wall substrate itself or a change in the location of the autolysin relative to sensitive bonds in the wall substrate could also be controlling factors and have not yet been ruled out. At any rate, with this organism, it becomes clear that autolysin and activation of autolysin by proteolytic enzymes can contribute significantly to apparent lysis of cells and walls by lysozyme.

It should be remembered that tests for lysozyme and autolysin sensitivity are of necessity usually performed with cells removed from the environment in which they can grow. We have designated those cells that possess the capability of autolyzing under these secondary conditions as "autolysis-prone cells."[41] Exponentially growing cultures are obviously not autolyzing, but when removed from the growth medium are "autolysis-prone".[41, 42] It is of interest to note that when *S. faecalis* is growing exponentially in a synthetic medium, the rate and extent of growth are virtually unaffected by the presence of as much as 1 mg/ml of lysozyme[47] or by 10 μg/ml of trypsin. In fact, the presence of trypsin (10 μg/ml) did not significantly affect growth curves observed in the complete growth medium, valine-, threonine-, or lysine-limited medium, the effect of chloramphenicol (50 μg/ml)[40] or lysis of exponential phase cells observed after the addition of penicillin (16.7 μg/ml) to the growth medium.[44] However, in the last case, lysis was so rapid that a catalytic effect of trypsin might not have been observed. Under conditions which do not provide an adequate nutritional environ-

ment for continued wall peptidoglycan synthesis, lysis of autolysis-prone Log phase cells is observed (providing suitable conditions of buffer concentration and pH are present).[41, 42]

The absence of cellular autolysis could be a result of (*a*) the lack of enzymatic hydrolysis, (*b*) enzymatic hydrolysis and repair, or (*c*) enzymatic hydrolysis of the wall peptidoglycan with other environmental or structural factors continuing to hold the cell together. The last may involve dissolution of the peptidoglycan but preservation of the protoplast by the external osmotic pressure of the environment or as a heat-coagulated or "fixed" body. Another example is the Nakamura effect. There are numerous instances, with many bacterial species, of the absence of visible cellular lysis upon lysozyme treatment, except when, after treatment, the pH is raised to 10.5 or higher. The cells then lyse almost instantaneously. An example of a situation that resembles the Nakamura effect is shown in Figure 24.5. In this case, Log phase *S. faecalis* cells were incubated in distilled water where only very slow cellular autolysis could be seen; damage to the wall structure was detected, however, when samples were removed and brought to pH 11.5. The alkali resistance of the cells decreased at a much more rapid rate than was apparent from the slow autolysis observed. Probably, autolysin-sensitive bonds in the wall peptidoglycan had been cleaved during this time but the environmental conditions were not such that rapid cellular lysis could take place. Salton[36] has shown that the release of reducing substances parallels turbidity reduction of walls from several lysozyme-sensitive bacteria under near optimum conditions. It should be of interest to correlate the release of reducing substance or, even better, of Morgan-Elson positive acetylhexosamines[10] with increase in alkaline sensitivity, under less than optimum conditions. The release of Morgan-Elson positive fragments could indicate enzymatic damage to the polysaccharide "backbone" of the peptidoglycan in the absence of actual cellular or wall lysis.

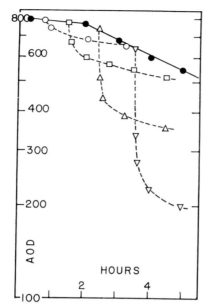

Figure 24.5. Increased sensitivity of Log cells to high pH with the time of incubation in water at 38°C. *Solid line:* change in turbidity of the washed Log cells with time. At the starting points of the descending *dashed lines,* samples were brought to pH 11.5 by the addition of 0.4 N NaOH; the dashed lines show the subsequent course of the turbidity of these samples. (From Shockman, Conover et al.[41])

There is evidence from other laboratories indicating that both proteolytic enzymes and autolysins may contribute to the observed effects of lysozyme. Most of these experiments deal with treatments that influence the lysis of whole cells of both lysozyme-sensitive and resistant species. Obviously, whole cell experiments introduce factors unrelated to the action of lysozyme or to its substrate. It is, therefore, often difficult to interpret clearly these results in terms of current knowledge of lysozyme action on the wall peptidoglycan. It is perhaps easiest to interpret treatments subsequent to the action of lysozyme, such as the exposure to high pH discussed above. Warren and collaborators[50, 51, 52, 54] have found, with normally lysozyme- and trypsin-resistant *S. aureus* cultures, as well as with certain other Gram-positive bacteria, that cells grown in the presence of subinhibitory concentrations of certain penicillins are not lysed by trypsin, are lysed only slowly by lysozyme (20 μg/ml), but are much more rapidly lysed by the addition of both lysozyme and trypsin. More recently, Warren & Gray[53] have found that younger nafcillin-treated, *S. aureus* cultures (four-hour) were more sensitive to lysis by trypsin plus lysozyme than were older cultures (18-hour). In the presence of trypsin plus lysozyme, non-antibiotic treated four-hour control cells showed a significant decrease in turbidity (over 40 per cent in three hours) while the 18-hour control cells showed only a small drop in turbidity (less than 20 per cent in three hours). Neither type, treated or untreated, lysed significantly in the absence of one or both enzymes. Heating (60° C for 15 minutes) abolished autolysis of the nafcillin-treated cells and substantially decreased the rate of lysis of cells treated with lysozyme (20 μg/ml) plus trypsin (10 μg/ml). Other proteolytic enzymes (e.g., pronase and ficin) were found to work nearly as well as trypsin. From this, the investigators concluded, "These marked differences indicate that the increase in lysis of lysozyme and nafcillin treated cells apparently depends in part on the activity of an autolytic factor."[53]

Other factors which influence lysozyme sensitivity of bacteria have been described. These include: (1) Growth of certain anthrax strains in the presence of high levels of bicarbonate and CO_2.[11] (2) Growth of *S. aureus* in the presence of 0.06 M bicarbonate.[53] (3) Growth of several enterococci in the presence of 0.05 M carbonate.[6] (4) Lysis of *E. coli* by the combined action of serum-complement and lysozyme[49] or enhancement of complement and specific antibody lysis (or the bactericidal effect) by lysozyme.[2, 28] It is of interest to note that Wardlaw[49] observed the formation of spheroplasts during the process of complement-plus-lysozyme lysis. (5) Exposure of *Brucella melitensis* to glycine (0.3 M) results in susceptibility to lysozyme and to a lysozyme-like agent from rabbit monocytes.[33] Some investigations considered the contribution of bacterial autolysis to lysozyme sensitivity. Wardlaw[49] considered activation of an autolysin, but proteolytic activation was not tested. Since reactions with lysozyme are usually rapid, suitable controls for relatively short incubation times might not reveal slow autolysis which might contribute, to a greater than expected extent, to lysozyme sensitivity, especially when speeded by proteolytic activation.

There are other examples of conditions which result in bacterial lysis or osmotic fragility that do not appear to involve lysozyme, but perhaps involve autolysins or activation of autolysins. These include: the addition of such things as one of a variety of D-amino acids;[17, 18] a high concentration of glycine;[16] specific inhibitors of peptidoglycan synthesis such as penicillin, or deprivation of a nutritionally indispensable amino acid that is a major wall peptidoglycan component. Examples of the latter are deprivation of diaminopimelic acid with certain *E. coli* mutants[21, 22] and deprivation of D-alanine, aspartic and glutamic acids, L-lysine or glucose with *S. faecalis* 9790.[40, 41] Osmotic fragility of *S. faecalis* has been shown to occur when both wall and protein syntheses were inhibited, such as after lysine exhaustion[43] or the addition of penicillin to Log phase cells in a "wall medium" which lacks many nutrients required for protein synthesis but not for wall synthesis.[39, 46] The occurrence or inhibition of protein synthesis seems to be incidental. When protein synthesis is inhibited, inhibiting the peptidoglycan synthetic reactions should not result in cellular lysis unless degradation of existing peptidoglycan occurs, such as by autolysin action. We have previously postulated[40, 41, 45, 48] that the *S. faecalis* autolysin functions in cell wall growth by cleaving bonds in existing peptidoglycan so that additional disaccharide peptide units can be inserted.

It then seems clear, in at least some *in vitro* situations, that autolysins, especially after activation with proteolytic enzymes, can play a role in cell dissolution and sensitivity to lysozyme. On the basis of current information the following statements can be made: (1) Despite the fact that lysozyme dissolves only a relatively few Gram-positive species, lysozyme-sensitive peptidogly-

can is present in many species. (2) Peptidoglycan is responsible for cell rigidity, shape and integrity, probably completely for Gram-positive bacteria and at least in part for Gram-negative bacteria. (3) Hydrolysis of lysozyme-sensitive bonds may not always result in immediate cell lysis, but may result in wall damage that can be revealed by subsequent treatment (e.g., exposure to high pH). (4) Many (perhaps all) bacteria, especially those taken from the exponential growth phase, possess wall autolytic systems. (5) Proteolytic enzymes can activate autolysins and speed autolysis. Some of these points are not as well established as others. However, the overall picture is sufficiently strong to provoke speculation.

In the tissues and fluids of the body, activators of bacterial autolysins are likely to exist. Proteolytic enzymes and proenzymes are known to occur in blood and tissues.[9] Upon inhibition of wall peptidoglycan synthesis (for example, from nutritional deprivation or with specific inhibitors, either physiological or therapeutic), activator, autolysin, and tissue lysozyme, acting together, may not cause total bacterial lysis of all pathogenic species, but may be able to cause enough damage to the wall peptidoglycan to allow other enzymes or factors further to damage or destroy many pathogenic species. The mechanism by which bacteria are converted to protoplasts, spheroplasts or L-forms, by a variety of agents, *in vitro* or *in vivo*, could involve a combination of similar factors.

The gap between experimental observations of relatively well-defined systems in the test tube and the many ill-defined events that occur upon infection of an animal is extremely wide. We hope, however, that our speculative extensions of experiments with only one bacterial species will stimulate experimentation that might help to narrow this gap as well as provide some new approaches, both practical and theoretical, to a complex problem.

SUMMARY

Apparent differences in lysozyme sensitivity of *Streptococcus faecalis* 9790 cells and cell walls have been, in part, attributed to the presence of a wall autolysin. Exponential phase cells and walls possess an autolysin which can be further activated by low concentrations of trypsin and other proteolytic enzymes. The presence of autolysin in some walls which autolyzed only very slowly could be detected after trypsin activation. Heat or detergent inactivation resulted in a disproportionate decrease in lysozyme sensitivity. The hypothesis has been proposed that autolysins and proteolytic or other activators can enhance lysozyme sensitivity *in vitro* and *in vivo*.

REFERENCES

1. Abrams, A.: O-acetyl groups in the cell wall of *Streptococcus faecalis*. *J. Biol. Chem.* **230**: 949, 1958.
2. Amano, T., Inai, S., Seki, Y., Kashiba, S., Fujikawa, J., and Nishimura, S.: Studies on the immune bacteriolysis. I. Accelerating effect on the immune bacteriolysis by lysozyme-like substance of leucocytes and egg-white lysozyme. *Med. J. Osaka Univ.* **4**: 401, 1954.
3. Bleiweis, A. S., and Krause, R. M.: The cell walls of group D streptococci. I. The immunochemistry of the type 1 carbohydrate. *J. Exp. Med.* **122**: 237, 1965.
4. Brumfitt, W.: The mechanism of development of resistance to lysozyme by some Gram-positive bacteria and its results. *Brit. J. Exp. Path.* **40**: 441, 1959.
5. Brumfitt, W., Wardlaw, A. C., and Park, J. T.: Development of lysozyme-resistance in *Micrococcus lysodeikticus* and its association with an increased O-acetyl content of the cell wall. *Nature* **181**: 1783, 1958.
6. Chesbro, W. R.: Lysozyme and the production of osmotic fragility in enterococci. *Canad. J. Microbiol.* **7**: 952, 1961.
7. Conover, M. J., Thompson, J. S., and Shockman, G. D.: Autolytic enzyme of *Streptococcus faecalis*: release of soluble enzyme from cell walls. *Biochem. Biophys. Res. Commun.* **23**: 713, 1966.
8. Fleming, A.: On a remarkable bacteriolytic element found in tissues and secretions. *Proc. Roy. Soc. London B* **93**: 306, 1922.
9. Fruton, J. S., and Simmonds, S.: *General Biochemistry* (2nd ed.). Wiley, New York, 1958.
10. Ghuysen, J.-M., Tipper, D. J., and Strominger, J. L.: Enzymes that degrade bacterial cell walls. In: *Methods in Enzymology, Vol. 8: Complex Carbohydrates* (S. P. Colowick and W. O. Kaplan, Eds.) Academic Press, New York, 1966: p. 685.
11. Gladstone, G. P., and Johnston, H. H.: The effect of cultural conditions on the susceptibility of *Bacillus anthracis* to lysozyme. *Brit. J. Exp. Path.* **36**: 363, 1955.
12. Grula, E. A., and Hartsell, S. E.: Lysozyme action and its relation to the Nakamura effect. *J. Bact.* **68**: 302, 1954.
13. ———: Lysozyme in the bacteriolysis of Gram-negative bacteria. I. Morphological changes during use of Nakamura's technique. *Canad. J. Microbiol.* **3**: 13, 1957.
14. ———: Lysozyme in the bacteriolysis of Gram-negative bacteria. II. Factors influencing cleaving during the Nakamura treatment. *Canad. J. Microbiol.* **3**: 23, 1957.
15. Hughes, R. C.: The isolation of structural components present in the cell wall of *Bacillus licheniformis* N.C.T.C. 6346. *Biochem. J.* **96**: 700, 1965.
16. Jeynes, M. H.: Growth and properties of bacterial protoplasts. *Nature* **180**: 867, 1957.
17. Lark, C., and Lark, K. G.: The effects of D-amino acids on *Alcaligenes fecalis*. *Canad. J. Microbiol.* **5**: 369, 1959.
18. ———: Studies on the mechanism by which D-amino acids block cell wall synthesis. *Biochim. Biophys. Acta* **49**: 308, 1961.
19. Mandelstam, J.: Isolation of lysozyme-soluble mucopeptides from the cell wall of *Escherichia coli*. *Nature* **189**: 855, 1961.
20. Martin, H. H.: Composition of the mucopolymer in cell walls of the unstable and stable L-form of *Proteus mirabilis*. *J. Gen. Microbiol.* **36**: 441, 1964.
21. McQuillen, K.: Bacterial "protoplasts": effects of diaminopimelic acid deprival and penicillin addition compared in *Escherichia coli*. *Biochim. Biophys. Acta* **27**: 410, 1958.
22. Meadow, P. E., Hoare, D. S., and Work, E.: Interrelationships between lysine and αε-diaminopimelic acid and their derivatives and analogues in mutants of *Escherichia coli*. *Biochem. J.* **66**: 270, 1957.
23. Mitchell, P., and Moyle, J.: Autolytic release and osmotic properties of 'protoplasts' from *Staphylococcus aureus*. *J. Gen. Microbiol.* **16**: 184, 1957.
24. Mohan, R. R., Kronish, D. P., Pianotti, R. S., Epstein, R. L., and Schwartz, B. S.: Autolytic mechanism for spheroplast formation in *Bacillus cereus* and *Escherichia coli*. *J. Bact.* **90**: 1355, 1965.
25. Montague, M. D. The enzymic degradation of cell walls of *Streptococcus faecalis*. *Biochim. Biophys. Acta* **86**: 588, 1964.
26. Muñoz, E., Ghuysen, J.-M., Leyh-Bouille, M., Petit, J.-F., Heymann, H., Bricas, E., and Lefrancier, P. The peptide subunit Nα-(L-

alanyl-D-isoglutaminyl)-L-lysyl-D-alanine in cell wall peptidoglycans of *Staphylococcus aureus* strain Copenhagen, *Micrococcus roseus* R27, and *Streptococcus pyogenes* group A, type 14. *Biochemistry* (Washington) **5**: 3748, 1966.

27. Muñoz, E., Ghuysen, J.-M., Leyh-Bouille, M., Petit, J.-F., and Tinelli, R.: Structural variations in bacterial cell wall peptidoglycans studied with *Streptomyces* F₁ endo-N-acetyl-muramidase. *Biochemistry* (Washington) **5**: 3091, 1966.

28. Muschel, L. H., and Jackson, J. E.: Activity of the antibody-complement system and lysozyme against rough Gram negative organisms. *Proc. Soc. Exp. Biol. Med.* **113**: 881, 1963.

29. Perkins, H. R.: Substances reacting as hexosamine and as N-acetylhexosamine liberated from bacterial cell walls by lysozyme. *Biochem. J.* **74**: 186, 1960.

30. ———: The action of hot formamide on bacterial cell walls. *Biochem. J.* **95**: 876, 1965.

31. Petit, J.-F., Muñoz, E., and Ghuysen, J.-M.: Peptide cross-links in bacterial cell wall peptidoglycans studied with specific endopeptidases from *Streptomyces albus* G. *Biochemistry* (Washington) **5**: 2764, 1966.

32. Prasad, A. L. N., and Litwack, G.: Growth and biochemical characteristics of *Micrococcus lysodeikticus,* sensitive or resistant to lysozyme. *Biochemistry* (Washington) **4**: 496, 1965.

33. Ralston, D. J., Baer, B. S., and Elberg, S. S.: Lysis of Brucellae by the combined action of glycine and a lysozyme-like agent from rabbit monocytes. *J. Bact.* **82**: 342, 1961.

34. Repaske, R.: Lysis of Gram-negative bacteria by lysozyme. *Biochim. Biophys. Acta* **22**: 189, 1956.

35. Salton, M. R. J.: Cell structure and the enzymic lysis of bacteria. *J. Gen. Microbiol.* **9**: 512, 1953.

36. ———: Studies of the bacterial cell wall. V. The action of lysozyme on cell walls of some lysozyme-sensitive bacteria. *Biochem. Biophys. Acta* **22**: 495, 1956.

37. ———: Studies of the bacterial cell wall. VIII. Reaction of walls with hydrazine and with fluorodinitrobenzene. *Biochim. Biophys. Acta* **52**: 329, 1961.

38. ———: *The Bacterial Cell Wall.* Elsevier, Amsterdam, 1964.

39. Shockman, G. D.: Reversal of cycloserine inhibition by D-alanine. *Proc. Soc. Exp. Biol. Med.* **101**: 693, 1959.

40. ———: Symposium on the fine structure and replication of bacteria and their parts. IV. Unbalanced cell-wall synthesis: autolysis and cell-wall thickening. *Bact. Rev.* **29**: 345, 1965.

41. Shockman, G. D., Conover, M. J., Kolb, J. J., Phillips, P. M., Riley, L. S., and Toennies, G.: Lysis of *Streptococcus faecalis. J. Bact.* **81**: 36, 1961.

42. Shockman, G. D., Conover, M. J., Kolb, J. J., Riley, L. S., and Toennies, G.: Nutritional requirements for bacterial cell wall synthesis. *J. Bact.* **81**: 44, 1961.

43. Shockman, G. D., Kolb, J. J., and Toennies, G.: Relations between bacterial cell wall synthesis, growth phase, and autolysis. *J. Biol. Chem.* **230**: 961, 1958.

44. Shockman, G. D., Thompson, J. S., and Conover, M. J.: Replacement of lysine by hydroxylysine and its effects on cell lysis in *Streptococcus faecalis. J. Bact.* **90**: 575, 1965.

45. ———: The autolytic enzyme system of *Streptococcus faecalis.* II. Partial characterization of the autolysin and its substrate. *Biochemistry* (Washington) **6**: 105, 1967.

46. Smith, W. G., Newman, M., Leach, F. R., and Henderson, L. M.: The effect of hydroxylysine on cell wall synthesis and cell stability in *Streptococcus faecalis. J. Biol. Chem.* **237**: 1198, 1962.

47. Toennies, G., Iszard, L., Rogers, N. B., and Shockman, G. D.: Cell multiplication studies with an electronic particle counter. *J. Bact.* **82**: 857, 1961.

48. Toennies, G., and Shockman, G. D.: Growth chemistry of *Streptococcus faecalis.* In: *Proceedings of the Fourth International Congress of Biochemistry,* Vienna, 1958, Vol. 13: p. 365.

49. Wardlaw, A. C. The complement-dependent bacteriolytic activity of normal human serum. I. The effect of pH and ionic strength and the role of lysozyme. *J. Exp. Med.* **115**: 1231, 1962.

50. Warren, G. H., and Gray, J.: Production of a polysaccharide by *Staphylococcus aureus.* II. Effect of temperature and antibiotics. *Proc. Soc. Exp. Biol. Med.* **114**: 439, 1963.

51. ———: Production of a polysaccharide by *Staphylococcus aureus.* III. Action of penicillins and polysaccharides on enzymic lysis. *Proc. Soc. Exp. Biol. Med.* **116**: 317, 1964.

52. ———: Effect of sublethal concentrations of penicillins on the lysis of bacteria by lysozyme and trypsin. *Proc. Soc. Exp. Biol. Med.* **120**: 504, 1965.

53. ———: Influence of nafcillin on the enzymic lysis of *Staphylococcus aureus. Canad. J. Microbiol.* **13**: 321, 1967.

54. Warren, G. H., Rosenman, S. B., and Horwitz,

P.: Production of polysaccharide by *Staphylococcus aureus*. IV. Correlation of lytic response with penicillin activity. *Proc. Soc. Exp. Biol. Med.* **117**: 730, 1964.

55. Weidel, W., and Pelzer, H.: Bagshaped macromolecules—a new outlook on bacterial cell walls. *Adv. Enzym.* **26**: 193, 1964.

56. Young, F. E. Autolytic enzyme associated with cell walls of *Bacillus subtilis*. *J. Biol. Chem.*, **241**: 3462, 1966.

57. Zinder, N. D., and Arndt, W. P.: Production of protoplasts of *Escherichia coli* by lysozyme treatment. *Proc. Nat. Acad. Sci. USA* **42**: 586, 1956.

25

Kinetics of Serum Bactericidal Action and Some Properties of Serum Spheroplasts*

Starkey D. Davis, Diethard Gemsa, Antoinette Iannetta and Ralph J. Wedgwood

UNIVERSITY OF WASHINGTON SCHOOL OF MEDICINE

SEATTLE, WASHINGTON

The first clear description of the transformation of bacteria to spheroplasts was made in 1895 by Pfeiffer,[26] who injected suspensions of *Vibrio cholerae* into the peritoneal space of guinea pigs and examined samples of the peritoneal fluid under the microscope. He described what he saw: 'The vibrios are first rapidly immobilized. Then they begin swelling and become round, dense structures. Some of the newly developed, round structures are motile. The vibrios behave like candles which soften and melt in hot water. The spheres then become paler, lose their sharp contour and staining quality with aniline dyes, and finally vanish without remnant in the exudate.' †

Many studies have since been done on this reaction.[4, 9, 19, 22] It has been shown that bacteria are killed by an antibody-complement system[17, 20, 21, 25, 27] which may be identical with the hemolytic antibody-complement system. After bacteria are killed by antibody and complement, lysozyme converts the bacteria to spheroplasts and ghosts.[2, 10, 14, 22, 30] Dienes and associates[7] grew serum spheroplasts in culture on soft horse serum agar. Bacteria have also been converted to spheroplasts by treatment with penicillin and other reagents.[13, 16, 18, 24]

The bactericidal reaction of serum has been studied by colony counts,[17] photometric growth assay,[23] or release of P[32]-labeled compounds.[28] The bacteriolytic reaction has been studied by determining changes in optical density (O.D.)[30] or release of nucleic acid.[2] Few studies have been done of both reactions simultaneously, and the kinetics of spheroplast and ghost formation have not been established.

Other studies have indicated that spheroplasts may play a role in disease in humans. In 1951, Voureka[29] observed unusual bacterial forms in the urine of patients treated with chloramphenicol. Later, Braude and associates[3] reported the observation of round, osmotically fragile forms in the urine of a patient with *Proteus* pyelonephritis dur-

* A portion of this investigation was carried out under the sponsorship of the Commission on Immunization of the Armed Forces Epidemiological Board and was supported in part by the Office of the Surgeon General, Department of the Army (Contract DA-49-193-MD-2308), U.S. Public Health Service Grants 5 TI AI-227-05 and 1 RO1-A 106882-02, and State of Washington Initiative 171 Funds for Research in Biology and Medicine.

† Translated from the original German[26] by the author.

ing penicillin therapy. Then, in 1965, Gutman and associates[12] were able to recover filterable bacterial variants from the urine of 11 patients with chronic bacteriuria.

These studies were designed to determine the kinetics of the bactericidal and bacteriolytic reactions of serum, and some properties of serum spheroplasts. A portion of this work has previously been reported,[5, 6] and a detailed description of the culture and reversion of *V. cholerae* spheroplasts will be published elsewhere.*

For purposes of this report, a *spheroplast* is defined as a dense, spherical form produced by the action of serum on Gram-negative bacteria.

MATERIALS AND METHODS

SERUM

Serum was obtained from five healthy adults and stored at −64°C until used.

BACTERIA

Escherichia coli 0127, 0111, and 055 were obtained from Dr. W. H. Ewing, Communicable Disease Center. *E. coli* B and C are the host strains for T and ϕX 174 bacteriophages. *Shigella boydii* and *Salmonella typhosa* 0901 were obtained from the American Type Culture Collection. *Salmonella typhimurium* was isolated from a patient at Babies and Children's Hospital, Cleveland. *V. cholerae* types Hikojima, Inaba, and Ogawa were obtained from the National Collection of Type Cultures, London.

MEDIA

All cultures, except those of cholera, were maintained on blood agar base plates (Baltimore Biological Laboratory) in the refrigerator and were transferred at regular intervals. For most experiments the organisms were cultured overnight on blood agar base and were then subcultured for several hours in brain-heart infusion broth (Baltimore Biological Laboratory) to insure that the organisms were in rapid

* A. Iannetta and R. J. Wedgwood, to be published in the *Journal of Bacteriology*.

growth phase. For cultures of cholera, 5 g NaCl and 1 g dextrose were added per liter of blood agar base, and the pH was adjusted to 8 with 1 M Tris [tris (hydroxymethyl) aminomethane] from Sigma. For cholera broth cultures, the pH of brain-heart infusion broth was adjusted to 8 with 1 M Tris.

For cultures of spheroplasts, the L-form agar medium described by Gutman and associates[12] was used. This medium contained the following (g/liter): sucrose, 100; phytone, 20; NaCl, 5; $MgSO_4 \cdot 7H_2O$, 2.5; yeast extract, 10; cholesterol, 0.04 dissolved in 10 ml 95% ethanol; and Ionagar $\#2$ (Oxoid), 8. The pH was adjusted to 7.8 with 1 N NaOH, and the medium was autoclaved for 15 minutes at 121°C. Horse serum (Microbiological Associates) was heat-inactivated and added to a final concentration of 25% after the medium was autoclaved.

BACTERIAL COUNTS

Numbers of viable bacteria were determined using a colony count assay which has been previously described.[6] Briefly, serial dilutions of the bacterial suspensions were made in 0.15 M NaCl, and 0.1 ml samples of each dilution were streaked on agar plates. The plates were incubated overnight and the colonies counted. The O.D. of the bacterial suspensions was measured spectrophotometrically at 650 mμ. Total and differential counts of bacterial rods, spheroplasts, and ghosts were made on samples fixed in 2% formalin using a phase contrast microscope (Carl Zeiss, West Germany). Total counts were made on samples in an improved Neubauer counting chamber (Max Levy).

EXPERIMENTAL PROCEDURES

Bacterial suspensions were adjusted to a final O.D. of 0.30 (2×10^8 organisms/ml) after the addition of serum. For most experiments the broth suspension of organisms was rapidly chilled and the appropriate volume of serum was added. The O.D. was determined and samples were taken for colony and microscopic counts. The suspension was then incubated at 37°C and was agitated frequently with a vortex shaker. At intervals, samples were taken for colony and microscopic counts, and the O.D. was determined.

For studies on the influence of sucrose, bacteria were collected by centrifugation and resuspended in 0.58 M sucrose in 0.15 M. NaCl. For studies with calcium or magnesium ions, concentrated reagents were added to broth suspensions.

BENTONITE-ABSORBED SERUM

Serum was absorbed with bentonite as described by Inoue et al.[14] except that absorption was with 1 mg (wet weight) of washed bentonite per ml of serum for 10 minutes at 4°C. Absorbed serum did not cause significant lysis of *Micrococcus lysodeikticus* after 30 minutes of incubation at 37°C.

ABSORBED SERUM WITH ADDED LYSOZYME

Crystalline egg white lysozyme (Nutritional Biochemical Corporation) was added to bentonite-absorbed serum to a concentration of 2 μg/ml.

CMC-TREATED SERUM

A column was prepared with 30 g of carboxymethylcellulose resin (CMC, Bio-Rad Laboratories) which was equilibrated with a 0.05 M phosphate buffer at pH 7.4. A sample of 10 ml of human serum was applied to the top of the column and was eluted with the same phosphate buffer in 3 ml fractions using a Gilson refrigerated fraction collector.

ANTISERA

Rabbits were immunized with cell wall preparations from the cholera strains suspended in Freund's complete adjuvant. The rabbit antisera were made specific by cross-absorption with heterologous cell wall preparations. The absorbed antisera caused agglutination of the homologous strain only in slide agglutination tests.

RESULTS

MICROSCOPIC OBSERVATIONS

The predominant bacterial forms produced by the action of human serum on Gram-negative rods are illustrated in the figures. These forms were distinct and could be easily differentiated. Normal rods (Figure 25.1) were smooth in contour and intermediate in density. Forms intermediate between rods and spheroplasts were observed early in many reactions, but only in

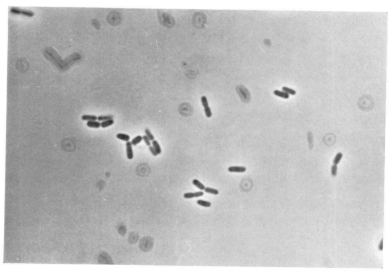

Figure 25.1. Appearance of *Escherichia coli* rods under phase contrast microscopy. × 1740.

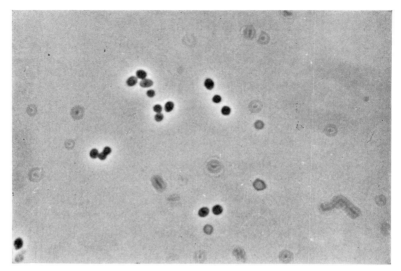

Figure 25.2. Serum spheroplasts of *Escherichia coli*, × 1750. The pale round forms are ghosts.

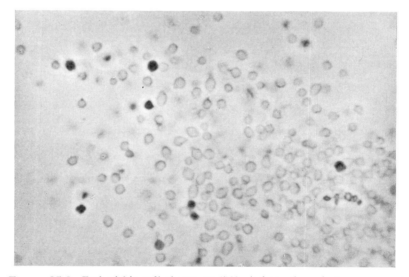

Figure 25.3. *Escherichia coli* ghosts, × 1760. A few spheroplasts are present.

small numbers. Spheroplasts (Figure 25.2) were spherical and denser than rods. In reactions with motile strains, a few spheroplasts were motile but most were not. Most spheroplasts were smooth in contour, but some appeared to have debris attached to the cell surface. Ghosts (Figure 25.3) were like spheroplasts in size and shape, but very pale. Some ghosts had dense material remaining within, or attached to the cell surface.

NORMAL SERUM

The results of a kinetic analysis of the action of normal serum on *E. coli* 0127 are illustrated in Figure 25.4. There was an initial lag phase followed by a simultaneous decrease in colony count and number of rod forms. Then spheroplasts appeared and increased, and subsequently ghosts appeared. The O.D. decreased when the number of spheroplasts decreased.

Similar results were obtained in kinetic

studies of the other strains of Gram-negative bacteria listed above. In every instance, the regular sequence of the transformation of rods to spheroplasts and
ghosts was observed. Most strains required
only 5 or 10% serum in the final reaction
volume to convert rapidly rods into spheroplasts and ghosts. *S. typhimurium* was
found to be the most serum-resistant of
these strains in that a final concentration of 40% serum was necessary for
prompt conversion. It was also observed
that any of the human sera were equally
effective against all the bacterial strains
except cholera. One serum produced rapid
transformation of cholera at low concentrations, and this serum was used for most
of the studies on cholera.

NORMAL SERUM WITH SUCROSE

The results of an experiment with *E.
coli* 0127 in 0.58 M sucrose with normal
serum are illustrated in Figure 25.5. The
results were similar to those obtained with
normal serum, except that all reactions
proceeded at a slower rate. Neither morphologic transformation was selectively inhibited. The O.D. decreased rapidly without a corresponding decrease in other
counts.[1]

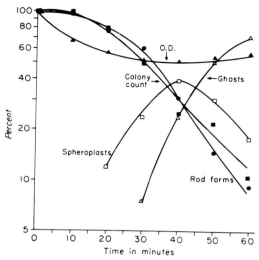

Figure 25.5. Effect on *Escherichia coli* of serum with 0.58 M sucrose. (From Davis, Gemsa &
Wedgwood.[5])

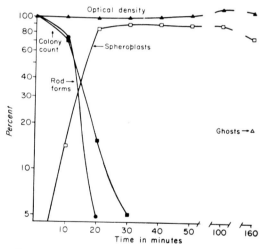

Figure 25.6. Effect on *Escherichia coli* of serum with added 0.005 M CaCl₂. (From Davis,
Gemsa & Wedgwood.[5])

NORMAL SERUM WITH ADDED DIVALENT CATIONS

The addition of either calcium or magnesium chloride in appropriate concentration was found to stabilize spheroplasts
selectively while allowing the transformation of rods to spheroplasts to proceed at a
normal rate. As an example, the effect of
serum on *E. coli* 0127 with added 0.005 M
calcium chloride is illustrated in Figure
25.6. The colony count and number of rod

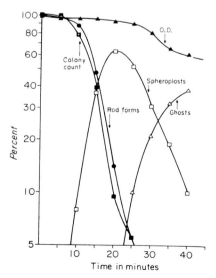

Figure 25.4. Kinetics of the action of normal
serum on *Escherichia coli*. (From Davis, Gemsa &
Wedgwood.[5])

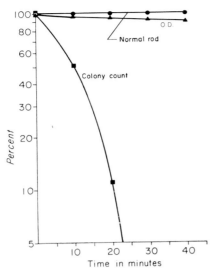

Figure 25.7. Effect of bentonite-absorbed serum on *Escherichia coli*. (From Davis, Gemsa & Wedgwood.[5])

forms decreased as with normal serum, but the number of spheroplasts remained high for a prolonged period of time. High concentrations of calcium or magnesium inhibited killing and low concentrations had no effect.

Spheroplasts of different Gram-negative strains were found to differ somewhat in optimal concentrations of divalent cations for stability. Spheroplasts of *E. coli* were fairly stable in 0.0025 M calcium chloride and 0.0025 M magnesium chloride; *S. boydii*, however, appeared to be more stable in 0.01 M magnesium chloride, while the cholera protoplasts were more stable in 0.01 M calcium chloride.

BENTONITE-ABSORBED SERUM

Kinetic study of the action of bentonite-absorbed serum on *E. coli* 0127 is presented in Figure 25.7. The colony count decreased rapidly but the number of rod forms was unchanged. When egg white lysozyme was added to the bentonite-absorbed serum, the results of a kinetic analysis were like those of normal serum, illustrated in Figure 25.4.

CMC-TREATED SERUM

The protein from 10 ml of human serum from the CMC column was eluted in a single peak. Fractions from the first half of the protein peak and the fractions from the second half were pooled separately and concentrated by pervaporation. The pooled fraction from the first half of the protein peak killed cholera and *S. boydii*, but did not cause conversion of rods to spheroplasts. When egg white lysozyme was added to this fraction, *S. boydii* rods were promptly converted to spheroplasts. The second half of the protein peak was found to have action like that of untreated serum in that rods were converted to spheroplasts.

SPHEROPLAST CULTURES

Attempts were made to culture spheroplasts on L-form agar from all of the strains of Gram-negative bacteria listed above. Spheroplasts were prepared by treatment of bacteria with serum with appropriate cations added for stability. The serum concentration chosen for each strain was one that would yield essentially complete conversion of rods to spheroplasts in 10 to 15 minutes. Egg white lysozyme, 10 µg/ml, was added to reaction mixtures to insure that killed rods were promptly converted to spheroplasts. Cholera spheroplasts were stabilized with 0.01 M calcium chloride. Spheroplast suspensions of *S. boydii* were stabilized with 0.01 M magnesium chloride. Spheroplasts of other Gram-negative bacteria were stabilized with 0.0025 M calcium chloride and 0.0025 M magnesium chloride. When the conversions of rods to spheroplasts appeared to be complete by inspection under the phase contrast microscope, samples from the reaction mixtures were taken and plated on conventional blood agar base and on the L-form agar. Cultures for spheroplasts were considered to be positive when no growth occurred on the conventional media and colonies appeared on L-agar media which were microscopically not classical rods.

Spheroplast colonies were regularly observed on L-form agar after treatment of the three cholera strains with serum. The colonies were similar to those of normal bacteria but were much smaller and appeared only after 48 hours of incubation.

After approximately four to five subcultures on L-form agar, the spheroplast colonies reverted to the classical bacterial form which could be cultured on conventional media. The identity of the reverted spheroplast colonies was confirmed by slide agglutination tests with specific rabbit antisera. During reversion, many pleomorphic forms were present.

Spheroplast cultures on L-form agar were also obtained from *S. typhimurium* and *S. typhosa* 0901. Spheroplast cultures of *Salmonella* 0901 appeared after approximately 48 hours and were much smaller than conventional colonies. The colonies reverted to the classical form after about three passages on L-form media. Spheroplast colonies were prepared from *S. boydii* which reverted after three passages on L-form agar.

In most experiments with *E. coli* 0127, and *E. coli* B and C, no spheroplast colonies were detected. However, in occasional experiments, tiny colonies of spheroplasts were seen, which grew slowly. Spheroplast colonies were not obtained from any of the other *E. coli* strains. No spheroplast colonies appeared in similar experiments using the media described by Landman, Altenbern & Ginoza.[15]

DISCUSSION

Considering the results of these and other studies, the sequence of serum action of Gram-negative bacteria seems well established: Gram-negative rods are converted to non-viable rods by the action of the antibody-complement system;[17, 21, 27] non-viable rods are then converted to spheroplasts by the action of lysozyme on the damaged cell wall;[10, 14, 22, 30] finally, the intracellular material is lost as spheroplasts are converted to ghosts. This sequence appeared to consist of consecutive first order reactions.[6] These reactions may be written as follows to conform to the terminology for the hemolytic antibody-complement system, using R for bacterial rod, R^* for non-viable rod, S for spheroplast, and G for ghost:

$$R \xrightarrow{AC'} R^* \xrightarrow{lysozyme} S \to G$$

Our earlier studies on the kinetics of serum action were done on one strain of *E. coli*.[5, 6] The present report extends those kinetic studies to other strains of *E. coli*, *Shigella*, *Salmonella*, and cholera. The morphologic changes of rods to spheroplasts and ghosts may well be a common response of all serum-sensitive Gram-negative bacteria to treatment with serum.

These studies provide the basis for a new and simple assay of serum bactericidal action. Provided that lysozyme is present in excess, the course of serum bactericidal action may easily be followed by differential counts of rods, spheroplasts, and ghosts. This type of assay has several advantages over the older methods: only small volumes of serum are needed; the results of experiments are available immediately; and, more important, tedious colony counts and photometric growth assays can be avoided. Many consecutive experiments can easily be done in one day, with great savings in time and effort.

These kinetic studies also permit more precise definitions for terms relating to serum action. Bactericidal action, which is mediated by the antibody-complement system, may be defined as cell damage which prevents bacterial multiplication on conventional media. This reaction is not accompanied by morphologic change which can be seen under phase contrast microscopy. Bacteriolytic action has been used to refer to a decrease in O.D. of a bacterial suspension.[30] As demonstrated in these studies, bacteriolysis represents the conversion of spheroplasts to ghosts.

The mechanism of bacteriolytic reaction is not known. Since divalent cations stabilized spheroplasts, it seemed possible that the cations activate essential enzyme systems in the spheroplasts.[8] To explore this possibility, a preliminary study was done on the influence of enzyme inhibitors on spheroplasts.† We predicted that, if enzyme systems were essential for stability, then one of a broad group of enzyme inhibitors would cause lysis. *E. coli* 0127 spheroplasts were prepared with serum, washed, and suspended in phosphate buffered saline with 0.01 M $CaCl_2$. Enzyme

† D. Gemsa and S. D. Davis, unpublished observations.

inhibitors were added to a concentration of 0.001 M, and changes in O.D. or microscopic appearance of the spheroplasts were noted. The inhibitors used included heavy metal poisons (arsenite, p-chloromercurisulfonic acid, cyanide), chelating agents (oxalate, tiron, versene), sulfhydril inhibitors (thiourea, iodoacetamide), an inhibitor of electron transport (sodium thiopental), and an inhibitor of calcium and magnesium dependent enzymes (sodium fluoride).

None of the inhibitors produced lysis of spheroplasts, though the chelating agents did cause agglutination. Tiron was the most effective and also agglutinated spheroplasts at 0.0001 M concentration. Tiron is a highly efficient chelator of iron; agglutination may have resulted from neutralization of a surface charge by binding of iron by tiron.

Another point to consider is that calcium and magnesium are often antagonistic in enzyme activation.[8] It therefore seems unlikely that calcium and magnesium act by activating enzymes. A more reasonable mechanism at present is that divalent cations may prevent lysis by forming "salt bridges" and protecting spheroplast surface proteins from denaturation.[11]

Although spheroplast cultures from cholera, Salmonella, and Shigella grew readily on the L-form media used, spheroplast cultures of E. coli grew poorly or not at all. Lederberg[16] reported in studies on penicillin spheroplasts that many strains of E. coli spheroplasts did not grow. Dienes and associates[7] were able to grow serum spheroplasts of Salmonella in cultures, but had little success with E. coli; it is not clear whether E. coli spheroplasts are inherently less viable or that a different L-form medium is required.

Although the role of lysozyme in the transformation of rods to spheroplasts is well documented, the possibility that other enzymes are present in serum with similar activity has not been excluded. For most of the studies presented, lysozyme was added in excess to insure the prompt conversion of killed rods to spheroplasts.

Some variation was found from day to day in the results of kinetic studies. Replicate experiments on the same day correspond more closely. Bacteria were tested only in rapid growth phase to reduce any variability in sensitivity to serum. Most experiments were designed to be completed in about one mean generation time to avoid any change in serum sensitivity of bacteria during incubation.

SUMMARY

Kinetic analysis of the action of serum on Gram-negative bacteria demonstrated that bacterial rods are quantitatively converted to spheroplasts and then to ghosts. Bacteria are killed by the antibody-complement system and changed to spheroplasts by lysozyme. Spheroplasts become ghosts by loss of intracellular contents. Calcium and magnesium, but not sucrose, protect spheroplasts from lysis.

Growth of spheroplast colonies on L-form agar was obtained from serum spheroplasts of cholera, Shigella boydii, and Salmonella typhimurium. All reverted to the rod form after subculture.

The conversion of spheroplasts to ghosts may not be a direct effect of serum action, but may result from instability of the spheroplast membrane.

REFERENCES

1. Abrams, A.: Reversible metabolic swelling of bacterial protoplasts. J. Biol. Chem. **234:** 383, 1959.
2. Amano, T., Fujikawa, K., Morioka, T., Miyama, A., and Ichikawa, S.: Quantitative studies of immune bacteriolysis. I. A new method of quantitative estimation. Biken's J. **1:** 13, 1958.
3. Braude, A. I., Siemienski, J., and Jacobs, I.: Protoplast formation in human urine. Trans. Ass. Amer. Physicians **74:** 234, 1961.
4. Carey, W. F., Muschel, L. H., and Baron, L. S.: The formation of bacterial protoplasts in vivo. J. Immun. **84:** 183, 1960.
5. Davis, S. D., Gemsa, D., and Wedgwood, R. J.: Kinetics of the transformation of Gram-negative rods to spheroplasts and ghosts by serum. J. Immun. **96:** 570, 1966.
6. Davis, S. D., and Wedgwood, R. J.: Kinetics of the bactericidal action of normal serum on Gram-negative bacteria. J. Immun. **95:** 75, 1965.

7. Dienes, L., Weinberger, H. J., and Madoff, S.: The transformation of typhoid bacilli into L forms under various conditions. *J. Bact.* **59:** 755, 1950.

8. Dixon, M., and Webb, E. C.: *Enzymes.* Academic Press, New York, 1958.

9. Freeman, B. A., Musteikis, G. M., and Burrows, W.: Protoplast formation as the mechanism for immune lysis of *Vibrio cholerae. Proc. Soc. Exp. Biol. Med.* **113:** 675, 1963.

10. Gemsa, D., Davis, S. D., and Wedgwood, R. J.: Lysozyme and serum bactericidal action. *Nature* **210:** 950, 1966.

11. Gurd, F. R. N., and Wilcox, P. E.: Complex formation between metallic cations and proteins, peptides, and amino acids. *Adv. Protein Chem.* **11:** 311, 1956.

12. Gutman, L. T., Turck, M., Peterdorf, R. G., and Wedgwood, R. J.: Significance of bacterial variants in urine of patients with chronic bacteriuria. *J. Clin. Invest.* **44:** 1945, 1965.

13. Guze, L. B., and Kalmanson, G. M.: Persistence of bacteria in "protoplast" form after apparent cure of pyelonephritis in rats. *Science* **143:** 1340, 1964.

14. Inoue, K., Tanigawa, Y., Takubo, M., Satani, M., and Amano, T.: Quantitative studies on immune bacteriolysis. II. The role of lysozyme in immune bacteriolysis. *Biken's J.* **2:** 1, 1959.

15. Landman, O. E., Altenbern, R. A., and Ginoza, H. S.: Quantitative conversion of cells and protoplasts of *Proteus mirabilis* and *Escherichia coli* to the L-form. *J. Bact.* **75:** 567, 1958.

16. Lederberg, J.: Bacterial protoplasts induced by penicillin. *Proc. Nat. Acad. Sci. USA* **42:** 574, 1956.

17. Maaløe, O.: *On the Relation Between Alexin and Opsinin.* Munksgaard, Copenhagen, 1946.

18. McQuillen, K.: Bacterial protoplasts. In: *The Bacteria, Vol. I.: Structure.* (I. C. Gunsalus and R. Y. Stanier, Eds.). Academic Press, New York, 1960: p. 249.

19. Michael, J. G., and Braun, W.: Serum spheroplasts of *Shigella dysenteriae. Proc. Soc. Exp. Biol. Med.* **100:** 422, 1959.

20. ———: Analysis of sequential stages in serum bactericidal reactions. *J. Bact.* **87:** 1067, 1964.

21. Muschel, L. H.: Immune bactericidal and bacteriolytic reactions. In: *Ciba Foundation Symposium on Complement* (G. E. W. Wolstenholme and J. Knight, Eds.). Churchill, London, 1965: p. 155.

22. Muschel, L. H., Carey, W. F., and Baron, L. S.: Formation of bacterial protoplasts by serum components. *J. Immun.* **82:** 38, 1959.

23. Muschel, L. H., and Treffers, H. P.: Quantitative studies on the bactericidal actions of serum and complement. I. A rapid photometric growth assay for bactericidal activity. *J. Immun.* **76:** 1, 1956.

24. Noller, E. C., and Hartsell, S. E.: Bacteriolysis of *Enterobacteriaceae.* I. Lysis by four lytic systems utilizing lysozyme. *J. Bact.* **81:** 482, 1961.

25. Osler, A. G.: Functions of the complement system. *Adv. Immun.* **1:** 132, 1961.

26. Pfeiffer, R.: Differentialdiagnose der Vibrionen der Cholera asiatica mit Hülfe der Immunisierung. *Z. Hyg. Infektionskr.* **19:** 75, 1895.

27. Rother, K., Rother, U., Petersen, K. F., Gemsa, D., and Mitze, F.: Immune bactericidal activity of complement; separation and description of intermediate steps. *J. Immun.* **93:** 319, 1964.

28. Spitznagel, J. K., and Wilson, L. A.: Normal serum cytotoxicity for P^{32}-labeled smooth *Enterobacteriaceae.* I. Loss of label, death, and ultrastructural damage. *J. Bact.* **91:** 393, 1966.

29. Voureka, A.: Bacterial variants in patients treated with chloramphenicol. *Lancet* **1:** 27, 1951.

30. Wardlaw, A. C.: The complement-dependent bacteriolytic activity of normal human serum. I. The effect of pH and ionic strength and the role of lysozyme. *J. Exp. Med.* **115:** 1231, 1962.

26

Bacterial L-Forms as Immunogenic Agents*

Raymond J. Lynn and Gary J. Haller

UNIVERSITY OF SOUTH DAKOTA SCHOOL OF MEDICINE
VERMILLION, SOUTH DAKOTA

Stable L-forms have been described for a number of bacterial species. The observation that these L-forms are not susceptible to many of the antibiotics has initiated extensive investigation as to their possible role in disease. Many L-forms were found to be avirulent, particularly if virulence for the parent bacterium was closely related to cell wall substances.[3, 5, 6] Investigations of stable L-forms of bacteria whose virulences are related to exotoxins or endotoxins indicated that, at least in some instances, such L-forms could produce disease.[10, 13] Also, it has been reported that a latent infection was probably due to a transitory L-form reverting to its virulent bacterial form.[6] Our principal interest has been to investigate the possibility that stable L-forms could initiate or "trigger" sequelar reactions based on immunological mechanisms. These studies were initiated at the University of Pittsburgh in 1958 in collaboration with Dr. A. H. Stock. His extensive knowledge of the streptococcal extracellular substances was invaluable in our early studies of the streptococcal L-forms.

The use of the term *L-form* in this presentation is patterned after that suggested by Klieneberger-Nobel.[6] The organisms

can be propagated in pure culture indefinitely in the absence of any bacterial inhibitors without reverting to a bacterial form. No cell wall material was detected by immunological analyses.

This presentation will indicate that the L-forms studied are immunogenic in the rabbit, with several different antigenic determinants being expressed. It will also be demonstrated that the use of such L-forms as immunizing agents will permit the expression of a greater diversity of membrane and cytoplasmic immunogens than will similar preparations of the bacterial form.

MATERIALS AND METHODS

All of the stable L-forms described in this study were prepared by treatment of the parent organism with penicillin. The L-form isolates GL-8-L, ADA-L, and the group A beta hemolytic streptococci, GL-8, ADA, and AED, were obtained from Dr. L. Dienes' laboratory in 1958. The stable L-forms AED-L, LG-1-L and Cook B-L were isolated by one of us (RJL) in 1961 from group A beta hemolytic streptococci. The Cook B-L is an erythrogenic B toxin producer described elsewhere.[12] The LG-1-L streptococcus was isolated in our laboratory from a rheumatic fever patient in 1961. The Campo L organism is a stable L-form prepared in Dr. Dienes' laboratory from a diphtheroid isolated from a

* Investigation supported by a Public Health Service research grant, HE-07004, from the National Heart Institute.

Mycoplasma culture.[11] All of these L-forms were maintained in our laboratory on a brucella medium (Difco) to which 3% NaCl was added. No serum enrichment was necessary for the propagation of these strains.

Antisera were prepared in New Zealand red and white rabbits as previously described.[8] Approximately 100 mg of cellular protein estimated by the method of Lowry and associates[7] was given to each animal. All of the animals were bled by cardiac puncture prior to, and at selected intervals during, immunization.

Complement fixation titers were estimated using a modified Kolmer technique.[1] A 50 per cent endpoint was used in all instances. The latex agglutination test has been described previously.[8] Growth inhibition studies were conducted in a manner similar to those practiced with the *Mycoplasma*, utilizing filter paper disks saturated with immune serum.[2] All of the sera tested were heat-inactivated at 56° C for one hour. Disc electrophoresis of various preparations was employed, using the apparatus of Canalco with their packaged chemicals (Canal Industrial Corp., Rockville, Maryland). Immunodiffusion and immunoelectrophoresis were conducted on microscope slides utilizing the Agafor II apparatus (Egatonag, Berne, Switzerland) and techniques described by Ouchterlony[9] and Grabar & Williams.[4]

TABLE 26.1

Agglutination Titers of Antisera to Various L-Forms and Their Parent Bacteria

Antiserum	Latex Agglutination Titers*			
	Antigens			
	ADA	ADA-L	GL-8	GL-8-L
ADA	5120	40	640	80
ADA-L	320	2560	5120	10240
GL-8	320	80	10240	40
GL-8-L	80	320	10240	10240
LG 1	80	<20	160	<20

* Reciprocal of the highest dilution of serum permitting definite agglutination of latex coated with 150 μg of antigen protein.

TABLE 26.2

Various Fractions of a Streptococcus as Serological Antigens in Complement Fixation Tests with Antisera to the Streptococcus and Its L-Form

GL-8 Antigen Preparation	Antigen Dilution	Complement Fixation Titer*	
		Antiserum	
		GL-8	GL-8-L
Whole cell	1:160	1280	2560
Ribi fraction, $S_{27,000}$	1:160	40	2560
Ribi fraction, $R_{27,000}$	1:80	1280	2560
Ribi fraction, S_{480}	1:80	640	640
Ribi fraction, R_{480}	1:320	5120	160

* Reciprocal of the highest dilution of serum permitting 50% binding of complement.

TABLE 26.3

Various Fractions of a Streptococcal L-Form as Serological Antigens in Complement Fixation Tests with Antisera to the L-Form and Its Parent Streptococcus

GL-8-L Antigen Preparation	Antigen Dilution	Complement Fixation Titer*	
		Antiserum	
		GL-8	GL-8-L
Whole cells	1:640	40	>5120
Ribi fraction, $S_{27,000}$	1:640	80	2560
Ribi fraction, $R_{27,000}$	1:640	<20	1280
Ribi fraction, S_{480}	1:640	<20	5120
Ribi fraction, R_{480}	1:80	80	1280

* Reciprocal of the highest dilution of serum permitting 50% binding of complement.

Disrupted cell preparations were prepared by subjecting the organisms to pressure in a Ribi Cell Fractionator (Servall, Norwich, Conn.). The streptococci and diphtheroids were disrupted by 30,000 psi pressure, whereas the L-forms easily broke at 12,000 psi. In some instances, where membrane fractions were desired, the L-forms were lysed in deionized water and the membranes sedimented from the lysate by centrifugation at 59,000 G in the Spinco Model L ultracentrifuge. These membrane preparations were then solubilized with dodecyl sulfate and dialyzed against deionized

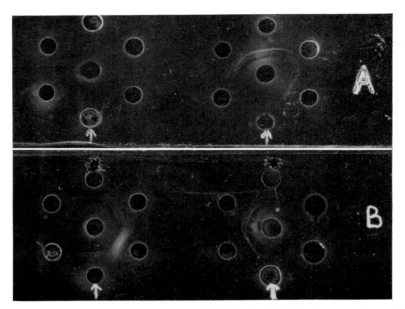

Figure 26.1. Immunodiffusion studies with GL-8-L Ribi fractions against antistreptococcal and anti L-form sera.

A. *Center well:* GL-8-L Ribi fraction, $S_{27,000}$.

    Outer wells (counterclockwise, starting at arrow):

Left side: anti GL–8 serum from:	Right side: anti GL-8-L serum from:
1) Rabbit #30 at 19 days	1) Rabbit #9 at 15 days
2) " #31, preimmune	2) " #9 at 29 days
3) " #31 at 3 days	3) " #9 at 106 days
4) " #31 at 8 days	4) " #10 at 15 days
5) " #31 at 19 days	5) " #10 at 106 days
6) " #31 at 30 days	6) " #10, preimmune

B. *Center well:* GL-8-L Ribi fraction, $R_{27,000}$

    Outer wells (counterclockwise, starting at arrow):

Left side: anti GL-8-L serum from:	Right side: anti GL-8-L serum from:
1) Rabbit #11 at 15 days	1) Rabbit #12 at 106 days
2) " #11 at 29 days	2) " #13, preimmune
3) " #11 at 106 days	3) " #13 at 15 days
4) " #12, preimmune	4) " #13 at 29 days
5) " #12 at 15 days	5) " #13 at 106 days
6) " #12 at 29 days	6) " #13 at 130 days

water. The dialysis resulted in some precipitation of the preparations. Partial solubilization of this precipitate with the detergent and immunoelectrophoresis indicated that several antigens were still present in this material. We are continuing to work on this problem of solubilization of the membrane so as to allow further study of these antigens.

Results

That L-forms can be immunogenic is illustrated by the results of various serological studies with rabbit sera after injection with viable L-forms. The results of typical latex-agglutination reactions with rabbit antisera directed toward the streptococcus and its stable L-form are presented in Table 26.1. In most instances, the antisera prepared against the L-form reacted to a high titer with either the streptococcal or L-form antigen. Conversely, the antistreptococcal sera reacted to only a low titer with the L-form antigens, but to high titers with homologous antigen. This was interpreted to indicate that the membrane

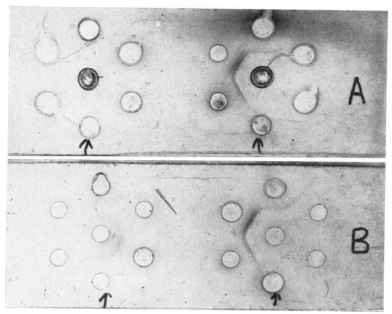

Figure 26.2. Immunodiffusion studies with Ribi fraction of GL-8 versus antisera to GL-8-L. *A*. Center well: GL-8 Ribi fraction, $R_{27,000}$. *B*. Center well: GL-8 Ribi fraction, $S_{27,000}$.

Outer wells same in both A and B: undiluted GL-8-L antiserum (counterclockwise, starting at arrow) from:

on left side:	on right side:
Rabbit #11 at 15 days	Rabbit #12 at 106 days
" #11 at 29 days	" #13, preimmune
" #11 at 106 days	" #13 at 15 days
" #12, preimmune	" #13 at 29 days
" #12 at 15 days	" #13 at 106 days
" #12 at 29 days	" #13 at 130 days

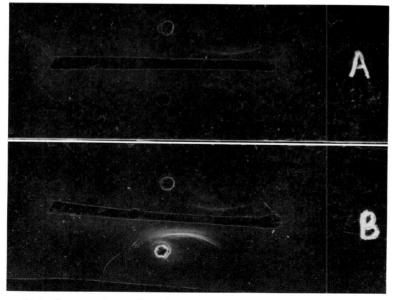

Figure 26.3. Immunoelectrophoresis study indicating extracellular and membrane antigens of GL-8-L. *A:* Center trough: anti GL-8; *B:* center trough: anti GL-8-L. In both *A* and *B:* bottom well, GL-8-L F_{ld}; top well, GL-8-L membrane fraction.

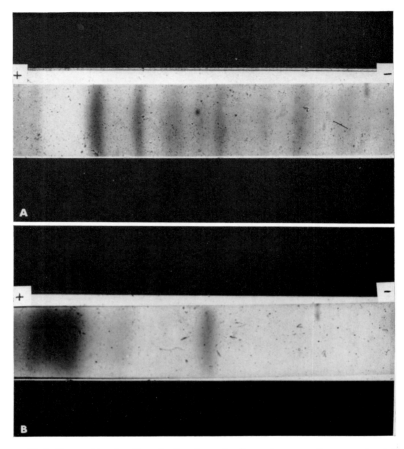

Figure 26.4. Separation by disc electrophoresis of membrane and supernatant fractions of lysates of GL-8-L. *A:* Separation of 50 $\mu\mu$g of supernatant fraction of GL-8-L. *B:* Separation of 50 $\mu\mu$g of membrane of GL-8-L. Agar was stained with amido black after electrophoresis.

and intracellular antigenic substances are not expressed as potent immunogens when introduced to the animal as intact streptococci.

Introduction of the L-form, however, resulted in antibodies being formed against such antigenic determinants. Further evidence for this is demonstrated in Tables 26.2 and 26.3. The streptococcal isolate GL-8 and its stable L-form were disrupted in a Ribi cell fractionator as described above. The disrupted material was separated into four fractions by differential centrifugation. Supernatant and residue fractions were obtained by centrifugation at 480 G for 10 minutes (S_{480} and R_{480}). An aliquot of this supernatant was re-

centrifuged for 20 minutes at 27,000 G, yielding two more fractions ($S_{27,000}$ and $R_{27,000}$). These fractions were tested for their ability to fix complement in the presence of immune sera utilizing a grid arrangement in which both antigen and antibody are diluted. The titers reported in Tables 26.2 and 26.3 reflect the highest dilution of serum at which 50 per cent lysis of sensitized sheep erythrocytes occurs. The antigen dilution is the highest dilution that permits the maximum titer with homologous antiserum.

The results indicate that the antisera prepared to whole streptococcal cells do not react strongly with the soluble fraction ($S_{27,000}$) of the streptococcus (Table 26.2).

These same sera react poorly with all the fractions of the L-form (Table 26.3). Also, these L-form fractions do not react visibly with such antisera in immunodiffusion studies (Figure 26.1). Multiple precipitin bands are produced with these fractions when reacted with antisera prepared against whole viable L-forms. Similar fractions of the streptococcus react in immunodiffusion with the L-form antisera (Figure 26.2).

Animals immunized with viable L-forms also showed the presence of precipitating antibodies directed against a number of extracellular antigens of the streptococcus (Figure 26.3). This figure is representative of results obtained with these antigens and antisera obtained against viable L-forms and heat-killed streptococci. When acetone-dried L-forms were used as immunizing agents, the results were similar to those obtained with antistreptococcal sera. The top wells in Figure 26.3 contained a thousandfold concentrate of the extracellular antigens of the GL-8 strain of streptococcus.[12] The bottom wells contained a membrane fraction of GL-8-L obtained by lysis of the L-form with deionized water and centrifugation at 12,000 G for 10 minutes. The supernatant fraction was recentrifuged at 59,000 G for 30 minutes. The residue was treated with deoxyribonuclease and ribonuclease, and washed three times at 59,000 G for 30 minutes. It was then solubilized with dodecyl sulfate and dialyzed against deionized water. After 10 minutes of electrophoresis in agar gel at 40 V, the center trough of A was filled with undiluted anti-L-form serum (anti-GL-8-L), while that of B received undiluted antiserum to the streptococcus (anti-GL-8).

Figure 26.4 shows the patterns obtained on disc electrophoresis of this membrane fraction and of the supernate obtained by centrifugation of the L-form lysate at 59,000 G. Preliminary immunodiffusion studies following disc electrophoresis indicated that many of these fractions will react serologically with antisera to the L-form.

It was of interest to determine the ability of these various antisera to inhibit the growth of both homologous and heterolog-

TABLE 26.4
Growth Inhibitory Activity of Antisera to Various L-Forms and the Bacteria from Which They Were Derived

Antiserum	Inhibition of L-form Isolates						
	GL-8-L	ADA-L	AED-L	LG-1-L	Cook B-L	Campo L	D-5-L
GL-8-L.........	+	+	±	0	0	0	0
GL-8...........	0	0	0	0	0	0	0
ADA-L.........	+	+	0	0	+	0	0
ADA...........	+	+	0	0	0	0	0
AED-L.........	0	0	+	0	0	0	0
AED...........	±	±	+	0	±	0	0
LG-1-L........	0	0	0	+	0	0	0
LG-1..........	+	0	0	0	0	0	0
Cook B-L......	+	+	0	+	+	0	0
Campo L.......	0	0	0	0	0	+	+
Campo D.......	0	0	0	0	0	0	0

+ : all immune sera tested inhibited growth in a zone measuring at least 3 mm from the outer edge of the saturated disk.

± : inhibition was demonstrated by only a few sera of the appropriate organism.

0 : no visible inhibition.

ous L-forms. The results of such a study are shown in Table 26.4; these data suggest that there may be multiple antigenic determinants involved in this reaction. It can be noted that, whereas antiserum to the L-form (Cook B-L) inhibits the growth of four of the five streptococcal L-forms tested, the L-form (Cook B-L) is inhibited only by antisera against two of them (Cook B-L and ADA-L). In some instances, antistreptococcal sera inhibited the growth of various L-forms.

The two L-forms of diphtheroids indicated in this table were inhibited only by antisera directed against one of them (Campo-L). None of the parent bacterial forms of these L-forms were inhibited by any antisera tested.

The type of growth inhibition exhibited by such L-form antisera is illustrated in Figure 26.5. A liquid culture of the L-form was streaked over the dry surface of agar plate and allowed to dry. Disks of filter paper were saturated with the appropriate antiserum, pressed against the wall of a vial to eliminate excess fluid, and placed on the surface of the medium. After three

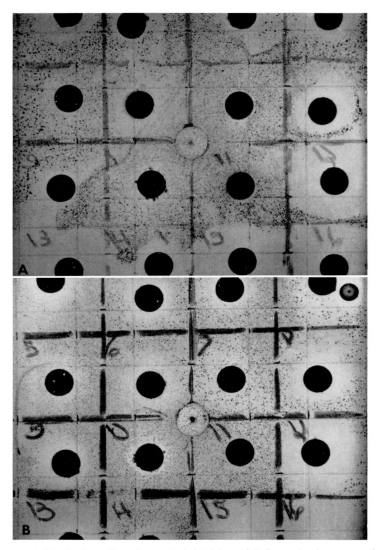

Figure 26.5. Typical results of growth inhibition of L-forms by immune rabbit sera. *A:* L-form isolate LG-1-L. *B:* L-form isolate Cook-B-L. Discs were saturated with the following sera and placed on the surface of freshly streaked plates of *Brucella* agar with 3% NaCl (from top, left to right):

1) anti LG-1-L	9) anti-AED
2) anti GL-8-L	10) anti AR-41 (type 12 streptococcus)
3) anti AED-L	11) anti GL-8
4) anti Cook B-L	12) anti LG-1; skin inoculated with GL-8
5) anti ADA-L	13) anti GL-8-L; skin inoculated with GL-8
6) anti LG-1	14) anti GL-8-L; skin inoculated with GL-8
7) anti ADA	15) anti GL-8-L; skin inoculated with GL-8
8) anti Cook B	16) anti GL-8-L; skin inoculated with GL-8

days the plates were examined for areas of inhibition. Definite zones of inhibition measuring from 2 to 20 mm from the outer edge of the disks have been noted.

A comparison of the antibody response of rabbits to a diphtheroid and its stable L-form is presented in Table 26.5. This diphtheroid had been isolated from a culture of *Mycoplasma* (PG-27), so that it was of interest to determine the degree of antigenic cross reactivity among the diphtheroid, its L-form, and the *Mycoplasma*. *Mycoplasma* strain 39 is quite similar antigenically to the PG-27 strain*. From these data it appears that there is a sharing of some antigenic determinants among these organisms. The immune response of rabbits to the L-form of the diphtheroid is shown in Figure 26.6. Serum samples were collected at intervals during the immunization procedure and reacted in immunodiffusion with a disrupted antigen preparation of the L-form. Precipitating antibodies did not appear until after the second injection of antigen (day 19). No attempt was made to determine a precipitin titer with these sera.

DISCUSSION

L-forms are capable of introducing into rabbits several immunogenic substances that are not evident when the parent bacteria are utilized as immunizing agents. This is probably due to the osmotically labile nature of the L-form. Some of these L-forms have been utilized in implantation studies† which indicate that these organisms are not recoverable from diffusion chambers after four weeks in the peritoneal cavity of rabbits. Whether this reflects inadequate methods of culturing or loss of viability is still uncertain. However, the observation that animals injected with viable (but not heat- or acetone-treated) L-forms have antibodies to extracellular antigens suggests that there may be some growth of the organism after injection, or at least some expression of these substances extracellularly.

Antibodies which inhibit the growth of L-forms are produced in rabbits in response to injection with L-forms, and in some instances by heat-killed streptococci. The specificity of the reaction does not appear to be related to the typing protein of the streptococcus. Antiserum prepared against the extracellular products of a streptococcus does not appear to inhibit

* Unpublished results.
† Reported in pp. 352–355.

TABLE 26.5

Complement Fixing and Growth Inhibitory Activity of Antisera to a Diphtheroid, its Stable L-Form, and Two Mycoplasma *Isolates*

Antiserum	Antigens							
	Growth Inhibition				Complement Fixation Titers*			
	Campo D	Campo L	PG-27	39	Campo D	Campo L	PG-27	39
Campo D	0	+	0	0	1280	160	40	40
Campo L	0	+	0	0	640	2560	160	80
PG-27	0	0	+	+	40	40	2560	1280
39	0	±	+	+	40	80	1280	2560

+: all immune sera tested inhibited growth in a zone measuring at least 3 mm from the outer edge of the saturated disk.

±: inhibition was demonstrated by only a few sera.

0: no visible inhibition.

* Reciprocal of the highest dilution of serum permitting 50% binding of complement with 50 μg antigen protein.

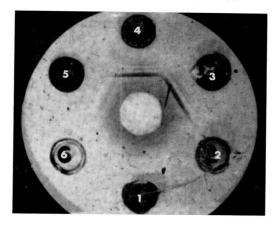

Figure 26.6. The immune response of a rabbit injected with an L-form of a diphtheroid as evidenced by precipitin bands in immunodiffusion. *Center well:* disrupted cells of Campo L. *Outer wells:* undiluted sera taken at (1) 6 days, (2) 11 days, (3) 16 days (animal boosted on day 14), (4) 21 days, (5) 49 days, (6) preimmune.

the growth of the stable L-form of that organism.

Disc electrophoresis and immunoelectrophoresis reveal a multitude of antigens present in membrane and soluble fractions of lysates of these L-forms. At present, efforts are being made to isolate such antigens and determine whether they are involved in the specificity of the growth inhibitory antibody.

It is of interest to note that immunization of rabbits with whole bacteria usually resulted in most of the antibodies produced being specific for cell wall antigens, with relatively few antibodies being capable of reacting with intracellular or membrane antigens.

Further investigations are warranted to determine if the membrane or intracellular antigens as exposed in the L-form are associated with sequelar reactions of acute bacterial infections.

SUMMARY

Antisera directed against bacteria and their stable L-forms were prepared in rabbits. The antisera against the L-forms showed greater reactivity with intracellular and membrane antigens. These antisera were also capable of inhibiting the growth of homologous and some heterologous L-forms.

A diphtheroid, its stable L-form and two *Mycoplasma* isolates were shown to share a few common antigenic determinants.

REFERENCES

1. Campbell, D. H., Garvey, J. S., Cremer, N. E., and Sussdorf, D. H. (Eds.): *Methods in Immunology*. Benjamin, New York, 1963.
2. Clyde, W. A., Jr.: Mycoplasma species identification based upon growth inhibition by specific antisera. *J. Immunol.* **92:** 958, 1964.
3. Freundt, E. A.: Experimental investigations into the pathogenicity of the L-phase variant of *Streptobacillus moniliformis*. *Acta Path. Microbiol. Scand.* **38:** 246, 1956.
4. Grabar, P., and Williams, C. A., Jr.: Méthode immuno-électrophorétique d'analyse de mélanges de substances antigéniques. *Biochem. Biophys. Acta* **17:** 67, 1955.
5. Klieneberger, E.: Further studies on *Streptobacillus moniliformis* and its symbiont. *J. Path. Bact.* **42:** 587, 1936.
6. Klieneberger-Nobel, E.: L-forms of bacteria. *In: The Bacteria, Vol. I: Structure* (I. C. Gunsalus and R. Y. Stanier, Eds.). Academic Press, New York, 1960: p. 361.
7. Lowry, O. H., Rosebrough, N. J., Farr, A. L., and Randall, R. J.: Protein measurement with folin phenol reagent. *J. Biol. Chem.* **193:** 265, 1951.
8. Lynn, R. J., and Muellenberg, M. B.: Immunological properties of an L-form of a group A beta hemolytic streptococcus. *Antonie Leeuwenhoek* **31:** 15, 1965.
9. Ouchterlony, Ö.: Antigen-antibody reactions in gels. IV. Types of reactions in coordinated systems of diffusion. *Acta Path. Microbiol. Scand.* **32:** 231, 1953.
10. Scheibel, I., and Assandri, J.: Isolation of toxigenic L-phase variants from *Cl. tetani*. *Acta Pathol. Microbiol. Scand.* **46:** 333, 1959.
11. Smith, P. F., and Rothblat, G. H.: Relation of PPLO to bacteria. *Ann. N. Y. Acad. Sci.* **79:** 461, 1960.
12. Stock, A. H., and Lynn, R. J.: Preparation and properties of partially purified erythrogenic toxin B of group A streptococci. *J. Immunol.* **86:** 561, 1961.
13. Tulasne, R., and Lavillaureix, J.: Pouvoir pathogène expérimental, pour la Souris, d'une souche de formes L des bactéries. *C. R. Soc. Biol.* (Paris) **148:** 2080, 1954.

27

Immunochemical Properties of the Protoplast Membrane of Group A Streptococci

Earl H. Freimer

THE ROCKEFELLER UNIVERSITY
NEW YORK, NEW YORK

A well-developed body of information on the streptococcal cell has been derived from the study of its surface structures. Interest in these surface structures is in part due to their dominant role in the interaction between the organism and the defense mechanism of the host. Under suitable growth conditions, the vast majority of strains of Group A streptococci possess a capsular envelope consisting of a gel of hyaluronic acid salts. The true protective exoskeleton, however, is the three-layered cell wall. The bacterial surface is largely defined by the nature of the morphological, chemical, and serological properties of this rigid cell wall which is absent in the mechanically and osmotically fragile derivative forms of bacteria, protoplasts and L-forms. These bacterial variants, capable of many of the biological functions of the intact bacterial cell, are subcellular units enclosed in a distinct cytoplasmic membrane.

The isolation, growth, and bacteriological characteristics of protoplasts prepared from Group A streptococci have been described, and chemical and immunological studies have demonstrated that these streptococcal protoplasts are essentially free of group-specific carbohydrate and M protein, two important antigens of the streptococcal cell wall.[7] This report is concerned with the isolation of streptococcal protoplast membranes free of both cell wall and cytoplasmic material, and with the immunochemical properties of these cytoplasmic membranes.

MATERIALS AND METHODS

STRAINS OF STREPTOCOCCI

The streptococcal strains used in these experiments were all from the Rockefeller University collection. The other Gram-positive cocci were also from this collection.

SEROLOGICAL IDENTIFICATION

The serological identification of the strains used in these experiments was confirmed with the capillary tube precipitin test using streptococcal group and type-specific rabbit antisera.[18]

PREPARATION OF GROUP C PHAGE-ASSOCIATED LYSIN

The partially purified phage-associated lysin was prepared by a modification of the method first described by Krause.[5, 10, 20]

ANALYTICAL METHODS

Rhamnose was determined by the method of Dische & Shettles.[3] Quantitative glucosamine determinations were done by a modification of the Elson and Morgan procedure.[16] Quantitative glucose analyses were done by a modified method employing glucose oxidase (glucostat) available from the Worthington Biochemical Corporation, Freehold, New Jersey. Microdeterminations of phosphorus were performed by the method of Chen.[1] Total nitrogen was determined by the micro-Kjeldahl technique. Ribonucleic acid was determined by the orcinol reaction. Total nucleic acid content and protein concentrations were determined by the absorption of solutions at 260 and 280 mμ respectively in the Beckman UV spectrophotometer.

PREPARATION OF CELL WALLS

The cell walls were prepared by the method of Salton, in which streptococci are disrupted in a Mickle disintegrator.[17] The cell walls are separated from residual cellular material by centrifugation, washed with distilled water until free of debris, and then lyophilized.

PREPARATION OF IMMUNODIFFUSION SLIDES

Double diffusion was performed by a modification of the Ouchterlony method. Slides for immunoelectrophoresis were prepared by a modified Scheidegger technique.[6]

PREPARATION OF STREPTOCOCCAL PROTOPLAST MEMBRANES

Membranes were prepared by the following modifications of the original procedure.[6, 7, 20]

Group A streptococci were harvested during the logarithmic growth phase, washed with saline, and incubated for one hour at 37°C with Group C phage-associated lysin in M/100 phosphate buffer (pH 6.5) containing 7% sodium chloride. Following a 7% sodium chloride wash, the protoplasts, free of cell wall carbohydrate as shown by chemical and serological analysis, were ruptured by suspension in M/100 phosphate buffer (pH 7.3) containing 0.2 mg/ml of magnesium-activated DNase to reduce viscosity of released DNA. This suspension was incubated at 37°C for 30 minutes, and the protoplast membranes were collected by centrifugation at 8000 G, and washed in phosphate-buffered saline. These membranes were incubated at 37°C for 30 minutes in phosphate buffer (pH 7.2) containing 0.02 mg/ml of both RNase and DNase, and washed twice with phosphate-buffered saline.

The partially washed protoplast membranes were reincubated at 37°C with phage-associated lysin in M/15 phosphate-buffered saline (pH 6) for one hour. This second treatment with lysin insured the removal of the last traces of cell wall carbohydrates from the membranes. After re-treatment with RNase and DNase, the membranes were washed three times in phosphate-buffered saline, twice with distilled water at 4°C, lyophilized, and stored in a vacuum desiccator at 4°C. The soluble supernatant that remained after the protoplasts had been osmotically ruptured and the protoplast membranes removed by centrifugation, was dialyzed against distilled water, and lyophilized. In subsequent studies, this cytoplasmic material proved useful for comparison with the other cell fractions.

Electron microscopic examinations demonstrated that protoplast membranes remained intact after enzymatic treatment. These thin structures were free of the large electron-dense granules associated with freshly isolated membranes. It should be emphasized that, although membranes and ribosomes may be intimately associated in the intact bacterial cell and separation of these structures may be artificial, these preparations of protoplast membranes, essentially free of intracellular components, have proved to be uniform material for chemical and immunological studies.

PREPARATION OF STREPTOCOCCAL MEMBRANES BY MECHANICAL DISRUPTION

After streptococci were mechanically disrupted in a Mickle disintegrator, cell walls were recovered by centrifugation.[12]

Subsequent high speed centrifugation of the cell wall supernatant also yielded a membrane fraction.

The cell walls of disrupted streptococci were collected by centrifugation at 3500 G for 60 minutes, washed several times with distilled water, and lyophilized. One gram of cell walls was obtained from 18 liters of overnight growth in beef heart infusion broth. To remove remaining cell wall particles, the cell wall supernatant was centrifuged for two hours at 4000 G. The resulting supernatant was centrifuged at 15,000 rpm (20,000 G) in a No. 30 rotor of the Spinco preparative ultracentrifuge, and the pellet which contained the membrane fraction was recovered. The pellet was washed several times with saline, and incubated at 37°C for 30 minutes in M/100 phosphate buffer (pH 7.4) that contained 0.04 M NaCl, 0.005 M $MgCl_2$, and 0.02 mg/ml of both DNase and RNase. The membrane fraction was collected by centrifugation, washed twice with saline, twice with distilled water at 0°C, and lyophilized. The final product, a white powder, weighed 600 mg.

Chemical analysis and immunological studies of the membrane fraction demonstrated that it was essentially free of cell wall carbohydrate and cytoplasmic constituents. Although electron micrographs revealed that the membrane material collected from mechanically disrupted cells was more fragmented than the membranes obtained by lysis of protoplasts, both were similar in chemical composition and antigenic properties.

PREPARATION OF ANTISERA

Sera with antibodies directed against the three streptococcal fractions were prepared in the following manner: A saline suspension of 5 mg of lyophilized membranes was injected intravenously into New Zealand Red rabbits three times a week for five weeks. The rabbits were bled after a five-day rest period, and the sera were tested in capillary precipitin tubes with extracts of membranes. In general, antisera which gave strong precipitin reactions were obtained after four to six weeks of immunization.

Group A streptococcal antisera, containing antibodies to the group-specific carbohydrate of the cell wall, were prepared in the usual manner.[18]

Antisera to cytoplasmic material were obtained by a weekly subcutaneous injection of 20 mg of lyophilized cytoplasmic material suspended in 1 ml of incomplete Freund's adjuvant.

RESULTS

Enzymatic removal of the cell wall from a living bacterium under conditions which prevent disruption of the cell releases the underlying spherical protoplast. Protoplasts of Group A streptococci have been obtained by means of a phage-associated lysin, which dissolves the streptococcal cell wall.[7, 9] The muralytic action of this lysin has been visualized by phase contrast microscopy. After the typical chain of streptococci (Figure 27.1A) are incubated with lysin, only debris remains. However, if the streptococci are suspended in hypertonic sodium chloride before addition of lysin, individual phase-dense spherical protoplasts persist (Figure 27.1B). The hypertonic environment has protected these osmotically fragile structures from rupture after dissolution of the cell wall.

Although osmotically fragile protoplasts lyse when the hypertonicity of the environment is reduced, the ruptured cytoplasmic membrane remains as a distinct structure. These membranes have been isolated, and adherent intracellular material removed, by treatment with nucleases. Figure 27.2A is an electron micrograph of streptococcal membranes. The membranes, which retain the size and shape of the protoplasts, are more delicate structures than the streptococcal cell walls, shown in Figure 27.2B.

CHEMICAL STUDIES OF THE PROTOPLAST MEMBRANES

A comparison of the chemical composition of the membrane to that of the cell wall demonstrates essential differences which confirm earlier morphological stud-

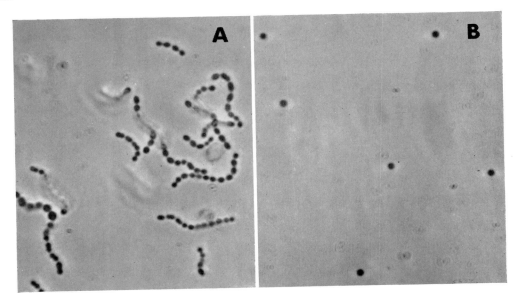

Figure 27.1. Photomicrographs taken by phase microscopy; × 1400. *A:* Typical chains of Group A streptococci in 7% NaCl; micrograph taken just before addition of Group C phage-associated lysin. *B:* Typical spherical protoplasts of Group A streptococci in 7% NaCl; micrograph taken one hour after addition of phage-associated lysin.

ies indicating that membranes are distinct from the cell wall.

The results of a typical analysis of protoplast membranes and cell walls isolated from the same streptococcal strain are recorded in Table 27.1. In general, cell membranes are largely lipoprotein, and it is apparent that a lipid-protein complex comprises more than 95 per cent of the streptococcal membrane.

A major chemical difference between the membrane and the cell wall is the presence of a considerable amount of lipid in the membrane. In contrast, the lipid content of the cell wall preparation is less than two per cent, and even this small amount of lipid is due to membrane fragments which have remained in close association with the cell wall fraction. Another striking difference is the absence of more than traces of rhamnose and hexosamine in the membranes. These two sugars, which are combined in the Lancefield group carbohydrate haptene, comprise more than 44 per cent of the streptococcal cell wall. These analytical results are in agreement with quantitative precipitin analyses of

extracts of protoplast membranes, which have shown that cell wall carbohydrate comprises less than 0.05 per cent of the membrane.[7] The membrane does contain two per cent glucose, a sugar detectable only in trace amounts in the cell wall.

The nitrogen-containing compounds of the cell wall are N-acetylglucosamine, N-acetylmuramic acid, and four amino acids. In contrast, the membranes, as shown by quantitative amino acid analysis, contain a wide variety of amino acids, thus suggesting a protein component.

The chemical determinations listed in Table 27.1 have been performed on 12 lyophilized preparations of streptococcal membranes. In general, all preparations of protoplast membranes appeared similar when examined by electron microscopy, and contained only trace amounts of cell wall carbohydrate. Analyses of four protoplast membrane preparations obtained from two streptococcal types are recorded in Table 27.2. The small amount of RNA detectable in each preparation suggests that the membranes are essentially free of intracellular material. The content of ni-

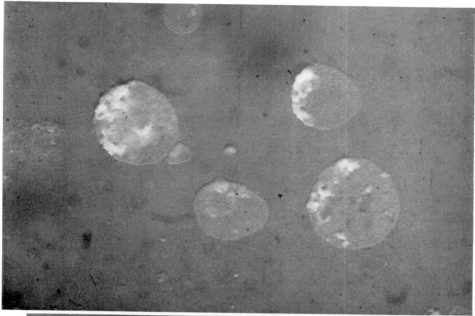

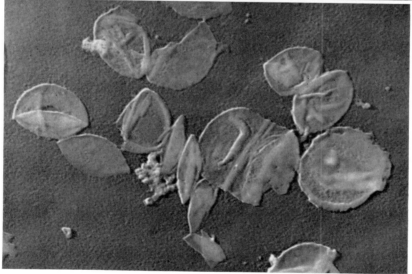

Figure 27.2. Membrane and cell wall specimens examined and photographed in a Phillips EM100 electron microscope; approximately × 7500. *Top:* Trypsin-treated protoplast membranes of streptococcal strain S43FL; the preparation was mounted on carbon-coated No. 150 mesh copper grids and shadowed with metallic chromium at a 16° angle; the membranes are delicate structures, much thinner than the cell walls shown below. *Bottom:* Trypsin-treated cell walls of hemolytic streptococci, isolated by a modification of the method of Salton[17] (in which bacteria are disrupted in a Mickle disintegrator); the preparation was mounted on copper grids by a method similar to that used for the membranes. (From Freimer, Krause & McCarty.[7])

TABLE 27.1

Chemical Composition of Membranes and Cell Walls of Streptococcal Strain T25/41FP

(Percentages)

	Total Lipid	Total Protein	Glucose	Rham- nose	Hexos- amine
Protoplast membranes	26.3	72.0	2.2	<0.1	0.1
Cell walls	<2.0	—	<0.3	28.4	16.2

TABLE 27.2

Chemical Analyses of Streptococcal Membranes

(Percentages)

Strain	Lot No.	Total Lipid	Nitro- gen	Phos- phorus	Glucose	RNA
T12	1	19.1	11.4	1.09	1.9	3.0
T25	4	23.7	10.8	1.00	2.1	1.9
,,	5	25.0	10.9	1.06	2.1	2.0
,,	6	24.3	10.7	1.08	2.3	1.8
Mean		23.0	10.9	1.06	2.1	2.2

trogen, phosphorus, glucose, and lipid is similar for each lot of membranes, indicating that the method of preparation is reproducible.

The semipermeable nature of the cell membrane is probably a function of layers of lipid and protein. Physicochemical studies which suggested that a similar selective osmotic barrier existed in bacteria had assumed the presence of a lipoprotein structure.[15] Because the cell walls of Gram-positive bacteria contain only small amounts of lipid and protein, and because the protoplasts, free of the rigid cell wall, are very sensitive to osmotic change, it appears likely that the membrane of the protoplast functions as the osmotic barrier in bacteria. Analyses of protoplast membranes from *Bacillus megaterium*[19] and from *Micrococcus lysodeikticus*[8] have indicated that these structures are essentially lipoprotein complexes. The lipoprotein complex of the streptococcal membrane has been studied and its lipid components partially characterized.

Most of the membrane lipid is easily extracted by such lipid solvents as a mixture of chloroform and methanol, while the remainder requires more vigorous extraction. The chloroform-methanol soluble lipid is extracted from membranes by a modification of the method devised by Folch[4] for the isolation and purification of lipids from biological sources; in this procedure, the lipid extract is washed with a dilute aqueous salt solution to remove non-lipid substances.

Almost 90 per cent of the extractable lipid is removed by the Folch procedure, while the remainder is extractable only after partial acid hydrolysis.[6] These two lipid extracts have been combined, and the content of phosphorus, nitrogen, and glucose in the total lipid has been determined. Roughly half of the total phosphorus of the membrane is found in the lipid, present largely as phosphoric acid in various phospholipids. Four per cent of the phospholipid molecule is phosphorus, and thus the lipid phosphorus content of 1.85 per cent indicates that phospholipids comprise almost 50 per cent of the total lipid. A similar phosphatide content has been reported for the lipid fraction obtained from disrupted cells of *Staphylococcus aureus*.[14] In contrast, phospholipids represent almost 90 per cent of the total lipid isolated from membranes of *B. megaterium* and *M. lysodeikticus*. Only traces of nitrogen are detectable in the phospholipid fraction of these two species, suggesting that a phosphatidic acid complex is the major phosphatide.[8, 19] On the other hand, the presence of nitrogen in roughly equimolar proportion to phosphorus in the lipid of the streptococcal membrane indicates the presence of phosphatides that possess a nitrogenous base. The demonstration of choline in the lipid is further evidence for the presence of one of the common phosphatides, phosphatidylcholine (lecithin). In addition, the presence of glucose in the lipid fraction suggests the presence of glycolipids.

Partial separation and identification of the lipid substances present in streptococcal membranes have been obtained by means of ascending chromatography using thin layers of silicic acid. Two solvent systems have been employed, a nonpolar solvent composed of 30% ethyl ether and

70% petroleum ether (40–60°), as well as a polar solvent containing a 3:1 mixture of chloroform and water-saturated methanol. The chromatograms prepared with the nonpolar solvent disclosed the presence of free fatty acids, diglycerides (both the 1,2 and the 1,3), and traces of triglyceride and an esterified hydroxy acid. It is of interest that sterols and sphingomyelin have not been detected in the membrane lipid. Use of the polar solvent system has revealed the presence of phospholipids and glycolipids. One large spot containing both phosphorus and choline had an R_f value very similar to that of phosphatidyl choline. In addition, several ninhydrin-positive spots which contain phosphorus correspond to those formed by phosphatidyl serine and phosphatidyl ethanolamine. Finally, two large glucose-containing spots had no phosphorus, and were ninhydrin-negative. These had the same R_f value as the common cerebrosides.

Additional studies have been concerned with the fatty acid composition of the total membrane lipid. After conversion to their respective methyl esters, the fatty acids have been separated by gas-liquid chromatography.[6] Although 16- and 18-carbon fatty acids predominate, a wide variety of saturated and unsaturated fatty acids were present. It is clear that the pattern of fatty acids found in the lipid of streptococcal membranes was quite similar to that described for human adipose tissues. In contrast, there is no evidence for the presence of branched fatty acids, which have been demonstrated in membrane lipids of other bacterial species.

These chemical studies have disclosed the lipoprotein nature of the streptococcal membrane, and demonstrated the similarity of membranes isolated either from mechanically disrupted cells or from protoplasts. The following immunological studies indicate that membranes of Group A streptococci possess a common antigen which is unrelated to the antigens of the cell wall or the cytoplasm.

IMMUNOLOGICAL STUDIES OF STREPTOCOCCAL MEMBRANES

In the following experiments, the antigenic nature of the streptococcal membrane was compared to that of other components of the streptococcus. Antisera were prepared to each streptococcal fraction, the cell wall, the membrane, and cytoplasmic material. Soluble antigens extracted by various techniques from these fractions were employed with the antisera in precipitin tests, in double diffusion studies in agar gel, and in immunoelectrophoresis.

Soluble antigen preparations suitable for precipitin analysis with these antisera were obtained by treating the membranes with proteolytic enzymes. Antigen-containing extracts of cell fractions were prepared with the enzymes produced by *Streptomyces albus*, which have proteolytic activity as well as the capacity to dissolve the Group A streptococcal cell wall. Similar immunologically reactive extracts were prepared by treating the membranes with other proteolytic enzymes, such as trypsin or chymotrypsin. In addition, extracts of membranes prepared by boiling for ten minutes at pH 2 also contain antigenic material.

In most of the following experiments, extracts have been prepared with trypsin or the enzymes of *S. albus*. Lyophilized membranes, suspended in M/15 phosphate buffer (pH 7.4) were mixed with an equal volume of saline containing 20 μg trypsin per ml, and incubated at 37°C for six hours. When extracts were prepared with the enzymes of *S. albus*, the suspension was buffered at pH 7.85 and incubated at 45°C. The insoluble residue was removed by centrifugation, and the supernatant was employed in precipitin tests.

Capillary precipitin tests employing soluble antigens of the cell wall, the membrane, and cytoplasmic material, and antisera to each of these fractions, indicated that the membrane contains an antigen distinguishable from those in the other fractions. The results of some of these precipitin tests are recorded in Table 27.3. Cell walls and protoplast membranes from three Group A streptococcal Types 6, 12, and 25, were extracted with the *S. albus* enzymes. Each of these extracts, as well as phosphate-buffered solutions of cytoplasmic material from each strain, was tested with antiserum to the group carbo-

TABLE 27.3

Serological Specificity of Streptococcal Cell Fractions

Soluble Antigens from	Rabbit Antisera to				
	Killed Group A streptococci	Protoplast membrane			Cytoplasmic material
		Type 6	Type 12	Type 25	
Cell wall					
Type 6	4+*	+	tr	tr	tr
Type 12	4+*	tr	+	tr	tr
Type 25	4+*	tr	tr	+	tr
Protoplast membrane					
Type 6	tr	4+	4+	4+	tr
Type 12	tr	4+	4+	4+	tr
Type 25	tr	4+	4+	4+	tr
Cytoplasmic material					
Type 6	+	+	+	+	4+
Type 12	+	+	+	+	4+
Type 25	+	+	+	+	4+

* This precipitate represents the interaction of Lancefield Group A carbohydrate and group-specific antiserum.

tr: trace reaction.

Data from Freimer.[6]

hydrate of the cell wall, antisera to each of the three membrane preparations, and antiserum to cytoplasmic material.

It is clear that each membrane extract produced a strong precipitin reaction with each of the three membrane antisera, while only trace reactions appeared with either the cell wall antiserum or the antiserum to cytoplasmic antigens. Extracts of freshly isolated membranes which had been insufficiently washed, and therefore contained adherent nucleoprotein, reacted strongly with cytoplasmic antisera. However, during treatment of the membranes with nucleases, the RNA-protein substances that react with cytoplasmic antisera were released into solution. Extracts of the final membrane preparation, therefore, gave only trace reactions with cytoplasmic antisera. The soluble antigens present in the other two fractions reacted strongly only with sera directed against the specific

fraction, and produced only faint reactions with membrane antisera. Thus, the precipitin reaction that develops between membrane antigen and membrane antiserum is specific, and supports the chemical evidence which suggests that the streptococcal membrane preparations are essentially free of other cellular components.

Serological studies using capillary precipitin tests have shown that soluble antigens can be extracted from membranes by several proteolytic enzymes. Immunodiffusion experiments demonstrated that the same antigen was released from the membrane by a variety of proteolytic enzymes, and that this antigen was distinct from antigens present in the cell wall and in the cytoplasm.

Proteolytic extracts of membranes isolated from many different serological types produced strong precipitin reactions with different membrane antisera in capillary precipitin tubes. Diffusion experiments designed to investigate further the antigenic relationships of membranes from different types of Group A streptococci demonstrated that these membranes contained an antigen in common. Two representative experiments are pictured in Figure 27.3. In A, the central well contained antiserum prepared with membrane from Type 25 streptococci; trypsin extracts of five membrane preparations, each from a different serological type of Group A streptococcus, were placed in five peripheral wells; the sixth well contained a trypsin extract of membranes isolated from an A-variant Type 14 streptococcus. The precipitin lines which appeared between the antiserum and each of the six extracts have formed a circular band of identity.

In the experiment illustrated in Figure 27.3B, the positions of the antigen and antiserum were reversed. Antisera to membranes isolated from many different serological types of Group A streptococci were prepared, and each of the five peripheral wells contained a different membrane antiserum. The central well was filled with a trypsin extract of T25 membranes. As expected, precipitin lines developed between the membrane extract and each serum, and these lines have merged to form

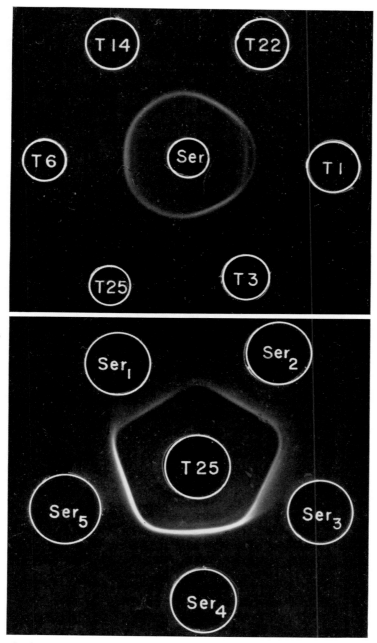

Figure 27.3. *Top:* Serological identity of membranes from various types of Group A streptococci. Central well: antiserum to Type 25 membranes. Peripheral wells: trypsin extracts of membranes from streptococci of Types 1, 3, 6, 22, and 25; well T14 contains extract of membranes from Type 14, Group A-variant streptococci. *Bottom:* The formation of an identity band between a membrane extract and antisera to membranes from different types of Group A streptococci. The center well contains a trypsin extract of T25 membranes; Ser 1 to 5: antisera prepared with membranes from streptococci of Types 6, 12, 14, 25 and 50, respectively. (From Freimer.[6])

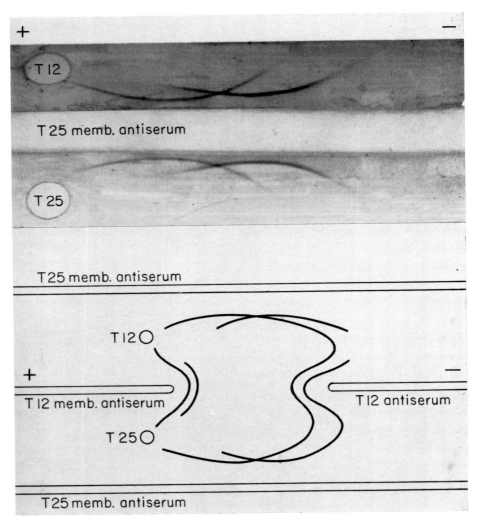

Figure 27.4. *Top:* Immunoelectrophoretic comparison of trypsin extracts of membranes from Type 12 and Type 25 streptococci; patterns developed with antiserum to Type 25 membranes. *Bottom:* Drawing of a modified immunoelectrophoretic experiment showing the precipitin arcs which develop with extracts of Type 12 and 25 membranes, and antisera to each of these membrane preparations; the antigenic identity of the membranes is demonstrated by the fusion of the precipitin lines. (From Freimer.[6])

a continuous pentagonal figure. Similar patterns appeared when extracts of membranes isolated from a wide variety of serological types of Group A and Group A-variant streptococci were studied. The formation of these bands of identity is evidence for the presence of an antigen common to the membranes of all Group A streptococci.

Immunoelectrophoretic analyses of proteolytic extracts of membranes were performed on ammonium sulfate-fractionated material by the usual methods. These studies indicated the presence of antigenic substances that migrated towards the cathode, and development with membrane-specific antisera revealed these antigens as a pair of overlapping precipitin arcs, as shown in

Figure 27.4A. Membranes isolated from different serological types of Group A streptococci formed similar precipitin arcs when extracts were prepared under standard conditions. In the modified immunoelectrophoretic experiment drawn in Figure 27.4B, extracts of T12 and T25 membranes had been electrophoresed; subsequent development with antisera to each of these membrane preparations produced typical precipitin arcs, and the antigenic identity of these membranes was clearly demonstrated by the fusion of the precipitin lines.

MEMBRANE OF OTHER BACTERIAL SPECIES

With the demonstration of common antigens in the membranes of Group A streptococci, it seemed of interest to compare the serological relationship of these membranes to those from other Grampositive cocci. In general, cell wall-dissolving enzymes suitable for the preparation of protoplasts have not been available for most bacterial species. However, by means of mechanical disruption of the bacterial cells, membranes were isolated from strains of hemolytic streptococci, *Streptococcus viridans*, and *S. aureus*, and rabbit serum was prepared against each of these membranes. When these antisera were compared in capillary precipitin tubes with trypsin extracts of membranes, each serum reacted strongly with its homologous membrane extract. The results of these studies are recorded in Table 27.4.

Streptococci of Groups A, C, and G have a number of biological characteristics in common, and therefore it is not surprising to find cross-reactions among these strains. Extracts of Group C and Group G membranes react with antisera to Group A membranes, and extracts of Group A and Group G membranes react with serum prepared against Group C membranes. On the other hand, immunodiffusion studies have shown that the antigenic substances in the membranes of these groups are only partially related. In the microdiffusion experiment shown in Figure 27.5A, trypsin extracts of membranes from Groups A, C, and G have been compared by means of antisera to Group A membranes; each

TABLE 27.4

Species Specificity of Bacterial Membranes

Soluble Antigens from Membranes of	Rabbit Antisera to Membranes of					
	Group A	Group C	Group D	*Streptococcus viridans*		*Staphylococcus aureus*
				SBE 154	B 683	
Group A	4+	2+	0	0	0	0
Group B	0	tr	0	tr	0	0
Group C	2+	4+	0	0	0	0
Group D	2+	2+	4+	0	0	0
Group G	+	+	0	tr	0	0
S. viridans						
SBE 154	0	0	0	4+	tr	0
B 683	0	0	0	+	4+	0
S. aureus	0	0	0	0	0	4+

tr: trace reaction.
Data from Freimer.[6]

membrane extract formed a precipitin line with each antiserum, and these lines have partially fused into bands of identity. The precipitin lines of the Group C and the Group G extracts formed spurs with the lines of the Group A extract, suggesting that the antigens of these three groups possess only partial identity. In other experiments using antisera to Group C membranes some of the precipitin lines intersected, indicating non-identity of the antigens. Thus, although the membranes of these three groups are related, they contain antigens which are similar but not identical.

Although extracts of Group D membranes react with antisera to membranes of Group A and Group C, it is evident that this is a one-way cross, since antisera to Group D membranes do not react with membrane preparations of other groups. In addition, double diffusion studies have clearly demonstrated that the antigens of Group D membranes are unrelated to those present in Group A, C, or G membranes. In the experiment illustrated in Figure 27.5B, extracts of two Group A membranes, T12 and T25, were analyzed with two Group A membrane antisera. The precipitin lines developed, and fused into a common band of identity that entered the well containing the extract of Group D

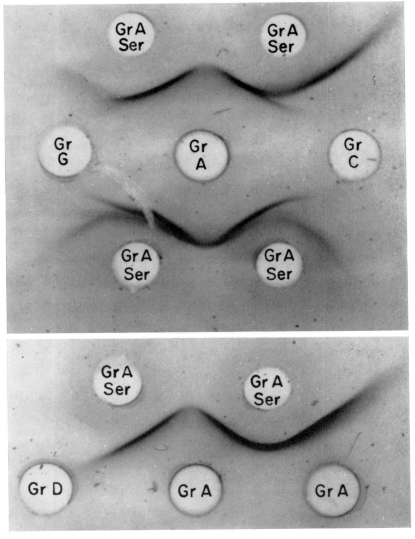

Figure 27.5. Wells labeled Gr A Ser contain antisera to membranes from two Group A strains. Wells labeled Gr A, Gr C, Gr D, and Gr G contain trypsin extracts of membranes from each of these groups. *Top:* Comparison of membranes from Groups A, C, and G streptococci; *bottom:* Of membranes from Groups A and D streptococci. (From Freimer.[6])

membranes. Although Group D extracts formed a precipitin line with some antisera to Group A membranes, no reaction developed with this Group A membrane antiserum. In those experiments in which a precipitin line formed between Group D membranes and Group A membrane antiserum, the line intersected the one formed with Group A membranes.

The experiment illustrated in Figure 27.6 clearly demonstrated the non-identity of membranes isolated from two serologically unrelated species, Group A streptococci and *S. aureus;* the lines of precipitate formed between each of these membrane preparations and their respective antisera intersected to form an X. Similar experimental results were obtained when extracts of membranes from strains of *S. viridans* were compared with those from the Group A streptococci. These serological studies strongly suggest that the membranes of Group A streptococci have no serological relationship to the membranes of other species of Gram-positive cocci.

DISCUSSION

The identification and classification of a bacterial species is usually determined by the specific nature of its cell surface. It is evident that such distinguishing characteristics as morphology and the capacity to take the Gram stain are dependent upon the presence of the rigid cell wall. The immunochemical properties of the bacterial cell wall have been extensively studied, and the evidence strongly suggests that the serological specificity of a bacterial species is determined by the chemical nature of its cell wall.[2, 11, 12, 13] Studies have shown that this rigid cell wall is absent in the mechanically and osmotically fragile derivative forms of bacteria, protoplasts and L-forms. These bacterial variants, which are capable of many of the biological functions of the intact bacterial cell, are subcellular units enclosed in a distinct cytoplasmic membrane.

Although properties of bacterial membranes are not as well established as those of the cell wall, bacterial membranes have specific chemical composition. It is evident that the membrane of the streptococcus is distinct from those isolated from other bacterial species. In addition, the serological studies which have demonstrated the specificity of the Group A membrane indicate that specific antigens may be present in membranes of other bacterial species.[6] A serological basis for identification of bacterial membranes is of value in studies of the relationships among bacterial species, as well as in determining the specific bacterial origin of those cell wall-free derivatives which have been isolated free in nature.

Investigations of the nature of bacterial membranes have been limited to those few bacterial species for which cell wall-dissolving enzymes suitable for the preparation of protoplasts have been available. The isolation from mechanically disrupted bac-

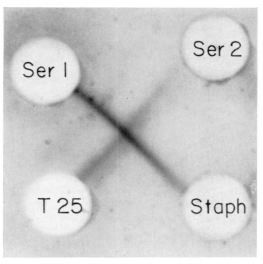

Figure 27.6. Serological non-identity of membranes from Group A streptococci and *Staphylococcus aureus*. *Staph:* trypsin extract of membranes from *S. aureus*; *Ser 1:* antiserum to these membranes. *T25:* An extract of Group A membranes; *Ser 2:* antiserum to membranes of this strain. (From Freimer.[6])

teria of a membrane fraction with chemical and serological properties of the protoplast membrane has removed this restriction, and membrane material can now be obtained from those bacteria for which there are no known muralytic enzymes.

SUMMARY

Intact bacterial membranes have been isolated from protoplasts prepared from Group A streptococci by a cell wall-dissolving enzyme. A membrane fraction with identical chemical and serological properties has been obtained by differential centrifugation of mechanically disrupted streptococci. The membrane is chemically distinct from the cell wall, and is composed of **72** per cent protein, **26** per cent lipid, and **2** per cent carbohydrate. Capillary precipitin tests and analysis by microdiffusion have demonstrated that the membrane contains antigens distinct from those of the cell wall and from those of the cytoplasm which it envelops. Evidence is presented which demonstrates that this antigenic material is common to the membranes of Group A streptococci, and that it can be distinguished by immunodiffusion from related antigenic substances present in membranes of several other serological groups of hemolytic streptococci. This antigenic material does not cross-react with the membrane antigens of other Gram-positive cocci.

REFERENCES

1. Chen, P. S., Jr., Toribara, T. Y., and Warner, H.: Microdetermination of phosphorus. *Anat. Chem.* **28:** 1756, 1956.
2. Cummins, C. S., and Harris, H.: The chemical composition of the cell wall in some Gram-positive bacteria and its possible value as a taxonomic character. *J. Gen. Microbiol.* **14:** 583, 1956.
3. Dische, Z., and Shettles, L. B.: A specific color reaction of methylpentoses and a spectrophotometric micromethod for their determination. *J. Biol. Chem.* **175:** 595, 1948.
4. Folch, J., Lees, M., and Sloane Stanley, G. H.: A simple method for the isolation and purification of total lipides from animal tissues. *J. Biol. Chem.* **226:** 497, 1957.
5. Fox, E. N.: Intracellular M protein of group A *streptococcus*. *J. Bact.* **85:** 536, 1963.
6. Freimer, E. H.: Studies of L forms and protoplasts of Group A streptococci. II. Chemical and immunological properties of the cell membrane. *J. Exp. Med.* **117:** 377, 1963.
7. Freimer, E. H., Krause, R. M., and McCarty, M.: Studies of L forms and protoplasts of Group A streptococci. I. Isolation, growth, and bacteriologic characteristics. *J. Exp. Med.* **110:** 853, 1959.
8. Gilby, A. R., Few, A. V., and McQuillen, K.: The chemical composition of the protoplast membrane, of *Micrococcus lysodeikticus*. *Biochim. Biophys. Acta* **29:** 21, 1958.
9. Gooder, H., and Maxted, W. R.: Protoplasts of Group A beta-haemolytic streptococci. *Nature* **182:** 808, 1958.

10. Krause, R. M.: Studies on the bacteriophages of hemolytic streptococci. II. Antigens released from the streptococcal cell wall by a phage-associated lysin. *J. Exp. Med.* **108:** 803, 1958.
11. Krause, R. M., and McCarty, M.: Studies on the chemical structure of the streptococcal cell wall. II. The composition of Group C cell walls and chemical basis for serologic specificity of the carbohydrate moiety. *J. Exp. Med.* **115:** 49, 1962.
12. McCarty, M.: Variation in the group-specific carbohydrate of Group A streptococci. II. Studies on the chemical basis for serological specificity of the carbohydrates. *J. Exp. Med.* **104:** 629, 1956.
13. ———: Further studies on the chemical basis for serological specificity of Group A streptococcal carbohydrate. *J. Exp. Med.* **108:** 311, 1958.
14. Mitchell, P., and Moyle, J.: The glycerophospho-protein complex envelope of *Micrococcus pyogenes*. *J. Gen. Microbiol.* **5:** 981, 1951.
15. ———: Osmotic function and structure in bacteria. *Symp. Soc. Gen. Microbiol.* **6:** 150, 1956.
16. Rondle, C. J. M., and Morgan, W. T. J.: The determination of glucosamine and galactosamine. *Biochem. J.* **61:** 586, 1955.
17. Salton, M. R. J., and Horne, R. W.: Studies of the bacterial cell wall. II. Methods of preparation and some properties of cell walls. *Biochim. Biophys. Acta* **7:** 177, 1951.
18. Swift, H. F., Wilson, A. T., and Lancefield, R. C.: Typing Group A hemolytic streptococci by M precipitin reactions in capillary pipettes. *J. Exp. Med.* **78:** 127, 1943.
19. Weibull, C.: The lipids of a lysozyme sensitive *Bacillus* species (*Bacillus* "M"). *Acta Chem. Scand.*, **11:** 881, 1957.
20. Zabriskie, J. B., and Freimer, E. H.: An immunological relationship between the Group A streptococcus and mammalian muscle. *J. Exp. Med.* **124:** 661, 1966.

28

Serum Bactericidal Activity Against Protoplasts*

George M. Kalmanson,

VETERANS ADMINISTRATION CENTER
AND UCLA SCHOOL OF MEDICINE
LOS ANGELES, CALIFORNIA

Earl G. Hubert

VETERANS ADMINISTRATION CENTER
LOS ANGELES, CALIFORNIA

John Z. Montgomerie and Lucien B. Guze

VETERANS ADMINISTRATION CENTER
AND UCLA SCHOOL OF MEDICINE
LOS ANGELES, CALIFORNIA

The effect of mammalian serum on protoplasts† becomes important in any consideration of the possible pathogenicity of these forms. The fact that serum is commonly used to enrich media for cultivation of protoplasts might suggest a lack of significant cidal activity on the part of serum for protoplasts of both Gram-negative and Gram-positive bacteria. The observation that protoplasts can be pro-

* Research supported by U.S. Public Health Service Grants Nos. AI 02257 and AI 03310.

† As used in this paper, *protoplasts* are osmotically fragile microbial forms in which the amount of cell wall present was not determined. Under certain conditions, these forms grow on solid media as characteristic *L-colonies*. Some authors have used "spheroplasts", "L-forms", "L-colonies", "L-phase growth", "microbial variants", etc. without defining these terms. In the references cited, we have followed the authors' usage and have assumed these terms to be interchangeable.

duced in kidneys of rats with acute enterococcal pyelonephritis by treatment with penicillin[27] suggested that these organisms were either sequestered from normal serum cidal activity (intracellular) or were resistant to its action. However, when efforts were made to produce disease in the kidney by either injecting protoplasts directly into that organ or by intravenous inoculation, protoplasts could not be recovered one hour later. Although this could have been due entirely to osmotic shock, it was possible that other factors were important. Because of these considerations, studies were designed to evaluate the effect of serum on protoplasts *in vitro.*

MATERIALS AND METHODS

ORGANISMS

Most studies were done with a strain of *Streptococcus faecalis* previously described,[26] which had been used for production of protoplasts *in vivo*. For certain experiments, the following organisms were used: Beta hemolytic *Streptococcus pyogenes*, Type 1, kindly sent by Dr. K. Vosti; coagulase-positive *Staphylococcus aureus* (laboratory designation 61); *S. faecalis* F24 and its lysozyme-produced L-form, kindly sent by Dr. H. Gooder; *Escherichia coli* (laboratory designation Yale); and *Proteus mirabilis* (laboratory designation 5).

MEDIA

The basic media were brain heart infusion broth and agar (Difco). For growth of protoplasts, 0.5 M sucrose was used as osmotic stabilizer and 40 μM MgSO$_4$ and 2% bovine serum albumin (Armour) were added. "Biphasic medium" consisted of osmotically stabilized broth over a slant of osmotically stabilized agar.

PREPARATION OF PROTOPLASTS

An aliquot of 0.1 ml of 18-hour broth culture was spread on the surface of an osmotically stabilized agar plate containing either penicillin or methicillin: Potassium penicillin G, 1000 units/ml for *S. faecalis*, 100 units/ml for *S. pyogenes*, 10,000 units/ml for *E. coli* and *P. mirabilis*; methicillin, 200 units/ml for *S. aureus*. No penicillin was necessary for the lysozyme-produced protoplasts of *S. faecalis* F24, as these had not originally been prepared with penicillin and have been stable for over a year on serial passage without lysozyme. All incubations were at 37°C. At approximately one week, when L-colonies had appeared, a portion of the plate was homogenized in osmotically stabilized broth, and an aliquot spread on a similar plate with antibiotic. The protoplasts were maintained by serial transfer at intervals of four to seven days. The number of serial passages on antibiotic media have been designated "T" with a subnumeral—for example, "T$_9$" means nine serial passages. When a liquid suspension was necessary, the homogenate was inoculated into biphasic medium. Two to three days later the liquid phase was passed

through glass wool to remove particles of agar and, after suitable dilution, used in the cidal test. The liquid growth usually contained 10^5 to 10^6 protoplasts per ml by plate count assay. Most experiments with *S. faecalis* were done with the ninth such transfer (T$_9$). At this stage, the protoplasts were unstable, as they would revert promptly to the bacterial form on removal from penicillin. Other studies were done with T$_{53}$ protoplasts: at the fifty-third passage, the protoplasts were serially transferred without penicillin at least 30 times prior to use in the cidal tests, with no reversion to bacterial form (stable protoplasts). The protoplasts made from *S. pyogenes* had been transferred eight times (T$_8$), those from the *S. aureus*, 121 times (T$_{121}$), from *E. coli*, 55 times (T$_{55}$), and from *P. mirabilis*, 57 times (T$_{57}$) in media containing antibiotic; these latter protoplasts were unstable.

SERA

The following sera were used: A pool prepared from clotted blood of normal random-bred Wistar rats (rat serum); sera obtained from clotted blood of healthy volunteers (human serum); and commercial human, horse, and fetal calf sera (Hyland Laboratories, Los Angeles, California).

CIDAL TEST

The effect of sera on protoplasts or bacteria in liquid milieu was studied by mixing protoplasts or bacteria at final concentration of 10^3/ml with an appropriate dilution of serum and incubating at 37°C. Samples were taken at intervals and assayed for surviving organisms by plate counts. Osmotically stabilized medium was used for studies of protoplasts. When the bacterial form was tested, although the test was carried out in the same diluent used with protoplasts, the survivors were plated on standard (non-osmotically stabilized) medium without penicillin. Controls consisted of diluent and organism without added serum.

In earlier experiments, the diluent was sucrose in water. Experiments were done at 310 mOsm/liter, the osmolality of serum, and at 730 mOsm/liter, the osmolality of broth with 0.3 M sucrose which had been used in *in vivo* studies. Subsequently, osmotically stabilized broth (0.5 M sucrose) at 950 mOsm/liter was used for better protection against osmotic shock.

The effect of serum on growth of protoplasts in osmotically stabilized agar was studied by inoculation of approximately 10^3 protoplasts in plates to which the sera had been added to desired concentration. After incubation at 37°C for four to seven days, the colony count was compared to that of the identical inoculum on osmotically stabilized plates with 2% bovine serum albumin. The latter count was considered to be 100 per cent survival.

An Advanced Osmometer (Advanced Instrument Company) was used, calibrated for direct readings up to 1000 mOsm/liter. Solutions of higher osmolality were appropriately diluted with water for measurement, and osmolality calculated from the dilution factor.

RESULTS

EFFECT OF RAT SERUM

These experiments were carried out with unstable (T_9) protoplasts of S. *faecalis* in liquid milieu. Preliminary experiments indicated that the serum pool killed 50–70 per cent of the bacterial form inoculum in 120 minutes at 37°C (310 mOsm/liter) in 0.5% peptone water diluent. Since protoplasts were subsequently tested at 310 mOsm/liter (the osmolality of rat serum) and 730 mOsm/liter to protect them from osmotic shock, the test with the bacterial form was repeated in sucrose-water diluent at 730 mOsm/liter. In this second experiment, the bacterial form was killed at essentially the same rate as had been noted at 310 mOsm/liter. The effects of rat serum against protoplasts (at both 310 and 730 mOsm/liter in sucrose water diluent) are shown in Table 28.1.* The protoplasts were killed at both osmolalities studied

* Data for Tables 28.1, 28.2, 28.4 and 28.6 from Kalmanson, Hubert et al.[35a] and from Guze, Hubert et al.[26a]

TABLE 28.1

Effect of Rat Serum* on Unstable (T9) Penicillin Protoplasts of Streptococcus faecalis

| Time (minutes) | Osmolality (mOsm/liter) (% inoculum surviving) | | | |
| | 310 | | 730 | |
	With serum	Control (no serum)	With serum	Control (No serum)
1	16	40	58	101
5	8	37	49	77
10	5	34	51	74
15	5	30	48	64
20	6	31	43	60
30	4	30	40	46
90	1	27	28	47

* Final dilution 1:2 in sucrose water diluent.

TABLE 28.2

Effect of Human Serum* on Killing of Stable (T53) and Unstable (T9) Penicillin Protoplasts of Streptococcus faecalis

| Time (minutes) | Surviving Inoculum (%) | | | |
| | Stable protoplasts (T53) | | Unstable protoplasts (T9) | |
	With serum	No serum (control)	With serum	No serum (control)
1	<1	100	0	107
5	<1	107	0	99
10	<1	93	0	89
15	<1	89	0	105
20	<1	74	0	81
30	<1	77	0	85
60	<1	59	0	73
90	<1	56	0	74

* Final dilution 1:2 in sucrose water diluent. Test done at 730 mOsm/liter.

more rapidly than could be accounted for by osmotic shock alone (controls) and most of the killing occurred in the first minute.

EFFECT OF HUMAN SERUM ON PROTOPLASTS

These experiments were done in liquid. The unstable (T_9) and stable (T_{53}) protoplasts of S. *faecalis* were rapidly killed when exposed to human serum (Table 28.2). The effects of human serum on the penicillin protoplasts of S. *pyogenes* and

TABLE 28.3

Effect of Human Serum* on Penicillin Protoplasts of Streptococcus pyogenes *and* Staphylococcus aureus

Time (minutes)	Surviving Inoculum (%)			
	S. pyogenes protoplasts		S. aureus protoplasts	
	With serum	No serum (control)	With serum	No serum (control)
10	0.4	105	4	100
30	0	96	1	99
60	0	99	0	101

* Final dilution 1:2. Diluent: osmotically stabilized broth. Test done at 950 mOsm/liter.

TABLE 28.4

Effect of Human Serum* on Lysozyme Protoplasts of Streptococcus faecalis *F24*

Time (minutes)	Surviving Inoculum (%)	
	With serum	No serum (control)
1	0	63
5	0	52
10	0	42
15	0	34
20	0	27
30	0	32
60	0	14
90	0	7

* Final dilution 1:2. Diluent: sucrose in water. Test done at 730 mOsm/liter.

S. aureus are shown in Table 28.3. These protoplasts were also rapidly killed by human serum. The better survival in the no-serum controls was due to the use of osmotically stabilized broth as diluent. It should be noted that, when identical studies were done simultaneously with the bacterial form, the bacterial forms of *S. faecalis, S. pyogenes,* and *S. aureus* were completely resistant to the cidal activity of serum under the conditions tested.

Since lysozyme produces protoplasts by enzymic removal of cell wall while penicillin inhibits its synthesis, experiments were carried out in liquid medium to determine if protoplasts formed by lysozyme activity would react to serum similarly to those produced by penicillin. Table 28.4 indicates prompt killing of lysozyme protoplasts of *S. faecalis* F24 by serum. The bacterial form of this strain was also resistant to serum activity.

The previous experiments were done with protoplasts of Gram-positive organisms. Further tests were carried out with protoplasts and bacterial forms of *E. coli* and *P. mirabilis* (Table 28.5). The results with *E. coli* were similar to those obtained with the Gram-positive forms, i.e., protoplasts were killed while bacterial forms were unaffected. However, with *P. mirabilis,* the findings were reversed: the protoplasts were resistant while the bacterial forms were killed.

TABLE 28.5

Effect of Human Serum* on Bacterial Forms and Penicillin Protoplasts of Escherichia coli *and* Proteus mirabilis

Time (minutes)	Surviving Inoculum (%)							
	E. coli				P. mirabilis			
	Protoplasts		Bacteria		Protoplasts		Bacteria	
	With serum	No serum (control)	With serum	No serum (control)	With serum	No serum (control)	With serum	No serum (control)
10	45	108	105	94	113	82	90	89
30	21	90	105	94	117	88	34	95
60	11	105	102	97	115	98	14	120

* Final dilution 1:2. Diluent: osmotically stabilized broth. Test done at 950 mOsm/liter.

TABLE 28.6

Effect of Dilution of Human Serum* on Killing of Penicillin Protoplasts (T9) of Streptococcus faecalis

Time (minutes)	Surviving Inoculum (%)					
	Final serum dilution					None (control)
	1:2	1:4	1:8	1:16	1:32	
1	2	91	107	118	95	82
10	1	0	42	89	93	84
20	1	0	4	74	79	58
30	1	0	2	63	67	54
60	0	0	0	19	56	40

* Test done at 730 mOsm/liter in sucrose water diluent.

TABLE 28.7

Effect of Heating Human Serum* on Killing of Penicillin Protoplasts (T9) of Streptococcus faecalis

Time (minutes)	Surviving Inoculum (%)		
	Unheated serum	Heated serum	No serum (control)
15	83	93	101
30	40	105	105
60	12	93	102

* Serum inactivated at 56° C for 30 minutes prior to test. Final serum dilution: 1:16. Diluent: osmotically stabilized broth. Test done at 950 mOsm/liter.

Additional studies of the cidal activity of human serum were performed using unstable (T_9) penicillin protoplasts of *S. faecalis* in liquid medium. Table 28.6 demonstrates that serial dilution of serum diminished the cidal activity. The cidal activity was abolished by heating at 56°C for 30 minutes (Table 28.7). Previous results[31] had indicated that increasing osmolality (sucrose) had an adverse effect on human serum cidal activity against a susceptible strain of bacterial form of *E. coli*. To test whether similar inhibition might occur in the protoplast cidal system, stable (T_{53}) and unstable (T_9) protoplasts were exposed to serum at osmolalities of 950 and 1250 mOsm/liter (Table 28.8). In this experiment, the diluent was the osmotically stabilized broth used previously (950 mOsm/liter), with additional sucrose to produce the higher osmolality. The protoplast cidal activity of serum against both test organisms was inhibited at the higher osmolality.

EFFECT OF HORSE SERUM

These experiments were done in liquid medium; the results are shown in Table 28.9. In general, the findings were similar to those obtained with human serum, except that the killing of protoplasts by horse serum was slower and less complete than that demonstrated by human serum. In addition, the bacterial form of *P.*

TABLE 28.8

Effect of Osmolality on Killing of Stable (T53) and Unstable (T9) Penicillin Protoplasts of Streptococcus faecalis by Human Serum*

Time (minutes)	Surviving Inoculum (%)							
	Stable protoplasts (T53) mOsm/liter				Unstable protoplasts (T9) mOsm/liter			
	950		1250		950		1250	
	With serum	No serum (control)	With serum	No serum (control)	With serum	No serum (control)	With serum	No serum (control)
10	116	100	116	117	106	104	100	100
30	37	97	93	94	50	104	95	93
60	6	89	107	107	21	100	78	98

* Final serum dilution: 1:16. Diluent: osmotically stabilized broth.

TABLE 28.9

Effect of Horse Serum* on Protoplasts and Bacteria

Organism	Test	Inoculum Surviving (%)		
		10 min.	30 min.	60 min.
Streptococcus faecalis				
Unstable penicillin protoplasts (T9)	Serum	49	8	<1
	No serum (control)	101	98	101
Stable penicillin protoplasts (T53)	Serum	95	2	<1
	No serum (control)	100	101	99
Bacteria	Serum	86	119	268
	No serum (control)	114	103	183
S. faecalis F24				
Lysozyme protoplasts	Serum	74	19	2
	No serum (control)	90	104	105
Bacteria	Serum	94	102	92
	No serum (control)	98	104	109
Escherichia coli				
Penicillin protoplasts	Serum	88	74	26
	No serum (control)	102	109	88
Bacteria	Serum	85	99	107
	No serum (control)	93	111	100
Proteus mirabilis				
Penicillin protoplasts	Serum	99	106	126
	No serum (control)	89	95	110
Bacteria	Serum	73	95	83
	No serum (control)	102	114	132

* Final dilution: 1:2. Diluent: osmotically stabilized broth. Test done at 950 mOsm/liter.

mirabilis was less susceptible to horse serum than to human serum (Table 28.5).

EFFECT OF VARIOUS SERA ON GROWTH OF PROTOPLASTS IN AGAR

Serial propagation of protoplasts is most frequently done on solid media, although some species can be grown in broth. Table 28.10 shows the effects of various mammalian sera on growth of protoplasts on agar. Equal inocula of protoplasts were placed on osmotically stabilized agar and on similar plates containing, in addition, 2% bovine serum albumin (BSA). These were compared with plates containing 10 or 20% final concentration of the mammalian serum to be tested. In another set of plates, the mammalian sera were inactivated with heat (56°C for 30 minutes) prior to incorporation into the agar. The colony count in the presence of 2% bovine serum albumin was considered 100 per cent, and for each organism the growth in the presence of various sera was recorded as a percentage of this figure. The results indicated that the addition of mammalian protein (BSA) resulted in a greater recovery of protoplasts, as compared to growth on osmotically stabilized agar without any added mammalian protein. In these experiments, human serum and, to a lesser extent, horse serum inhibited growth of T9 and T53 protoplasts of *S. faecalis* and the lysozyme protoplasts of *S. faecalis* F24. The other effects noted were variable and less intense than those obtained in the cidal test in liquid milieu. In this regard, it is important to note that the final concentrations of mammalian sera used in these agar experiments were considerably less than those employed in the liquid cidal studies. This may have accounted for the lesser inhibition recorded. As an example of variability, horse serum markedly inhibited unstable *S. faecalis* (T9) protoplasts but was considerably less active

TABLE 28.10

Effect of Mammalian Sera on Growth of Protoplasts in Osmotically Stabilized Agar

Protoplasts	Serum Tested	Inactivated*		Not Inactivated		2% BSA	No Serum
		10%	20%	10%	20%		
Streptococcus faecalis unstable (T9)	Horse	0.4†	0.3†	0.3†	0.0†	100.0	87.3
	Human (c)	41.6	23.1	29.4	24.2		
	Human	1.1	—	1.1	—		
	Fetal calf	79.7	56.5	60.1	33.7		
S. faecalis stable (T53)	Horse	47.7	36.4	39.6	28.5	100.0	80.7
	Human (c)	101.9	59.6	89.6	87.1		
	Human	44.8	42.8	0.6	0.0		
	Fetal calf	108.7	97.5	85.7	85.7		
S. faecalis F24 lysozyme-produced	Horse	98.3	71.4	100.0	30.6	100.0	99.1
	Human (c)	170.2	127.6	300.0	204.2		
	Human	84.2	39.1	34.8	0.7		
	Fetal calf	272.3	263.8	272.3	195.7		
Escherichia coli	Horse	84.0	85.2	48.0	48.0	100.0	90.4
	Human (c)	144.0	118.4	109.6	129.6		
	Human	120.4	78.0	114.4	103.2		
	Fetal calf	92.8	96.8	124.0	83.2		
Proteus mirabilis	Horse	103.5	86.4	80.9	95.4	100.0	51.1
	Human (c)	82.2	98.7	103.2	103.2		
	Human	85.7	86.0	85.1	87.0		
	Fetal calf	91.9	91.5	77.0	87.3		

* 56° C for 30 minutes.

† Percentage of colonies, with the value for 2% BSA taken as 100%.

BSA: Bovine serum albumin.

(c): Commercial.

against the other protoplasts. For any given protoplast, the source of serum had considerable influence on the colony count. In general, with all protoplasts studied, human serum prepared in the laboratory was most inhibitory, and commercially obtained horse and human sera less active. Fetal calf serum appeared to have the least inhibitory effect.

DISCUSSION

These studies demonstrated that human serum was rapidly, and horse serum slowly, cidal for all protoplasts studied except those prepared from *P. mirabilis*. The bacterial forms of *S. faecalis*, *S. pyogenes*, *S. aureus* and *E. coli* were resistant to serum, while *P. mirabilis* was susceptible. The method of production of protoplasts, whether by lysozyme, penicillin, or methicillin, did not influence this serum activity. Preliminary investigations were made of the cidal substance in human serum: it lost its activity on dilution, was inactivated by moderate heat, and was inhibited by increased osmolality. Rat serum was cidal for both penicillin protoplasts and bacterial forms of *S. faecalis*. This suggests the possible presence of two factors in rat serum, one lethal for bacteria and one which kills protoplasts, while human serum would appear to contain only one protoplast cidal factor.

Inhibition of protoplasts by serum has been noted by other investigators. Dienes[16, 17] described L-forms of a Gram-positive spore-bearing bacillus and of strains of *Clostridium tetani* which grew better in the absence of serum than when it was present. Similarly, Mattman and associates[37] found that either inactivated horse serum or PPLO serum fraction (Difco) inhibited L-colony formation of various strains of *Proteus*. Hamburger & Carleton[28] noted that 10% normal human serum enhanced the growth of staphylococcal protoplasts, while 50% serum was inhibitory. Muschel & Jackson[46] studied killing of lysozyme spheroplasts of *E. coli* and protoplasts of *Bacillus subtilis* by normal rabbit serum; both were destroyed, and when the serum was heated, it lost its activity against *E. coli* but not against *B. subtilis*. Further studies indicated that, in addition to the heat-stable substance active against the protoplasts of *B. subtilis*, complement also played a role; the authors felt that the heat-stable cidal substance was related to basic proteins in serum (possibly histones); it was not considered identical to beta-lysins as serum allowed to clot in the absence of cellular elements was as active against protoplasts of *B. subtilis* as serum obtained from clotted whole blood. However, Amano and associates[3, 5] demonstrated that platelet extracts, which may be similar to beta-lysins, killed protoplasts of *Bacillus megaterium*. The findings of Dienes[15] on the effect of horse serum on growth of L-forms of *Proteus* may be pertinent to the role of beta-lysins (or other agents in serum derived from cellular elements); this author routinely used "10 percent red-colored horse serum, obtained by defibrination of the blood." Serum obtained from clotted blood, however, was unsatisfactory and was unimproved by the addition of laked horse blood. It may be speculated that the serum obtained from clotted blood contained lethal factors not present in that obtained from defibrinated blood.

These demonstrations of the protoplast inhibitory activity of serum need to be reconciled with other reports which have used serum to make protoplasts from *Proteus vulgaris*,[24] *Salmonella typhosa*,[20] *E. coli*, *Vibrio tyrogenus* and *Vibrio comma*,[4] rough strains of *E. coli* and *S. typhosa*,[45] *E. coli*,[56] *Vibrio cholerae*[21] and *V. comma*.[7] Furthermore, various sera have been employed to enrich media used for growth of protoplasts. A partial review of this use is given in Table 28.11. It may be seen that a wide variety of protoplasts, from both Gram-negative and Gram-positive bacteria, have been grown in the presence of different sera.

Speculation can be made regarding the factors which might be important in this apparently paradoxical use of serum to grow, make, or kill protoplasts. Outcome may vary relative to the inter-relationship between serum, species or strain of protoplast, and medium.

ROLE OF SERUM

Although serum has commonly been used to "enrich" media, it may actually serve to neutralize some toxic component of the medium. This was pointed out by Medill & O'Kane[40] and studied in some detail by Weibull & Lundin.[58] Different sera or differently prepared sera may vary in this neutralizing activity. Regardless of the mode of action of serum, enriching or neutralizing, the animal source may be significant. Weinberger and associates[59] noted that protoplasts of strains of *Salmonella* could not grow in guinea pig or mouse serum, grew initially with difficulty in rabbit serum, and grew well in horse or human serum. Tulasne[55] noted variations in growth with beef, rabbit, horse, and human serum, depending on the protoplast; mouse and guinea pig sera were ineffective. In the present study, the protoplast cidal activity of human serum was greater than that of rat serum (Tables 28.1 and 28.2). In addition to the source of the serum, its mode of preparation may be significant. In the present study, human sera prepared in the laboratory were more cidal than that which was commercially obtained (Table 28.10). The studies of Dienes,[15] comparing sera from coagulated and defibrinated horse blood, have been mentioned. Factors known to play a role in serum cidal activity include plakin or beta-lysins,[3, 5] lysozyme,[33] leucocyte extracts,[6] pH,[31, 56] osmolality, urea, sodium and potassium chlorides,[31] and excessive amounts of gamma globulin.[52] Thus, the final effect of serum might depend on the

TABLE 28.11

Use of Sera in Propagation of Protoplasts

Reference	Organism(s)	Sera*
Dienes[12]	*Bacteroides funduliformis*	Rabbit serum
Heilman[29]	*Streptobacillus moniliformis*	20% horse serum
Brown & Nunemaker[8]	*S. moniliformis*	Horse, rabbit, beef and swine sera. Seitz filtered.
Dienes[13]	Hemolytic parainfluenza bacillus	Horse blood
Dienes[14]	*Hemophilus influenzae*	Blood
Dienes[15]	*Proteus*	10% horse plasma from defibrinated blood
Dienes et al.[20]	*Salmonella typhosa*	Horse serum from defibrinated blood
Dienes et al.[19]	*Proteus*	Horse, rabbit sera
Weinberger et al.[59]	*Salmonella* and *Shigella*	Horse serum
Tulasne[55]	Various	Horse, human, beef, rabbit sera
Moustardier et al.[44]	Various	Human or animal serum
Carrère et al.[9]	*Salmonella typhimurium*	Horse serum
Medill & O'Kane[40]	*Proteus*	Horse plasma
Dienes & Sharp[18]	Beta and alpha hemolytic streptococci, staphylococci	10% inactivated horse serum
Sharp et al.[53]	*Streptococcus pyogenes*	Horse serum
Crawford et al.[10]	Streptococci	10% inactivated horse serum
Freimer et al.[22]	Group A streptococci	10% horse serum
Altenbern & Landman[1]	*Proteus mirabilis*	10% horse serum
Mattman et al.[39]	*Mycobacterium tuberculosis* var. *hominis*	Human, horse or guinea pig serum
Wittler et al.[61]	*Corynebacterium* Sp.	Rabbit, horse, human sera
Marston[36]	Staphylococci	20% inactivated horse serum
Godzeski et al.[23]	Various	Human or horse serum filtered through porcelain candle
Hijmans[30]	Group D streptococci	10% horse serum
Kagan et al.[34]	Staphylococci	Inactivated, filtered human plasma
Pease & Laughton[48]	Corynebacteria	10% human plasma or horse serum
Taubeneck[54]	*P. mirabilis*	10% bovine serum
Weibull[57]	Staphylococci and diphtheroids	10% inactivated horse serum
Kagan et al.[35]	Beta hemolytic streptococci	10% horse serum
Mikhailova[41]	Streptococci	20% horse serum
Diena et al.[11]	*Salmonella typhi*	Beef, horse sera
Gutman et al.[25]	Various Gram-negative bacteria and *Streptococcus faecalis*	20% inactivated horse serum
Mattman & Mattman[38]	*S. faecalis*	2% fresh horse serum
Mortimer[43]	*S. pyogenes*	10% horse serum
Nesbitt & Lennarz[47]	*Proteus*	10% inactivated horse serum
Rogul et al.[49]	*P. mirabilis*	16% human serum
Rotta et al.[50]	Group A streptococci	10% horse serum
Hamberger & Carleton[28]	Staphylococci	Human serum filtered through a Millipore filter
Willett & Thacore[60]	*Mycobacterium tuberculosis*	10% horse serum

* Details about sera are as given in the original reference.

relative influences of these various factors. The observations that smaller amounts of serum stimulate and large quantities inhibit protoplast growth[28] suggest that, while serum nutrients might increase growth, other factors present in smaller quantities are cidal to protoplasts when introduced in sufficient concentration.

SPECIES OR STRAIN OF PROTOPLAST

In this study protoplasts of *S. faecalis*, *S. pyogenes* and *S. aureus* were killed rapidly by human serum (Tables **28.2** and **28.3**). *E. coli* protoplasts were less susceptible, and those of *P. mirabilis* were unaffected (Table **28.5**). Weinberger and associates[59] noted that 3A colonies of *Salmonella* L-forms required serum, while 3B types did not. Similar differences between 3A and 3B colonies of L-forms of *Proteus* were noted.[15] It might be expected that variations in protoplast membrane structure would be differently affected by serum protocidal substances, whether these be antibodies, complement components, enzymes, etc.

MEDIUM

Although this has not been extensively investigated, raising of the osmolality in the present study from 950 to 1250 mOsm/liter inhibited serum cidal activity. In addition, variables of chemical composition, pH, etc., which are known to inhibit bactericidal activity, may be important in the killing of protoplasts. Similarly, the less intense reactions noted on agar (Table **28.10**) may be related to factors other than quantity of serum present. Also, the interaction of serum with various media, synthetic or undefined, may determine its ultimate net effect on protoplasts.[40, 58]

While the mechanism by which serum kills protoplasts is unknown, it may be that the active factor reacts with some component of the cell membrane and disrupts its integrity. Early studies by Amano and associates[2] of lysis of protoplasts (but not bacteria) by sodium desoxycholate suggested the structural importance of the lipids in cell membranes; more recent studies confirmed this (Ibbott

& Abrams,[32] Salton & Freer[51]). It is possible, therefore, that serum factor may be lipolytic and perhaps analogous to staphylococcal alpha-toxin and streptolysin S, which lyse a variety of protoplasts and were considered by Bernheimer & Schwartz[7] to act on the lipid structure of the membranes.

The demonstration in this study that the cidal substance in human serum cannot affect the bacterial form (except for *P. mirabilis*) while killing the protoplasts implicates the presence of cell wall in the resistance of the former. These results are analogous to findings previously reported from this laboratory (Montgomerie and associates[42]) on the effect of antibiotics. In those studies, protoplasts of *S. faecalis* were more sensitive to a variety of antibiotics than was the bacterial form. The simplest explanation would be that the cell wall interferes with access of the active substance (serum-cidal or antibiotic) to its reactive site on the cell membrane or within the cell. These findings suggest that the cell wall should probably not be regarded as an inert structure which only functions to provide structural rigidity to the bacteria. The failure of serum to kill protoplasts of *P. mirabilis* is puzzling. It may be that the receptors for the protoplast cidal substance are lost during protoplast formation.

Since serum contains a protoplast cidal substance, the question arises as to how these forms have been able to survive *in vivo* generally, and in the rat kidney in particular. Two alternatives present themselves: they may not be accessible to serum (intracellular) or something in the intrarenal milieu may influence host ability to dispose of protoplasts. In this study, elevated osmolality has inhibited serum cidal activity against protoplasts. In previous studies[31] we demonstrated that not only increased osmolality but other factors found in the kidney environment, such as increased concentrations of sodium or potassium chloride and urea, and increased acidity or alkalinity, can interfere with serum cidal activity against susceptible bacteria. Additional study of the host-parasite (protoplast) relationship in light of the present *in vitro* findings will be of interest.

SUMMARY

Human serum killed penicillin- or lysozyme-produced protoplasts of *Streptococcus faecalis* and penicillin produced protoplasts of *Streptococcus pyogenes*, *Staphylococcus aureus* and *Escherichia coli*, while it was ineffective against the bacterial forms. Penicillin protoplasts of *Proteus mirabilis* were not affected by serum, while the bacterial form was killed. Similar protoplast cidal activity was found in horse serum and to a lesser extent in other types of mammalian sera. This protoplast inhibitory activity varied not only with the source of serum, but also with the species or strain of protoplast studied, as well as with the medium in which the test was conducted. Protoplast cidal activity was inhibited by increasing the osmolality of the milieu or by inactivating the serum at 56°C for 30 minutes.

The serum killing of protoplasts of organisms whose bacterial forms were resistant suggests an important role of cell wall in protecting the organism from cidal activity, probably by preventing access of responsible substance(s) to the membrane or intracellular site of action.

REFERENCES

1. Altenbern, R. A., and Landman, O. E.: Growth of L-forms of *Proteus mirabilis* in liquid media. *J. Bact.* **79**: 510, 1960.
2. Amano, T., Fujikawa, K., Morioka, T., Miyama, A., and Ichikawa, S.: Quantitative studies of immune bacteriolysis. I. A new method of quantitative estimation. *Biken's J.* **1**: 13, 1958.
3. Amano, T., Kato, K., Okada, K., Tamatani, Y., and Higashi, Y.: Studies on the rôle of plakin. VII. Effects on the protoplast of *B. megatherium*. *Med. J. Osaka Univ.* **7**: 217, 1956.
4. Amano, T., Morioka, T., Seki, Y., Kashiba, S., Fujikawa, K., and Ichikawa, S.: Studies on the immune bacteriolysis. VIII. The mechanisms of the immune bacteriolysis. *Med. J. Osaka Univ.* **6**: 709, 1955.
5. Amano, T., Seki, Y., Kashiba, S., Fujikawa, K., Morioka, T., and Ichikawa, S.: The effect of leucocyte extract on Staphylococcus pyogenes. *Med. J. Osaka Univ.* **7**: 233, 1956.
6. Amano, T., Shima, M., and Kato, K.: Studies on the rôle of plakin. III. The damage of semipermeability of bacteria caused by plakin. *Med. J. Osaka Univ.* **4**: 277, 1953.
7. Bernheimer, A. W., and Schwartz, L. L.: Lysis of bacterial protoplasts and spheroplasts by staphylococcal α-toxin and streptolysin S. *J. Bact.* **89**: 1387, 1965.
8. Brown, T. M., and Nunemaker, J. C.: Rat-bite fever. A review of the American cases with reevaluation of etiology; report of cases. *Bull. Johns Hopkins Hosp.* **70**: 201, 1942.
9. Carrère, L., Roux, J., and Mandin, J.: A propos du cycle L des bactéries: obtention de formes naines, viables et filtrables, en milieu liquide. *C. R. Soc. Biol.* (Paris) **148**: 2050, 1954.
10. Crawford, Y. E., Frank, P. F., and Sullivan, B.: Isolation and reversion of L forms of beta-hemolytic streptococci. *J. Infect. Dis.* **102**: 44, 1958.
11. Diena, B. B., Wallace, R., and Greenberg, L.: Reversion and biological characteristics of Salmonella typhi spheroplasts. *Canad. J. Microbiol.* **11**: 427, 1965.
12. Dienes, L.: Isolation of L type growth from a strain of *Bacteroides funduliformis*. *Proc. Soc. Exp. Biol. Med.* **47**: 385, 1941.
13. ———: L type of growth in cultures of a hemolytic para-influenza bacillus. *Proc. Soc. Exp. Biol. Med.* **55**: 142, 1944.
14. ———: Isolation of pleuropneumonia-like organisms from *H. influenzae* with the aid of penicillin. *Proc. Soc. Exp. Biol. Med.* **64**: 166, 1947.
15. ———: The development of Proteus cultures in the presence of penicillin. *J. Bact.* **57**: 529, 1949.
16. ———: Isolation of an L type culture from a Gram positive spore-bearing bacillus. *Proc. Soc. Exp. Biol. Med.* **71**: 30, 1949.
17. ———: Isolation of L type cultures from Clostridia. *Proc. Soc. Exp. Biol. Med.* **75**: 412, 1950.
18. Dienes, L., and Sharp, J. T.: The role of high electrolyte concentration in the production and growth of L forms of bacteria. *J. Bact.* **71**: 208, 1956.
19. Dienes, L., Weinberger, H. J., and Madoff, S.: Serological reactions of L type cultures isolated from Proteus. *Proc. Soc. Exp. Biol. Med.* **75**: 409, 1950.
20. ———: The transformation of typhoid bacilli into L forms under various conditions. *J. Bact.* **59**: 755, 1950.
21. Freeman, B. A., Musteikis, G. M., and Burrows, W.: Protoplast formation as the mechanism of immune lysis of *Vibrio cholerae*. *Proc. Soc. Exp. Biol. Med.* **113**: 675, 1963.

22. Freimer, E. H., Krause, R. M., and McCarty, M.: Studies of L forms and protoplasts of group A streptococci. I. Isolation, growth, and bacteriologic characteristics. *J. Exp. Med.* **110**: 853, 1959.

23. Godzeski, C. W., Brier, G., and Pavey, D. E.: L-phase growth induction as a general characteristic of antibiotic-bacterial interaction in the presence of serum. In: *Antimicrobial Agents and Chemotherapy—1962* (J. C. Sylvester, Ed.). American Society for Microbiology, Ann Arbor, 1963: p. 843.

24. Grasset, E.: Observations comparées sur la production *in vivo* et *in vitro* de formes L de *Proteus vulgaris* et *Klebsiella pneumoniae* sous l'influence d'anticorps spécifiques. *Ann. Inst. Pasteur* (Paris) **89**: 111, 1955.

25. Gutman, L. T., Turck, M., Petersdorf, R. G., and Wedgwood, R. J.: Significance of bacterial variants in urine of patients with chronic bacteriuria. *J. Clin. Invest.* **44**: 1945, 1965.

26. Guze, L. B., Goldner, B. H., and Kalmanson, G. M.: Pyelonephritis. I. Observations on the course of chronic non-obstructed enterococcal infection in the kidney of the rat. *Yale J. Biol. Med.* **33**: 372, 1961.

26a. Guze, L. B., Hubert, E. G., Montgomerie, J. Z., and Kalmanson, G. M.: Observations on the killing of microbial protoplasts by serum. *Nature* **214**: 1343, 1967.

27. Guze, L. B., and Kalmanson, G. M.: Persistence of bacteria in "protoplast" form after apparent cure of pyelonephritis in rats. *Science* **143**: 1340, 1964.

28. Hamburger, M., and Carleton, J.: Staphylococcal spheroplasts and L colonies. I. Population curves of vegetative staphylococci and spheroplasts in methicillin-containing broth over long periods. *J. Infect. Dis.* **116**: 221, 1966.

29. Heilman, F. R.: A study of Asterococcus muris (Streptobacillus moniliformis). I. Morphologic aspects and nomenclature. *J. Infect. Dis.* **69**: 32, 1941.

30. Hijmans, W.: Absence of the group-specific and the cell-wall polysaccharide antigen in L-phase variants of group D streptococci. *J. Gen. Microbiol.* **28**: 177, 1962.

31. Hubert, E. G., Montgomerie, J. Z., Kalmanson, G. M., and Guze, L. B.: Effect of renal physico-chemical milieu on serum bactericidal activity. *Amer. J. Med. Sci.* **253**: 225, 1967.

32. Ibbott, F. A., and Abrams, A.: The phospholipids in membrane ghosts from *Streptococcus faecalis* protoplasts. *Biochemistry* (Washington) **3**: 2008, 1964.

33. Inoue, K., Tanigawa, Y., Takubo, M., Satani, M., and Amano, T.: Quantitative studies on immune bacteriolysis. II. The role of lysozyme in immune bacteriolysis. *Biken's J.* **2**: 1, 1959.

34. Kagan, B. M., Molander, C. W., and Weinberger, H. J.: Induction and cultivation of staphylococcal L forms in the presence of methicillin. *J. Bact.* **83**: 1162, 1962.

35. Kagan, G. Y., Levashev, V. S., and Komm, S. G.: Morphology of L-forms of beta-hemolytic streptococci. Communication I. Peculiarities in the growth and multiplication of the L-form of hemolytic streptococci. *Zh. Mikrobiol.* **41**(2): 122, 1964.

35a. Kalmanson, G. M., Hubert, E. G., Montgomerie, J. Z., and Guze, L. B.: Killing of microbial protoplasts by sreum. *Antimicrob. Agents Chemother.* 1966, p. 304.

36. Marston, J.: Observations on L forms of staphylococci. *J. Infect. Dis.* **108**: 75, 1961.

37. Mattman, L. H., Burgess, A. R., and Farkas, M. E.: Evaluation of antibiotic diffusion in L variant production by *Proteus* species. *J. Bact.* **76**: 333, 1958.

38. Mattman, L. H., and Mattman, P. E.: L forms of Streptococcus fecalis in septicemia. *Arch. Intern. Med.* (Chicago) **115**: 315, 1965.

39. Mattman, L. H., Tunstall, L. H., Mathews, W. W., and Gordon, D. L.: L variation in mycobacteria. *Amer. Rev. Resp. Dis.* **82**: 202, 1960.

40. Medill, M. A., and O'Kane, D. J.: A synthetic medium for the L type colonies of Proteus. *J. Bact.* **68**: 530, 1954.

41. Mikhailova, V. S.: Biological properties of revertants of streptococci from L-forms obtained by penicillin action. *Fed. Proc.* **23**: T989, 1964.

42. Montgomerie, J. Z., Kalmanson, G. M., Hewitt, W. L., and Guze, L. B.: Effectiveness of antibiotics against the bacterial and "protoplast" phases of pyelonephritis. In: *Antimicrobial Agents and Chemotherapy—1965* (G. L. Hobby, Ed.). American Society for Microbiology, Ann Arbor, 1966: p. 427.

43. Mortimer, E. A., Jr.: Production of L forms of group A streptococci in mice. *Proc. Soc. Exp. Biol. Med.* **119**: 159, 1965.

44. Moustardier, G., Brisou, J., and Perrey, M.: Milieu de culture pour l'isolement des organismes L dans les uréthrites amicrobiennes a inclusions. *Ann. Inst. Pasteur* (Paris) **85**: 515, 1953.

45. Muschel, L. H., Carey, W. F., and Baron, L. S.: Formation of bacterial protoplasts by serum components. *J. Immun.* **82**: 38, 1959.

46. Muschel, L. H., and Jackson, J. E.: The reactivity of serum against protoplasts and spheroplasts. *J. Immun.* **97**: 46, 1966.

47. Nesbitt, J. A., III, and Lennarz, W. J.: Comparison of lipids and lipopolysaccharide from the bacillary and L forms of *Proteus* P18. *J. Bact.* **89**: 1020, 1965.

48. Pease, P., and Laughton, N.: Observations on corynebacteria and related pleuropneumonialike organisms (PPLO). *J. Gen. Microbiol.* **27**: 383, 1962.

49. Rogul, M., McGee, Z. A., Wittler, R. G., and Falkow, S.: Nucleic acid homologies of selected bacteria, L forms, and *Mycoplasma* species. *J. Bact.* **90**: 1200, 1965.

50. Rotta, J., Karakawa, W. W., and Krause, R. M.: Isolation of L forms from group A streptococci exposed to bacitracin. *J. Bact.* **89**: 1581, 1965.

51. Salton, M. R. J., and Freer, J. H.: Composition of the membranes isolated from several Gram-positive bacteria. *Biochim. Biophys. Acta* **107**: 531, 1965.

52. Schneider, L. E., Miyama, A., Braun, W., Plescia, O. J., and Björklund, B.: Comparison of bactericidal and hemolytic serum systems. I. Inhibitory effects of normal human serum fractions. *Proc. Soc. Exp. Biol. Med.* **116**: 80, 1964.

53. Sharp, J. T., Hijmans, W., and Dienes, L.: Examination of the L forms of group A streptococci for the group-specific polysaccharide and M protein. *J. Exp. Med.* **105**: 153, 1957.

54. Taubeneck, U.: Demonstration of lysogeny in stable L forms of *Proteus mirabilis. J. Bact.* **86**: 1265, 1963.

55. Tulasne, R.: Les formes L des bactéries. *Rev. Immun.* (Paris). **15**: 223, 1951.

56. Wardlaw, A. C.: The complement-dependent bacteriolytic activity of normal human serum. I. The effect of pH and ionic strength and the role of lysozyme. *J. Exp. Med.* **115**: 1231, 1962.

57. Weibull, C.: Size of minimal reproductive units of bacterial L forms. *Proc. Soc. Exp. Biol. Med.* **113**: 32, 1963.

58. Weibull, C., and Lundin, B.: Factors influencing the growth of a stable L form of *Proteus mirabilis. J. Bact.* **81**: 812, 1961.

59. Weinberger, H. J., Madoff, S., and Dienes, L.: The properties of L forms isolated from Salmonella and the isolation of L forms from Shigella. *J. Bact.* **59**: 765, 1950.

60. Willett, H. P., and Thacore, H.: The induction by lysozyme of an L-type growth in Mycobacterium tuberculosis. *Canad. J. Microbiol.* **12**: 11, 1966.

61. Wittler, R. G., Malizia, W. F., Kramer, P. E., Tuckett, J. D., Pritchard, H. N., and Baker, H. J.: Isolation of a Corynebacterium and its transitional forms from a case of subacute bacterial endocarditis treated with antibiotics. *J. Gen. Microbiol.* **23**: 315, 1960.

29

The Susceptibility of Protoplast and Bacterial Forms of *Streptococcus faecalis* to Antibiotics

John Z. Montgomerie, George M. Kalmanson and Lucien B. Guze

VETERANS ADMINISTRATION CENTER
AND UCLA SCHOOL OF MEDICINE
LOS ANGELES, CALIFORNIA

The isolation of protoplasts* from patients and experimental animals[3] has raised questions of their significance as possible microbial persisters. An understanding of the pathogenicity of these forms would encompass their response to defense mechanisms and their resistance to antibiotics. In earlier studies we found that, in the rat kidney, protoplasts of *Streptococcus faecalis* were sensitive to erythromycin and kanamycin, antibiotics which were relatively ineffective against the bacterial form.[2, 5, 8] Previous *in vitro* studies of the antibiotic sensitivity of protoplasts of a variety of bacteria have demonstrated that protoplasts are insensitive to antibiotics which act on cell wall synthesis.[4, 13, 15, 16] Varying results, however, have been obtained with other antibiotics.[4, 6, 9, 12-16] Using penicillin-produced protoplasts of *S. faecalis*, we have compared the sensitivity of these forms and of the parent bacteria to a variety of antibiotics.

MATERIALS AND METHODS

The *S. faecalis* used in this study has been described previously.[1] The basic media were brain heart infusion agar and broth (Difco). Biphasic medium in which both broth and agar media were combined, with the agar present as a slope in the tube, was also used. Two per cent bovine serum albumin (Armour), 0.001% $MgSO_4 \cdot 7H_2O$, and 0.5 M sucrose were added to the media; where indicated, 0.86 M NaCl replaced 0.5 M sucrose as the osmotic stabilizer. Penicillin (potassium penicillin G, Squibb), 1000 units/ml, was used to produce protoplasts and was necessary to prevent reversion to the parent bacterial form.

L-colonies were produced by streaking 0.1 ml of an 18-hour culture of *S. faecalis* on agar medium containing penicillin. The colonies which appeared after 48 to 72 hours were transferred to fresh agar at weekly intervals. After more than ten transfers, the agar containing protoplasts was ground in broth with a tissue grinder (Tri R Co.) and inoculated into the broth

* The term *protoplast* as used in this paper indicates an osmotically fragile bacterial cell in which the amount of cell wall present has not been determined. Protoplasts may grow on solid media as characteristic *L-colonies*. In discussing results of other authors, it was assumed that the terms, "L-forms," "L-colonies" and "L-phase growth" were interchangeable.

phase of biphasic medium. After three days, the protoplasts in the biphasic medium were spread with a sterile cotton applicator on the surface of agar medium containing penicillin to prevent reversion. Protoplast and bacterial antibiotic sensitivities were compared at equivalent inocula by also streaking a 1:1000 dilution of an 18-hour culture of S. faecalis on the surface of agar medium without penicillin. Four antibiotic discs (BBL) were placed on each plate. The well method was used to determine the sensitivity of protoplasts to synthetic penicillins. Solutions of synthetic penicillin in concentrations up to 10,000 μg/ml were added in 0.1 ml amounts to wells cut in the agar medium. The diameter of the zone of growth inhibition was measured after incubation at 37°C for two to five days.

RESULTS

The results are shown in Table 29.1. All antibiotics tested except penicillin and synthetic penicillins were more active against protoplasts of S. faecalis than against the parent bacterial form. These differences were marked for bacitracin, chloramphenicol, erythromycin, kanamycin, neomycin, nitrofurantoin, novobiocin, oleandomycin, polymyxin, tetracyclines, and vancomycin. Less marked differences were observed with the remaining antibiotics. The synthetic penicillins (ampicillin, cloxacillin, oxacillin, and methicillin), in concentrations up to 10,000 μg/ml, had no effect on protoplasts.

The antibiotic sensitivity of protoplasts was also studied in medium containing 0.86 M NaCl (5%). The differences between the sensitivities of protoplasts and parent bacterial form were less marked than in sucrose medium. Protoplasts were only slightly more sensitive to tetracyclines, polymyxin, colistin, and ristocetin, while they were resistant to bacitracin. The experiments have been repeated using stable protoplasts of S. faecalis. These protoplasts were considered to be stable because they had been transferred to osmotically stabilized agar in the absence of penicillin without reversion to

TABLE 29.1

Sensitivity of Bacterial and Protoplast Forms of Streptococcus faecalis *to Antibiotics*

Antibiotic	Antibiotic Concentration (BBL) (μg or units)	Diameter of Inhibition Zone (mm)	
		Proto-plast form	Bacterial form
Bacitracin	10	20	10
Chloramphenicol	30	36	20
Chlortetracycline	30	22	13
Colistin	10	9	7*
Demethylchlortetra-cycline	30	30	15
Dihydrostreptomycin	10	10	7*
Erythromycin	15	33	22
Kanamycin	5	7*	7*
Kanamycin	30	19	12
Neomycin	30	17	9
Nitrofurantoin	100	35	19
Novobiocin	30	16	9
Oleandomycin	15	32	18
Oxytetracycline	20	25	11
Penicillin	10	7*	17
Polymyxin	300	15	7*
Ristocetin	30	17	13
Streptomycin	10	9	7*
Tetracycline	30	23	11
Vancomycin	30	22	14

* Since the disc diameter was 7 mm, these measurements indicate no inhibition of growth.

Data from Montgomerie, Kalmanson & Guze.[7a]

bacterial form; they have remained stable for more than 30 such transfers. In general, differences between the sensitivities of the bacterial and stable protoplast forms were similar to but not as marked as those noted with the unstable protoplasts. An exception was that the stable protoplasts were insensitive to bacitracin.

These studies were extended to examine the sensitivity of a number of strains of S. faecalis to lincomycin*. Protoplasts were produced with penicillin from cultures of S. faecalis which had been isolated from patients with urinary tract infection. Protoplasts of all strains were more sensitive to lincomycin than the parent bac-

* The lincomycin (Lincocin, Upjohn Co.) used in these experiments was generously supplied by Dr. Raymond DeHaan of the Upjohn Company.

TABLE 29.2

Sensitivity of Bacterial and Protoplast Forms of
Strains of Streptococcus faecalis
*to Lincomycin**

Strain No.	Diameter of Inhibition Zone (mm)	
	Protoplasts	Bacterial form
1	25	10
2	34	10
3	21	9
4	25	7†
5	23	10
6	20	7†

* Discs contained 30 μg lincomycin.

† Since the disc diameter was 7 mm, these measurements indicate no inhibition of growth.

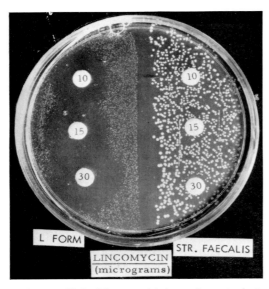

Figure 29.1. The sensitivity of protoplasts (L-forms) and bacterial forms of one strain of *Streptococcus faecalis* to 10, 15, and 30 μg discs of lincomycin.

terial form (Table 29.2 and Figure 29.1). A marked difference was noted with strain No. 6, in which the protoplast was sensitive even to a 10 μg disc. When the parent bacterial culture of strain No. 6 was studied by standard tube dilution methods, it was found that the bacterium was insensitive to 1600 μg of lincomycin per ml, the highest concentration tested.

DISCUSSION

Other investigators have studied the antibiotic sensitivity of protoplasts of a number of organisms with varying results. The various conditions used by the individual authors may account to some extent for the differences in their results.

Some workers did not find the protoplast to be more sensitive than the bacterial form. In a study of *Streptococcus, Proteus, Salmonella typhimurium,* and *Vibrio,* Ward and associates[16] concluded that, with the exception of penicillin and bacitracin, the sensitivity of L-forms and the parent bacteria was comparable. Similar conclusions were reached by Shakhovsky,[12] who examined the antibiotic sensitivity of L-forms of *Streptococcus hemolyticus, Salmonella typhosa, S. typhimurium,* and *Proteus vulgaris.* Shockman & Lampen[13] studied lysozyme-produced protoplasts of *S. faecalis* by measuring the turbidity of liquid media in the presence and absence of antibiotics; although some differences between protoplasts and intact bacteria were recorded, the authors concluded that, with the exception of penicillin and cycloserine, all antibiotics inhibited protoplasts and parent bacteria of *S. faecalis* at similar concentrations; penicillin and cycloserine, while effective against the bacterial phase, did not alter protoplasts.

Our results with *S. faecalis,* showing that penicillin-produced protoplasts were more sensitive than the bacterial form, are similar to those obtained by a number of other workers. The findings with L-forms of *Proteus morgani* and *P. vulgaris,*[15] *Proteus mirabilis,*[14] and five strains of *Staphylococcus aureus,*[4] all indicated that the L-forms were more sensitive than the parent bacteria. Observations by others[6, 9] support these conclusions.

These studies of the antibiotic sensitivity of microorganisms with deficient cell walls allow us to draw some conclusions concerning the action of certain antibiotics. For instance, observations that protoplasts were sensitive to bacitracin, vancomycin and ristocetin suggested that these antibiotics had some action in addition to the previously demonstrated inhibition of cell wall synthesis.[7, 10, 17] The lack of response by protoplasts to the synthetic penicillins studied (ampicillin, cloxacillin, oxacillin and methicillin) was confirmatory evidence that these antibiotics acted on cell wall synthesis.

The finding that NaCl inhibited the action of some antibiotics (especially bacitracin) on protoplasts is not explained, but emphasizes the importance of the type of media used in testing antibiotic sensitivities when protoplasts as well as bacterial forms are tested.

It has yet to be explained why S. faecalis became more sensitive to antibiotics when the cell wall was absent. It is not possible to be sure which of a number of means of altering drug resistance had been changed. The large number of antibiotics involved, however, including those with supposedly different actions, suggests that the sites of action of the antibiotics had become more accessible. If this was the case, it further suggests either that the cell wall acts as a barrier to antibiotics or that removal of the cell wall alters in some way the cell membrane, which has usually been regarded as the permeability barrier. The availability of a lincomycin-resistant bacterial form and sensitive protoplast form of S. faecalis will permit further studies of these alternatives.

The sensitivity of protoplasts to concentrations of antibiotics to which the intact bacterial form is resistant may indicate a means by which synergism occurs. Plotz & Davis[11] found that penicillin treatment of Escherichia coli increased the uptake and killing effect of streptomycin, and suggested that penicillin increased the permeability of the cell and permitted greater access of the second antibiotic. It has also been shown that noninhibitory concentrations of kanamycin for S. faecalis were synergistic with penicillin in vitro and in vivo, and killed protoplasts in vivo.[8] Erythromycin was also effective against protoplasts in the rat kidney, although it had little effect on the bacterial phase of infection.[2, 5]

Until the role of protoplasts in the pathogenesis of infectious diseases is defined, it will be difficult to relate these results to clinical therapy. It has been suggested that, when antibiotics which may produce protoplasts are used therapeutically, a course of a second antibiotic to which protoplasts are sensitive should follow.[4] Alternatively, the antibiotics may be used in combination. The killing of protoplasts of S. faecalis in the rat kidney with kanamycin or erythromycin following penicillin treatment, and the rapid elimination of the bacterial and protoplast populations by using either antibiotic in combination with penicillin, provide some experimental support to this line of reasoning. It should be pointed out, however, that these conclusions regarding clinical therapy are based on assumptions that protoplasts play a significant role in disease as microbial persisters, and that penicillin-produced protoplasts studied in vitro and in vivo are similar to protoplasts of a variety of other bacteria which may occur in disease processes. These points have yet to be established.

SUMMARY

The antibiotic sensitivities of penicillin-produced protoplasts and bacterial forms of Streptococcus faecalis were compared.

In general, protoplasts were more sensitive than the bacterial form to the antibiotics tested, with the exception of the synthetic penicillins. Protoplasts of six strains of S. faecalis were consistently more sensitive to lincomycin than the bacterial forms. The different sensitivities of protoplasts and parent bacterial forms provide some insight into the action of antibiotics and suggest a means by which antibiotic synergism may occur.

REFERENCES

1. Guze, L. B., Goldner, B. H., and Kalmanson, G. M.: Pyelonephritis. I. Observations on the course of chronic non-obstructed enterococcal infection in the kidney of the rat. Yale J. Biol. Med. 33: 372, 1961.

2. Guze, L. B., and Kalmanson, G. M.: Action of

erythromycin on "protoplasts" *in vivo. Science* **146:** 1299, 1964.

3. ————: Persistence of bacteria in "protoplast" form after apparent cure of pyelonephritis in rats. *Science* **143:** 1340, 1964.

4. Kagan, B. M., Molander, C. W., Zolla, S., Heimlich, E. M., Weinberger, H. J., Busser, R., and Liepnieks, S.: Antibiotic sensitivity and pathogenicity of L-phase variants of *Staphylococci.* In: *Antimicrobial Agents and Chemotherapy—1963* (J. C. Sylvester, Ed.). American Society for Microbiology, Ann Arbor, 1963: p. 517.

5. Kalmanson, G. M., and Guze, L. B.: Role of protoplasts in pathogenesis of pyelonephritis. *JAMA* **190:** 1107, 1964.

6. Lederberg, J., and St. Clair, J.: Protoplasts and L-type growth of *Escherichia coli. J. Bact.* **75:** 143, 1958.

7. Mandelstam, J., and Rogers, H. J.: The incorporation of amino acids into the cell-wall mucopeptide of Staphylococci and the effect of antibiotics on the process. *Biochem. J.* **72:** 654, 1959.

7a. Montgomerie, J. Z., Kalmanson, G. M., and Guze, L. B.: The effects of antibiotics on the protoplast and bacterial forms of *Streptococcus faecalis. J. Lab. Clin. Med.* **68:** 543, 1966.

8. Montgomerie, J. Z., Kalmanson, G. M., Hewitt, W. L., and Guze, L. B.: Effectiveness of antibiotics against the bacterial and "protoplast" phases of pyelonephritis. In: *Antimicrobial Agents and Chemotherapy—1965* (G. L. Hobby, Ed.): American Society for Microbiology, Ann Arbor, 1966: p. 427.

9. Moustárdier, G., Brisou, J., and Perrey, M.: Étude de la sensibilité aux antibiotiques d'organismes L isolés par culture d'urétrites amicrobiennes a inclusions; déductions thérapeutiques. *Rev. Immun.* (Paris) **17:** 359, 1953.

10. Park, J. T.: Inhibition of cell-wall synthesis in *Staphylococcus aureus* by chemicals which cause accumulation of wall precursors. *Biochem. J.* **70:** 2P, 1958.

11. Plotz, P. H., and Davis, B. D.: Synergism between streptomycin and penicillin: a proposed mechanism. *Science* **135:** 1067, 1962.

12. Shakhovsky, K. P.: Resistance of bacterial L-forms to the effect of antibiotics. *Antibiotiki* **9:** 220, 1964.

13. Shockman, G. D., and Lampen, J. O.: Inhibition by antibiotics of the growth of bacterial and yeast protoplasts. *J. Bact.* **84:** 508, 1962.

14. Taubeneck, U.: Susceptibility of *Proteus mirabilis* and its stable L-forms to erythromycin and other macrolides. *Nature* **196:** 195, 1962.

15. Tulasne, R., and Minck, R.: Sensibilité comparée des formes normales et des formes L de deux souches de Proteus vis-à-vis de quelques antibiotiques. *C. R. Soc. Biol.* (Paris) **146:** 778, 1952.

16. Ward, J. R., Madoff, S., and Dienes, L.: *In vitro* sensitivity of some bacteria, their L-forms and pleuropneumonia-like organisms to antibiotics. *Proc. Soc. Exp. Biol. Med.* **97:** 132, 1958.

17. Wise, E. M., Jr., and Park, J. T.: Penicillin: its basic site of action as an inhibitor of a peptide cross-linking reaction in cell wall mucopeptide synthesis. *Proc. Nat. Acad. Sci. USA* **54:** 75, 1965.

30

Relationship of the Antibiotic Sensitivity of Enterococci to Acquired Resistance in their L-Forms

William L. Hewitt, Stephen J. Seligman and Rosalyn A. Deigh

UCLA SCHOOL OF MEDICINE
LOS ANGELES, CALIFORNIA

The remarkable acceleration by streptomycin of the bactericidal action of penicillin upon enterococci is well known.[2] *In vitro* studies indicate this synergism to be marked with some strains of enterococci but relatively lacking in others. Our laboratory has previously reported[1] a relatively high level of resistance of the bacterial forms to streptomycin alone, in contrast to a much lower level of resistance of some of the penicillin-induced L-forms. The following data may further relate the level of streptomycin resistance of the penicillin induced L-forms to penicillin/streptomycin synergism on the bacterial forms.

MATERIALS

The media employed were trypticase soy broth (TSB) and trypticase soy agar (TSA). For the work with L-forms, 3% sodium chloride and 10% sterile inactivated agammaglobulinemic horse serum were added to the media (henceforth called serum-salt broth or serum-salt agar).

The organism used was a *Streptococcus faecalis var. zymogenes*. In previous studies this organism conformed to the usual sensitivity pattern with respect to streptomycin in that more than 100 μg/ml was required to inhibit all but a few members of the bacterial population. Marked sensitivity existed, on the other hand, to a combination of penicillin and a small concentration (20 μg/ml) of streptomycin.

METHODS AND RESULTS

A bacterial mutant with increased resistance to streptomycin was isolated by serial culture in increasing concentrations of this antibiotic and was picked from a plate containing 2000 μg/ml of streptomycin—henceforth called No. 31/S2000. Numerous attempts by various methods to isolate a streptomycin-resistant L-form directly from L-form cultures of the parent strain have so far been unsuccessful.

To demonstrate the extent of streptomycin resistance of the bacterial mutant compared with the parent strain, TSA plates were prepared containing concentrations of streptomycin from 25 μg/ml to 7500 μg/ml (Table 30.1). Each plate was inoculated with 0.05 ml of an undiluted 18 hour broth culture, and 0.05 ml of 100-

TABLE 30.1

Streptomycin Resistance of a Bacterial Population of the Parent Strain (No. 31) and the Streptomycin-Resistant Mutant

	Bacterial Colonies/ml*	
STM (μg/ml)	✳31	✳31/S2000
0	2×10^8	4×10^8
25	4×10^8	3×10^8
100	4×10^5	2×10^8
250	480	3×10^8
500	40	3×10^8
1000	0	3×10^8
7500	0	3×10^8

* The figures reflect colony-forming units appearing on TSA plates containing various concentrations of streptomycin.

fold dilutions of the same culture. The majority of the organisms in the parent strain were inhibited at streptomycin concentrations between 25 and 100 μg/ml, while the suspected mutant grew in undiminished numbers in up to 7500 μg/ml of streptomycin.

L-colonies were induced on serum-salt plates containing 1000 units/ml of penicillin G. Growth of the L-colonies occurred within three days. The colonies were subcultured by cutting out a block of agar and emulsifying it in 2 ml of serum-salt broth by squeezing it through an 18 gauge needle with a syringe; 0.05 ml of the undiluted suspension and tenfold dilutions were streaked with a pipette onto the surface of serum-salt plates containing 1000 units/ml of penicillin plus varying concentrations of streptomycin. After incubation the results indicated that the mutant, selected because of increased resistance of its bacterial form,

TABLE 30.2

Streptomycin Resistance of an L-Form Population Derived from the Parent Strain (No. 31) and the Streptomycin-Resistant Mutant

	L-Colonies/ml*	
STM (μg/ml)	✳31	✳31/S2000
0	8×10^5	8×10^3
25	4×10^3	4×10^4
100	0	4×10^4
250	0	2×10^4
500	0	2×10^4
1000	0	8×10^3

* The figures reflect colony-forming units appearing on TSA serum-salt plates with 1000 units/ml of penicillin and containing various concentrations of streptomycin.

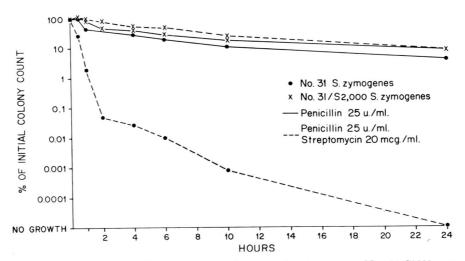

Figure 30.1. Viability of the streptomycin-resistant enterococcus No. 31/S2000 compared with the parent strain (No. 31) in broth containing penicillin singly and in combination with streptomycin. The effect of the antibiotic combination for the mutant 31/S2000 does not differ from that with penicillin alone, in contrast to the effect upon the parent strain No. 31.

also showed increased resistance in its L-form (Table 30.2). The majority of L-colonies from the parent strain were inhibited by 25 μg/ml streptomycin, while those from the mutant grew readily on plates containing 1000 μg/ml, the highest concentration tested.

For the viability counts, TSB reaction mixtures containing bacteria and single antibiotics or their combinations were incubated at 37°C. The number of surviving bacteria at selected times was estimated by colony counts from samples suitably diluted and plated on the surface of TSA (Figure 30.1). In broth containing streptomycin alone (20 μg/ml), the viability curves conformed closely to the normal growth curve, with no cumulative antimicrobial effect. Exposure of the culture (No. 31) to penicillin G alone (25 units/ml) resulted in a relatively slow decline in the number of viable bacteria, which was somewhat more rapid during the first four hours than subsequently. Marked acceleration of early bactericidal action occurred when the broth contained the penicillin/streptomycin combination: four hours after starting the reaction tubes, less than 0.1 per cent of the original inoculum remained viable, and after 24 hours no viable bacteria were recovered from the sample tested.

DISCUSSION

The viability curves for the highly streptomycin-resistant enterococcal mutant (No. 31/S2000) did not differ from that of the parent strain when exposed to penicillin alone. The acceleration of early bactericidal activity by penicillin/streptomycin was notably absent, and the effect of the antibiotic combination upon the mutant strain was the same as that following exposure to penicillin alone. In addition, the bacterial revertant derived from the L-forms of the streptomycin-resistant enterococcus conformed to the same pattern of resistance to the penicillin/streptomycin combination.

The mechanism by which streptomycin accelerates the bactericidal action of penicillin is unclear. Previous studies have shown that in spite of relative resistance of the bacterial culture to streptomycin alone, the presence of small concentrations of this agent with penicillin are sufficient to enhance bactericidal activity. This effect is not uniform, since some strains are very sensitive to the combination, whereas others are resistant.[1] An obvious speculation is that the effect of streptomycin is upon penicillin-induced cell wall deficient forms, which have increased permeability to streptomycin and which may be related to those viable units able to grow as L-colonies. Prior studies of naturally occurring strains of enterococci resistant to penicillin/streptomycin revealed marked streptomycin resistance of the penicillin-induced L-colonies of these bacteria.[1]

SUMMARY

The current study has shown that a bacterial mutant with increased resistance to streptomycin has become resistant to the synergistic bactericidal activity of the penicillin/streptomycin combination. In addition, passage of this streptomycin-resistant mutant through at least three cycles of L-form induction and bacterial reversion without alteration of its resistance suggests that spheroplasting had no effect on this property.

REFERENCES

1. Hewitt, W. L., Seligman, S. J., and Deigh, R. A.: Kinetics of the synergism of penicillin-streptomycin and penicillin-kanamycin for enterococci and its relationship to L-phase variants. J. Lab. Clin. Med. 67: 792, 1966.
2. Robbins, C. W., and Tompsett, R.: Treatment of enterococcal endocarditis and bacteremia; results of combined therapy with penicillin and streptomycin. Amer. J. Med. 10: 278, 1951.

31

Antibiotic Sensitivities of Staphylococcal L-Forms*

Benjamin M. Kagan

CEDARS-SINAI MEDICAL CENTER
AND UCLA SCHOOL OF MEDICINE
LOS ANGELES, CALIFORNIA

In the work to be described here, the terms *L-forms, protoplasts, spheroplasts,* and *L-form variants* have been considered to have essentially one and the same meaning. To avoid confusion because of terminology, their appearance, behavior, and conditions for development will be described in some detail. The forms to be discussed are known either to have been derived from bacteria, or in due course to have reverted to bacterial form. These forms are characterized by having the following differences from their parent bacterial cells; (1) smaller size of colonies, (2) slower growth of colonies to the point of being visible to the naked eye, (3) characteristic staining of L-form colonies by the Dienes methylene blue staining technique,[8, 9, 10] (4) very different appearance of cells under the microscope, (5) failure of the cells to take Gram stain as do their parent bacterial cells.

These L-forms are assumed to have lost all or most of their rigid cell wall. Since we have not proven that all of their cell wall has been lost, we have preferred to call them L-forms, reserving the term "protoplast" for those cells proven to have no cell wall. (This distinction is admittedly arbitrary.) These L-forms may revert to parent forms, but only after a very long period of time, and are therefore referred to as "stable L-forms".

The purpose of the following studies was to compare the sensitivities to various antibacterial agents of staphylococcal L-forms, and of the parent forms from which they were derived.

MATERIALS AND METHODS

All coccal and L-phase variants were grown on a medium containing the following: Brain heart infusion agar (Difco), 6.0 g; sodium chloride, 6.7 g; distilled water, 116 ml; human serum, 30 ml. The serum was prepared from plasma which was decanted from whole citrated blood. The plasma was centrifuged at 2500 rpm for 15 minutes at 4°C; it was then inactivated at 56°C and frozen overnight at $-20°C$ to precipitate the fibrin, after which it was recentrifuged. The serum was passed through diatomaceous earth and Schleicher and Schuell analytical filter paper No. 589 white ribbon, 604, and 602. It was then passed in sterile manner through a HAWP Millipore filter of 0.45 μ pore size and stored in sterile vaccine bottles in a refrigerator until used.[16−23] Induction of L-forms from penicillin

* The author wishes to acknowledge with gratitude the assistance in these studies of Susan Zolla, Dr. Charles W. Molander, Dr. Howard Weinberger, Dr. Elmo R. Martin and Shakila Hasan.

G-sensitive strains of staphylococci in a medium containing penicillin G and a high concentration of sodium chloride has been reported by several investigators.[11, 24]

In the following studies, penicillin G-sensitive and also penicillin G-resistant and methicillin-resistant strains were included.

The strains were inoculated on the solid agar medium described above, and methicillin, in amounts of up to 10,000 µg/ml, was added. Typical L-colonies developed after incubation for two to five days under aerobic conditions at 37°C. Stable colonies were produced by subculturing many times with high concentrations of methicillin until reversion did not occur in the absence of methicillin even after many transfers.

The antibiotics tested were in reagent form as provided for tube dilution testing; they were dissolved in sterile water. Two different techniques were used for the sensitivity tests: in the first, graduated concentrations of the antibiotics were mixed into the culture medium; in the second, deep wells were cut into the agar; the same volume of differing concentrations of antibiotic solutions was placed in each well.

Before inoculation, all culture plates were incubated overnight at 37°C. A generous loop from each slant of the coccal forms was suspended in 5 ml of sterile 5% saline. A 1-cm² block of agar containing the L-phase organisms was placed in 5 ml of sterile 5% saline and was allowed to stand, with periodic shaking, for about one hour before plating. Plates were inoculated with 0.05 ml of these saline suspensions, and the inoculum spread over the surface of the agar with a sterile glass rod.

In the second technique, plates were seeded in a similar manner. Five deep wells were cut into each plate and 0.1 ml of a freshly prepared distilled water solution containing a known concentration of antibiotic was placed into each well.

In the first method, observation was made for inhibition of growth of the L-forms in the plates. In the second method, rings of inhibition of varying sizes were observed surrounding the wells. The results with the two techniques were so close to each other that for the purpose of analysis the results can be presented as identical.

RESULTS

The results are shown in Table 31.1. In general, the following antibiotics inhibited the classical coccal forms but did not inhibit the L-phase variants: penicillin, methicillin, oxacillin, cephalothin, bacitracin, and vancomycin. It is well recognized that the primary site of action of all these agents is upon the cell wall.[5, 27] In contrast to the penicillins and cephalothin, bacitracin and vancomycin had some inhibitory effect upon certain L-forms. Also, the penicillins and cephalothin were found to induce L-forms readily, whereas bacitracin and vancomycin did not. It would therefore appear that, although the primary site of action of this group is indeed upon the cell wall, bacitracin[31] and vancomycin[14] probably have in addition some effect upon either the cell membrane or the protoplasmic body within the membrane.

The group that includes kanamycin, neomycin, gentamycin, and streptomycin had in general somewhat more effect upon the L-forms than it did upon the coccal forms. Davies and associates[6, 7] have shown that kanamycin, neomycin and streptomycin interfere with protein synthesis, which probably occurs within the protoplasmic body. Gentamycin, while distinctly different, is a member of this same deoxystreptamine family, and the action is probably likewise within the protoplasmic body.[28]

Polymyxin B had little effect upon either the coccal forms or the L-forms. In high concentration (50 µg/ml or above) it had, relatively, a little more effect on the L-forms. This agent is known to increase permeability of the cell membrane;[25, 26] its activity appears to depend upon an affinity for the phospholipid content of the cell membrane.[30] The relatively greater effect of polymyxin B upon the L-form may be due to the fact that the phospholipid content of the cell membrane is much higher than that of the cell wall.[29] It is of interest that Salton[29] found that the cell walls of Gram-negative bacteria, which in turn are

TABLE 31.1

Concentration of Antibiotic Required for Inhibition of Growth of Coccal (C) and L-Phase Variants (L) (μg/ml)

| Antibiotic | Strain of Staphylococcus | | | | | | | | | |
| | 6538P | | 292 | | 325 | | 212 | | 342A | |
	C	L	C	L	C	L	C	L	C	L
Penicillin G	<100	>500	<100	>500	<100	>500	>500	>500	>500	>500
Methicillin	<100	>500	<100	>500	<100	>500	<100	>500	<100	>500
Oxacillin	<100	>500	<100	>500	<100	>500	<100	>500	<100	>500
Cephalothin	<100	>500	<10	>500	<100	>500	<100	>500	<12.5	>500
Bacitracin	25.0	>500	25.0	>500	250	>500	<12.5	>500	<12.5	25.0
Vancomycin	3.0	>50	<1.0	>5.0	<1.0	>50	3.0	>50	<1.0	>50
Kanamycin	>10.0	5.0	>10.0	5.0	>10.0	10.0	>10.0	10.0	>10.0	2.5
Neomycin	>12.5	5.0	>12.5	5.0	>12.5	12.5	>12.5	12.5	>12.5	5.0
Streptomycin	40	20	>40	<10	>40	20	>40	>40	>40	>40
Gentamycin	>10.0	2.7	>10.0	2.7	7.5	2.7	>10.0	2.7	>10.0	2.0
Polymyxin B	>500	100	>500	50	>500	100	>500	250	>500	100
Lysostaphin	4	>2000	4	>2000	20	>2000	4	>2000	100	>2000
Novobiocin	0.5	0.5	0.5	0.5	0.5	0.5	0.5	0.5	0.5	0.5
Chloram-phenicol	3.0	3.0	3.0	3.0	3.0	3.0	>3.0	3.0	3.0	3.0
Erythromycin	>0.1	0.1	0.1	0.05	0.1	0.1	>0.1	0.1	0.1	0.05
Lincomycin	0.7	0.05	>0.7	0.1	>0.7	0.4	>0.7	0.05	>0.7	0.1
Oleandomycin	>0.5	0.5	0.5	0.1	0.5	0.5	>0.5	0.5	0.5	0.5
Tetracycline	0.5	<0.1	0.5	<0.1	0.5	<0.1	0.5	<0.1	>1.0	0.5

more sensitive to polymyxin B, are richer in lipoid than are those of Gram-positive organisms; this may be one explanation for the relative lack of effect of polymyxin B upon either the coccal or the derived L-forms of staphylococci.

Novobiocin and chloramphenicol had a different effect, in that they inhibited coccal and L-forms about equally. Novobiocin, in addition to its effect on the cell wall, has been shown to increase permeability of the cell membrane.[2, 3, 27] There is a considerable body of evidence which indicates that the primary action of chloramphenicol is to block protein synthesis by preventing growth of the peptide on the ribosomes.[1, 15, 34] The cell walls of the strains of staphylococci studied appear to offer no barrier to access to the site affected by novobiocin or chloramphenicol within the protoplasmic body.

The following agents, in contrast to all the others already mentioned, had more effect upon the L-form than upon the coccal form: erythromycin, lincomycin, oleandomycin, and tetracycline. All of these exert their primary influence by inhibiting protein synthesis within the cell protoplasm, and possibly also at the ribosome level, as does chloramphenicol. Their differential activity against coccal and L-forms would thus appear to be related to the effectiveness of the cell wall in preventing their penetration to the protoplasmic body. In addition, they are, microgram for microgram, more effective against the L-forms than are either chloramphenicol or novobiocin.[4, 12, 13, 32, 33] It would appear that the lesser effect upon the coccal form is due to the barrier posed by the cell wall itself to the passage of these agents to the interior of the cell. On the basis of these experiments alone, however, one cannot rule out the possibility that the methicillin which was used to induce the L-form modified the response of the protoplasmic body or membrane.

Additional information can be obtained by examining strains which are resistant to given antibiotics. For example, we have

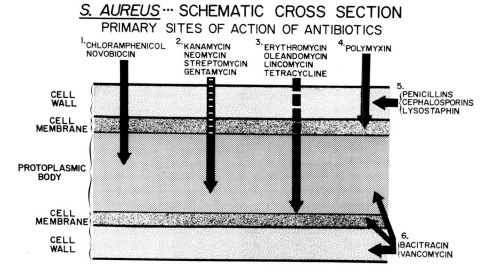

Figure 31.1. Schematic cross section of *Staphylococcus aureus*, showing primary sites of action of antibiotics. *1:* Cell wall has little, if any, effect; *2:* cell wall retards effect; *3:* principal effect on body; *4:* principal effect on cell membrane; *5:* principal effect on cell wall; *6:* principal effect on cell wall, some on body and membrane.

examined lincomycin-resistant strains of staphylococci and found that the derived L-forms were equally resistant. This is, of course, quite contrary to what would be expected with penicillin, and emphasizes again the fact that lincomycin has its primary effect on the protoplasmic body.

SUMMARY

To summarize, we might best refer to Figure 31.1, which presents a schematic cross section of a cell of *Staphylococcus aureus* and shows the primary sites of action of the various groups of agents. Thus it can be seen that (1) chloramphenicol and novobiocin have their primary effect upon the protoplasmic body and that the cell wall interferes slightly, if at all, with this effect. (2) The group containing kanamycin, neomycin, streptomycin, and gentamycin exert their primary effect also on the protoplasmic body, but that the cell wall has a variable effect in lessening their action upon the cell. (3) The third group, composed of erythromycin, oleandomycin, lincomycin and tetracycline, has its primary effect also upon the protoplasmic body, the effect of these agents upon the cell being modified to a variable degree by their ability to penetrate the cell wall; it was demonstrated that, when the cell is resistant to lincomycin, this resistance resides in the protoplasmic body itself rather than in the cell wall. (4) Polymyxin apparently has its major effect upon the protoplasmic membrane; in the case of the staphylococci tested, high concentrations have a slightly greater effect upon the L-forms than upon cells with intact cell walls. (5) Penicillin, cephalothin, and lysostaphin exert their primary influence upon the cell wall itself. (6) Bacitracin and vancomycin also exert their primary effect upon the cell wall, but in addition have some effect upon the protoplasmic membrane and the protoplasmic body.

A presentation such as this takes into account, of course, a tremendous amount of work by other authors, to which these studies of the sensitivity of coccal and L-forms are contributory.

REFERENCES

1. Brock, T. D.: Chloramphenicol. *Bact. Rev.* **25:** 32, 1961.
2. ———: The mode of action of novobiocin. *Bact. Proc.* **62:** 123, 1962.

3. Brock, T. D., and Brock, M. L.: Effect of novobiocin on permeability of *Escherichia coli. Arch. Biochem.* **85**: 176, 1959.

4. ———: Similarity in mode of action of chloramphenicol and erythromycin. *Biochem. Biophys. Acta* **33**: 274, 1959.

5. Chang, T.-W., and Weinstein, L.: Inhibition of synthesis of the cell wall of Staphylococcus aureus by cephalothin. *Science* **143**: 807, 1964.

6. Davies, J. E.: Studies on the ribosomes of streptomycin-sensitive and resistant strains of *Escherichia coli. Proc. Nat. Acad. Sci. USA* **51**: 659, 1964.

7. Davies, J., Gilbert, W., and Gorini, L.: Streptomycin, suppression and the code. *Proc. Nat. Acad. Sci. USA* **51**: 883, 1964.

8. Dienes, L.: L organisms of Klieneberger and Streptobacillus moniliformis. *J. Infect. Dis.* **65**: 24, 1939.

9. ———: The significance of the large bodies and the development of L type of colonies in bacterial cultures. *J. Bact.* **44**: 37, 1942.

10. ———: Morphology and nature of the pleuropneumonia group of organisms. *J. Bact.* **50**: 441, 1945.

11. Dienes, L., and Sharp, J.: The role of high electrolyte concentration in the production and growth of L forms of bacteria. *J. Bact.* **71**: 208, 1956.

12. Gale, E. F.: The nature of the selective toxicity of antibiotics. *Brit. Med. Bull.* **16**: 11, 1960.

13. Gale, E. F., and Folkes, J. P.: The assimilation of amino-acids by bacteria. 15. Actions of antibiotics on nucleic acid and protein synthesis in *Staphylococcus aureus. Biochem. J.* **53**: 493, 1953.

14. Jordan, D. C., and Inniss, W. E.: Selective inhibition of ribonucleic acid synthesis in *Staphylococcus aureus* by vancomycin. *Nature* **184**: 1894, 1959.

15. Julian, G. R.: [¹⁴C] lysine peptides synthesized in an *in vitro Escherichia coli* system in the presence of chloramphenicol. *J. Mol. Biol.* **12**: 9, 1965.

16. Kagan, B. M.: Staphylococcal L-forms—ecologic perspectives. *Ann. N. Y. Acad. Sci.* **128**: 81, 1965.

17. Kagan, B. M., Hasan, S., and Martin, E.: End point in antibiotic tube dilution tests: role of L forms. *Bact. Proc.*: 15, 1966.

18. Kagan, B. M., Martin, E., and Hasan, S.: Factors affecting induction of *Staphylococcus aureus* L forms. *Bact. Proc.*: 75, 1966.

19. ———: Site of action of lincomycin. *Bact. Proc.*: 15, 1966.

20. Kagan, B. M., Martin, E. R., and Stewart, G. T.: L form induction of naturally occurring methicillin-resistant strains of *Staphylococcus aureus. Nature* **203**: 1031, 1964.

21. Kagan, B. M., Molander, C. W., and Weinberger, H. J.: Induction and cultivation of staphylococcal L forms in the presence of methicillin. *J. Bact.* **83**: 1162, 1962.

22. Kagan, B. M., Molander, C. W., Zolla, S., Heimlich, E. M., Weinberger, H. J., Busser, R., and Liepnieks, S.: Antibiotic sensitivity and pathogenicity of L-phase variants of staphylococci. In: *Antimicrobial Agents and Chemotherapy—1963* (J. C. Sylvester, Ed.). American Society for Microbiology, Ann Arbor, 1964: p. 517.

23. Kagan, B. M., Zolla, S., Busser, R., and Liepnieks, S.: Sensitivity of coccal and L forms of *Staphylococcus aureus* to five antibiotics. *J. Bact.* **88**: 630, 1964.

24. Marston, J.: Observations on L forms of staphylococci. *J. Infect. Dis.* **108**: 75, 1961.

25. Newton, B. A.: Site of action of polymyxin on *Pseudomonas aeruginosa;* antagonism by cations. *J. Gen. Microbiol.* **10**: 491, 1954.

26. ———: The properties and mode of action of the polymyxins. *Bact. Rev.* **20**: 14, 1956.

27. Perkins, H. R.: Chemical structure and biosynthesis of bacterial cell walls. *Bact. Rev.* **27**: 18, 1963.

28. Rinehart, K. L.: *The Neomycins and Related Antibiotics.* Wiley, New York, 1964.

29. Salton, M. R. J.: The nature of the cell walls of some Gram-positive and Gram-negative bacteria. *Biochem. Biophys. Acta* **9**: 334, 1952.

30. ———: The anatomy of the bacterial surface. *Bact. Rev.* **25**: 77, 1961.

31. Smith, J. L., and Weinberg, E. D.: Mechanisms of antibacterial action of bacitracin. *J. Gen. Microbiol.* **28**: 559, 1962.

32. Taubman, S. B., Young, F. E., and Corcoran, J. W.: Antibiotic glycosides. IV. Studies on the mechanism of erythromycin resistance in Bacillus subtilis. *Proc. Nat. Acad. Sci. USA* **50**: 955, 1963.

33. Vasquez, D.: Antibiotics affecting chloramphenicol uptake by bacteria; their effect on amino acid incorporation in a cell free system. *Biochem. Biophys. Acta* **96**: 102, 1966.

34. Wolfe, A. D., and Hahn, F. E.: Mode of action of chloramphenicol. IX. Effects of chloramphenicol upon a ribosomal amino acid polymerization system and its binding to bacterial ribosome. *Biochem. Biophys. Acta* **95**: 146, 1965.

32

Protoplasts, Spheroplasts and L-Forms Viewed as a Genetic System*

Otto E. Landman

GEORGETOWN UNIVERSITY
WASHINGTON, D. C.

To the geneticist, spheroplasts, protoplasts and L-forms offer several intriguing problems for experimentation. For one, there is the possibility of using these wall-deficient cells in transformation, transduction or mating experiments—in this way, the role of the cell wall and the cell membrane in the transport of macromolecules can be explored. Many laboratories, including our own, have made studies in this area.

There is another aspect of the study of protoplasts and L-forms which, by contrast, has received rather little attention from geneticists and yet is of considerable genetic interest: the question of the nature of the heritable mechanism which accounts for the stability of stable L-forms. It

* Work supported by grants GB 1875 and GB 4506 from the National Science Foundation, and by grant AI 05972 of the National Institutes of Health.

Several collaborators have made important contributions to the work reviewed here. Mr. Herbert Ginoza carried out most of the experiments on reverting L-forms and *Salmonella* mutants; Mr. William Burchard and Mr. Lorell Angelety studied phage attachment sites. Mr. Sidney Halle and Mr. William Webster investigated induced reversion in *B. subtilis*. Dr. Irving Miller performed the experiments on the intermediate form of *B. subtilis*.

is principally this subject which is reviewed and discussed in the present paper.

To place the subject of stability into perspective, the relationship of stable L-forms to reverting L-forms is described. It is found that, although these two cell types often differ markedly in their properties, they are closely related in their origin. Further, in reviewing recent evidence concerning the induced reversion of stable L-forms or protoplasts to the bacillary state, it is concluded that there are important parallels between the physiological-phenotypic process represented by the reversion of spheroplasts and the quasi-genetic process of reversion from the stable L-state.

Neither gain nor loss of nucleic acid-borne information accompanies the mass-conversion of cells to the stable L-state or their reversion. Hence, the gene complement of stable L-forms is identical to that of their bacillary homologs. Nevertheless, genes play a decisive role in determining the properties of the L-forms. This conclusion is here illustrated by showing how mutation can modify many facets of the relationship between stable L-forms, reverting L-forms and bacillary forms.

In the concluding section, physical and conceptual points of contact between the special "feedback inheritance" displayed in the stable L-state and classical DNA inheritance are reviewed. In this discussion, the parallelism between feedback inheritance and the inheritance of organ-specific cell characteristics in differentiation is noted. Finally, the position of feedback inheritance as a stage in evolution is discussed.

MATERIALS AND METHODS

Strains and Procedures

The *Salmonella* strains used in these studies were derived from *Salmonella paratyphi* B777.[30] Bacillary inocula were grown overnight at 37°C in Brucella Broth (Albimi Co., Flushing, N. Y.), with shaking. Spontaneous penicillin-resistant mutants were obtained by plating a heavy inoculum of such cells on penicillin gradient plates[43] of Brucella Broth agar and incubating at 30°C. Resistant colonies, appearing after 48 hours, were streaked twice on selective media before further use. Incubation for L-form growth was always at 30°C; counts of L-colonies were made with the dissecting scope. Further procedural details are shown in footnotes to tables. Methods used in producing and handling L-forms have been described previously.[30]

The *Escherichia coli* strains were all K12 derivatives. Small colony mutants were obtained from a multiply marked F⁻ strain and an Hfr strain. Log phase growth from a Brucella Broth culture was inoculated into McLeod's synthetic medium[13] at pH 7.6 to a concentration of 10^6 cells/ml. Menadione was added to 25 μg/ml or 50 μg/ml, and incubation continued at 37°C with shaking in a series of tubes containing 2 ml samples. After 24 and 48 hours the samples were streaked on brain heart infusion agar (Difco). Following 72 hours incubation at room temperature, small colonies were picked, suspended and replated to check for persistence of the small colony characteristic and presence of biochemical markers. Only one isolate was made from each tube.

The strain of *Bacillus subtilis* used was the Marburg Strain, 168. The procedures used have been described.[31, 36*]

Media

The medium base used in studies with *Salmonella* and *E. coli* was Brucella Broth medium (28 g/liter) supplemented with 0.01 M $MgSO_4$. Sodium chloride, agar, penicillin G, 10% defibrinated horse serum, and other antibiotics were added as required. To avoid a lengthy description of the media used in each case, a code is used in which the variable components are listed in the order given. Thus, 0.2-1.0-200-S-O medium contains 0.2 M NaCl, 1% agar, 200 units/ml penicillin, 10% serum and no additional antibiotics.[30] This was the medium used routinely to grow *Salmonella* L-forms. (Subsequent to the performance of the experiments described in this paper, it was found that the growth of *Salmonella* L-forms improved in proportion to the amount of contamination of the horse serum with laked red blood cells. A hemoglobin-associated factor is responsible.)

The media used in work with *B. subtilis*, *Bacillus licheniformis* and *Bacillus megaterium* have been described previously,[22, 31] as have those used with *Proteus mirabilis*.[2, 3, 28]

RESULTS AND DISCUSSION

THE RELATIONSHIP OF STABLE L-FORMS TO REVERTING L-FORMS AND THE NATURE OF THE EVENT WHICH TRIGGERS COMMITMENT TO THE STABLE L-STATE

The Influence of Penicillin Concentration on the Ratio of Reverting to Stable L-Colonies

In several Gram-negative genera two distinctly different types of L-forms have been observed: the *reverting* L-forms which revert to the bacillary state promptly and en masse when the L-form inducing reagent—e.g. penicillin—is withdrawn, and the *stable* L-forms which continue to multiply as L-forms for successive generations after the removal of the L-form-inducing reagent.[30, 31] Some-

---

* See also, Ryter & Landman paper, p. 110.

TABLE 32.1

Conversion of Salmonella paratyphi B *to Reverting and Stable L-Forms on Soft Serum Agar**

Penicillin concentration units/ml	Number of colonies of Substrain A			Number of colonies of Substrain B		
	Bacillary	Reverting	Stable	Bacillary	Reverting	Stable
0	3.4×10^9	—	—	4.7×10^9	—	—
5	2.8×10^9	—	—	2.4×10^9	—	—
10	—	1.2×10^9	1.2×10^9	2.0×10^9	—	—
15	—	3.3×10^7	2.1×10^9	2.0×10^9	—	—
20	—	5.6×10^5	1.7×10^9	—	5.0×10^9	—
30	—	3.2×10^4	1.2×10^9	—	1.4×10^6	2.7×10^8
40	—	1.5×10^4	7.7×10^8	—	7.0×10^6	2.4×10^8
50	—	1.3×10^4	8.6×10^8	—	8.0×10^6	2.5×10^8
60	—	4.0×10^2	9.6×10^8	—	1.8×10^5	2.2×10^8
80	—	5.2×10^2	7.3×10^8	—	7.0×10^4	1.0×10^8
100	—	2.0×10^2	8.4×10^8	—	3.8×10^4	8.7×10^8
200	—	3.5×10^2	5.3×10^8	—	2.1×10^4	4.3×10^8

* Overnight cultures of strains A and B were serially diluted and plated on 0.2-1.0-$\times$-S-0 media ($\times$: varying concentrations of penicillin). Reverting colonies were counted after 3 days, stable ones after 7 days. The distinction between the two L-colony types was made on the basis of colony morphology and growth rate.

times, a change in a single constituent of the growth medium may determine whether reverting or stable L-colonies develop: For example, strains of *S. paratyphi* B give rise to a high yield of reverting L-colonies on soft serum agar containing low penicillin concentrations, and produce stable L-colonies on the same medium at higher penicillin concentrations.[30] The reverting L-colonies appear after three days of incubation and exhibit the familiar 3B "fried egg" morphology;[14] the stable L-colonies appear after seven to ten days and initially present a uniform aspect. In the experiment shown in Table 32.1, 35 per cent of the total number of the plated bacilli of strain A—and 50 per cent of the survivors—formed reverting L-colonies at ten units of penicillin/ml; at 15 units/ml, 62 per cent of the plated bacilli formed stable L-colonies. Evidently, a given cell may give rise to either type of L-colony, depending on the penicillin concentrations.

The properties of reverting and stable L-forms of *S. paratyphi* B are contrasted in Table 32.2.

Reverting L-Colonies Consist of a Mixture of Reverting and Stable L-Bodies

The close relationship between reverting and stable L-forms is also apparent when an individual reverting L-colony is examined for its content of reverting and stable L-bodies: In one such colony analysis, shown in Table 32.3, only a small minority of the L-bodies were capable of reverting to the bacillary state —the majority gave rise to stable L-colonies on penicillin-free medium. The ratio of stable to reverting L-bodies in reverting L-colonies is actually very variable. It depends on the original penicillin concentration, the state of penicillin decay at the time of resuspension, the presence of serum or other selecting ingredients in the agar medium, and the age of the colony. However, accurate data can only be obtained when the stable bodies predominate, otherwise the growth of the stable L-colonies in the assay plates is masked by bacillary colonies.

Reverting and Stable L-Forms in E. COLI

A relationship of reverting to stable L-forms quite analogous to that observed in *Salmonella* has also been found in certain slow growing "small colony" mutants of *E. coli*. While *E. coli* K12 strains of normal morphology have produced only reverting L-colonies in our hands,[28*] ten different

* O. E. Landman, unpublished results.

small colony mutant isolates (selected after incubation in synthetic media containing 25–100 μg/ml menadione[13]) all gave rise to stable L-colonies at high penicillin concentrations and to reverting ones at lower antibiotic levels.

A Transient Spheroplast-Like State in B. SUBTILIS

In our initial studies with the Grampositive *B. subtilis*, only stable L-forms were observed—more particularly, when the cell wall was removed by a 20-minute incubation with lysozyme, the resultant protoplasts quantitatively gave rise to stable L-colonies.[31] Since then, however, a more detailed study of the conversion process has revealed that, if lysozyme action upon the cell wall is interrupted by dilution before it is complete, an intermediate cell type can be detected which gives rise to bacillary colonies on the semisynthetic DP medium[36] but produces L-colonies on SD medium containing 600 μg/ml D-methionine[35, 36] (D-methionine inhibits the overgrowth of L-colonies by bacillary revertants but otherwise does not affect the plating properties of normal bacillary or protoplast inocula). If lysozyme action is stopped at the right moment, 30–40 per cent of the cell populations can be "trapped" in the intermediate form. The intermediate forms are osmotically sensitive and exhibit spherical morphology in the phase microscope. Electron microscopic examination of the intermediate populations show that many spherical cells retain large, thin fragments of cell wall on their surface. Such fragments are much less in evidence after a more prolonged lysozyme treatment.[36]*

* Analogous observations have been made with Streptococcus faecalis.[24]

(Colwell et al)

TABLE 32.2

Comparison of Some Properties of Stable and Reverting L-Forms of Salmonella paratyphi *B*

Characteristic	Reverting L-Form	Stable L-Form
Penicillin requirement for formation	Low concentrations	High concentrations
Ability to grow in liquid	Can grow at low penicillin concentration	No growth
Agar requirement for propagation	None at low penicillin concentration	Agar required
Serum requirement for propagation	None	Serum factors required
Growth in minimal medium	Yes	No—even when serum is added
Reversion	Prompt reversion upon penicillin removal	Very rare
Phage attachment sites	Present for all 7 phage strains tested	Very faint or absent
Growth rate	Attain near maximal size in 3 days	Can be counted under dissecting scope in 7–10 days
Colony morphology	Commonly show "fried egg" morphology	Young colonies have uniform aspect

TABLE 32.3

Analysis of a Reverting L-Colony for Stable and Reverting L-Bodies*

Medium	Penicillin	Number and Type of Colonies		
		Bacillary	Reverting	Stable
0.2-1.0-0-S-0	−	5.1×10^4	0	1.0×10^6
0.2-1.0-10-S-0	+	0	5.7×10^4	not counted

* A reverting L-colony of strain A was suspended in stabilizing fluid (0.5-0-0-S-0), serially diluted and plated on the two media shown. Plates were incubated at 30°C. Bacillary colonies and reverting L-colonies were counted after 3 days, stable L-colonies after 10 days.

Commitment Triggered by Near-Complete Wall Removal

The observations which we have cited, among others, have led us to postulate that the commitment to heritable stability in the L-state is triggered by a near-complete loss of the cell wall, and that the intermediate form of *B. subtilis*, as well as the reverting L-forms of *E. coli* and *Salmonella* represent a pre-commitment stage in which enough cell wall remains to prime the reconstitution of the full normal feedback system for cell wall formation[31, 41] upon lysozyme or penicillin removal. As cell wall disintegration proceeds under the impact of lysozyme action or penicillin inhibition, a point is reached where repair of the feedback system becomes impossible—this is when commitment to the stable L-state takes place.[30, 31] (Reinitiation of the interrupted feedback system—i.e., reversion from the *stable* L-state—will be discussed below.)

Mass-Conversion Stable L-forms Are Probably Completely Devoid of Cell Wall

If the hypothesis is correct that the extent of the cell wall removal determines commitment, it would be predicted that stable L-forms should always contain less polymerized cell wall than their homologous reverting forms or, more boldly and less certainly, that stable L-forms should be bounded solely by naked membrane.

The data which we have accumulated on this question in our laboratory are consistent with this prediction. In particular, our evidence comes from phage growth and absorption studies and from electron microscopy. In phage growth experiments with L- and bacillary forms of *E. coli*, spots of lysis at high phage dilutions showed that the reverting L-forms retained attachment sites for the phages to which their parent bacteria were sensitive. The stable L-forms were not susceptible to lysis. Data of this type are shown in Table 32.4 for the small colony strain SfC 4 of *E. coli* and phages T2, T3, T4 and T7. In *Salmonella*, spots of high titer lysates of six out of seven different phage strains occasionally produced clear-

TABLE 32.4

Sensitivity of Bacillary Form and L-Forms of Escherichia coli SfC 4* to Several T Phages

Phage strain spotted	Lowest phage dilution giving negative lysis reaction on			Presumed location of phage attachment site[49]
	Bacillary form	Reverting L-form	Stable L-form	
T2	10^4	10^2	10^0	Lipoprotein layer
T3	10^4	10^4	10^0	Lipopolysaccharide layer
T4	10^8	10^8	10^0	"
T7	10^{10}	10^9	10^0	"

* This small colony strain is resistant to phages T1, T5 and T6. It forms reverting L-colonies on agar containing 25 units/ml penicillin (medium 0.2-0.9-25-S-0) and stable L-colonies on the same medium containing 100 units/ml penicillin. Dilutions of the four T phages (10^0, 10^2, 10^4, 10^6, 10^8, 10^9, 10^{10}) were spotted on the bacillary lawn at the time of plating, on the reverting L lawn 24 hours after plating, and on the stable L lawn 72 hours after plating. Using spheroplasts and reverting L-forms of a K12 strain sensitive to all of the T phages, we have obtained clear evidence for the presence of adsorption sites for phages T2, T4 and T7 and, occasionally, positive evidence for T5 sites. T1, T3 and T6 sites were not demonstrated in K12 spheroplasts.

ing in layers of stable L-forms, but at least 10^6 phage per spot were required. Similarly, weak adsorption of phage from the supernatant was only irregularly demonstrable, even in dense stable L-form suspensions. By contrast, reverting L-forms and spheroplasts of *Salmonella*, produced at lower penicillin concentrations, retained attachment sites to all seven phages tested.[29] Adsorption data obtained with a spheroplast suspension of *Salmonella* are shown in Table 32.5.

In studies with the electron microscope, we have examined, in collaboration with Dr. A. Ryter, thin sections of stable L-colonies of *B. subtilis*, *B. licheniformis*[41] and, more recently, *S. paratyphi*. (Figure 32.1) In all three instances the stable L-forms were bounded only by a plasma membrane; not a trace of wall could be seen.

The observations that spheroplasts and reverting L-forms of Gram-negative bac-

TABLE 32.5

Adsorption of Various Phage Strains on Spheroplasts and Bacillary Forms of Salmonella paratyphi *B**

Phage Strain	Per cent of Phage Adsorbed in 10 Minutes by	
	Bacilli	Spheroplasts
PLT22 temperate†	92	95
1156 temperate	36	63
1334 temperate	82	88
R virulent	92	75
S virulent	85	92
777 virulent	94	99
1135 virulent	91	92

* A rejuvenated overnight culture was suspended in 0.5-0-0-0-0 medium (Brucella Broth + 0.5 M NaCl) at 37°C to a viable count of 3 × 10^8/ml; 0.1 volumes of phage suspension were then added. Multiplicities ranged from 0.04 to 13. After 10 minutes of shaking incubation at 37°C, the cultures were diluted 1:10 and centrifuged. The supernatant was assayed for unadsorbed phage. Spheroplasts (of Strain B) were produced by 4½ hour stationary incubation in the same medium containing 50 units penicillin/ml. They were centrifuged and resuspended to the same optical density as the bacilli before addition of phage. At this time, the viable count was 1.5 × 10^7.

† Phage PLT22 is known to adsorb on the lipopolysaccharide layer of *Salmonellae* (8). The location of the adsorption sites of the other phage strains (all isolated in our laboratory) are not known.

teria retain phage adsorption sites has been made by numerous workers.[11, 18, 29, 34] In addition, electron micrographs of these forms regularly show the presence of substantial amounts of wall material.[17, 38, 40, 45] By contrast, the question of whether stable L-forms retain wall material has been answered positively for *P. mirabilis* in some studies,[18, 37, 45, 47] while other investigators have obtained negative findings.[21, 44] We believe the explanation for the apparent inconsistency is to be sought in the different modes of origin of the various *Proteus* stable L-forms. Some widely used strains are probably cell wall mutants of different kinds, while others may have

originated by mass-conversion.* Our hypothesis, that commitment to heritable stability is triggered by loss of the cell wall, is of course only relevant to mass-conversion stable L-forms and does not apply to stable forms originating as cell wall mutations.

Commitment Is not Dependent on Any Particular Chemical Constituent of the Cell Wall

In summary, then, we hold to the opinion that near-complete cell wall removal is the critical event responsible for commitment. The chemical constitution of the cell wall fragments which are removed last does not appear to matter particularly: in *E. coli* and *Salmonella* these are the lipoprotein and lipopolysaccharide layers; in *B. subtilis*, teichoic acid and mucopolysaccharide seem to come off together;† in yeast, removal of mannan and glucan material initiates the corresponding stable state.[39]

THE STABLE L-STATE AND REVERSION FROM THE STABLE L-STATE

Stable Mass-Conversion L-Forms Revert-Reversion Proclivity Varies with Strain and Environment

In the present publication and earlier[31] we have operationally described the stable mass-conversion L-forms as those forms which continue to multiply in the L-state after removal of penicillin or lysozyme. Whether this multiplication in the L-state continues indefinitely or whether, and how soon, overgrowth of bacillary revertants occurs, depends on both the bacterial strains and the chemical and physical environment. In Table 32.6 the stability of

* In our laboratory, mass-conversion stable L-forms of *Proteus* never exhibited the inability to revert or the ability to grow in liquid media.[3, 4] Both properties are characteristics of the well-studied strains of stable *Proteus* L-forms. These differences further bolster our belief that such widely used strains as L9 and L52 are stable L-forms of mutational origin.

† I. L. Miller and O. E. Landman, unpublished observations, 1966.

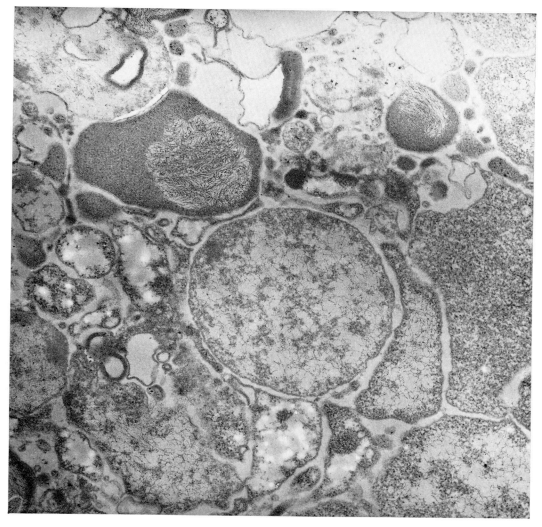

Figure 32.1. Thin section of a stable L-colony of *Salmonella paratyphi* B. All bodies are bounded by unit membranes only. × 32,000. (Electron micrograph by A. Ryter).

mass-conversion L-forms of a variety of bacterial strains is recorded. Only bona fide mass-conversion L-forms are considered—i.e., only strains are shown which were derived from their parent bacilli in high yield by a single treatment step. The table shows that the natural tendency of mass-conversion stable L-forms to revert to the bacillary form varies very widely—from "never" to "very rapid". It will be noted that this reversion tendency has been stated in quantitatively imprecise terms: Landman & Halle[31] have shown that the reversion of *B. subtilis* L-forms can be completely prevented—or induced with 100 per cent efficiency—by making appropriate changes in the environment. Similar, albeit less dramatic success in efforts to stimulate reversion of stable L-forms has been recorded for other organisms[3, 25, 39] as have reports of failures in other instances.[30] In view of the profound influence

TABLE 32.6

Reversion Frequency of Mass-Conversion Stable L-Forms under Ordinary Conditions of Laboratory Cultivation

Genus	Stable L-Form Produced by	Approximate Maximum Conversion Efficiency (%)	Reversion Frequency	Reference
Escherichia coli small colony forms	penicillin	20	nil	Landman*
Salmonella paratyphi B.	penicillin	60	very rare	Landman & Ginoza[30]
Proteus mirabilis	penicillin	1.5	moderate	Altenbern[3]
Bacillus subtilis	penicillin or lysozyme	100	moderate	Landman & Halle[31]
Bacillus licheniformis	lysozyme	20	rare	Landman*
Bacillus megaterium	lysozyme	15	very rapid	Kawakami & Landman[22] Miller & Landman*
Streptococcus pyogenes	enzyme	10	—	Gooder & Maxted[16]
Streptococcus faecalis	enzyme	50	moderate[25]	Gooder & King[15]

* Unpublished observations.

of the environment in stimulating reversion of some of the stable L-form strains, one can only speak of "reversion frequency as observed under ordinary conditions of cultivation." As to special conditions, further advances in the technology of reversion induction might at any time change the "never" in the *E. coli* column to "frequently". It is for this reason that we have eschewed Klieneberger-Nobel's definition of stable L-forms as those L-forms which "never revert".[26]

Current Concepts Concerning the Mechanism of Reversion of Stable L-Forms

What is the nature of the step which allows reversion from the stable L-state? Certainly, it is something more than repair of the damaged cells which is involved in reversion from the spheroplast (reverting L-) state. A special priming event is required to start up again the feedback system for wall formation and septum formation which had been lost during commitment.[31, 41] On the basis of recent electron microscopic studies of reversion of *B. subtilis* in gelatin media, which are partly reported in this symposium* we now believe that a crucial step in reversion from the stable L-state is the accretion of cell wall outside the cell membrane.[32, 39] Formation of the septum and

* See paper by Ryter & Landman, p. 110.

of mesosomes follows this first step. We hypothesize that the special physical conditions which stimulate reversion in *B. subtilis*—15–35% gelatin media, hard agar media or membrane filters[31]—do so by physically facilitating this wall accretion, in somewhat the same way in which the outer wall layers of Gram-negative spheroplasts or the residual wall fragments in the intermediate form of *B. subtilis* permit repair of the damaged wall-septum feedback system. Stable L-forms of *P. mirabilis* in penicillin medium actually pass through the reverting L-stage on their way to the bacillary form.[2]

In earlier publications, we have stressed the fact that L-forms are defective in two important functions, wall formation and septation, that the cell membrane plays a key role in both of these functions, and that, in our opinion, it is inhibition at membrane sites by penicillin which leads to the L-state.[30, 31] Our recent results indicate that, in returning to the full functions of the bacillary state, the formation of a supporting wall (the "exoskeleton" of the bacterial cell) precedes, and is required for, the reformation of septa and other intracellular membrane structures.

GENE MUTATIONS RELATING TO THE L-STATE

In the preceding discussion, we have focused our attention on the peculiar and rather unique mechanism which is responsible for the perpetuation of the mass-conversion stable L-state: the long-lasting consequence of a brief interruption of a self-dependent reaction sequence leading to organelle synthesis. Clearly, loss of nucleic acid-borne information cannot be directly involved in this feedback inheritance (as it is in mitochondrial and chloroplast mass-conversion inheritance systems), since protoplasts and L-forms can be mass-reverted to the bacillary state.

The absence of direct involvement of nuclear or cytoplasmic nucleic acid in this heritable system does not imply, of course, that wall and septum formation mechanisms are not subject to gene control. On the contrary, experience indicates —as one would expect—that spheroplast formation, commitment, stability of the L-forms, and reversion, can all be modified by mutation.

Mutations Simultaneously Affecting Spheroplasting and Commitment

An example of the effect of mutation on spheroplasting and commitment was shown in Table 32.1. The mutation which differentiates substrain B from substrain A has simultaneously boosted strain B's resistance both to spheroplasting and to commitment by penicillin. This dual effect is usually observed in penicillin resistance mutations. (Table 32.7; see also table 5 in Landman & Ginoza.[30]) In terms of our hypothesis that near-complete wall removal is required for commitment, the mutational interdependence between spheroplasting and commitment suggests that the loss of lipoprotein and lipopolysaccharide layers in penicillin medium may depend upon the prior disintegration of the rigid layer.

Mutations Selectively Affecting Commitment

By contrast, another type of mutation may occur which affects the spheroplasting response and the commitment response selectively. Such a mutation is represented by the small colony form of E. coli. The parental E. coli strains of normal morphology produce reverting L-col-

TABLE 32.7

Conversion of Penicillin-Resistant Mutants to Reverting and Stable L-Forms

| Strain | Penicillin Concentration (units/ml) | | | |
| | Bacillary form | | Mixture of stable and reverting L-colonies | Stable L-colonies predominate |
	Growth	No growth		
A	5	10	10	15
*A-1	10	20	20	30
*A-1′	50	70	70	100
†A-2	100	200	200	300
†A-2′	300	500	500	800

* First step mutants derived from A.
† Second step mutants derived from A-1′.

onies at 40, 100 as well as at 1000 units of penicillin per ml, but the slow-growing small colony mutants form only stable L-colonies at the latter two antibiotic levels. It appears that the tendency to lose the outer wall layers during penicillin treatment is enhanced by this mutation, although the sensitivity to penicillin killing (on non-stabilizing media) is not markedly altered by it.

Genetic Control of Reversion Proclivity

The ability of stable L-forms, once formed, to revert back to the bacillary form is also dependent on the genetic constitution of the bacteria. This conclusion clearly emerges from a comparison of the reversion proclivities of different bacterial genera shown in Table 32.6. However, no studies of this property have been made with mutants of a single species.

Genetic Blocks in Cell Wall Biosynthesis

Situations in which stability is entirely gene-determined are represented by cell wall biosynthesis mutants.[7, 34] In such mutants, the spherical shape and osmotic sensitivity of the cells, as well as their inability to return to the bacillary form, are all due to a mutational block in the biosynthesis of the rigid layer (e.g., inability to synthesize diaminopimelic acid[7]). The dap-less mutant produces stable L-colonies without the necessity of a commitment step. Obviously, stable L-forms of mutational origin are likely to be different in their properties from the mass-conversion stable L-forms.

Stability Resulting from the Combined Effects of Mutation and Mass-Conversion

In experimentation with L-forms, one is fairly likely to encounter situations where gene mutation and mass-conversion effects are superimposed. For example, after having transferred an isolate of lysozyme-induced L-forms of *B. subtilis* for three years in the L-state without any notable change in its properties, we suddenly noticed that we could no longer induce reversion by the usual gelatin medium procedure, or by any other method. In addition, microscopic examination revealed that the L-bodies of this new strain were now much larger than before and frequently contained other L-bodies. (However, the tryptophan requirement of the original isolate remained.) Apparently, a mutational block to reversion arose in our strain during the transfers in the L-state and the mutant was eventually selected.

We believe instances of superposition of mass-conversion stability and mutation-induced stability are encountered in many laboratories—whenever attempts are made to select a "truly stable" L-form by repeated transfers of mass-conversion stable L-forms. In our opinion, results obtained with stable L-strains emerging from such a procedure must be interpreted with great caution, since it is never clear whether the observed properties originated at the time of mass-conversion, or when mutation occurred, or later.

Mutations Selectively Affecting Wall Formation and Septum Formation

As we have discussed earlier in this paper, and elsewhere,[4, 30, 31] both wall formation and septation are inhibited in spheroplasts and are essentially absent in the stable L-state in our strains. Nevertheless, these two characteristics can be studied separately in physiological[33] and genetic[1, 27] experiments, and mutations have been identified which selectively affect the penicillin sensitivity of one or the other of the two mechanisms. One

such mutation in *Proteus* was described in detail by Altenbern & Landman.[4] Briefly, it was found that in our *Proteus* wild types septum forming capacity was more sensitive to penicillin than wall forming capacity. Consequently, filaments were formed at the lowest effective penicillin concentrations, and spheroplasts only appeared at higher antibiotic levels. Lacking the ability to septate, these spheroplasts required soft agar for growth and could not multiply in liquid medium.* In the strains which formed "centerless" L-colonies on hard agar, a mutation had occurred which had raised the penicillin resistance of the septum forming process, while leaving the sensitivity of the wall forming process at a lower level. As a result, centerless mutants could grow as spheres in liquid penicillin media by a septation process resembling budding.

Our *S. paratyphi* wild types resemble the centerless *Proteus* mutants in their response to penicillin. Spheroplasts are formed in the lowest range of effective penicillin concentrations. Up to about 12 units/ml, these spheroplasts retain their ability to form septa, and can consequently grow on hard agar, in gelatin media and in liquid medium.

On agar containing ten units penicillin/ml but lacking NaCl for osmotic stabilization, the spheroplasts lyse; however, a few colonies of penicillin-resistant mutants remain. Some of these are found to consist largely of long filaments. Apparently, a mutation has occurred in these strains in which wall resistance to penicillin has now leapfrogged septation re-

---

* The agar requirement has been explained by the assumption that herniation and pinching off of the burgeoning protoplasm of septation-incompetent cells, and hence increase in cell number, can occur in the agar gel, whereas such an artificial subdivision of the protoplasm cannot take place in liquid medium.[4, 31, 34] An outward manifestation of the agar requirement is the "fried egg" morphology of L-colonies, due to a small agar penetration area in the center, covered by a larger mound of enlarging, non-subdividing L-bodies on the agar surface. Centerless strains can achieve division without agar, hence they can grow without a center of agar penetration.[4]

TABLE 32.8

Wall Sensitivity and Division Sensitivity in Different Salmonella *Genotypes*

Plating	Strain	Medium Tonic-ity	Number and Type of Colonies*					
			Penicillin concentration (units/ml)					
			0	5	10	15	20	25
First round	Wild type (wall sensi-tive)	High	3.3×10^{-5} B	2.7×10^{-5} B	1.7×10^{-5} L	0	0	0
		Low	4.1×10^{-5} B	2.9×10^{-5} B	1† B + F	0	0	0
Second round	Mutant (division sensitive)	High	240 B	212 B	214 B	140 F	34 F	0
		Low	237 B	209 B	202 B	126 F	0	0

B = Bacillary colony; L = reverting L-colony; F = colony consisting of filaments.
* None of these media contain serum and hence they do not support the growth of stable L-colonies.
† Mutant.

sistance. These filamenting mutants of *Salmonella* resemble the *Proteus* wild type in showing sensitivity in their septation mechanism at the lowest effective penicillin concentration (Table 32.8).

RELATIONSHIPS BETWEEN FEEDBACK INHERI-
TANCE AND NUCLEIC ACID INHERITANCE

The delineation of a novel mode of inheritance affecting such vital cellular functions as cell wall formation and cell division raises several broad questions: What is the interplay of this inheritance with the nucleic acid-borne inheritance of bacteria? What is the evolutionary significance of feedback inheritance?

Reversion from the Stable L-State: a Complex Developmental Process

In reverting from the stable L-state to the bacillary state, a bacterium such as *S. paratyphi* or *P. mirabilis* must build *de novo*, and on the outside of its cell membrane, the mucopeptide, lipopolysaccharide and lipoprotein layers of the cell wall, flagellae and, sometimes, pili. Internally, it must establish the membrane machinery which is required for septation and organized separation of genomes. The information needed to perform these tasks is of course contantly present in the genes of the L-forms, but the priming event is required to call it forth. Reversion thus

offers many parallels to developmental processes in higher organisms. Future investigations will determine whether genes concerned with wall building functions are repressed in the stable L-state—as are the unemployed genes in development[9]—or whether they are constantly and ineffectually producing messages.

Is the Trigger Event in Reversion Localized —Is the DNA-Membrane Attachment Site Involved?

There is little experimental evidence concerning the manner of management of the complex organizational tasks which are set in motion by the priming event. More particularly, we do not know whether a chance agglomeration of a bit of wall anywhere on the surface of the protoplast starts off a self-sustaining assembly process for the whole complex wall or, by contrast, whether priming must occur at special locations at the cell surface and whether subsequent wall assembly involves coordinated activities of regulatory genes.

A straw in the wind is perhaps provided by Cole's studies[12] showing that wall synthesis is restricted to the area near the septa and, further, by the observation that penicillin sensitivity of the wall of growing cells is greatest in the same subcellular region.[34] (This accounts for the development of "rabbit forms" early in penicillin treatment.)

Cultures in which DNA synthesis is inhibited quite generally show filamentation.[6, 10, 23, 42, 46] Thus, there are indications that a localized control of wall synthesis (and membrane synthesis[20]) is coordinated with the controls of the DNA synthesis cycle. More precisely, we have observed that thymine starvation produces filamentation in *B. subtilis* cultures in which chromosome replication has been arrested by amino acid starvation.[5] Apparently, formation of complete cross walls must await a signal from the DNA replication machinery—presumably the DNA-membrane attachment site.

All these findings suggest the possibility that, in reversion, priming may occur at the DNA-membrane attachment site.

Speculations Concerning the Evolutionary Role of Feedback Inheritance

It has been pointed out that the site of DNA attachment to the membrane—normally at the mesosome[40]—simultaneously serves the bacteria as centromere and centriole.[19] The centriole (or genome separation) function is at least partially subject to disruption by the vagaries of feedback inheritance since, in protoplasts and in the L-state, the bacterial chromosome is no longer as neatly distributed to daughter cells as it is in the bacillary form.[41] (However, the centromere function remains undisturbed* and the coordinated distribution of episomes with chromosomes persists in the L-state.[22]) Moving this vital function to an intracellular location and endowing it with a more secure heritable continuity would constitute a clear evolutionary advance for the cell. It is plausible that the evolutionary development of the centriole—a shift from feedback inheritance to self-duplication—followed as a consequence of the disabilities manifested in the L-state. A similar argument applies to the development of mitochondria: in *Staphylococcus*, and perhaps in other bacteria with prominent mesosomes, an appreciable fraction

* See Ryter & Landman, p. 110.

of the oxidative enzymes of the cell may be lost in the L-state[48]—again, the development of an intracellular autonomous organelle, secure against the vagaries of feedback inheritance, would be a great evolutionary advance. The mesosome-imbedded DNA attachment point is certainly plausible as an evolutionary precursor of the membranous, DNA-containing mitochondrion.

SUMMARY

Having defined stable L-forms as "those forms which continue to divide in the L-state after withdrawal of the L-form-inducing reagent", and having shown earlier that, in *Bacillus subtilis*, every cell can give rise to a stable L-form and every stable L-body can regain the bacillary form,[31] attention is now focused on two key events: commitment—the event whereby the ability to form a bacillary form is lost, and reversion—the event which causes this ability to be regained. Commitment in *B. subtilis* occurs as the last traces of wall are removed by lysozyme. In *Escherichia coli* and in *Salmonella* commitment can be demonstrated for, respectively, 20 and 60 per cent of the cells at high penicillin concentrations; at low penicillin concentrations spheroplasts and reverting L-colonies are formed from almost all cells. Reverting spheroplast colonies consist of mixtures of reverting and stable L-bodies. Evidence is presented that phage attachment sites and a wall visible in the electron microscope are present in reverting L-forms and are absent in the stable ones —it is postulated that commitment occurs in these Gram-negative strains also as the last vestige of (lipoprotein-lipopolysaccharide) wall is lost. Stable L-forms of mutational origin are of course excluded from the generalization that wall loss triggers commitment.

Once committed to the stable L-state, strains of different bacterial genera exhibit very different proclivities to revert back to the bacillary state. In *B. subtilis* an important early step in reversion is the formation of a wall layer; formation of mesosomes follows much later. Evidence is discussed which suggests that the initial priming synthesis leading to the formation of this thin wall layer might be localized near the DNA-membrane attachment site.

Gene mutations are described which affect spheroplasting, commitment, stability of the stable L-state, wall biosynthesis and septum formation. Some insights concerning the inter-relationships of these processes emerge from a consideration of the properties of these mutants.

Keeping in mind that bacillary forms and L-forms contain the same genetic information, the persistence of the bacillary and stable L-states may be considered analogous to the persistence of nerve, liver or muscle cell states in metazoan growth and development—in this light, reversion is a developmental process at the cellular level.

REFERENCES

1. Adler, H. I., and Hardigree, A. A.: Analysis of a gene controlling cell division and sensitivity to radiation in *Escherichia coli. J. Bact.* **87**: 720, 1964.

2. Altenbern, R. A.: Critical factors influencing growth of L forms of *Proteus mirabilis. J. Bact.* **81**: 586, 1961.

3. ———: Reversion of 3A type L forms of *Proteus mirabilis. J. Bact.* **81**: 762, 1961.

4. Altenbern, R. A., and Landman, O. E.: Growth of L forms of *Proteus mirabilis* in liquid media. *J. Bact.* **79**: 510, 1960.

5. Anraku, N., and Landman, O. E.: To be published, 1967.

6. Barner, H. D., and Cohen, S. S.: The induction of thymine synthesis by T2 infection of a thymine-requiring mutant of *Escherichia coli. J. Bact.* **68**: 80, 1954.

7. Bauman, N., and Davis, B. D.: Selection of auxotrophic bacterial mutants through diaminopimelic acid or thymine deprival. *Science* **126**: 170, 1957.

8. Beckmann, I., Subbaiah, T. V., and Stocker, B. A. D.: Rough mutants of *Salmonella typhimurium.* (2) Serological and chemical investigations. *Nature* **201**: 1299, 1964.

9. Beermann, W., and Clever, U.: Chromosome puffs. *Sci. Amer.* **210** (4): 50, 1964.

10. Berrah, G., and Konetzka, W. A.: Selective and reversible inhibition of the synthesis of bacterial deoxyribonucleic acid by phenethyl alcohol. *J. Bact.* **83**: 738, 1962.

11. Böhme, H., and Taubeneck, U.: Die Wirkung von Bakteriophagen auf Normalformen und "Large Bodies" von *Proteus mirabilis. Naturwissenschaften* **45**: 296, 1958.

12. Cole, R. M., and Hahn, J. J.: Cell wall replication in *Streptococcus pyogenes. Science* **135**: 722, 1962.

13. Colwell, C. A.: Small colony variants of *Escherichia coli. J. Bact.* **52**: 417, 1946.

14. Dienes, L., and Weinberger, H. J.: The L forms of bacteria. *Bact. Rev.* **15**, 245, 1951.

15. Gooder, H., and King, J. R.: Growth as L colonies of protoplasts of *Streptococcus faecalis* F$_{24}$. *Bact. Proc.*: 71, 1964.

16. Gooder, H., and Maxted, W. R.: External factors influencing structure and activities of *Streptococcus pyogenes. Symp. Soc. Gen. Microbiol.* **11**: 151, 1961.

17. Hofschneider, P. H.: Zur Wandstruktur von *Escherichia coli* B Sphaeroplasten. In: *Proc. Eur. Reg. Conf. Electron. Microscopy*, Delft. Vol. II: 1028, 1960.

18. Hofschneider, P. H., and Lorek, H.: Studies on the residual cell wall structures of *E. coli-* and *B. megaterium* spheroplasts and of L-forms of *Proteus mirabilis.* In: *Fifth International Congress for Electron Microscopy*, Vol. 2 (S. S. Breese, Jr., Ed.). Academic Press, New York, 1962: RR9.

19. Jacob, F., Brenner, S., and Cuzin, F.: On the regulation of DNA replication in bacteria. *Cold Spring Harbor Symp. Quant. Biol.* **28**: 329, 1963.

20. Jacob, F., Ryter, A., and Cuzin, F.: On the association between *DNA* and membrane in bacteria. *Proc. Roy. Soc. London B* **164**: 267, 1966.

21. Kandler, O., and Zehender, C.: Über das Vorkommen von α,ε-Diaminopimelinsäure bei verschiedenen L-Phasentypen von *Proteus vulgaris* und bei den pleuropneumonieähnlichen Organismen. *Z. Naturforschg.* **12**b: 725, 1957.

22. Kawakami, M., and Landman, O. E.: Retention of episomes during protoplasting and during propagation in the L state. *J. Bact.* **92**: 398, 1966.

23. Kilgore, W. W., and Greenberg, J.: Filament formation and resistance to 1-methyl-3-nitro-1-nitrosoguanidine and other radiomimetic compounds in *Escherichia coli. J. Bact.* **81**: 258, 1961.

24. King, J. R., and Gooder, H.: Subsequent growth as L forms or Streptococci of lysozyme-damaged group D Streptococci. *Bact. Proc.*: 58, 1965.

25. ———: Comparison of Group D Streptococci

and their derived L forms. *Bact. Proc.*: 59, 1966.

26. Klieneberger-Nobel, E.: L-forms of bacteria. In: *The Bacteria, Vol. I. Structure* (I. C. Gunsalus and R. Y. Stanier, Eds.). Academic Press, New York, 1960: p. 361.

27. Kohiyama, M., Cousin, D., Ryter, A., and Jacob, F.: Mutants thermosensibles d'*Escherichia coli* K 12. I. Isolement et caractérisation rapide. *Ann. Inst. Pasteur* (Paris) **110**: 465, 1966.

28. Landman, O. E., Altenbern, R. A., and Ginoza, H. S.: Quantitative conversion of cells and protoplasts of *Proteus mirabilis* and *Escherichia coli* to the L form. *J. Bact.* **75**: 567, 1958.

29. Landman, O. E., Burchard, W. K., and Angelety, L. H.: Lysogeny and bacteriophage adsorption in stable and reverting L forms of *Salmonella paratyphi* B and *Escherichia coli.* *Bact. Proc.*: 58, 1962.

30. Landman, O. E., and Ginoza, H. S.: Genetic nature of stable L forms of *Salmonella paratyphi. J. Bact.* **81**: 875, 1961.

31. Landman, O. E., and Halle, S.: Enzymically and physically induced inheritance changes in *Bacillus subtilis. J. Mol. Biol.* **7**: 721, 1963.

32. Landman, O. E., and Ryter, A.: To be published.

33. Lark, K. G.: Abnormal growth induced by penicillin in a strain of *Alcaligenes fecalis.* *Canad. J. Microbiol.* **4**: 165, 1958.

34. Lederberg, J., and St. Clair, J.: Protoplasts and L-type growth of *Escherichia coli.* *J. Bact.* **75**: 143, 1958.

35. Miller, I. L., and Landman, O. E.: The effect of chloramphenicol pretreatment of *Bacillus subtilis* on its cell wall and lysozyme spheres. *Bact. Proc.*: 27, 1965.

36. Miller, I. L., Zsigray, R. M., and Landman, O. E.: *J. Gen Microbiol.,* 1967, in press.

37. Morrison, T. H., and Weibull, C.: The occurrence of cell wall constituents in stable *Proteus* L forms. *Acta Path. Microbiol. Scand.* **55**: 475, 1962.

38. Murray, R. G. E., Steed, P., and Elson, H. E.: The location of the mucopeptide in sections of the cell wall of *Escherichia coli* and other Gram-negative bacteria. *Canad. J. Microbiol.* **11**: 547, 1965.

39. Nečas, O.: The mechanism of regeneration of yeast protoplasts. II. Formation of the cell wall de novo. *Folia Biol.* (Praha) **11**: 97, 1965.

40. Ryter, A., and Jacob, F.: Étude morphologique de la liaison du noyau a la membrane chez *E. coli* et chez les protoplastes de *B. subtilis.* *Ann. Inst. Pasteur* (Paris) **110**: 801, 1966.

41. Ryter, A., and Landman, O. E.: Electron microscope study of the relationship between mesosome loss and the stable L state (or protoplast state) in *Bacillus subtilis. J. Bact.* **88**: 457, 1964.

42. Shiba, S., Terawaki, A., Taguchi, T., and Kawamata, J.: Selective inhibition of formation of deoxyribonucleic acid in *Escherichia coli* by mitomycin C. *Nature* **183**: 1056, 1959.

43. Szybalski, W., and Bryson, V.: Genetic studies on microbial cross resistance to toxic agents. I. Cross resistance of *Escherichia coli* to fifteen antibiotics. *J. Bact.* **64**: 489, 1952.

44. Taubeneck, U.: Die Phagenresistenz der stabilen L-Form von *Proteus mirabilis.* *Z. Naturforsch.* **16b**: 849, 1961.

45. Thorsson, K. G., and Weibull, C.: Studies on the structure of bacterial L forms, protoplasts and protoplast-like bodies. *J. Ultrastr. Res.* **1**: 412, 1958.

46. Webb, M., and Nickerson, W. J.: Differential reversal of inhibitory effects of folic acid analogs on growth, division and deoxyribonucleic acid synthesis of microorganisms. *J. Bact.* **71**: 140, 1956.

47. Weibull, C.: Chemical analyses elucidating the structure of bacterial L forms. *Acta Path. Microbiol. Scand.* **42**: 324, 1958.

48. Weibull, C., and Gyllang, H.: Metabolic properties of some L forms derived from Gram-positive and Gram-negative bacteria. *J. Bact.* **89**: 1443, 1965.

49. Weidel, W., Frank, H., and Martin, H. H.: The rigid layer of the cell wall of *Escherichia coli* strain B. *J. Gen. Microbiol.* **22**: 158, 1960.

33

Identification of L-Forms:
Problems and Approaches*

Ruth G. Wittler, Zell A. McGee, Carol O. Williams,
Carroll Burris

WALTER REED ARMY INSTITUTE OF RESEARCH
WASHINGTON, D. C.

Richard L. Cohen

UNIVERSITY OF MARYLAND
COLLEGE PARK, MARYLAND

and Richard B. Roberts

WALTER REED ARMY INSTITUTE OF RESEARCH
WASHINGTON, D.C.

Stabilized L-forms of unknown or dubious parental derivation present a multitude of problems to the bacteriologist who attempts to identify them precisely. The initial sorting procedures customarily employed to determine genus and species of classical bacteria have little if any applicability to L-forms. Gram staining does not neatly sort an L-form into one or the other of the two large categories of Gram-positive or Gram-negative genera; all L-forms are Gram-negative. Microscopic examination of an L-form gives no hint of differential morphologic features which would place it among either bacillary or coccal species, among species arranged in clusters or in chains, among species containing or lacking spores, capsules or flagella.

* This investigation was supported in part by Public Health Service Research Grant AI 02332 from the National Institute of Allergy and Infectious Diseases.

The first level at which any characterization of an L-form can be made is that pertaining to its biochemistry. The few L-forms which have been compared with their respective bacterial parents have been found to retain many, but not necessarily all, of the enzymatic activities of the parent. An L-form could not, therefore, be identified with certainty on the basis of biochemical activities alone.

Serologic identification of an L-form may yield highly reliable results but has many serious limitations. In the first place, few if any laboratories would be prepared to test an unidentified L-form against a whole library of antibacterial reference serums. Secondly, those serologic identifications which are dependent on the presence of antigenic components associated with the cell wall are inapplicable to identification of L-forms, which have no cell walls. Thirdly, non-species specific antigenic components shared by different genera of bacteria could lead to improper serologic identification of L-forms if data derived from other characterization techniques were not considered.

Identification at present rests, therefore, on the ability to achieve reversion of the L-form to its bacterial form and thence to identify the reverted bacterium. For highly stabilized L-strains, reversion may be unobtainable or too time-consuming for even the most research-oriented diagnostic laboratory.

A fresh approach to the problem of identification of L-forms is suggested by the current application of molecular genetic techniques to problems of bacterial taxonomy. The molecular genetic approach to the determination of relationships among bacterial species is based on the principle that the precise composition and sequence of nucleotide bases of the chromosomal deoxyribonucleic acid (DNA) determines the identity of an organism. Dowell and associates[4] in 1964 were the first to show that a bacterium, *Sphaerophorus necrophorus*, and its variant "large body" form were indistinguishable with respect to nucleotide base composition. Furthermore, they showed that another organism, an L-form tentatively identified as *Sphaerophorus* sp., was not a closely related species, since it differed from the first pair by seven per cent guanine plus cytosine (G+C). (A difference of greater than ten per cent G+C indicates that there is little if any genetic relatedness.[16])

Panos[13] in 1965 found that a group A streptococcus and its stable L-form also had similar nucleotide base compositions.

A system of identification of L-forms cannot utilize base composition data to prove genetic identity. This data can only serve to exclude from consideration those species which are not closely related, and to select those which, having the same base composition, may be genetically similar to the L-form. The determination of the degree of genetic relatedness between these organisms and the L-form must be done by molecular hybridization techniques. Such an identification system, utilizing genetic comparison

between L-forms and suspected parent organisms, assumes that an L-form and its parent species have identical genetic constitutions.

Our laboratory has been concerned with the formulation of this systematic genetic approach to the identity of L-forms, with the testing of its assumptions and, in addition, with the utilization of biochemical tests for characterizing L-forms as a correlative approach to identification.

Materials and Methods

Definitions

The term *L-form* is here used to designate morphologic variants which grow on agar in colonies having the so-called "fried egg" configuration. The elements composing the colonies are granules and large or small bodies which lacked rigid cell walls. These variants can be propagated indefinitely in serial passage under specified conditions without reversion to bacterial form. Three degrees of stability of the L-forms are here distinguished: (1) *stable L-forms*, signifying strains which in broth or on agar media in the absence of penicillin never reverted to bacterial form; (2) *relatively stable L-forms*, signifying strains which in the absence of penicillin did not revert on agar but which might, on occasion, revert when passed in large volumes of broth; (3) *unstable L-forms*, signifying strains which reverted to bacterial form as soon as penicillin was removed from the medium.

Organisms and Media

Most of the cultures were obtained from the American Type Culture Collection (ATCC) and in general were cultivated on media recommended by the ATCC. Origin and cultivation of a number of strains employed here have been described in previous publications: for *Proteus mirabilis* 9 (ATCC ⋕14273) and its stable L-form, L9 (ATCC ⋕14168), see Rogul and associates;[15] for *Streptococcus* MG9 (ATCC ⋕9895) see McGee and associates;[10] for *Streptococcus faecalis* F24 (ATCC ⋕19634) and its stable L-form, F24-L (ATCC ⋕19635), see Gooder & King;[6] for *Neisseria subflava* (ATCC #11076) see Catlin & Cunningham;[1] for *Neisseria meningitidis* parent cocci (P), L-forms (L) and revertant cocci (R) see Roberts & Wittler.[14] For this investigation *Streptococcus faecalis* F24 and F24-L were cultivated in Albimi Brucella Broth containing 0.4 M ammonium chloride and 0.5% dextrose.

Meningococci used in the present study were as follows: group B, strain 55-P, freshly isolated from a meningitis case; 55-L (ATCC #19578), a relatively stable L- harvested for these studies after 100 to 150 passages in the L-form; and 55-R, the revertant obtained from the 60th serial passage of the L-form. Also used was an older group B "laboratory strain" Ne15-P; Ne15-L (ATCC #17935), an unstable L- used after 55 passages in the L-form; and Ne15-R, the revertant obtained after 140 serial passages of the L-form. The group C meningococcus used was 47-P, freshly isolated from the blood of a meningitis case by Mr. J. R. Evans of our laboratory; 47-L (ATCC #19577), an unstable L- used after 82 passages in the L-form; and 47-R, the revertant obtained from the 70th serial passage of the L-form. Harvests of P, L and R forms were made from agar-grown organisms in all instances, except for the isotopically labeled 55-L, which was grown in and harvested from broth. Harvested organisms were checked for purity and identified by the phenotypic and serologic criteria employed previously.[14]

TESTS FOR BIOCHEMICAL CHARACTERIZATION

Tests for enzymatic activities, such as utilization of carbohydrates, reduction or hydrolysis, were carried out by methods described in the Army and Air Force technical manual[3] or in the manual of Cowan & Steel.[2] Slight modifications were made in the standard tests to permit growth of serum-requiring L-forms. For *N. meningitidis* and its variants the methods of Roberts & Wittler[14] were used.

DNA EXTRACTION

Bacteria and L-forms grown either on agar or in broth were harvested and their DNA extracted by methods previously used by our laboratory.[10, 11, 15] *Proteus* DNA was isotopically labeled with C^{14}-uracil. The DNA of other species was labeled with tritiated thymidine or adenine (DNA-H^3) and had a specific activity of 700 to 10,000 counts per minute per microgram. Labeled and unlabeled DNA from *S. faecalis* F24 and its L-form were prepared in collaboration with Dr. Harry Gooder.*

BASE RATIO DETERMINATION

DNA base ratio determinations, expressed as the molar ratio of guanine + cytosine $\times$ 100/adenine + thymine + guanine + cytosine (per cent G+C), were performed by the thermal denaturation method of Marmur & Doty[8] with the exceptions noted previously.[11]

AGAR COLUMN HYBRIDIZATION

The degree of genetic relatedness, expressed as percentage relative homology, was estimated by the agar column hybridization method of McCarthy & Bolton[9] with the modifications specified by McGee and associates.[11]

RESULTS AND DISCUSSION

As a model system for the relationship between a bacterium and its stable L-form, we chose to study *P. mirabilis*, strain 9, and its stable L-form, L9. Dr. Marvin Rogul,† in collaboration with our laboratory, showed that the base compositions of the two forms were nearly identical, i.e., 39.5 per cent G+C for the parent and 39.7 per cent G+C for the L-form.[15] To establish the degree of genetic relatedness of these two forms of *Proteus*, agar column hybridization studies were performed, and the genomes of the two organisms were found to be genetically indistinguishable.

These results were in good agreement with the results of other studies in which we confirmed the similarity in enzymatic activities of the two forms of *Proteus*. Both parent and L-form produced acid from galactose, glucose, glycerol, maltose, trehalose, and xylose. Neither form produced

* University of North Carolina, Chapel Hill.

† Department of Veterinary Microbiology, Walter Reed Army Institute of Research.

TABLE 33.1

Relatedness of Neisseria meningitidis *Strains, Parents (P), L-Forms (L) and Revertants (R)*

Radio-active "Donor" DNA	"Recipient" DNA in Agar	% G + C of DNA of "Recipient"[a]	% Labeled DNA Bound[b]	% Relative Homology
55-L	55-L	50.7 ± 0.2	43.8 ± 4.6	100
"	55-P[c]	50.4 ± 0.1	45.3 ± 11.1	103.5
"	55-R	50.6 ± 0.1	50.1 ± 14.5	114.6
"	Ne15-L	50.7 ± 0.2	n.d.	n.d.
"	Ne15-P[d]	50.6 ± 0.1	n.d.	n.d.
"	Ne15-R	51.9 ± 0.03	42.4 ± 14.2	96.8
"	47-L	50.3 ± 0.1	46.5 ± 7.4	106.3
"	47-P[e]	50.8 ± 0.1	43.2 ± 6.1	98.6
"	47-R	50.6 ± 0.1	43.6 ± 4.4	99.5
"	Blank Agar	—	0.7 ± 0.1	0

[a] Mean per cent G + C determined from 3 or more thermal denaturation curves with standard deviation of mean.

[b] Mean per cent binding determined from 3 or more agar column hybridization preparations with standard deviation of mean.

[c] Group B, fresh isolate.

[d] Group B, laboratory strain.

[e] Group C, fresh isolate.

n.d.: Not determined.

acid from arabinose, dulcitol, fructose, inulin, lactose, mannitol, mannose, raffinose, salicin, sorbitol, or sucrose. Both forms produced catalase and hydrogen sulfide, both hydrolyzed urea and reduced nitrates. Neither form produced indole and neither liquified gelatin.

Thus it is evident that this old and stable L-form is still genetically indistinguishable from and biochemically similar to its parent *Proteus*, and evident too that conversion to a different morphologic form did not produce a detectable change in its species identity.

Using a similar approach, we examined a different genus for relatedness of parents and L-forms. Here, however, the experiments were designed to answer the following additional questions: (1) Do revertant bacterial forms retain the species identity of their respective parent and L-forms? (2) Are fresh isolates of a given species homologous with old laboratory reference strains

of that species? (3) To what extent are different serologic groups of a given species homologous? To answer these questions we used *N. meningitidis*, another Gram-negative organism, but a coccus instead of a rod. Among the meningococci employed were parent, L- and revertant strains, fresh isolates from cases, an older laboratory strain, and serologic group B and group C strains.

As shown in Table 33.1, all of the meningococci and their variants had similar base compositions, which fell within a range of 50.3 to 51.9 per cent G+C.

Agar column hybridizations were performed using strain 55-L DNA-H^3 as the "donor", and unlabeled DNA from the other strains or variant forms in turn as the "recipient". Compared with the homologous reaction between 55-L DNA-H^3 versus 55-L DNA (100 per cent relative homology), the heterologous reactions showed between 96.8 and 114.6 per cent relative homology (Table 33.1).

The results indicate that for these organisms there is no significant loss of species identity, whether the variant is a relatively stable or unstable L-form or a revertant, whether the variant is derived from a fresh isolate or a laboratory culture, or whether the variant is derived from the same or a different serologic group. This high degree of relatedness also indicates that any differences which may exist in the genomes of these variant forms of the same species are too small to be detected by the methods here employed.

In contrast, a different species, *N. subflava*, reported to have a G+C of 50.5 per cent,[1] showed only approximately 25 per cent relative homology with *N. meningitidis*, strain 55-L, and thus was clearly not closely related.

Roberts & Wittler[14] had shown that glucose and maltose utilization, serologic group, and sulphadiazine sensitivity of parents and respective revertant meningococci were identical. In contrast, the L-forms were non-groupable and at times showed only weak acid production from glucose and maltose. Had these meningococcal L-forms been nonrevertable, the loss of group specificity and the paucity of differential enzymatic activities would have made accurate identification by routine diagnostic tests extremely difficult if not impossible. In cases such as this, the value of data derived from the molecular genetic approach to identification is obvious.

Investigation of the relationship between a Gram-positive coccus and the L-form derived from it demonstrated the importance of choosing well-documented parent-L-form pairs as models before attempting to test assumptions concerning the genetic relationship between L-forms and their parents.

We chose for study the Gram-positive species *S. faecalis* F24-P and the stable lysozyme-induced L-form, F24-L, derived in the absence of antibiotics from this streptococcus. According to H. Gooder and J. R. King,* this L-form was passed for some time on serum-free agar before good growth was obtained. Then continuous serial passage of this L-form was required to adapt it to grow in broth. At each agar passage of the L-form, colonies were selected which were capable of growth at progressively lower percentages of agar, until finally a strain, F24-L, was obtained which was capable of growth in broth containing no agar at all.

A comparison of the enzymatic activities of F24-P and F24-L revealed that both parent and L-form produced acid from arabinose, fructose, galactose, glucose, glycerol, lactose, maltose, mannitol, mannose, and trehalose. Both produced ammonia from arginine. Both forms were negative for catalase, hydrogen sulfide and indole production, nitrate reduction, hydrolysis of urea and liquifaction of gelatin. The L-form, however, showed only a very weak acid reaction on salicin, and gave only slight and delayed reduction of triphenyltetrazolium chloride and potassium tellurite, both of which partially inhibited its growth. The parent organism gave strongly positive reactions in these three tests.

Similar nucleotide base ratios were found for F24-P and F24-L, 38.1 and 37.9

* Personal communication.

TABLE 33.2

Relatedness of Streptococcus faecalis *F24-P to Stable L-Form F24-L Compared with Lack of Relatedness to* Streptococcus *MG9**

Radio-active "Donor" DNA	"Recipient" DNA in Agar	% G + C of DNA of "Recipient" [a]	% Labeled DNA Bound [b]	% Relative Homology
F24-P	F24-P	38.1 ± 0.3	59.3 ± 0.9	100
"	F24-L	37.9 ± 0.3	42.4 ± 3.3	71.2
"	Blank Agar	—	0.7 ± 0.3	0
F24-L	F24-L	37.9 ± 0.3	57.2 ± 2.0	100
"	F24-P	38.1 ± 0.3	32.8 ± 2.0	57.0
"	Blank Agar	—	0.5 ± 0.02	0
Strep. MG9	Strep. MG9	39.3 ± 0.2*	50.2 ± 3.0*	100
"	F24-P	38.1 ± 0.3	3.3 ± 0.3	0
"	Blank Agar	—	6.4 ± 2.0*	0

[a] Mean per cent G + C from 3 thermal denaturation curves with standard deviation of mean.

[b] Mean per cent binding determined from 2 or more agar column hybridization preparations with standard deviation of mean.

* Data from McGee and associates[10].

per cent G+C respectively, as shown in Table 33.2. Hybridization experiments using F24-P DNA-H³ as the "donor" and F24-L DNA as the "recipient" showed 71.2 per cent relative homology. The reciprocal hybridization, using F24-L DNA-H³ as the "donor" and F24-P DNA as the "recipient", gave an even lower relative homology, only 57.0 per cent.

The differences in these two strains are perhaps not surprising, considering the manner in which F24-L was derived from F24-P. If F24-L is a "mutant" of F24-P, then the results of hybridization tests indicate that it has undergone rather extensive genetic changes and is an evolutionary product of the bacterium rather than a simple phenotypic variant. On the other hand, it is conceivable that F24-L is not a mutant but, instead, a contaminant picked up during the course of serial selection. If it is a contaminant, then the contaminant must be of a species very closely related to the F24-P strain of *S. faecalis*, as indicated by the finding of partial homology between the two. In contrast, another streptococcus species, strain MG9, with a base ratio of 39.3 per cent G+C,[10] showed no homology with F24-P (Table 33.2). If F24-L is a contaminant, it may represent an instance of cross-contamination at the laboratory bench while working with another related *S. faecalis* strain.

Thus, the choice of organisms to be used for testing the assumptions concerning parent-L-form relationships has to be made with great care and has to take into account the history of the strains employed for testing.

DNA hybridizations, as well as base ratio determinations, have proved useful in our laboratory for demonstrating lack of relatedness between strains purported to be parent-L-form pairs. In this way McGee and associates[10] showed that *Mycoplasma pneumoniae* was not an L-form of *Streptococcus* MG. Rogul and associates[15] showed that neither *Mycoplasma gallisepticum* nor *Mycoplasma gallinarum* were L-forms of *Hemophilus gallinarum*. McGee, Rogul & Wittler[11] pointed out that it is unlikely that all of the mycoplasmas represent permanently stabilized L-forms of bacteria, since the G+C ratios of most *Mycoplasma* species are so much lower than those of most bacterial species. These investigators examined most of the mycoplasma-bacterial pairs proposed as evidencing a relationship between mycoplasmas and bacteria or bacterial L-forms; using genetic techniques, they failed to find any support for such a theory.

Molecular genetic techniques have already been used successfully to define the genus and species of an unidentified microbial agent. In collaboration with our laboratory, O'Malley and associates[12] employed base composition determinations and molecular hybridization to identify the A-1 agent isolated from human icterogenic plasma and formerly believed to be a virus; using genotypic tests only, its species identity as *M. gallisepticum* was established.

On the basis of the foregoing data, the formulation of a systematic approach to identification of stable L-forms is here proposed. The step-by-step procedure is as follows:

(1) Determine the G+C ratio of the unidentified L-form.

(2) From the literature[7] determine which genera contain species having G+C ratios similar to that obtained for the L-form.

(3) Select three or four biochemical reactions which will aid in differentiating the genera chosen in step (2). These may be catalase production, cytochrome oxidase production, hydrolysis of urea, or any other reaction of differential diagnostic value.

(4) Test the L-form for the biochemical activities chosen in step (3) in order to narrow the choice of genera to which the L-form may belong. Several further biochemical tests may be required to narrow the possibilities to one most probable genus.

(5) Considering the source of the L-form, select the species of the genus determined in step (4) to which the L-form may belong. The number of possible species in certain genera may be quite large, as in *Salmonella* or in *Streptococcus*, or the species in the genus may be poorly defined, as in *Corynebacterium*. In such cases, choice of probable species may be narrowed by further biochemical reactions.

(6) For laboratories unequipped to perform DNA hybridizations, serologic examination by complement fixation, gel diffusion, fluorescent antibody or other tests will generally be of most help in identifying the species of the L-form. Also useful at this step will be tests for immunological specificity of extracellular products of the L-form, such as proteins or enzymes specific for the species. Even laboratories equipped for hybridizations will find these methods useful.

(7) Only when all other characterization data show good agreement as to the one most probable species of the L-form, is it worthwhile to confirm the tentative identification by agar column hybridization, which is highly specific but involves considerable work when many organisms need to be tested.

In conclusion, identification of stabilized L-forms is at best a difficult and time-consuming problem. For the present, an approach which utilizes molecular genetic characterization along with biochemical and serologic characterization offers increased opportunities for reaching a precise identification.

SUMMARY

Identification of stable L-forms may be unreliable when phenotypic characterization or serologic analysis alone are employed. Data based on the composition and sequence of base nucleotides of the chromosomal DNA increase the possibility of making an accurate identification of L-forms of unknown parentage. Using *Proteus mirabilis* and its L-form as the model for genetic identity of parent and L-form of Gram-negative species, a similar relationship was found to exist among several *Neisseria meningitidis* strains, their L-forms and revertants, which had similar DNA base ratios and a high degree of homology of base sequences. Thus, on the basis of genetic homology alone, their identification as *N. meningitidis* strains could have been made with certainty. The applicability of these model relationships to L-forms derived from Gram-positive genera requires further investigation, since the species studied to date, *Streptococcus faecalis*, and its L-form showed only partial homology. A step-by-step procedure employing molecular genetic, biochemical and serologic techniques for identifying L-forms is suggested.

REFERENCES

1. Catlin, B. W., and Cunningham, L. S.: Transforming activities and base contents of deoxyribonucleate preparations from various Neisseriae. *J. Gen. Microbiol.* **26:** 303, 1961.
2. Cowan, S. T., and Steel, K. J.: *Manual for the Identification of Medical Bacteria.* Cambridge Univ. Press, London, 1965.
3. Departments of the Army and the Air Force: *Methods for Medical Laboratory Techni-*

cians. TM 8-227—AFM 160-14. U.S. Government Printing Office, Washington, D.C., 1951.
4. Dowell, V. R., Jr., Loper, J. C., and Hill, E. O.: Constancy of deoxyribonucleic acid base composition in the transition of *Sphaerophorus necrophorus* from bacilli to large bodies. *J. Bact.* **88:** 1805, 1964.
5. Falkow, S.: Nucleic acids, genetic exchange and bacterial speciation. *Amer. J. Med.* **39:** 753, 1965.
6. Gooder, H., and King, J. R.: Growth as L colonies of protoplasts of *Streptococcus faecalis* F$_{24}$. *Bact. Proc.:* **71,** 1964.
7. Hill, L. R.: An index to deoxyribonucleic acid base compositions of bacterial species. *J. Gen. Microbiol.* **44:** 419, 1966.
8. Marmur, J., and Doty, P.: Determination of the base composition of deoxyribonucleic acid from its thermal denaturation temperature. *J. Mol. Biol.* **5:** 109, 1962.
9. McCarthy, B. J., and Bolton, E. T.: An approach to the measurement of genetic relatedness among organisms. *Proc. Nat. Acad. Sci. USA* **50:** 156, 1963.
10. McGee, Z. A., Rogul, M., Falkow, S., and Wittler, R. G.: The relationship of *Mycoplasma pneumoniae* (Eaton agent) to *Streptococcus* MG: application of genetic tests to determine relatedness of L-forms and PPLO to bacteria. *Proc. Nat. Acad. Sci. USA* **54:** 457, 1965.
11. McGee, Z. A., Rogul, M., and Wittler, R. G.: Molecular genetic studies of relationships among mycoplasmas, L-forms and bacteria. *Ann. N. Y. Acad. Sci.* In press.
12. O'Malley, J. P., McGee, Z. A., Barile, M. F., and Barker, L. F.: Identification of the A-1 agent as *Mycoplasma gallisepticum*. *Proc. Nat. Acad. Sci. USA* **56:** 895, 1966.
13. Panos, C.: Cellular physiology during logarithmic growth of a streptococcal L-form. *J. Gen. Microbiol.* **39:** 131, 1965.
14. Roberts, R. B., and Wittler, R. G.: The L form of *Neisseria meningitidis*. *J. Gen. Microbiol.* **44:** 139, 1966.
15. Rogul, M., McGee, Z. A., Wittler, R. G., and Falkow, S.: Nucleic acid homologies of selected bacteria, L forms and *Mycoplasma* species. *J. Bact.* **90:** 1200, 1965.
16. Sueoka, N.: Variation and heterogeneity of base composition of deoxyribonucleic acids: a compilation of old and new data. *J. Mol. Biol.* **3:** 31, 1961.

34

Discussion

Drs. Morton Hamburger and A. Frederick Rasmussen, Jr.,
CO-CHAIRMEN.

Drs. Monroe D. Eaton, Harry Gooder, William L. Hewitt,
Gladys L. Hobby, Benjamin M. Kagan, Otto E. Landman,
H. H. Martin, John Z. Montgomerie, Robert G. E. Murray,
James T. Park, Jack L. Strominger

DR. MURRAY: I have a comment in reference to Dr. Hamburger's presentation.* In inducing L-forms in various media, it is important to determine whether there is an antagonism between divalent and monovalent cations. Large amounts of sodium chloride, for instance, might possibly provide strong competition for sites that, for stability, would normally be taken up by divalent cations. It would be important to know, in this instance, whether one is really dealing with hypertonicity or sodium requirement of some metabolic sort, or whether it is competition for some ionic linkage also required for stability.

DR. HAMBURGER: I am sure I do not know the answer; I am not a biochemist. All I can say from our experience is that when we first began out studies we were able to grow L-colonies very well in flasks, and then suddenly, under apparently the same conditions, we would not get the growth; we did not know why. Finally, it turned out that the still in which our distilled water was made had not been cleaned for a while; it was full of concretion. The question arose as to what we were missing. At that point a more knowledgeable person suggested we add magne-

* Pages 221–229.

sium sulfate; from then on we were able to grow L-colonies quite well. Whether this has any relevance to your question, I do not know.

DR. MURRAY: In our laboratory, *Spirillum serpens*, whose cell wall sensitivity I would suspect is similar to that of the *Neisseriae*, will suffer calamitous lysis in aerated broth cultures directly it runs out of calcium. This is potentiated by sodium: addition of sodium chloride results in a quicker calamitous lysis. It is prevented quite specifically by calcium, and not by magnesium. So, it is possible that in your system, for instance, the magnesium sulfate also present is not actually protecting. It would be interesting to know if calcium prevented or reduced the conversion.

Interestingly, when *S. serpens* mutates, as I suppose one might call it—mutation through the loss of the lipoprotein on the surface (the outer 100 Å of the cell wall)—sensitivity to calcium deprivation is also lost. The organism no longer suffers calamitous lysis when calcium runs out. I just mention this as the physiological mechanism.

DR. HAMBURGER: We never studied calcium. We noticed that, in magnesium-containing flasks flooded with spheroplasts from broth cultures, the L-colonies de-

Mg, Ca requirement

veloped distinctly faster than in flasks which did not contain magnesium, even though the number of L-colonies was the same.

DR. MURRAY: Magnesium is essential to the stability of most plasma membranes.

DR. HOBBY: I would like to ask Dr. Hewitt if his group has produced L-forms from organisms resistant, say, to a drug such as one of the tetracyclines, and then has subsequently tried to maintain these L-forms in the presence of other, antibiotic-sensitive organisms. Is there any relationship of protoplasts to the phenomena of drug transfer factor and transfer of drug resistance? It is a very exciting field, and I am curious to know if there is any relationship.

DR. HEWITT: We have not tried to do that. I agree, it is a very exciting proposal.

DR. GOODER: Probably I should not say anything, since we have not done a systematic study of antibiotics. However, we have induced a large number of streptococcal L-forms using a large variety of different antibiotics. Every antibiotic (such as novobiocin, bacitracin, cycloserine and, of course, the penicillins and cephalothins) whose presumed site of action is in the biosynthesis of the streptococcal cell wall has, in fact, induced L-forms. We made a large number of mutants resistant to other antibiotics, such as tetracycline, and every induced L-form was resistant to the antibiotic in the same way as the parent organism.

I was struck by some of the methods being used to test antibiotic sensitivity of the L-forms, the methods which depend upon the diffusion of the antibiotic. All our L-forms have a much slower growth rate than the bacterial culture, and I wonder if some of the presumed sensitivities of the L-form to the antibiotic are not due simply to the fact that the antibiotic has diffused a much greater distance during the time it takes the L-colony to develop and show itself on the culture medium.

DR. KAGAN: I think that is a troubling facet of the entire problem. There is no doubt that what you are saying is true. That is what we tried to approach with

our two different techniques;* we still have no answer. When a clear inhibition area is produced, it shows up quite clearly, and could be due to the antibiotic having had more time to penetrate. This is not the case, however, when the antibiotic is put on the entire plate. But this does not answer your question.

DR. MONTGOMERIE: I cannot give a direct answer, either. However, I would like to point out that we do see very marked differences, and it seems unlikely that these are due solely to different diffusion intervals.

DR. KAGAN: In reference to Dr. Gooder's question, I would further like to state that, with lysostaphin, the differences in the sensitivities of the parent form and the L-form can be of the order of 2 μg as compared with 10,000 μg. This is not accounted for by a diffusion problem.

DR. MARTIN: Dr. Landman, you mentioned massive appearance of L-forms in *Escherichia coli* with penicillin concentration as low as 10 gamma/ml. If I recall correctly, Lederberg & St. Clair[4] noted on the gradient plate that at low concentrations of penicillin there was only spheroplast or large body formation, or formation of organisms unable to reach the L-form stage.

DR. LANDMAN: I said there was parallelism between *Salmonella* and *E. coli*†. This is true, but it does not extend to the aspect of penicillin concentration. The *E. coli* stable L-forms are formed at higher concentrations. The main point, however, is that we made the same findings as Lederberg & St. Clair[4] and, in fact, published them about the same time.[3] But the only strains in which stable L-form formation is observed are mutants of *E. coli*, special mutants which, then, by virtue of a gene mutation, are susceptible to penicillin in such a way that they produce stable L-forms.

DR. STROMINGER: I would like to ask a question that relates to an observation made by Eagle[1, 2] a long time ago, namely that some organisms are killed more

stable forms of E. coli

* See Dr. Kagan's presentation, p. 314.
† Pages 319–332.

rapidly at low penicillin concentrations than at high ones. Lederberg & St. Clair's paper[4] also contains the interesting observation that L-forms do not survive well at low penicillin concentrations on a gradient plate: there is a zone in which no survival of L-forms is seen, and in that zone only mutants without blocked cell wall synthesis survive. Then, at much higher penicillin concentrations, the L-forms do survive. I have no explanation for that phenomenon. Perhaps Dr. Landman would comment on it.

DR. LANDMAN: We have also made that observation, but we have noted that it is not true for all media; it happens on some media—others do not show the L-form-free zone.

We have also made some experiments involving variation of various components, such as the concentration of salt or of agar in the medium. Under certain combinations of circumstances, penicillin seems to stabilize the L-form. My interpretation of this is that the penicillin combines with the cell membrane, where it does its work and acts as a stabilizing agent.

DR. PARK*: I should like to comment on a point that has come up several times during these discussions, namely the origin and nature of stable L-forms. It seems certain and obvious that a process of mutation and selection must occur during the repeated transfer of such cultures, whether the initial mass conversion to L-forms was mediated by penicillin or by lytic enzymes.

It has been stated that the repeated transfer of L-forms in the presence of penicillin selected mutants defective in murein synthesis, and therefore these mutants were stable because they could not revert to the bacterial form. However, to my mind, the selective pressure at work in a population of L-form cells repeatedly transferred in the presence of penicillin is *not* primarily one that selects mutants defective in murein synthesis. On the contrary, it is difficult to see any advantage such cells would have over the

original L-forms growing in penicillin medium. A more understandable pressure at work under these conditions is that which selects L-forms which resist rupture of their membranes for relatively extended periods. I believe the average L-form cell, at least during the first days following mass conversion, lives barely long enough to divide: the balance between survival of the population and death is narrow. Those cells which are "tougher" and hence can survive longer without dividing will be selected relatively rapidly. Obviously, the stable L-forms selected may be the result of multiple mutations or, if recovered without isolating individual colonies at each transfer, may consist of a mixed culture of many different mutants, each of which is better able to preserve cellular integrity than the parent cells.

Dr. Panos presented evidence that the lipid content of certain L-forms is strikingly different from that of the protoplast membranes from their parent bacteria, and he also observed that the membranes of the L-forms seem tougher or more rigid than those of the protoplasts; this could be an example of the type of mutant one would expect to survive. Dr. Rothstein suggested another type which might adapt to extended survival without walls by learning to grow and multiply with a lowered internal osmotic pressure; such cells would be able to withstand their environment without tougher membranes, but it is questionable whether all of their essential enzymes would function effectively and with coordination if the internal ion concentration were reduced markedly. Hence, in my opinion, the most likely "stable" L-form is one such as that observed by Dr. Panos to have a tougher membrane. The principal selective pressure is destruction of the cellular integrity of the fragile L-form or protoplast membrane, and the simplest mutation would be one which made the membrane less fragile. It is quite possible that the resulting alteration of membrane structure would be such that the membranes could no longer form a useful crosslinked murein even though all of the necessary enzymes were still

* Added after the Conference.

present. Hence, phenotypically, these mutants might appear to be cell wall mutants, while in fact, they are probably something quite different.

MYCOPLASMAS, L-FORMS AND EVOLUTION

DR. EATON: I would like to present some aspects of my work which are related to some of this session's presentations.*

L-forms may be intermediates in the evolution of mycoplasmas from bacteria, and this has been given special consideration in relation to *Mycoplasma pneumoniae* and *Streptococcus* M.G. The streptococcus was originally isolated from the lungs in two fatal cases of atypical pneumonia where, we may assume, it was associated with the mycoplasma. The existence of an antigen in common has been demonstrated in several laboratories, but when the streptococcus is changed to its L-form the common antigen is lost. To the present, a relation between the mycoplasma and the streptococcus, evolutionary or otherwise, has not been demonstrated by nucleic acid homology. There is one other approach to this problem which I should like to outline briefly.

The use of biochemical reactions of microorganisms as a basis for taxonomy is fundamental and well known, and should be useful in exploring the relationships between L-forms, bacteria, and mycoplasmas. If the presence or absence of constitutive enzymes reflects the presence or absence of corresponding genes in the L-form and its parent, then there are innumerable biochemical tests, many of them very simple, by which homology can be indicated and possible evolutionary relationships established. Unique metabolic features are of course the most interesting. Table 34.1 lists a few.

Consider first catalase, which is absent from streptococci, pneumococci, anaerobes, and many species of mycoplasmas. The relation of *M. pneumoniae* to anaerobes is at once ruled out because aerobic con-

*Expanded after the Conference.

TABLE 34.1

Metabolic Features that Might Help in Establishing Possible Evolutionary Relationship

	Myco-plasma pneu-moniae	Strepto-coccus M.G.	Strepto-coccus faecalis
Catalase	0	0	0
Aerobic stimulation (glucose)	+	n.d.	+
α Glycerophosphate $\rightarrow H_2O_2$ + lactate	+	0	+
Arginine $\rightarrow$ ornithine, NH_3, ATP	0	+?	+
Methylene blue tolerance (%)	0.02	0.005	0.1

n.d.: Not determined.

ditions in the presence of glucose stimulate growth of this organism, as well as of *Streptococcus faecalis* (taken as a representative of group D) and of *Mycoplasma mycoides*. Most catalase-negative organisms also have deficiencies in, or complete lack of, the cytochrome system, and have instead cyanide-insensitive respiration by flavines or quinones.

Dr. I. E. Low in my laboratory has been interested in the similarities between glycerol utilization by *M. pneumoniae* and group D streptococci. In *S. faecalis*, glycerol enters the triose-phosphate cycle and is oxidized to lactic acid and H_2O_2 with absence of NAD linkage. *M. pneumoniae* also forms measurable quantities of H_2O_2 during aerobic incubation with glycerol, and respiration is markedly stimulated by the addition of catalase or pyruvate, which react non-enzymatically with H_2O_2. Since *Streptococcus* M.G. does not ferment glycerol to lactic acid, this becomes a point where it is not related to *M. pneumoniae*.

Another intriguing set of enzymes is that concerned with the utilization of arginine. There are at least two different pathways by which microorganisms may produce ammonia from arginine. Many species of mycoplasmas, but not *M. penumoniae*, use arginine as a source of energy by way of citrulline, carbamylphosphate, and ATP. This type of arginine metabolism apparently occurs in streptococci and, although *Streptococcus* M.G. produces ammonia, the exact mechanism is not known.

M. pneumoniae is more resistant to methylene blue than most other species of mycoplasmas, and this property is shared by group D streptococci.

Obviously, tests of nucleic acid homology cannot be done with all species of mycoplasmas or supposed stable L-forms against all bacteria, and it is hoped that disclosure of unique metabolic properties such as those discussed will be useful in selecting the organisms most likely to give positive results in such homology measurements.

REFERENCES

1. Eagle, H.: A *paradoxical zone* phenomenon in the bactericidal action of penicillin *in vitro*. *Science* **107**: 44, 1948.
2. Eagle, H., and Musselman, A. D.: The rate of bactericidal action of penicillin *in vitro* as a function of its concentration, and its paradoxically reduced activity at high concentrations against certain organisms. *J. Exp. Med.* **88**: 99, 1948.
3. Landman, O. E., Altenbern, R. A., and Ginoza, H. S.: Quantitative conversion of cells and protoplasts of *Proteus mirabilis* and *Escherichia coli* to the L form. *J. Bact.* **75**: 567, 1958.
4. Lederberg, J., and St. Clair, J.: Protoplasts and L-type growth of *Escherichia coli*. *J. Bact.* **75**: 143, 1958.

IV.
ROLE OF PROTOPLASTS, SPHEROPLASTS AND L-FORMS IN DISEASE

George Gee Jackson
Robert G. Petersdorf
CO-CHAIRMEN

35

The Production of L-Forms of Group A Streptococci in Mice*

Edward A. Mortimer, Jr.

THE UNIVERSITY OF NEW MEXICO SCHOOL OF MEDICINE
ALBUQUERQUE, NEW MEXICO

Sharp in 1954[7] first reported the production of reproducing L-forms from group A streptococci. The technique by which these bacteria were induced to assume the L-form involved the inoculation of streptococci onto a solid medium of high osmolarity containing a gradient of penicillin. After several days' incubation, typical L-form colonies could be identified. Propagation was achieved by the serial transfer of blocks of agar to media containing high concentrations of penicillin. After propagation, reversion to the original strain of group A streptococci was achieved by repeated transfer to penicillin-free media.

Sharp's observations have subsequently been confirmed and extended by others. Employing the penicillin gradient technique many strains of group A streptococci can be converted to the L-form. These forms have been shown to possess most of the characteristics of the organism from which they were derived, except for the ability to construct the mucopeptide portion of the cell wall.[1] Although not all the extracellular enzymes produced by parent bacterium have been studied in relation to the L-form, it is assumed that their production is not altered by loss of the cell wall. In addition, the L-form continues to produce the appropriate M protein[1] and hyaluronic acid† (in the case of encapsulated mucoid strains of streptococci). Production of the group A polysaccharide has not been demonstrated, however. Whether this carbohydrate is antigenically incomplete as a result of its close biochemical relationship with the mucopeptide portion of the cell wall and accordingly not recognized, is not known. Thus, the major and probably the sole defect exhibited by the L-form is failure to construct the mucopeptide skeleton of the cell wall. Without the mucopeptide, the L-form is insusceptible to antibiotics that affect the parent bacterium by interfering with synthesis of the cell wall. Thus the group A streptococcal L-form grows well in the presence of penicillin or bacitracin in concentrations many times greater than those to which the parent bacterium is susceptible.

However, in spite of hypotheses con-

* Studies conducted under the sponsorship of the Commission on Streptococcal and Staphylococcal Diseases, Armed Forces Epidemiological Board, and supported by the Office of the Surgeon General, Department of the Army, Washington, D.C.

Mrs. Dorothy Simon, Miss Ellen Vastine, Mr. Charles Vinocur and Mr. Kevin O'Brien provided technical assistance. Drs. Alan Hinman and Frank Calia participated in some of the studies described.

† Unpublished observations.

cerning possible roles that the L-form might play in group A streptococcal infections, their suppurative and non-suppurative sequelae, and the response to therapy, the participation of the L-form in the natural history of streptococcal infections has not been demonstrated. Thus, their significance, other than as a curious laboratory phenomenon, is not known.

METHODS AND RESULTS

RECOVERY OF L-FORMS FROM INFECTED MICE

A recent observation[5] has provided a model which offers some promise as a means by which the L-form may be studied in relation to possible biologic activities *in vivo*. In the course of attempts to enhance the virulence of two strains of group A streptococci (type 14 and type 3, the Richards strain) by repeated mouse passage, peritoneal exudate and heart's blood from mice succumbing subsequent to intraperitoneal injection were inoculated onto solid media appropriate for the isolation and propagation of L-forms, as well as onto standard bacteriologic medium. The L-form medium comprised brain heart infusion, 2% salt, 10% horse serum, 1000 units of penicillin/ml, and 1.2% agar. From both heart's blood and peritoneal exudate L-forms were recovered, in addition to streptococci on standard media. These L-form colonies were readily propagated by serial transfer, and formed typical fried-egg colonies visible macroscopically. As the two strains of streptococci developed enhanced virulence for mice as a consequence of repeated mouse passage, L-forms were no longer recovered from the mouse infections.

After propagation it was possible to identify the L-forms as indeed being derived from the original streptococcus. This was achieved by demonstrating the production of homotypic M protein by immunodiffusion.[1] In addition, continued serial propagation after withdrawal of penicillin from the medium resulted in reversion of one or more colonies of each L-form strain to the original group A

streptococcus. Subsequent experiments with other M protein types have shown that the ability to assume the L-form *in vivo* in mice is not unique to the two original strains.

After reversion of one of these strains of type 14 L-forms to the parent streptococcus, it was found that this reverted strain displayed a remarkable propensity to assume the L-form after inoculation into mice. Indeed, as many as one L-form colony for every four bacterial colonies has been recovered from inoculated mice. This type 14 streptococcus, designated the PCA strain, has been employed in most subsequent experiments.

Of major importance was the question of whether these L-forms actually were produced in the mouse, or whether the inoculation of profuse streptococci in blood and exudate onto L-form medium resulted in their *in vitro* production by penicillin contained in the medium. The low rate of yield of L-forms by Sharp's gradient technique suggested that this latter mechanism was unlikely; in addition, simultaneous inoculation of cultures into mice and directly onto L-form medium yielded many L-forms from the mice after death, but only rare colonies on the plates inoculated directly.

Final proof that the L-forms were produced in the mice was achieved by growing the L-forms in the absence of penicillin. This was accomplished by differential filtration. Exudate and blood from infected mice were suspended in Todd-Hewitt broth containing 0.6 M sucrose and the suspensions passed through Millipore filters of 0.65 and 0.45 μ pore sizes. It was anticipated that the plasticity and relatively small size of L-form colony-producing units (as small as 0.125 μ compared to 0.80 μ for the streptococcus) would permit some of these smaller forms to pass through the filter, whereas the larger bacterial forms would be retained. The filtrates were inoculated into penicillin-free L-form medium and into other media appropriate for the growth of the parent bacteria. From many of the filtrates of blood and exudate L-forms were recovered on the penicillin-free medium in the absence of streptococci, indicating that they had indeed existed *in vivo* in the mice.

MECHANISM OF PRODUCTION OF L-FORMS *IN VIVO*

Subsequent observations* obtained by sacrificing mice at various intervals following inoculation with the PCA strain indicated that some hours of residence within the mouse were required for conversion of the streptococcus to the L-form. By serial dilutions and quantitation of streptococci and L-forms it was obvious that the appearance of L-forms was not simply a matter of quantitatively more streptococci being present later in the infection. The fact that L-forms usually began to appear only after the infection had existed for some time suggested that their production was the result of some host response, and might represent a stage in the degradation of the streptococcus by the host. Disruption of the cell wall would most likely be accomplished by lysozomal enzymes, chief among which would be glucosaminadase, which would interfere with synthesis of the mucopeptide. Survival, at least transiently, of these fragile forms *in vivo* might depend on some other host factor, such as the polyamines,[2] that might afford protection against osmotic lysis.

Nevertheless, the fact that the L-forms were shown to have been produced *in* the mice does not mean they were produced *by* the mice. Instead, it is possible that they represent variants that occur in the course of multiplication of large bacterial populations. In the usual fluid media of low osmolarity such variants would promptly lyse and be unrecognized. It is conceivable that *in vivo* these naturally occurring variants might be protected against osmotic lysis by some substance provided by the host, such as the polyamines. This mechanism would require no active participation by the host in removal of the cell wall.

Various experiments, designed to test

* Unpublished.

these two alternative hypotheses directly and indirectly, have thus far failed to demonstrate active disruption of the cell wall by processes within the mouse. Most of these experiments have been based on the seemingly logical assumption that active participation by the mouse would entail participation by the reticuloendothelial system. If this assumption were correct, it should be possible to demonstrate alterations in the rates of production of L-forms *in vivo* in mice prepared with substances known to influence the reticuloendothelial system, such as endotoxin, thorotrast, cortisone and stilbestrol.[4, 6, 9]

In all of these experiments, it was necessary to compare the rates of production of L-forms from streptococci in the experimental preparations to rates in control preparations. This was accomplished by pour plate techniques employing serial dilutions in both L-form medium and trypticase-soy agar. The L-form medium in these more recent studies comprised brain heart infusion (Difco), 10% horse serum, 2% salt (0.3 M), 10% sucrose (0.3 M), 1000 U of penicillin per ml, 0.5% yeast (Oxoid) and 1.2% agar. Initial dilutions of peritoneal exudate and heart's blood were made in Todd-Hewitt broth to which sucrose was added in a final concentration of 0.6 M. All pour plates were incubated at 37°C. Streptococcal colonies were counted on the trypticase-soy agar plates after incubation for 48 hours, and L-form colonies were counted after seven days. The rates of production of L-forms were expressed as the number of L-colonies per 10^8 streptococci, and rates from the experimental preparations compared with simultaneous control preparations.

One such experiment is shown in Table 35.1, and represents the effect of 7.5 mg of hydrocortisone intravenously 24 to 36 hours prior to intraperitoneal inoculation of a lethal dose of the PCA strain on the production of L-forms in 20 mice compared to 19 mice who received diluent without hydrocortisone. The table shows no difference between treated and control mice in the rates of production of L-forms.

Similar studies, employing 150γ of

TABLE 35.1

Effect of Hydrocortisone (7.5 mg) on Production of L-Forms of Group A Streptococci by Mice

L-Colonies per 10^8 Streptococci	Number of Mice			
	Heart blood		Peritoneal exudate	
	Cortisone	Control	Cortisone	Control
10^1–10^2	0	0	2	0
10^2–10^3	0	0	5	6
10^3–10^4	7	5	6	7
10^4–10^5	11	9	6	3
10^5 or more	1	5	1	3
Total	19*	19	20	19

* One specimen lost.

Salmonella typhosa endotoxin intraperitoneally immediately prior to inoculation with streptococci, yielded no alteration in L-form production. Likewise, the administration of the same endotoxin in increasing doses at three-day intervals to produce endotoxin tolerance to 450γ resulted in no alteration in rates of L-form production following challenge with the PCA strain, although the mice became strikingly more resistant to the streptococcus. Thorotrast, 0.25 to 0.5 cc, given intravenously from a few minutes to four days prior to inoculation with the PCA strain, failed to influence the rates of L-form production. When given within 24 hours of inoculation with the streptococcus, thorotrast did markedly increase susceptibility to infection. Finally, stilbestrol, which is known to induce hyperplasia of the reticuloendothelial system[6] was given in 0.1 mg doses daily for seven days prior to infection; no effect on the rates of L-form production was recognized.

Table 35.1, in addition to demonstrating no difference between L-form production by hydrocortisone-prepared mice compared to control mice, also indicates the marked variability in the rates of L-form production by mice in the same experiment. Ten thousand or hundred thousand-fold differences are not uncommon; no explanation for these discrepancies is apparent.

Other attempts to influence the rates of production of L-forms by the mice have likewise failed to shed light on the mechanism by which they are produced. Among these are the induction of leukopenia by nitrogen mustard, the production of prior chemical peritonitis, preparation by inoculation with a killed vaccine of the homologous strain of streptococci, and the administration of type-specific antibody.

In other efforts to approach the problem of the mechanism by which these L-forms occurred *in vivo*, various fractions of fresh mouse and human blood and the leukocytes of several species were studied *in vitro*. A four- to eight-hour broth culture of the PCA strain was added to tubes containing varying concentrations of Todd-Hewitt broth and the blood fraction in question. The tubes were incubated at 37°C and rotated eight times per minute to ensure satisfactory mixing as with the bactericidal test.[8] Aliquots were made into pour plates of L-form and standard media at intervals up to four hours, and again at 18 to 24 hours. The rates of L-form production were compared with control preparations in Todd-Hewitt broth. Mouse serum and white cells, human whole blood, serum and white cells, and rabbit blood, peritoneal macrophages and neutrophiles, failed to influence L-form production, although mouse whole blood resulted usually in a hundred-fold increase in numbers of L-forms. From most preparations, including controls, approximately 10^2 L-forms were recovered per 10^8 streptococci; this increase from mouse whole blood represents 10^4 L-forms per 10^8 streptococci. The significance and mechanism of this apparent induction of L-forms at a low rate by mouse blood is not apparent. Finally, the addition of type-specific immune serum to these preparations yielded no alteration in rates of recovery of L-forms.

EFFECT OF PENICILLIN *IN VIVO*

The fact that group A streptococci can be converted to the L-form *in vitro* by penicillin suggested that similar conversion might occur *in vivo*. Three different types of experiments were performed employing the mouse as a model in an effort to determine whether such might indeed occur.

In the first of these experiments, mice were inoculated intraperitoneally with a Type 3 or a Type 6 streptococcus, both known to produce L-forms in mice at a low rate. Procaine penicillin, 3000 units, was given daily subcutaneously following inoculation. The mice were sacrificed at one-day intervals up to four days after infection. No evidence of induction of L-forms by the penicillin was recognized on culture.

In the second set of experiments, advantage was taken of the unique ability of the Type 50 group A streptococcus to produce upper respiratory disease in laboratory mice.[3] Such respiratory infections are transmissible between mice housed in the same or adjacent cages, and are associated with a clinical illness that includes weight loss, lethargy, cervical adenitis and persistently positive throat cultures. Pneumonia, sepsis and death frequently occur. This organism produces L-forms at a low rate when inoculated intraperitoneally into mice. In these experiments mice were inoculated intranasally with 0.1 ml of an eight-hour broth culture of Type 50 streptococci. Daily throat cultures were obtained, employing sterile cotton swabs made from toothpicks, and inoculated onto the surface of sheep blood agar plates and L-form medium containing penicillin. Of 127 mice so inoculated, 82 (64 per cent) developed persistently and markedly positive throat cultures. Fifteen mice were given daily subcutaneous injections of 3000 units of procaine penicillin for periods up to seven days; this therapy resulted in the disappearance of the streptococcus within 24 to 48 hours, as determined by twice-daily throat cultures. From throat cultures of none of these mice, treated or untreated, were Type 50 streptococcal L-forms recovered.

Finally, penicillin was administered to mice with Type 50 streptococcal abscesses of the abdominal wall induced by subcutaneous inoculation two to four days previously. Aqueous crystalline penicillin was administered intraperitoneally one-half to six hours prior to sacrifice and culture of the abscesses of some mice; other mice received 3000 units of procaine penicillin subcutaneously 18 to 24 hours prior to sacrifice. L-forms of the Type 50 streptococcus were recovered from 12 (21 per cent) of 58 mice so treated, but also from three (19 per cent) of 16 untreated control mice. Thus these experiments have failed to demonstrate conversion of group A streptococci in mice as a consequence of the action of penicillin.

DISCUSSION

Many gaps exist in our knowledge of the natural history of group A streptococcal disease, as well as other bacterial diseases. For example, in the case of group A streptococcal disease it is not known how the human host kills the organism. In streptococcal disease and in other bacterial diseases persistence of infection has been demonstrated; explanations for such persistence are not entirely clear. Why penicillin given for approximately ten days is required to eradicate the group A streptococcus from man, in spite of the fact that the organism is extremely sensitive to this antibiotic, is not known. Finally, although it is well established that the group A streptococcus is the causative agent of rheumatic fever and acute glomerulonephritis, the exact mechanism or mechanisms by which these nonsuppurative sequelae are produced has not been determined. These unknowns have stimulated interest in the L-form of bacteria because of the possibility that these forms, devoid of cell wall, might play a role in the natural history of streptococcal and other bacterial diseases.

The present studies have demonstrated that the L-form of the group A streptococcus exists in mice infected with the group A streptococcus. Accordingly, the appearance of L-forms in mice infected with streptococci has provided a model by which it might be possible to study some of these unknowns in the natural history of streptococcal disease.

The first problem examined was that of the mechanism by which the streptococcus was converted to the L-form in the mouse. It seemed logical that such conversion would result from action of lysozomal enzymes elaborated by the cells of the mouse. The initial studies, which indicated that residence of the streptococcus within the mouse was required for some hours prior to the appearance of L-forms, served as further evidence that the inflammatory response was in some way responsible for this phenomenon. Accordingly, *in vivo* studies were undertaken in which mice were exposed to substances known to alter the reticuloendothelial system. These included thorotrast, which blocks the reticuloendothelial system,[4] cortisone, which inhibits the release of lysozomal enzymes,[4, 9] and stilbestrol, which induces hyperplasia of the reticuloendothelial system.[6] The effects of endotoxin administered acutely were also studied; this increases the susceptibility of mice to infections and is probably associated with the release of lysozomal enzymes.[9] Finally, endotoxin-tolerant mice were also studied; endotoxin tolerance inhibits the release of the lysozomal enzymes.[4, 9] None of these techniques altered the production of L-forms by the mice. More recent studies, in which lysozomal enzymes extracted from mouse liver by the techniques of Weissmann & Thomas[9] have been studied *in vitro* in relation to their ability to convert the streptococcus to the L-form, have been unsuccessful, but these studies have been fraught with difficulties both in extracting the lysozomal enzymes and in dealing with the L-form. Finally, various preparations of mouse, human and rabbit blood with and without type-specific antibody have shed no light on how these L-forms are produced.

The fact that active participation by the mouse in the disruption of the cell wall has not been demonstrated in these studies suggests that the mouse may play more of a passive role in the appearance of L-forms *in vivo*. Such a role might well be that of providing some defense for the L-form against osmotic lysis. According to such a concept, the L-forms might be naturally occurring variants which appear in the course of rapid multiplication of streptococci, or perhaps simply dying streptococci.

Other studies employing these mouse infections as a model have similarly failed to show that the streptococcus is converted to the L-form *in vivo* by the action of penicillin, or that persistence of a streptococcal infection in the presence of penicillin is related to the appearance of L-forms.

Thus, it has as yet not been possible to assign a significant role to L-forms in the natural history of streptococcal infections in mice. Whether such a role will be demonstrated by further studies and by improved techniques of isolation and identification remains a subject for conjecture.

SUMMARY

From mice infected with group A streptococci, L-forms of the streptococcus have been recovered. Studies *in vivo* in the mice, employing substances known to modify the reticuloendothelial system, have suggested that this system does not participate in the mechanism by which L-forms are produced. Likewise, *in vitro* studies utilizing blood and blood fractions from mice and other species have not demonstrated L-form production. Finally, the administration of penicillin to mice did not result in increased appearance of L-forms *in vivo* in mice infected with group A streptococci.

REFERENCES

1. Freimer, E. H., Krause, R. M., and McCarty, M.: Studies of L forms and protoplasts of group A streptococci. I. Isolation, growth and bacteriologic characteristics. *J. Exp. Med.* **110:** 853, 1959.
2. Gooder, H.: L-type growth of streptococcal protoplasts. *Bact. Proc.:* 60, 1964.
3. Hook, E. W., Wagner, R. R., and Lancefield, R. C.: An epizootic in Swiss mice caused by a group A streptococcus, newly designated Type 50. *Amer. J. Hyg.* **72:** 111, 1960.
4. Janoff, A., and Zweifach, B. W.: Effect of endo-

toxin-tolerance, cortisone, and thorotrast on release of enzymes from subcellular particles of mouse liver. *Proc. Soc. Exp. Biol. Med.* **114:** 695, 1963.

5. Mortimer, E. A., Jr.: Production of L forms of group A streptococci in mice. *Proc. Soc. Exp. Biol. Med.* **119:** 159, 1965.

6. Nicol, T., Bilbey, D. L. J., Cordingley, J., and Druce, C.: Response of the reticulo-endothelial system to stimulation with oestrogens. *Nature* **192:** 978, 1961.

7. Sharp, J. T.: L colonies from hemolytic streptococci: new technique in the study of L forms of bacteria. *Proc. Soc. Exp. Biol. Med.* **87:** 94, 1954.

8. Stollerman, G. H., Kantor, F. S., and Gordon, B. D.: Accessory plasma factors involved in the bactericidal test for type-specific antibody to group A streptococci. I. Atypical behavior of some human and rabbit bloods. *J. Exp. Med.* **108:** 475, 1958.

9. Weissmann, G., and Thomas, L.: Studies on lysozomes. I. The effects of endotoxin, endotoxin tolerance, and cortisone on the release of acid hydrolases from a granular fraction of rabbit liver. *J. Exp. Med.* **116:** 433, 1962.

36

The Response Observed in Rabbits Following Implantation of Diffusion Chambers Containing L-Forms of Group A Beta Hemolytic Streptococci*

Gary J. Haller and Raymond J. Lynn

UNIVERSITY OF SOUTH DAKOTA SCHOOL OF MEDICINE
VERMILLION, SOUTH DAKOTA

Several workers have implanted diffusion chambers containing viable microorganisms or their products into experimental animals, under the assumption that this technique may represent a valid experimental model.[3, 4] The response of rabbits following the implantation of diffusion chambers containing beta-hemolytic streptococci into their peritoneal cavity was the subject of a previous study.[2] In that study, diffusion chambers containing group A, type 12, strain AR-41, beta-hemolytic streptococci were implanted into the peritoneal cavity of 17 rabbits, five of which received daily injections of 100,000 units of penicillin. Viable streptococci were recovered from seven of the chambers taken from rabbits as long as six months after implantation. However, neither viable streptococci nor streptococcal L-forms could be recovered from the chambers taken from rabbits that received penicillin. Viable organisms could not be recovered from the tissues of the implanted rabbits. No febrile response was observed in any

of the implanted rabbits. It should be noted that the LD_{50} for mice of the organisms recovered from the chambers was increased 300-fold when compared to that of the organisms introduced into the chambers. Significant anti-streptolysin O titers, as high as 2500 Todd units, were observed.

Through these studies it was determined that the optimal Millipore filters used for constructing the diffusion chambers had an average pore diameter of 0.22 μ. It was postulated that the streptococci were too large to penetrate through the filter, so that L-forms of these organisms were possibly the agents responsible for the antibody production attained.

The present study was undertaken to determine if L-forms would retain viability in such chambers; also, to determine if stable L-forms would revert to the bacterial form in such an environment. In addition, the immune response of the rabbits to cellular and extracellular antigens of the L-form was noted.

METHODS AND MATERIALS

The organisms used throughout the present experiments were a group A beta-

* Investigation supported by a Public Health Service research grant, HE-07004, from the National Heart Institute.

hemolytic streptococcus, strain LG1, and its penicillin derived L-form, LG1-L. LG1 was grown in Todd-Hewitt broth (Difco), and LG1-L was grown in brucella broth to which 3% NaCl was added (Difco).

The diffusion chambers were a modification of the Eschenbrenner-Francis chamber.[1] The chambers were ring-shaped and constructed from plexiglass, being 10 mm thick with an outer diameter of 30 mm and an inner diameter of 20 mm. Glass tubing was cemented into a hole drilled into the chambers. Onto both sides of the chambers

Figure 36.1. The diffusion chamber utilized in the present study.

were cemented Millipore filters (Millipore Filter Corp., Bedford, Mass.) with an average pore diameter 0.22 μ. The chambers (Figure 36.1) were sterilized by dry heat, and filled by introducing 1–2 ml of a 24-hour broth culture of LG1 or a 48-hour broth culture of LG1-L through the glass tubing into the chamber; the tubing was then sealed with a flame.

The sterile filled chambers were aseptically implanted into the peritoneal cavity of anesthetized albino rabbits. Twenty seven rabbits were implanted with diffusion chambers containing LG1 or LG1-L according to Table 36.1. In addition, certain rabbits were given 1000 units of penicillin in a single, weekly intramuscular injection for the first four weeks of the implantation period. Also, certain animals were injected intramuscularly with viable LG1 (10 mg protein) plus complete Freund's adjuvant (Difco) four weeks before implantation, and with viable LG1 (10 mg protein) plus incomplete Freund's adjuvant two weeks before implantation (Table 36.1).

The diffusion chambers were left in the rabbits for five to six months. The rabbits were bled by cardiac puncture and sacrificed, after which the spleen, heart, kidneys, and diffusion chamber were removed. The tissues were examined for gross pathology. Sections of the removed tissues were homogenized in a glass tissue grinder

TABLE 36.1
Protocol and Results of Serological Tests

Number of Rabbits	Organism in Chamber	Injected with LG1*	Injected with Penicillin†	No. of ppt. Bands against LG1-L Membrane	No. of ppt. Bands against LG1-L f₁d‡
4	LG1	+	+	2, 2, 2, 2	1, 4, 2, 4
5	LG1	+	−	1, 3, 1, 1, 0	3, 0, 3, 3, —
3	LG1	−	+	0, 1, 1	1, 0, 0
2	LG1	−	−	1, 2	0, 1
4	LG1-L	+	+	2, 1, 2, 2	0, 1, 1, 0
3	LG1-L	+	−	1, 1, —	3, 2, —
3	LG1-L	−	+	1, 1, 1	1, 0, 0
3	LG1-L	−	−	0, 1, 0	0, 1, 0

* Rabbit injected with LG1 plus complete Freund's adjuvant 4 weeks before implantation, and with LG1 plus incomplete Freund's adjuvant 2 weeks before implantation.

† Rabbit receiving 1000 units of penicillin per week.

‡ Ammonium sulphate precipitate of the supernatant fluids of a broth culture of LG1-L.

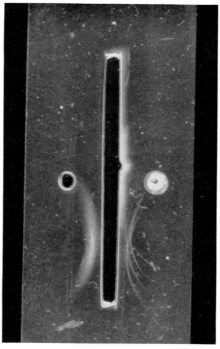

Figure 36.2. The immune response of an immune rabbit implanted with a diffusion chamber containing LG1. *Center trough:* serum; *left well:* LG1-L membrane antigen; *right well:* LG1-L f₁d antigen.

the solubilized membranes against deionized water resulted in a precipitate that would not go back into solution. The LG1-L f₁d fraction was prepared by bringing the supernatant fluid of a centrifuged broth culture of LG1-L to 0.57 saturation with ammonium sulfate; the resulting precipitate was removed by filtration, dissolved in phosphate buffer (pH 7.5), and dialyzed in the cold against running tap water for 18 hours. A 100-fold concentration was achieved.

The immunoelectrophoresis studies were carried out on agar slides. The agar slides were prepared from ion agar No. 2 (Difco) in a barbital buffer at pH 8.2. The antigens, LG-1L membranes, and LG1-L f₁d fraction, were placed in the outer wells and subjected to a current of 40 volts for 10 minutes. The undiluted antiserum was then placed in the center trough. The slides were incubated at room temperature

and 0.1 ml amounts of each tissue and each diffusion chamber content was spread onto plates of blood agar and brucella with 3.5% NaCl. The plates were incubated for 24 to 72 hours, and periodically examined for growth.

EKG's were taken with a Sanborn 500 Viso Cardiette (Hewlitt Packard, Sanborn Div., Waltham, Mass.) previous to experimentation with the rabbits, after the rabbits were injected and implanted, and prior to final cardiac bleeding.

Membrane antigens from LG1-L were prepared according to the modified procedure of Razin.[5] In addition to the procedures mentioned in his paper, the membrane material was treated with RNase and DNase. The membrane material was solubilized in sodium lauryl sulphate (SLS), by adding 0.15 ml of a 0.1 M SLS solution to each ml of membrane material. It should be noted that dialyzing

Figure 36.3. The immune response of a nonimmune rabbit implanted with a diffusion chamber containing LG1-L. *Center trough:* serum; *left well:* LG1-L membrane antigen; *right well:* LG1-L f₁d antigen.

for 24 hours and observed for precipitin bands.

RESULTS

As previously indicated, the diffusion chambers were left in the rabbits for five to six months. In only one of the 27 implant contents examined were viable Gram-positive beta-hemolytic organisms found: the diffusion chamber had been filled with LG1 and implanted into a rabbit which did not receive penicillin or preimplantation injections of LG1. No gross pathology of the removed tissue was observed.

A comparison of the EKG patterns taken before and after implantation did not reveal any gross abnormalities.

As can be seen from Table 36.1, the sera from the rabbits that were injected with LG1 previous to implantation produced a larger number of precipitin bands against the two antigen preparations. The rabbits produced detectable antibodies against three components of the LG1-L membrane antigen and against four components of the LG1-L f_{ld} antigen (Figure 36.2). The sera of rabbits that were not injected with LG1 and contained LG1-L in the diffusion chambers produced single precipitin bands against both antigens (Figure 36.3). No attempt was made to determine the identity of the precipitin bands.

DISCUSSION

The strain of streptococcus used in this study was not re-isolated at the termination of the intraperitoneal implantations as readily as was the type 12, AR-41 strain previously examined. We have been unsuccessful in our attempts to obtain stable L-forms of this strain.

The inability to recover LG1-L from the diffusion chambers may be due to the fragile nature of these organisms. Also, the culture conditions may not have been "sufficiently rich" for growth of the L-forms that have been in a diffusion chamber implanted in an animal for a long period of time.

The fact that detectable antibodies were observed in the sera of rabbits implanted with diffusion chambers containing LG1-L and not injected with LG1 is significant.

Work still to be completed includes the study of sections of the removed tissues utilizing fluorescent antibody techniques and expansion of the serological studies to include, for example, the determination of anti-streptolysin O titers.

SUMMARY

The viability of streptococci in diffusion chambers implanted in rabbits varies with the strain of streptococci employed. L-forms could not be recovered from the chamber contents or tissues of rabbits implanted with diffusion chambers. Rabbits implanted with diffusion chambers containing LG1-L, the penicillin-derived L-form of group A beta-hemolytic streptococcus, strain LG1, produced antibodies directed against the membrane and extracellular antigens of this L-form.

REFERENCES

1. Eschenbrenner, A. B., and Francis, R. D.: Growth of monkey kidney cells in diffusion chambers in mice; effect of poliomyelitis virus. *Fed. Proc.* **15:** 514, 1956.
2. Haller, G. J., and Lynn, R. J.: Immune response of rabbits to streptococci grown in intraperitoneal diffusion chambers. *Bact. Proc.:* **46,** 1965.
3. Kelly, D. K., and Winn, J. F.: Renal lesions produced by group A, type 12, streptococci. *Science* **127:** 1337, 1958.
4. Markowitz, A. S., Armstrong, S. H., and Kushner, D. S.: Immunological relationships between the rat glomerulus and nephritogenic streptococci. *Nature* **187:** 1095, 1960.
5. Razin, S., Morowitz, H. J., and Terry, T. M.: Membrane subunits of *Mycoplasma laidlawii* and their assembly to membranelike structures. *Proc. Nat. Acad. Sci. USA* **54:** 219, 1965.

37

An Immunological Relationship Between the Protoplast Membrane of Group A Streptococci and the Sarcolemma, the Cell Membrane of Cardiac Muscle

Earl H. Freimer and John B. Zabriskie

THE ROCKEFELLER UNIVERSITY
NEW YORK, NEW YORK

Although the available evidence clearly indicates that the Group A streptococcus represents the probable etiological agent of acute rheumatic fever, its role in the pathogenesis of this disease remains obscure. One of the widely considered theories suggests that some individuals become sensitized to one or more streptococcal antigens during an infection with this microorganism, and that the acute rheumatic process stems from the interaction between these antigens and antibodies within the tissues of the host. This concept of hypersensitivity has led to many studies of the antigens of Group A streptococci. In spite of the accumulation of a large body of information about these antigens, however, the pathogenesis of rheumatic fever remains an enigma. No specific antigen has been identified, and the manner by which the inflammatory reaction is invoked and sustained is unknown at this time.

Kaplan[4, 5] has reported that a number of the antisera prepared by immunizing rabbits with cell walls of certain Group A streptococci bound to heart muscle, and that protein-containing extracts of these cell walls blocked the binding of this streptococcal antibody. He suggested that these cell walls contained a "cross-reactive" protein antigen similar in some chemical features but immunologically distinct from streptococcal type-specific M protein. He also detected antibodies cross-reactive with heart muscle in sera obtained from patients either with recent streptococcal infections or with the non-suppurative sequelae of streptococcal infection.[6]

Studies in our laboratory also provided evidence that antibody to a Group A streptococcal antigen reacted with cardiac muscle, and that this heart-reactive antigen was widely distributed among Group A streptococci.[10]

This report contains a description of the immunofluorescent staining of cardiac muscle by this streptococcal antibody, and the results of serological studies which showed that this heart-reactive antigen is present in all strains of Group A streptococci and that it is absent in unrelated Gram-positive cocci. Furthermore, chemical and immunological studies localize this streptococcal antigen in the cell (protoplast) membrane of the Group A streptococcus, and indicate that this cross-reaction represents an immunological relationship between the streptococcal membrane and the sarcolemma, the complex membrane structure of striated muscle cells.

MATERIALS AND METHODS

The strains of streptococci, their serological identification, the preparation of Group C phage-associated lysin, of protoplast membranes, and of cell walls, and the analytical methods used have been described earlier.*

PREPARATION OF FLUORESCEIN-LABELED GLOBULINS

The gamma globulins were isolated from various sera as follows: Each antiserum was dialyzed for 16 hours at 4°C in 0.015 M phosphate buffer (pH 7.1), passed over DEAE-cellulose (Serva), 0.6 mEq/g, at 25°C, and then eluted with the same buffer. To prevent overloading the column, it was important not to add more than 0.8 ml of serum to each gram of DEAE-cellulose. The eluted gamma globulin was concentrated by ultrafiltration in S & S collodion bags, and its purity confirmed by cellulose acetate paper electrophoresis.

At 4°C, the solution containing 15 mg of gamma globulin/ml was brought to pH 9.5 by the addition of 0.1 N NaOH. Crystalline fluorescein isothiocyanate, 0.03 mg/mg of protein, was added slowly while the globulin solution was stirred continuously. During the first two hours of the reaction the pH was maintained between 9.2 and 9.5 by means of a Radiometer type PHM 28 titrator 11. The vessel was then stoppered, and the reaction allowed to proceed for 18 hours without pH control.

Following coupling of the globulin, unconjugated fluorescein isothiocyanate was removed by passage through a Sephadex G-25 column which had been equilibrated with 0.05 M phosphate-buffered saline (pH 7.5). Each ml of conjugated globulin, containing 15 mg of protein, was absorbed with 8 mg of a rabbit liver powder to remove nonspecific fluorescence, and stored at 4°C.

* See paper by E. H. Freimer, pp. 279–292.

TISSUE SPECIMENS

The tissues used in the immunofluorescent studies were obtained at surgery from individuals with inactive rheumatic heart disease or with congenital heart defects. Biopsy specimens from the left auricular appendages or from ventricular myocardium were quickly frozen to −70°C within 60 minutes of surgical removal and stored at −70°C in a CO_2 box. Representative sections of frozen as well as of formalin-fixed tissues were stained with hematoxylin and eosin. In addition, sections were prepared from biopsies of heart, lung, liver, uterus, spleen, intestine, and synovia obtained either at surgery or at necropsy from patients dying of unrelated diseases.

IMMUNOFLUORESCENT STAINING TECHNIQUES

Representative sections cut at 4 or 6 $m\mu$ at −20°C in a cryostat, were fixed for two minutes in acetone, and washed twice in 0.05 M phosphate-buffered saline (pH 7.5). After removal of excess moisture, the sections were stained by one of the following methods.

Direct Technique

Each tissue section was covered with several drops of fluorescein-conjugated globulin, and incubated for 30 minutes in a moist chamber at 25°C.

Indirect Technique

Each section was incubated with unlabeled rabbit or human antiserum for 30 minutes as above. After two five-minute washes with buffered saline, fluorescein-conjugated sheep anti-rabbit or rabbit anti-human IgG globulin was applied. Then the section was incubated for an additional 30 minutes.

Following either procedure, the stained sections were washed twice in phosphate-buffered saline for five minutes each, mounted in glycerol buffered at pH 7.5, and examined. Although minor variations in the intensity and degree of staining were observed, both the direct and the indirect techniques produced essentially the same pattern of fluorescent staining.

FLUORESCENCE MICROSCOPY

Sections were examined with a Reichert "Biozet" microscope, using a HBO-200 mercury lamp with a red excluding filter as the ultraviolet light source. In crucial experiments, serial photomicrography was employed; each section was photographed under identical exposure conditions, and contact prints of these serial photomicrographs were used to evaluate the degree and intensity of immunofluorescent staining.

SPECIFIC ABSORPTION TECHNIQUE

In a typical experiment using the direct staining technique, a solution containing fluorescein-labeled antibodies to membranes of Group A streptococci was diluted to a concentration that still produced bright staining of representative heart sections. Weighed amounts of antigen were added to 0.2 ml aliquots of this dilute globulin solution, and each mixture was incubated, first at 37°C for 60 minutes and then at 4°C for 18 hours. As a control, 0.2 ml of the same globulin solution was incubated without any antigen. After centrifugation, a portion of each supernatant was applied to a heart section. The sections then were incubated, washed, and examined by the methods described above.

ISOLATION OF SARCOLEMMAL SHEATHS

A "normal" human heart, obtained at autopsy and preserved after rapid freezing at −60°C, was defrosted. After grossly trimming away most of the connective tissue and fat, the ventricular myocardium was minced into small blocks and suspended in cold 0.05 M $CaCl_2$. This suspension was chopped in a Waring blendor at 0°C for 15 seconds, and then filtered through fine mesh cheese cloth.

The fine sediment in the filtrate was collected by centrifugation, washed several times with cold 0.025 M NaCl, and incubated at 37°C in this dilute salt solution for 30 minutes. After further washing at room temperature, the particulate material was resuspended in distilled water; at this point marked swelling occurred. Following several additional washes with water, the pellet decreased in volume, and on resuspension appeared granular. The material then was washed with phosphate-buffered saline until the wash was free of any substances that gave a reading at 260 or 280 mμ. Finally, after several rinses in distilled water, the pellet was lyophilized. Approximately 100 g of heart muscle yielded 3.5 g of a light brown granular powder.

RESULTS

NATURE OF THE IMMUNOFLUORESCENT STAINING OF CARDIAC MUSCLE WITH GROUP A STREPTOCOCCAL ANTIBODY

When a section of human heart tissue is incubated with rabbit antiserum to Group A streptococci, streptococcal antibody is bound to the cardiac muscle cells. If fluorescein-labeled antibody is used, this antigen-antibody reaction can be visualized by fluorescence microscopy.

A distinctive pattern of immunofluorescent staining is seen, in which the bright apple-green fluorescence of the muscle fibers stands out in contrast to the blue autofluorescence of unstained connective tissue. Although fluorescent staining patterns are better reproduced in color, good contrast can be obtained in a black-and-white photograph. One such pattern with diffuse staining of the sarcoplasm is illustrated in Figure 37.1A. When a serum without heart-reactive antibody is incubated with cardiac tissue, the myofibers remain unstained and appear dark brown (Figure 37.1B).

In some sections, such as the one shown in Figure 37.1C, the cross-striations of cardiac muscle are clearly outlined, at times creating a scalloped effect along the margin of the myofiber. The most intense staining is found in the region of the sarcolemma, the complex membrane structure which surrounds the muscle cell (Figure 37.2). Although this observation suggested that the sarcolemma is the site at which the streptococcal antibody was bound, precise definition has not been obtained at the limit of resolution of fluorescence microscopy.

The immunofluorescent staining reaction

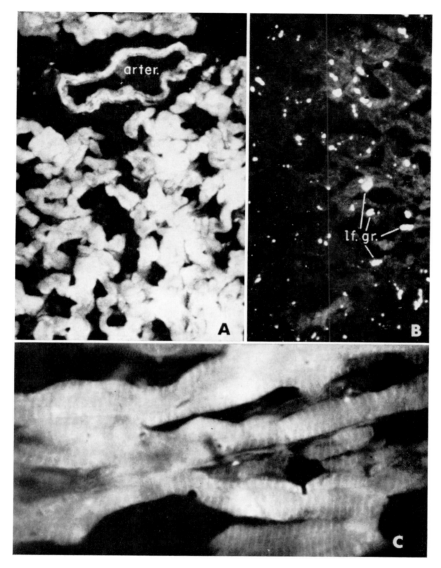

Figure 37.1. *A:* Immunofluorescent staining of cardiac tissue showing diffuse sarco-plasmic staining; a small arteriole (*arter.*) is also stained. This section was incubated first with unlabeled rabbit antiserum to membranes of Group A streptococci, and then with fluorescein-tagged sheep anti-rabbit globulin; the specimen was a left auricular appendage from a patient undergoing surgery for mitral valvular disease. The black open spaces are artifacts due to sectioning ($\times$ 277). *B:* The absence of specific fluorescence when another section from the heart specimen shown in *A* was incubated with antiserum that did not contain heart-reactive antibody; the bright granular areas (*lf. gr.*) represent lipofuschin granules ($\times$ 277). *C:* Cross-striational staining pattern in a longitudinal section of cardiac muscle from a left auricular biopsy specimen of an individual with rheumatic heart disease; fluorescein-labeled antimembrane globulin was used ($\times$ 691). (From Zabriskie & Freimer.[10])

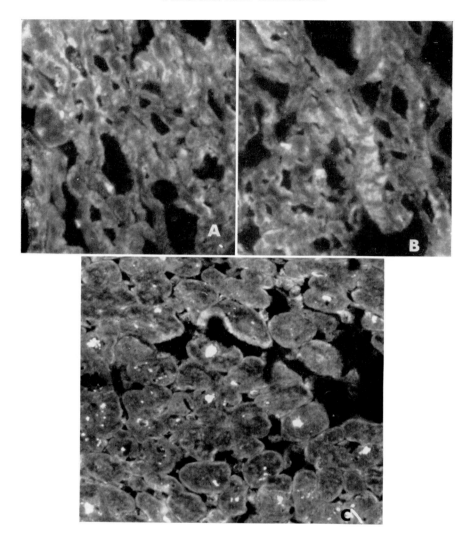

Figure 37.2. Demonstration of sarcolemmal staining by antisera to membranes of Group A streptococci, using the indirect staining technique ($\times$ 1000). *A* and *B:* Longitudinal sections of muscle cells from the left ventricle of a 4-year-old child who died of leukemia. *C:* Cross-section of muscle cells from the left auricle of another patient with rheumatic heart disease. (From Zabriskie & Freimer.[10])

was not limited to cardiac muscle, for specimens of skeletal muscle obtained from a number of different voluntary muscles also bound streptococcal antibody. In general, smooth muscle cells did not react, but the layer of smooth muscle in the media of the endocardium, and smooth muscle elements in the medial wall of medium-sized arterioles in other areas of the body as well as those in the heart, stained brightly when labeled streptococcal antibody was applied. Staining of such an arteriole in heart muscle is seen in Figure 37.3. Although arterioles always stained in sections of such tissues as the synovial lining of joint spaces, the other cellular elements of this tissue as well as those of liver, spleen, and portions of the genitourinary tract did not react. In contrast to this tissue specificity, the reaction of strep-

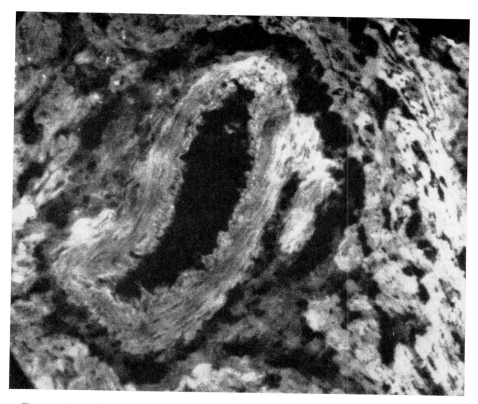

Figure 37.3. Direct immunofluorescent staining of the smooth muscle layer of an arteriole, as well as of the striated muscle in a section from a biopsy of the left auricle of a nonrheumatic human heart; the fluorescein-labeled globulin was prepared against protoplast membranes of Group A streptococci ($\times$ 250). (From Zabriskie & Freimer.[10])

tococcal antibody with muscle cells was not species specific, and heart sections from normal rabbits or from normal guinea pigs showed the same staining patterns as those from human hearts.

DISTRIBUTION OF THE HEART-REACTIVE ANTIGEN AMONG HEMOLYTIC STREPTOCOCCI

Turning to an investigation of the streptococcal antigen involved in the reaction with heart tissue, a study of its distribution within the various groups of hemolytic streptococci was begun. As the distribution of this antigen among the many serological types of Group A streptococci was of special significance, rabbit antisera to a wide variety of Group A streptococcal types, in addition to those representing most of the other streptococcal groups, were tested. Antisera to other Gram-positive cocci were used as controls. Since whole killed bacterial suspensions were used for immunization, each serum contained antibodies directed against many of the cellular antigens. However, specific antisera were also prepared to the protoplast membrane and to cytoplasmic materials. The presence of heart-reactive antibody in each serum was determined by both the direct and indirect fluorescent staining techniques, and the intensity of each staining reaction was graded from 4+ to 0.

The average intensity of immunofluorescent staining reactions between a large series of bacterial antisera and heart sections are recorded in Table 37.1. These data clearly demonstrate that the heart-staining antibody was present in antisera to Group A and A variant streptococci. Although the intensity varied from one serum

TABLE 37.1

Demonstration of the Heart-Staining Antibody in Antisera to Group A Streptococci[*]

Rabbit Antisera to Whole Cells of	Number of Sera	Immunofluorescent Reactions		
		Number positive	Number negative	Intensity of staining[a]
Hemolytic strepto-cocci				
Group A	48[b]	47	1[c]	2+/3+
A var.	3	3	0	2+/3+
B	4	0	4	0
C	6	4	2	1+/2+
D	4	0	4	0
E	3	0	3	0
F	6	1[d]	5	+
G	6	0	6	0
H	2	0	2	0
L	1	0	1	0
M	1	0	1	0
N	1	0	1	0
Staphylococcus aureus	1	0	1	0
Staphylococcus albus	1	0	1	0
Diplococcus pneumoniae	2	0	2	0
Pre-immune serum controls	15	0	15	0

[a] These results represent the average staining reaction of each antiserum after absorption with rabbit liver powder.

[b] The 48 group antisera were unabsorbed, and represented 21 different serological types as well as two strains, J17A4 and S43 glossy, that had no type-specific M protein.

[c] This serum was prepared with strain B514, originally isolated from a mouse infection.

[d] This serum was prepared with strain H127 isolated from a human throat infection.

[*] Data from Zabriskie & Freimer.[10]

to another, 50 unabsorbed Group A and A variant antisera representing 21 different serological types produced strong staining reactions. Only one Group A serum, prepared with strain B514 originally isolated from a mouse infection, failed to stain the heart sections. This immunofluorescent reaction evidently did not involve antibody to type-specific M protein, since a variety of serological types as well as Group A strains that contained little or no M pro-

tein produced identical reactions. Furthermore, six antisera prepared by Dr. Eugene Fox[2] to highly purified M protein antigens failed to react with the heart sections.

In contrast to Group A antisera, only a few of the other group-specific antisera showed positive reactions. These reactions, mainly with Group C antisera, were weaker in intensity than those of Group A. The antisera to the other groups of hemolytic streptococci and to the other Gram-positive cocci failed to react at all.

When sera prepared by immunization with purified protoplast membranes[3] were examined for the presence of heart-staining antibodies, the results were even more striking. All of the antisera to Group A streptococcal membranes produced extremely bright (4+) staining patterns. In contrast, antisera to membranes from other streptococcal groups as well as from other Gram-positive cocci did not react. The results of several of these studies are recorded in Table 37.2.

These immunofluorescent studies show that antisera to Group A streptococci contain an antibody which reacts with cardiac tissue, and indicate that this antibody is formed in response to an antigen localized in the membrane of the streptococcal cell.

TABLE 37.2

Immunofluorescent Reactions which Demonstrate the Heart-Staining Antibody in Antisera to Membranes of Group A Streptococci[*]

Rabbit Antisera to Membranes of	Number of Sera	Immunofluorescent Reactions		
		Number positive	Number negative	Intensity of staining
Hemolytic Strepto-cocci				
Group A	15	15	0	4+
C	2	0	2	0
D	3	0	3	0
Streptococcus viridans	2	0	2	0
Staphylococcus aureus	1	0	1	0
Pre-immune serum controls	15	0	15	0

[*] Data from Zabriskie & Freimer.[10]

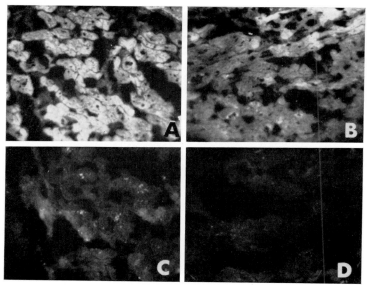

Figure 37.4. Quantitative absorption of heart-reactive antibody by increasing weights of antigen. This fluorescein-labeled globulin was prepared against whole Group A streptococci. The sections of heart muscle were from the left auricle of another patient with rheumatic heart disease. Each section was photographed under identical conditions ($\times$ 200). *A:* Bright (4+) staining produced by the unabsorbed globulin. *B* and *C:* Progressive removal of heart-staining antibody. *D:* Absence of staining (0) after this antibody had been completely removed. (From Zabriskie & Freimer.[10])

SPECIFIC ABSORPTION STUDIES DEMONSTRATING THE LOCALIZATION OF HEART-REACTIVE STREPTOCOCCAL ANTIGEN IN THE CELL MEMBRANE

In light of the indications that heart-reactive antigen was part of the streptococcal membrane, the ability of various streptococcal cellular components to absorb heart-staining antibody from Group A streptococcal antisera and from membrane antisera was examined.

The degree of absorption of heart-reactive antibody by a given weight of an antigen was evaluated by comparing the intensity of the fluorescent reaction produced by an absorbed globulin with that of an unabsorbed globulin. An example of quantitative absorption of heart-reactive antibody by increasing weights of antigen is shown in Figure 37.4. The brightest intensity (4+) of staining (Figure 37.4A) was produced by unabsorbed globulin. Partial absorption of heart-reactive antibody resulted in decreased staining (Figure

37.4, B and C); Figure 37.4D shows the absence of staining (0) that resulted when all of the antibody had been removed.

Antigenic fractions were obtained from strains representing many of the serological groups of hemolytic streptococci, and from strains of *Streptococcus viridans* and *Staphylococcus aureus*. Lyophilized preparations of cell walls and membranes from each strain, and preparations of cytoplasmic material and whole cells from several strains were examined for the presence of antigens capable of absorbing heart-reactive antibody.

The results summarized in Table 37.3, demonstrate the complete absorption of heart-reactive antibody by membranes of Group A streptococci. In most experiments, absorption with as little as one mg of purified membrane abolished the staining reaction. Membranes from 35 strains of Group A and A variant streptococci, representing 14 different serological types and several non-typeable strains, proved

TABLE 37.3

Absorption of Heart-Reactive Antibody by Membranes of Group A Streptococci*

Antigens Prepared from	Number of Strains	Absorption with							
		Whole cell		Cell wall		Cell membrane		Cytoplasmic material	
		wt. (mg)	Int.	wt. (mg)	Int.	wt. (mg)	Int.	wt. (mg)	Int.
Hemolytic Streptococci									
Group A	33	10	2+	5	+/2+	1	0	10	4+
A var.	3	10	2+	5	+/2+	1	0	10	4+
C	4	10	4+	10	4+	5	2+	10	4+
D	3			10	4+	10	4+		
E	1			10	4+	10	4+		
F	1			10	4+	10	4+		
G	2			10	4+	5	2+		
Streptococcus viridans	2			10	4+	10	4+		
Staphylococcus aureus	1			10	4+	10	4+		
Unabsorbed globulin control			4+		4+		4+		4+

Int. = Intensity of the immunofluorescent staining reaction after absorption.

Group A membranes used were prepared from the following types: 1, 3, 4, 5, 6, 12, 14, 19, 22, 24, 26, 30 and 50 and several non-typeable strains. Of the 33 strains tested, only one, A236 (a strain isolated from mice) failed to absorb the heart-reactive antibody.

* Data from Zabriskie & Freimer.[10]

equally effective in removing this antibody. Only the membranes from a Group A strain originally isolated from a mouse infection failed to block the fluorescent staining reaction.

Although membranes from some strains of Group C and Group G streptococci partially absorbed the immunofluorescence, at least 5 mg of these membranes were necessary to produce 50 per cent inhibition (2+). Membranes from the other streptococcal groups and from the Gram-positive cocci produced no detectable decrease in imunofluorescence, although as much as 10 mg of antigen was added to the antibody globulin.

Absorption with either 5 mg of cell walls or 10 mg of whole cells from Group A streptococci did significantly reduce the intensity of staining (2+). As the cell membrane represents about ten per cent of the dry weight of the streptococcus, it seems likely that the absorption of the heart-staining antibody by whole cells is a reflection of the presence of the cell membrane. This concept is supported by serological

evidence which has shown that almost all sera prepared against whole cells of Group A streptococci contained membrane antibodies.[10]* On the other hand, the absorption of heart-reactive antibody from membrane antisera by cell walls was perplexing.

However, chemical and immunological studies demonstrated that all of our preparations of "purified" Group A streptococcal cell walls contained a considerable proportion of cell membrane (at times as much as 40 per cent). Thus, the absorption of heart-staining antibody by streptococcal cell walls might be explained by persistence of contaminating membrane antigens. To examine the significance of this membrane contamination, the insoluble residues obtained by enzymatic lysis of a number of cell wall preparations were studied both chemically and serologically.

Treatment of the cell walls with Group C phage-associated lysin, a muramidase which splits bonds in the mucopeptide of the cell wall, leads to solution of almost 80 per cent of the wall. The soluble ma-

* See paper by Freimer (p. 279).

terial contains 96 per cent of the cell wall sugars, rhamnose and glucosamine, while the insoluble residue has a chemical composition similar to that of streptococcal protoplast membranes and quite distinct from that of the original cell wall preparation.

Absorption studies which compared the effectiveness of equal weights of original cell wall preparation, soluble and insoluble fractions of enzyme treated walls, and protoplast membranes in removing the heart-staining antibody from streptococcal antisera, showed that as little as one mg of insoluble residue was as effective as protoplast membranes in abolishing all immunofluorescent reactivity. This insoluble residue, representing only one-fifth of the weight of the cell wall, was more than five times as active as the wall in quenching fluorescence. The soluble fraction of the wall did not contain membrane antigens and did not absorb heart-reactive antibody. Thus it is evident that the absorptive capacity of cell wall is due to that portion of the cell membrane which remains associated with the wall during the isolation process.

A SARCOLEMMAL FRACTION FROM CARDIAC MUSCLE WHICH REACTS WITH STREPTOCOCCAL ANTIBODY

As the sarcolemma seemed to be the part of the cardiac muscle cell which stained with streptococcal antibody, an investigation of this structure was begun. A fraction, isolated from human heart muscle by modification of a method used to obtain the sarcolemma of skeletal muscle,[8] was found by phase contrast microscopy to consist largely of flattened cross-striated sheath-like structures. When these sheaths were examined by electron microscopy (Figure 37.5A) the cross-striation was still present but the cytoplasmic structures usually seen in a section of mammalian cardiac muscle (Figure 37.5B), were absent. In addition, these "sarcolemmal sheaths" appeared chemically similar to the sarcolemma of skeletal muscle;[7] they contained less than one per cent nucleic acid, 70 per cent protein, and 15 per cent lipid.

The cross reaction between streptococci and heart tissue was supported by the fact that as little as one mg of these sarcolemmal sheaths absorbed the heart-staining antibody from streptococcal antisera. HCl extracts of sarcolemma were also active in blocking this reaction. Treatment of sarcolemmal sheaths with collagenase or defatting did not alter the ability of the residues to absorb heart-staining antibody. Furthermore, antisera prepared by Rothbard & Watson[9] to various mammalian collagens did not stain the heart sections, and antisera to streptococcal membranes used in this study did not stain collagen in the immunofluorescent test system employed by Rothbard & Watson.

These experiments suggested that neither collagen nor lipid was involved in the serological reaction between streptococci and sarcolemma, since the streptococcal-related antigen remained after removal of these components. It is likely that the sarcolemmal residue still contained the so-called amorphous fraction, considered to be in part a mucopolysaccharide complex; immunochemical studies of this fraction of the sarcolemma are in progress. Although the experimental evidence is preliminary, it seems possible that the immunological cross-reaction described in this report involves a "membrane structure" of cardiac muscle as well as the cell membrane of Group A streptococci.

HEART-REACTIVE ANTIBODY IN HUMAN SERA

The recognition that rabbit antibody to protoplast membranes of Group A streptococci is capable of binding to cardiac muscle suggested that similar antibodies might be found in the serum of patients with uncomplicated streptococcal infections and with acute rheumatic fever. When serum of several patients with any of these two disorders was examined, the presence of heart-reactive antibodies was confirmed. Furthermore, these human sera produced bright immunofluorescent staining patterns indistinguishable from those that occurred with antisera to streptococcal membranes.

To establish the extent to which heart-staining antibodies were present in diseases other than those of streptococcal

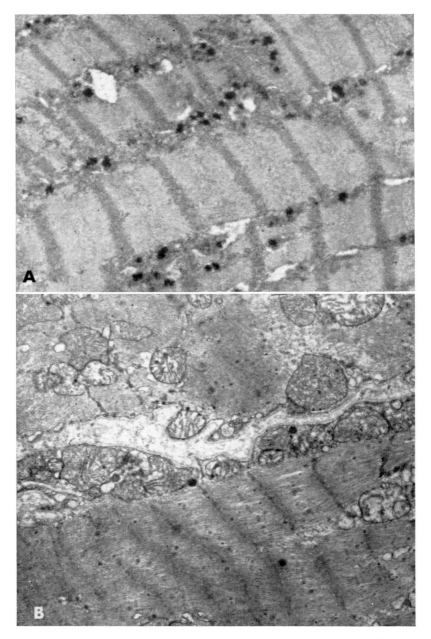

Figure 37.5. Electron micrographs of thin sections stained with uranyl acetate ($\times$ 11,680). *A:* Section through "sarcolemmal sheath" isolated from human ventricular muscle; the presence of cross-striations and the absence of other intracellular structures is apparent; this section was further stained with lead. *B:* Section through "normal" human ventricular myocardium; the typical intracellular organization can be seen.

origin, serum samples were collected from several hundred individuals with a number of different clinical disorders. As undiluted serum from a number of "healthy" individuals bound to cardiac tissue, each sample of serum was tested at a dilution of 1:5 to eliminate "nonspecific" staining. The presence of heart-reactive antibody in these sera was determined by the indirect immunofluorescent staining technique. Using this method, the intensity of each staining reaction was graded from 4+ to 0. For each clinical disorder, the average of the individual staining reactions was established; these data are recorded in Table 37.4.

It is evident that sera from more than 80 per cent of individuals with either a streptococcal infection or with rheumatic fever contained an antibody which reacted with human heart tissue. In contrast, not one serum from 55 individuals with a clinical disorder involving a gamma globulinopathy produced a heart-staining reaction. Furthermore, although half of the sera of individuals with rheumatic heart disease, and all of the sera of patients who had undergone cardiac surgery for repair of scarred valves or a congenital defect, stained intensely the heart sections, these heart-reactive antibodies were different from those present in the serum of acute rheumatic fever, as shown by absorption studies.

Although sera from the group of patients with acute rheumatic fever generally gave staining reactions four times more intense than those from the group with an uncomplicated streptococcal infection, sera from several patients with rheumatic fever produced weak (1+) staining, while a few sera from patients with a streptococcal infection produced extremely bright (4+) staining. These observations were based on serum dilutions of 1:5, and with further dilution of the serum it was noted that the individual variations within each group tended to disappear. Indeed, at a dilution of 1:10, none of the sera from patients with a simple streptococcal infection produced staining.

These results suggested that patients who developed acute rheumatic fever had higher titers of heart-reactive antibody than those with uncomplicated streptococcal infections. To investigate this concept, sera from a carefully controlled patient population were examined. During an epidemic of scarlet fever among recruits at the Great Lakes Naval Training Center in 1944, sera were obtained from a large

TABLE 37.4

Demonstration of Heart-Reactive Antibody in Sera from Individuals with Streptococcal Infections, Acute Rheumatic Fever, and Rheumatic Heart Disease

Clinical Disorder	Number of Patients	Per cent with Antibody	Intensity of Staining*
Streptococcal infection	38	81	+
Acute rheumatic fever	80	87	4+
Rheumatic heart disease	50	47	1+/2+
Post-cardiotomy	12	100	3+/4+
Lupus erythematosus	20	0	0
Rheumatoid arthritis	15	0	0
Multiple myeloma	10	0	0
Sarcoidosis	10	0	0

* These results represent the average of the individual staining reactions for each clinical disorder. The staining reaction is graded from 0 (no staining) to 4+ (maximum brightness).

number of patients in whom the clinical diagnosis of scarlet fever had been supported by microbiological and serological studies. These sera were collected from each patient on admission to the hospital and at weekly intervals thereafter. The sera and clinical records of several hundred of these patients have been preserved in our laboratory. This set of serial bleedings of patients from a single epidemic of scarlet fever occurring among young adult males in an era prior to the general use of antimicrobial agents has proved invaluable in further evaluation of the levels of heart-reactive antibodies in acute rheumatic fever.

From this series of scarlet fever patients it was possible to select two comparable groups. Group 1 was composed of individuals who subsequently developed typical rheumatic fever. Group 2 contained individuals who did not develop rheumatic fever. Two serum samples were chosen from each patient's file. The first serum had been drawn within two weeks of the onset of scarlet fever in both groups. The second serum had been collected from patients in Group 1 at the onset of rheumatic fever, and at a comparable time from patients in Group 2. Serial dilutions of each serum were prepared, and the staining reactions

Table 37.5

Heart-Reactive Antibody Titers in Sera of Scarlet Fever Patients With and Without Subsequent Rheumatic Fever

Clinical Disorder	Number of Patients	Onset of Scarlet Fever*			Onset of Rheumatic Fever†			Average ASO Titer
		Serum dilutions						
		1:5	1:10	1:20	1:5	1:10	1:20	
Scarlet fever with rheumatic fever (Group 1)	20	3+	2+	0	4+	2+	+	700
Scarlet fever without rheumatic fever (Group 2)	20	2+	+	0	+	0	0	260

At each dilution of serum, the results represent the average of 20 individual staining reactions The intensity of the staining reaction is graded from 0 (no staining) to 4+ (maximum brightness).

* Serum samples obtained within 14 days of onset of scarlet fever.

† Serum samples obtained at onset of rheumatic fever.

produced by the 1:5, 1:10, and 1:20 dilutions were observed. For each dilution of serum, the average of 20 individual staining reactions was calculated both for Group 1 and for Group 2. These data are recorded in Table 37.5. It can be seen that, at the onset of scarlet fever, the group of patients who eventually developed rheumatic fever (Group 1) had titers of heart-reactive antibody twice as high as the group without rheumatic fever (Group 2). Furthermore, at the onset of rheumatic fever the titers of Group 1 were still rising, while those of Group 2 had already fallen off.

The average ASO response of each group is included in Table 37.5, and the higher average titers in the group that developed rheumatic fever is consistent with the reported findings of many other studies.[1] On the other hand, a number of the patients in this study with ASO titers of more than 1000 had no detectable heart-reactive antibodies and did not develop rheumatic fever.

The presence of high titers of heart-reactive antibody in the serum of patients at the onset of acute rheumatic fever led to an investigation of the persistence of these antibodies. In this study, serum samples were collected weekly from patients during the acute and convalescent stages of a rheumatic attack, and tested for the presence of heart-reactive antibody at dilutions of 1:5, 1:10 and 1:20. Monthly serum

samples from each of 39 patients, most of whom had been followed at the Rockefeller University Hospital for periods from six months to five years following the initial attack of rheumatic fever, were examined in this manner. The average of the staining reactions observed in each group of serum dilutions was calculated.

In Figure 37.6, these results are plotted against the time following the onset of the acute rheumatic process. It can be seen that the highest titers of heart-reactive antibody occur during the first two months, and that after the third month of the disease the level of antibody gradually declines. At the end of three years, only a weak (1+) reaction remains at a 1:5 dilution. Unless a streptococcal infection or a recurrence of rheumatic fever occurred during this period, the vast majority of the patients had little or no detectable heart-reactive antibody at the end of four to five years. Examination of several sera drawn up to ten years after the initial attack of rheumatic fever were also unreactive.

By means of absorption studies, a clearer understanding of the nature of the various heart-staining antibodies was obtained. These experiments were performed by the same method used to absorb heart-reactive antibodies from rabbit antisera to protoplast membranes. The bright (4+) staining reaction of 15 sera from patients with acute rheumatic fever was completely absorbed with as little as one mg of either

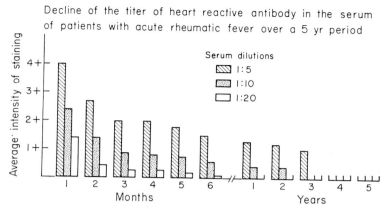

Figure 37.6. The titer of heart-reactive antibody in the serum of patients with acute rheumatic fever followed up to 5 years after the onset of the rheumatic process. Each bar represents the average of 39 individual staining reactions for a group of serum dilutions.

streptococcal protoplast membranes or human cardiac sarcolemmal sheaths. In contrast, as much as 10 mg of protoplast membranes failed to absorb the antibody present in ten sera from patients with chronic rheumatic heart disease, and in six sera from patients with heart who had just undergone cardiac surgery. In all 16 sera the heart-reactive antibodies were absorbed with 1–2 mg of the sarcolemma.

DISCUSSION

The existence of an immunological relationship between the hemolytic streptococcus and mammalian tissue is now well established.[4, 5, 6, 10] In the studies reported here, antisera to Group A and A variant streptococci from a wide variety of serological types were shown to contain an antibody which reacted with heart muscle. Not only did the cardiac myofibers stain with the fluorescein-labeled streptococcal antibody, but smooth muscle present in the endocardium and in the media of arterioles also reacted. Although intense staining was observed in the region of the sarcolemma, exact localization of the antibody-binding site within the muscle cell was not possible.

Heart-reactive antibody was found in most Group A and A variant and some Group C antisera, but was not present in sera to other streptococcal groups and other Gram-positive cocci. Antisera to streptococcal membranes produced extremely bright staining of cardiac tissue, an indication that the cell membrane was the site of the antigenic determinant of the heart-reactive antibody. These findings, coupled with the experimental evidence reviewed below, clearly showed that this antigen was indeed a unique property of the cell membrane of the Group A streptococcus.

First, antisera to purified membranes of Group A streptococci, free of cell wall and cytoplasmic constituents, had high titers of heart-reactive antibody; in contrast, antisera to membranes from other streptococcal groups and other Gram-positive cocci did not react with heart tissue. Second, this immunofluorescent staining reaction was extinguished by absorbing the antisera either with small amounts of purified Group A streptococcal membranes or with soluble antigenic extracts of these membranes. Third, not only do streptococci of Groups A, C, and G have a number of biological characteristics in common, but their membranes are immunologically related to each other.[3] Thus, the detection of heart-reactive antibody in a number of Group C antisera was not surprising, and its absorption from Group A sera by membranes of Groups C or G lends further credence to localization of the antigen within the cell membrane.

Finally, antisera absorbed with cytoplasmic material still stained brightly, and although absorption with cell walls of Group A streptococci did appear to inhibit immunofluorescent staining, even the purest of cell wall preparations were shown to contain large amounts of cell membrane. After the cell wall preparation was dissolved with a muralytic enzyme, the insoluble residue, chemically and serologically very similar to the cell membrane, absorbed the heart-staining antibody, while the soluble portion of the cell wall did not. This experiment was the final link in the chain of evidence which pointed to the streptococcal membrane as the locus of this heart-reactive antigen.

The recognition that rabbit antisera to Group A streptococci contained a heart-reactive antibody led to the detection of similar antibodies in the serum of patients with uncomplicated streptococcal infections and with rheumatic fever. Specific absorption studies have demonstrated that these antibodies are related to the streptococcal membrane as well as to the sarcolemma of human cardiac muscle. In contrast, the heart-reactive antibody present in sera of patients with myocardial damage can only be absorbed with sarcolemma. These findings suggest that there are at least two heart-reactive human antibodies, one reactive with antigens common to both the Group A streptococcal membrane and the sarcolemma, the other reactive with a sarcolemmal antigen unrelated to the streptococcus.

Neither the significance of the immunological relationship between Group A streptococci and mammalian muscle cells nor the exact nature of the specific antigens is known. However, the appearance of a heart-reactive antibody in response to a streptococcal infection is obviously of great interest, and the presence of high titers of this antibody may prove of value in the diagnosis of acute rheumatic fever. Although the information about the nature of this antibody and its possible role in the pathogenesis of rheumatic fever is fragmentary, the discovery that a bacterial cellular membrane is immunologically related to a cell membrane structure of mammalian tissue may prove to be of broad biological significance.

SUMMARY

By means of the immunofluorescent staining technique, antisera to a wide variety of serological types of Group A and A variant streptococci were found to contain an antibody which reacted with mammalian striated muscle, both skeletal and cardiac, as well as with smooth muscle in the endocardium and in the media of arterioles. Similar heart-reactive antibodies were not present in antisera to most other groups of hemolytic streptococci and to other Gram-positive cocci. Chemical and serological studies clearly pointed to the cell (protoplast) membrane of the Group A streptococcus as the locus of the antigenic determinant of this heart-reactive antibody. In addition, studies suggested that the reaction between this streptococcal antibody and cardiac tissue represented an immunological relationship between the sarcolemma, the membrane of a mammalian muscle cell and the cell membrane of a bacterium, the hemolytic streptococcus. Finally, a similar antibody has been found in the sera of patients with uncomplicated streptococcal infections, and in higher titer in those individuals with acute rheumatic fever.

REFERENCES

1. Anderson, H. C., Kunkel, H. G., and McCarty, M.: Quantitative antistreptokinase studies in patients infected with Group A hemolytic streptococci: a comparison with serum antistreptolysin and gamma globulin levels with special reference to the occurrence of rheumatic fever. *J. Clin. Invest.* **27**: 425, 1948.
2. Fox, E. N., and Wittner, M. K.: The multiple molecular structure of the M proteins of group A streptococci. *Proc. Nat. Acad. Sci. USA* **54**: 1118, 1965.
3. Freimer, E. H.: Studies of L forms and protoplasts of group A streptococci. II. Chemical and immunological properties of the cell membrane. *J. Exp. Med.* **117**: 377, 1963.
4. Kaplan, M. H.: Immunologic relation of streptococcal and tissue antigens. I. Properties of an antigen in certain strains of group A streptococci exhibiting an immunologic

cross-reaction with human heart tissue. *J. Immunol.* **90**: 595, 1963.

5. Kaplan, M. H., and Meyeserian, M.: An immunological cross-reaction between group-A streptococcal cells and human heart tissue. *Lancet* **1**: 706, 1962.

6. Kaplan, M. H., and Svec, K. H.: Immunologic relation of streptococcal and tissue antigens. III. Presence in human sera of streptococcal antibody cross-reactive with heart tissue; association with streptococcal infection, rheumatic fever, and glomerulonephritis. *J. Exp. Med.* **119**: 651, 1964.

7. Kono, T., Kakuma, F., Homma, M., and Fukuda, S.: The electron-microscopic structure and chemical composition of the isolated sarcolemma of the rat skeletal muscle cell. *Biochim. Biophys. Acta* **88**: 155, 1964.

8. McCollester, D. L.: A method for isolating skeletal-muscle cell-membrane components. *Biochim. Biophys. Acta* **57**: 427, 1962.

9. Rothbard, S., and Watson, R. F.: Immunologic relations among various animal collagens. *J. Exp. Med.* **122**: 441, 1965.

10. Zabriskie, J. B., and Freimer, E. H.: An immunological relationship between the Group A streptococcus and mammalian muscle. *J. Exp. Med.* **124**: 661, 1966.

38

Role of L-Forms in Staphylococcal Infection*

Benjamin M. Kagan

CEDARS-SINAI MEDICAL CENTER
AND UCLA SCHOOL OF MEDICINE
LOS ANGELES, CALIFORNIA

L-phase variants of bacteria, characterized by absence of usual cell walls, have been known for over 30 years. They lack rigidness and uniform shape and appear, rather, as variously shaped particles of "naked" protoplasm, sometimes called spheroplasts or protoplasts.

Evidence suggesting the possible infectious nature of L-phase bacteria has appeared in the literature with increasing frequency.[1-3, 8, 11-15, 18-20, 27, 35, 39, 42, 43]

Overt infection and subsequent death of egg embryo and test animals challenged with bacterial L-phase organisms have resulted in isolation of "parent" organisms.[6, 8-10]

Streptococcus faecalis L-forms were reported in two cases in which septicemia became increasingly severe during antibiotic therapy. Routine blood cultures were repeatedly negative.[27]

Godzeski and associates[8] reported isola-

tion of staphylococcal L-forms from 11 patients with past histories of chronic staphylococcal infections. The L-forms reverted to "parent" staphylococci after continued subculture.

Charache & Kaslick[3] reported finding protoplasts in the tissues of ten patients (*Staphylococcus aureus* in five: one in endocarditis, two from pus, two from pyarthrosis; one *Staphylococcus albus* in pyarthrosis; one *S. faecalis* in sepsis; one *Hemophilus influenzae* in pyarthrosis; one *Listeria monocytogenes* in meningitis; and one unidentified Gram-positive rod in septicemia).

Wittler and associates[42, 43] reported that a corynebacterium persisted as a "transition form" in a patient with bacterial endocarditis following antibiotic therapy. She reported that some of these forms resembled L-phase growth in their colony and morphological characteristics. She also reported[42] the isolation of transitional and L-forms, possibly of the streptococcus, from the blood during attacks of rheumatic fever. All patients were receiving penicillin. G. Kagan[21] reported isolation of streptococcal L-forms from blood of patients with "rheumatism" and endocarditis.

Guze & Kalmanson[12] reported the persistence of "protoplasts" of *S. faecalis*

* The author wishes to thank Mrs. Shakila Hasan for her untiring efforts in the laboratory studies, Dr. Chun I. Wang of the Children's Hospital of Los Angeles for her superb cooperation in the study of patients with cystic fibrosis of the pancreas at that hospital, and Dr. Kenneth Elconin, who directed the clinical work involved in the patients with chronic osteomyelitis.

following penicillin therapy in enterococcal pyelonephritis.

Gutman and associates[11] reported isolation of L-forms from the urine of 15 per cent of patients with chronic bacteriuria. Urine samples were mixed with sucrose to provide osmotic stability and then passed through a 0.45 μ filter to exclude classic bacteria. L-forms were found with and without the presence of classic bacterial forms and in the presence and absence of antibiotic therapy. When L-forms isolated from the urine reverted to classic bacteria, the latter were found to be identical with the original infecting organisms.

G. Kagan, in her review[20] of literature on pathogenicity of L-forms, cited many references between the years 1949 and 1959 implicating L-forms of a number of bacteria in disease processes. There appears to be considerable variability in the pathogenicity of different strains of L-forms. She concluded that L-forms and their reversion occur not only *in vitro* but *in vivo*, and that L-forms are found in some diseases of man characterized by relapses.

The facts that the Eaton agent which causes atypical pneumonia is a PPLO, and that L-forms of some bacteria may be important in the pathogenesis of human disease[7, 22-26, 28-32, 36-38, 40, 41] further stimulated our desire to study the L-phase variants of staphylococci. The tendency of staphylococcal disease to persist and to recur is well known.

MATERIAL AND METHODS

Control media were plain blood agar in plates and plain brain heart infusion agar and broth (Difco).

Medium for induction or for maintenance of non-stable L-forms was Salt Serum Methicillin Agar (SSMA): 30.0 g brain heart infusion agar (BHI, Difco) 33.5 g sodium chloride, 580.0 ml distilled water; autoclaved at 121°C at 15 lb pressure for 15 minutes and cooled to 50°C in a water bath; to this were added 150 ml of heat-inactivated sterile human serum, and methicillin to a final concentration of 500 μg/ml.

The human serum was prepared from citrated plasma obtained from the hospital blood bank and prepared for use by one hour of heat inactivation at 56°C, refrigeration for 24 hours, centrifugation in an International refrigerated centrifuge (25,000 rpm) for one hour, and sterilization by Seitz filtration. Whole plasma or whole blood has been used by others in place of serum, but we prefer serum because then the agar is more clear and colonies are more readily observed.

The SSMA medium described above was used to maintain L-forms when a state of stability was desired for further studies of an individual strain. An increased concentration of methicillin and repeated transfers were sometimes required in order to obtain a stable L-form culture. The stable L-strains were then maintained on media without antibiotic (see SSA below).

The antibiotic-free medium for L-forms was Salt Serum Agar (SSA), prepared in the same way as SSMA, but without methicillin.

Liquid medium for L-forms was Salt Serum Broth (SS): 36.5 g brain heart infusion broth (Difco), 56.0 g sodium chloride, and 965.0 ml distilled water, also autoclaved at 121°C and 15 lb pressure for 15 minutes and cooled to 50°C in a water bath. Human heat-inactivated sterile serum (250 ml), prepared as described for SSMA above, was then added.

Our success with broth cultures of L-forms has made it possible to demonstrate coagulase and hemolysin activity of both stable and non-stable L-forms. Among other advantages gained by use of this liquid culture is prolonged viability (up to 60 days, or approximately twice as long as by the agar block seeding method).

We called L-forms those we saw in colonies with L-form morphology which later reverted to typical coccal colonies. We also observed classic colonies of *S. aureus* in L-form media, but none in control media, and these we called "L-forms" on the assumption that they had reverted after passing through the L-phase, and therefore required L-form media. Sometimes we saw typical G-form colonies and these were recorded as such; these G-forms have been previously described by us and others.[17, 44]

RESULTS

This report includes systematic studies done between December 18, 1964, and October 31, 1966; 312 cultures on 201 patients are included. Of these, 62 were cultures of bone from 51 patients with chronic osteomyelitis, and 116 were cultures of sputum from 54 patients with proven cystic fibrosis of the pancreas. Prior to December, 1964, an approximately equal number of cultures of human tissues were studied, none of which revealed staphylococcal L-forms. However, in one patient with cystic fibrosis of the pancreas who died during that period of time, typical L-form colonies were found in a lung culture obtained at autopsy; this culture was not maintained because it was lost in the process of staining with the Dienes methylene blue technique.[4, 5]

With the exception of those from patients with cystic fibrosis of the pancreas, it is very easy to report on all the cultures: most of them were negative for staphylococcal L-forms. In one leukemic patient all specimens from the blood and a rib were sterile, yet staphylococci were grown after some delay from SS broth but not from control media. From another leukemic patient, staphylococci were likewise grown from SS broth after some delay, but not from control media. When these staphylococci were then inoculated into control media, they grew readily. One might speculate that these were L-forms which eventually reverted, and therefore we called them "L-forms".

One patient with cervical adenitis of several weeks' duration yielded a pure culture of *Pseudomonas* L-forms. Two patients with leukemia yielded blood cultures positive for L-forms of diphtheroids; in one of the latter, the culture was also positive for diphtheroid L-forms from the thymus gland and the bone marrow, both obtained during life.

The data from patients with cystic fibrosis of the pancreas are more convincing. Of the 116 cultures of sputum from 54 patients, 33 cultures from 13 patients

revealed either L-forms, "L-forms", or G-forms as described above. In eight of these cultures from four patients, typical L-form colonies were observed before they reverted to classic coccal colonies. In three cultures from two patients, G-colonies were observed, which later reverted to classic coccal colonies. One of the latter patients also had L-colonies as well as G-colonies. In 22 cultures from 28 patients, "L-form" growth, as defined above, was found. If it were not for the definite evidence of L-forms in some of these cultures, one might be somewhat skeptical in evaluation of these "L-forms", one reason being the fact that the high salt content of the L-form media might inhibit growth of *Pseudomonas*, so common in this sputum, thus permitting observation of classic coccal colonies which might otherwise not be seen; it is not possible at this time to evaluate the role of this factor. We plan now to add polymyxin to an additional control plate in the hope of depressing the growth of *Pseudomonas* and thus to observe whether classic coccal colonies will appear in the absence of the high salt content of the L-form media.

In one patient, G-forms were found twice. In two patients, L-form colonies were found twice over a period of two weeks and five months, respectively. One of these is of special interest because her course suggests the possibility that L-forms might not only explain persistence or recurrence of staphylococcal disease, but also might be pathogenic themselves under certain circumstances. This is a seven year-old girl (Figure 38.1) who was known to have cystic fibrosis since six months of age. She had extensive pulmonary pathology. She had been receiving continuous antibiotics for a long period of time. On this admission, she was 6½ years old and considered to be critically ill. Her temperature curve was septic in nature. Because her previous sputum cultures revealed *S. aureus* and *Pseudomonas*, she was given polymyxin B by aerosol and intravenously, and methicillin intravenously. Her clinical condition became worse; her fever remained unchanged. Several observers at this time thought she was pre-

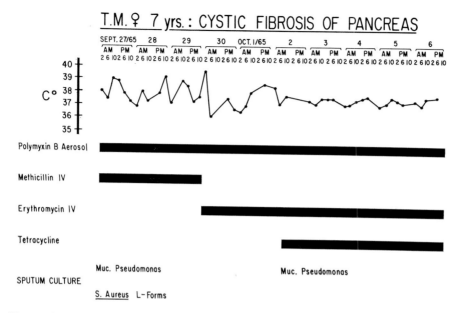

Figure 38.1. Course of a case of cystic fibrosis of the pancreas which suggests pathogenicity of L-forms.

terminal. Sputum obtained on the day after admission was found to show no classical *S. aureus* but numerous colonies of morphologically typical L-forms, which later reverted to typical *S. aureus* colonies. The L-forms grew only on L-form media, both solid and broth, and no *S. aureus* appeared on routine control media. Once reversion occurred, however, these colonies of staphylococci grew readily on control media as well as on L-form media.

The methicillin in this case was discontinued, and intravenous erythromycin given. Her response was dramatic. Her temperature became normal and she responded clinically. A few days later, because of a slight rise in temperature and anxiety over the fact that she had been so critically ill, tetracycline was also given intravenously. Her temperature became normal soon thereafter and remained so. She was discharged within a week and has remained in much better condition. It is of interest, however, that we were able to culture typical L-forms from her sputum five months later in spite of the fact that she had been receiving erythromycin orally over this entire period. The reason

for continuing erythromycin administration was that we had previously found that L-forms of staphylococci were quite sensitive to this antibiotic, as they are also to tetracycline, oleandomycin and lincomycin.

We had hoped to find staphylococcal L-forms in two other circumstances, but were not successful. The first, a situation easy to recognize clinically, is that of the patient (or of the family), who has recurrent episodes of staphylococcal disease. These patients, when treated with effective penicillin agents, often become clinically free of staphylococcal disease only to have the disease return within a matter of weeks after treatment has been discontinued. These recurrences are often of the same phage type. It was theorized that during the intervals between active episodes of staphylococcal disease the organism might be present in the L-form. We have now studied 14 families in which recurrent disease was proven.

In each of these there had been repeated episodes of staphylococcal disease after a number of courses of various antibiotics, mostly oxacillin. Each time the patients would improve with oxacillin, only to have the infection recur. To be admitted to this study the patient must have had at least three recurrences of proven staphylococcal disease. Based upon the theory cited above we chose to give a course of ten days of oxacillin followed by a seven-day course of tetracycline. We chose tetracycline for this experiment, rather than erythromycin or lincomycin, because the parent forms are not infrequently also sensitive to either of these agents. We were primarily interested at this time in testing the basic theory. Therapy was given to every person in the home and also to any cats or dogs in the house. Briefly, in 11 of the 14 experiments thus far, this program has been successful. The follow up periods for 12 of these experiments range from 16 to 30 months. The three failures occurred in this group of 12 as follows: One patient did not follow the course of oxacillin directly with the starting dose of tetracycline; there was a lapse of 24 hours. Another failure occurred in a family situation in which we learned later of probable irregularity in administration of the drugs. The third failure occurred quite recently after a two-and-a-half year interval following the experimental approach. At this time two members of the family developed infection due to beta hemolytic streptococci, and at the same time a few pustules appeared on the skin which revealed staphylococci. The longest period of freedom from infection (30 months) was in a patient with an extensive burn who, prior to this experiment, had spent eight consecutive months in the hospital because of numerous recurrent episodes of staphylococcal infection.

Although the clinical response is impressive, we have not been able to support the theory by laboratory evidence. Cultures were taken from the nose and throat and from active lesions during the pre-experimental period and during administration of the oxacillin. None was positive for L-forms.

A somewhat similar situation is well known in chronic osteomyelitis. The onset may be with a definite acute staphylococcal osteomyelitis. This infection may go on for years and, at various times after the initial cultures, repeat routine type of cultures often no longer reveal the staphylococcus. It was thought that here we might have an opportunity to demonstrate L-forms. Although we have attempted this in 62 cultures from 51 patients with chronic osteomyelitis, no L-forms have been found.* Based on the theory that persistence of this condition was caused by L-forms, we gave patients courses of lincomycin, since this drug is known to achieve good concentrations in bone and is very effective against staphylococcal L-forms. The clinical results, to be reported elsewhere by Dr. Elconin, have been impressive. Our failure to demonstrate L-forms in this disease does not rule out the possibility of their presence. It may well be that some modifications of our culture technique are needed, and we are currently experimenting with this.

SUMMARY

We have demonstrated L-forms of staphylococci in the sputum of patients with cystic fibrosis of the pancreas. We have found staphylococcal L-forms and L-forms of other bacteria in a few other situations. We have not been able to demonstrate staphylococcal L-forms in tissues of patients with other recurrent staphylococcal disease or in chronic osteomyelitis.* It may be that modifications of the technique used will be more successful in demonstrating these forms in the latter or other situations.

The demonstration of staphylococcal "L-forms" in 24 per cent, direct visualization of L-forms in seven per cent, and presence of G-forms in a few of the patients with cystic fibrosis of the pancreas suggest that this is an important aspect of the chronicity and persistence as well as recurrence of staphylococcal infection in this disease. On the basis of limited clinical experience it would appear that

---

* Since the presentation of this paper, "L-forms" have been found in one case of chronic osteomyelitis.

attention to this aspect may be of importance to the survival of some of these patients.

REFERENCES

1. Brier, G., Ellis, L., and Godzeski, C. W.: Survival *in vivo* (in ovo) of L-phase bacteria. *Ann. N. Y. Acad. Sci.* **79**: 854, 1960.
2. Carey, W. F., Muschel, L. H., and Baron, L. S.: The formation of bacterial protoplasts *in vivo*. *J. Immunol.* **84**: 183, 1960.
3. Charache, P., and Kaslick, D.: Isolation of protoplasts in human infection. *Clin. Res.* **13**: 293, 1965.
4. Dienes, L., and Sharp, J. T.: The role of high electrolyte concentration in the production and growth of L forms of bacteria. *J. Bact.* **71**: 208, 1956.
5. Dienes, L., and Weinberger, H. J.: The L forms of bacteria. *Bact. Rev.* **15**: 245, 1951.
6. Edward, D. G. ff.: Biology of the pleuropneumonialike organisms. *Ann. N. Y. Acad. Sci.* **79**: 305, 1960.
7. Edwards, J., and Panos, C.: Streptococcal L forms. V. Acid-soluble nucleotides of a group A *Streptococcus* and derived L form. *J. Bact.* **84**: 1202, 1962.
8. Godzeski, C. W., Brier, G., Griffith, R. S., and Black, H. R.: Association of bacterial *L*-phase organisms in chronic infections. *Nature* **205**: 1340, 1965.
9. Godzeski, C. W., Brier, G., and Pavey, D. E.: Bacterial L-phase growth as a possible complicating factor in certain bacteriological procedures. *Life Sci.* **1**: 565, 1962.
10. ———: L-phase growth induction as a general characteristic of antibiotic-bacterial interaction in the presence of serum. In: *Antimicrobial Agents and Chemotherapy—1962* (J. C. Sylvester, Ed.). American Society for Microbiology, Ann Arbor, 1963: p. 843.
11. Gutman, L. E., Turck, M., Petersdorf, R. G., and Wedgwood, R. J.: Bacterial variants in urinary tract infections. *J. Pediat.* **67**: 909, 1965.
12. Guze, L. B., and Kalmanson, G. M.: Persistence of bacteria in "protoplast" form after apparent cure of pyelonephritis in rats. *Science* **143**: 1340, 1964.
13. Hannoun, C., Vigouroux, J., Levaditi, J., and Nazimoff, O.: Études des formes L des bactéries appareus spontanément *in vivo*. III. Histopathologie comparée des lésions provoquées par la bactérie normale et par ses formes modifiées. *Ann. Inst. Pasteur* (Paris) **92**: 231, 1957.
14. Jordan, D. C.: Effect of chalcomycin on protein synthesis by *Staphylococus aureus*. *Canad. J. Microbiol.* **9**: 129, 1963.
15. Kagan, B. M.: Staphylococcal L-forms—ecologic perspectives. *Ann. N. Y. Acad. Sci.* **128**: 81, 1965.
16. Kagan, B. M., and Martin, E. R.: On the site of inhibition of *Staphylococcus aureus*: studies of the effect of chalcomycin on parent forms and L phase variants. In press, 1966.
17. Kagan, B. M., Martin, E. R., and Stewart, G. T.: L form induction of naturally occurring methicillin-resistant strains of *Staphylococcus aureus*. *Nature* **203**: 1031, 1964.
18. Kagan, B. M., Molander, C. W., and Weinberger, H. J.: Induction and cultivation of staphylococcal L forms in the presence of methicillin. *J. Bact.* **83**: 1162, 1962.
19. Kagan, B. M., Molander, C. W., Zolla, S., Heimlich, E. M., Weinberger, H. J., Busser, R., and Liepnieks, S.: Antibiotic sensitivity and pathogenicity of L-phase variants of staphylococci. In: *Antimicrobial Agents and Chemotherapy—1963* (J. C. Sylvester, Ed.). American Society for Microbiology, Ann Arbor, 1964: p. 517.
20. Kagan, G.: The problem of the pathogenicity of L-form bacteria; review of literature. *Klin. Med.* (Moscow) **39**(3): 12, 1961.
21. Kagan, G. Y.: L-forms of β-haemolytic streptococcus and their pathogenetic role. In: *VIII International Congress of Microbiology* (Abstracts), 1962: p. 125.
22. Klieneberger-Nobel, E.: Filterable forms of bacteria. *Bact. Rev.* **15**: 77, 1951.
23. ———: Micro-organisms of the pleuropneumonia group. *Biol. Rev.* **29**: 154, 1954.
24. ———: *Pleuropneumonia-Like Organisms (PPLO): Mycoplasmataceae.* Academic Press, New York, 1962.
25. Marston, J.: Cultivation of staphylococcal L forms in a liquid medium. *J. Bact.* **81**: 832, 1961.
26. ———: Observations on L forms of staphylococci. *J. Infect. Dis.* **108**: 75, 1961.
27. Mattman, L. H., and Mattman, P. E.: L forms of *Streptococcus fecalis* in septicemia. *Arch. Intern. Med.* (Chicago) **115**: 315, 1965.
28. Mattman, L. H., Tunstall, L. H., and Rossmoore, H. W.: Induction and characteristics of staphylococcal L forms. *Canad. J. Microbiol.* **7**: 705, 1961.
29. Panos, C.: Streptococal L forms. IV. Comparison of the metabolic rates of a *Streptococcus* and derived L form. *J. Bact.* **84**: 921, 1962.
30. Panos, C., and Barkulis, S. S.: Streptococcal L forms. I. Effect of osmotic change on viability. *J. Bact.* **78**: 247, 1959.

31. Panos, C., Barkulis, S. S., and Hayashi, J. A.: Streptococcal L forms. II. Chemical composition. *J. Bact.* **78**: 863, 1959.

32. ———: Streptococcal L forms. III. Effects of sonic treatment on viability. *J. Bact.* **80**: 336, 1960.

33. Pease, P.: Evidence that *Streptobacillus moniliformis* is an intermediate state between a corynebacterium and its L-form or derived PPLO. *J. Gen. Microbiol.* **29**: 91, 1962.

34. Pease, P., and Bisset, K. A.: Effect of parasitism on Gram-positive bacteria, with reference to the origin of certain types of virus. *Nature* **196**: 357, 1962.

35. Pease, P., and Laughton, N.: Observations on *Corynebacteria* and related pleuropneumonia-like organisms (PPLO). *J. Gen. Microbiol.* **27**: 383, 1962.

36. Prozorovsky, S. V.: Conditions for the formation of stabilized cultures of L-forms of pathogenic staphylococci and their biological properties. *Zh. Mikrobiol. Epidemiol. Immunobiol.* **30**: 117, 1959.

37. Schönfeld, J. K.: "L" forms of staphylococci; their reversibility; changes in the sensitivity pattern after several intermediary passages in the "L" phase. *Antonie Leeuwenhoek* **25**: 325, 1959.

38. ———: "L" forms of staphylococcus. II. Studies on the morphology of the transformation and on the reversibility. *Antonie Leeuwenhoek* **27**: 139, 1961.

39. Tulasne, R., and Lavillaureix, J.: Mécanisme de l'action pathogène d'une forme L des bactéries d'origine vibrionniene. *C. R. Soc. Biol.* (Paris) **149**: 178, 1955.

40. Weibull, C., and Gyllang, H.: Metabolic properties of some L forms derived from Gram-positive and Gram-negative bacteria. *J. Bact.* **89**: 1443, 1965.

41. Williams, R. E. O.: L forms of *Staphylococcus aureus*. *J. Gen. Microbiol.* **33**: 325, 1963.

42. Wittler, R. G., Malizia, W. F., Kramer, P. E., Tuckett, J. D., Pritchard, H. N., and Baker, H. J.: Isolation of a corynebacterium and its transitional forms from a case of subacute bacterial endocarditis treated with antibiotics. *J. Gen. Microbiol.* **23**: 315, 1960.

43. Wittler, R. G., Tuckett, J. D., Muccione, V. J., Gangarosa, E. J., and O'Connell, R. C.: Transitional forms and L forms from the blood of rheumatic fever patients. In: *VIII International Congress of Microbiology* (Abstracts), 1962: p. 125.

44. Youmans, G. P., Williston, E. H., and Simon, M.: Production of small colony variants of *Staphylococcus aureus* by the action of penicillin. *Proc. Soc. Exp. Biol. Med.* **58**: 56, 1945.

39

In Vivo Persistence of L-Phase Bacteria*

Carl W. Godzeski

LILLY RESEARCH LABORATORIES
INDIANAPOLIS, INDIANA

The ability of a microbe to survive an adverse environment has been and is yet a primary concern to chemotherapeutic medicine. In 1958, McDermott[18] suggested that microbial persistence may occur at different levels of detectability, and one such level may include the L-phase of bacterial growth. The bacterial L-phase has yet to be included in laboratory routine diagnostic procedures. Even a cursory examination of the published literature concerned with bacterial L-phase involvement in various disease states would indicate that it is time for the clinical laboratories to be aware of and to look for certain unusual morphological and biochemical variants of the suspected microbes.

Although the bacterial L-phase cell has not been indisputably proven to be the etiological agent in any specific disease state, the increasing number of reported isolations of these forms in association with chronic or relapsing diseases raises many questions concerning their possible role in the prolongation of such infections. Antibiotic therapy has not been shown to be very efficacious in the eradication of persisting infection, even with the advent of more potent and wide-spectrum antibiotic agents.

In our laboratory, we use the term *L-phase bacteria* to describe the cell wall modified, osmotically sensitive, propagating spheroplast form that is capable of reversion to classic parental bacteria upon removal of the inducing agent or induction environment. We do not equate this with the bacterial *L-form*, which we define as the stable, non-reverting, propagating protoplast,[2] nor do we believe that the variety of L-phase cells that can arise from a multitude of known inducing conditions or agents are equivalent structures. The bacterial L-phase has been designated, at one time or another, the "transitional form" or "soft-walled bacteria" and we accept these descriptions as valid for the L-phase. This definition may even include, by extrapolation, many of the so-called "pleomorphic" forms which many bacteria can assume in diverse environments. For brevity and descriptive association, however, we prefer the term L-phase to any of the others that have been proposed.

Since the physiology and biochemistry of L-phase bacteria are relatively un-

* The studies reported involved the intimate cooperation of Dr. R. S. Griffith, Dr. H. R. Black, Mr. G. Brier, Mr. J. Farran, and Miss Nancy Balsbaugh of the Lilly Research Laboratories, and Dr. W. W. L. Glenn of Yale University School of Medicine, Department of Surgery. The author is sincerely appreciative of their cooperation and support.

explored subjects, the current general concept that these organisms are avirulent and non-pathogenic is premature and, in fact, may be quite misleading. Not too long ago researchers considered L-phase bacteria as bothersome pests in their search for the true etiological agent, and some reports even stated that it was desirable to prove the existence of L-phase organisms in the genito-urinary tract so that "attention could then be turned from these non-pathogenic variants to the normal pathogenic cultivable form".[1] As knowledge and interest in these bacterial forms has increased, we notice fewer such statements. The recent experimental studies of many investigators emphasize the potential importance of L-phase bacteria in a variety of infectious diseases.[9, 10, 25, 27, 29]

Our laboratory has contributed to this area via isolation of L-phase staphylococci associated with persisting infections usually ascribed to staphylococci[7] and, more recently, by the discovery of L-phase bacteria in heart muscle tissue taken from open heart surgical procedures performed on individuals with a history of rheumatic heart disease.[6]

METHODS

ISOLATION FROM BLOOD

Blood samples in 10 ml volumes were drawn after the disappearance of clinical signs of infection. The sample was divided so that 5.0 ml were inoculated into 5.0 ml of double strength Mattman modified Medill-O'Kane L-phase medium,[17] and the remaining 5.0 ml were placed into 50 ml of Difco brain heart infusion (BHI) medium containing 0.1% agar. The L-phase medium was incubated in a N_2-CO_2 (95:5) atmosphere until a growth reaction was noticed by overt changes in the medium. The routine culture was incubated aerobically in a normal manner and was examined for classic bacterial forms over a two-week period. Growth of the L-phase cells was generally apparent by five to seven days of incubation.

Transfers from the original L-phase culture were inoculated in 0.5 ml amounts into 4.5 ml of fresh medium, so that dupli-

cate inoculated tubes could be incubated both aerobically and under the N_2-CO_2 atmosphere. Propagating spheroplasts usually appeared in both cultures but were more numerous in the N_2-CO_2 chamber incubation. Subsequent transfers to fresh medium were incubated aerobically. Transfers were not attempted until maximum growth occurred. Reversion to classic bacteria occurred by daily transfers into BHI broth and onto Difco "110" medium agar slopes. Growth on the "110" medium was initially thin and grey in color, but successive transfers went through the changes from thin and white to luxuriant, golden yellow colonial growth forms.

The original BHI-0.1% agar inoculation for classic bacteria remained sterile throughout this period. The reverted staphylococci from the "110" medium were capable of excellent growth in the "sloppy" BHI medium; therefore, if classic staphylococci were present in the initial blood sample, they should have been able to grow in this control medium.

Positive L-phase culture was noted when the L-phase isolation process produced propagating cells and no classic bacteria developed in the normal, classic bacterial isolation medium. Uninoculated medium controls always remained sterile.

ISOLATION FROM HEART TISSUE

Heart muscle tissue removed during open heart surgery was placed into a test tube containing 10 ml of a sterile 10% sucrose solution. The tubes were marked by serial number only, so that the examining laboratory had no prior knowledge of the patient's history. Since congenital heart defects were also repaired during the surgical schedule, the laboratory was unable to ascertain what sort of sample[6] was being tested.

Bacteriological examination of the heart tissues was conducted for both classic parental bacterial forms and for L-phase variants. The original sucrose diluent, tissue washes, sliced tissue, and tissue homogenates were examined for bacterial forms. Tissue homogenates were performed by cutting away all external portions and removing a small piece from the center core.

This bit of core tissue was aseptically placed in a smooth ground-glass test tube homogenizer and was lightly macerated for a few minutes. The ground bits were suspended in sterile 10% sucrose and cultured for bacteria.

Culture techniques for both L-phase cells and classic parental forms utilized a variety of media, since the laboratory did not know what type of organism might arise. Preliminary isolation media included the modified Medill-O'Kane, BHI broth plus or minus 5% sodium chloride, Difco PPLO broth, and thioglycollate broth. All media were prepared with and without 20% pre-incubated human serum and, after inoculation, were incubated both aerobically and under N_2-CO_2 (95:5) atmosphere as before. Uninoculated media controls were routinely negative.

The L-phase cells that arose were recognized by phase microscopy. Multiple transfers were required to revert these isolates to classic parental bacterial forms. Growth in osmotically stabilized media of typical spheroplast microscopic forms without concomitant classic growth in ordinary media was considered a positive L-phase isolation. Only when such isolates were obtained from the tissue homogenates and not from the suspending fluid or tissue washings were the tissues considered as harboring L-phase organisms. Mixed cultural types were suspected as arising externally.

Reversion media for subsequent transfers used a variety of bases and included eosin methylene blue (EMB) agar, and MacConkey agar, as well as BHI broth and agar, Difco "110" agar, blood agar base, and thioglycollate broth.

RESULTS

Isolations were attempted from blood of patients who were carefully chosen for their history of chronic infections, generally involving boils and other staphylococcal problems. The patients were treated in the hospital and had undergone symptomatic remission when the blood samples were taken. Antibiotic therapy had ceased at this time, although there may have been some residual assayable

blood level remaining. The immediate dilution of the sample and the long-term incubation was sufficient to lower any residual antibiotic activity to non-determinable levels.

Positive L-phase cultures which slowly reverted to *Staphylococcus aureus* strains were obtained from each of 11 such patients tested. The individual strains varied in their antibiotic sensitivity patterns and were indistinguishable from the cultures originally isolated from the patients on admission. Medium controls remained negative, as did ordinary culture for classic staphylococci.

As a further control on the methodology, 22 hospital staff members with no sign of apparent infection were studied with blood cultures. Of these, 20 were negative. The two individuals that gave positive cultures were negative when retested one week later. Transient subacute infection or sample contamination during the blood withdrawal may have accounted for these two isolations. It is reasonable to assume that all persons are subacutely infected from time to time, and the host resistance mechanisms deal with these situations

TABLE 39.1

Isolate Types from Either Rheumatic Heart Disease or Congenital Heart Defect Patients

Sample #	Patient	Isolate*
1	Rheumatic	Staphylococcus
2	Rheumatic	Mixed staphylococcus and enterococcus
3	Congenital	Negative
4	Rheumatic	Staphylococcus, microaerophilic
5	Rheumatic	Negative
6	Congenital	Mixed culture (contaminants)
7	Rheumatic	Staphylococcus
8	Rheumatic	Negative
9	Rheumatic	Gram-variable rod
10	Congenital	Negative
11	Congenital	Negative
12	Congenital	Negative
13	Rheumatic	Gram-negative rod
14	Rheumatic	Negative

* Determined after the culture grew out in classic bacterial form.

TABLE 39.2

*Antibiotic Sensitivity Patterns of the Isolates**

Antibiotic	Isolate #					
	1	2	4	7	9	13
Erythromycin (2 μg)	+	+	−	+	+	−
Chloramphenicol (5 μg)	+	+	+	+	+	+
Novobiocin (5 μg)	+	+	+	+	−	+
Tetracycline (5 μg)	+	+	−	−	+	+
Lincomycin (2 μg)	+	+	+	+	−	+
Streptomycin (2 μg)	+	+	+	−	+	+
Pen G (2 μg)	+	+	+	+	−	+
Neomycin (5 μg)	+	+	+	+	+	+

* Disc sensitivities performed on brain heart infusion agar (Difco).

most effectively. Perhaps these two positive controls represented such subclinical infection. Follow-up of these individuals did not reveal any symptomatic infectious process.

Samples of heart tissue removed during open heart surgery were taken with great

TABLE 39.3

Characteristic Reactions of the Isolated Staphylococci

Isolate #	Mannitol	Coagulase	Hemolytic
1	+	−	−
2	+	−	−
4	+	+	α
7	+	−	−

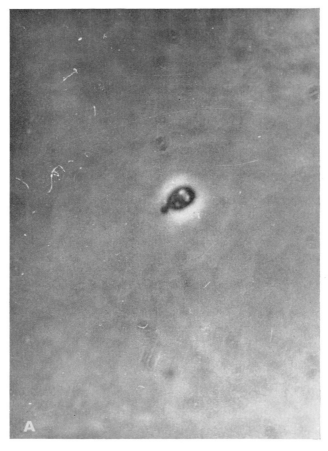

Figure 39.1. Phase micrographs of the sequential reversion of heart tissue isolate #9 from L-phase growth to classic bacterial forms.

A–C: Represent the second transfer from the initial culture.

precaution to prevent external contamination of the site and tissues concerned. The tissue was received in our laboratory within 24 hours after surgery with no identification label other than a surgery sequence number and the date taken. Thus, the laboratory could not tell whether the tissue was from a patient with congenital or rheumatic disease defects. Fourteen such samples were examined for L-phase and classic bacteria. Classic bacteria were isolated using the routine bacteriological procedures from sample #6. The sucrose diluent and tissue washes yielded positive cultures. A summary of the isolations is presented in Table 39.1. Other limited observations are tabulated in Tables 39.2 and 39.3.

Of particular interest was the staphy-

lococcal isolate from sample #4, which on primary reversion grew on EMB agar as tiny, microaerophilic, gonidial, G-type colonies.[12, 23, 26] The cells were Gram-positive, in grape-like clusters and typically staphylococci, but colonies were smooth, bright white. Subsequent transfers onto "110" medium slowly turned yellow and would no longer grow on the EMB medium. The culture, however, remained microaerophilic throughout the propagation period. Initial isolations of this culture grew only under the increased CO_2 tension incubation.

Isolation of L-phase bacteria from sample #2 yielded both an apparent enterococcus and a staphylococcus. The enterococcal cells grew for two additional transfers after reversion but died out and the culture was lost.

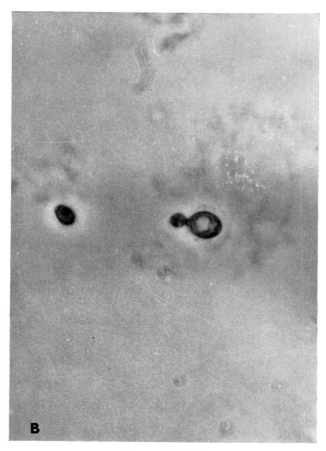

Figure 39.1 *B.*

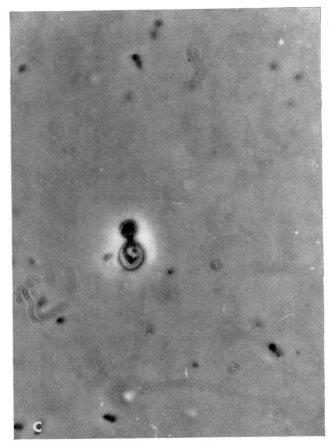

Figure 39.1 *C*.

No isolations were made from four of the five samples taken from congenital heart defect patients. We considered the positive isolation from the one sample of this series as contaminated, since cultures were obtained from the original sucrose diluent and the tissue washes, and the bacteria were large Gram-positive rods, Gram-positive cocci and small Gram-positive rods. These were isolated as classic bacteria and were not initially in the L-phase or spheroplast form.

The reverted L-phase isolates demonstrated variable antibiotic sensitivity patterns (Table 39.2), and the aforementioned sample #4 was coagulase positive and α-hemolytic (Table 39.3). The sequential reversion process for sample #9 was photographed (Figure 39.1).

DISCUSSION

The etiological role of L-phase bacteria in chronic or recurring infectious disease processes has been obscured by both semantics and the unexpected diversity of morphological and physiological forms that bacteria can assume under various environmental conditions.[21] Previous reports from our laboratory[8] have essentially substantiated earlier views held by Dienes and his associates[4] and Pulvertaft[22] concerning the ability of a variety of antibiotics to induce morphological variants in many bacterial cultures. We believe that the induction ability depends upon the cultural history of the bacterial species, the immediate environment during and after exposure to the inducing agent, and

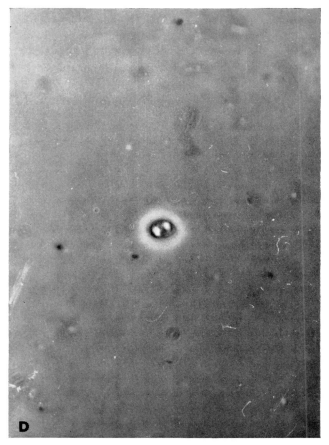

Figure 39.1 *D:* The third transfer.

the subsequent manipulative experimental techniques that are utilized.[20, 28]

Kagan[14] reviewed much of the L-phase isolation data in 1961, and the reported isolations of L-phase bacteria from infections have steadily increased since then. Mattman & Mattman[16] have reported on streptococcal L-phase isolations from septicemias, and their paper considered similar isolations from earlier reports. That L-phase bacteria occur *in vivo* has been well documented in the studies of Wittler's group,[30] and more recently by Mortimer,[19] Godzeski and his associates,[5, 6] and Gutman and colleagues.[9] There is no longer any doubt that these forms of bacterial growth are more than laboratory phenomena.

Our data concerning the association of L-phase staphylococci in certain selected cases of persisting infections requires confirmation from clinical laboratories that have access to large numbers of such infections under study. Epidemiological studies carried out in the general uninfected population might also be of interest. The data suggest that similar studies should be performed on specific problem patients. Negative blood cultures from patients with obvious symptomatic indications should be suspected of harboring the L-phase of the suitable organism. Naturally, the L-phase of the suspected microbe may be located in the tissue and not necessarily in the blood. Repeated culture should reveal the culprit, however, since blood is the transport system to and from most tissues.

Cooper and associates[3] recently com-

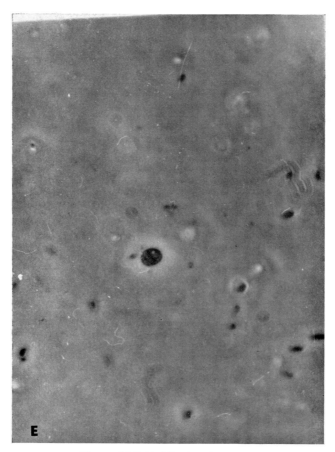

Figure 39.1 *E:* The fourth transfer.

mented on pitfalls in the diagnosis of bacterial endocarditis, and their data emphasize the possibilities of delayed diagnosis of this disease via autopsy examinations (autopsy seems a remarkably inappropriate time for diagnosis). The authors state that *S. aureus* has replaced *Streptococcus viridans* as the most common causative agent, and they note the large number of patients with bacterial endocarditis who had completely negative blood cultures. The reasons for this are numerous, but L-phase involvement was postulated as a distinct possibility. Heavy antibiotic therapy of patients for other associated diseases serves only to compound the difficulty. Lerner & Weinstein's comprehensive coverage of this problem[15]

should be consulted for further information concerning endocarditis.

We were mildly surprised upon examining the laboratory findings from the heart tissue samples, for we thought the surgeon had misunderstood our intentions to examine rheumatic heart muscle for L-phase contamination, and that he was sending endocarditis tissue. We fully expected a series of streptococcal isolates.

Our isolates became more intriguing as the samples were studied, for we were struck with the consistency of the procedures. Obviously, our surgeon, Yale's Dr. W. W. L. Glenn, was a scrupulous performer, as single culture isolates were generally obtained, and these only from deep tissue homogenates. The cultures

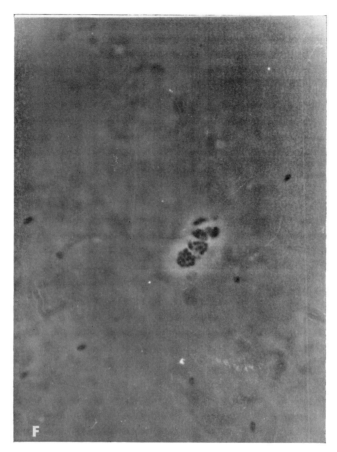

Figure 39.1 *F:* The fifth transfer.

could not have penetrated so deeply without contaminating the wash fluids and suspending solution if they had dropped in, so to speak, during the operation. Certainly, the patients were on heavy antibiotic cover before and during the operation, yet a recent infection would not likely be so slow in reverting to classic bacteria as were these. Our experience with L-phase isolates from animals or humans has been consistent in that long-term infections demonstrate slow reversion after isolation, oxygen sensitivity on primary cultures, and some rather unusual cultures during the first few transfers—as an example, staphylococci that grow on EMB agar as G-type colonies.[12]

The data on the admittedly too few samples do allow us the speculation that unsuspected underlying bacterial endocarditis may be masked in some cases of rheumatic fever in humans. Certainly, open heart surgery is a drastic diagnostic measure. Perhaps intermittent antibiotic therapy would allow reversion of these cultures *in vivo* so that positive blood cultures could be obtained. This could be done under close observation; antibiotic withdrawal for any extended period of time might not be necessary nor, of course, advisable. Antibiotic therapy may be masking more infectious problems *in vivo* than is currently suspected. Alternating and/or combined antibiotic therapy may be at least a partial, if not a complete, answer to some of these problem diseases.[13]

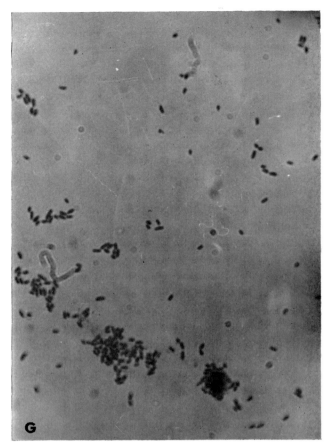

Figure 39.1 *G:* The sixth transfer.

Thus, continuing studies in our laboratory have convinced us that any bacterial species may be induced into a stage of existence closely resembling the propagating spheroplast. These observations, combined with the published experience of others, lead us to conclude that the ability to shed at least a part of the rigid outer matrix and exist in the spheroplast state is an inherent property of all bacteria; this state can be called a "phase" of growth. Environmental conditions determine the phase of growth observed in the laboratory, the phase can be shifted via environmental alteration, and the phase usually studied in ordinary bacteriological media may or may not relate to the phase that occurs *in vivo.* The L-phase of bacterial growth can be induced by a wide variety of agents which include certain amino acids, antibiotics, enzymes, host resistance factors and even specific inorganic salts. To consider the forms of cellular growth obtained from these diverse inducing agents as essentially equivalent structures seems, at the very least, naive. The pathogenicity or virulence of L-phase bacteria is a problem ready for immediate investigation. Our studies[5] on the *in vivo* induction of L-phase *Salmonella typhimurium* have indicated increasing virulence for the mouse when animal passage was attempted. We have maintained *S. typhimurium* L-phase bacteria in mice for six weeks without reversion, and the mice are sickly but not dying. When environmentally stressed (exposure to 4°C for eight hours), the subacutely infected mice die of overt classic *S. typhi-murium* infection.*

We also feel that Mortimer's[19] suggestion that virulence is correlated with L-phase inducibility has merit and should be more thoroughly examined. Serum resistance, virulence, ease of L-phase induction, effect of antibody-complement and phagocytic action are likely correlated in some as yet unknown manner.

Pulvertaft[22] stated that "it may be that the life cycles of bacteria are far more complex than is usually believed, and that growth on conventional media and examination by conventional methods have obscured the facts." They have. Salton[24] said that "it would be unfortunate for man if these forms also synthesize endo- and exotoxins responsible for the pathogenicity of particular organisms." They do, and it is.

Summary

The L-phase of staphylococci have been isolated from 11 patients selected for their history of chronic recurring infections usually associated with staphylococci. Twenty of 22 controls were negative and the two positives were negative on retest.

Bacterial L-phase organisms have been isolated from heart tissues removed from rheumatic fever patients during open heart surgery, and it was concluded that a possible underlying masked bacterial endocarditis may exist in at least some patients suffering from rheumatic fever. The six isolated and reverted L-phase cultures consisted of four strains of *Staphylococcus aureus*, a Gram-negative rod, and a small Gram-variable rod from a total of nine rheumatic heart samples. Congenital heart defect samples did not yield L-phase isolates.

The significance of L-phase bacteria in persisting infections was discussed.

REFERENCES

1. Amies, C. R., and Jones, S. A.: A description of *Haemophilus vaginalis* and its L forms. *Canad. J. Microbiol.* **3**: 579, 1957.

2. Brenner, S., Dark, F. A., Gerhardt, P., Jeynes, M. H., Kandler, O., Kellenberger, E., Klieneberger-Nobel, E., McQuillen, K., Rubio-Huertos, M., Salton, M. R. J., Strange, R. E., Tomcsik, J., and Weibull, C.: Bacterial protoplasts. *Nature* **181**: 1713, 1958.

3. Cooper, E. S., Cooper, J. W., and Schnabel, T. G., Jr.: Pitfalls in the diagnosis of bacterial endocarditis. *Arch. Intern. Med.* (Chicago) **118**: 55, 1966.

4. Dienes, L., Weinberger, H. J., and Madoff, S.: The transformation of typhoid bacilli into L forms under various conditions. *J. Bact.* **59**: 755, 1950.

5. Godzeski, C. W., Brier, G., and Farran, J. D.: The interaction of antibiotics, bacteria, and the bacterial L-phase *in vivo*. *Ann. N. Y. Acad. Sci.*, 1967 (in press).

6. Godzeski, C. W., Brier, G., and Glenn, W. W. L.: L-phase bacteria in human heart tissue. *Life Sci.*, in press.

7. Godzeski, C. W., Brier, G., Griffith, R. S., and Black, H. R.: Association of bacterial L-phase organisms in chronic infections. *Nature* **205**: 1340, 1965.

8. Godzeski, C. W., Hisker, R. M., and Brier, G.: Predominant characteristics of the growth of some antibiotic-induced L-phase bacteria. In: *Antimicrobial Agents and Chemotherapy—1963* (J. C. Sylvester, Ed.). American Society for Microbiology, Ann Arbor, 1964: p. 507.

9. Gutman, L. T., Turck, M., Petersdorf, R. G., and Wedgwood, R. J.: Significance of bacterial variants in urine of patients with chronic bacteriuria. *J. Clin. Invest.* **44**: 1945, 1965.

10. Guze, L. B., and Kalmanson, G. M.: Action of erythromycin on "protoplasts" *in vivo*. *Science* **146**: 1299, 1964.

11. ———: Persistence of bacteria in "protoplast" form after apparent cure of pyelonephritis in rats. *Science* **143**: 1340, 1964.

12. Hadley, P., Delves, E., and Klimek, J.: The filtrable forms of bacteria. I. A filtrable stage in the life history of the Shiga dysentery bacillus. *J. Infect. Dis.* **48**: 1, 1931.

13. Hewitt, W. L., Seligman, S. J., and Deigh, R. A.: Kinetics of the synergism of penicillin-streptomycin and penicillin-kanamycin for enterococci and its relationship to L-phase variants. *J. Lab. Clin. Med.* **67**: 792, 1966.

14. Kagan, G. Y.: The problem of pathogenicity of L-form bacteria; review of literature. *Klin. Med.* (Moscow) **39**: 12, 1961 (in Russian).

15. Lerner, P. I., and Weinstein, L.: Infective endocarditis in the antibiotic era. *New Eng. J. Med.* **274**: 388, 1966.

_____

* Unpublished results.

16. Mattman, L. H., and Mattman, P. E.: L-forms of *Streptococcus fecalis* in septicemia. *Arch. Intern Med.* (Chicago) **115**: 315, 1965.

17. Mattman, L. H., Tunstall, L. H., and Rossmoore, H. W.: Induction and characteristics of staphylococcal L forms. *Canad. J. Microbiol.* **7**: 705, 1961.

18. McDermott, W.: Microbial persistence. *Yale J. Biol. Med.* **30**: 257, 1958.

19. Mortimer, E. A., Jr.: Production of L forms of group A streptococci in mice. *Proc. Soc. Exp. Biol. Med.* **119**: 159, 1965.

20. Muschel, L. H., Carey, W. F., and Baron, L. S.: Formation of bacterial protoplasts by serum components. *J. Immunol.* **82**: 38, 1959.

21. Nativelle, R., and Deparis, M.: Formes évolutive des bactéries dans les hémocultures. *Presse Méd.* **68**: 571, 1960.

22. Pulvertaft, R. J. V.: The effect of antibiotics on growing cultures of *Bacterium coli*. *J. Path. Bact.* **64**: 75, 1952.

23. Quie, P. G.: Atypical colony forms in patients with staphylococcal disease. *J. Lab. Clin. Med.* **66**: 1013, 1965.

24. Salton, M. R. J.: *The Bacterial Cell*. Elsevier, Amsterdam, 1964.

25. Schegolev, A. G., and Starshinova, V. S.: Isolation of L-form bacteria from typhoid patients and carriers. *Zh. Mikrobiol. Epidemiol. Immunobiol.* **41**(7): 15, 1964 (in Russian).

26. Spink, W. W., Osterberg, K., and Finstad, J.: Human endocarditis due to a strain of CO_2-dependent penicillin-resistant staphylococcus producing dwarf colonies. *J. Lab. Clin. Med.* **59**: 613, 1962.

27. Timakov, V. D., and Kagan, G. Y.: Pathogenic properties of the L forms of bacteria and of the *Mycoplasmataceae* family and their role in infectious pathology. *Zh. Mikrobiol. Epidemiol. Immunol.* **43**(3): 3, 1966 (in Russian).

28. Waisbren, B. A., and Brown, I.: Effect of wide-spectrum antibiotics on bactericidal activity of human serum: *in vitro* and *in vivo*. *Amer. J. Med. Sci.* **248**: 56, 1964.

29. Wittler, R. G.: The L form of *Haemophilus pertussis* in the mouse. *J. Gen. Microbiol.* **6**: 311, 1952.

30. Wittler, R. G., Tuckett, J. D., Muccione, V. J., Gangarosa, E. J., and O'Connell, R. C.: Transitional forms and L forms from blood of rheumatic fever patients. In: *Eighth International Congress of Microbiology* (Abstracts), 1962: p. 125.

40

The Role of Bacterial Variants in Experimental Pyelonephritis*

Laura T. Gutman, Richard H. Winterbauer, Marvin Turck,
Ralph J. Wedgwood and Robert G. Petersdorf

UNIVERSITY OF WASHINGTON SCHOOL OF MEDICINE
AND KING COUNTY HOSPITAL

SEATTLE WASHINGTON

Determining the relation of spheroplasts, protoplasts, and L-forms (henceforth called bacterial variants) to human infection is exceedingly difficult because the parent organism is frequently isolated concomitantly with the variant. Therefore, in order to relate variants to disease in the host, they must be isolated unaccompanied by classical bacteria, preferably in the absence of antibiotic therapy, indicating that the variant alone is capable of inducing disease. Whether this occurs in renal infections in man is not known. This report deals with the role of apparently stable *Escherichia coli* variants in experimental pyelonephritis in rats.

MATERIALS AND METHODS

Variants of a strain of *E. coli* serogroup 06 were induced by exposure to penicillin, and aliquots were subsequently passed at weekly intervals in the absence of further inducing agents without reverting to the parent strain. The method for inducing

and culturing the variants has been described in detail.[5] Criteria for variant growth will be discussed elsewhere in this volume.*

Female Sprague-Dawley rats were used in all experiments. Initial studies had demonstrated that intracardiac inoculation of variants, followed by renal massage, failed to establish infection in the kidney, and variants were not recovered from liver, spleen, blood or kidney when this route was used. These results were interpreted to mean that the variants were not reaching the kidney in sufficient numbers to establish an infection, or were being killed rapidly. Therefore, it was decided to inject the variants directly into the medulla of the left kidney under direct vision. Animals were sacrificed at varying intervals after inoculation of variants, the left kidney was removed under aseptic conditions and cultured for variants and classical bacteria. In addition to being studied bacteriologically, kidneys were examined microscopically, employing standard histologic techniques.

RESULTS

Initially it seemed important to determine if variants would survive and pro-

* This investigation was supported by Public Health Service Training Grants AI146-07 and AI227-04, and Grants AI-06311-02 and AI-06882-01 from the National Institutes of Health.

The authors express their gratitude to several members of the Pathology Department of the University of Washington, who kindly reviewed the histological sections.

* See Turck, Gutman, Wedgwood & Petersdorf (p. 415).

TABLE 40.1

Frequency of Isolation of Escherichia coli *06 Variant and Reverted Parent Following Intramedullary Injection, in the Absence of Penicillin**

Time of Sacrifice	Number of Animals	Frequency of Isolation of Classical *E. coli* 06	Frequency of Isolation of *E. coli* 06 Variants
1 minute	4	0	2/4
1 hour	4	0	2/4
2 hours	4	0	2/4
4 hours	4	0	4/4
8 hours	4	4/4	—
12 hours	4	4/4	—
1 day	4	4/4	—
4 days	4	4/4	—
7 days	4	4/4	—

* Data from Winterbauer et al.[5]

TABLE 40.2

Frequency of Isolation of Escherichia coli *06 Variant and Reverted Parent Following Intramedullary Injection in the Presence of Penicillin**

Time of Sacrifice	Number of Animals	Frequency of Isolation of Classical *E. coli* 06	Frequency of Isolation of *E. coli* 06 Variants
1 minute	4	0	1/4
1 hour	4	0	4/4
2 hours	4	0	2/4
4, 8, 12 hours, 1, 4, and 7 days	78	0	0/78
Alternate days, 4 days through 4 weeks	28	0	0/28

* Data from Winterbauer et al.[5]

liferate in the kidney in the absence of penicillin, following direct intramedullary injection (Table 40.1). No classical bacteria were found in any group of animals sacrificed less than four hours after injection, and only variants were cultured within this period. In contrast, all animals sacrificed between eight hours and seven days after injection demonstrated abundant growth of the parent *E. coli* from their renal homogenates. These results indicate that variants could survive following intramedullary injection but reverted rapidly to the parent in renal tissue. These observations *in vivo* are contrary to *in vitro* studies with the same variant strain,

which did not revert in broth following weekly passage in the absence of penicillin.

Treatment of rats with penicillin at time of injection resulted in the suppression of reversion from the variant to the classical form (Table 40.2). Variants were recovered from the left kidney of seven of 12 animals sacrificed between one minute and two hours after injection. Variants were not isolated from any animal sacrificed four hours to four weeks after injection, and no classical forms could be cultured. In addition, pretreatment with penicillin prevented reversion to the parent strain. These results indicate that in rat renal tissue penicillin-induced variants of this particular serogroup of *E. coli* either reverted to classic forms in the absence of penicillin or, if penicillin was administered concurrently, were destroyed rapidly. Late reversion did not occur.

The relative hypertonicity of kidney, when compared to the isotonicity of liver, spleen and other tissues, has been suggested as a possible factor favoring renal medullary survival of variants.[1-4] An experiment was therefore designed to compare survival and reversion of classical and variant forms of *E. coli* 06 in three visceral organs, kidney, liver and spleen. Following direct injection of variants in liver, spleen and renal medulla, the number of reverting variants recovered from the kidney greatly exceeded that isolated

TABLE 40.3

Quantitation of Escherichia coli *06 Isolated Following Inoculation of Variant or Classical* E. coli *06 into Kidney, Liver and Spleen**

Site of Inoculation	Variants Injected Average number classical *E. coli* 06/g tissue Sacrifice group		Classical *E. coli* 06 Injected Average number classical *E. coli* 06/g tissue Sacrifice group	
	Day 1	Day 4	Day 1	Day 4
Kidney	10^7	10^5	10^7	10^5
Liver	10^3	0	10^6	10^5
Spleen	10^3	0	10^7	10^5

* Data from Winterbauer et al.[5]

from either liver or spleen, when animals were sacrificed both one and four days after injection. In contrast, the number of classical *E. coli* 06 cultured following injection of classical *E. coli* was similar in kidney, liver and spleen (Table 40.3).

In addition to culturing organs for classical and variant forms of bacteria, excised tissue was examined for macroscopic and histologic lesions. The severity of gross lesions was graded from 0 (minimal) to 2+ (marked). Grossly, a pronounced visible lesion occurred in over 70 per cent of kidneys when either classical *E. coli* 06 or variant forms which had reverted were injected (Table 40.4). On the other hand, marked macroscopic responses were seldom produced by variants which did not revert to classical bacteria (exemplified by forms which were prevented from reverting by penicillin), a penicillin-induced non-reverting variant, L-form broth without variants, endotoxin, and heat-killed 06 variants (Table 40.5).

Figure 40.1 (bottom) depicts two sections of renal tissue into which classical *E. coli* had been injected, or in which *E. coli* variants had reverted. The histological reaction following the medullary injection of classical *E. coli* and *E. coli* 06 variants which reverted to the classical form was an acute and widespread pyelonephritis. The normal architecture of the medulla was grossly distorted with sheets of infiltrating polymorphonuclear neutrophils. Tubular lumena frequently contained white cell casts, and often proteinaceous debris. The acute inflammatory process involved 25 to 75 per cent of the total area of the section. Suspensions which did not lead to infection with classic organisms produced an intense fibrosis with a mild chronic inflammatory reaction in both medulla and cortex. Polymorphonuclear leukocytes were virtually absent and there was a moderate round cell infiltration. This cicatrizing reaction was usually found in areas contiguous to the needle tract and extended only a few millimeters from the site of trauma. Some sections disclosed dendritiform spread of the reaction at the depth of the tract, which might represent a cleavage plane caused by

TABLE 40.4

Incidence of Macroscopic Renal Lesions Four Days Following Injection; Classical Escherichia coli Present*

Suspension Injected	Number of Animals	Frequency 0+ Reaction	Frequency 1+ Reaction	Frequency 2+ Reaction
Classical *E. coli*	16	2 (12%)	3 (19%)	9 (66%)
06 variants without penicillin	16	2 (12%)	0 (0%)	14 (88%)

* Data from Winterbauer et al.[5]

TABLE 40.5

Incidence of Macroscopic Renal Lesions Four Days Following Injection; Classical Escherichia coli Not Present*

Suspension injected	Number of Animals	Frequency 0+ Reaction	Frequency 1+ Reaction	Frequency 2+ Reaction
06 variants with penicillin	30	15 (50%)	8 (27%)	7 (23%)
0 undetermined without penicillin	16	10 (62%)	3 (19%)	3 (19%)
L-form broth	25	14 (56%)	5 (20%)	6 (24%)
0 111 endotoxin	48	28 (58%)	8 (17%)	12 (25%)
Heat killed 06 variants	16	9 (56%)	3 (19%)	4 (25%)

* Data from Winterbauer et al.[5]

the injected material. The total area involved almost never exceeded 15 per cent of the section. Areas with purulent exudation were rarely seen. Kidneys obtained seven days after injection showed clearing of the round cell infiltrate and only minimal fibrosis remained.

DISCUSSION

The experiments described above can be summarized as follows: (1) *E. coli* variants rapidly reverted after injection into the renal medulla in the absence of penicillin; this occurred in spite of the apparent stability of these forms *in vitro*. (2) Variants failed to survive in the kidney when the animals were treated with penicillin concomitantly or prior to inoculation;

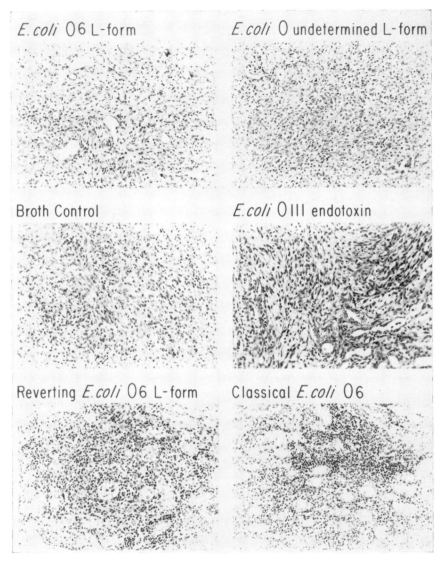

Figure 40.1. Histological response to each of the 6 test solutions of *Escherichia coli* (× 240). Identical reactions of moderate fibrosis and chronic inflammation contiguous to the needle tract were elicited by non-reverting 06, 0 undetermined L-forms which did not revert, L-form broth without variants, and 0 111 endotoxin. In contrast, reverted 06 L-forms and classical *E. coli* 06 produced an intense, widespread acute pyelonephritis. (From Winterbauer, Gutman et al.[5])

furthermore, late reversion of variants did not occur. (3) Compared with liver and spleen, variants injected into the renal medulla tended to survive; in contrast, when classical organisms were injected into the three organs, they were recovered in approximately equal numbers. (4) The histological response to reverting variants and classical *E. coli* was characterized by an acute, granulocytic infiltrate typical of acute pyelonephritis. (5) In contrast, the histological response to non-reverting variants, media, and killed variants was similar and was characterized primarily by a fibrotic reaction with moderate round cell infiltration.

These results indicate that, under the condition of this experiment, variants did not produce infection unless reversion took place. Moreover, the possibility that variants may cause a persistent inflammatory response in renal tissue already damaged by previous pyelonephritis has not been excluded. Most importantly, these studies in rats do not clarify whether variants play a pathogenetic role in man. It well may be that conditions in the human kidney differ sufficiently from those in the rat kidney to make these results inapplicable. Nevertheless, the available information best supports the thesis that bacterial variants may be responsible for persistence of microorganisms in the kidney but not for the inflammatory process *per se*.

Summary

Stable variants of *Escherichia coli* 06 were used to produce experimental pyelonephritis in rats. Infection did not occur unless reversion to the parent form took place. The implications of this observation are discussed briefly.

REFERENCES

1. Alderman, M. H., and Freedman, L. R.: Experimental pyelonephritis. X. The direct injection of *E. coli* protoplasts into the medulla of the rabbit kidney. *Yale J. Biol. Med.* **36:** 157, 1963.
2. Braude, A. I., Siemienski, J., and Jacobs, I.: Protoplast formation in human urine. *Trans. Ass. Amer. Physicians* **74:** 234, 1961.
3. Gutman, L. T., Turck, M., Petersdorf, R. G., and Wedgwood, R. J.: Significance of bacterial variants in urine of patients with chronic bacteriuria. *J. Clin. Invest.* **44:** 1945, 1965.
4. Guze, L. B., and Kalmanson, G. M.: Persistence of bacteria in "protoplast" form after apparent cure of pyelonephritis in rats. *Science* **143:** 1340, 1964.
5. Winterbauer, R. H., Gutman, L. T., Turck, M., Wedgewood, R. J., and Petersdorf, R. G. The role of penicillin-induced bacterial variants in experimental pyelonephritis. *J. Exp. Med.* **125:** 607, 1967.

41

Spheroplasts in Human Urine*

Abraham I. Braude, Jennie Siemienski and Kathleen Lee

UNIVERSITY OF PITTSBURGH

PITTSBURGH, PENNSYLVANIA

Bacteria in the kidney and urine encounter osmotic pressures that exceed those in all other extracellular fluids, reaching 1300 mOsm/liter, or approximately four times the osmotic pressure of plasma. Because this osmotic pressure is more than enough to prevent lysis of spheroplasts,[†] they might be more likely to persist in the urinary tract than elsewhere. In addition to its capacity for reaching a high osmotic pressure, infected urine also contains lysozyme, antibodies, antibiotics, glycine, bacteriophage, and other agents than can weaken the cell wall of Gram-negative bacilli and allow spheroplasts to develop. Accordingly, the following study was undertaken to determine under what conditions, if any, spheroplasts could develop in human urine. The demonstration of spheroplasts in urine might account for the clinical observation that urinary infections have a tendency to recur after antibiotic treatment or after spontaneous recovery; such recurrences could be explained by the reversion of spheroplasts to bacterial forms.

MATERIALS AND METHODS

Uninfected dilute and concentrated urines were collected from healthy volun-

teers during different stages of diuresis and antidiuresis. Their osmolarities were measured in the Fiske osmometer, and their pH in the Beckman pH meter. Sodium was determined by photometry and urea by urease nesslerization. Sterile urines were mixed with suspensions of spheroplasts obtained in 10% sucrose broth prepared according to the Lederberg & St. Clair formula.[3] Seventy milliliters of an 18–20 hour Penassay broth (Difco) culture of bacteria were inoculated into a liter of the sucrose broth containing 0.2% $MgSO_4$ and 1000 units/ml of benzyl penicillin. After incubation for 20 hours at 37°C, the spheroplasts were separated by centrifugation at 2000 rpm. Appropriate concentrations of spheroplasts were made by diluting the sediment with sucrose broth, and their number was determined in a hemocytometer.

Infected urines were collected, from men by midstream catch and from women by catheter, with strict aseptic techniques previously described.[1] These urines were cultured by conventional methods and colony counts determined in pour plates. The infected urines were centrifuged at 1000 rpm for five minutes and the sediment fixed on glass slides with absolute methyl alcohol before staining with methylene blue, Wright's stain, and Gram's stain. In spite of the fact that the staining reagents contained hypotonic solutions, methyl alcohol fixation prevented the dis-

* Investigation supported by Grant H-3220 from the U.S. Public Health Service.

† The term *spheroplasts* in this paper denotes osmotically fragile spherical forms of Gram-negative bacilli.

tortion and destruction of spheroplasts observed after air fixation.

Osmotic fragility tests on infected urine were performed by comparing plate counts after mixing the urine with water and 10% sucrose broth. This was done by delivering 0.5 ml of urine into 100 ml of sterile distilled water and 0.5 ml into 10% sucrose broth. Then 0.5 ml was transferred again from each into 100 ml of the corresponding fluid, to a final dilution of 1:40,000. Pour plates were made by adding 0.1 ml of each 1:200 dilution and 1:40,000 dilution to 10% sucrose agar plates.[3] The plate counts were made after incubation for 48 hours and again at one week. The plating error was calculated from a series of 40 cultures, in trypticase soy broth, of *Pseudomonas aeruginosa, Escherichia coli, Klebsiella pneumoniae,* and *Aerobacter aerogenes.* The plate counts obtained from such cultures were in the general range of those obtained with infected urines (i.e., 10^5–10^8 bacteria/ml).

Results

FORMATION OF SPHEROPLASTS BY URINARY BACTERIA

In order to form an idea of the morphology of spheroplasts developing from urinary bacteria in different stages of formation, as well as of their relative susceptibility to spheroplast transformation under the influence of penicillin, a systematic survey was made of ten strains each of bacteria listed in Table 41.1. Each strain had been isolated from human urine. An 18-hour culture of each strain in Penassay broth was inoculated into 10% sucrose broth containing M/600 benzyl penicillin, to give approximately 10^8 bacteria/ml. The sucrose-penicillin broth was examined up to 20 hours during incubation at 37°C for conversion of bacterial to spherical forms. Spheroplasts were identified by their microscopic appearance in wet preparations and in Gram stains, and by their osmotic fragility (demonstrated by lysis of spheroplasts upon transfer to water).

Among the urinary bacteria examined, spheroplasts developed most readily from

TABLE 41.1

Susceptibility of Pathogenic Urinary Bacteria to Spheroplast Transformation in 10% Sucrose Broth Containing 0.1% Benzyl Penicillin After 20 hr Incubation at 37°C

	Total Number of Bacterial Strains		
	Transformation of nearly all bacillary forms to spheroplasts	Transformation of a few bacillary forms to spheroplasts	Spheroplasts not formed
Proteus mirabilis	10	0	0
Klebsiella pneumoniae	7	3	0
Aerobacter aerogenes	5	5	0
Escherichia coli	3	7	0
Pseudomonas aeruginosa	0	0	10

Proteus mirabilis. Nearly all bacillary forms from each of the ten strains of this species underwent conversion to spheroplasts within 20 hours. The bacillary forms of seven strains of *K. pneumoniae*, five of *A. aerogenes*, and three of *E. coli* also exhibited nearly universal transformation to spheroplasts, while the remaining strains in these species were transformed to spheroplasts in small numbers. No spheroplasts developed from the ten strains of *P. aeruginosa*, and only rarely from *Proteus rettgeri*. Serial observations disclosed that bacteria changed to spheroplasts by developing osmotically sensitive swellings that enlarged to form a sphere equal in diameter to the original length of the rod. Bacilli did not become spheres under these conditions when chloramphenicol, streptomycin, kanamycin, and sulfisoxazole were substituted for penicillin in the same concentration. A few spherical forms developed from *E. coli* and *K. pneumoniae* upon incubation with tetracycline, but their osmotic fragility was not clearly established.

The minimal amount of penicillin needed to induce spheroplast formation from a strain of *E. coli* (0113) and a strain of *P. mirabilis* was determined in 10% sucrose broth containing serial dilutions of penicillin. As little as one unit of penicillin produced a small number of spheroplasts

TABLE 41.2

Osmotic Fragility of Spheroplasts Induced in Hypertonic Human Urine in Vitro

Urine No.	Osmolarity	Sodium mM/L	Urea mM/L	pH	Viable Bacteria/ml Before and After Lysis in Water			
					Proteus mirabilis		*Escherichia coli*	
					Before lysis	After lysis	Before lysis	After lysis
1	500	108	230	7.9	19,300	1,420	200	20
2	1126	165	529	5.6	345,600	10,000	11,600	2,600
3	1016	264	351	6.0	88,200	2,820	7,000	860
4	1012	214	479	6.5	16,600	10	2,300	470
5	996	226	522	5.6	55,500	2,060	15,000	3,200
6	1056	226	416	5.4	3,024,000	18,500	2,148,000	548,000
7	980	146	399	5.3	70,300	27,300	810,000	12,400
8	480	105	406	6.6	7,500	0	3,200	4,000
9	820	49	288	5.8	51,000	10	800	0
10	904	217	293	6.1	12,400	1,860	2,470	160

from each organism after 20 hours incubation at 37°C, but 10–25 units were necessary to convert the majority of bacillary forms to spheroplasts. In the range from 1 to 25 units, many intermediate forms between bacilli and spheroplasts were seen; these had usually the appearance of spindle-shaped filaments with large osmotically-sensitive central swellings. These results show that a certain proportion of bacterial cells are more susceptible than others to spherical transformation. They also indicate that approximately 10^{10} molecules of penicillin are needed for complete transformation to spheroplasts of the average bacterial cell of these two strains.

FORMATION OF SPHEROPLASTS IN HUMAN URINE *IN VITRO*

The osmolarity of 10% sucrose broth is 650. Osmolarities greater than 600 were found in 51 per cent of urines collected in the evening from 200 patients with urinary infections. Accordingly, sterile human urines with osmolarities in this range or higher were examined for their capacity to promote spheroplast formation. The osmolarities, as well as the concentrations of sodium, urea, and hydrogen ion of these urines are given in Table 41.2. Penicillin was added to each urine to a concentration of 1 mg/ml. Spheroplasts of *E. coli* (O113) and *P. mirabilis* (North

strain) were readily induced by inoculating 0.1 ml of the sediment from 18-hour nutrient broth cultures into each hypertonic sterile urine, and incubating at 37°C for 16 hours. The spheroplasts were seen in large numbers under the microscope and their osmotic fragility was demonstrated by reduction in viable counts after lysis in water. The viable bacteria in the spheroplast suspensions in urine were counted in agar plates containing 10% sucrose without penicillin and the results compared with plate counts made simultaneously with aliquots transferred to water. In each case, exposure to water induced lysis so that a sharp drop in viable bacteria occurred, as indicated in Table 41.2.

Direct comparisons were next made of spheroplast survival in concentrated and dilute urine containing M/600 penicillin. Figure 41.1 shows little change in the number of *Proteus* spheroplasts in hypertonic urine over a period of 6½ hours, and complete lysis of the same spheroplasts in hypotonic urine from a different subject. The formation of spheroplasts of *P. mirabilis* was also compared in hypertonic and hypotonic urines obtained from the same subjects. Table 41.3 demonstrates that bacillary forms were almost completely transformed to spheroplasts by three hours in morning urines with osmolarities of 877 to 1096. In urines

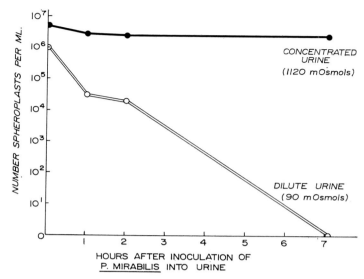

Figure 41.1. Survival of spheroplasts in dilute and concentrated urine. The hypertonic urine contained 169 mEq/liter sodium and 517 mOsmols urea; the hypotonic urine, 26 mEq/liter sodium and 50 mOsmols urea; both contained M/600 benzyl penicillin. The two urines were incubated at 37° C and the number of spheroplasts determined by direct hemocytometer chamber counts at 0, 1, 2, and 6½ hours after the spheroplasts were added to the hypertonic urine.

obtained from the same three subjects after they had imbibed water, so that osmolarities fell below 217, no spheroplasts developed in the presence of M/600 penicillin.

ANALYSIS OF URINARY CONSTITUENTS CONTRIBUTING TO SPHEROPLAST FORMATION

As shown in Tables 41.2 and 41.3, sodium and urea were primarily responsible for the high osmolarity of the concentrated urines that promoted formation of spheroplasts. A study was undertaken, therefore, to determine the relative importance of these and other urinary solutes in spheroplast formation and protection against osmotic lysis.

Urea was examined first for its ability to restore to diluted human urine the capacity to support spheroplast formation. Concentrated morning urines, capable of supporting full transformation of *P. mirabilis* to spheroplasts, were diluted serially with water beyond the point at which these spheroplasts would develop. Each set of dilutions was divided in two, urea was

TABLE 41.3

Comparison of Spheroplast Formation in Vitro from Proteus mirabilis in Hypertonic and Hypotonic Urines Obtained from the Same Normal Men Before and After Drinking Water

Subject	Osmolarity	Sodium (mM/L)	Urea (mM/L)	Bacilli Transformed to Spheroplasts in 3 hrs. (%)
AB*	992	198	200	>99
CO*	1096	n.d.	467	>99
SH*	877	264	234	>99
AB†	217	62	53	0
CO†	183	42	53	0
SH†	120	4.8	53	0

Each urine contained M/600 penicillin and was incubated at 37° C after bacterial inoculation.

* Before drinking water
† After drinking water
n.d.: Not determined

added to one of the sets to raise the osmolarity to approximately 1000, and penicillin added to all preparations in a concentration of 1 mg/ml. The dilutions with and without urea were again divided into duplicate 10 ml aliquots; to one series of

TABLE 41.4
Restoration by Urea of Spheroplast Formation in Diluted Urines*

Subject	Dilution	Supplement of Urea	Tonicity	Bacilli Transformed to Spheroplasts† approx. %	Spheroplasts Withstanding Lysis‡ approx. %
J.C.	0	0	867	>99	100
	1:2	0	420	0	50
	1:2	+	840	>99	75
	1:4	0	224	0	0
	1:4	+	860	25	50
H.D.	0	0	434	>99	100
	1:2	0	220	0	25
	1:2	+	478	>99	50
	1:4	0	112	0	0
	1:4	+	510	50	25
C.H.	0	0	950	>99	100
	1:2	0	475	75	75
	1:4	0	255	0	25
	1:4	+	958	0	75
	1:8	0	130	0	0
	1:8	+	980	0	50
J.S.	0	0	888	75	100
	1:2	0	460	0	75
	1:2	+	920	>99	100
	1:4	0	234	0	0
	1:4	+	900	>99	75

* Each urine contained 1 mg/ml penicillin.

† Spheroplast formation from Proteus mirabilis in 5 hours.

‡ Ability of spheroplasts added to the diluted urines to withstand lysis.

aliquots was added the sediment from an 18 hour Penassay broth culture of P. mirabilis, and to the other 0.1 ml of the sediment from an 18-hour penicillin-sucrose broth culture of P. mirabilis spheroplasts. Smears were made after 0, 3, and 5 hours incubation at 37°C in order to determine the approximate number of bacillary forms converting to spheroplasts, and of spheroplasts undergoing lysis. As shown in Table 41.4, hypertonic urea restored to urines from three subjects the capacity to support spheroplast formation after this capacity had been lost by dilution. Hypertonic urea also helped prevent lysis of spheroplasts in diluted urines from all subjects. This finding indicated that, in contrast to mammalian cell membranes, urea in urine is not freely diffusible

across spheroplast membranes under certain conditions.

The conditions governing the preservation of spheroplasts by urea were next studied in the company of other urinary solutes. The object of these experiments was to determine if other solutes were necessary in order for urea to prevent lysis of spheroplasts.

Table 41.5 illustrates that urea reduced the lysis of spheroplasts of a strain of P. mirabilis (North) and E. coli (0113) in hypotonic solutions of NaCl. Without NaCl, urea was ineffective in preventing lysis. The lysis of spheroplasts of two other strains of E. coli was not reduced by urea in these hypotonic solutions of NaCl. Table 41.5 also indicates that Proteus spheroplasts were more susceptible than E. coli spheroplasts to lysis in hypotonic NaCl. As shown in Table 41.6, this dif-

TABLE 41.5

Reduced Lysis of Spheroplasts After Addition of Urea to Hypotonic NaCl solutions Containing M/600 Benzyl Penicillin

NaCl (mM/L)	Urea (mM/L)	Spheroplasts/ml*	
		Proteus mirabilis	Escherichia coli
100	0	61,000	264,000
100	937	263,000	2,984,000
0	920	0	0

Spheroplast counts made in a hemocytometer chamber.

* Three hours (at 37°C) after inoculation of 9×10^6 spheroplasts per ml of test solution (pH adjusted to 6.0).

TABLE 41.6

Preservation of Escherichia coli Spheroplasts by Isotonic Saline

Strain of Bacteria	Isotonic Saline	H₂O
Proteus mirabilis (North)	19,000	0
E. coli (0113)	2,580,000	0
E. coli (5536)	4,064,000	0
E. coli (Shoemaker)	1,030,000	0

Spheroplasts/ml after 3 hour incubation at 37°C in isotonic NaCl or water containing M/600 penicillin; 9×10^6 spheroplasts of each strain were inoculated at the start of incubation.

ference was even more striking in isotonic NaCl: *E. coli* spheroplasts were well preserved while *P. mirabilis* spheroplasts were rapidly lysed.

In addition to NaCl and urea, observations were made on the effect of creatinine on spheroplast lysis. In concentrations found in the urine (17 mEq/liter), creatinine retarded lysis of *P. mirabilis* spheroplasts in the presence of 900 mM/liter urea in water or hypotonic (100 mM/liter) NaCl.

SPHEROPLAST FORMATION IN PATIENTS

Spheroplasts were searched for in patients with urinary infections by examining stained preparations and by demonstrating osmotic fragility.

Spheroplasts in Stained Specimens of Infected Urine

Urine sediments fixed with absolute methyl alcohol and stained with methylene blue, Wright's stain or Gram's stain occasionally contained unmistakable spheroplasts in large numbers. Organisms in the urine in all stages of transition from bacillary to spherical forms were identical in appearance to those found in 10% sucrose broth and left no question that they were spheroplasts. Spheroplasts have been seen in urine under three circumstances:

1) Patients receiving no antibiotics: Figure 41.2 shows the appearance of spheroplasts of *E. coli* in midstream voided urine of a subject receiving no treatment at the time the specimen was collected. The tonicity of this urine was 740 mOsm/liter. Spheroplasts are seen in all stages of transition from *E. coli* rod forms.

2) Voided midstream urine during penicillin treatment: Figure 41.3 shows large numbers of fully developed spheroplasts in urine infected with *P. mirabilis*. Shortly after the subject was given 600,000 units of penicillin intramuscularly, he voided; numerous spheroplasts had developed. Since there were such small numbers of bacillary forms, the numerous spheroplasts could be easily missed by someone not looking for them.

3) Urine obtained from indwelling catheters in patients receiving penicillin: these offer an opportunity for serial studies of spheroplasts, as treatment, urinary osmolarity and urinary solutes shift over a period of time. Figure 41.4 shows the appearance of *P. mirabilis* spheroplasts and intermediate conversion forms in the urine of a patient with indwelling catheter and receiving intramuscular penicillin.

Demonstration of Osmotically Fragile Forms in Infected Urine

The organisms in 100 consecutive urines infected with more than 10^5 bacteria/ml were examined for osmotic fragility by comparing bacterial counts after mixing aliquots of the urine in water and 10% sucrose broth. The count fell in 17 specimens; in five of these the percentage fall was more than two standard deviations beyond the mean obtained in 14 broth cultures that also showed a drop in viable bacterial count after suspension in water. As shown in Table 41.7, three of the five urines showing significant osmotic fragility received no antibiotics.

DISCUSSION

From these studies it would appear that three major variables affect the development of spheroplasts in human urine: the bacterial strain or species, the antibiotic or other agent weakening the cell wall, and the relative concentration of different solutes. These factors interact simultaneously and spheroplasts develop and resist lysis only if all three are in proper relationship. The variable interaction between bacillus and antibiotic is brought out by the different susceptibility of each bacterial species to spheroplast formation from penicillin. All strains of *P. mirabilis* are easily converted to spheroplasts by that drug, most strains of *E. coli* partially resist such transformation, and all strains of *P. aeruginosa* completely resist spheroplast formation by penicillin. Yet large numbers of osmotically fragile forms of *P. aeruginosa* were found in urine of a patient receiving no antibiotics.

Even after the cell wall is weakened, however, the development and preservation

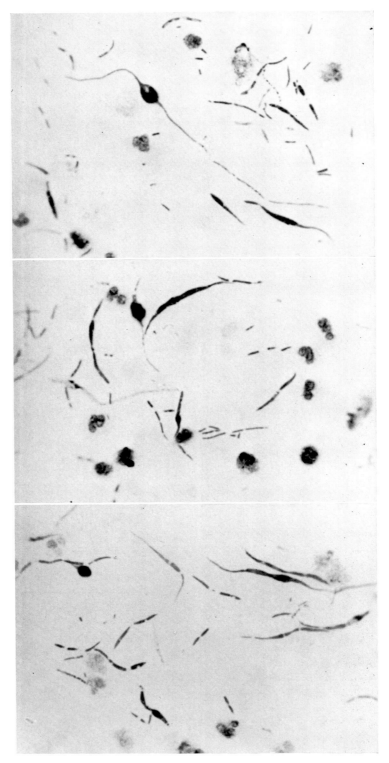

Figure 41.2. Spheroplasts of *Escherichia coli* in midstream voided urine of a man receiving no antibiotics. The tonicity of this urine was 740 mOsm/liter. Spheroplasts are seen in all stages of transition from *E. coli* rod forms. (Top and center, × 900, bottom, × 1260.)

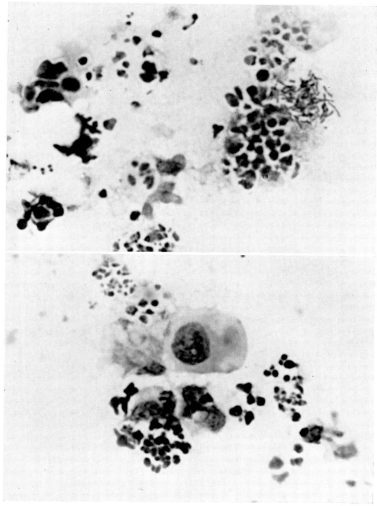

Figure 41.3. Spheroplasts in midstream urine infected with *Proteus mirabilis,* voided shortly after the subject had received 600,000 units of penicillin intramuscularly; numerous spheroplasts have developed. × 1260.

of spheroplasts depends on a favorable balance of solutes in the urine. Generally speaking, spheroplasts develop in hypertonic but not in hypotonic urines. Both urea and sodium help prevent lysis of spheroplasts, but urea does so only if small amounts of sodium are present as well. Isotonic concentrations of NaCl, on the other hand, can prevent lysis in the absence of any other solute. This protective effect of isotonic NaCl on spheroplasts was seen, however, only with strains of *E. coli* and not with *P. mirabilis*. These findings

demonstrate a more complex function for these solutes than simple osmolarity. The protective effect of hypertonic urea in the presence of hypotonic NaCl, but not in water, must indicate that sodium prevents free diffusion of urea across spheroplast membranes, a surprising observation in view of the ease with which urea diffuses across mammalian cells.

The role of other urinary solutes in spheroplast formation seems relatively unimportant compared to sodium and urea. The concentration of hydrogen ions has

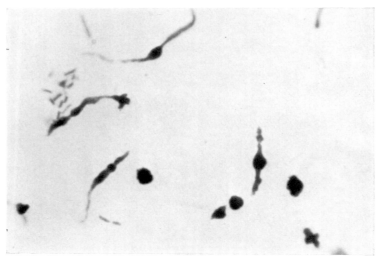

Figure 41.4. Spheroplasts of *Proteus mirabilis* and intermediate conversion forms in the urine of a patient with an indwelling catheter and receiving intramuscular penicillin. × 1260.

TABLE 41.7

Osmotic Fragility of Organisms in Urines of 5 Patients

Sub-ject	Total Drop in Bacterial Count	Drop %	Bacterial Species	Antibiotics Given at Time of Culture
1	9,560,000	99	*Escherichia coli*	Neomycin
2	180,000	69.5	*E. coli*	Penicillin
3	460,000	88	*Pseudomonas aeruginosa*	None
4	96,000,000	75	*Proteus mirabilis*	None
5	590,000	80	*E. coli*	None

little effect on spheroplasts.[2] *E. coli* spheroplasts are best preserved in the acid range. Slight destruction occurs in the range found in alkaline urines, but massive destruction has been found only at a pH higher than that encountered in human urine. *Proteus* spheroplasts are even more resistant to pH changes.[2]

In view of these observations, it is not surprising that all the conditions necessary for spheroplast development are encountered only occasionally in human urine. The large numbers of spheroplasts portrayed in Figures 41.2, 41.3 and 41.4 are an exceptional finding in smears of hu-

man urine. Spheroplasts are sometimes readily destroyed by smears and staining even after methyl alcohol fixation. Examination of wet preparations will sometimes disclose spheroplasts that would be missed in stained preparations. A truer estimate of the frequency of spheroplasts or protoplasts in human urine can probably be made from our finding of osmotically fragile forms in five per cent of infected urines.

The significance of spheroplasts in human urinary infections is not yet clear. In experimental animals, it has been shown that spheroplasts are well preserved in phagocytic cells in the bladder, and even appear to proliferate within them.[2] In the renal medulla of rats and rabbits, the spheroplasts have been found to revert to bacillary forms. It seems reasonable, therefore, that spheroplasts may survive the effects of antibiotics and immune processes and produce recurrent urinary infections in some patients. In the present study, osmolarities greater than 600 were found in 51 per cent of urines collected between 5:00 p.m. and 8:00 p.m. from 200 hospitalized patients with urinary infections. In the morning, the incidence of hypertonic urines is even higher. Since spheroplasts are well preserved in such hypertonic urines, it may be necessary to insist that patients drink large amounts of fluid during treatment of urinary infection in order to maintain dilute urines as a precaution against recurrences.

SUMMARY

If the bacterial cell wall is weakened by penicillin or other agents, spheroplasts develop and persist in human urine only if there is a favorable balance of solutes. In general, spheroplasts develop in hypertonic urines but not in hypotonic urines. Both urea and sodium help prevent lysis of spheroplasts, but urea does so only if small amounts of sodium are present as well. The protective effect of hypertonic urea in the presence of hypotonic NaCl, but not in water, indicates that sodium prevents free diffusion of urea across spheroplast membranes. The conditions favorable to spheroplast formation occasionally produce large numbers of spheroplasts visible in infected human urines. The incidence of infected human urines containing osmotically fragile organisms was five per cent. Maintenance of a dilute urine to produce lysis of spheroplasts is advocated as a precaution against the possibility that they may survive the effects of antibiotics and immune processes and produce recurrences.

REFERENCES

1. Braude, A. I., and Berkowitz, H.: Detection of urinary catalase by disk flotation. *J. Lab. Clin. Med.* **57**: 490, 1961.
2. Braude, A. I., Siemienski, J., and Jacobs, I.: Protoplast formation in human urine. *Trans. Ass. Amer. Physicians* **74**: 234, 1961.
3. Lederberg, J., and St. Clair, J.: Protoplasts and L type growth of *Escherichia coli. J. Bact.* **75**: 143, 1958.

42

Pyelonephritis: Isolation of Protoplasts from Human Kidney Tissue*

George M. Kalmanson and Lucien B. Guze

VETERANS ADMINISTRATION CENTER
AND UCLA SCHOOL OF MEDICINE
LOS ANGELES, CALIFORNIA

Previous studies from our laboratory[13] demonstrated that it was possible to isolate protoplasts† from the kidneys of rats with experimental hematogenous enterococcal pyelonephritis after treatment with penicillin. It was found that adequate early therapy with penicillin eradicated the infection, as judged by absence of bacteria when kidneys were cultured on standard media. However, when renal tissue was cultured on osmotically stabilized media (0.3 M sucrose), protoplasts were recovered as revertants to the original bacterial form. In view of the obvious implications of persistence of bacteria in altered form after apparently adequate therapy, a search for the presence of these forms in human kidney was performed.

* The authors wish to express their thanks to Dr. Victor Rosen, of the Department of Pathology, Wadsworth Hospital, Veterans Administration Center, Los Angeles, for his help in examining the sections of kidney tissue.

† As used in this paper, *protoplasts* are osmotically fragile microbial forms in which the amount of cell wall present was not determined. Under certain conditions, these forms grow on solid media as characteristic *L-colonies*. Some authors have used "spheroplasts", "L-forms", "L-colonies", "L-phase growth", microbial variants", etc., without defining these terms. In the references cited, we have followed the authors' usage and have assumed these terms to be interchangeable.

MATERIALS AND METHODS

PATIENTS

The patients were all middle-aged or elderly males hospitalized at the Wadsworth Hospital, Veterans Administration Center, Los Angeles, California. A portion of kidney tissue was obtained from consecutive patients undergoing genitourinary surgery in which the kidney was exposed, regardless of the preoperative diagnosis.

EXAMINATION OF TISSUE

Each piece of kidney tissue was divided into three parts. A slice was taken from the middle and placed in neutral formalin. Subsequent histologic study was performed by a pathologist who did not know the clinical findings nor the results of bacteriological examination.

The method of culturing kidney tissue was that described for rat kidneys.[12] One of the remaining two kidney portions was ground (Tri-R Grinder, Tri-R Instruments, New York) in distilled water and quantitatively cultured on standard medium (blood agar base, BBL). The other was ground in heart infusion broth (Difco) containing 0.3 M sucrose as osmotic stabilizer, 40 μM $MgSO_4$ and 2% bovine serum albumin (Armour), and plated on the blood agar base with 0.3 M sucrose, $MgSO_4$ and bovine serum albumin. The number of protoplasts was represented by the difference in colony counts obtained on stabilized and unstabilized media.

Whenever possible, urine was obtained from the patients studied prior and subsequent to surgery for quantitative culture on the same media. In addition, results of routine urine cultures performed by the hospital laboratory were available.

RESULTS

Twenty-six specimens from 25 patients were studied. In one instance, two separate specimens were taken by the surgeon from one kidney. The patients could be divided into three groups: (1) Those from whom only protoplasts were isolated; the patient from whom two separate specimens were studied is included in this group, as protoplasts were found in one portion, while bacteria were found in the other. (2) Those from whom bacteria were isolated; in this group, counts on stabilized and unstabilized media were the same, and identical species were isolated from both pieces. (3) Those with sterile kidneys.

Table 42.1 shows the bacteriologic findings in the kidneys of seven patients in whom protoplasts were found. In two instances, coagulase positive *Staphylococcus aureus* was isolated; twice, *Staphylococcus* sp. coagulase negative; twice, beta hemolytic streptococci, not group A; once, alpha hemolytic streptococci; and once, *Streptococcus faecalis*. When attempts were made to subculture the alpha hemolytic streptococci from the osmotically stabilized agar plates used for primary isolation, these organisms grew poorly in liquid media (heart infusion broth, Difco). Only after several passages on unstabilized agar could they be grown readily in unstabilized liquid media. It was additionally noted that initially the streptococci Gram-stained poorly, appearing Gram-variable. On further subculture, they became consistently Grampositive. Of particular interest is Patient 6; in addition to having *S. faecalis* protoplasts in the kidney, the bacterial form was simultaneously isolated from the urine. This patient had been treated with penicillin for *S. faecalis* bacteriuria 14 months prior to the

TABLE 42.1

Bacteriologic Findings in Kidneys of Patients from Whom Protoplasts were Isolated

Patients	Protoplast Culture			Bacterial Culture		
	Tissue weight (g)	Quantity*	Species	Tissue weight (g)	Quantity*	Species
1	0.1925	2.36	*Staphylococcus* sp. coagulase negative	0.1695	None	—
2	0.2187	2.90	Alpha hemolytic streptococci	0.1770	None	—
3	0.0407	2.87	*Staphylococcus aureus* coagulase positive	0.0434	None	—
4	0.1610	1.18	Beta hemolytic streptococci not Group A	0.1501	None	—
5	0.1910	2.70	*S. aureus* coagulase positive	0.1780	None	—
6	0.0211	3.15	*Streptococcus faecalis*	0.1390	None	—
7a†	0.3250	1.18	Beta hemolytic streptococci not Group A	0.2917	None	—
7b†	0.2498	2.18	Beta hemolytic streptococci not Group A and *Staphylococcus* sp. coagulase negative	0.2301	4.54	*Bacillus* sp. and diphtheroids

* Log No. organisms/g of tissue.

† Two separate specimens at same time.

TABLE 42.2

Bacteriologic Findings in Urine of Patients

Found in Patients' Kidneys	No. of Patients Studied	No. with Bacteria in Urine	No. with Significant Bacteriuria	No. with Same Organism in Kidney
Protoplasts	7	7	0	2*
Bacteria	5	5	4	3 (2†)
Sterile	13	7	2	—

* Patients No. 5 and 6, Table 42.1.

† More than 100,000 organisms/ml urine.

TABLE 42.3

Summary of Data on Patients

	Patients with Protoplasts (7)		Patients with Bacteria (5)		Patients with Sterile Kidneys (13)	
	No.	%	No.	%	No.	%
Histological evidence of pyelonephritis	5	71	2	40	2	15
Significantly* positive urine	2	29	5	100	2	15
Renal insufficiency†	2	29	2	40	0	0
History of previous infection	3	43	3	60	4	31
Prior chemotherapy	5	71	4	80	5	38

* More than 100,000 bacteria/ml.

† Creatinine greater than 1.5 mg %.

TABLE 42.4

Findings in Patients With and Without Histological Evidence of Pyelonephritis

	With Pyelonephritis (9)		Without Pyelonephritis (16)	
	No.	%	No.	%
Protoplasts in kidneys	5	56	2	12
Bacteria in kidneys	2	22	3	19
Sterile kidneys	2	22	11	69
Prior chemotherapy	8	89	5	31
History of infection	6	67	5	31
Renal insufficiency*	4	44	0	0

* Creatinine greater than 1.5 mg %.

isolation of *S. faecalis* protoplasts from his kidney.

Table 42.2 gives the results of urine cultures obtained on each patient just prior to or shortly after surgery. It should be noted that, in all instances, the bacteria were isolated from the urine in classical form, i.e., in no case did the organism grow only on stabilized media. It may be seen that bacteria were isolated from the urine of all seven patients with protoplasts in their kidneys, albeit none in significant numbers (10^5/ml urine). In two instances, the organism in the urine was the same species as that isolated from the kidney tissue (*S. faecalis* and beta hemolytic streptococci). The urines of all five patients with bacteria in the kidney were positive, four in significant numbers. In three of these, the organism was the same species as had been isolated from the kidney. Seven of 13 patients with sterile kidneys had bacteriuria. In two of these the bacteria were present in significant numbers.

Comparison has been made of the various aspects of the three groups of patients (Table 42.3). Five of seven (71 per cent) patients with protoplasts had histologic evidence of pyelonephritis, compared with two of five (40 per cent) patients with bacteria and two of thirteen (15 per cent) patients with sterile kidneys. Table 42.4 analyzes these data in another way and compares patients with and without histologic evidence of pyelonephritis. Among nine patients with pyelonephritis, five (56 per cent) had protoplasts in their kidneys, compared with two of sixteen (12 per cent) in those without pyelonephritis. History of infection, prior chemotherapy and renal insufficiency were more common in the group with pyelonephritis.

Additional studies were performed to determine if the results obtained could be due to technical factors rather than to protoplasts being present in the kidney. In order to investigate whether grinding and diluting the kidneys in distilled water could affect the intact organism, 18-hour broth cultures of the isolates from kidneys were serially diluted through distilled water or broth and plated on standard media. In no case was the count of the broth-diluted cultures higher than that of the water-diluted. Another possibility considered was that the sucrose used for osmotic stabilization was nutritive and would lead to higher counts on sucrose agar. This possibility was made more cogent by the finding that, in six of seven instances, the organism isolated from the kidney tissue was able to ferment sucrose. However, when counts of broth cultures of the organisms were compared on standard and sucrose agars, they were identical. Furthermore, it should be pointed out that the strain of *S. faecalis* used to produce protoplasts in rat kidneys after treatment with penicillin does not ferment sucrose.

Additional studies were done to investigate whether kidney tissue *per se* was deleterious to protoplasts. Normal rat kidney was ground in osmotically stabilized broth and added to osmotically stabilized agar plates, which were then inoculated with a variety of protoplasts. The following were studied: Penicillin-produced protoplasts of *S. faecalis*, *Escherichia coli* (Yale) and *Proteus mirabilis* (Lab. No. 5) and stable lysozyme-produced L-forms of *S. faecalis* (F24).*

Protoplasts were produced by streaking the bacterial forms of *S. faecalis* on osmotically stabilized agar containing 1000 units penicillin per ml. L-colonies thus produced were maintained by serial transfer on osmotically stabilized agar containing penicillin. The number of serial passages on antibiotic media was designated "T" with a subnumeral. In these experiments, T_9 protoplasts were used. These readily revert to the bacterial form when plated on osmotically stabilized medium without antibotic ("unstable" protoplasts). Other studies were done with T_{53} protoplasts. At the 53rd passage, these protoplasts were serially transferred without penicillin at least 30 times without reversion to bacterial form ("stable" protoplasts). *E. coli* (Yale) and *P. mirabilis* (Lab. No. 5) protoplasts were produced by streaking the bacterial form on osmotically stabilized medium containing 10,000 units penicillin per ml. The T_{55} protoplast of *E. coli* and the T_{57} protoplasts of *P. mirabilis* were used. These protoplasts were unstable. Table 42.5 indicates that rat kidney inhibited the growth of all protoplasts studied. The most marked effects were noted with protoplasts of *S. faecalis* (T_9), *P. mirabilis* and stable protoplasts of *S. faecalis* F24.

* Kindly supplied by Dr. Harry Gooder.

TABLE 42.5

Effect of Kidney Tissue on Growth of Protoplasts on Agar

Protoplasts	Concentration of Kidney Tissue*	
	1%	2%
Streptococcus faecalis, T_9	0.47	—
S. faecalis, T_{53}	21.68	19.21
S. faecalis (F24)	0.43	0.43
Escherichia coli (Yale)	60.60	60.80
Proteus mirabilis (Lab. No. 5)	0.43	0.41

* Normal rat kidney was ground in osmotically stabilized broth and incorporated in osmotically stabilized agar plates.

Results are expressed as percentage of growth on control plates of osmotically stabilized agar containing 2% bovine serum albumin but without kidney tissue.

DISCUSSION

In the present study, it was possible to isolate protoplasts from the kidneys of seven of 25 patients, selected only on the basis that they were undergoing surgery in which the kidney was accessible. The protoplasts were recognized by the fact that no growth appeared on standard medium; however, when an aliquot of the biopsy specimen was cultured on the same medium osmotically stabilized with 0.3 M sucrose, the protoplasts survived, reverted, and grew into classic bacterial form. The alpha hemolytic streptococcus (from Patient 2, Table 42.1) appears to have still been in protoplast form on primary isolation, as indicated by Gram-variability and poor growth early in isolation. It is tempting to consider, but unproved, that the patient from whom *S. faecalis* protoplasts were isolated harbored these forms in his kidney for 14 months subsequent to his initial treatment with penicillin. It may be that the factors in the kidney which keep microbes in protoplast form no longer operate when the organisms are released into the urine. This would explain the two instances (Patients 5 and 6, Table 42.1) in which the same species was present in the kidney in protoplast form and in the urine in bacterial form.

The failure to demonstrate protoplasts of

Gram-negative bacteria, which are the usual cause of human pyelonephritis, is puzzling. It is possible this was due to technical reasons. Our criterion for protoplasts has been osmotic fragility. Since some protoplasts of Gram-negative bacteria can grow on media not osmotically stabilized, differences in counts between standard and osmotically stabilized media may not have occurred despite the presence of protoplasts. It is further possible that, for unknown reasons, the media used may not have been suitable for demonstration of protoplasts in the state in which they were present in the kidney. Pertinent to this point are some studies made of a stable protoplast of a strain of *Proteus* kindly supplied by Dr. Ruth Wittler, together with the formula of the medium used for its growth. This medium is enriched with 20% human serum but is not osmotically stabilized. The *Proteus* protoplasts have grown well in this medium but not in the osmotically stabilized medium with 2% bovine serum albumin used in the present study.

The fact that kidney tissue was inhibitory to a variety of protoplasts (Table 42.5) is another factor which complicates efforts to isolate protoplasts. That protoplasts can survive *in vivo* in the kidney but were destroyed by kidney homogenates suggests they were protected *in vivo*. It may be that this protection is related to an intracellular location of protoplasts or to the fact that the renal milieu interferes with this protoplast cidal activity in a manner not unlike that noted for interference with bactericidal activity.[14]

Other studies have reported protoplasts from the genitourinary tract. Moustárdier and associates[24] studied patients with "nonbacterial" urethritis and noted four instances in which, on serial passage, primary atypical isolates reverted to bacterial form; twice to *S. faecalis*, once to *Alcaligenes faecalis,* and once to *P. mirabilis*. The medium was enriched with ascitic fluid, serum ("animal or human"), and contained 1% salt. Barile and associates[3] used a medium composed of brain heart infusion, yeast extract, agar, distilled water, and human blood to culture organisms from a wide variety of clinical material. and were

able to isolate four L-forms from the genitourinary tract. Two were variants of *Corynebacterium hofmannii* and *Hemophilus hemolyticus,* isolated from the urethrae of patients with non-gonococcal urethritis. Variants of an alpha hemolytic streptococcus and *Neisseria gonorrhea* were recovered from the urethrae of patients with gonorrhea. In a further study,[2] these workers speculated that failure of penicillin treatment of gonorrhea may be due to L-form transformation of *N. gonorrhea*. This was based on successful *in vitro* transformation by penicillin.

Gutman and associates[11] examined 146 samples of urine from 57 patients with chronic bacteriuria, 73 samples from 59 patients with other renal disease, and 15 samples from 15 consecutive admissions for other than renal disease. Protoplasts were demonstrated in 11 of the 57 (19 per cent) with chronic bacteriuria. One patient in whom *E. coli* protoplasts were found in urine also had classical *E. coli* in renal biopsy tissue. None of the patients with other renal disease nor the consecutive non-renal patients demonstrated protoplasts.

Braude and associates[4] were able to produce *in vitro* in urine, by means of a number of antibiotics, protoplasts from a variety of Gram-negative bacteria causing pyelonephritis. In addition, they studied the phenomenon *in vivo*. Protoplasts occurred in urine following systemic treatment with penicillin and, in one case, chloramphenicol. Reversion of *P. mirabilis* protoplasts produced *in vitro* to classical bacterial forms occurred when the protoplasts were instilled into the rat bladder.

Neither the findings of protoplasts in clinical material nor their deliberate induction *in vivo* proves that they can cause disease. However, it is important to consider the possible mechanisms by which these forms could produce disease in order to design meaningful clinical experiments.

DIRECT HOST-PARASITE INTERACTION

Carrère and associates[6] prepared L-forms of *Salmonella typhimurium in vitro* in peptone medium with plasma and penicillin. After three days' growth, the culture was passed through a Chamberland L3 filter and filtrate deposited on the chorioallantoic membrane of a ten-day egg. After four days, the membranes showed hemorrhagic macroscopic plaques. Microscopic examination revealed the L-forms to be growing both extra- and intracellularly in these plaques; and, in one instance, three serial passages on egg were successful. The L-forms did not cause death of the embryos. Alderman & Freedman[1] found that, while intracutaneous injection of 10^7 or more bacillary forms of E. coli produced induration of greater than 0.5 cm in all of six rabbits, protoplasts produced similar reaction in only one of six instances.

Kagan & Rakovskaya[16] studied the effect of stable L-forms from a strain of Salmonella typhosa and three strains of hemolytic streptococci on tissue cultures. It was found that L-forms had varying degrees of cytopathogenicity, depending on the species of organism used and the origin of the cell line used for culture. Similarly, Freeman & Rumack[9] found that spheroplasts of Brucella were more destructive to guinea pig monocytes in tissue culture than were the unaltered bacteria. Diena and associates[7] produced spheroplasts of Salmonella typhi with glycine. These forms were toxic, as judged by both intracutaneous inoculation in rabbits and intraperitoneal injection in mice, although less so than the parent bacteria.

Kagan and associates[15] injected L-forms of hemolytic streptococci into the peritonsillar areas of Macacus speciosus monkeys. Various degrees of clinical infection persisted from 3 to 22 days; in one instance, L-forms were isolated from the blood. Koptelova and associates[20] developed a model of experimental meningitis in rabbits by suboccipital injection of streptococcal and staphylococcal L-forms. The clinical picture, while somewhat more torpid than that produced with the corresponding bacterial forms, usually resulted in death on the 7th through 15th day. Histologic findings were characteristic of severe meningitis.

Mattman & Mattman[22] described two patients with septicemia from whom L-forms of S. faecalis were isolated from the blood. One of these also had the same L-forms in the spinal fluid. The L-forms were found at a time when classic bacteria were not present. The authors felt that active infection was present during the periods when only L-forms were isolated, suggesting their responsibility for treatment failure.

B. M. Kagan* cultured sputum from 54 children with cystic fibrosis and recovered hemolytic S. aureus protoplasts as bacterial revertants on osmotically stabilized medium from approximately 30 per cent of patients. In a few instances, the microbial variants were isolated as L-colonies on osmotically stabilized agar. On serial transfer, these L-colonies reverted to the bacterial form of hemolytic S. aureus.

TOXIC PRODUCTS ACTING DIRECTLY OR IMMUNO-LOGICALLY

Dienes[8] found that L-forms of Clostridium tetani did not produce tetanus in mice. Scheibel & Assandri,[25] however, in an in vitro study were able to induce toxin-producing L-phase variants from four toxigenic strains of C. tetani. Minck & Fruhling[23] compared the reaction in the skin of rabbits of parent bacteria and L-forms of a Vibrio cholerae and a strain of Proteus. The Vibrio bacterial form produced only transitory edema and slight necrosis; the Proteus bacterial form produced intense edema and congestion, usually with eventual death of the animal. On the other hand, reactions to the L-forms of both organisms were identical: there was an intense local reaction with eventual production of a caseous lesion from which the L-forms could not be recovered. The authors could reproduce the lesions with chloroform extracts of the Proteus L-forms and considered the reaction to be a response to irritating fatty substances. Tulasne & Lavillaureix[26] studied the pathogenicity of a "fixed L-form of a water vibrio". When injected by various routes into mice, death usually occurred within hours and, in most cases, the authors were able to recover the organism as L-forms. They noted that the pathology was identical to that produced by endotoxin; and, in a subsequent report,[27] they found the same pathological picture could be induced with killed or extracted L-forms.

* Personal communication.

Lynn & Muellenberg[21] indicated the possible presence of an antigen in L-forms not existing in the parent bacteria, having found that in antisera to L-forms specific antibodies were present which could not be absorbed with the parent *Streptococcus*. Karakawa and associates[19] demonstrated the presence of M protein in colonies of streptococcal L-forms by means of immunofluorescence technique. The pathologic significance of the presence of these antigens is suggested by the studies of Kantor,[18] who found that intravenous injection of Type 1 streptococcal M protein in mice and rats produced lesions confined to the renal glomeruli. Thrombi of eosinophiles and amorphous material were seen to occlude glomerular capillaries and were shown to contain M protein and fibrinogen. Gradual regression of the morphologic lesions occurred during the three weeks following injection. Initial abnormal proteinuria and azotemia returned to control levels by the end of the first week. A secondary rise in urinary protein excretion and urea retention was demonstrated in some rats, coincident with the appearance of an anti-M protein antibody. This was not accompanied by increased morphologic changes.

REVERSION TO THE CLASSIC BACTERIAL FORM

Wittler and associates[28] repeatedly studied a child with subacute bacterial endocarditis. Prior to the initiation of therapy, the "conventional bacillary form" of *Corynebacterium* species was present in the blood and bone marrow. In addition, in one blood culture, a filamentous Gram-negative pleomorphic variant was found, which eventually reverted to a small Gram-positive rod resembling *Corynebacterium*. During a period of several years, at times when antibiotics were administered, a variety of non-bacillary "transitional" forms were isolated, whose microscopic and colonial morphology resembled L-forms; these could be reverted to the conventional bacillary form. At times when antibiotics were discontinued, relapses of clinical disease occurred, and the conventional bacilli reappeared in the blood.

Brier and associates[5] prepared L-phase organisms *in vitro* from staphylococci, *E. coli,* and *Proteus* sp. These were inoculated into egg embryos and could be held in L-phase by treatment with antibiotics. When the antibiotics were discontinued, reversion to classic bacterial form occurred with concomitant overt infection and subsequent death of the embryo. Alderman & Freedman[1] prepared protoplasts of *E. coli* by penicillin treatment and inoculated them directly into the renal medulla of rabbits. The bacterial form was recovered from the protoplast-injected kidney in 11 of 17 animals in four to five days. In two instances, lesions of experimental pyelonephritis were found. Godzeski and associates[10] reported the isolation of L-phase staphylococci from the blood of individuals subject to recurrent "boils and staphylococcal problems" after remission of the clinical symptoms of disease had been brought about by antibiotics. It was suggested that these forms were responsible for clinical relapse at times when host resistance was lowered.

Studies from this laboratory indicated that protoplasts can remain in the kidney tissue for many months.[13] Although it was not possible experimentally to induce reversion to the parent bacteria *in vivo* with consequent recrudescence of clinical disease,[17] the rapid reversion which occurred when the kidney tissue was cultured *in vitro* indicated the possibility of this recurrence *in vivo* under appropriate, but as yet undefined, conditions. That reversion may occur is suggested by findings in the present studies, in which the organism was found in tissue in protoplast form while the same species was isolated from the urine as classic bacterial form. Perhaps the protoplast was intracellular and reverted rapidly to the parent form when released into the urine, at which time whatever factors were operating intracellularly no longer served to prevent reversion. The patient (Patient 6, Table 42.1), who had been treated for a *S. faecalis* urinary tract infection with penicillin 14 months prior to isolation of *S. faecalis* protoplasts from his kidney, is of particular interest in this regard.

The relationship of the finding of protoplasts in the kidneys of seven patients to the pathogenesis of chronic pyelonephritis is not known. Five of the seven (71 per cent) had histologic evidence of pyelonephritis, while this was the case in two of 13 (15 per cent) patients with sterile kidneys. Viewed another way, nine of the patients studied had pyelonephritis and protoplasts were demonstrated in five (56 per cent), while among the remaining 16 with no histologic evidence of pyelonephritis, protoplasts were found in only two (12 per cent). It is attractive to speculate that protoplasts may contribute to the development of chronic pyelonephritis by any of the mechanisms described. This possibility may provide a partial explanation for some cases of the often puzzling finding of sterile kidneys in patients with histologic evidence of chronic pyelonephritis.

SUMMARY

Protoplasts were demonstrated in the kidneys of seven of 25 consecutive patients who had surgical biopsies. Five of seven (71 per cent) patients with protoplasts had histologic evidence of pyelonephritis as compared with similar findings of disease in only two of 13 (15 per cent) with sterile kidneys. Viewed another way, nine of the 25 patients had histologic evidence of pyelonephritis, and protoplasts were found in five (56 per cent), while only two of the 16 (12 per cent) patients without such evidence of pyelonephritis had protoplasts. Two of the seven patients with protoplasts in their kidneys had the same species in classic bacterial form in the urine.

The role of protoplasts as etiologic agents of disease and a cause of recurrence of infection after therapy has been discussed. In addition, speculation has been made concerning the possibility that protoplast persistence may explain development of chronic pyelonephritis in the absence of demonstrable classic bacterial forms.

REFERENCES

1. Alderman, M. H., and Freedman, L. R.: Experimental pyelonephritis. X. The direct injection of *E. coli* protoplasts into the medulla of the rabbit kidney. *Yale J. Biol. Med.* **36:** 157, 1963.
2. Barile, M. F., Van Zee, G. K., and Yaguchi, R.: The occurrence of failures in penicillin-treated gonorrheal urethritis. I. The significance of L-form transformation of *Neisseria gonorrhoeae* to penicillin resistance. *Antibiot. Med. Clin. Ther.* **6:** 470, 1959.
3. Barile, M. F., Yaguchi, R., and Eveland, W. C.: A simplified medium for the cultivation of pleuropneumonia-like organisms and the L-forms of bacteria. *Amer. J. Clin. Path.* **30:** 171, 1958.
4. Braude, A. I., Siemienski, J., and Jacobs, I.: Protoplast formation in human urine. *Trans. Ass. Amer. Physicians* **74:** 234, 1961.
5. Brier, G., Ellis, L., and Godzeski, C. W.: Survival *in vivo* (in ovo) of L-phase bacteria. In: *Antimicrobial Agents and Chemotherapy —1962*, (J. C. Sylvester, Ed.). American Society for Microbiology, Ann Arbor, 1963: p. 854.
6. Carrère, L., Roux, J., and Mandin, J.: Culture des organismes L sur membrane chorio-allantoïde d'embryon de Poulet. *C. R. Soc. Biol.* (Paris) **149:** 777, 1955.
7. Diena, B. B., Wallace, R., and Greenberg, L.: Immunologic studies of glycine-induced spheroplasts of *Salmonella typhi. Canad. J. Microbiol.* **10:** 555, 1964.
8. Dienes, L.: Isolation of L type cultures from Clostridia. *Proc. Soc. Exp. Biol. Med.* **75:** 412, 1950.
9. Freeman, B. A., and Rumack, B. H.: Cytopathogenic effect of *Brucella* spheroplasts on monocytes in tissue culture. *J. Bact.* **88:** 1310, 1964.
10. Godzeski, C. W., Brier, G., Griffith, R. S., and Black, H. R.: Association of bacterial L-phase organisms in chronic infections. *Nature* **205:** 1340, 1965.
11. Gutman, L. T., Turck, M., Petersdorf, R. G., and Wedgewood, R. J.: Significance of bacterial variants in urine of patients with chronic bacteriuria. *J. Clin. Invest.* **44:** 1945, 1965.
12. Guze, L. B., Goldner, B. H., and Kalmanson, G. M.: Pyelonephritis. I. Observations on the course of chronic non-obstructed enterococcal infection in the kidney of the rat. *Yale J. Biol. Med.* **33:** 372, 1961.
13. Guze, L. B., and Kalmanson, G. M.: Persistence of bacteria in "protoplast" form after apparent cure of pyelonephritis in rats. *Science* **143:** 1340, 1964.
14. Hubert, E. G., Montgomerie, J. Z., Kalmanson, G. M., and Guze, L. B.: Effect of renal physico-chemical milieu on serum bactericidal activity. *Amer. J. Med. Sci.* **253:** 229, 1967.
15. Kagan, G. Y., Koptelova, E. I., Prozorovsky, S. V., Mikhailova, M. S., Dzhikidze, E. K., Akbroit, E. Y., Doroftienko, S. F., Chirko-

vich, E. M., Simovanyan, V. G., and Dzobakhidze, L. V.: Experience with experimental infection of monkeys macacus with L-forms of hemolytic streptococcus. *Vestn. Akad. Med. Nauk. SSSR* **20**(8): 54, 1965.

16. Kagan, G. Y., and Rakovskaya, I. V. The cytogenic action of the L-forms of some pathogenic bacterial species in tissue cultures. *Biull. Eksp. Biol. Med.* **57**(6): 69, 1964 (in Russian).

17. Kalmanson, G. M., and Guze, L. B.: Role of protoplasts in pathogenesis of pyelonephritis. *JAMA* **190**: 1107, 1964.

18. Kantor, F. S.: Fibrinogen precipitation by streptococcal M protein. II. Renal lesions induced by intravenous injection of M protein into mice and rats. *J. Exp. Med.* **121**: 861, 1965.

19. Karakawa, W. W., Rotta, J., and Krause, R. M.: Detection of M protein in colonies of streptococcal L forms by immunofluorescence. *Proc. Soc. Exp. Biol. Med.* **118**: 198, 1965.

20. Koptelova, E. I., Pokrovsky, V. I., and Gorshkova, E. Y. P.: A model of experimental meningitis in rabbits produced by L-forms of streptococci and staphylococci. *Vestn. Akad. Med. Nauk. SSSR* **20**(8): 60, 1965 (in Russian).

21. Lynn, R. J., and Muellenberg, M. B.: Immunological properties of an L-form of a group A beta hemolytic streptococcus. *Antonie Leeuwenhoek.* **31**: 15, 1965.

22. Mattman, L. H., and Mattman, P. E.: L-forms of *Streptococcus faecalis* in septicemia. *Arch. Intern. Med. (Chicago)* **115**: 315, 1965.

23. Minck, R., and Fruhling, L.: Obtention chez le Lapin de lésions dermiques après inoculation de formes L. *C. R. Soc. Biol.* (Paris) **148**: 2091, 1954.

24. Moustárdier, G., Brisou, J., and Perrey, M.: Transformation en bactéries normales d'organismes L isolés par culture à partir d'uréthrites amicrobiennes à inclusions. *Ann. Inst. Pasteur* (Paris) **85**: 520, 1953.

25. Scheibel, I., and Assandri, J. Isolation of toxigenic L-phase variants from *Cl. tetani. Acta Path. Microbiol. Scand.* **46**: 333, 1959.

26. Tulasne, R., and Lavillaureix, J.: Pouvoir pathogène expérimental, pour la Souris, d'une souche de formes L des bactéries. *C. R. Soc. Biol.* (Paris) **148**: 2080, 1954.

27. ———: Mécanisme de l'action pathogène d'une forme L des bactéries d'origine vibrionnienne. *C. R. Soc. Biol.* (Paris) **149**: 178, 1955.

28. Wittler, R. G., Malizia, W. F., Kramer, P. E., Tuckett, J. D., Pritchard, H. N., and Baker, H. J.: Isolation of a Corynebacterium and its transitional forms from a case of subacute bacterial endocarditis treated with antibiotics. *J. Gen. Microbiol.* **23**: 315, 1960.

43

Significance of Bacterial Variants in Urinary Tract Infections

Marvin Turck, Laura T. Gutman, Ralph J. Wedgwood
and Robert G. Petersdorf

UNIVERSITY OF WASHINGTON SCHOOL OF MEDICINE
AND KING COUNTY HOSPITAL
SEATTLE, WASHINGTON

Infections of the urinary tract often recur following cessation of antimicrobial therapy. The precise bacteriologic and serologic identification of enterobacteriaceae, particularly the characterization of the somatic and flagellar antigens of *Escherichia coli,* has made possible the differentiation between two patterns of recurrent infection.[19] Most often, recurrences are due to a different bacterial species or strain than was present originally, and in all likelihood represent exogenous reinfection. In some instances, however, recrudescence of infection takes place with the same species or serologic strain of organism which was present at the outset of treatment. This type of recurrence has been defined as relapse and may be due in part to the ability of organisms to remain viable in the kidney in the form of bacterial variants, often termed "protoplasts", "L-forms", or "spheroplasts". These variants can be induced *in vitro* by most antibiotics as well as serum factors,[5] lysozyme,[22] and leukocyte granules.[2]

Protoplasts and L-forms may fall along a continuum, and it is often difficult to separate one from the other by their morphological or physiochemical properties. For the purposes of this paper, *protoplasts* and *L-forms* are used interchangeably and are defined as osmotically fragile, filtrable bacterial forms that appear as granular or budding bodies in broth, grow as distinct colonies on a medium modified for pleuropneumonia-like organisms (PPLO), and may or may not revert to the parent, classical bacterial form on repeated subcultures.

This paper deals with the demonstration of bacterial variants in some patients with chronic bacteriuria, and the results suggest that L-forms and protoplasts may be one cause of recurrent infection in these patients.

METHODS

The methods for processing the urine specimens, and the culture procedures for isolation of bacterial variants have been described previously.[8] Briefly, urine was added to a 20% sucrose solution for osmotic stabilization, as suggested by Lederberg.[13] The urine was then passed through a 0.45 μ Millipore filter. Because of their plasticity, variants usually pass through this pore size, whereas their classical parent forms will generally be retained by the filter.[11] The urine filtrate was then processed as follows: (1) 0.25 ml was inoculated into an L-form medium pour plate; (2) 0.25 ml was inoculated into an L-form medium pour plate containing **25** μg/ml tetrazolium red indicator; (3) 0.1 ml was inoculated onto a standard sheep blood agar plate; (4) a drop was examined directly by phase contrast microscopy; (5) the remainder of the filtrate was inoculated into biphasic L-form medium, that is, the broth and agar media were combined, with the agar layered as a slope on the bottom of the tube. All plates were incubated aerobically at 37°C. The blood agar plates served as a check on contamination by classical bacterial forms, and the samples were discarded if urine filtrates produced growth on the blood plate. Only those samples that showed growth of colonies in L-form medium agar plates, including colonies that were macroscopically visible in the agar and colonies that reduced the indicator dye to visible pink and red, were considered positive. Forms that could be identified only in the broth or forms that were visible in the agar only by microscopy were not accepted because of possible artifacts.

Results

The number of patients from whom L-forms could be identified is shown in Table

Table 43.1
*Total Experience in Culturing for Bacterial Variants**

Cases	Total No.	Positive for Variants	
		No.	%
Patients with chronic bacteriuria or pyelonephritis			
Patients	57	11	19
Urine samples	146	23	16
Patients with renal disease other than chronic bacteriuria or pyelonephritis			
Patients	59	0	0
Urine samples	73	0	0
Consecutive admissions for medical reasons other than renal disease			
Patients	15	0	0
Urine samples	15	0	0

*Data from Gutman, Turck, Petersdorf & Wedgwood.[8]

Table 43.2
Routine Urine Cultures at Time of Positive Variant Culture

Case	Routine Culture		Reversion	Concurrent Antimicrobial Therapy
	Organism	No.		
1	Negative		None	Ampicillin
	Escherichia coli	$>10^3$	None	Ampicillin
2	E. coli	$>10^5$	None	Ampicillin
	Klebsiella	$<10^2$	None	Ampicillin
	Klebsiella	$<10^2$	None	Ampicillin
3	E. coli and Proteus mirabilis	$>10^4$	E. coli	Ampicillin
4	E. coli	$>10^5$	None	Ampicillin
	E. coli	$<10^2$	None	Ampicillin
	Negative		None	Ampicillin
	E. coli	$>10^5$	E. coli	Ampicillin
	E. coli	$<10^2$	E. coli	Ampicillin
	Negative		E. coli	Ampicillin
5	E. coli	$>10^5$	None	None
6	Streptococcus faecalis	$>10^5$	S. faecalis	None
7	Negative		None	None
8	E. coli	$>10^5$	E. coli	Cephalothin
	Negative		E. coli	Cephalothin
9	E. coli	$>10^5$	None	Chloramphenicol
10	Negative		None	None
11*	Negative		None	None
	Negative		None	None
	Negative		None	None
	Negative		None	None
	Negative		None	None

* A renal biopsy from this patient was positive for variants, which subsequently reverted to *P. mirabilis*.

43.1. A total of **234** urine cultures was processed from **131** patients; bacterial variants were demonstrated from 11 of 56 patients with the clinical diagnosis of chronic bacteriuria or pyelonephritis. They were not cultured from the urine of any of 59 patients with renal disease other than chronic urinary tract infection, nor from 15 consecutive patients admitted to the hospital for reasons other than renal disease.

The bacteriologic and clinical data of the 11 patients from whom L-forms or protoplasts were recovered are summarized in Table 43.2. Bacterial variants were usually demonstrated at a time when the patient had significant bacteriuria and was receiving concurrent antimicrobial therapy. However, cultures positive for variants were also obtained from five patients who had not received therapy for at least six weeks, or had not been treated at all. In all, 23 samples from these 11 patients showed L-form growth and in seven instances the variant subsequently reverted to a classical bacterial form. When reversion occurred, the same species or serogroup of organism with which the patient was initially infected invariably reappeared. Variants were more likely to revert when they were isolated in relation to antibiotic treatment. Urine samples from three patients (cases No. 7, 10, and 11) were positive for variants at a time when the routine bacteriologic culture was negative and the patient was not receiving concurrent chemotherapy. Patient No. 11 was admitted to the hospital because of progressive azotemia of unknown etiology, and renal biopsy was performed which showed histologic evidence of pyelonephritis. Bacterial variants which ultimately reverted to classical *Proteus mirabilis* were cultured from homogenates of the tissue specimen. Urinary L-forms were demonstrated on four separate occasions, but failed to revert. However, passage of these apparently stable variants resulted in isolation of forms that readily reverted to *P. mirabilis*. Renal tissue obtained at post mortem also grew L-forms that failed to revert.

An additional patient (No. 4) had been followed for the past five years in the "pyelonephritis" clinic at King County Hospital for asymptomatic bacteriuria, and consistently harbored the same strain of *E. coli* 016-62. During this period of observation she had remained completely asymptomatic despite persistent bacteriuria. Because L-forms were demonstrated in her urine during treatment with ampicillin, she was admitted to the hospital for further study and treatment. Percutaneous renal biopsy was performed and classical *E. coli* 016-62 was cultured from the tissue homogenate, although L-forms could only be identified in the urine. A course of parenteral ampicillin was administered, and the urine was sterilized promptly. Erythromycin was also

TABLE 43.3

*Patients Studied for Bacterial Variants While Receiving Antimicrobial Therapy**

Case	Infecting Organism	Variant Culture	After Therapy
1	*Streptococcus faecalis*	+	*S. faecalis*
	Escherichia coli 04		*E. coli* 04
2	*E. coli* 07	+	*E. coli* 07
4	*E. coli* 016/62	+	*E. coli* 016/62
9	*E. coli*	+	*E. coli*
12	*E. coli*	−	*Klebsiella*
13	*E. coli*	−	No relapse
14	Intermediate coliform	−	*Proteus mirabilis*
15	*E. coli*	−	No relapse
16	*E. coli* 075	−	*E. coli* 075

* Data from Gutman, Turck, Petersdorf & Wedgwood.[8]

added because of apparent *in vitro* susceptibility of the L-form to this drug. However, relapse of infection with the same serologic strain occurred again shortly following cessation of therapy.

Nine patients were studied for the presence of variants before, during, and after treatment with antibiotics (Table 43.3). This was a selected group because not all patients were studied serially in relation to chemotherapy. All but one had received several courses of antimicrobials for chronic urinary tract infection in the past, and all were either refractory to treatment or had recurrences with the same or different strains after cessation of therapy. Although all nine patients became abacteriuric during therapy, only two remained free from significant infection for at least six weeks. Of note is the fact that recurrences of infection among the four patients in whom L-forms were demonstrated during therapy were characterized by relapse with the same organism or serogroup of *E. coli* present prior to therapy, whereas recurrence did not occur or was due to a different bacterial species among the patients without L-forms. Although relapse of infection with the same strain of *E. coli* 075 was also found in one patient from whom variants were not grown, this patient had nephrolithiasis and relapse was not unexpected.

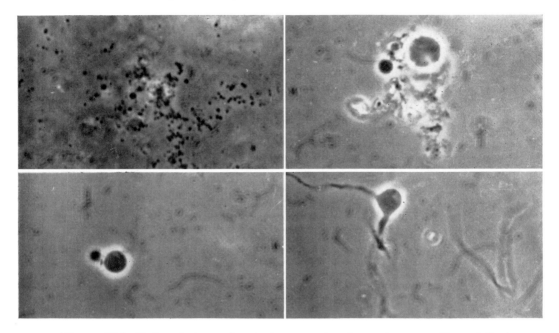

Figure 43.1. Various features of variants as seen by phase microscopy. *Upper left:* A variant colony within an agar block; note the cluster of organisms in the center of the colony; these organisms were obtained from Patient 4, and reverted to *Escherichia coli* (agar smash × 300). *Upper right:* A stable L-form or protoplast isolated from the urine of Patient 11; note the large body surrounded by granules and spheres in various stages of development, which mature to become variants (wet mount of broth culture × 3000). *Lower left:* A budding protoplast obtained from Patient 3; these variants reverted to *E. coli* (wet mount of broth culture × 3000). *Lower right:* A variant during the process of reversion to *Proteus mirabilis*, isolated from the kidney biopsy of Patient 11; the long filamentous extensions from the central round body undergo segmentation to become bacilli (wet mount of broth culture × 3000). (From Gutman, Turck, Petersdorf & Wedgwood.[8])

Figure 43.1 depicts characteristic examples of an agar smash of a variant colony, stable granular variant forms, budding, and filamentous forms identified from patients in this study.

DISCUSSION

The treatment of urinary tract infections has been generally unsatisfactory, and these patients' long histories of repeated instrumentation and multiple courses of antimicrobial therapy interspersed with flare-ups characterized by classical symptoms of "cystitis" or "pyelonephritis" attest to the refractoriness of these infections. Why infections of the urinary tract have been so notoriously resistant to attack with both medical and surgical therapeutic maneuvers

is not entirely clear.[14] Among the possible reasons are: failure to remedy obstruction to urine flow; emergence of antibiotic-resistant mutants during or after treatment; presence of "mixed infections" in which only the sensitive pathogens are eliminated while resistant strains persist; choice of the incorrect antimicrobial, use of a drug in inadequate dosage or for too brief a period; inability of a drug to achieve antibacterial levels in renal tissue as well as urine; a milieu unfavorable to optimal action of antibiotics within the renal parenchyma; the possibility that local and humoral defense mechanisms are poor in the kidney, when compared to other loci. An additional reason is that some persistent and recurrent bacterial infections of the urinary tract may result from the ability of organisms to remain viable in the kidney as bacterial variants.

In the present study approximately 20 per cent of a selected group of patients with chronic bacteriuria had bacterial variants demonstrated in the urine at some time in their course. It should be emphasized that variants are probably not responsible for most instances of recurrent bacteriuria. Many failures that follow antimicrobial treatment of chronic bacteriuria are related to reinfections with new resistant strains rather than relapse with the initial pathogen.[12, 15]

In attempting to relate variants to the pathogenesis of infection in the kidney, it may be worthwhile to attempt to distinguish protoplasts from L-forms. There is evidence that L-forms are not as osmotically fragile as are protoplasts,[17] and the greater osmotic stability of the L-form may in part explain its survival in the isotonic environment of the body. Distinct from L-forms, protoplasts may lyse in an isotonic milieu, and only the renal medulla may be sufficiently hypertonic to support their growth. It is also conceivable that protoplasts are formed in the renal medulla during infection and subsequently develop into stable L-forms that can be recovered from the urine. Other factors besides hypertonicity of the renal medulla, which may influence survival of bacterial variants within kidney tissue, include inactivation of the fourth component of complement by ammonia,[3] and the delayed leukocyte mobilization which follows thermal injury of the renal medulla.[18]

In previous studies direct microscopy has shown round, bizarre forms in the urine of patients with bacteriuria receiving antimicrobial agents.[4, 20] The present study differs from those previously reported because bacterial variants were grown as well as observed microscopically.

In 1951, Voureka[20] observed bizarre bacterial forms in the urine of patients who were treated with chloramphenicol and also noted their reversion to the parent form after repeated subcultures. In the present study, variants were also cultured from one patient with recurrent E. coli pyelonephritis

during treatment with chloramphenicol. Variants can be induced in vitro by most antimicrobials, regardless of their mode of action, and it has been found that most antibiotics in low concentration can induce L-form formation in the presence of serum or other body fluids.[6]

Braude, Siemienski & Jacobs[4] reported a patient with Proteus pyelonephritis, in whose urine round, osmotically fragile forms were found during therapy with penicillin. When these organisms were injected into the bladders of rats, a Proteus pyelonephritis was produced seven to eight days later. In the present study, variants were cultured from the urine of a patient with multiple myeloma who was not receiving antimicrobial treatment concurrently. Although these urinary variants, which were demonstrated on four separate occasions, failed to revert to classical bacterial forms, passage of these stable variants into rats resulted in isolation of forms that readily reverted to P. mirabilis. More recently we have demonstrated[23] that penicillin-induced L-forms of E. coli 06 which were made stable in vitro rapidly reverted in vivo after injection into renal medullary tissue. These observations are similar to those of Alderman & Freedman,[1] who injected E. coli protoplasts produced by contact of the parent with penicillin into the renal medulla and into the skin of rabbits. The animals developed E. coli pyelonephritis, presumably due to reverted protoplasts; however, the protoplasts injected into the dermis failed to produce infection. It was inferred from these data that the higher osmolality of the renal medulla favored survival and reversion of protoplasts, whereas the organisms in the isotonic dermis had lysed. The effect of urinary osmolality on isolation of bacterial variants from patients has not been settled.

Guze & Kalmanson[9] incriminated protoplasts in the persistent infection that characterizes Streptococcus faecalis pyelonephritis in rats. In their studies, the kidneys were often sterile on routine media, while a significant number of colonies, presumably representing reverted protoplasts, occurred on the osmotically stabilized media.

It should be pointed out that in most

experimental infections L-forms and protoplasts *per se* did not produce infection, and tissue injury was produced only after there was reversion to the classical bacterial form. We have not been able to produce experimental disease with stable *E. coli* L-forms; these microorganisms either revert *in vivo* to the parent or are not recoverable at all.[23]

The finding that the antibiotic sensitivity pattern of a variant usually differs from that of its parent[10, 16, 21] has opened up new therapeutic considerations in patients with chronic relapsing bacteriuria. Results of *in vitro* studies have shown that variants are usually sensitive to antibiotics which affect the cytoplasmic membrane and intermediary metabolism, such as kanamycin, erythromycin, and tetracycline. Variants are, however, usually resistant to penicillin and cephalothin, antimicrobials which act primarily on the cell wall. Guze & Kalmanson[10] have demonstrated that when rats with *S. faecalis* pyelonephritis are treated with penicillin followed by erythromycin, protoplasts fail to persist. In the present study this approach failed in the one patient in whom it was tried. More recently, Gutman, Schaller & Wedgwood[7] reported the successful eradication of recurrent bacteriuria with ampicillin followed by erythromycin in a child with lupus erythematosus from whose urine filtrable bacterial variants, which subsequently reverted to *P. mirabilis,* were recovered.

Finally, although bacterial variants may play a role in certain recurrent infections of the urinary tract, there is insufficient information to recommend routinely combined antimicrobial treatment aimed against both the parent strain and L-form. Instead, the major effort should be aimed at ruling out structural abnormalities of the urinary tract which are probably a much more frequent cause of persistent and recurrent infections than are bacterial variants. Even when a recurrent infection is characterized by relapse with the same strain that was present prior to chemotherapy, in a patient with no demonstrable structural abnormalities of the collecting system, an extended course

with a drug directed against the parent strain is probably preferable to a regimen consisting of combined or sequential therapy against the variant.

SUMMARY

L-forms or protoplasts were demonstrated from 11 of 57 patients with chronic urinary tract infection. Patients from whom variants were identified during treatment with antibiotics were shown to relapse with the original parent strain when therapy was completed. The results on the occurrence of bacterial variants in renal disease suggest that L-forms and protoplasts may be one cause of persistent or chronic infection of the urinary tract.

REFERENCES

1. Alderman, M. H., and Freedman, L. R.: Experimental pyelonephritis. X. The direct injection of *E. coli* protoplasts into the medulla of the rabbit kidney. *Yale J. Biol. Med.* **36:** 157, 1963.
2. Amano, T., Seki, Y., Fujikawa, K., Kashiba, S., Morioka, T., and Ichikawa, S.: The isolation and characterization of protoplasts from *Escherichia coli* B with the treatment of leucocytes extract. *Med. J. Osaka Univ.* **7:** 245, 1956.
3. Beeson, P. B., and Rowley, D.: The anticomplementary effect of kidney tissue: its association with ammonia production. *J. Exp. Med.* **110:** 685, 1959.
4. Braude, A. I., Siemienski, J., and Jacobs, I.: Protoplast formation in human urine. *Trans. Ass. Amer. Physicians* **74:** 234, 1961.
5. Dienes, L., Weinberger, H. J., and Madoff, S.: The transformation of typhoid bacilli into L forms under various conditions. *J. Bact.* **59:** 755, 1950.
6. Godzeski, C. W., Brier, G., and Pavey, D. E.: L-phase growth induction as a general characteristic of antibiotic-bacterial interaction in the presence of serum. In: *Antimicrobial Agents and Chemotherapy—1962* (J. C. Sylvester, Ed.). American Society for Microbiology, Ann Arbor, 1963: p. 843.
7. Gutman, L. T., Schaller, J., and Wedgwood. R. J.: Bacterial L-forms in relapsing urinary tract infection. *Lancet* **1:** 464, 1967.
8. Gutman, L. T., Turck, M., Petersdorf, R. G., and Wedgwood, R. J.: Significance of bacterial variants in urine of patients with

chronic bacteriuria. *J. Clin. Invest.* **44:** 1945, 1965.

9. Guze, L. B., and Kalmanson, G. M.: Persistence of bacteria in "protoplast" form after apparent cure of pyelonephritis in rats. *Science* **143:** 1340, 1964.

10. ———: Action of erythromycin on "protoplasts" in vivo. *Science* **146:** 1299, 1964.

11. Klieneberger-Nobel, E.: On Streptobacillus moniliformis and the filtrability of its L-form. *J. Hyg.* (London) **47:** 393, 1949.

12. Kunin, C. M.: Microbial persistence versus reinfection in recurrent urinary tract infection. In: *Antimicrobial Agents and Chemotherapy —1962* (J. C. Sylvester, Ed.). American Society for Microbiology, Ann Arbor, 1963: p. 21.

13. Lederberg, J.: Bacterial protoplasts induced by penicillin. *Proc. Nat. Acad. Sci. USA* **42:** 574, 1956.

14. Lindemeyer, R. I., Turck, M., and Petersdorf, R. G.: Factors determining the outcome of chemotherapy in infections of the urinary tract. *Ann. Intern Med.* **58:** 201, 1963.

15. McCabe, W. R., and Jackson, G. G.: Treatment of pyelonephritis; bacterial, drug and host factors in success or failure among 252 patients. *New Eng. J. Med.* **272:** 1037, 1965.

16. Montgomerie, J. Z., Kalmanson, G. M., and Guze, L. B.: The effects of antibiotics on the protoplast and bacterial forms of *Streptococcus faecalis. J. Lab. Clin. Med.* **68:** 543, 1966.

17. Razin, S., and Argaman, M.: Lysis of mycoplasma, bacterial protoplasts, spheroplasts and L-forms by various agents. *J. Gen. Microbiol.* **30:** 158, 1963.

18. Rocha, H., and Fekety, F. R., Jr.: Delayed granulocyte mobilization in the renal medulla. In: *Progress in Pyelonephritis* (E. H. Kass, Ed.). Davis, 1965: p. 211.

19. Turck, M., Anderson, K. N., and Petersdorf, R. G.: Relapse and reinfection in chronic bacteriuria. *New Eng. J. Med.* **275:** 70, 1966.

20. Voureka, A.: Bacterial variants in patients treated with chloramphenicol. *Lancet* **1:** 27, 1951.

21. Ward, J. R., Madoff, S., and Dienes, L.: *In vitro* sensitivity of some bacteria, their L forms and pleuropneumonia-like organisms to antibiotics. *Proc. Soc. Exp. Biol.* **97:** 132, 1958.

22. Weibull, D.: The isolation of protoplasts from Bacillus megaterium by controlled treatment with lysozyme. *J. Bact.* **66:** 688, 1953.

23. Winterbauer, R., Gutman, L. T., Turck, M., Wedgwood, R. J., and Petersdorf, R. G.: The role of penicillin-induced bacterial variants in experimental pyelonephritis. *J. Exp. Med.* **125:** 607, 1967.

44

Some Aspects of Investigations of the Pathogenic Potentialities of L-Forms of Bacteria

*G. Y. Kagan**

THE GAMALEYA INSTITUTE FOR EPIDEMIOLOGY AND
MICROBIOLOGY
MOSCOW, USSR

The role of different bacterial variants with cell wall defects in infectious disease pathology is one of the most important problems of contemporary microbiology, and the subject of much experimental research. The basic aspects of these investigations are related to studies of the possibility of spheroplast production and L-transformation of pathogenic species of microorganisms *in vitro* and *in vivo*, L-form stabilization, persistence and reversion *in vivo*, experimental studies of the pathogenicity of L-forms and their revertants, and clinical-laboratory observations on the isolation of L-form and spheroplast-like variants in some pathological processes.

The study of these problems is of great interest, as demonstration of the pathogenic potentialities of different microbial variants with cell wall defects could possibly change substantially our ideas of the biology and life forms of etiologic agents and the conditions of their persistence in the host organism.

We have used the following differentiation criteria for the identification of bacte-

rial variants with defective cell walls known as "spheroplasts", "protoplasts", "transitional forms", "unstable" and "stable" L-forms: (1) causes inducing their emergence; (2) capacity to grow on nutrient media and character of growth; (3) morphology of microstructures; (4) capacity to multiply and character of multiplication; (5) capacity to resynthesize cell wall and reversion to the original bacterial species.

It is known that spheroplasts are produced under the influence of agents blocking cell wall synthesis in environmental conditions of increased osmotic pressure; perhaps spheroplasts are initial phases of L-transformation. However, L-form genesis is not limited to the spheroplast-production phase; it is more complicated and has different morphological expressions. L-forms differ from spheroplasts by a number of inherent markers, such as: (1) growth on solid media as characteristic L-colonies, composed of spherical bodies of different size and different optical density, ranging from huge 10 μ forms to submicroscopic filterable granules of 150 mμ, vacuolized bodies and filaments, granular unformed masses; (2) capacity to be transferred in subcultures on solid, semisolid, and fluid media containing

* Dr. Kagan was unfortunately unable to attend the Conference. The other participants, therefore, had no opportunity to discuss her paper.

the L-transforming agent for unstable L-forms, and without its presence for stable L-forms; (3) plural ways of multiplication (budding, division, disintegration into elemental reproducing bodies); (4) capacity of unstable L-forms to revert into bacterial forms and loss of this capacity in stable L-forms.

As transitional forms, we identified several changed bacterial variants with defective cell walls (including spheroplasts) capable of converting into L-forms or reverting to bacteria, depending on the conditions of culture.

In the present communication we shall review briefly the results of studies on bacterial L-form pathogenicity conducted in our laboratory between 1956 and 1966, involving investigation of the possibility of L-transformations of pathogenic microorganisms *in vitro* and *in vivo*, studies of pathologic reactions of the host in response to infection by L-forms, and clinical-laboratory observations of the possibility of L-form isolation directly from patients.

MATERIALS AND METHODS

L-TRANSFORMATION *IN VITRO*

The investigations were conducted on *Salmonella typhi, Salmonella typhimurium, Neisseria gonorrhoeae, Neisseria meningitidis, Streptococcus hemolyticus, Staphylococcus aureus,* and *Treponema pallidum.* Positive results were recorded by L-colony growth.

The basal medium for the production of the different species of L-forms was semi-solid agar (0.3%), tryptic digest of beef cardiac muscle, pH 7.6, with addition of different concentrations of penicillin and 10–20% of normal horse serum.

The composition and concentration of compounds added to provide osmotic stabilization of the medium varied with the species of microorganism transformed into L-form. Detailed descriptions of the methods can be found in the works of G. Y. Kagan and associates,[12, 14, 17] S. V. Prozorovsky[33] and L. M. Ustimenko.[36]

L-TRANSFORMATION *IN VIVO*

In the first series of experiments, the L-transforming effect of penicillin on *S. typhi* was examined in white mice. A 48-hour culture with 500 million/ml density of viable cells on optical standards in a volume of 0.25 ml was injected into the peritoneal cavity of white mice weighing 18–20 g. Immediately after the introduction of the culture, intraperitoneal injections of 2 ml of penicillin were made in doses of 100, 500, 2000 and 4000 units/g body weight.

At different intervals after the injection of cultures and penicillin, the exudate was taken from the peritoneal cavity and examined with the phase contrast microscope. In each preparation, 15–20 fields were examined. Results of all the experiments were documented with microphotographs.

In another series of experiments, the action of sera of syphilitic patients on *T. pallidum* was investigated.[36] Sera of patients receiving penicillin (penicillin concentration in their blood was 0.96 units), biochynol (iodine-bismuth-quinine, 8% suspension in neutral peach oil), or neoarsenol were used as transforming agents to obtain L-forms. These sera were added to 0.3% tryptic digest agar containing up to 20% normal horse serum.

PATHOLOGIC REACTIONS OF ANIMALS INFECTED BY L-FORMS OF BACTERIA

The following aspects of the pathogenicity of L-form bacteria were studied: (1) the character of the direct reaction of animals after infection and the period of persistence of the infecting agent in the host;[20] (2) cytopathic effect in tissue cultures;[19] (3) sensitizing effect of antigenic complexes of L-forms; (4) experimental models of pathologic processes.[18, 24]

As a model for investigation of sensitizing antigens extracted from L-form bacteria, we chose the Shwartzman phenomenon. Antigens were obtained by alternate freeze-thawing (ten times at −70°C and +37°C) of aqueous suspensions of L-forms of group A beta-hemolytic streptococci, their parental cultures and the revertant strains. As controls, washings of culture media were used, treated similarly. Experiments were conducted in 79 rabbits weighing 3.5 kg apiece.

The sensitizing substrate was injected (2.0 ml) into the knee joint of one of the rabbit's hind legs, and 18 hours later a resolving dose of the antigen was injected intravenously. The reaction was recorded 24 hours after the resolving injection. Results were evaluated by the following schedule: Reaction −: joint unchanged; Reaction +: a small serous exudate in the joint pouch, and moderate infiltration of the surrounding tissue; Reaction ++: turbidity of the surface of joints, significant serous exudate in the joint pouch, moderate infiltration of surrounding tissues; Reaction +++: turbid surfaces of joints, much sero-purulent exudate, strongly infiltrated surrounding tissues; Reaction ++++: a net swelling in the joint region, turbid surfaces of joints, a great quantity of sero-purulent or purulent-bloody exudate in the joint pouch, extensive infiltration of tissues; after cutting tissues surrounding the joints, a serous fluid flows out.

In order to investigate pathologic processes during infection of animals with L-forms, we tried to produce experimental angina in monkeys and experimental meningitis in rabbits.

Experimental Angina of Monkeys

Two methods of infection were used: intravenous, and direct injection into paratonsillar cellular tissue. The infection was carried out in cycles, with intervals of four to six months. Each cycle consisted of three to four injections six to seven days apart.

The infecting agent was a mixture of four L-form cultures: a stable L-form of group A type 2 beta-hemolytic streptococci obtained in experiments in vitro, a stable L-form of streptococcus isolated by us from the blood of a patient with rheumocarditis, and two foreign L-form strains, of type 12 beta-hemolytic streptococcus (AED L) and type 19 (gl. 8L).

A suspension of washed L-forms containing two billion organisms/ml (optical standards), and consisting of equal quantities of the four strains was injected; 0.5 ml was used in the paratonsillar infection, and 2.0 ml in the intravenous route. Suspensions of bacterial forms were prepared similarly, and the same doses used. The group infected

with L-forms paratonsillarly was designated L + L + L + L p/t; the intravenously infected group, L + L + L + L i/v. The corresponding groups infected by streptococci were designated S + S + S + S p/t, and S + S + S + S i/v.

In the first series of experiments were 11 Macacus speciosus monkeys, three to five years old; in the second group, 20 Macacus rhesus monkeys no older than one year. In total, 31 monkeys were used. One month before each cycle of infection and one month after it, the monkeys were thoroughly examined, clinically, electrocardiographically and roentgenologically. We studied the indices of inflammatory processes: erythrocyte sedimentation rate (ESR), C-reactive protein (CRP), and leucocytosis; specific immunologic indices: antistreptolysin O (ASO), precipitins to antigens isolated by the hydrochloric acid extraction method of Lancefield (HAE), and extraction by freezing and thawing of aqueous suspensions (FTE), in relation to streptococcal L-forms (LP) and streptococci (SP). Clinical observations were made every day and two days after each infection; all the other examinations were made once a week. Postmortem histological examinations were made.

Experimental Meningitis of Rabbits

In this work an experimental model of rabbit meningitis was used as originally described by Zdrodowsky.[42] The animals were suboccipitally infected in the subarachnoidal space by the following L-cultures: beta-hemolytic streptococci (32 rabbits), S. aureus (18), S. typhi (18). Parental cultures of streptococci were injected into 18 rabbits, of staphylococci into 12, of S. typhi into 12. Six control rabbits were injected with washings of culture media, and three received punctures without infection. L-form suspensions and suspensions of parental cultures were washed. For infection, all cultures were used in 0.5 ml volumes and density of 1 billion/ml. Examinations were made every day during three weeks. Bacteriological and laboratory examinations of spinal fluid were made 2, 5, 12, and 20 days after infection.

Post-mortem histological examinations were made.

DIRECT ISOLATION OF L-FORMS FROM PATIENTS

We worked with different diseases that gave negative results on bacteriological examination,[13, 16] choosing rheumatic fever, septic endocarditis, protracted purulent meningitis and meningoencephalitis because of the following considerations: in one instance (rheumatic fever and septic endocarditis) a chronic pathologic process was related to only one species of infectious agent—the streptococcus; the pathogenetic significance of the latter in connection with its inconstant isolation from blood is based on results of experimental and immunologic investigations. In another instance (protracted purulent meningitis) a polyetiologic disease gave negative bacteriological results that could be due to the persistence of the agent in the host as an L-form. The blood in the first instance and the spinal fluid in the second were cultured at 37°C for 21 days. As a rule, the studies were discontinued after four to six transfers.

Transfers on media containing the L-transforming agent were made to obtain optimal conditions for L-colony isolation and maintenance of these colonies in artificial conditions of culture. Photographic records and careful microscopic study of these cultures helped to determine the morphological characteristics of L-forms isolated from patient materials and the course of transformation of transitional forms isolated from these material into L-forms. Transfers on media without the transforming agent were carried out to obtain the optimal conditions for reversion of L-forms and transitional forms to bacteria and for isolation of bacterial forms. L-colonies were revealed in the first, second and third passages, transitional forms in the first and second passages, reverted forms in the fourth to sixth passages, bacterial forms in the first and second passages.

The results are recorded on the basis of

TABLE 44.1

Evaluation of Results when Testing Materials from Patients for L-Forms

Case	Results of Analysis of Cultivation on Media		Evaluation of Results
	Containing L-transforming agent	Without L-transforming agent	
1	L-forms	L-forms	Positive. L-forms isolated
2	L-forms	No growth	Positive. L-forms isolated
3	No growth	L-forms	Positive. L-forms isolated
4	L-forms	Transitional and bacterial forms	Positive. L-forms isolated, reverting to bacterial forms
5	L-forms	Bacterial forms	Positive. Isolation of mixed culture of bacterial and L-forms, or of bacterial forms changing on medium with transforming agent to L-forms, or of L-forms changing on medium without transforming agent to bacterial forms. Exact evaluation of analysis impossible
6	Transitional forms	Transitional forms	Positive. Transitional forms isolated
7	Transitional forms	No growth	Positive. Transitional forms isolated
8	No growth	Transitional forms	Positive. Transitional forms isolated
9	Transitional forms	Bacterial forms	Positive. Isolation of mixed culture of bacterial and transitional forms. Exact evaluation of analysis impossible (see 5)
10	Bacterial forms	Bacterial forms	Positive. Bacterial forms isolated
11	Bacterial forms	No growth	Positive. Bacterial forms isolated
12	No growth	Bacterial forms	Positive. Bacterial forms isolated
13	No growth	No growth	Negative

TABLE 44.2

Frequency of L-Colony Production in Different Microorganisms

Species	No. of Strains Tested	L-Form Production	Authors
Salmonella	52	Stable and unstable (49)	Kagan & Levashov[14]
Neisseria gonorrhoeae	94	Unstable (76)	Kagan & Pesina[17]
Neisseria meningitidis	21	Unstable (3)	Koptelova[25]
Streptococcus hemolyticus	64	Stable (12)	Kagan[12]
Staphylococcus aureus	10	Stable (8)	Prozorovsky[33]
Treponema pallidum	7	Unstable (4)	Ustimenko[36]

L-colony isolation in Table 44.1, the patients being divided accordingly into the following groups: (1) Patients from whom only L-forms were isolated directly (Table 44.1: №1–3); if the isolated L-forms did not revert into bacteria after passages *in vitro* we could not identify them as stable L-forms or *Mycoplasmas*. (2) Patients from whom mixed cultures were isolated, i.e., L-forms on media containing the L-transforming agent and transitional forms on media without the transforming agent (№4) and bacterial forms on media without the transforming agent (№5); in this latter case it was unclear whether the L-forms found in the patients were the outcome of *in vitro* transformation of bacteria present in the patients, or whether the bacteria were the outcome of *in vitro* reversion of L-forms present in the patients. (3) Patients from whom transitional forms or mixed cultures of bacterial and transitional forms were isolated (№6–9); in №9 it was likewise impossible to say whether the given transitional forms were the outcome of *in vitro* transformation of bacteria present in the patients, or whether the bacteria represented reversion of transitional forms present in the patients. (4) Patients from whom only bacteria were isolated (№10–12). (5) Patients from whom neither bacteria nor their changed variants were isolated (№13).

RESULTS

L-TRANSFORMATION OF SOME SPECIES OF PATHOGENIC MICROORGANISMS

L-Transformation In Vitro

Summarized data about the frequency of L-colony production in different pathogenic microorganisms are given in Table 44.2 and Figure 44.1. These data demonstrate that all the species of microorganisms we investigated are capable of L-transformation. L-transformation of pathogenic microorganisms depends on (1) the character of the L-transforming effect, its intensity and duration; (2) conditions of cultivation; (3) species of microorganism, and (4) individual susceptibility of particular strains and even of cells of the population to the L-transforming effect. Strains were found which formed no L-colonies but were capable of forming spheroplasts, strains which formed L-colonies directly in response to the first action of penicillin, and other strains which formed L-colonies after spheroplast formation. Depending on the dose of the transforming agent, the same strain produced spheroplasts, formed L-colonies, or died. Each population was heterogenous in relation to capacity for L-transformation: in each population there were cells easily transformed into L-forms, cells with a limited capacity for L-transformation, and nonviable cells which died quickly after the action of the agent. The trends of L-formation of *T. pallidum* were similar to the trends of L-transformation of the pathogenic bacteria we investigated. The period of L-colony appearance varied from six to 40 days.

L-Transformation In Vivo

Figure 44.2 shows the L-transforming action of penicillin on *S. typhi*. It was found that penicillin injection of 100 U/g body weight disturbed cell division during two or three hours; long, undivided individual cells were produced, and a swelling of rods into partly vacuolized spheroplast-like forms was noted; five hours later these were transformed into typical L-forms (Figure 44.2B). Careful microscopic study of these preparations did not find bacteria; ghosts

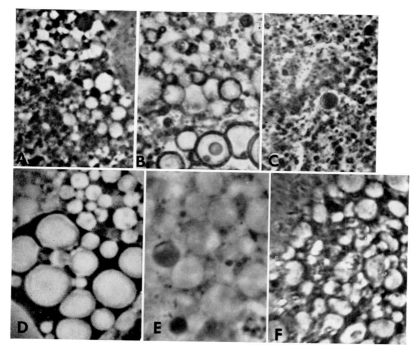

Figure 44.1. Microstructure of L-forms of some pathogenic microorganisms. A: *Salmonella typhi;* B: *Corynebacterium diphtheriae;* C: *Neisseria gonorrhoeae;* D: *Streptococcus hemolyticus;* E: *Neisseria meningitidis;* F: *Treponema pallidum.* × 1850.

of dead rods were seldom found; 24 hours later all the mice of this group were dead, and in the exudate rods, identified as *S. typhi*, were found (C). This leads us to suppose that reversion *in vivo* of the latter from the L-form is possible.

One and one-and-a-half hours after the injection of high concentrations of penicillin (1000–4000 units/g body weight), the transformation of rods into small spherical bodies was noted (D). These spheroplast-like forms very quickly disintegrated into a multiplicity of granular forms (E), which were intensely phagocytized (F), and completely disappeared from the exudate three to five hours later. All mice in this group survived.

The possibility of L-transformation of *T. pallidum in vivo* was suggested by the work of L. M. Ustimenko,[36] who demonstrated L-form production after exposure of some strains of *T. pallidum* to sera of syphilitic patients. Fourteen sera of patients in diverse stages of the illness were tested; of these, four sera had been obtained during treat-

ment with penicillin, six during treatment with biochynol and neoarsenol, two during treatment with biochynol only, one before penicillin treatment, and one after penicillin cure. Of the 14 sera, six had L-transforming activity. In four cases, transformation of all the population into typical L-forms with subsequent growth of L-colonies was observed, in two cases mixed cultures composed of L-forms and treponema were obtained. Transformation of all the population of treponemas into L-forms was observed with serum obtained in three cases during treatment with penicillin, and in one case during treatment with biochynol and neoarsenol. A partial L-transforming effect was produced by serum of a patient treated with penicillin, and by serum of another patient treated with biochynol and neoarsenol.

Sera from 15 healthy controls were tested and found to have no L-transforming effect. In a complementary control series, the L-transforming activity of sera of 14 patients with other diseases treated with penicillin was tested. Additional controls consisted of

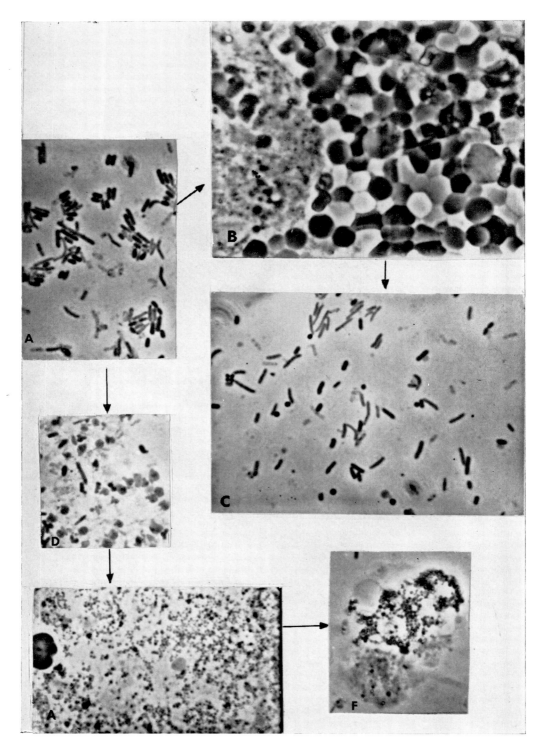

Figure 44.2. L-transformation of *Salmonella typhi in vivo. A:* Initial culture of *S. typhi* at the moment of contact with penicillin; *B:* production of typical L-forms 5 hours after penicillin injection, 100 U/g body weight; *C:* bacterial forms reverted from these L-forms 24 hours later; *D:* production of spheroplast-like forms 60–90 minutes after injection of 2000–4000 U/g body weight of penicillin; *E* (marked "A", lower left): disintegration of these spheroplasts into a multiplicity of granular forms; *F:* phagocytosis of these granular forms.

sera of healthy people, to which penicillin in varying concentrations (0.96–7.68 U/ml) was added before the experiment; in the penicillin-treated controls, L-forms were obtained after the action of six sera. All normal human sera with added penicillin produced an L-transforming effect at 1.25–2.0 U/ml penicillin concentration. Even though indirect, these experiments provide a basis to conclude that *in vivo* L-transformation of *T. pallidum* is possible.

PATHOLOGIC REACTION OF ANIMALS INFECTED WITH L-FORMS

Study of the virulence of L-forms of different pathogenic bacteria tested by us (*S. typhi, S. typhimurium, S. hemolyticus, Proteus vulgaris*) by infection of laboratory animals (mice, rabbits) revealed that strains virulent enough to cause death of the animals are very seldom encountered. However, investigation of these practically non-virulent strains demonstrated that they are far from being innocuous to the host. Experiments with L-forms of *P. vulgaris* showed that these strains are capable of prolonged persistence in the host and infrequently revert into bacterial forms.

Immunization studies with L-forms of *S. typhi* and *S. typhimurium* revealed some immunizing effect, greater with the latter. The immunizing effect of L-forms, however, was accompanied by severe reaction of the animals in the form of severe, protracted, non-healing sterile abscesses; the reaction was more severe during immunization with L-forms of *S. typhimurium* than with those of *S. typhi*. Immunization with bacterial forms did not produce increased reaction in response to the introduction of the vaccine, and death of animals during the immunization cycle was rarely observed. Injection of L-cultures was accompanied by an increased reaction after the second and third injection. Out of 120 mice, 57 survived, 35 of the latter having severe protracted sterile abscesses which did not heal for a long time. Results of these experiments demonstrated that the immunizing effect in L-forms is accompanied by an increased reactivity of the host in the form of abscesses and even death of the animals.

These observations served as a basis for investigations of sensitizing properties of antigens obtained from L-form bacteria. Results of experiments involving production of the Shwartzman phenomenon in knee joints of rabbits showed that injection of antigens of streptococcal L-forms into the joint pouch, with their subsequent introduction into the blood, was accompanied by strong reaction of the joints (++ and +++). Sensitizing properties of antigens of bacterial forms of hemolytic streptococci were much greater than L-form antigens (+++ and ++++). In all the experiments, a cross-sensitizing effect was noted between bacterial and L-form antigens.

Experimental Angina in Monkeys

Figure 44.3 presents the results of four cycles of infection of *Macacus speciosus* monkeys, showing that introduction of streptococcal L-forms into the paratonsillar region produced angina in four of five monkeys in the first cycle of infection. In the subsequent cycles all the monkeys became ill, and the clinical course of infection was more severe. Angina was complicated by the phenomenon of cardiac pathology. In one of the monkeys, diffuse changes of the cardiac muscle were demonstrated electrocardiographically. A certain increase of indices of inflammatory processes (rate of erythrocyte sedimentation—ESR, C reactive protein—CRP, leucocytosis), of antistreptolysin O (ASO), and of specific precipitins was noted. In three monkeys, L-forms were isolated from the blood during the first cycle of infection.

Intravenous injections of L-forms into two monkeys were also accompanied by the occurrence of angina, more severe in the third cycle of infection. In one monkey, clinical and electrocardiographic changes of the cardiac muscle were noted. Paratonsillar injections of bacterial forms of beta-hemolytic streptococci into three monkeys did not produce angina in the first cycle of infection, but one of two monkeys reacted with severe anginas accompanied by cardiac complications in subsequent cycles of infection. Intravenous injections of streptococci

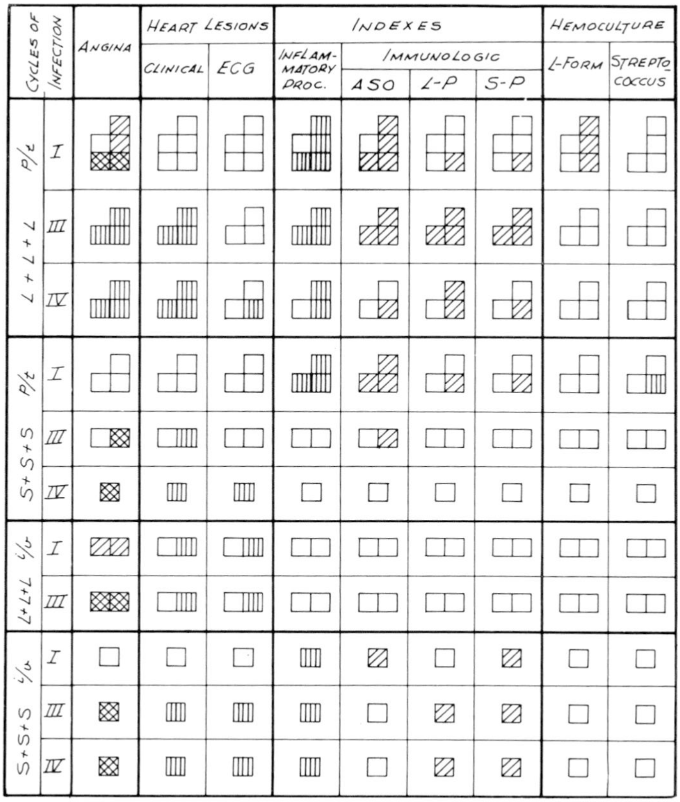

Figure 44.3. Summarized results of 4 cycles of infection of *Macacus speciosus* by L-
and bacterial forms of β-hemolytic streptococci. Each square represents a monkey. *Angina
registration:* − (blank squares): normal larynx and tonsils; + (diagonal hatching): moderate and limited hyperemia of arcs and little tongues; ++ (cross hatching): moderate and
confluent hyperemia of arcs, little tongues, tonsils, and insignificant edema of tonsils; +++
and ++++ (vertical hatching): strong confluent hyperemia and edema of arcs, little
tongues and tonsils; purulent or necrotic foci in ++++. *Heart lesions* (−, blank squares,
and +, vertical hatching): clinical—tachycardia, diminished tones; electrocardiographically
expressed lesions (ECG). *Indices of inflammatory processes* (−, blank squares, and +, vertical hatching): rate of erythrocyte sedimentation (ESR), leucocytosis, C-reactive protein
(CRP). *Immunologic indices* (−, blank squares, and +, diagonal hatching): antistreptolysin
O (ASO); precipitin to L-form (L-P) and to streptococcus (S-P). *Hemoculture* (−, blank
squares, and +, diagonal or vertical hatching): L-forms and streptococci.

into monkeys produced a similar reaction. Results of this series of experiments, conducted on a limited number of monkeys, demonstrated that multiple injections of L-forms and streptococci produced a pathologic reaction such as angina independently of the site of injection, with intensification of the reaction in the following cycles of infection. This finding must be extended and controlled in a greater number of monkeys of the same age.

In connection with this, a second series of experiments was conducted on **20** *Macacus rhesus* monkeys. Figure 44.4 presents the results of the first cycle of this series, and suggests that, independent of their route of introduction into the host (i.e., whether paratonsillarly or intravenously), streptococcal L-forms always provoked protracted and severe anginas, which appeared most often after the second infection and were accompanied by prolonged cardiac lesions.

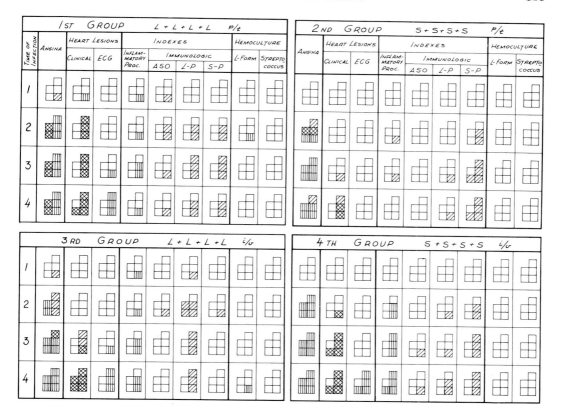

Figure 44.4. Summarized results of the first cycle of infection of *Macacus rhesus* by L- and bacterial forms of β-hemolytic streptococci. Each square represents a monkey. Symbols as in Figure 44.3., except for *Heart lesions:* clinical—tachycardia (diagonal hatching), diminished tones and tachycardia (cross hatching), and electrocardiographical (vertical hatching).

The anginas and the cardiac reaction were intensified after each subsequent infection, so that, after the fourth infection of the first cycle, clinical lesions of the heart were observed in four of five monkeys in the group of paratonsillar infection. In three monkeys, electrocardiographic examination revealed stable, diffuse myocardial lesions, lasting about a month. A similar reaction was observed in monkeys following intravenous injection of L-forms.

Paratonsillar and intravenous injection of streptococci also provoked angina reactions which were little different from the response of monkeys to L-form injection in terms of the severity and period of illness and the dynamics of intensification in subsequent infections. Cardiac lesions that could be recorded clinically and electrocardiographi-

cally were observed in four of five monkeys infected intravenously. After paratonsillar injection of streptococci, lesions of cardiac muscle were not revealed by electrocardiographic examination; clinically, diminished heart tones were noted for a short time in three monkeys. Hence, the results of the second series of experiments confirmed the presence of pathologic reactions in the form of angina as response to the introduction of streptococcal L-forms into the host. *Macacus rhesus* monkeys were more susceptible than *Macacus speciosus*, probably due not only to their species pecularities but also to the age of the animals. Isolation of L-forms and streptococci was very seldom observed. Indices of inflammatory processes and increased ASO and precipitins to the L-form (L-P) and to the streptococcus were noted occasionally, and were higher in adult *Macacus speciosus* monkeys. Histological investigations of individual monkeys which died later of causes unrelated to the experimental infections revealed changes in two monkeys (one of Group L + L + L + L i/v and one of Group S + S + S + S i/v) in the form of cardiosclerosis and intensive development of connective tissue, which could have resulted from earlier myocarditis.

Experimental Meningitis and Meningo-Encephalitis in Rabbits

Suboccipital infections of rabbits with bacterial and L-forms produced a meningeal syndrome characterized by a temperature reaction, weight decrease, increased nervous excitation, flow of tears, edema of the mucous tissue of the eyes, adynamia, paresis and paralysis of pelvic organs and hind legs, leucocytosis (15,000–20,000 white blood cells/mm³), and changes of cytosis

and proteins in the spinal fluid. The summarized results (Table 44.3) demonstrate that the meningeal syndrome during L-form infection developed slowly and differed from infection with bacterial forms by a more prolonged and inert course. In animals infected with bacteria the most severe courses were observed in the groups infected with *S. typhi* and *S. aureus*. In groups infected with L-forms these differences did not occur.

During infection with L-cultures, L-forms were isolated from the spinal fluid in about 50 per cent of the cases; these would grow as single L-colonies and could not be subcultured. Patho-histological investigations confirmed the presence of acute confluent meningo-encephalitis in rabbits infected by L-forms and by parental cultures (Figure 44.5). During the first five days, hyperemia of the membranes, turbidity and edema were noted. Microscopic investigations of brain sites far from the site of injection

TABLE 44.3

Summarized Results of Suboccipital Infection of Rabbits by Bacterial (B) and L-Forms (L) of Different Species of Bacteria

Infection		Died		Illness				Indices of Cytosis in Spinal Fluid (ml)				
				Dura-tion (days)	Clinical symptoms			Before infec-tion (25)	After infection			
Organism	No. Anim.	No.	Time (days)		Fever	Con-vulsions	Paresis and paral-ysis		2–5 days		12 days	
									100–500	500–2000	<100	>100
β-hemolytic strep-tococci												
L	32	4	2–10	up to 20	20	15	15	32	15	15	9	18
B	18	7	2–3	5–7	12	12	12	18	8	10	2	4
Staphylococcus aureus												
L	18	2	2–15	up to 20	8	12	12	18	2	16	2	12
B	12	10	2–5	2–5	12	12	12	12	—	12	—	—
Salmonella typhi												
L	18	4	11–20	up to 20	5	7	7	18	7	10	8	4
B	12	12	1–3	1–3	12	12	12	12	nt	nt	nt	nt
Controls:												
Injection of cul-ture media	6	—	—	—	—	—	—	6	—	—	—	—
Puncture without injection	6	—	—	—	—	—	—	3	—	—	—	—

nt: not tested.

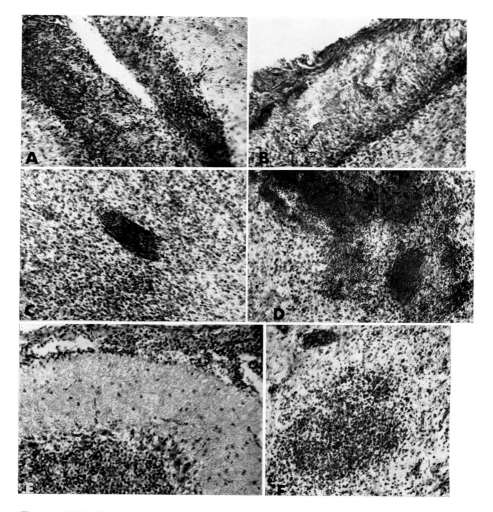

Figure 44.5. Character of changes after suboccipital infection by streptococcal L-forms. *A–D:* On 5th day. *A:* Multiple foci of hemorrhages with inflammatory infiltrations around them; *B:* diffuse inflammatory infiltration in the white substance of the medulla; *C:* infiltration of brain membranes with fibrin leakage; *D:* purulent meningitis, infiltrations of soft brain membranes. *E* and *F:* On 12th day. *E:* Purulent meningitis, moderate infiltrations of soft brain membranes, accumulation of inflammatory elements in the region of the cerebellum. *F:* Multiple abscesses with necrotic foci in the white substance of the medulla.

(S-P) showed a pattern of acute meningoencephalitis: the brain was soft; membranes were defibrinated and markedly thickened because of acute inflammatory infiltrations, as well as being hyperemic with paretic enlarged blood vessels overfilled with blood; many hemorrhages of the brain were seen; occasional leakage of fibrin was noted.

During this time, a morphologically expressed pattern of encephalitis was observed in all rabbits: foci of hemorrhage of the brain with surrounding acute inflammatory reaction, multiple perivascular acute inflammatory infiltrations, and paretic hyperemia. These phenomena were attenuated at 15–20 days. The reparative phenomenon during infection with L-forms was slower; in most of the animals a moderate focal infiltration of membranes remained on the 15th–20th days. Swelling of nerve cells, dispersed, oc-

TABLE 44.4

Analysis of the Blood of Patients with Endocarditis and Rheumatic Fever

Clinical Diagnosis	No. of Patients Examined	Positive Results					Negative Results
		Isolation of				Total	
		Cultures of α- and β-hemolytic streptococci	Mixed cultures of streptococci and L-forms	Transitional forms	L-forms		
Rheumatic fever	20	2	0	4	13	19	1
Septic endocarditis	14	3	3	1	6	13	1
Control group of practically healthy subjects	16	—	—	—	—	—	16

casional packed glyose nodules, and perivascular infiltrations were noted in the brain substance even in the late period after infection (12–20 days).

CLINICAL LABORATORY INVESTIGATIONS OF THE POSSIBILITY OF ISOLATING FORMS WITH DEFECTIVE CELL WALLS DIRECTLY FROM PATIENTS

Septic Endocarditis and Rheumatic Fever

From the data presented in Table 44.4 it may be seen that L-form cultures were isolated from the blood of rheumatic fever patients in most of the cases (13 out of 20); transitional forms were isolated in four patients. Only in two cases were cultures of alpha-hemolytic streptococci isolated from the first blood platings. L-forms also appeared fairly frequently in endocarditis (6 cases out of 14); the transitional forms were somewhat less common; in three cases, mixed L-form cultures and streptococci were isolated (two alpha-hemolytic and one beta-hemolytic strains).

The isolated L-cultures sometimes grew, in the first passage, as typical L-colonies. More frequently, they grew in the second passage on media containing an L-transforming agent (Figures 44.6–44.9). Simultaneous platings on media without the L-transforming agent ended on the fourth to sixth passages by reversion of streptococci (Figures 44.6C and 44.7E). In the first and second passages, transitional forms grew, composed of huge globular bodies, frequently in groups or chains of elongated, pear-shaped

and dumb-bell shaped cells (Figure 44.8A); their passages on media containing an L-transforming agent terminated in L-colony formation (Figure 44.8B); on penicillin-less media, in reversion to streptococci (Figure 44.8C). Of 24 L-form cultures and transitional forms, 20 reverted into streptococci; four did not revert after six to eight passages on media without penicillin (Figure 44.9).

Of 20 reverted streptococcal cultures, ten grew in subcultures; these cultures were highly polymorphic in the first phases of reversion. The beginning of reversion was indicated by the appearance of a delicate halo around the L-colony in semisolid media. Under the microscope, the reverted forms looked like elongated, swollen, dumb-bell-like structures, spheroplasts and big globular bodies, infrequently grouped into chains (Figure 44.8, A and C). They did not grow on blood agar and were Gram-negative. The fourth-to-fifth passage cultures in semi-solid agar without penicillin were morphologically similar to streptococci but contained chains of spheroplast-like cells and did not stain or stained defectively; they consisted of Gram-positive and Gram-negative cells in chains. After many passages, the morphological patterns became normal, and growth on blood agar was observed only in subcultures of the fifth to sixth passage. Six strains gave alpha-hemolysis and three grew as mixed cultures, composed of colonies of streptococci that gave alpha and beta-hemolysis.

The enzymatic activity of reverted strep-

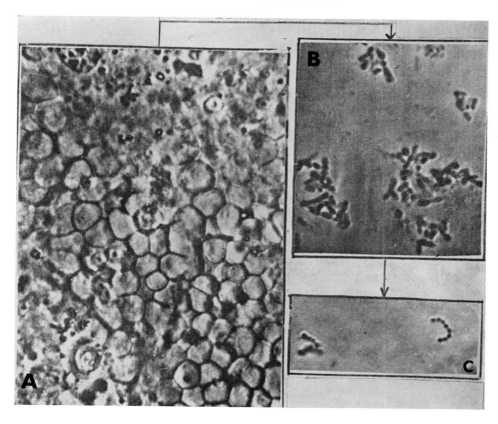

Figure 44.6. L-form culture isolated from the blood of a patient with rheumatic endocarditis. *A:* Structure of L-colonies; *B:* reversion forms of streptococci after multiple passages on media without penicillin; *C:* reversion to streptococci.

tococci was decreased. They were unable to produce streptolysin O and produced small quantities of streptokinase, hyaluronidase and an erythrogenic toxin. Reduction of the Lancefield polysaccharide antigen (group A) was demonstrated in four of seven strains examined.

Meningitis and Meningo-Encephalitis

Spinal fluid examinations in patients with meningitis and meningo-encephalitis, presented in Table 44.5, demonstrate the following results: Bacterial forms of different species with the prevalence of cocci were noted in 14 per cent of patients. In three cases, transitional forms were isolated, which reverted into bacterial cultures (staphylococci, lancet-like diplococci and an hemophilus rod); in one case a culture of unstable L-forms was isolated, which reverted into staphylococci; in five patients, mixed cultures of bacteria and unstable L-forms of the coccus group were isolated.

Stable L-forms or PPLO were isolated in 15 per cent of the patients. In semifluid media, a diffuse growth of minute granular forms and refractory light bodies that could not be identified by the conventional criteria for identification of different bacterial variants with defective cell walls were isolated from 23 per cent of the patients. Stable L-forms and cultures consisting of granules were subcultured in two to three cultures and then died. Bacterial and L-colonies could not be plated out from the spinal fluid of the patients in the control group. Figure 44.10 shows examples of isolated L-forms. The isolated transitional forms were characterized by marked polymorphism, and during passages on media

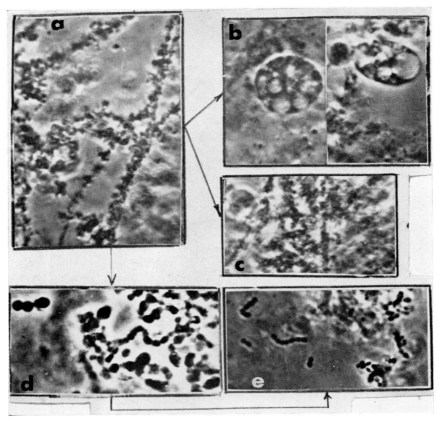

Figure 44.7. L-forms isolated from the blood of a patient with septic and rheumatic endocarditis. *a:* Filaments and granular structure in the first plating; *b* and *c:* L-colony structure in the second passage on a penicillin-containing medium; *d:* reversion forms of streptococci after multiple passages on media without penicillin; *e:* reversion to streptococci.

without antibiotics reverted into bacterial forms.

Comparison of the character of the disease with the periods of L-form isolation from the spinal fluid allowed division of the patients with positive results into the following groups:

a. Patients (8) with typical and rapid course of disease. L-form isolation was early at the beginning of the illness, before antibiotic treatment. In these patients, treatment with massive doses of penicillin (200,-000 U/kg body weight) was effective.

b. Patients (7) with a severe and protracted course of disease. L-forms were isolated from these patients later on, after a prolonged treatment with antibiotics. In these patients, isolation of L-forms replaced

the preliminary isolation of bacterial forms. In five out of seven of these patients, treatment with penicillin was ineffective. In two patients, combined treatment with penicillin and other antibiotics was initiated on the 30th and 63rd day of disease; their recovery was very slow.

c. Patients (8) with brain abscesses and purulent meningitis due to rupture of abscesses into the subarachnoid space. In these patients, L-forms were isolated very frequently, as a rule in the periods of clinical and spinal fluid deterioration. Antibiotic therapy of this group of patients was ineffective. Of six patients from whom bacterial forms were isolated from the spinal fluid, one became negative on repeated platings. In five of these six patients unidentified

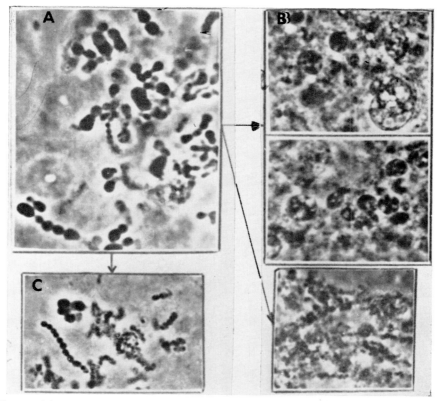

Figure 44.8. Transitional forms isolated from the blood of a patient with rheumatic endocarditis. *A:* Transitional forms isolated directly from the blood in the first passage; *B:* transformation of these forms into typical L-forms during passages on penicillin-containing media; *C:* reversion into streptococci on media without penicillin.

granular forms continued to be isolated. The clinical course of the disease was sluggish and protracted, convalescence corresponding to negative plating results. In one of three patients from whose spinal fluid transitional and unstable L-forms were isolated, replated examination of the spinal fluid revealed no growth. Stable L-forms (PPLO), were as a rule isolated from patients with brain abscesses on many occasions and for a long time.

DISCUSSION

Current ideas about the etiology and pathogenesis of many diseases of a yet unclear infectious character cannot be restricted by the limited frames of the conventional orders, families and species of the agents, and the forms in which they exist. Investigations in the field of infectious dis-

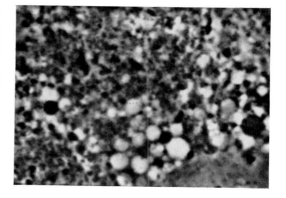

Figure 44.9. Stable L-forms isolated from the blood of a rheumatic fever patient.

ease pathology can no longer be fruitful if they are not complemented by data about other infectious agents not yet studied, such

TABLE 44.5

Results of Analyses of the Spinal Fluid of Patients with Meningitis

Clinical Diagnosis	Patients Examined	Forms Isolated				
		Bacterial Forms	Mixed cultures of bacterial and L-forms	Non-stable L-forms and transitional forms	Stable L-forms or PPLO	Granular forms
Purulent meningitis	144	21	5	4	22	34
Controls:*	25					
Group A	7	3				3
Group B	18		0	0	0	

* Group A: patients with tuberculous meningitis.
  Group B: patients with serous meningitis.

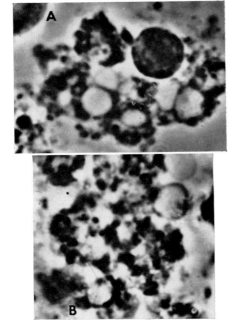

Figure 44.10. L-forms isolated from the spinal fluid of patients with purulent meningitis.

as mycoplasmas or the different microorganism forms with cell wall defects. Because of these considerations, the hypothesis of the possible role in pathology of bacterial variants with defective cell walls is now the subject of much interest. This hypothesis has won more and more adherents, and is supported by an increasing number of facts. Essential aspects of the investigations in this field are studies of the possibility of production of variants with cell wall defects and L-transformation of pathogenic microorganisms *in vitro* and *in vivo*, of their pathogenic potentialities in experimental conditions, and of clinical-microbiological observations in relation to certain pathologic processes, the infectious character of which is not always clear.

Many antibiotic and chemotherapeutic compounds which have the microbial cell wall as their site of action may lead to production of spheroplast-like variants and L-forms, which are highly resistant to these agents, are plastic, physiologically mobile, and unrevealed by conventional methods of laboratory analysis.[2, 7, 8, 11] L-forms of *Mycobacterium tuberculosis* have been obtained,[23, 29] and Ustimenko[36] demonstrated L-transformation of *T. pallidum* under the influence of penicillin, biochynol, neoarsenol and other preparations, showing these compounds to be active factors of L-transformation not only *in vitro*, but *in vivo*, i.e., in the sera of treated patients.

Data about L-transformation *in vivo* presented in this report and observations of other authors[6, 7, 40] regarding the possibility of production of L-forms and related bacterial variants under the influence of antibiotics in the host, their prolonged persistence and their possible reversion into the original bacteria are in our opinion most convincing proof of the need to reconsider the role of the infectious agents' different forms of life in disease pathology. The trends of production of different variants with cell wall defects, their biological characteristics, and an increasing awareness of the factors in their induction suggest that such variants are regular forms of existence, deserving great attention; investigations from many points of view must be conducted on this subject. It is known that unstable L-forms may be subcultured indefinitely in the presence of L-transforming agents, and that when the action of the agent ceases the unstable L-forms revert, with restoration of all the characteristics of the original bacterium, including virulence. The alternating existence of disease-causing agents as bacterial-revertants and L-forms may have an essential influence on the entire course of the infectious process and may play an important role in relapsing infections. This alternating existence may complicate the infectious process, lower the effectiveness of therapeutic measures, promote the carrier state, and produce uncontrollable infectious foci.

Investigations of the pathogenic potentialities of L-forms have also demonstrated that these forms are not without effect on the host organism. There have been reports of isolation of L-forms which retained the parent culture's initial degree of pathogenicity, such as, for example, virulent L-forms of strains of cholera vibrios,[31] Clostridium tetani[34] and Clostridium perfringens.[1] We have presented data demonstrating that multiple injections of stable L-forms produced at the same time a small immunizing effect and a changed pathologic reaction of the host, such as severe, protracted, slowly healing sterile abscesses (L-forms of Salmonella). Some increase of the immunizing effect of S. typhimurium L-forms in comparison with S. typhi L-forms was accompanied by intensification of the pathologic response, as revealed by the death of 63 out of 120 mice after the second and third S. typhimurium L-form injection. These data were confirmed in a series of experiments demonstrating the sensitizing properties of antigens extracted from L-forms of beta-hemolytic streptococci by alternating freezing and thawing (Shwartzman phenomenon production in the knee joints of rabbits).

Of great interest in this regard are the data of Freimer and his associates[3, 4] describing the presence in streptococcal L-

forms of an M protein which diffuses into the medium. Freimer investigated the immunochemical nature of the cytoplasmic membrane of streptococcal L-forms and showed its antigenic relationship with human cardiac tissue. Preservation in L-forms of many biosynthetic functions of the bacterial forms, i.e., capacity to produce hemolysin, streptokinase and deoxyribonuclease in streptococcal L-forms, coagulase in staphylococcal L-forms,[30] and neuroaminidase in L-forms of cholera vibrios,[27] suggests the preservation of many pathogenic features in these forms. The pathogenic potentialities of L-form bacteria was demonstrated by our data[19] on the cytopathic effect of L-forms of S. typhi and S. hemolyticus in certain tissue cultures, by the work of Lavillaureix[26] on the cytopathic action of the L-form of cholera vibrios, and by the data of Hatten & Sulkin[10] on the persistence of Brucella L-forms in cells.

Of great importance for the study of the pathogenic potentialities of L-forms of bacteria is the construction of experimental models of pathologic processes, with introduction of different etiologic agents, which is not always easy. For these experiments the choices of the experimental animals, of the site of injection, and of the dose and subsequent multiplication of the infectious agent introduced can be crucial. Many other factors not at present recognized are also probably essential.

The response of monkeys to experimental infections was studied by many workers with the aim of reproducing the rheumatic process. Because of the similarity of the connective tissues of men and monkeys, plus the latter's natural susceptibility to streptococcal infections, primates seemed ideal subjects for such experiments; the results, however, failed to demonstrate the production of characteristic changes, such as Aschoff-Talalaev granuloma in primate cardiac tissue.[5, 9, 22, 35, 37, 39] Experimental streptococcal infection of monkeys was not always successful; it may be acute or subclinical and was sometimes accompanied by increased ESR and leucocytosis and specific antibodies in the blood; heart lesions were infrequently observed. Reaction in the form of chronic tonsillitis in one monkey was demonstrated by Friou[5] during pharyngeal infection of three chimpanzees.

In an attempt to produce angina in monkeys, we injected streptococcal L-forms into the paratonsillar cellular tissue; and L-forms were injected intravenously to reveal the general reaction. Control groups were infected by the parent strains of streptococci. The results of this investigation showed that it was possible to produce angina in monkeys independent of the site of injection (intravenous or paratonsillar). No essential difference was observed in response to infection by L-form or parent cultures, and in some monkeys angina was complicated by diffuse myocardial lesions in instances of infection both by L-forms and parent cultures of streptococci. The data provided by these yet unfinished experiments, however, are not an indication that it is possible to produce a model of the pathologic processes in L-form infection.

This possibility was demonstrated in a series of experiments designed to produce meningitis in rabbits, where it was possible to follow differences in the pathologic process produced by L-forms in comparison with those due to parent cultures: independent of their specific species origin, L-forms injected suboccipitally produced a meningeal syndrome characterized by a more sluggish and prolonged course; the acute period and the healing phase began late, and death of a lesser number of animals was observed.

Results of these experiments permit the conclusion that, by using different species of animals and different methods of infection, corresponding models of pathologic processes may be reproduced. Reversion to bacteria of the initial species could not be observed. Construction of experimental models of pathologic processes has great importance from the point of view of the elucidation of the pathogenic potentialities of L-forms, and of approaching the most rational methods of therapy for diseases where L-forms may play an essential role in etiology and pathogenesis. Of great interest in this connection are the works of Guze and Kalmanson,[7, 8, 21] who succeeded in obtaining an experimental model of chronic

pyelonephritis in rats, and produced protoplasts in vivo under the influence of penicillin treatment. The authors showed the advisability of combined treatment of processes such as pyelonephritis by a combination of antibiotics of the penicillin and erythromycin or kanamycin types; the latter two antibiotics were ineffective against intact bacterial cells, but penetrated intracellularly into protoplasts (where cell wall synthesis had been blocked by penicillin); under these circumstances, erythromycin and kanamycin killed protoplasts.

Of undoubted significance for the solution of the problem of the role of L-forms in infectious disease pathology is the isolation of L-forms directly from patients. Fundamental for such bacteriological analysis are simultaneous primary plating of the material tested and subsequent passages, on media containing an L-transforming agent for the isolation of L-forms and related variants, and on a medium without L-transforming agents for the isolation of transitional, reverting and bacterial forms. As early as 1951, Nelson & Pickett[32] noted L-forms of *Brucella* in the blood of patients. Later on, an L-form of *Corynebacterium* was isolated from the blood of a child with subacute endocarditis,[40] and L-forms of *S. typhi* from a typhoid fever case.[23] Our observations and those of other authors[28, 38] suggest that in septic endocarditis L-forms and similar variants reverting *in vitro* to streptococci are noted with great constancy. Supporting data on isolation of streptococcal L-forms from the blood of rheumatic fever patients were obtained in our laboratory and by Wittler and associates.[41]

In the case of purulent meningitis and meningoencephalitis, different species of bacteria and transitional, unstable and stable L-forms were isolated from the spinal fluid. The latter were practically indistinguishable from *Mycoplasmas*. With a particular constancy, stable L-forms were isolated in severe and protracted cases of meningitis, meningo-encephalitis and brain abscess in which treatment with antibiotics had little effect. L-forms could not be plated out from the spinal fluid in periods of convalescence. Comparison of these data with the results of experimental models of meningitis in rabbits during their infection with stable L-forms of diverse species of bacteria would seem to prove the pathogenic action of L-forms.

SUMMARY

Many species of pathogenic microorganisms are capable of L-transformation and spheroplast production.

There is substantial proof of the possibility of production, persistence and reversion of L-forms *in vivo*.

The alternating existence of the infectious agent as transitional and unstable L-forms and reverted bacteria may be important for the course of the pathological process, the L-forms affording prolonged persistence of the agent, and their reversion into bacteria causing relapses.

Pathogenic potentialities of stable L-forms are expressed in their retention of some pathological characteristics, such as cytopathic action in tissue cultures, sensitizing properties, and capacity to produce pathological responses after artificial infections. Experimental models of pathological processes produced by stable L-forms have a number of peculiarities. Thus, experimental angina in monkeys emerged as a response to multiple infections by streptococcal L-forms independent of the site of introduction of the infectious agent (intravenous or paratonsillar), and was frequently complicated by myocardial lesions. Angina was similarly produced by infections with L-forms or with streptococci. The model of meningitis and meningo-encephalitis in rabbits, produced by injection of L-forms and independent of their specific species origin, was different from meningitis produced by the bacteria in that the disease had a delayed onset and a more protracted course, and healing was late in starting.

Clinical and laboratory observations demonstrated the possibility of occurrence of the infectious agent as L- or transitional forms in certain pathologic processes. Thus, in rheumatic fever and septic endocarditis, relatively stable L-forms were frequently isolated, reverting only after many passages on media without the inducing agent and always into the same bacterial species— streptococci. In purulent bacterial meningitis and meningo-encephalitis unstable L-forms and transitional forms which reverted to bacteria *in vitro*, and stable L-forms practically indistinguishable from *Mycoplasma* were noted simultaneously. These forms were isolated from patients unsuccessfully treated with antibiotics.

While investigations of the pathogenic potentialities of L-form bacteria began relatively recently, there is now enough evidence to suggest the importance of continued and many-sided investigations of the role of these forms in infectious disease pathology.

REFERENCES

1. Bittner, J., and Vionesco, V.: Formes "L" toxigenes du *Clostridium perfringens*. In: *IX International Congress for Microbiology* (Abstracts). Moscow, 1966: p. 353.
2. Dienes, L., and Weinberger, H. J.: The L forms of bacteria. *Bact. Rev.* **15**: 245, 1951.
3. Freimer, E. H.: Studies of L forms and protoplasts of group A streptococci. II. Chemical and immunological properties of the cell membrane. *J. Exp. Med.* **117**: 377, 1963.
4. Freimer, E. H., Krause, R. M., and McCarty, M.: Studies of L forms and protoplasts of group A streptococci. I. Isolation, growth and bacteriologic characteristics. *J. Exp. Med.* **110**: 853, 1959.
5. Friou, G. J.: Experimental infection of the upper respiratory tract of young chimpanzees with group A hemolytic streptococci. *J. Infect. Dis.* **86**: 264, 1950.
6. Godzeski, C. W., Brier, G., and Farran, J. D.: The interaction of antibiotics, bacteria and bacterial L-phase *in vivo. Ann. N. Y. Acad. Sci.*, 1967 (in press).
7. Guze, L. B., and Kalmanson, G. M.: Persistence of bacteria in "protoplast" form after apparent cure of pyelonephritis in rats. *Science* **143**: 1340, 1964.
8. ———: Action of erythromycin on "protoplasts" in vivo. *Science* **146**: 1299, 1964.
9. Hamilton, T. R., Dascomb, H. E., and Syverton, J. T.: Experimental cardiovascular disease in monkeys and rabbits. *Fed. Proc.* **9**: 332, 1950.
10. Hatten, B., and Sulkin, S. E.: Intracellular production of *Brucella* L forms. I. Recovery of L forms from tissue culture cells infected with *Brucella abortus. J. Bact.* **91**: 285, 1966.
11. Kagan, B. M., Molander, C. W., Zolla, S.,

Heimlich, E. M., Weinberger, H. J., Busser, R., and Liepnieks, S.: Antibiotic sensitivity and pathogenicity of L-phase variants of staphylococci. In: *Antimicrobial Agents and Chemotherapy—1963* (J. C. Sylvester, Ed.). American Society for Microbiology, Ann Arbor, 1963: p. 517.

*12. Kagan, G. Y.: *Biologic Characteristics of L-Forms of Some Pathogenic Types of Bacteria.* Thesis, Moscow, 1963.

13. Kagan, G. Y., Koptelova, E. I., and Pokrovsky, B. M.: Isolation of pleuropneumonia-like organisms, L-forms and heteromorphous growth of bacteria from the cerebrospinal fluid of patients with septic meningitis. *J. Hyg. Epidemiol. Microbiol. Immunol.* (Praha) **9**: 310, 1965.

14. Kagan, G. Y., and Levashev, V. S.: Biological properties of typhoid bacilli cultures after reversion from L-form. *Izmench. Mikroorg.* **2**: 373, 1957 (in Russian).

15. ————: The L-transforming action of some antibiotics in *in vivo* experimental conditions. *Antibiotiki* **6**: 383, 1961 (in Russian).

16. Kagan, G. Y., and Mikhailova, V. S.: Isolation of L-forms of streptococci from the blood of patients with rheumatism and endocarditis. *J. Hyg. Epidemiol. Microbiol. Immunol.* (Praha) **7**: 327, 1963.

17. Kagan, G. Y., and Pesina, Z. A.: The isolation and study of certain morphological peculiarities of L-form gonococcus. *Vestn. Derm. Vener.* **33**(4): 54, 1959 (in Russian).

*18. Kagan, G. Y., Prozorovsky, S. V., Koptelova, E. Y., Mikhailova, V. S., Danko, L. V., Cherkovich, G. M., Mezentsev, A. M., Simovonian, V. G., and Kavtaradze, K. N.: Results of experimental infection of primates by L-forms of group A β-haemolytic streptococci. In: *International Symposium on Biology and Pathology, Studies of Human Disease in Experiments of Monkeys.* Sunhumi, 1966: p. 58.

19. Kagan, G. Y., and Rakovskaya, I. V.: Cytopathogenic action of the L-forms of certain pathogenic bacterial species in tissue culture. *Byul. Eksp. Biol. Med.* **57**(6): 69, 1964 (in Russian).

20. Kagan, G. Y., Schegolev, A. G., and Prozorovsky, S. V.: Pathogenic and immunogenic properties of *S. typhimurium* L-forms obtained under the action of penicillin. *Antibiotiki* **9**(8): 722, 1964 (in Russian).

21. Kalmanson, G. M., and Guze, L. B.: Role of protoplasts in pathogenesis of pyelonephritis. *JAMA* **190**: 1107, 1964.

22. Kennedy, D. R., Hamilton, T. R., and Syverton. J. T.: Effects on monkeys of introduction of hemolytic streptococci into root canals. *J. Dent. Res.* **36**: 496, 1957.

23. Kochemasova, Z. N., Dykhno, M. M., Prozorovsky, S. V., Kassirskaya, N. G., Burmistrovich, S. E., Savenkova, V. T., Schegolev, A. G., and Starshinova, V. S.: L-forms of some pathogenic bacteria types. *Vestn. Akad. Med. Nauk SSSR* **20**(8): 39, 1965 (in Russian).

24. Koptelova, E. I., Pokrovsky, V. I., and Gorshkova, E. P.: A model of experimental meningitis of rabbits caused by streptococcal and staphylococcal L-forms. *Vestn. Akad. Med. Nauk SSSR* **20**(8): 60, 1965 (in Russian).

*25. Koptelova, E. I. et al.: In press, 1966.

26. Lavillaureix, J.: Action de formes L pathogènes sur des cultures de cellules cancéreuses. *C. R. Acad. Sci.* (Paris) **244**: 1098, 1957.

27. Madoff, M., Annenberg, S., and Weinstein, L.: Production of neuraminidase by L forms of *Vibrio cholerae. Proc. Soc. Exp. Biol. Med.* **107**: 776, 1961.

28. Mattman, L. H., and Mattman, P. E.: L forms of *Streptococcus faecalis* in septicemia. *Arch. Intern. Med.* (Chicago) **115**: 315, 1965.

29. Mattman, L. H., Tunstall, L. H., Mathews, W. W., and Gordon, D. L.: L-variation in mycobacteria. *Amer. Rev. Resp. Dis.* **82**: 202, 1960.

30. Mattman, L. H., Tunstall, L. H., Rossmoore, H. W.: Induction and characteristics of staphylococcal L forms. *Canad. J. Microbiol.* **7**: 705, 1961.

31. Minck, R., and Lavillaureix, J.: La transformation L des bactéries *L'Année Biol.* **6**: 153, 1956.

32. Nelson, E. L., and Pickett, M. J.: The recovery of L-forms of Brucella and their relation to brucella phage. *J. Infect. Dis.* **89**: 226, 1951.

33. Prozorovsky, S. V.: Obtaining L-form of pathogenic staphylococci following administration of penicillin. *Antibiotiki* **3**(6): 86. 1958 (in Russian).

34. Scheibel, I., and Assandri, J.: Isolation of toxigenic L-phase variants from *Cl. tetani. Acta Path. Microbiol. Scand.* **46**: 333, 1959.

*35. Smirnov, P. V., Beletskaya, L. V., and Borodiuk, N. A.: Experimental streptococcal infection of monkeys (*Macacus rhesus*); (on the nature of rheumatic fever and rheumatoid diseases). *Zh. Mikrobiol. Epidemiol. Immunobiol.* **30**(5): 61, 1959.

36. Ustimenko, L. M.: L-forms of Treponema pertenue. *Vestn. Akad. Med. Nauk SSSR* **20**(8): 46, 1965 (in Russian).

37. Vanale, P. W.: Experimental streptococcal in-

* Unverified reference.

fection in the rhesus monkey; care and diseases of the research monkey. *Ann. N. Y. Acad. Sci.* **85:** 910, 1960.

38. Vigouroux, J., and Hannoun, C.: Apparition spontanée in vivo de formes L des bactéries; leur importance possible en pathologie infectieuse. *C. R. Acad. Sci.* (Paris) **242:** 2603, 1956.

39. Watson, R. F., Rothbard, S., and Swift, H. F.: Type-specific protection and immunity following intranasal inoculation of monkeys with group A hemolytic streptococci. *J. Exp. Med.* **84:** 127, 1946.

40. Wittler, R. G., Malizia, W. F., Kramer, P. E., Tuckett, J. D., Pritchard, H. N., and Baker, H. J.: Isolation of a corynebacterium and its transitional forms from a case of subacute bacterial endocarditis treated with antibiotics. *J. Gen. Microbiol.* **23:** 315, 1960.

41. Wittler, R. G., Tuckett, J. D., Muccione, V. J., Gangarosa, E. J., O'Connell, R. C., and Washington, D.: Transitional forms and L forms from the blood on rheumatic fever patients. In: *VIII International Congress for Microbiology* (Abstracts). Montreal, 1962: p. 125.

42. Zdodrowsky, P. F.: Cerebrospinal meningitis in the light of excitement. *Sov. Med. Gaz.* **6:** 323, 1932.

45

Streptococcus sanguis in the Pathogenesis of Recurrent Aphthous Stomatitis

Michael F. Barile, Thomas C. Francis and Edward A. Graykowski

NATIONAL INSTITUTES OF HEALTH

BETHESDA, MARYLAND

Recurrent aphthous stomatitis (recurrent aphthae) is a disease of man characterized by painful, recurrent, single or multiple necrotizing ulcerations of the oral mucosal tissues. The etiology is unknown and there is no specific therapy. Recurrence is associated with hormonal changes in women, physical or psychic stress, oral trauma and mucosal exposure to chemical irritants.[2, 31, 44] The disease may have an immunological basis[36] and a familial tendency.[42] The severe form of recurrent aphthae (periadenitis aphthae) may have clinical and histopathologic features in common with Bechet's, Steven-Johnson's, and Reiter's syndromes; periadenitis aphthae is often confused with oral *Herpesvirus hominis*[55] (*Herpes simplex*) infections. The combined problems of unknown etiology, lack of specific therapy, and frequent recurrence have made eradication of this disease and the management of these patients a difficult challenge.

The clinical, histopathological, and skin hypersensitivity findings in patients with recurrent aphthae observed over a four-year period at the National Institutes of Health Clinical Center have been reported.[16] This report will briefly review the microbiologic aspects of recurrent aphthae and will summarize our* findings on the possible role of *Streptococcus sanguis* in the pathogenesis of this disease.

HISTORICAL ASPECTS OF MICROBIOLOGY

Herpesvirus hominis

Some clinicians believe that the clinical aspects of recurrent aphthae and recurrent labial herpes are similar.[2] Since *H. hominis* is known to cause recurrent labial herpes,[40] numerous laboratory attempts were made to establish the possible role of viruses in recurrent aphthae, but with negative results: *Herpesvirus* was not isolated from aphthous lesions;[5, 12, 13, 43] patients did not develop a rise in antibody titer to *Herpesvirus* nor respond to a *Herpesvirus* skin test;[47] histologic examination of aphthous lesions did not show the intranuclear inclusion bodies and the "ballooning" degeneration characteristic of *Herpesvirus* infection of epithelial tissues.[5, 40]

---

* The study group at the National Institutes of Health includes M. F. Barile, T. C. Francis, E. A. Graykowski, H. R. Stanley, W. B Lee, C. DeJong, T. Coyne, M. W. Grabowski and D. B. Riggs.

Toxoplasmosis

Sedallian et al.[41] reported two cases of toxoplasmosis with associated buccal ulcerations, but Sircus[45] showed that patients with recurrent aphthous stomatitis did not develop increased antibody titers for toxoplasma.

Bacillus crassus

Early studies dealt with the possible role of B. crassus as the cause of recurrent aphthae and with the similarities in the clinical appearance of recurrent aphthae and Vincent's angina. In 1910, Löblowitz isolated a staphylococcus, a streptobacillus (B. crassus) and the spirochete of Vincent's angina from aphthous lesions;[27] Löblowitz believed that B. crassus was a morphologic variant of Vincent's fusiform and that recurrent aphthae was an unusual manifestation of Vincent's disease. In 1911 Sutton[48] isolated both of Vincent's organisms from aphthous lesions and supported Löblowitz's contentions. In 1959, Lang et al.[25] reported that specimens from aphthous lesions produced pox-like formations in the chorioallantoic membrane of developing chick embryos; histologically, the lesions showed infiltration of giant cells, destruction of blood vessel walls, and a large number of fusiform-like organisms. Lang et al. concluded that fusiforms may cause recurrent aphthae.

MATERIALS AND METHODS

Specimens

The procedures necessary for successful isolation of the pleomorphic S. sanguis agent from aphthous lesions have been reported.[17] We emphasized that: (a) the specimen should be obtained early, during the acute phase of the disease—the organism was more difficult to recover in pure culture from lesions more than two days old; (b) the pseudomembrane should be removed and the specimen obtained from the surface of the denuded lesion—the abraded cells from the base and marginal areas of the lesion were the desired specimen (a sterile cotton-tipped applicator was used); and (c) the specimens should be inoculated immediately and directly onto the recommended media. We have also shown that biopsied tissue from the aphthous lesions obtained during onset of disease is an excellent specimen for culture.

Specimens were obtained also from nonaphthous lesions and from saliva of patients with no history of recurrent aphthae; these were processed in the same manner as the specimen from the aphthous lesions.

Media

The original approach was to establish whether Mycoplasma sp. was present in aphthous lesions. Two broth and agar media were used: a human blood medium[4] and the Eaton-agent medium.[7] Antibiotic and antibacterial agents were not incorporated in these media. Multiple specimens from each lesion were taken and inoculated in broth and onto agar medium, in duplicate. Half of the media were incubated aerobically and the other half in an atmosphere of 5% CO_2 in nitrogen, both at $36 \pm 1°C$ for at least three days. In addition, primary rabbit kidney cell culture and Hela cell culture tubes were inoculated in duplicate and observed for cytopathic changes consistent with virus infection, in particular with Herpesvirus infection.[40]

Isolations

Representative Streptococcus strains from each lesion and saliva specimen were selected and stored in a frozen state (−20°C) or maintained by subculture in Todd-Hewitt broth until tested for identity.

Test for Identity

Identification of the group specific carbohydrate ("C" substance) was used to characterize the Streptococcus isolates. Serologic group identification was determined by the precipitin test as described by Lancefield[24] by use of reference beta-hemolytic Streptococcus Group antisera (Group A through Q inclusive from Burroughs-Wellcome Laboratories, England); and reference Streptococcus Group strains (Groups A, B, C, D, E, F, G, H, K, M, N,

O, and Q from R. M. Cole, Bethesda, Md.). The reference alpha-hemolytic *S. sanguis* and *Streptococcus* Group H strains used were: *S. sanguis* type I[53] (ATCC #10556), type I–II (ATCC #10558), and type II (ATCC #10557) obtained from the American Type Culture Collection, Rockville, Md.; *Streptococcus* Group H strain *Challis* and *Streptococcus* strain *SBE* from R. M. Cole, Bethesda, Md.; and *Streptococcus* Group H strains *Chanon*, 6180, 5042, 3315, H455, 3437, E-91 and *Col* from J. S. Porterfield, Mill Hill, London.

RESULTS

MICROBIOLOGIC FINDINGS

Incidence

Mycoplasma species were not isolated from these specimens; the cell cultures did not show gross cytopathic changes suggestive of viral infections, and fusiforms and spirochetes were not seen in stained tissue scrapings of aphthous lesions.

A pleomorphic *Streptococcus*, designated strain 2A, was isolated in pure culture (one colony type) from an aphthous lesion in patient AL.[3] Similar organisms were isolated frequently in pure-colony culture from aphthous lesions or found as the predominant organism in cultures. A total of 70 *Streptococcus* strains were isolated and examined: 50 were isolated from 30 patients with recurrent aphthae; ten from five patients with non-aphthous ulcerations, and ten from the saliva of five patients with no history of recurrent aphthae. The morphologic, biochemical, and serologic properties of these *Streptococcus* isolates are described below.

S. sanguis *strain 2A*

Strain 2A represents the prototype *Streptococcus* strain.[3] The original isolation plates from patient AL are shown in Figures 45.1, A and B. On the human blood medium, colonies were embedded, star-shaped and produced an alpha-type of hemolysis (Figure 45.1C). On the Eaton-agent medium, colonies were smaller (0.2 to 0.4 mm), partially embedded and nodular (Figure 45.1D).

These colonies consisted of Gram-nega-tive amorphous material interspersed with pleomorphic organisms: large (1–5 μ) round Gram-negative cells which appeared fragile (Figure 45.2A); clumps containing small (0.2–0.4 μ) delicate Gram-negative coccal forms, in pairs with occasional short chains (Figure 45.2B), diphtheroids (Figure 45.2C), and Gram-positive and Gram-negative bacilli occasionally resembling fusiform-like structures (Figure 45.2D).

PPLO broth medium[4] cultures were turbid and had sediments which contained particulate matter. Initially, little to no chain-formation was seen. On subculture to ordinary media, the organism grew without difficulty, produced either glossy or matt colonies with alpha-hemolysis, were morophologically uniform, and appeared as Gram-positive diplococci in short chains. In dextrose broth, the organism appeared as a typical chain-forming *Streptococcus* (Figure 45.3).

When specimens from aphthous lesions were inoculated directly onto ordinary media and 5% sheep blood agar, glossy and matt colonies with alpha-hemolysis typical of streptococci were isolated.

Biochemical Properties

The *Streptococcus* strains isolated from the aphthous lesions showed a similar biochemical and serologic pattern of reactivity. They produced alpha type hemolysis on 5% sheep blood agar, gave negative reactions for catalase production, failed to reduce nitrate to nitrite, did not grow in 6.5% sodium chloride broth, produced ammonia from arginine, and produced acid and curdling with reduction in litmus milk broth. Many strains (45 per cent) gave positive reactions in methylene blue milk broth. All strains produced acid in broth containing dextrose, lactose, maltose, mannose, and sucrose. Most strains produced acid in broth containing inulin (67 per cent), salicin (71 per cent), raffinose (52 per cent), starch (90 per cent), and trehalose (71 per cent). They rarely produced acid with glycerine (10 per cent) and sorbitol (5 per cent), and none produced acid in broth containing arabinose, inositol, mannitol, and xylose. Dextran was

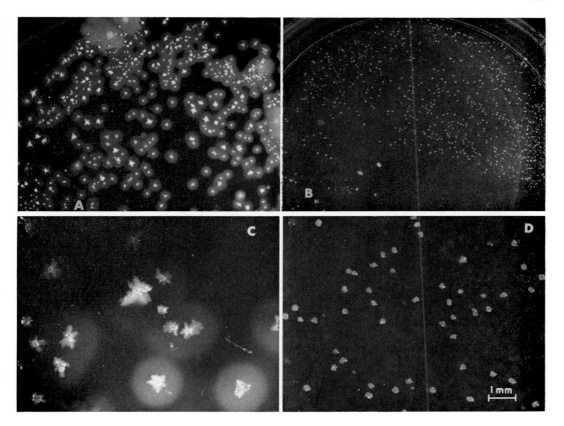

Figure 45.1. Original primary isolation plates from Patient AL, illustrating growth of *Streptococcus sanguis* strain 2A on (*A*) human blood medium (× 1.2), and (*B*) Eaton-agent medium (× 2.0). *C:* On human blood medium,[3] colonies were embedded, star-shaped, and produced an alpha type of hemolysis (× 6.0). *D:* On Eaton-agent medium,[3] colonies were smaller, partially embedded and nodular.

produced by 30 of 45 strains tested (67 per cent).

Serologic Group Identification

The "C" substance of the prototype *Streptococcus* strains 2A and 14A, isolated from aphthous lesions, gave positive precipitin reactions with the reference antiserum to *Streptococcus* Group H and a weak positive reaction with the reference antiserum to *Streptococcus* Group O. Strain 14A reacted with antiserum to strain 2A, but not vice versa. Eleven of 13 reference *S. sanguis* and *Streptococcus* Group H strains tested gave positive precipitin reactions with antisera to strains 2A and 14A. Strain 10557 reacted only with anti-serum to strain 2A. Strains 10556, 6180, 5042, 3315, H455 and *Col* reacted only with antiserum to strain 14A. Strains 10558, *Challis* and *SBE* reacted with antisera to both strains 2A and 14A. Aphthous *Streptococcus* strain 2A appears to be related to or identical with a *S. sanguis*, type I,[53] and strain 14A appears to be *S. sanguis*, type II.[53] Strain *Channon* gave a positive reaction with antiserum to Group H initially, but after freeze-drying it gave a negative reaction with antiserum to Group H and a positive reaction with antiserum to Group O. The remaining two Group H strains (3437 and E-91) did not react with strain 2A, strain 14A, Group H and Group O antisera.

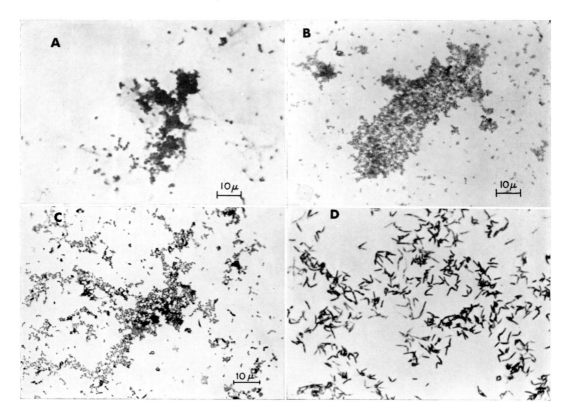

Figure 45.2. Colonies of pleomorphic organisms[3] from Patient AL. *A:* Large protoplast-like structures with fragile cell walls; *B:* small, delicate Gram-negative coccal forms, in pairs with occasional short chains; *C:* diphtheroids; *D:* long filamentous Gram-negative and Gram-positive bacilli occasionally resembling fusiform-like structures (× 850).

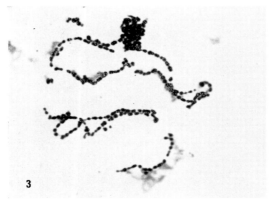

Figure 45.3. On subculture of specimens from aphthous lesions to dextrose broth, the morphology became uniform and the organism appeared as a typical chain-forming streptococcus. × 850.

The Group specific "C" substance of the 50 *Streptococcus* isolates from aph-thous lesions gave positive precipitating reactions with antisera to *Streptococcus* strains 2A (64 per cent), strain 14A (48 per cent), strain Group H (46 per cent), and strain Group O (32 per cent). These findings showed that the strepto-cocci isolated from aphthous lesions were related to *Streptococcus* Group H and Group O, and were *S. sanguis*. Like orga-nisms were found in mixed cultures from non-aphthous lesions in two of five pa-tients, and a few colonies were found in mixed cultures of the saliva of four of five patients with no history of recurrent aph-thae.

Histopathology

The histopathologic aspects of recur-rent aphthae have been published.[16, 17, 44] The salient features are summarized as follows: (a) each aphthous lesion represents an individual entity displaying its own rate and extent of tissue breakdown and subsequent repair; (b) aphthous ulcers present all of the pathologic manifestations of typical ulcers; (c) the surface epithelium is necrosed and sloughed, and is replaced by a fibropurulent plaque or membrane made of fibrin, necrotic and degenerating leukocytes, epithelial cells and debris; (d) small colonies of microorganisms may be present; (e) early aphthous lesions are usually associated with and possibly the result of epithelial disturbances of ducts of minor salivary glands; (f) disruption of marginating and ductal tissues appears to initiate at the basal layer of the epithelium and progresses upward with inflammatory cells infiltrating the edge canals; (g) there is a preponderance of mononuclear cells in the inflammatory response of early lesions, which persists peripherally even after neutrophils become predominant in the central region of ulceration; (h) prominent vascular channels are present in the papillary layers running perpendicular to the surface and in the reticular layer parallel to the surface; some vessels are congested with neutrophils and erythrocytes; (i) the inflammatory infiltrate in the deeper tissues are perivascular and reveal an increase in number of mononuclear cells; occasionally eosinophil and mast cells are present.

Microorganisms in Microscopic Section

Fifteen aphthous and ten non-aphthous lesions, plus 32 specimens of oral mucosa obtained at autopsy were biopsied, sectioned, stained by the Giemsa method, and examined[46] for microorganisms showing the morphologic appearance of the *Streptococcus* strain 2A described above. Although many pleomorphic forms were seen, the predominant form was a diplococcoid structure which occasionally appeared in short chains (Figure 45.4). Microorganisms morphologically consistent with the pleomorphic *Streptococcus* strain 2A were found[46] in the majority of aphthous lesions (94 per cent), and less frequently in non-aphthous lesions (40 per cent) and

normal oral mucosa (47 per cent) obtained at autopsy.

ANIMAL STUDIES

Experimentally Produced Skin Lesions

Representative *S. sanguis* isolates were inoculated in the skin of guinea pigs and rabbits. In animals, lesions were produced which had many features typical of the aphthous lesions in patients (Figure 45.5).[17] The lesions in animals were large, extensive, and nodular with necrosis and crusting (Figure 45.6). Histologically, the lesions showed an acute necrotic ulcerative inflammatory reaction of the epithelial tissues. In both man and animals, the mononuclear cells predominated.

Experimentally Produced Oral Lesions

Rizzo & Ashe[35] reported a procedure for producing intraoral herpetic lesions in rabbits. In collaboration with Dr. A. Rizzo, representative *S. sanguis* strains and Group specific "C" substance were inoculated into the buccal mucosa, lip, and tongue of rabbits and guinea pigs. Intraoral lesions were produced which had many features in common with the aphthous lesions of man (Figure 45.7). The severity of the intraoral lesions produced appeared to parallel the severity of the skin lesions produced.

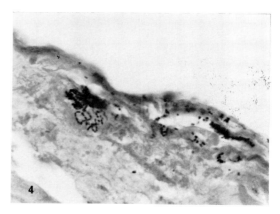

Figure 45.4. In histologic sections of aphthous lesions,[46] the appearance of the organism was varied, but a diplococcoid structure resembling a small dumbbell was the most predominant form, and occasionally appeared in short chains. × 850.

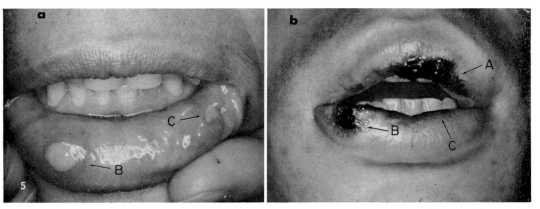

Figure 45.5. Patients with recurrent periadenitis aphthae[16] had large single or multiple deep mucosal erosive ulcerations (*a*), with elevated margins surrounded by diffuse erythema, extensive local edema, serosanguineous crusting[17] (*b*), and scar formation.

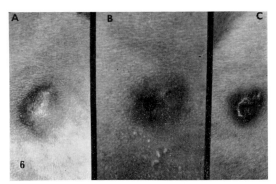

Figure 45.6. Lesions on rabbits following inoculation with *Streptococcus sanguis*. A: Skin lesions[12] developed 12 hours after inoculation; *B*: ulcers developed at the pericentral site in 4 days; *C*: the ulcer extended over the entire nodule in 7 days.

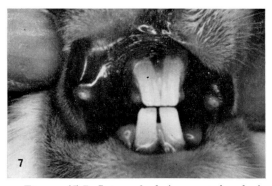

Figure 45.7. Intraoral lesions produced in guinea pigs with *Streptococcus sanguis*.

Lesion-Producing Capacity of S. sanguis strains

The following streptococcal preparations were inoculated into the skin of guinea pigs: (*a*) *Streptococcus* cells washed free of culture media and heated at 60°C for one hour to destroy viability; (*b*) acid-soluble *Streptococcus* group "C" substance as used for the Lancefield precipitin test; and (*c*) the sediments of the acid-extracted *Streptococcus* cells described in *b*, neutralized with 1.0 N sodium hydroxide and washed. The most severe lesions were produced by viable and heat-killed *Streptococcus* cells and by the acid-soluble cell wall material. Lesions were produced equally well by viable and heat-killed *S. sanguis* cells. A minimum of 10^7 viable or heat-killed *Streptococcus* cells were required to produce a necrotizing lesion. The chain-forming *S. sanguis* cells contained more cell wall substance and produced a more severe skin ulcer than did the freshly-isolated, pleomorphic, ("transitional") *Streptococcus* cells. *Streptococcus* cell-free broth culture filtrates produced erythema and edema but no ulcerations. Uninoculated broth medium did not produce a skin reaction. The least reactive material tested was *Streptococcus* cells containing less cell wall substance, i.e., the *Streptococcus* cell sediments following the Lancefield acid extraction procedure.

Our preliminary experiments have indicated that protoplasts prepared by phage C enzymatic lysates[15, 29, 30] do not produce severe lesions. The reference beta-hemolytic *Streptococcus* Group strains were also tested for their lesion-producing capacity. Moderate skin reactions were produced by strains Group B, Group F, and at times Group C. Severe ulcerating lesions were not produced by *Streptococcus* strains Groups A, D, E, G, K, M, N, and Q.

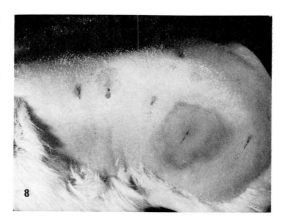

Figure 45.8. Severe delayed-type skin hypersensitivity reaction developed on skin test with *Streptococcus sanguis* in immunized guinea pigs.

HYPERSENSITIVITY REACTIONS

Skin Reactions

Guinea pigs were immunized with viable *S. sanguis* cells in incomplete Freund's adjuvant (3:2 parts), 2 ml of an emulsion containing 10^9 streptococci were inoculated subcutaneously in the nape of the neck, and the animals were skin challenged three to seven weeks later. A severe delayed type of skin hypersensitivity, or an Arthus type of reaction developed: the central site of the lesion became blanched and a purulent papule developed, which was surrounded by extensive erythema and edema. Necrosis with crusting followed (Figure 45.8). *S. sanguis* cells and cell wall material produced similar skin lesion reactions. Animals were immunized with alpha-hemolytic *S. sanguis* strain 2A, and were challenged with the reference beta-hemolytic *Streptococcus* Group strains. Only strain Group K produced a more severe reaction in the immunized animals than in the non-immunized animals.

Anaphylactic Reactions

Guinea pigs were immunized with *S. sanguis* cells and with the cell wall material in incomplete Freund's adjuvant, and were challenged by intracardiac puncture with high concentrations of *S. sanguis* cells or with cell wall material. Thirty-three of 95 guinea pigs tested (35 per cent) developed typical anaphylactic reactions and died within ten minutes. The surviving guinea pigs had ruffled fur, appeared hyperirritable, showed difficulty breathing, and 32 (53 per cent) developed transitory inflammatory arthritic "stiff joints". The "stiff joints" developed within 24 to 48 hours following challenge and were present for a period of only three to seven days. Anaphylaxis was transferred passively with serum. Non-immunized animals did not produce anaphylactic reactions following the intracardial *Streptococcus* challenge. Nine of our patients (14 per cent) reported histories of arthritic symptoms.[16]

Skin Testing of Patients with Recurrent Aphthae

Forty-four patients were skin tested with the *S. sanguis* vaccine: 32 with aphthae, 6 with non-aphthae lesions (4 lichen planus, 1 amyloidosis, and 1 oral keratosis), and 6 with no history of aphthae; 0.1 ml of the vaccine was injected intradermally into one forearm, and saline solution, used as control reagent, was injected at the same time in the other forearm. The injection sites were observed for a minimum of three days.

Twenty-eight of 32 patients with recurrent aphthae (88 per cent) produced a delayed-type hypersensitivity skin or an Arthus reaction with a peak intensity between 24 and 48 hours[16] (Figure 45.9). The diameter of the erythema and edema reactions usually measured 2 cm, occasion-

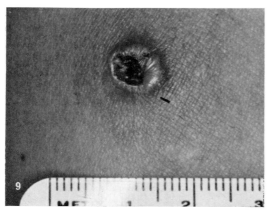

Figure 45.9. Delayed-type skin hypersensitivity reaction developed in patients with recurrent aphthae with the skin test *Streptococcus sanguis* vaccine.

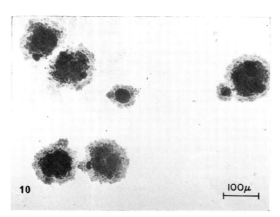

Figure 45.10. L-form-like colonies that grew out[3] during a quiescent period from cultured biopsied scar tissue of a previous lesion of Patient AL; colonies stained by Dienes method, approximately 100 μ in diameter.

ally 4 cm, and, in one patient, 16 cm. The severity of the skin test reaction tended to parallel the severity of the oral aphthous lesions. In four cases with lesions that developed scar formation (periadenitis aphthae), the skin test lesions developed necrosis and scar formation. Patients reported pain and pruritus at the skin lesion site. In five patients, a severe flare of the oral lesions followed the skin test.

Of the six patients tested with nonaphthous lesions, two of the four patients with lichen planus had moderate skin re-

actions; the one patient with oral keratosis had a positive skin reaction, and the one patient with amyloidosis had a negative reaction.

Of the six patients with no history of aphthae, only one patient had a positive skin reaction, and he reported a long history of chronic sore throats.

Before the skin test studies can be considered meaningful, the number of control subjects must be increased, and for this reason the skin test studies are being continued and extended.

Discussion

A possible association has been suggested[16] between *S. sanguis* and the pathogenesis of recurrent aphthous stomatitis. A pleomorphic *S. sanguis* agent was isolated, frequently in pure culture, from the lesions of 30 patients examined. Recovery of the organism in pure culture from the base and marginal areas of an acute, advancing, necrotizing lesion may be meaningful since the oral mucosa is constantly bathed in a rich mixed microbial flora. In Patient AL, *S. sanguis* strain 2A, the prototype organism, was isolated in pure culture from numerous lesions during six exacerbations studied over a four-year period. During two of these exacerbations, a *S. sanguis* bacteremia occurred. During a quiescent period, biopsied scar tissue of a previous lesion was cultured and L-form-like colonies grew out (Figure 45.10). The L-form growth could not be maintained on subculture to standard mycoplasma media without addition of penicillin or high salt content. On histologic examination, microorganisms morphologically consistent with the pleomorphic *S. sanguis* strain 2A were present in the ulcers of most patients studied (94 per cent). The streptococcus strains isolated from aphthous ulcers were related antigenically to *Streptococcus* strains Group H and Group O. The *S. sanguis* isolates appeared to have several variant forms; one variant was more pathogenic than the other. The chain-forming streptococcus had more cell wall substance and produced a more severe lesion than the pleomorphic streptococcus obtained on primary isolation or the streptococcus cell sediment following acid extraction. The skin lesion-producing capacity of *S. sanguis* appeared to be related to the acid-soluble cell wall material containing the group and type specific cell wall substance. Available data do not permit precise definition of the chemical structure of the toxic moiety. Schwab and associates[9, 30, 38, 39] have produced an "intermitting multinodular lesion" of dermal connective tissue with the "C" polysaccharide of Group A streptococcus. L-forms which contain no "C" substance did not produce lesions,[39] were not virulent,[30] and the protoplasts had minimal "C" substance and produced small lesions.[30] The lesions produced with Group A *Streptococcus* do not appear to be the same as ulcers produced with *S. sanguis* strain 2A.

The aphthous *Streptococcus* strains appeared similar to the streptococcal organisms isolated from some patients with subacute bacterial endocarditis (SBE).[1, 28, 33] Similar streptococci were isolated from dental plaques.[6] The SBE organisms were bizarre diphtheroid streptococci[23, 32, 37] and pleomorphic transitional corynebacteria.[54] Both aphthae and SBE streptococcal strains were pleomorphic on primary isolation, produced an alpha type of hemolysis, were related antigenically to *Streptococcus* Group H,[10, 34] were identified as *S. sanguis*,[53] and were dextran producers. Dextran production has been associated with the virulence[19, 20] of *S. sanguis*. L-forms of *S. sanguis* were isolated from patients with SBE by Kagan,[21] Vigouroux & Hannoun,[51, 52] and Frenkel & Hirsch,[14] who concluded that the presence of these forms in SBE could explain the unsolved difficulties in the diagnosis and treatment of the disease. These organisms produced vasculo-sanguinous lesions in developing chick embryos.[18] Aphthous lesions may appear serosanguinous,[17] and histologic sections of aphthous lesions may present a marked perivascular infiltrate.[16, 17, 44]

Viable and heat-killed *S. sanguis* cells and the acid-soluble cell wall material produced lesions in the skin (Figure 45.6) and oral mucosa (Figure 45.7) of guinea pigs and rabbits[17] which had clinical (Figure 45.5) and histologic features typical of aphthous ulcers. These streptococcal materials also produced a similar but more severe delayed-type skin hypersensitivity or Arthus reaction in immunized guinea pigs (Figures 45.6 and 45.8) and in patients with aphthous stomatitis (Figure 45.9). Skin ulcers were produced in patients by the *S. sanguis* skin test vaccine (Figure 45.9) which had many clinical and histopathologic features typical of oral ulcers (Figure 45.5B). These findings may suggest an immunologic basis as the possible etiologic mechanism for recurrent aphthae. Lymphocyte transformation studies[11] on cells from five aphthous and two non-aphthous patients exposed to *S. sanguis* strain 2A "C" substance showed that the mean tritiated thymidine uptake determination was five times greater in lymphocytes from aphthous patients than from non-aphthous patients.* Several investigators have suggested that food hypersensitivity can cause recurrent aphthae.[50] Lehner[26] showed that the sera of patients with aphthous ulcers caused specific agglutination of red blood cells coated with normal oral mucosal tissue, and he proposed that the part played by an autoimmune reaction or by an antibody cross-reacting with an infectious agent and oral mucosa deserves further consideration. Immunologic cross-reactions between Group A streptococcal cells and mammalian tissues and a relationship to induction of autoimmunity in rheumatic fever has been suggested by Kaplan.[22] Taylor *et al.*[49] reported that patients with recurrent aphthae show significant antibody titers to milk proteins.

The mechanism which governs recurrence of attacks in aphthous stomatitis is not yet known. An "L-form theory" was postulated[3] and proposes than an organism having both a pathogenic and a nonpathogenic variant could provide a mechanism to explain the recurrences and remissions in aphthous stomatitis. The cell wall material of *S. sanguis* strain 2A is toxic, and an L-form does not have a cell wall; thus, an L-form of *S. sanguis* could represent a nonpathogenic variant. The bac-

---

* C. W. Trygstad, personal communication.

terial form of *S. sanguis* containing the lesion-producing cell wall material could represent the pathogenic variant. The L-form would be present during quiescence, whereas the pleomorphic ("transitional") and bacterial *S. sanguis* variants containing more of the toxic cell wall material would appear during exacerbation. Since patients produce an ulcerating reaction to the *S. sanguis* skin test vaccine, an aphthous ulcer may represent the result of a similar reaction in the oral mucosal tissues in patients with aphthous stomatitis. In aptients with recurrent aphthae, predisposing factors[2, 16] have been shown to induce recurrence of attacks; thus, for example, recurrence of lesions has been associated with trauma.[2, 16] Trauma can provide an opportunity to expose oral mucosal tissues to available *S. sanguis* cells or cell wall material which may be present in saliva or freed from mucosal tissue. Recurrence of lesions has been associated also with hormonal changes, including onset of menarche,[8, 55] menses,[8] and menopause.[45] Remission often occurs during pregnancy, with recurrence one month post-partum.[2, 16] In one of our patients, more than 100 distinct lesions erupted three days following parturition. Such findings led Zondek[56] to suggest that patients with aphthae may develop a hypersensitivity to endogenous hormones or their derivatives. Steroid therapy, either the topical use of cortisone or the parenteral use of prednisone, can reduce lesion pain and healing time.[2, 13] Moreover, the effectiveness of steroids and the ineffectiveness of antihistamines may be of interest, since these findings are consistent with those reported for other diseases characterized by delayed-type hypersensitivity.

Summary

The preliminary findings suggest a possible association between *Streptococcus sanguis* and recurrent aphthous stomatitis. This association is based on the isolation of *S. sanguis* from aphthous lesions, the production of lesions with *S. sanguis* in the skin and oral mucosa of nonimmunized animals and of severe ulcers in immunized animals and patients, the histologic similarities of lesions produced in animals and in patients, and the presence of microorganisms in histologic sections of lesions. An immunologic basis is proposed as a possible etiologic mechanism of this disease, and an "L-form theory" is suggested to provide a mechanism to explain recurrence of attacks in aphthous stomatitis. Clearly, however, further investigations must be made before the exact nature of these relationships can be properly established.

REFERENCES

1. Alture-Werber, E., and Loewe, L.: Prophylactic immunization against *Streptococcus sanguis*. *J. Bact.* **56:** 391, 1948.
2. Barile, M. F., and Graykowski, E. A.: Primary herpes, recurrent labial herpes, recurrent aphthae, and periadenitis aphthae: a review with some new observations. *J. Dist. Columbia Dent. Soc.* **38:** 7, 1963.
3. Barile, M. F., Graykowski, E. A., Driscoll, E. J., and Riggs, D. B.: L form of bacteria isolated from recurrent aphthous stomatitis lesions. *Oral Surg.* **16:** 1395, 1963.
4. Barile, M. F., Yaguchi, R., and Eveland, W. C.: A simplified medium for the cultivation of pleuropneumonia-like organisms and the L-forms of bacteria. *Amer. J. Clin. Path.* **30:** 171, 1958.
5. Blank, H., Burgoon, C. F., Coriell, L. L., and Scott, T. F. M.: Recurrent aphthous ulcers. *JAMA* **142:** 125, 1950.
6. Carlsson, J.: Zooglea-forming streptococci, resembling *Streptococcus sanguis*, isolated from dental plaque in man. *Odontologisk Revy* **16:** 348, 1965.
7. Chanock, R. M., Hayflick, L., and Barile, M. F.: Growth on artificial medium of an agent associated with atypical pneumonia and its identification as a PPLO. *Proc. Nat. Acad. Sci. USA* **48:** 41, 1962.
8. Collings, C. K., and Dukes, C. D.: Recurrent herpetic stomatitis treated by intradermal injections of influenza A and B virus vaccine. *J. Periodont.* **23:** 48, 1952.
9. Cromartie, W. J.: Reactions of connective tissue to cellular components of group A streptococci. In: *The Streptococcus, Rheumatic Fever and Glomerulonephritis* (J. W. Uhr, Ed.). Williams & Wilkins, Baltimore, 1964: p. 187.
10. Dodd, R. L.: Serologic relationship between Streptococcus group H and *Streptococcus sanguis*. *Proc. Soc. Exp. Biol. Med.* **70:** 598, 1949.
11. Ehrich, W. E.: Lymphoid tissues: their morphology and role in the immune response.

In: *Immunological Diseases* (M. Samter and H. L. Alexander, Eds.). Little, Brown; Boston, 1965: p. 251.

12. Farmer, E. D.: Recurrent aphthous ulcers. *Dent. Practitioner* **8**: 177, 1958.

13. Fraser-Moodie, W.: The treatment of aphthous ulceration with gamma-globulin; the results obtained in a controlled series. *Brit. Dent. J.* **108**: 326, 1960.

14. Frenkel, A., and Hirsch, W.: Spontaneous development of L forms of streptococci requiring secretions of other bacteria or sulphhydryl compounds for normal growth. *Nature* **191**: 728, 1961.

15. Gooder, H., and Maxted, W. R.: Protoplasts of group A beta-haemolytic streptococci. *Nature* **182**: 808, 1958.

16. Graykowski, E. A., Barile, M. F., Lee, W. B., and Stanley, H. R., Jr.: Recurrent aphthous stomatitis: clinical, therapeutic, histopathologic and hypersensitivity aspects. *JAMA* **196**: 637, 1966.

17. Graykowski, A. E., Barile, M. F., and Stanley, H. R.: Periadenitis aphthae: clinical and histopathologic aspects of lesions in a patient and of lesions produced in rabbit skin. *J. Amer. Dent. Ass.* **69**: 118, 1964.

18. Hannoun, C., Vigouroux, J., Levaditi, J., and Nazimoff, O.: Étude des formes L des bactéries apparues spontanément *in vivo*. III. Histopathologie comparée des lésions provoquées par la bactérie normale et par ses formes modifiées. *Ann. Inst. Pasteur* (Paris) **92**: 231, 1957.

19. Hehre, E. J.: Dextran-forming streptococci from the blood in subacute endocarditis and from the throats of healthy persons. *Bull. N. Y. Acad. Med.* **24**: 543, 1948.

20. Hehre, E. J., and Neill, J. M.: Formation of serologically reactive dextrans by streptococci from subacute endocarditis. *J. Exp. Med.* **83**: 147, 1946.

21. Kagan, G. Y.: The problem of the pathogenicity of L-form bacteria; review of literature. *Klin. Med.* (Moscow) **39**(3): 12, 1961.

22. Kaplan, M. H.: Immunologic cross-reactions between group A streptococcal cells and mammalian tissues—possible relationship to induction of autoimmunity in rheumatic fever. In: *The Streptococcus, Rheumatic Fever and Glomerulonephritis* (J. W. Uhr, Ed.). Williams & Wilkins, Baltimore, 1964: p. 169.

23. Lamanna, C.: A non-life cycle explanation of the diphtheroid streptococcus from endocarditis. *J. Bact.* **47**: 327, 1944.

24. Lancefield, R. C., and Todd, E. W.: Antigenic differences between matt hemolytic streptococci and their glossy variants. *J. Exp. Med.* **48**: 769, 1928.

25. Lang, D., Francis, L. E., and McCallum, L.: The recurrent aphthous lesion. *Canad. Dent. Ass. J.* **25**: 767, 1959.

26. Lehner, T.: Recurrent aphthous ulceration and autoimmunity. *Lancet* **2**: 1154, 1964.

27. Löblowitz, J.: Ulcus neuroticum mucosae oris (chronische Aphthen). *Arch. Belg. Dermat. Syph.* **102**: 191, 1910.

28. Loewe, L., Plummer, N., Niven, C. F., Jr., and Sherman, J. M.: Streptococcus s.b.e. in subacute bacterial endocarditis. *JAMA* **130**: 257, 1946.

29. Maxted, W. R.: The active agent in nascent phage lysis of streptococci. *J. Gen. Microbiol.* **16**: 584, 1957.

30. ———: Streptococcal bacteriophages. In: *The Streptococcus, Rheumatic Fever and Glomerulonephritis* (J. W. Uhr, Ed.). Williams & Wilkins, Baltimore, 1964: p. 25.

31. McMichael, J. et al.: Oral ulceration. *Proc. Roy. Soc. Med.* **58**: 453, 1965.

32. Mellon, R. R.: Antigenic relationships between M, S, and R phases of streptococci and their diphtheroid descendants. *J. Immun.* **60**: 91, 1948.

33. Niven, C. F., Jr., and White, J. C.: A study of streptococci associated with subacute bacterial endocarditis. *J. Bact.* **51**: 790, 1946.

34. Porterfield, J. S.: Classification of the streptococci of subacute bacterial endocarditis. *J. Gen Microbiol.* **4**: 92, 1950.

35. Rizzo, A. A., and Ashe, W. K.: Experimental herpetic ulcers in rabbit oral mucosa; clinical, cultural and histologic studies of primary lesions. *Arch. Oral Biol.* **9**: 713, 1964.

36. Samitz, M. H., and Weinberg, R. A.: Recurrent aphthous stomatitis; concepts in pathogenesis. *Postgrad. Med.* **39**: 221, 1966.

37. Schneierson, S. S.: Serological and biological characteristics and penicillin resistance of nonhemolytic streptococci isolated from subacute bacterial endocarditis. *J. Bact.* **55**: 393, 1948.

38. Schwab, J. H., and Cromartie, W. J.: Studies on a toxic cellular component of group A streptococci. *J. Bact.* **74**: 673, 1957.

39. Schwab, J. H., Gooder, H., and Maxted, W. R.: Further studies on toxic C polysaccharide complexes of the β-haemolytic streptococci. *Brit. J. Exp. Path.* **43**: 181, 1962.

40. Scott, T. F. M., and Tokumaru, T.: The *Herpesvirus* group. In: *Viral and Rickettsial Infections of Man* (F. L. Horsfall, Jr., and I. Tamm, Eds.). Lippincott, Philadelphia, 1965: p. 892.

41. Sedallian, P., Garin, J. P., and Faure, P.:

Toxoplasmose humaine acquise; angine, aphthose et porte d'entrée buccopharyngée. *Press Méd.* **62**: 850, 1954.

42. Ship, I. I.: Inheritance of aphthous ulcers of the mouth. *J. Dent. Res.* **44**: 837, 1965.

43. Ship, I. I., Ashe, W. K., and Scherp, H. W.: Recurrent "fever blister" and "canker sore" tests for herpes simplex and other viruses with mammalian cell cultures. *Arch. Oral Biol.* **3**: 117, 1961.

44. Ship, I. I., Merritt, A. D., and Stanley, H. R.: Recurrent aphthous ulcers. *Amer. J. Med.* **32**: 32, 1962.

45. Sircus, W., Church, R., and Kelleher, J.: Recurrent apthous ulceration of the mouth; a study of the natural history, aetiology and treatment. *Quart. J. Med.* **26**: 235, 1957.

46. Stanley, H. R., Graykowski, E. A., and Barile, M. F.: The occurrence of microorganisms in microscopic sections of aphthous and non-aphthous lesions and other oral tissues. *Oral Surg.* **18**: 335, 1964.

47. Stark, M. M., Kibrick, S., and Weisberger, D.: Studies on recurrent aphthae: evidence that herpes simplex is not the etiologic agent, with further observations in the immune response in herpetic infections. *J. Lab. Clin. Med.* **44**: 261, 1954.

48. Sutton, R. L.: Periadenitis mucosa necrotica recurrens. *J. Cutan. Dis.* **29**: 65, 1911.

49. Taylor, K. B., Truelove, S. C., and Wright, R.: Serologic reactions to gluten and cow's milk proteins in gastrointestinal disease. *Gastroenterology* **46**: 99, 1964.

50. Tuft, L., and Ettleson, L. N.: Canker sores from allergy to weak organic acids (citric and acetic); case report and clinical study. *J. Allergy* **27**: 536, 1956.

51. Vigoroux, J., and Hannoun, C.: Étude des formes L des bactéries apparues spontanément *in vivo*. I. Propriétés biologiques et pouvoir pathogéne. *Ann. Inst. Pasteur* (Paris) **91**: 912, 1956.

52. ———: Étude des formes L des bactéries apparues spontanément *in vivo*. II. Caractéres particuliers des éléments granulaires. *Ann. Inst. Pasteur* (Paris) **92**: 112, 1957.

53. White, J. C., and Niven, C. F., Jr.: Streptococcus S.B.E.; a streptococcus associated with subacute bacterial endocarditis. *J. Bact.* **51**: 717, 1946.

54. Wittler, R. G., Malizia, W. F., Kramer, P. E., Tuckett, J. D., Pritchard, H. N., and Baker, H. J.: Isolation of a corynebacterium and its transitional forms from a case of subacute bacterial endocarditis treated with antibiotics. *J. Gen. Microbiol.* **23**: 315, 1960.

55. Woodburne, A. R.: Herpetic stomatitis (aphthous stomatitis). *Arch. Derm.* **43**: 543, 1941.

56. Zondek, B., and Bromberg, Y. M.: Endocrine allergy; clinical recations of allergy to endogenous hormones and their treatment. *J. Obst. Gynaec. Brit. Emp.* **54**: 1, 1947.

46

Possible Role of *Brucella* L-Forms in the Pathogenesis of Brucellosis*

Betty A. Hatten and S. Edward Sulkin

THE UNIVERSITY OF TEXAS SOUTHWESTERN MEDICAL SCHOOL
DALLAS, TEXAS

McDermott,[37] and later Smadel,[46] suggested that persistent infections could be the result of *in vivo* production of altered bacterial forms which were more resistant to humoral factors and therapeutic agents than conventional microorganisms. Evidence has been provided to substantiate this theory in some reports on chronic pyelonephritis,[5, 8, 15, 28, 39] bacterial endocarditis,[17, 34, 56] tubercular meningitis[35] and in certain types of aseptic meningitis.[33] While the chronicity of many *Brucella* infections, their resistance to treatment, and the difficulties experienced in isolating the causative agents are well known,[10, 47] only two accounts on the occurrence of *Brucella* L-forms in recent isolates have come to our attention.[9, 40]

The purpose of the present study was to determine whether a virulent strain of *Brucella abortus* could convert into an altered form under simulated *in vivo* conditions, such as those provided by a tissue culture system. In the discussion of this work all organisms which did not morphologically resemble the parent bacteria and did not produce a bacterial-type colony, are designated as *L-forms*. Organisms

designated as typical L-forms were capable of producing minute colonies similar to those described for other bacterial L-forms and *Mycoplasma* strains. A second type, referred to as *large or small round bodies* was larger and less dense than the parent bacteria. Some of these bodies appeared to be capable of reproduction and reversion to the bacterial form. The term *granular bodies* was used to describe the very dense forms seen both intracellularly and on artificial media which apparently did not revert to the typical L-type or bacterial form. The granular bodies are also referred to as *T-types* since they resemble the T-forms first described by Shepard.[45] The terms "protoplast" and "spheroplast" are avoided in this presentation since they imply that the presence or absence of certain cell wall constituents, osmotic fragility and viability of the forms have been specifically defined.

MATERIALS AND METHODS

A virulent strain of *B. abortus*, 3183, originally obtained from the laboratory of Dr. Wesley Spink, was used throughout this study. Table 46.1 summarizes the procedures used for infection of tissue cultures with this strain, and subsequent reisolation and identification of *Brucella* L-forms from infected tissue culture cells after varying periods of time. More de-

* This investigation was supported by Public Health Service Training Grant 5 T1 A1 142 from the National Institute of Allergy and Infectious Diseases, and a General Research Support Grant (FR-5426) from the National Institutes of Health.

TABLE 46.1

Technique for Tissue Culture Growth and Reisolation of Brucella abortus *L-Forms*

Several drops of heavily suspended stock *B. abortus* cultures inoculated into TSB* tubes
↓
Incubated 7 days at 37°C in 5 to 10% CO_2 tension
↓
Broth centrifuged, organisms resuspended in Hank's BSS, pH 7.8
(3.2 × 10⁹ organisms/ml)
↓
Suspended organisms absorbed for 5 hrs to HKC, cells rinsed once with Hank's BSS
(0.5 ml organism/Leighton tube or 2.5 ml/4 oz. prescription bottle)
↓
Cultures maintained in Hank's LAH medium with 5% calf serum, pH 7.4 and
varying concentrations of antibiotics
↓
Antibiotics removed from medium at intervals and pH adjusted to 7.8
↓
Primary sedimented tissue culture material subcultured to artificial medium after 10 days
(0.1 ml/tube)
↓

L-Form Cultures	*Bacterial Cultures*
Thioglycollate medium cultures examined after 7 days by MGG and FA stains	Number of positive TSB cultures recorded at 7 days
↓	↓
Doubtful positive cultures subcultured to BYE agar	Subcultured to blood agar plates
↓	↓
Agar block preparations examined for organisms	Origin of organisms confirmed by agglutination tests with *B. abortus* antiserum

* TSB, trypticase soy broth; BSS, balanced salt solution; HKC, hamster kidney cells; LAH, lactalbumin hydrolysate; MGG, May-Grunwald-Giemsa; FA, fluorescent antibody; and BYE, Barile, Yaguchi and Evelyn.

tailed information regarding these techniques is given in previous publications.[18, 19]

Hamster kidney cells (HKC) were prepared for electron microscopy by the glutaraldehyde-osmic acid fixation technique described by Anderson and associates,[2] and were embedded in maraglas. *B. abortus* 3183, grown for 96 hours in trypticase phosphate broth containing 0.3 M sucrose in the presence or absence of antibiotics, was centrifuged and then treated in a similar manner. Ultrathin sections were also made of L-form microcolonies cut in small wedges of agar from inoculated plates and fixed by the same technique. Sections were examined in an RCA EMU-3G electron microscope.

RESULTS

CHARACTERISTICS OF L-FORMS RECOVERED FROM HAMSTER KIDNEY CELLS

It soon became apparent after initiation of these studies that the characteristics of recovered L-forms varied with the length of their intracellular survival. Table 46.2 shows the type of L-forms recovered from HKC after varying periods of time when 2.5 mcg/ml each of penicillin and streptomycin were added to the tissue culture medium, and indicates the frequency of reversions to the bacterial form from each type. It can be seen that typical L-forms were recovered with decreasing frequency during the first few days and were not recovered after this time. After the first 24

TABLE 46.2

Variation of L-Form Characteristics with Duration of Intracellular Growth

Period of Intracellular Growth*	Type of L-Forms Recovered	Bacterial Reversions†
24 hrs	Predominance of typical L-forms—white, flocculent or granular growth in thioglycollate medium and microcolonies on agar medium within 24 to 72 hrs	Numerous—smooth colonial types resembling parent strain
24 to 72 hrs	Some typical L-forms mixed with small round bodies —growth in thioglycollate medium varying from granular to opaque. Microcolonies less numerous on agar plates	Frequent—small, flat and slightly spreading colonies
5 to 7 days	Round bodies and granular forms—growth in thioglycollate opaque. Usually no microcolonies seen on agar plates	Occasional—moist, coalescent colonies with foul odor
Over 7 days	Granular forms and few large round bodies—opaque growth in thioglycollate medium. No microcolonies on agar plates. Prolonged incubation sometimes necessary to detect growth	Usually none

* Hamster kidney cells infected with *Brucella abortus* strain ⚥3183 and maintained in medium with 2.5 mcg/ml penicillin and streptomycin added.

† All colony types agglutinated with *Brucella* (AMS) antiserum.

hours, round bodies were seen which usually began as smaller bodies at less than $2-3\mu$ in diameter and increased in size until at five to seven days some were approximately $5-6\mu$. The round bodies tended to decrease in number with time and were replaced by granular or "T-type" forms. The ability of the recovered L-forms to revert to bacteria declined during the same time, and after the first 24 hours most of the bacterial colonies were not characteristic of the stock *B. abortus* strain. Although later experiments using single antibiotics or other combinations of antibiotics showed considerable variations in the time intervals at which each type was recovered, the sequence of events appeared to be the same provided adequate inhibition of bacterial organisms was attained.

The morphology of various L-types observed in tissue cultures and upon recovery in artificial media by conventional microscopic methods is illustrated in Figure 46.1. Small bacterial colonies appeared as dark blue homogeneous masses in May-Grunwald-Giemsa (MGG) stains of agar block preparations (*a* in Figure 46.1), and with higher magnification typical coccobacillary organisms were visible about the periphery of the colony (*b* in the figure). Typical L-form microcolonies prepared in the same manner appeared as flattened, vacuolated masses with density and staining characteristics which varied within a single colony (*d*). Upon higher magnification the latter colonies were found to consist of a vacuolated, blue matrix with an amorphous appearance and round bodies with staining reactions which varied from pink to dark blue (*c*). Round bodies from broth cultures and from the supernatant tissue culture medium of infected hamster kidney cells resembled those from agar plates (*e, f, g*). The staining properties of these bodies also ranged from pale blue to light pink with MGG stain. It can be seen that some contained dark granular material.

Increased granulation of equivalent forms observed in tissue culture after removal of antibiotics from the medium suggested that they were capable of reverting to the bacterial form or other L-types. This process was also noted on agar plates, where it appeared that granulation spread from the periphery of the round body outward and became increasingly greater until the central body could no longer be seen (Figure 46.1, *g, h, i, j*). The central

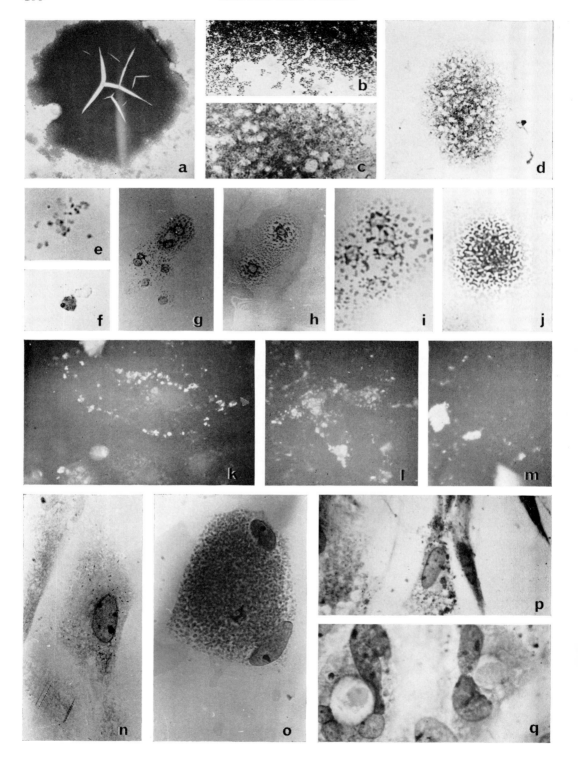

portion contained dark granular forms resembling those seen within infected tissue culture cells after prolonged incubation. The outer areas were stained light pink and the individual forms resembled the round bodies already described. The presence of microcolonies and bacterial colonies similar to those shown in Figure 46.1, a, b, c, d shortly after this process was observed suggested that the round bodies had developed into typical L-forms or had reverted to the bacterial form.

Shortly after infection with B. abortus 3183, hamster kidney cells had about the periphery of the cytoplasm a predominance of typical microorganisms which stained with specific fluorescein-conjugated antiserum (k in Figure 46.1). Following exposure of the infected cells to antibiotics, typical intracellular bacteria were less frequently observed as the duration of treatment increased, and by the fifth to seventh days they had been replaced with fluorescent areas of varying sizes and shapes (l in the figure). The intracellular fluorescent masses resembled those obtained when L-forms from thioglycollate medium were stained by the fluorescent antibody technique (m). When hamster kidney cells were stained by the MGG technique immediately after infection, typical bacterial organisms could be seen within the cytoplasm (n). Infected cells which contained predominantly normal bacteria throughout the observation period did not show signs of abnormality even when heavily infected. Round bodies seen in tissue culture cells within 24 hours after infection and exposure to antibiotics were similar in size and staining characteristics to the ones obtained in artificial media. Occasionally the cytoplasm of infected cells which had been exposed for several days to antibiotics was filled with these forms (o). After prolonged periods of exposure to antibiotics, granular forms (p) or a mixture of granular forms and larger round bodies (q) were the predominant intracellular forms observed.

RECOVERY OF L-FORMS AFTER INTRACELLULAR EXPOSURE TO SEVERAL ANTIBIOTICS

Results of experiments to determine whether L-forms could survive following intracellular exposure to penicillin, streptomycin, combined penicillin and streptomycin, tetracycline, and combined tetracycline and penicillin or streptomycin are given in Figures 46.2 and 46.3. Neither penicillin nor streptomycin alone completely eradicated B. abortus from the infected hamster kidney cells, but a significantly greater percentage of positive L-form cultures over bacterial cultures were obtained when 20 or 40 mcg/ml penicillin

Figure 46.1. a: Small bacterial colony from an agar plate, fixed agar block preparation, MGG stain; × 60. b: Periphery of colony in a showing cocco-bacillary forms; MGG stain; × 400. c: Periphery of L-form microcolony in d showing amorphous, vacuolated matrix and round bodies with variable staining characteristics; fixed agar block preparation, MGG stain; × 400. d: L-form microcolony from an agar plate; MGG stain; × 60. e: Round bodies from thioglycollate medium, some of which have areas of dark chromatin-like material; MGG stain; × 400. f: Round bodies similar to those in thioglycollate medium, seen in supernatant tissue culture medium of infected HKC; MGG stain; × 950. g: Round bodies from an agar plate, showing small amount of granulation about the periphery of the central body; MGG stain, fixed agar block preparation; × 400. h: Round bodies from an agar plate with increased amount of granulation; MGG stain; × 400. i: Higher magnification of round bodies in about the same stage of development as those in h; MGG stain; × 800. j: Final stage of granulation process in which central round body is obscured by a mass of dark-stained granules and surrounded by small, light pink, round bodies; MGG stain; × 800. k: Intracellular microorganisms in the peripheral cytoplasm of HKC shortly after infection; FA stain; × 270. l: Large masses of microorganisms in the cytoplasm several days after HKC infection; FA stain; × 270. m: Similar masses of specifically stained microorganisms from thioglycollate medium; FA stain; ×270. n: Bacterial organisms in cytoplasm of normal-appearing HKC; MGG stain; × 400. o: Small, round bodies in cytoplasm several days after infection; MGG stain; × 400. p: Granular bodies seen in increasing numbers after the first few days of infection; MGG stain; × 400. q: Large, round inclusion seen in cytoplasm of cells 5 to 7 days after infection; MGG stain; × 400.

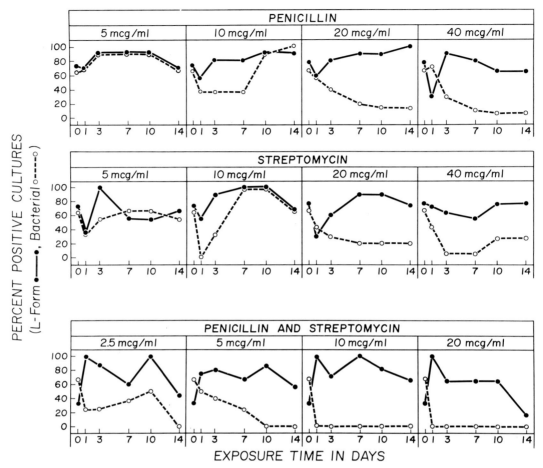

Figure 46.2. Percentage of positive L-form and bacterial cultures obtained from infected hamster kidney cells which had been exposed to from 5 to 40 mcg/ml penicillin or
streptomycin, and 2.5 to 20 mcg/ml each penicillin and streptomycin for various periods of
time.

or streptomycin were incorporated into the
tissue culture medium for 7 to 14 days.
Combination of 10 and 20 mcg/ml each
penicillin and streptomycin reduced the
survival time of the bacteria to less than
one day, but 67 and 17 per cent, respectively, of the L-form cultures were still
positive at the end of 14 days exposure of
infected cells to these concentrations. Although 2.0 mcg/ml tetracycline eliminated
bacterial organisms from the cultures after
10 days, L- forms were still present in 10
per cent of the cultures after 14 days. When
combined with penicillin or streptomycin,
0.5 to 2.0 mcg/ml tetracycline inhibited bac-

terial growth after the first day. Survival of
L-forms was greatly reduced by the tenth
day by a combination of penicillin and
tetracycline and by the seventh to tenth
day by streptomycin and tetracycline. The
percentage of positive L-form cultures
varied and was not dependent upon the
concentration of tetracycline. Approximately 86 per cent of the cultures contained both bacteria and L-forms throughout a 10-day period of intracellular growth
when no antibiotics were added to the culture medium. None of the cultures had
bacterial growth when thallium acetate
was added in a concentration of 1:5000 to

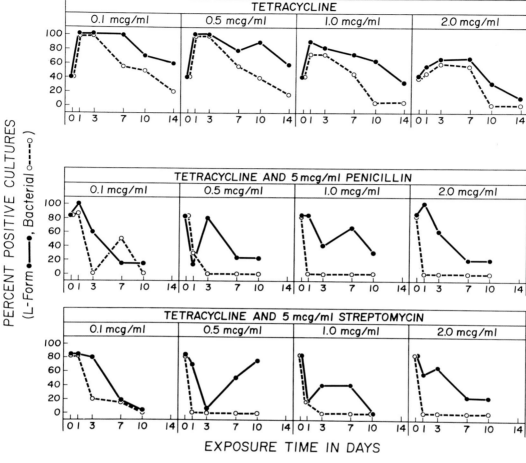

Figure 46.3. Percentage of positive L-form and bacterial cultures obtained from infected hamster kidney cells which had been exposed to from 0.1 to 2.0 mcg/ml tetracycline, and tetracycline with 5 mcg/ml penicillin or streptomycin for various periods of time.

the tissue culture medium at various periods of time after infection, but about 43 per cent still contained a few L-forms.

ANTIBIOTIC SENSITIVITY OF *B. ABORTUS* RECOVERED FROM HAMSTER KIDNEY CELLS

The antibiotic sensitivity of bacterial organisms recovered from HKC after intracellular treatment with antibiotics was compared with that of the stock *B. abortus* 3183. The results are summarized in Table 46.3. Several organisms recovered after intracellular exposure for different periods of time to each antibiotic were tested. The antibiotic sensitivity was not related to the concentration of antibiotic in the culture medium or the duration of exposure. Sensitivity to penicillin decreased from 5 to 10 mcg/ml when the bacteria had been exposed to penicillin, streptomycin, or tetracycline intracellularly. Tetracycline sensitivity decreased from 0.1 to 0.5 mcg/ml when the bacteria had been previously treated with penicillin or tetracycline. Streptomycin sensitivity was altered only in those organisms which had been exposed to streptomycin intracellularly, where a significant increase in resistance from 5 to 40 mcg/ml occurred. An increase in resistance to combined penicillin and strepto-

TABLE 46.3

Antibiotic Sensitivity of Brucella abortus *Before and After Intracellular Exposure to Antibiotics‡*

	Level of Antibiotic Resistance*					
	P	S	PS	T	TP	TS
Tetracycline						
0.1 mcg/ml						
24 hrs	10	<5	<2.5	0.5	<0.1	0.1
72 hrs	10	<5	<2.5	0.5	<0.1	0.1
10 days	10	<5	<2.5	0.5	<0.1	0.1
14 days	10	<5	<2.5	0.5	<0.1	0.1
1.0 mcg/ml						
72 hrs	10	<5	<2.5	0.5	<0.1	0.1
5 days	10	<5	<2.5	0.5	<0.1	0.1
10 days	10	<5	<2.5	0.5	0.1	0.1
Penicillin						
40 mcg/ml						
14 days	10	<5	<2.5	0.5	0.1	0.1
Streptomycin						
10 mcg/ml						
10 days	10	>40	5.0	<0.1	0.1	0.1
40 mcg/ml						
10 days	10	>40	5.0	<0.1	0.1	0.1
14 days	10	>40	5.0	<0.1	0.1	0.1
Original Culture†	5	<5	<2.5	<0.1	<0.1	0.1
Subculture	5	<5	<2.5	<0.1	<0.1	0.1

* The amounts given are maximum concentrations of antibiotic or combinations of antibiotics allowing bacterial growth. The range of concentrations used were: 5.0 to 40 mcg/ml penicillin (P) or streptomycin (S); 2.5 to 20 mcg/ml each penicillin and streptomycin (PS); 0.1 to 2.0 mcg/ml tetracycline (T) or tetracycline with 5 mcg/ml penicillin (TP); or tetracycline with 5 mcg/ml streptomycin (TS).

† B. abortus strain 3183.

‡ Data from Hatten & Sulkin.[19]

mycin from 2.5 to 5.0 mcg/ml was also observed in the latter bacteria. No changes in sensitivity to combined antibiotics was noted following intracellular exposure to penicillin or tetracycline.

EXAMINATION OF L-FORMS AND INFECTED HAMSTER KIDNEY CELLS BY ELECTRON MICROSCOPY

L-forms from broth cultures and agar plates which resembled intracellular forms observed in MGG stains of infected HKC were used in electron microscopy studies for comparison with intracellular organisms. In preliminary experiments, *B. abortus* L-forms were induced in broth containing 0.3 M sucrose by addition of 10 or 20 mcg/ml penicillin and on agar plates by 20 or 40 mcg/ml penicillin. After 96 hours exposure to penicillin, the broth cultures contained viable organisms similar to round bodies seen intracellularly and recovered from infected tissue culture cells, and the agar plates had typical microcolonies. Both types grew when transferred to fresh penicillin-containing media or reverted to bacteria upon removal of the antibiotic. Electron micrographs of these forms are shown in Figure 46.4. While a few organisms had retained a typical bacterial structure in broth cultures with penicillin added, the majority were enlarged and irregularly shaped (Figure 46.4 *a–d*). It can be seen that the amount of cell wall and internal material in the latter forms varied considerably. Occasionally, dense forms were also seen which had some differentiation of their internal structures. Small dense bodies resembling aggregates of chromatin material were seen internally or about the periphery of some forms.

B. abortus cultured in artificial media or tissue culture in the absence of antibiotics were generally uniform in size and appearance. Several normal bacteria and a dying organism are shown in Figure 46.4*e* for comparison with the L-forms. Electron micrographs of sections of the microcolonies also revealed structures which varied markedly in appearance and size. Some difficulty was encountered in sectioning the L-form colonies, but the structures shown in Figure 46.4, *f–j* came from the outer edge of a microcolony. While some forms such as those seen in *f* had a moderately dense homogeneous internal structure and were surrounded by a definite membrane, others were minute dense forms occurring in several sizes and shapes (*g, h*). A third structure observed had no detectable membrane and was present in a wide range of sizes. The smallest structures of this type were round dense bodies similar to some of the ones shown in *g* and *h* in Figure 46.4. As

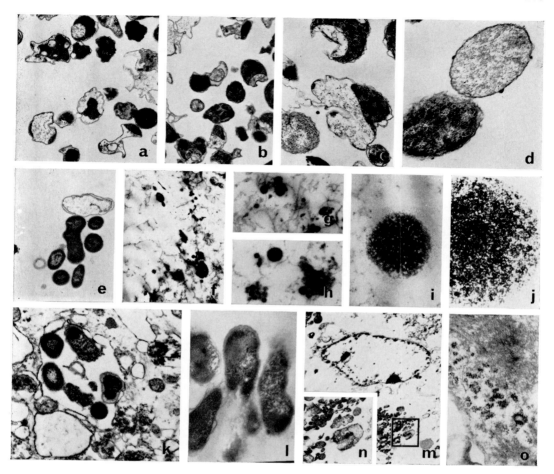

Figure 46.4. *a:* Ultrastructure of L-forms induced by penicillin in broth medium with 0.3 M sucrose; 96 hours culture, glutaraldehyde-osmic acid fixed section; × 5000. *b:* L-forms induced and fixed in the same manner as those in *a,* showing further variations in size and shape; × 5000. *c:* Higher magnification of L-forms induced in broth medium, showing dense material contained in one area of the organism; × 11,000. *d:* Two L-forms from broth medium showing variation in density of organisms of the same size and shape, and the concentration of chromatin-like material often seen about the periphery or within these forms; × 11,000. *e:* Several normal bacteria typical of those seen in untreated HKC or in artificial media without penicillin; × 11,000. *f:* Larger forms with membranes from section through the edge of an L-form microcolony; gluteraldehyde-osmic acid fixed; × 4000. *g:* Smaller forms from section through the edge of an L-form microcolony; × 17,000. *h:* Forms similar to those in *g,* showing variations in configuration of the small round structures; × 17,000: *i:* Finely granulated round body typical of those seen in sections from an L-form microcolony; × 11,000. *j:* Coarsely granulated round body also from an L-form microcolony; × 17,000. *k:* Normal appearing bacteria within a membrane-enclosed cytoplasmic vacuole; 24 hours after infection and treatment with 10 mcg/ml penicillin; × 11,000. *l:* Bacteria in process of disintegration seen in HKC infected and treated with 10 mcg/ml penicillin for 96 hours; × 20,000. *m:* Cluster of intracellular forms resembling those shown in *f;* × 3000. *n:* Slightly higher magnification of structures shown in *m* insert; × 5000. *o:* Formations of small bodies which are similar in configuration to those shown in *g* and *h;* × 4000.

they increased in size they began to show fine granulation and small vacuoles (*i*), and the largest round forms had definite aggregation of dense chromatin-like material (*j*).

Initial attempts to study the relationship of *B. abortus* L-forms to the infected host cell have been limited so far by obvious difficulties in differentiating possible L-forms from altered cellular components or even from normal cellular structures. Within the first 24 hours after infection and treatment of HKC with 10 mcg/ml penicillin, numerous bacteria with little signs of morphological alteration could be found just outside of the kidney cells or within cytoplasmic vacuoles which were enclosed by a limiting cellular membrane (*k*). Although some apparently normal bacteria were still present at 96 hours, many had begun to show signs of disintegration (*l*). Recognizable bacteria were rarely seen by the seventh day after infection and treatment with 10 mcg/ml penicillin, even though bacteria and L-forms could generally be recovered from similar cultures at this time. Many cells contained dense cytoplasmic inclusions throughout the experimental period, but their direct relationship to the infection, if any, cannot be ascertained at this time. Occasional cells from seven-day cultures did contain clusters of forms, each of which had a limiting membrane and size and density similar to those shown in *h* from an L-form microcolony. Figure 46.4*m* shows a cluster of these forms lying in a vacuolated area of the cytoplasm adjacent to the nucleus of the cell; no cellular membrane is detectable about the vacuole in this electron micrograph. A higher magnification of some of the forms seen in *m* is shown in *n*. In addition to the larger inclusions, formations of very small particles were seen in a number of cells which also resembled the small structures observed in sections from an L-form colony (*o*).

Discussion

Nelson & Pickett[40] recovered *Brucella* L-forms from recent human blood culture isolates and suggested that frequent difficulties in recovering the causative agent from patients suffering from brucellosis might be due to their presence. Later Spink[48] stated that he found no evidence to substantiate their proposal during his studies of numerous cases of brucellosis, but did describe the presence of minute colonies, referred to as "G colonies," in one case of human brucellosis.[16] The G colonies grew after incubation for four to five days, were approximately 0.1 mm in diameter, and died quickly unless subcultured frequently in large numbers; they resisted the bactericidal action of human serum and of streptomycin in concentrations up to 7500 mcg/ml. Growth was poor in tryptose phosphate broth and agar, and was not visible in agar pour plates before 8 to 11 days incubation. Microscopic examination of Gram-stained preparations revealed faint tiny coccoid or bizarre amorphous organisms as well as large red-staining coccoid forms. In other respects the microorganisms were characteristic of *B. abortus*, requiring CO_2 for growth, and were serologically and biochemically identical to the brucellae originally isolated from the patient. Other accounts of recovery of G colonies from human and bovine sources have been given,[20, 22] and at least two reports of their recovery from infected tissue cultures are known.[7, 42] In all instances the microcolonies were less virulent and grew more slowly on artificial media than smooth, virulent strains.

Chronicity of *Brucella* infections in man and experimental animals indirectly suggests that L-forms may be produced *in vivo*. Dalrymple-Champneys[10] reported that the duration of infection was over six months in 127 (10.4 per cent) of 1215 cases studied, and that in 18 of these the duration of symptoms was over three years. Spink[47] estimated that three-fourths of the human cases in the United States are caused by *B. abortus*, and later reported that 19 per cent of all treated cases and 46 per cent of the untreated ones had symptoms of illness one year after onset of infection. Difficulty in freeing the host of the infecting brucellae by antibiotic therapy has been encountered not only in clinical brucellosis but also in experimental animal and tissue culture infections.[42, 49] While mice are less susceptible to initial infection than man or other laboratory animals, the pathology of the disease is quite similar in all species studied.[4] It has been observed that the brucellae are present in the sinusoids of the spleen and liver within a few hours after infection and that the microorganisms begin to proliferate in the macrophages and Kuppfer cells shortly thereafter.[4, 49] Formation of granulomata, the typical lesions produced in *B. abortus* infections, was noted about one week after infection and coincided with the rapid disappearance of macrophages and microorganisms from the lesion. Since in experimental studies treatment was instigated immediately after infection without apparent decrease in the number of relapses,[6, 27] protection of organisms within the granulomatous lesions does not seem likely. No antibiotic-resistant brucellae have been recovered from experimentally infected animals, but one human case has been described in which streptomycin resistance developed.[16] Development of resistance in this case was not considered to be a valid explanation for therapeutic failures after short periods of therapy, since resistance developed only after a long course of treatment with streptomycin.

The results of the present study lend support to the theory that *in vivo* L-form production may be an important factor in persistent *Brucella* infection. While we did not attempt initially to characterize the altered forms recovered from infected hamster kidney cells, their morphology and growth characteristics were typical of those generally associated with other L-forms[11, 30, 53] and were similar to *Brucella* L-forms described by Nelson & Pickett[40] and Carrère & Roux.[9] Changes in morphology of intracellular brucellae were similar to and coincided with morphological changes in the recovered L-forms. Increased difficulty in obtaining bacterial reversions after prolonged intracellular survival suggests stabilization of the L-forms. Atypical bacterial colonies obtained from L-forms recovered after several days of intracellular survival resembled the "porteuse" or coalescent, lysogenic brucellae isolated by Nelson & Pickett[40] and Renoux & Suire.[41] Large round bodies seen in infected hamster kidney cells had a striking resemblance to intracellular inclusions of *Mycoplasma pneumoniae* demonstrated by Eaton and associates,[12] not only in morphology but in their frequent location adjacent to the cell nucleus. Photographs of the round bodies on agar plates indicate that they multiplied through the formation of granules which began about the periphery of the original body. Spread of the granulation outward suggests that the granules fragmented and gave rise to smaller round bodies, which presumably were capable of continuing the cycle until a large dense granular mass was formed. Microcolonies and bacterial colonies seen later in the same cultures imply that further development of these forms gave rise to typical L-form growth or to bacterial growth. The dark granules seen in the central portion of these formations resembled granular forms seen intracellularly. Although granular forms were found in cultures from hamster kidney cells at times when they were the predominant intracellular form, they were never directly observed to give rise to any other type of growth and did not reproduce themselves to any great extent in artificial media.

Results of experiments with *B. abortus* 3183 are in agreement with reports of several workers who have shown that virulent brucellae are capable of prolonged intracellular growth without apparent damage to the host cell,[7, 13, 21] and confirm Richardson & Holt's[42] findings concerning the ineffectiveness of penicillin and streptomycin in eliminating brucellae from infected tissue culture cells. Differences in the percentage of positive bacterial and L-form cultures after 7 to 10 days intracellular exposure to the highest concentrations of penicillin or streptomycin indicated that the L-forms were not inhibited by these antibiotics. Increased resistance of recovered bacteria to penicillin demonstrated in agar plate sensitivity tests corresponds to the high percentage of bacterial cultures obtained after several days exposure of infected cells to 10 mcg/ml of this antibiotic, but does not explain continued recovery of bacteria when higher concentrations were employed. Recovery of streptomycin-resistant bacteria from streptomycin-treated cells probably accounts for continued presence of bacteria in these cultures. A continuous conversion and reversion process which favors conversion to L-forms when higher concentrations of antibiotics are present in the tissue culture medium is also feasible.

L-forms and bacterial organisms were recovered in approximately the same percentage of cultures when no antibiotics were added to the tissue culture medium. Combined streptomycin and penicillin effectively inhibited bacterial growth. A significant reduction in the percentage of positive L-form cultures was not seen, however, until 14 days of intracellular exposure of the organisms to 20 mcg/ml each of penicillin and streptomycin. These results suggest that L-forms were resistant to the combined antibiotics, and were able to survive for a significant time after bacterial forms were inhibited. The gradual decrease in the percentage of positive L-form cultures following inhibition of bacterial growth may indicate, however, that periodic reversions are necessary for long term infection to occur.

A similar trend was observed when combinations of tetracycline and penicillin or streptomycin were incorporated into the tissue culture medium. Recovery of L-forms was greatly reduced by the 10th to 14th day whenever tetracycline was present in the medium, whether in combination with another antibiotic or alone. Better inhibition of B. abortus L-forms by tetracycline was expected, since mycoplasmae and L-forms are usually inhibited by antibiotics which are known to be active against internal metabolic processes.[24, 38, 51] Tetracycline or a combination of tetracycline and streptomycin has been found to be the most effective therapy in clinical brucellosis, significantly decreasing the relapse rate when given over a period of two to three weeks.[49]

B. abortus 3183 L-forms were induced in broth cultures for electron microscopy by a method similar to that employed by Freeman & Rumack[14] to induce spheroplast formation by a Brucella suis strain. Electron micrographs of the B. suis spheroplasts resembled those of the B. abortus L-form but were less dense, having little internal structure. In addition, the B. suis spheroplasts were for the most part nonviable structures which had no endotoxic activity when inoculated into rabbits, but which caused lysis of tissue culture monolayers within a few hours. Although we have occasionally observed spontaneous lysis of infected hamster kidney cells, particularly following five to seven days of treatment with penicillin or streptomycin, the relationship of intracellular L-form production to this phenomenon has not been established. The B. abortus L-forms were viable, giving rise within 24 to 48 hours to more L-forms in antibiotic-containing media, or to bacteria upon removal of the penicillin. The B. abortus L-forms more closely resembled those reported by Weibull,[52] who showed identical characteristics in several L-forms from morphologically distinct parental species. The wide variations in the appearance of B. abortus L-forms from broth cultures made it difficult to identify comparable structures in infected tissue cultures. The electron micrographs of possible L-forms within an infected cell not only resemble some of the structures seen in a B. abortus L-form microcolony, but are also similar in appearance to mycoplasmae shortly after infection of several cell types.[57] The intracellular mycoplasmae were always seen in a membrane-enclosed capsule, while the suspected Brucella L-forms varied in this respect. Brucellae present in early infections of treated cells or organisms observed throughout the observation period, when no antibiotics were added to the culture medium, were generally seen in vacuoles surrounded by a cellular membrane and resembled electron micrographs of intracellular brucellae.[26]

A number of L-forms are now known to produce toxins or antigenic substances associated with virulence of the parent bacteria. Group A streptococcal L-forms are capable of producing both streptolysin and M proteins,[32, 43] L-forms of *Clostridium tetani* generally elaborate tetanus toxin, and *Vibrio* L-forms have been found to retain the ability to produce neuraminadase.[31, 44] Catalase activity, which is associated with virulence of strains of *Brucella* and *Mycobacteria*,[3, 23] has been detected in some staphylococcal and *Proteus* L-forms.[36, 54] *Vibrio, Salmonella* and *Proteus* L-forms were observed some time ago to have a rapid destructive effect upon tissue culture cells,[29, 50] and similar results were recently obtained with *B. suis* spheroplasts.[14] *Escherichia coli* protoplasts have been induced by normal serum factors *in vitro* and protoplast formation was observed within a short time after injection of the bacteria intraperitoneally into laboratory animals.[8, 39] *E. coli* protoplasts were later shown to survive for a considerable period of time in the medulla of rabbit kidneys.[1] This confirmed a report by Braude and associates,[5] who suggested that protoplasts of Gram-negative organisms were being formed in human urine. Similar reports have been made regarding the presence of streptococcal protoplasts in kidneys of rats with chronic pyelonephritis due to *Enterococcus* infection.[15, 25] *Corynebacterium* and *Streptococcus sanguis* L-forms have been implicated in bacterial endocarditis, and Group A streptococcal and staphylococcal L-forms in Reiter's disease, rheumatic fever, rheumatoid arthritis, and osteomyelitis.[17, 28, 34, 55, 56]

From the references just cited it becomes apparent that increasing evidence has accumulated to indicate that L-forms from a wide variety of bacteria are potentially involved in several types of chronic diseases. Results of the present studies with *B. abortus* L-forms suggest that such forms may also play a role in the persistence of *Brucella* infections. The destructive effect of *B. suis* spheroplasts upon tissue culture cells[14] may also indicate that L-form production *in vivo* is related to production of the lesions seen in brucellosis, since virulent brucellae have not been found to have a destructive effect upon infected cells.[7, 13, 21] We believe, however, that unequivocal evidence of a direct relationship of *Brucella* L-forms to the infection must come from *in vivo* studies.

SUMMARY

Microorganisms resembling L-forms were isolated from tissue cultures infected with *Brucella abortus* upon disintegration of the cells. Morphology of recovered L-forms changed with the duration of intracellular survival from typical L-form microcolonies to round bodies and eventually to granular bodies. Corresponding change in the morphology of intracellular organisms was noted. Ability of recovered L-forms to revert to bacteria decreased as the duration of intracellular existence increased, and after several days reversion to the parental colony type was rare.

Penicillin or streptomycin alone did not eliminate bacteria or L-forms from infected tissue culture cells during a 14-day period of treatment, but a significantly greater percentage of L-form cultures were positive after 7 to 14 days intracellular exposure to these antibiotics. A combination of penicillin and streptomycin effectively controlled bacterial growth. A small percentage of L-form cultures were still positive after 14 days of treatment with 20 mcg/ml of each of these antibiotics.

Tetracycline alone or in combination with streptomycin or penicillin inhibited both bacterial and L-form growth, although L-forms usually survived for several days longer than bacteria. Concentrations of tetracycline required to inhibit the L-forms were not critical, particularly when combined with penicillin or streptomycin.

Bacteria recovered from hamster kidney cells after intracellular exposure to streptomycin had developed a marked resistance to this antibiotic and slight resistance to combined penicillin and streptomycin. Only slight increases in resistance to penicillin and tetracycline were detected in recovered bacteria, and generally no increased resistance to combined antibiotics was noted following intracellular exposure to either of these two antibiotics.

Preliminary results of electron microscopy studies were presented which reveal similarities between some intracellular forms and *B. abortus* L-forms induced in artificial media by penicillin.

REFERENCES

1. Alderman, M. H., and Freedman, L.: Experimental pyelonephritis. X. The direct injection of *E. coli* protoplasts into the medulla of the rabbit kidney. *Yale J. Biol. Med.* **36:** 157, 1963.

2. Anderson, D. R., Hopps, H. E., Barile, M. F., and Bernheim, B. C.: Comparison of the ultrastructure of several rickettsiae, ornithosis virus, and *Mycoplasma* in tissue culture. *J. Bact.* **90:** 1387, 1965.

3. Bloch, H.: Biochemical properties of virulent and avirulent strains of *Mycobacterium tuberculosis*. *Ann. N. Y. Acad. Sci.* **88:** 1075, 1960.

4. Braude, A. I.: Studies in the pathology and pathogenesis of experimental brucellosis. I. A comparison of the pathogenicity of *Brucella abortus*, *Brucella melitensis*, and *Brucella suis* for guinea pigs. *J. Infect. Dis.* **89:** 76, 1951.

5. Braude, A. I., Siemienski, J., and Jacobs, I.: Protoplast formation in human urine. *Trans. Ass. Amer. Physicians* **74:** 234, 1961.

6. Braude, A. I., and Spink, W. W.: The action of aureomycin and other chemotherapeutic agents in experimental brucellosis. *J. Immun.* **65:** 185, 1950.

7. Braun, W., Pomales-Lebrón, A., and Stinebring, W. R.: Interactions between mononuclear phagocytes and *Brucella abortus* strains of different virulence. *Proc. Soc. Exp. Biol. Med.* **97:** 393, 1958.

8. Carey, W. F., Muschel, L. H., and Baron, L. S.: The formation of bacterial protoplasts *in vivo*. *J. Immun.* **84:** 183, 1960.

9. Carrère, L., Roux, J.: Obtention de formes L de *Brucella melitensis*. *Ann. Inst. Pasteur* (Paris) **84:** 796, 1953.

10. Dalrymple-Champneys, W.: *Brucella Infection and Undulant Fever in Man*. Oxford Univ. Press, London, 1960.

11. Dienes, L., and Weinberger, H. J.: The L forms of bacteria. *Bact. Rev.* **15:** 245, 1951.

12. Eaton, M. D., Farnham, A. E., Levinthal, J. D., and Scala, A. R.: Cytopathic effect of the atypical pneumonia organism in cultures of human tissue. *J. Bact.* **84:** 1330, 1962.

13. Freeman, B. A., Kross, D. J., and Circo, R.: Host-parasite relationships in brucellosis. II. Destruction of macrophage cultures by brucella of different virulence. *J. Infect. Dis.* **108:** 333, 1961.

14. Freeman, B. A., and Rumack, B. H.: Cytopathogenic effect of *Brucella* spheroplasts on monocytes in tissue culture. *J. Bact.* **88:** 1310, 1964.

15. Guze, L. B., and Kalmanson, G. M.: Persistence of bacteria in "protoplast" form after apparent cure of pyelonephritis in rats. *Science* **143:** 1340, 1964.

16. Hall, W. H., and Spink, W. W.: *In vitro* sensitivity of *Brucella* to streptomycin: development of resistance during streptomycin treatment. *Proc. Soc. Exp. Biol. Med.* **64:** 403, 1947.

17. Hannoun, C., Vigouroux, J., Levaditi, J., and Nazimoff, O.: Étude des formes L des bactéries apparues spontanément *in vivo*. III. Histopathologie comparée des lésions provoquées par la bactérie normale et par ses formes modifiées. *Ann. Inst. Pasteur* (Paris) **92:** 231, 1957.

18. Hatten, B. A., and Sulkin, S. E.: Intracellular production of *Brucella* L forms. I. Recovery of L forms from tissue culture cells infected with *Brucella abortus*. *J. Bact.* **91:** 285, 1966.

19. ———: Intracellular production of *Brucella* L forms. II. Induction and survival of *Brucella abortus* L forms in tissue culture. *J. Bact.* **91:** 14, 1966.

20. Henry, B. S.: Dissociation in the genus brucella. *J. Infect. Dis.* **52:** 374, 1933.

21. Holland, J. J., and Pickett, M. J.: Intracellular behavior of brucella variants in chick embryo cells in tissue culture. *Proc. Soc. Exp. Biol. Med.* **93:** 476, 1956.

22. Huddleson, I. F., and Baltzer, B.: The characteristics and dissociation pattern of type G (micro-colony type) of *Brucella abortus*. Studies in brucellosis III, part 2. *Mich. Agr. Exp. Sta. Mem.* **6:** 64, 1952.

23. Huddleson, I. F., and Stahl, W. H.: Catalase activity of the species of *Brucella* as a criterion for virulence. Studies in brucellosis II. *Mich. Agr. Exp. Sta. Tech. Bul.* **182:** 57, 1943.

24. Kagan, B., Zolla, S., Busser, R., and Liepnieks, S.: Sensitivity of coccal and L forms of *Staphylococcus aureus* to five antibiotics. *J. Bact.* **88:** 630, 1964.

25. Kalmanson, G. M., and Guze, L. B.: Role of protoplasts in pathogenesis of pyelonephritis. *JAMA* **190:** 1107, 1964.

26. Karlsbad, G., Kessel, R. W. I., de Petris, S., and Monaco, L.: Electron microscope observations of *Brucella abortus* grown within monocytes *in vitro*. *J. Gen. Microbiol.* **35:** 383, 1964.

27. Knight, V., Ruiz-Sanchez, F., Ruiz-Sanchez,

A., and McDermott, W.: Aureomycin in typhus and brucellosis. *Amer. J. Med.* **6:** 407, 1949.

28. Kuzell, W. C., and Mankle, E. A.: Cultivation of pleuropneumonialike organisms in Reiter's disease, including one instance of laboratory cross infection. *Ann. N.Y. Acad. Sci.* **79:** 650, 1960.

29. Lavillaureix, J.: Action de formes L pathogènes sur des cultures de cellules cancéreuses. *C.R. Acad. Sci.* (Paris) **244:** 1098, 1957.

30. Lederberg, J., and St. Clair, J.: Protoplasts and L-type growth of *Escherichia coli*. *J. Bact.* **75:** 143, 1958.

31. Madoff, M. A., Annenberg, S. M., and Weinstein, L.: Production of neuraminidase by L forms of *Vibrio cholerae*. *Proc. Soc. Exp. Biol. Med.* **107:** 776, 1961.

32. Maruyama, Y., Sugai, S., and Egami, F.: Formation of streptolysin *S* by streptococcal protoplasts. *Nature* **184,** suppl. 11: 832, 1959.

33. Mattman, L., and Karris, G.: L and transitional forms in meningitis. *Bact. Proc:* p. 49, 1966.

34. Mattman, L. H., and Mattman, P. E.: L forms of *Streptococcus fecalis* in septicemia. *Arch. Intern. Med.* (Chicago) **115:** 315, 1965.

35. Mattman, L. H., Tunstall, L. H., Mathews, W. W., and Gordon, D. L.: L variation in mycobacteria. *Ann. Rev. Resp. Dis.* **82:** 202, 1960.

36. Mattman, L. H., Tunstall, L. H., and Rossmoore, H. W.: Induction and characteristics of staphylococcal L forms. *Canad. J. Microbiol.* **7:** 705, 1961.

37. McDermott, W.: Microbial persistence. *Yale J. Biol. Med.* **30:** 257, 1958.

38. Montgomerie, J. Z., Kalmanson, G. M., and Guze, L. B.: The effects of antibiotics on the protoplast and bacterial forms of *Streptococcus faecalis*. *J. Lab. Clin. Med.* **68:** 543, 1966.

39. Muschel, L. H., Carey, W. F., and Baron, L. S.: Formation of bacterial protoplasts by serum components. *J. Immun.* **82:** 38, 1959.

40. Nelson, E. L., and Pickett, M. J.: The recovery of L forms of brucella and their relation to brucella phage. *J. Infect. Dis.* **89:** 226, 1951.

41. Renoux, G., and Suire, A.: Spontaneous lysis and phage-carrier state in *Brucella* cultures. *J. Bact.* **86:** 642, 1963.

42. Richardson, M., and Holt, J. N.: Synergistic action of streptomycin with other antibiotics on intracellular *Brucella abortus in vitro*. *J. Bact.* **84:** 638, 1962.

43. Rotta, J., Karakawa, W. W., and Krause, R. M.: Isolation of L forms from Group A streptococci exposed to bacitracin. *J. Bact.* **89:** 1581, 1965.

44. Rubio-Huertos, M., and Gonzalez-Vasquez, C.: Morphology and pathogenicity of L forms of *Clostridium tetani* induced by glycine. *Ann. N. Y. Acad. Sci.* **79:** 626, 1960.

45. Shepard, M. C.: T-form colonies of pleuropneumonialike organisms. *J. Bact.* **71:** 362, 1956.

46. Smadel, J. E.: Some aspects of intracellular infections. *J. Immun.* **84:** 1, 1960.

47. Spink, W. W.: What is chronic brucellosis? *Ann. Intern. Med.* **35:** 358, 1951

48. ———: *The Nature of Brucellosis.* Univ. of Minnesota Press, Minneapolis, 1956.

49. ———: Host-parasite relationships in brucellosis. *Lancet,* **2:** 161, 1964.

50. Tulasne, R., and Lavillaureix, J.: Pouvoir pathogène expérimental, pour la Souris, d'une souche de formes L des bactéries. *C.R. Soc. Biol.* (Paris) **148:** 2080, 1954.

51. Ward, J. R., Madoff, S., and Dienes, L.: *In vitro* sensitivity of some bacteria, their L forms and pleuropneuomina-like organisms to antibiotics. *Proc. Soc. Exp. Biol. Med.* **97:** 132, 1958.

52. Weibull, C.: Structure of bacterial L forms and their parent bacteria. *J. Bact.* **90:** 1467, 1965.

53. Weibull, C., and Beckman, H.: Growth of bacterial L forms and bacterial protoplasts. *J. Bact.* **79:** 638, 1960.

54. Weibull, C., and Hammarberg, K.: Occurrence of catalase in pleuropneumonia-like organisms and bacterial L forms. *J. Bact.* **84:** 520, 1962.

55. Wittler, R. G.: Possible pathogenic implications for L forms and transitional forms. *Bact. Proc.:* p. 60, 1964.

56. Wittler, R., Malizia, W. F., Kramer, P. E., Tuckett, J. D., Pritchard, H. N., and Baker, H. J.: Isolation of a corynebacterium and its transitional forms from a case of subacute bacterial endocarditis treated with antibiotics. *J. Gen. Microbiol.* **23:** 315, 1960.

57. Zucker-Franklin, D., Davidson, M., and Thomas, L.: The interaction of mycoplasmas with mammalian cells. II. Monocytes and lymphocytes. *J. Exp. Med.* **124:** 533, 1966.

47

L-Forms Isolated From Infections*

Lida H. Mattman

WAYNE STATE UNIVERSITY

DETROIT, MICHIGAN

It is interesting that the phenomenon of L-forms in infectious disease has been discovered independently by many investigators, in most instances unaware of each other's work.[1, 13, 16, 21, 25, 29, 30, 31, 43, 46] In this paper I shall refer to many publications concerned with L-forms and pathogenesis, but undoubtedly additional "discoveries" remain in the literature, unknown to me because the foreign journal was unlisted in English-language abstracts.

The L-stages found occurring alone in infection have included the variant of *Candida albicans* in septicemia,[34] of *Escherichia coli*, *Proteus*, and a yeast-like fungus in gall bladder disease,[20] in addition to *E. coli* in pyelonephritis,[11, 19] the tubercle bacillus, and the pyogenic cocci which have been the most commonly encountered. The L-stage of *Clostridia* may be of importance, as toxin formation can be increased in some *Clostridium tetani* L-colonies,[35] or be undiminished in variants of *C. tetani*[38] and *Clostridium perfringens*.[3] Variants of the typhoid bacillus may be clinically significant, since they retain their pathogenicity in some instances.[22]

Using the terms *L-form, L-stage, L-variant* as synonyms, I shall further include under L-type any growth which might revert to the classical stage. While the term

fixed L-form is a useful one for strains that have been carried in culture for several years without reversion, there can be a question of whether the term "transitional" should be based upon reversibility of a strain. We have found that strains of staphylococcal L-forms which appear stable as they are successively transferred during six months can revert to cocci if they are cultured in the presence of N-acetyl glucosamine and yeast extract. Therefore, it might be wise to reserve the term "transitional" or a similar descriptive term for organisms which morphologically or biochemically are not as distinctive as the fixed L-growth. In the case of L-forms from infection, when the colonies assume areas with Gram-positive cocci, or have areas with acid-fast bacilli, this is truly an intermediate type of growth rather than the characteristic L-stage. L-forms from infections may initially show a minimal amount of intermediate type morphology, or give such clues to their identity only after months of serial passage.

And, again hoping for some changes in contrast to the present trend, one can wish that the term *spheroplast* would be returned to its original meaning of the spherical units of growth existing as part of the extremely divergent structures found in growth of any L-strain. Otherwise we shall have to employ such descriptions as L-bodies, large bodies, round forms, budding yeast-like forms, etc.

* The study of the leukemia patient was supported in part by a grant from the Michigan Cancer Foundation.

Materials and Methods

Serum Agar (Similar to Chanock's Medium[6])

PPLO broth, the weight for 100 ml, is placed in 70 ml of distilled water; if the pH is not 7.8 this adjustment is made with NaOH, and 1.4 g of agar is added. Each lot of agar, purified or otherwise, is tested for possible toxicity to L-growth. After autoclaving, 10 ml of Fleischmann's yeast extract and 20 ml of not inactivated fresh or frozen horse serum are added. To prepare yeast extract, 250 g of Fleishmann's 20–40 yeast are boiled in 750 ml of distilled water to make a paste; this is centrifuged and the almost clear supernate adjusted to pH 8.0, autoclaved in 12 ml amounts, and stored in the frozen state; when added to the medium the supernate is decanted from sedimented debris.

N-Acetyl Glucosamine Reversion Medium[36]

Prepared as the above antibiotic sensitivity medium with the additives of Fleischmann's yeast and horse serum, but with dehydrated nutrient broth (Difco) instead of PPLO broth. No agar is added. The pH of the components is kept at 7.3–7.5. Just before use, a filter-sterilized solution of N-acetyl glucosamine is added to give a concentration of 200 mcg/ml. A filter-sterilized solution of yeast extract (Difco 0127) is also added to give a concentration of 0.2%.

Modified Medium of Medill and O'Kane[28]

The following salts are mixed, homogenized by grinding, and stored at 4°C: 40 g $MgSO_4 \cdot 7H_2O$, 2 g NaCl, 2 g $FeSO_4 \cdot 7H_2O$, 8 g $MnSO_4 . 4H_2O$). A stock combination of the salts, buffer and casamino acids is prepared as follows and stored in a closed container at 4°C: 2 g salt mixture, 5 g vitamin free casamino acids (Difco), 9 g K_2HPO_4. To prepare 100 ml of the medium, the following are mixed and sterilized by filtration: 1.6 g of the stock combination of salts, buffer and casamino acids, 50 ml distilled water, 0.15 g glucose, 1 ml stock solution of nicotinamide.* This is aseptically bottled in 25 ml amounts. The mixture is stable for at least six months at 4°C. On the day the blood culture is to be made, the following are autoclaved together: 46 ml distilled water, 4 ml 60% sodium lactate, 10 g sucrose, 0.05 g agar (a pretested lot). After cooling to 60°C it is added aseptically in 25 ml quantities to the filtered mixture.

Medium for Morphological Reversion

Veal infusion broth and 0.5% soluble starch (Difco) are dissolved in distilled water, the pH adjusted with NaOH to 7.8, tubed in 6 ml amounts and autoclaved. Sucrose is autoclaved in a 40% solution and 2 ml added to each tube of broth. This medium is apparently not adequate per se, as 0.5 ml of blood culture must be added to assure growth. If the medium is used the day of preparation it will usually give growth of L-colonies with some morphologically classical bacteria by 24 hours.

Production of Mycobacterium tuberculosis L-Form Antigen with Cycloserine

To produce L-form antigen, six strains of M. tuberculosis var. hominis were checked for purity by four successive platings of single colonies on Tarshis[41] medium without antibiotic. The L-phase was induced by culturing each strain on 10 ml slants of Kirchner's agar containing 50 μg/ml of cycloserine; 10 ml of Kirchner's broth with cycloserine were employed as an overlay. The tubes, in a slanted position with liquid over the entire surface, were incubated for 10 days. The resultant growth was successively subcultured to the same medium two additional times with 10 days of incubation intervening. Media inoculated with each transfer to check for contamination included Thiol broth (Difco) and blood agar plates. The final L-form growth was examined by stained preparations and phase optics to ascertain that a minimum of 95 per cent of the growth was non-bacillary. The organisms were sedimented from the liquid by centrifugation, washed

---

* The stock solution of nicotinamide contains 100 μg/ml, is sterilized by filtration and stored at 4°C.

three times in 10% sucrose at pH 7.2, then killed by 48-hour exposure to 1% formalin in 10% sucrose. They were finally suspended in 0.5% formalin in 10% glucose and adjusted to a nephelometer standard representing 10^8 organisms. A composite antigen, of equal volumes of the six L-forms suspensions, was stored at 4°C in aliquots.

Immunization of Rabbits to M. tuberculosis L-Form Antigen

To obtain antibody to the L-form antigen, rabbits were first injected intravenously at 48-hour intervals with seven injections of 0.5 ml antigen followed by five injections of 0.25 ml and an intradermal injection of 0.5 ml after 25 days of rest. At this point the animals' sera demonstrated no antibody by Oudin,[14] Ouchterlony, or Middlebrook-Dubos indirect bacterial hemagglutination methods.[32] Therefore, immunization was resumed using Freund's incomplete antigen (Difco), diluted 1:1 with antigen. Injections (1 ml) were given intramuscularly eight times at 72-hour intervals, followed by an injection after 14 days; 72 hours later, two of three animals had demonstrable antibodies and were bled for 50 ml amounts.

Fluorescent Antibody Study of Sputum Samples

The indirect fluorescent antibody (FA) technique of Weller & Coons[44] was utilized for examination of sputum for the presence of normal and variant forms of the tubercle bacillus. Slides containing sputum were placed in a moist chamber and covered with a 1:10 dilution of L-form antiserum or a comparative dilution of H37Ra antiserum, and incubated at 37°C for 30 minutes. The slides were washed twice in buffered saline for a total of ten minutes, drained, replaced in the moist chamber, and reacted with a balanced dilution of FA antisera for an additional 30 minutes at 37°C. Following washing of the slides, the Flazo orange counterstain of Hall & Hansen[12] was applied for three minutes, and the slides washed ten minutes in buffered saline. The specimens were protected with mounting medium and coverslips and observed with an ultraviolet microscope for typical reactive forms.

Controls for autofluorescence of the antigen and positive and negative sera were included in all determinations. A constant level of fluorescent reactivity was maintained by adjusting dilution titers when new lots of FA or H37Ra antisera were introduced into the system. Some lots of commercial goat antiglobulin contained variable levels of reactivity for mycobacterium species, perhaps resulting from use of complete adjuvant in the immunization process. Thus, it was necessary to absorb some FA antiglobulin with mycobacteria as follows: The FA reconstituted globulin was diluted, 1:4 with buffered saline and added to a tube containing an equal volume of washed packed cells of *M. tuberculosis* H37Ra. After mixing the contents, the tube was left overnight at 4°C. The supernatant was then clarified by centrifugation and stored in the frozen state. It also proved necessary to absorb the specific sera and the antiglobulin sera with staphylococci and streptococci. Six cultures of staphylococci and six of streptococci from sputa were pooled and used for this purpose.

Optical Equipment

For fluorescent microscopy, a Zeiss GFL model microscope was used with an Osram HB200 mercury burner. The exciter filter was a 3 mm Schott BG 12, and the barrier filters Schott OG 4 and OG 5.

Method for Examination of Spinal Fluids

Each spinal fluid was centrifuged for 10 minutes at 40,000 rpm and the sediment used to prepare six smears and duplicate 100 mm plates of blood agar, chocolate agar and serum agar plates. The duplicate plates permitted incubation in both 2% CO_2 and anaerobically, using phosphorus to remove O_2.

The fluorescent staining of *Hemophilus influenzae* was done by the direct method,[7] employing *H. influenzae* antiserum coupled with Fluorescein Isothiocyanate (Difco). This serum was applied to a fixed smear for 30 minutes; after washing with cold saline for 10 minutes, Flazo orange counterstain[12] was applied for three minutes. Smears of *H. influenzae* type B culture were included in each examination as positive controls. For the blocking test to indicate the specificity of the reaction between serum and L-variants, untagged *H. influenzae* rabbit serum (Difco or Hyland) was applied for 15 minutes, followed by a 30-minute application of fluorescene-tagged goat antirabbit serum (BBL).

Concentration of L-Forms from Blood Cultures

A blood culture which is thought to contain L-growth is prepared for antibiotic sensitivity testing by transferring 10 ml to a conical tube and centrifuging just long enough to clear of erythrocytes. The supernate is transferred to a second tube and subjected to 13,000 rpm (20,200 G) for 30 minutes. All but one ml of the supernate is discarded. The sediment is suspended in this minimal liquid and spread with a bent glass rod over the surface of Serum Agar. After incubation for 24 or 48 hours the plates are read microscopically with a magnification of × 200.

RESULTS

BLOOD CULTURES

The impression that an L-form in a blood culture will be encountered only in extreme rarity is still commonly held by workers in the field of infectious disease. In contrast, Nativelle & Deparis[30] reported that three times as many hospital blood cultures develop L-growth as the recognized classical stage. They found the species represented were predominantly staphylococci and streptococci, though contaminants in the L-stage were also encountered.

In our laboratory we have surveyed 328 blood cultures for L-forms; these consisted of 164 blood samples cultured in duplicate aerobically and anaerobically in standard media (BBL or Difco) from eight Detroit area hospitals, representing patients from upper and lower economic strata. Of these, a total of 39 per cent showed growth, 11

per cent classical bacteria and 28 per cent L-forms. After 14 days incubation these unselected cultures were surveyed to obtain L-form strains for teaching and research. In the instances where reversion occurred, the spectrum of organisms resembled the classical species commonly encountered, including hemolytic coagulase positive staphylococci, alpha-hemolytic streptococci, pneumococci, *E. coli, Corynebacterium acnes*, and a micrococcus occurring after cardiac surgery. The order of frequency was staphylococci, alpha-hemolytic streptococci, and pneumococci. There was one notable peculiarity: beta-hemolytic streptococci were not encountered. This then agrees with the finding[18, 21, 37] that L-forms in the blood of scarlet fever and rheumatic fever patients revert to alpha-hemolytic streptococci. To date, the data suggest that beta-hemolytic streptococci which have grown *in vivo* in the L-stage have altered characteristics when they assume classical morphology.

Cultures with L-growth had characteristic forms in smears stained by Gram's and Seller's[39] methods, and characteristic growth in either Chanock's Serum Agar or Reversion medium. In Gram stain a great variety of forms are encountered in the same specimen: large budding spheres, fine and coarse branching strands, and often faintly staining cocci appearing along filaments. The color micrographs of Nativelle & Deparis[30] illustrate the common possibilities.

We have found interpretation of a Gram stain time-consuming. For a more rapid screening method, Seller's stain is applied to a methanol-fixed slide. With this stain, fine L-growth cannot be differentiated from fibrin and cellular debris, but large spheres, 20 μ or more in diameter, with a deeply staining rim, are numerous in positive cultures. These rings, which occur singularly or in small groups, stain dark blue and are easily sighted against the pink background with × 200 magnification. (A colony of such spheroplasts in liquid is shown in Figure 47.1.) One or two such spheroplasts per slide should be ignored, as should any L-type structure found in minimal incidence, since some L-forms contaminate most distilled and deionized water,* and their morphology is unchanged by autoclaving.

Some patients had repeated cultures, all positive for L-forms. In other cases successive cultures showed intermittently L-forms and classical organisms. In the clinical data available in our series there was no evidence that patients with L-forms only were less seriously ill than those with classical bacteria. This was also the interpretation of Nativelle & Deparis.[30]

When the Reversion medium was used, morphologically classical organisms appeared along with L-growth in 18 hours if the strain was a staphylococcus, streptococcus, or pneumococcus. Attempts to demonstrate the identity of a strain as staphylococcus by testing for coagulase or clumping factor were negative in the 16 L-variants of staphylococcus tested, although it is known that L-strains produced in vitro retain the ability to make coagulase.[27, 45] Conceivably, the inability to demonstrate the enzyme may be correlated with the minimal growth of the L-phase when it is from an in vivo source.

L-forms from septicemia, as from other infections, revert slowly and uncertainly. Recommended methods to hasten the process include serial passage in chick embryo,[21] intracerebral inoculation of mice, growth with Sarcina lutea or other organisms, and addition to the culture of unheated yeast extract with N-acetyl glucosamine[36] (See Materials and Methods). We have found that a simple veal infusion-sucrose me-

* The L-forms in water, which may number as high as 30,000/ml, presumably consist mainly of fine granules, since centrifuged sediment shows relatively few rods and colonies. Nevertheless, occasional dead L-colonies are seen in all media. Precautions we use to avoid mistaking dead colonies for growth include microscopic examination of inoculated plates before incubation; placing duplicate plates in the refrigerator (Pseudomonas aeruginosa L-forms are the only ones we have found to give growth in seven days of refrigeration); incubating duplicates in an atmosphere saturated with phenol, where no growth occurs; identification of species with fluorescent antibody; subculture; staining with vital dyes.

dium (Medium for Morphological Reversion) gives morphological reversion of streptococci, staphylococci or pneumococci, often in 24 hours. The bacteria, with characteristic Gram reaction and morphology, appear at the periphery of rhizoid colonies of L-phase growth. Although at this stage their reaction with fluorescent antibody is marked and specific, these bacteria will not colonize, and for several transfers are "L-dependent", growing only on soft Serum Agar which supports the L-growth. Reversion medium has practical application because the clinician often can determine the site of the infection by learning the identity of the etiological agent.

The presence of the L-form of streptococci in the blood of scarlet fever cases has been studied intensively by Klodnitskaia,[21] and similar organisms have been isolated in blood cultures of rheumatic fever.[47] Kagan et al.[18] have produced myocarditis and tonsillitis in monkeys injected intravenously with these strains. It is feasible that the streptococci found by Scheff et al.[37] in blood cultures in rheumatic fever were reverted forms, since their appearance was delayed.

The interesting role of L-variants in blood cultures in latency of infection has been noted by Nelson & Pickett[31] for brucellosis, for staphylococci by Godzeski, for C. acnes by Wittler.[46] One possible site for residence of latent variants was demonstrated as we found developmental stages of the organism within erythrocytes.[27] The growth of the variant of Brucella[15] and Borrelia[40] within tissue cells may also be typical of latency for many species.

L-FORMS IN CASES OF TUBERCULOSIS

Examination of unfixed samples of sputum usually reveals L-forms among the bacteria. It has been shown that the pneumococcus is one bacterium encountered in the L-phase in such specimens.[33] Our experience, however, concerns the tubercle bacillus, as described below.

The paucity of Ziehl-Neelsen staining bacilli in many cases of pulmonary tuberculosis has always suggested the existence of a variant form in this disease.[5] Even before antibiotic therapy, some authors[4] reported that 38 per cent of cases considered active tuberculosis were consistently negative in smear and culture. Our *in vitro* studies have indicated that L-type growth is only occasionally acid-fast; nevertheless, we have observed at times acid-fast organisms with the morphology of L-forms in sputum of tuberculosis cases.[26] Therefore, a pilot study to determine whether variants have diagnostic value seemed worthwhile. Such a project, employing fluorescent antibody, was conducted in our laboratory by D. F. Garvin.[9]

Sputum specimens from 45 patients hospitalized for pulmonary tuberculosis were compared with samples from a similar series of patients hospitalized for non-tuberculous respiratory conditions. An additional type of control was sputum pooled from healthy laboratory workers. The study tested the feasibility of detecting L-forms of the tubercle bacillus by fluorescent antibody[7] and by auramine-rhodamine (AR) staining.[10, 42] Antiserum versus the bacillary stage of H37Ra, made commercially, was compared with antiserum to the L-stage, prepared in our laboratory by immunization of rabbits. To constitute antigen for immunizing rabbits, six freshly isolated strains of the tubercle bacillus were induced into the L-stage with cycloserine and pooled. Details of antigen preparation, immunization schedule and technique for fluorescent antibody are given in the section on Materials and Methods.

Table 47.1 shows that false positives did not constitute a problem when fluorescent antibody was employed. In the entire non-tuberculosis series only one questionable organism was seen, a rod which appeared to be a diphtheroid and with staining less definite than in the organisms from cases. This table does show, also, that auramine-rhodamine cannot be used to recognize variant forms of the tubercle bacillus, as 39 per cent of the specimens from non-tubercular individuals had pleomorphic forms staining with these fluorescent dyes. The much higher number, 65 per cent, of variant forms reacting in the tuberculosis series indicates that L-variants of the tubercle

TABLE 47.1

L-Variants and Bacilli in Control and Tuberculous Sputa Reacting with Auramine Rhodamine (AR) and Fluorescent Antibody (FA)

	Non-tuberculosis Cases (46)	Tuberculosis Cases (45)
	%	%
AR Reactions		
Rods	0	67
Pleomorphic forms	39	65
FA Reactions		
Rods	*	11
Pleomorphic forms	0	33

* One rod with diphtheroid morphology in one specimen exhibited a faint reaction.

bacillus do stain with auramine-rhodamine, but they have no characteristics to distinguish them from the nonspecific reactions in the control series.

Table 47.1 shows that specific immune fluorescence was found in samples from tuberculosis cases, involving both bacillary and pleomorphic forms. Since no reactions occurred in the control series, it was concluded that fluorescent staining is a specific reaction for detection of both the tubercle bacilli and the variant.

The specific immune reaction with antibody utilized the indirect method, giving a green-gold halo at the periphery of the organism. The L-forms consisted of large round bodies from which emerged thin filamentous strands, small spheres with a diameter approximately the length of the tubercle bacilli, or very fine rhizoid colonies.

With the technique employed, FA was insensitive compared to AR. It is believed that the reactivity of FA can be greatly increased, since it was noticed that, if the fluorescent antibody was applied to wet organisms in tubes rather than to fixed smears, approximately ten times as many organisms showed specific fluorescence. It is now known that many FA reactions require native rather than fixed antigens.

Table 47.2 shows that commercial antiserum to the bacillary stage was as functional in detecting the L-variant as was antiserum versus the variant. This is for-

TABLE 47.2

Comparison of Antiserum to Entire Organism (H37Ra) with L-Form Antiserum

(Sputum from 45 tuberculosis cases)

	H37Ra Serum %	L-Form Serum %
Rods	14	3
Pleomorphic forms	31	25

TABLE 47.3

Specific Reactions Detected with Fluorescent Antibody Only

No rods stained by AR, but FA-staining L-forms: 3 specimens

No acid-fast rods, but FA-staining L-forms: 4 specimens

Total tuberculosis cases: 45

Number positive by at least one method (Kinyoun's Acid fast; AR, FA): 42

Percentage of positives detected only by FA-reacting L-forms: 7.1.

tunate, since preparing an antibody to the L-stage proved difficult. The figures suggest that the L-stage serum was inferior for reacting with bacilli, but this may be a sampling artifact, as the immune sera were not tested with identical specimens in each instance.

Table 47.3 shows that 7 per cent of the specimens found to contain forms of the tubercle bacillus would have been missed had not the variant been revealed by fluorescent antibody.

Although 39 of the 45 samples were positive by direct smear when studied in our laboratory, the sanatorium reported only four instances of growth after acid-digestion, in accordance with the finding of others that organisms from treated cases do not resist routine digestion procedures. Although no conclusion can be drawn from such a small series, the fact that all positive cultures came from samples showing specific L-forms, and in one instance in the absence of any bacilli detected by antibody, AR or Kinyouns, arouses speculation about the relative resistance of the "delicate" L-stage.

In summary, we have shown that the L-stage is found in 25–30 per cent of cases of pulmonary tuberculosis, in some instances without acid fast rods. The L-stage can be detected reliably with the indirect method of fluorescent antibody. The relative efficiency of auramine-rhodamine versus fluorescent antibody for detecting the *bacillary* stage of the organism remains to be deciphered by future studies.

We have recently studied cultures from a patient who appeared to have a typical L-form septicemia. The man was known to have leukemia, at the time in remission. Two blood cultures taken in our modification of Medill & O'Kane's medium,[28] showed growth of L-forms after overnight incubation. Four cultures taken previously in standard medium and incubated two weeks showed variants also. All six cultures have behaved identically in subsequent examination. When the six isolates were put in the Medium for Morphological Reversion, which usually reveals cocci in 18 hours, the L-growth remained actinomyces-like. On all media tested, growth was better at pH near 8.0 than at pH 6.0, and better anaerobically than in 2% CO_2. On the Serum Agar used for the antibiotic sensitivity plates, the growth, if sparse, consisted of vacuolated colonies or, if confluent, of a fishnet sheet. With continued incubation the growth did not extend, but the vacuoles gradually filled with granules or by widening of their peripheral membranes. This growth pattern on Serum Agar is typical of every L-strain we have isolated from blood cultures.

Before the antibiotic sensitivity tests were done, the cultures were freed of most of their blood cells and also concentrated by differential centrifugation as described in Methods. A check of the sediments after high speed centrifugation revealed colonies of spheroplasts as shown in dark field in Figure 47.1

The antibiotic sensitivity tests, unlike those for any other L-form strain we have ever tested, were almost entirely negative. When a heavy inoculum was used there was no sensitivity to any antibiotic tested, namely the low concentration discs of ampicillin, vancomycin, chloramphenicol, erythromycin, declomycin, dihydrostreptomycin, cephalosporin, chlortetracycline, polymyxin B, colymycin, nitrofurantoin, kanamycin, lincomycin, bacitracin, novobiocin, triple sulfonamides, amphotericin B, and nystatin. The last two agents were tested because the patient's sputum was reported to contain *C. albicans*. With an inoculum barely enough to give a sheet of growth, there was marked inhibition by one agent only, triple sulfonamides.

After three addition weeks of incubation, reversion began on all media, including the original blood cultures. In broth, the fine strands in colonies became stiff and straight and exhibited right-angle branching. Groups of rods developed on the plates. Varying degrees of acid-fastness existed in the rods and filaments and re-examination of the original spheroplasts in culture sediments showed that some walls had acid-fast segments. After six weeks more acid-fast bacilli were found (Figures 47.2 and

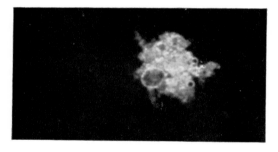

Figure 47.1. Spheroplasts in blood culture of a tuberculosis case.

47.3). It is interesting that more rods were AR-staining than acid-fast.

The patient expired before any clue to the identity of the organism was obtained, and at autopsy was found to have advanced pulmonary tuberculosis. Now that it is known that the L-stage of the tubercle bacillus can be grown from the blood in 24 hours, it is hoped that testing of more pertinent antimicrobial agents can be done in the next similar case. The sensitivity of this strain to sulfonamides is in accord with the *in vitro* sensitivity of the bacillary stage to these agents, and, of course, has no meaning for therapy.

MENINGITIS

L-forms were found in the spinal fluid in meningitis as long ago as 1945.[1] They were also studied by Barile, Yaguchi & Eveland in 1958.[2] That L-forms *per se* play the most significant role in the common aseptic meningitis was learned only recently in Kagan's laboratory[17] in Moscow, and in our laboratory.[24, 25]

Several years ago, when "negative" cultures from three problem cases of meningitis were referred to our laboratory, it was found that the L-stage of the pneumococcus was present in each, even before antibiotic therapy. Initially, growth was obtained on chocolate agar or glucose ascites medium (Difco). Using clear Serum Agar, the inhibition spectrum for antibiotics was determined and the patients, none of whom had responded to penicillin alone, were

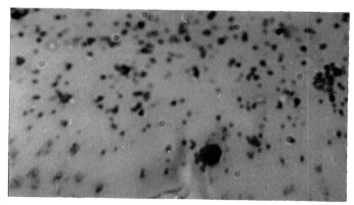

Figure 47.2. Reverting L-forms from blood culture of same patient as in Figure 47.1.

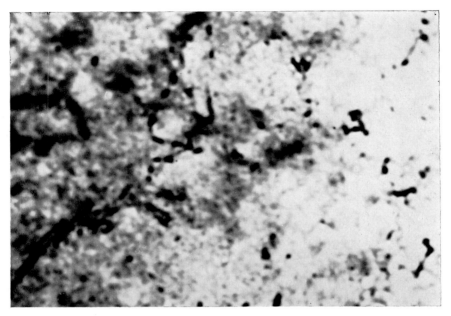

Figure 47.3. Reversion of culture from the same patient as in Figures 47.1 and 47.2. The filaments and rods were acid-fast.

successfully treated. In at least one instance it was necessary to give the patient an antibiotic for the classical pneumococcus as well as one directed against the L-form. This follows the tenet of Nativelle & Deparis[30] that therapy should be directed against "the entire organism".

We also surveyed 45 spinal fluids from meningitis cases and compared them with 23 spinal fluids from non-infectious cases. As has been suggested by the work of others, L-variants occurred in association with meningococci, pneumococci, beta hemolytic streptococci, *H. influenzae*, staphylococci, *E. coli* and *Cryptococcus neoformans*. In a chronic drug resistant case of tuberculous meningitis, the numerous L-colonies were rapidly agglutinated by rabbit serum to H37Ra and not by other immune rabbit sera.

Because of this experience it was considered worthwhile to examine minutely a small series of meningitis cases to determine the relative incidence of the L-stage, and to learn whether fluorescent antibody could facilitate recognition of species of the pathogens. Gregory Karris, in our labora-

tory, made a careful analysis of organisms in ten samples of spinal fluid from eight meningitis cases; spinal fluid from four non-meningitis cases served as control (see Materials and Methods).

This study, summarized in Table 47.4, indicates several points. Of primary interest is the fact that of eight unselected cases, three had aseptic meningitis from which bacteria later developed from the L-stage; these cases had spinal fluids showing a pleocytosis predominately neutrophilic; in each instance, the reverting bacteria were cocci. It has been shown by Koptoleva and associates[23] that intrathecal inoculation of fixed L-strains of staphylococci and streptococci into rabbits can produce meningitis.

Secondly, it was found that the L-variant of *H. influenzae* could be identified with specific serum, using fluorescent antibody (see CSF #9, Table 47.4). The specificity of the reaction was shown by blocking the staining with untagged specific serum. There was no crossing with the L-form of the staphylococcus from patient #12.

Thus, at least two species of L-variants can be recognized by direct application of fluorescent antibody procedures with the clinical specimen. The second species is the tubercle bacillus, as described earlier in this paper. Furthermore, we believe that with high titered grouping serum it should be possible to identify the L-variants of pneumococci, as we have been able to agglutinate L-forms in spinal fluid from pneumococcal meningitis and from peritoneal cavity infections of mice with specific grouping sera.

We have made a preliminary study of peripheral blood in meningitis. In two cases with pneumococci in the spinal fluid, but with negative blood cultures, we have found L-forms in blood culture and followed their reversion to pneumococci. If meningitis is commonly accompanied by a septicemia with the L-stage, this will have diagnostic value and may be related to the mechanism of meningeal invasion.

With the tubercle bacillus, the pneumococcus and with *H. influenzae* in Karris' series, the L- and the classical stages usually occurred unbalanced, with a preponderance of one or the other. This may be related to the finding that the classical stage tends to inhibit the other.[8] Another related fact is that some bacteria, inoculated into an experimental animal, multiply for long periods exclusively in the L-form.[13]

SUMMARY

Of 164 blood samples cultured in duplicate, 11 per cent showed classical bacteria and 28 per cent L-forms. The variants were demonstrated by Gram's and Seller's stains, and by characteristic fishnet growth on Serum Agar, or development in Reversion medium. The species demonstrated in the instances where reversion occurred included staphylococci, streptococci, pneumococci, *Escherichia coli*, *Corynebacterium acnes* and a micrococcus. In comparison with the spectrum of organisms recovered in the classical stage in blood cultures, beta hemolytic streptococci were conspicuously absent.

In pulmonary tuberculosis L-forms were

TABLE 47.4

Smears and Cultures of Spinal Fluid Sediment

Case No.	Growth on L-Variant Medium	Antibiotic Therapy Before Culture	Direct Smear: FA Reaction to *Hemophilus influenzae* Serum
3	*H. influenzae* classical	No	Fluorescing classical rods
4	*H. influenzae* classical	No	Fluorescing classical rods
5 a.	*H. influenzae* and L-forms	No	Fluorescing classical rods*
b.	(after therapy): no growth	Yes	Negative
6	*H. influenzae* and L-forms	Yes	(Not done)
9	*H. influenzae* and L-forms	No	Fluorescent classical rods and L-variants
12 a.	L-colonies, reverted to staphylococci	No	Negative
b.	(after therapy) L-colonies, reverted to staphylococci	Yes	Negative
14	L-colonies, reverted to staphylococci		(Not done)
19	L-colonies, reverted to streptococci		(Not done)
Four controls (not meningitis)	No growth	No	

In every instance where growth of classical *H. influenzae* appeared, it also developed on the blood agar and chocolate agar plates.

* This specimen had only a few L-colonies on culture.

demonstrated by the use of fluorescent antibody in sputum of 33 per cent of known cases. Seven per cent of all positive samples revealed L-forms exclusively. It remains to be determined whether fluorescent antibody should be reserved for problem cases negative by auramine-rhodamine staining, or used routinely.

In a patient with fever of unknown origin, all of six blood cultures showed L-forms which gradually reverted to acid-fast bacilli. The patient expired and at autopsy exhibited gross pathology characteristic of advanced pulmonary tuberculosis. The noteworthy point is that this variant grew out in 24 hours on the special casamino acid medium; in future similar cases appropriate sensitivity tests can be done.

In a series of eight meningitis cases with neutrophilic pleocytosis in the spinal fluid, three were aseptic but showed growth of L-forms after varied periods of incubation. In two cases these L-forms reverted to staphylococci, and in one to streptococci. The five cases with classical bacteria had *Hemophilus influenzae*, with or without L-variants. Specific identification of the *H. influenzae* L-form was made by the direct fluorescent antibody method.

REFERENCES

1. Alexander-Jackson, E.: A hitherto undemonstrated zoogleal form of *Mycobacterium tuberculosis*. *Trans. N. Y. Acad. Sci.* **7**: 81, 1945.
2. Barile, M. F., Yaguchi, R., and Eveland, W. C.: A simplified medium for the cultivation of pleuropneumonia-like organisms and L-forms of bacteria. *Amer. J. Clin. Path.* **30**: 171, 1958.
3. Bittner, J., and Vionesco, V.: Formes "L" toxigenes du Clostridium perfringens. In: *IX International Congress of Microbiology* (Abstracts), Moscow, 1966: p. 353.
4. Bogen, E., and Bennett, E. S.: Tubercle bacilli in sputum; criteria for negativity, and the significance of the number of bacilli found. *Amer. Rev. Tuberc.* **39**: 89, 1939.
5. Calmette, A., and Valtis, J.: Les éléments virulents filtrables du bacille tuberculeux. *Ann. Méd.* **19**: 553, 1926.
6. Chanock, R. M., Hayflick, L., and Barile, M. F.: Growth on artificial medium of an agent associated with atypical pneumonia and its identification as a PPLO. *Proc. Nat. Acad. Sci. USA* **48**: 41, 1962.
7. Coons, A. H., and Kaplan, M. H.: Localization of antigen in tissue cells. II. Improvements in a method for the detection of antigen by means of a fluorescent antibody. *J. Exp. Med.* **91**: 1, 1950.
8. Fodor, M., and Rogers, H. J.: Antagonism between vegetative cells and *L*-forms of *Bacillus licheniformis* strain 6346. *Nature* **211**: 658, 1966.
9. Garvin, D. F.: *Immunofluorescent Identification of Mycobacterial Variants.* M.S. Thesis, Wayne State University, Detroit, 1966.
10. Gray, D. F.: Detection of small numbers of mycobacteria in sections by fluorescent microscopy. *Amer. Rev. Tuberc.* **68**: 82, 1953.
11. Gutman, L., Turck, M., Petersdorf, R. G., and Wedgwood, R. J.: Significance of bacterial variants in urine of patients with chronic bacteriuria. *J. Clin. Invest.* **44**: 1945, 1965.
12. Hall, C. T., and Hansen, P. A.: Chelated azo dyes used as counterstains in the fluorescent antibody technic. *Zbl. Bakt.* (Orig.) **184**: 548, 1962.
13. Hannoun, C., Vigoroux, J., Levaditi, J., and Nazimoff, O.: Étude des formes L des bactéries apparues spontanément *in vivo*. III. Histopathologie comparée des lésions provoquées par la bacterie normale et par ses formes modifiées. *Ann. Inst. Pasteur* (Paris) **92**: 231, 1957.
14. Harris, T. N., Harris, S., and Ogburn, C. A.: Gel-precipitation of streptococcal culture supernates with sera of patients with rheumatic fever and streptococcal infection. *Proc. Soc. Exp. Biol. Med.* **90**: 39, 1955.
15. Hatten, B. A., and Sulkin, S.: Intracellular production of *Brucella* L forms. II. Induction and survival of *Brucella abortus* L forms in tissue culture. *J. Bact.* **91**: 14, 1966.
16. Hauduroy, P.: Mécanisme de formation des formes filtrables et invisibles. *Ann. Inst. Pasteur* (Paris) **86**: 395, 1954.
17. Kagan, G. Y., Koptelova, E. I., and Pokrovsky, B. M.: Isolation of pleuropneumonia-like organisms, L-forms and heteromorphous growth of bacteria from the cerebrospinal fluid of patients with septic meningitis. *J. Hyg. Epidemiol. Microbiol. Immunol.* (Prague) **9**: 310, 1965 (in Russian).
18. Kagan, G. Y., Koptelova, E. I., Prosorovsky, S. V., Petrosova, V. N., Mikhailova, V. S., Raskova, T. M., Danko, L. V., Cherkovich, T. M., Mesenzev, A. M., and Simovonian, V. G.: Some results of experimental investigations of the pathogenicity of L-forms of

β-hemolytic streptococci. In: *IX International Congress of Microbiology* (Abstracts), Moscow, 1966: p. 353.

19. Kalmanson, G. M., and Guze, L. B.: Role of protoplasts in pathogenesis of pyelonephritis. *JAMA* **190:** 1107, 1964.

20. Kazancheva, A. M.: On the formation of L-forms of microbes in the organism. *Klin. Med.* (Moscow) **40**(3): 32, 1962 (in Russian).

21. Klodnitskaia, N. S.: On the problem of the etiology of scarlet fever. IV. Isolation of the L-form of streptococcus from penicillin-treated patients with scarlet fever and experience in the production of ovohemocultures. *Zh. Mikrobiol.* **33**(5): 31, 1962 (in Russian).

22. Koptelova, E. I.: The production of filterable forms of typhoid bacilli by harmful treatments *in vitro* and *in vivo. J. Microbiol. Epidemiol. Immunobiol.* **28:** 858, 1957.

23. Koptelova, E. I., Pokrovsky, V. I., and Gorshkova, E. P.: A model of experimental meningitis in rabbits caused by streptococcal and staphylococcal L-forms. *Vestn. Akad. Med. Nauk. SSSR* **20**(8): 60, 1965.

24. Mattman, L., and Karris, G.: L and transitional forms in meningitis. *Bact. Proc.:* p. 49, 1966.

25. Mattman, L. H., and Mattman, P. E.: L forms of *Streptococcus fecalis* in septicemia. *Arch. Intern. Med.* (Chicago) **115:** 315, 1965.

26. Mattman, L. H., Tunstall, L. H., Mathews, W. W., and Gordon, D. L.: L variation in mycobacteria. *Amer. Rev. Resp. Dis.* **82:** 202, 1960.

27. Mattman, L. H., Tunstall, L. H., and Rossmoore, H. W.: Induction and characteristics of staphylococcal L forms. *Canad. J. Microbiol.* **7:** 705, 1961.

28. Medill, M. A., and O'Kane, D. J.: A synthetic medium for the L type colonies of *Proteus. J. Bact.* **68:** 530, 1954.

29. Moustárdier, G., Brisou, J., and Perrey, M.: Transformation en bactéries normales d'organismes L isolés par culture à partir d'uréthrites amicrobiennes à inclusions. *Ann. Inst. Pasteur* (Paris) **85:** 520, 1953.

30. Nativelle, R., and Deparis, M.: Formes évolutives des bactéries dans les hémocultures. *Presse Méd.* **68:** 571, 1960.

31. Nelson, E. L., and Pickett, M. J.: The recovery of L forms of brucella and their relation to brucella phage. *J. Infect. Dis.* **89:** 226, 1951.

32. Neter, E.: Bacterial hemagglutination and hemolysis. *Bact. Rev.* **20:** 166, 1956.

33. Perelli, C.: "Formazioni L" di "Diplococcus pneumoniae". *Igiene Mod.* **51:** 985, 1958.

34. Rosner, R.: Isolation of *Candida* protoplasts from a case of *Candida* endocarditis. *J. Bact.* **91:** 1320, 1966.

35. Rubio-Huertos, M., and Gonzalez-Vazquez, C.: Morphology and pathogenicity of L forms of *Clostridium tentani* induced by glycine. *Ann. N. Y. Acad. Sci.* **79:** 626, 1960.

36. Salowich, L., and Mattman, L.: Factors in reversion of microbial L forms. *Bact. Proc.:* p. 141, 1966.

37. Scheff, G. J., Marienfeld, C. J., and Hackett, E.: Blood culture studies in rheumatic fever patients. *J. Infect. Dis.* **103:** 45, 1958.

38. Scheibel, I., and Assandri, J.: In vitro investigation into sensitivity of different strains of *Cl. tetani* to antibiotics. *Acta Path. Microbiol. Scand.* **47:** 435, 1959.

39. Sellers, T. F.: A new method for staining Negri bodies of rabies. *Amer. J. Pub. Health* **17:** 1080, 1927.

40. Sidorov, V. E.: The body cavity of argasid ticks as habitat of spirochaetes and brucella. *Zh. Mikrobiol. Epidemiol. Immunobiol.* **31**(6): 91, 1960 (in Russian).

41. Tarshis, M.: Blood media for the cultivation of *Mycobacterium tuberculosis*. IV. Effect of adding penicillin. *J. Lab. Clin. Med.* **40:** 628, 1952.

42. Truant, J. P., Brett, W. A., and Thomas, W., Jr.: Fluorescence microscopy of tubercle bacilli stained with auramine and rhodamine. *Henry Ford Hosp. Med. Bull.* **10:** 287, 1962.

43. Tulasne, R., and Lavillaureix, J.: Mécanisme de l'action pathogène d'une forme L des bactéries d'origine vibrionnienne. *C. R. Soc. Biol.* (Paris) **149:** 178, 1955.

44. Weller, T. H., and Coons, A. H.: Fluorescent antibody studies with agents of Varicella and Herpes zoster propagated *in vitro. Proc. Soc. Exp. Biol.* **86:** 789, 1954.

45. Williams, R. E. O.: L forms of *Staphylococcus aureus. J. Gen. Microbiol.* **33:** 325, 1963.

46. Wittler, R. G., Malizia, W. F., Kramer, P. E., Tuckett, J. D., Pritchard, H. N., and Baker, H. J.: Isolation of a corynebacterium and its transitional forms from a case of subacute bacterial endocarditis treated with antibiotics. *J. Gen. Microbiol.* **23:** 315, 1960.

47. Wittler, R. G., Tuckett, J. D., Muccione, V. J., Gangarosa, E. J., and O'Connell, R. C.: Transitional forms and L forms from blood of rheumatic fever patients. In: *VIII International Congress of Microbiology* (Abstracts), Montreal, 1962: p. 125.

48

Atypical Bacterial Forms in Human Disease

Patricia Charache

JOHNS HOPKINS UNIVERSITY, UNIVERSITY OF MARYLAND
AND BALTIMORE CITY HOSPITALS
BALTIMORE, MARYLAND

Many workers in recent years have looked for fragile bacterial forms in isolates from patients with suspected sepsis. Major interest has been directed toward culture of blood in patients with subacute bacterial endocarditis, acute rheumatic fever, or fever of unknown origin.[5-10] More recently, isolations have been described from other body fluids.[3, 4]

This paper will be concerned with studies in our laboratory designed to assess the role of atypical bacterial forms in the pathogenesis or persistence of human infection, and studies directed toward the development of more reliable procedures for culture and identification of these forms in clinical material.

The phrase *atypical bacterial forms* (ABF) is intended to be an inclusive term used to describe all organisms which have altered morphology and altered cultural characteristics consistent with damage to, or absence of, their cell wall structure. The term includes spheroplasts, protoplasts, L-forms, and non-spherical forms which are too fragile to grow on solid media with or without L-colony morphology.

MATERIALS

MEDIA

Cultures were processed routinely, using trypticase soy broth, heart infusion broth, thioglycolate broth, blood agar, chocolate agar, and desoxycholate agar. In addition, selected cultures were processed in hypertonic liquid or solid media, prepared as follows: 100 ml heart infusion broth (Baltimore Biological Laboratory—BBL), 1 ml 1 N $MgSO_4$, and 11.4 g sucrose are mixed and autoclaved at 15 lbs pressure for 10 minutes; a Seitz filtrate of 10 ml serum plus 10 ml bacterial extract is added after cooling; the mixture is tubed and incubated for sterility for 48 hours, with random samples being selected for further incubation and sterility checks. Serum sources being evaluated include horse, rabbit, and fetal calf; that currently being employed is from immature rabbits. The bacterial extract is a supernatant of a 48 hour heart infusion broth culture of a spore-bearing, Gram-positive bacillus, which has been shown to enhance the growth of fragile forms and to encourage reversion to parent bacteria. The appearance of this organism is illustrated in Figure 48.1. The medium has been shown to support the growth of 14 bacterial species, excluding *Pneumococcus*. Solid medium is prepared by adding the above solution to washed BBL agar, giving a final agar concentration of one per cent.

GLASSWARE

Glass tubes and pipettes are used throughout isolation and identification pro-

Figure 48.1. Gram-positive spore-bearing rod used to prepare bacterial extract for hypertonic media. × 1500.

cedures. Petri dishes are both glass and plastic.

CLINICAL MATERIAL

Specimens studied include samples of blood, urine, cerebrospinal fluid, ascitic, pleural, and synovial fluids, pus aspirates, and biopsy material from liver, skin, and lymph nodes.

Patients studied come from three groups of cases:

Selected Cases

Patients are selected for study if their clinical presentation suggests that a search for atypical forms is likely to be of diagnostic or therapeutic value, or if the diagnosis is of research interest to the laboratory.

Laboratory Referral Cases

Cultures are evaluated if routine processing in the main hospital bacteriology laboratory yields a culture which appears positive, but in which specific pathogens cannot be identified.

General Screening Cases

In order to train technicians, to develop improved methods for the processing of cultures in a hospital laboratory setting, and to evaluate the reliability of the processing procedures, a major screening study was instituted. In this group, all joint, pleural, and ascitic fluids submitted to the Johns Hopkins Hospital laboratory over an eight-month period were processed both for atypical bacterial forms and for classical bacteria.

RESULTS

BACTERIAL ISOLATION TECHNIQUES

Three groups of positive cultures have been obtained, as summarized in Table 48.1. In Group 1, atypical organisms are seen on smear, and organisms with atypical morphology grow slowly in routine culture media, reverting on subculture to classical bacterial forms; up to 19 subcultures have been required to complete reversion of some of these forms. With few exceptions, when atypical bacteria have been isolated from mammalian isotonic sources such as blood or spinal fluid, they have survived in routine thioglycolate broth. They are fragile when compared to parent bacterial forms, are lysed by distilled water, and will not survive subculture to ordinary solid media. Subculture survival of the morphologically identified fragile forms, and reversion to bacteria with normal cell walls, have been enhanced by hypertonic media.

Positive cultures in this group appear sterile when the usual processing techniques of subculture and Gram stain

TABLE 48.1
Atypical Bacterial Isolate Techniques

1) Atypical Forms Seen on Smear
   Routine culture positive for atypical forms, reverting on subculture to normal bacteria.
2) Atypical Forms Seen on Smear
   Routine culture sterile
   Hypertonic medium grows bacteria
3) Atypical Forms Seen on Smear
   Routine culture sterile
   Hypertonic medium grows atypical forms, reverting on subculture to normal bacteria.

are employed. With routine processing, turbid cultures are subcultured on ordinary solid media, which remain sterile. Heat-fixed, Gram-stained slides of such cultures are usually thought to show no organisms. We have found that many readily identifiable fragile forms are heat labile, but can be readily recognized if air dried samples are prepared. Figure 48.2 illustrates the appearance of such a preparation, showing (A) an air dried specimen taken from a thioglycolate broth culture of a patient with symptoms of subacute bacterial endocarditis; forms of streptococci can be seen readily. The ap-

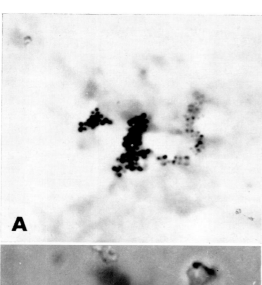

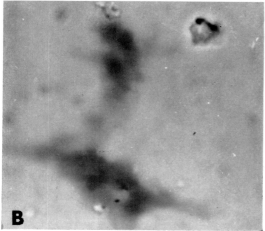

Figure 48.2. Atypical *Streptococcus viridans.* A: Air-dried Gram stain smear; B: heat-fixed Gram stain smear. × 1900.

pearance of the same culture after minimal heat fixation, usually employed in Gram staining, is shown in B; only bacterial debris is visualized, resembling Gram stain precipitation. Since this Gram-variable, fragile organism failed to grow on routine subculture, this culture, and 13 similar samples from the same patient were thought to be sterile by five competent bacteriology technicians, although all specimens contained *Streptococcus viridans.*

In the second and third groups, routine media are sterile, and hypertonic isolation must be employed. In the second group, air-dried smears show atypical bacterial forms; initial isolation in hypertonic media yields bacteria; on subculture, the organisms which on initial isolation grew only in hypertonic media, grow equally well without hypertonic protection.

In the third group, organisms grow only in hypertonic media, but as atypical forms which revert to parent bacterial forms only after subculture.

CRITERIA FOR ISOLATION OF ATYPICAL BACTERIAL FORMS

Because this study involves clinical material, subject to all of the problems involved in procuring the processing bacterial specimens in rich media over extended periods of time, rigid controls have been adopted and rigid criteria have been applied to all research cases. The following criteria are used to establish that the organism was resident in the patient in atypical form and was related to his disease: The atypical organisms must be visualized on smear; they must have cultural characteristics consistent with atypical forms, and must fail to grow under conditions which will support the growth of the parent bacterium; the organism must be reverted to a classical bacterium so that it can be characterized; it must be shown to have come from the patient, either by repeated isolation of the same organism, or through the use of immunological techniques; the clinical course of the patient should be consistent with the bacteriological findings.

In the processing of routine hospital material, repeated sampling is not always possible, and the above criteria cannot always be filled. Additional controls have therefore been developed to increase the validity of single isolate material. These include the following:

a. Media and laboratory controls. Multiple samples of hypertonic sucrose and thioglycolate broth media are cultured weekly, and are repeatedly subcultured to help insure sterility of media and glassware. Contaminant checks are made at intervals, recording cultures positive for *Bacillus subtilis, Staphylococcus albus,* and diphtheroids. Laboratory contamination noted with these techniques has involved less than five culture tubes per month.

b. Simultaneous culture controls. Fifty or more cultures from different patients are simultaneously processed; if more than one patient develops cultures positive with the same organism at the same time, the cultures would be considered suspect. To date, this has not occurred.

c. Source controls. For each clinical source studied, a series of source controls is being obtained; these include over 75 negative blood cultures from normal individuals, and 95 negative pleural, ascitic, and joint fluids from non-infected patients.

d. Unknown controls. Physicians obtaining material for atypical bacterial cultures have been requested to include occasional coded samples from normal individuals; this insures that the laboratory cannot know in advance whether a given culture should be positive or negative.

Through the use of these controls, it has been possible to determine the reliability of individual culture samples and to obtain information of clinical value.

CLINICAL ISOLATIONS

To date, atypical bacterial isolations have been made in over 160 cultures from 41 patients who meet the research criteria outlined. These include 21 patients with septicemia (including nine with subacute bacterial endocarditis), seven with positive abscess cultures, seven with pyarthrosis, five empyema, and one positive skin biopsy culture. In each case, routine hospital laboratory cultures had given the impression that the clinical material was sterile. In 38 of the patients, the full bacteriological diagnosis was helpful in defining patient care.

Review of individual case material has demonstrated that a search for atypical bacterial forms can be useful in demonstrating the presence or persistence of sepsis. A few examples of the type of material obtained may be summarized as follows:

Case #1

The patient was a two-year-old white male with a history of severe, recurrent neck swellings of a year's duration. An older sibling had died of staphylococcal cervical, pulmonary, and liver abscesses. The patient was placed on prednisone therapy for three months prior to admission because of a diagnosis of Still's disease. On admission, he had cervical, hepatic, and probably splenic abscesses. Aspiration of cervical abscesses revealed *Staphylococcus aureus* on smear and routine culture. On long-term penicillin and methicillin therapy, the abscesses became sterile on routine culture, although new lesions continued to form, and the patient remained markedly febrile. Gram stain smears of these aspirates revealed Gram-negative spherical forms, some with Gram-positive stippling. Hypertonic culture of the pus grew Gram-negative spheres, and intact *S. aureus*, indicating that sepsis had persisted. Addition of chloramphenicol resulted in defervescence to normal for the first time in six months. Smears and cultures of a residual cervical fluctuent area were sterile. A hepatic abscess aspiration revealed Gram-negative spherical forms which remained viable over a six-month period but never reverted to the parent pathogen. In this case, when chloramphenicol was discontinued by the mother after hospital discharge, the child relapsed and eventually died of staphylococcal hepatic disease. This suggested that even after protracted therapy using an apparently effective drug (in this case, more than two months of chloramphenicol), complete bacteriological cure may not readily occur in a susceptible individual infected with an organism which can survive in damaged form.

Case #2

The patient is a 16-year-old white female with congenital heart disease. Two years prior to admission, an atrial septal defect was repaired with a teflon patch. Two and one-half weeks prior to admission the patient's right proximal thumb joint became painful, hot and swollen. Two weeks prior to admission she developed a transient, pruritic generalized rash and sustained high fever, weakness and anorexia. On admission, a change in the previous murmur was noted. Eleven blood cultures were negative on routine bacteriologic processing. Eight days of penicillin therapy failed to alter the febrile course, and the drug was discontinued on the ninth hospital day because of the appearance of an acute allergic reaction to penicillin. Because of progressive splenomegaly, anemia, leukocytosis and one month of fever, cultures of blood were processed for atypical bacterial forms. These revealed that four out of four cultures were positive in both trypticase soy broth and thioglycolate broth for atypical forms of coagulase-negative staphylococcus, resistant to penicillin. Therapy with methicillin was successfully completed despite difficulties with allergic manifestations. The patient became well, and has remained asymptomatic for more than seven months.

Case #3

The patient is a 12-year-old white boy with a history of congenital heart disease corrected by a Blalock-Taussig shunt. Six months prior to admission he developed fever, weakness, weight loss, arthritis, and splenomegaly controlled by administration of oral Bicillin (Wyeth Laboratories). Repeated blood cultures over the first 20 days of admission after cessation of Bicillin were sterile; two subsequent blood cultures grew atypical streptococci. During the period of study of the atypical organisms,

on hospital days 24–26, three additional cultures grew classical forms of *Streptococcus faecalis*. It was presumed that falling levels of Bicillin permitted recognition of fragile forms before drug levels fell sufficiently to allow more osmotically resistant forms to appear.

Case #4

The patient is a 41-year-old white male in whom an anterolateral myocardial infarction was diagnosed electrocardiographically on admission. On the sixth hospital day, infectious disease consultation was requested because of persistent daily fever spikes of 102° F or more, associated with leukocytosis of 20–25,000 and a generally toxic appearance. The fever curve is summarized in Figure 48.3. He was thought to be septic by the infectious disease consultant, and blood cultures were recommended. Three separate blood cultures were referred by the main hospital laboratory for atypical bacterial processing; all six samples had become turbid, but routine processing was unrevealing; all samples were positive for atypical forms of coagulase-positive *S. aureus*. Laboratory control checks revealed that other blood cultures being processed simultaneously from the patient's ward or elsewhere were not positive for any form of *Staphylococcus*. By the time the bacteriologic diagnosis had been established, the patient had defervesced spontaneously, as seen in Figure 48.3. He recovered uneventfully thereafter. This case is included to indicate that, in some cases, cultures for atypical bacterial forms have raised questions which cannot be answered at present. In this case, a young man with an infarction seemed septic clinically and grew *S. aureus* from repeated blood cultures, but subsequently became well with no therapy. We can speculate that the fact that organisms were in atypical form meant that the patient could partially control them, and that subsequently he was able to control the pathogen completely. At present, however, such a case can only be collected, reserving final interpretation until further cases can be documented.

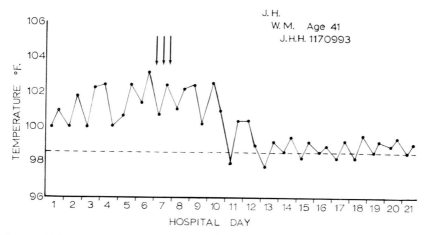

Figure 48.3. Temperature chart of Case ⚭4. Cultures were obtained at intervals marked by arrows; the temperature spontaneously returned to normal on day 10.

Case ⚭5

A search for atypical bacterial forms can be helpful in defining pathology in specific disease states. A review case of Whipple's disease can give an example of such an approach.[1]

Whipple's disease is a chronic, formerly fatal disorder characterized by episodic fever, weight loss, arthritis and polyserositis, progressing to diarrhea and malabsorption syndrome. The major diagnostic feature of the disease is the presence of characteristic macrophages found in many tissues, but most prominent within jejunal villae. These macrophages contain PAS-staining particles in their cytoplasm. In 1961, Yardley & Hendrix,[11] and independently Chears & Ashworth[2] demonstrated in jejunal biopsies the presence of bacillary bodies in and around the macrophages. These findings, in association with reports of successful antibiotic therapy of Whipple's disease, have stimulated attempts to isolate bacteria and a search for specific pathogens. Only rod-shaped bacteria have been considered significant, although samples studied have often been heavily contaminated by a variety of organisms including streptococci, neisseria, pneumococci, and enteric bacilli.

The patient is a 45-year-old white male with a six-year history of progressively severe arthralgia weakness, weight loss, fever, pleural effusion, abdominal pain, hepatosplenomegaly and leukocytosis. Repeated evaluations including multiple cultures, and biopsies of liver, muscle, skin lymph node, and kidney were nondiagnostic. Therapy with steroids for a diagnosis of collagen vascular disease and with isoniazid failed to interrupt his downhill course. A diagnosis of Whipple's disease was confirmed by jejunal biopsy.

Three blood cultures had been processed for six days prior to the establishment of the diagnosis. All looked positive, but were considered to be negative when routine Gram stain was negative, and subcultures on blood agar plates were sterile. Repeat smears of the same specimens showed that all six (three trypticase soy flasks and three thioglycolate tubes) were, in fact, positive for atypical bacterial forms.

Atypical bacteria presented as clumps of Gram-positive, and Gram-negative cocci or rods often, in initial samples, adherent to strands of debris. On subculture, some isolates again appeared as Gram-negative rods. In other subcultures, Gram-positive characteristics became apparent, with Gram-positive cocci, and Gram-positive stippling of Gram-negative rods and pleomorphic forms being noted.

All samples, regardless of presenting

morphology, eventually reverted to a beta hemolytic enterococcus, Lancefield Group D. Between three and eight subcultures were required to complete reversion in different samples.

Since the original cultures had been obtained during a febrile episode, three additional cultures were obtained during an afebrile period to determine if the initial positive samples were related to a transient infection with bacteremia. Again, all three trypticase soy broth and all three thioglycolate cultures were positive for atypical forms of beta-hemolytic enterococcus.

A repeat sterile biopsy of two lymph nodes adjacent to each other was obtained, cut into 19 pieces, and each piece was cultured individually. Sections of both nodes were shown to be positive for PAS-containing macrophages. Nine samples cultured on routine solid media (blood agar, chocolate agar and desoxycholate), two in trypticase soy broth, and one in hypertonic medium were sterile. Seven cultures, two in hypertonic sucrose agar, two in hypertonic sucrose broth and three in thioglycolate broth, were positive for the atypical enterococcus.

Although 19 samples from this patient grew the same beta-hemolytic enterococcus, that organism was not cultured from hundreds of other samples being processed simultaneously, in the same manner, using the same media, and being evaluated by the same personnel.

TABLE 48.2

Serologic Studies in Patient with Whipple's Disease Reciprocal of Agglutination Titers of Patient and Control Sera

| Sera | Antibody Titer | | | |
| | Bacterial Antigen | | | |
	T. Strep.	Group A Strep.	Streptococcus albus	Escherichia coli
1. Patient T	*128	*2	*2	*2
2. Control 1	2	32	2	4
3. Control 2	4	4	2	32
4. Control 3	0	8	0	8
5. Control Pool	0	2	2	64

* Reciprocal of serum dilution.

The enterococcus reverted spontaneously to atypical forms and was difficult to maintain as a Gram-positive streptococcus. When the cell wall was deliberatedly damaged with penicillin, the enterococcus acquired the form of Gram-negative spheres or rods, depending upon the concentration of penicillin and length of incubation. These atypical forms were unusually stable, even in relatively hypotonic media and in the presence of high concentrations of penicillin.

Human polymorphonuclear leukocytes, monocytes and lymphocytes readily phagocytized the enterococcus *in vitro*, and intracellular bacteria showed a variety of sizes, shapes and staining properties. The smallest particles measurable by light microscopy and seen within leukocytes were approximately 0.2 μ in diameter, or within the size range of the intracellular bodies seen on electron microscopy of the biopsies from the patient with Whipple's disease.

PAS staining of intracellular organisms phagocytized *in vitro* by leukocytes showed PAS-staining bodies similar to those seen in impression smears of lymph node tissue obtained from the patient. The bacterium itself was shown to be PAS-positive when fixed and stained on a glass slide.

Antibody studies revealed that the patient had an elevated agglutinin titer to the isolated organism, as seen in Table 48.2, contrasting to his antibody titer with other test organisms (Group A *Streptococcus, Escherichia coli, S. albus*).

Antibiotic sensitivity studies were obtained only after the patient had been discharged from the hospital. They showed that the enterococcus was resistant to tetracycline and streptomycin, and sensitive to chloramphenicol, penicillin, erythromycin and novobiocin. The patient had been placed on tetracycline five days prior to discharge; this therapy did not influence his febrile course in the hospital. He was continued on tetracycline for about two months, during which time his status deteriorated rapidly. Treatment was then changed to chloramphenicol, followed by erythromycin, with a dramatic response: he gained 20 pounds in weight within three weeks and has since returned to work.

This patient with documented Whipple's disease met our criteria for demonstration of infection due to atypical bacterial forms. The organism in this case was a Group D enterococcus which had the capacity to take the size, shape and staining properties of forms previously identified in pathologic specimens of Whipple's disease. We believe that the patient, over a period of years, was able to control partially but not completely his infection, and that during this time microbial persistence was responsible for the pattern of symptoms observed. Failure to identify this pathogen in the past may readily be explained by its presentation in atypical form.

Since in most cases in which atypical bacterial forms could be documented the bacteriologic information has been clinically useful, studies have been undertaken to evaluate the reliability and practicality of applying atypical bacterial isolation techniques in a general hospital laboratory. In this program, pleural, ascitic and joint fluids were processed blindly over an eight-month period routinely and for atypical bacterial forms, without laboratory knowledge of diagnosis. The results of this study are now being evaluated. During the first three months of the program, 31 cultures taken from patients thought to have no sepsis showed only one positive. Of 30 cases in which the patient had fever, leukocytosis, or other signs of infection, 24 samples were positive. Of these, 14 were positive for organisms which in the past would probably have remained unrecognized. These data are currently being further assessed.

BACTERIAL ISOLATIONS

Bacterial species isolated are summarized in Table 48.3. Over three fourths of the recognized ones have been *Streptococcus* or *Staphylococcus* species; *Candida* was isolated in atypical form in one culture only; the remaining bacterial species isolates have been recovered from two or more samples.

The appearance of the bacterium varies with the species, the culture source, and

TABLE 48.3
Bacterial Species Isolated in Atypical Form

Candida sp.
Corynebacterium
aerobic
anaerobic
Escherichia coli
Herellae
Hemophilus influenzae
Klebsiella
Listeria
Proteus
Staphylococcus
albus
aureus
Streptococcus
enterococcus
faecalis
microaerophilic
viridans

the media on which it is placed; some of these forms are illustrated in Figure 48.4.

Streptococci have shown particular variability, ranging in size from large yeast-like forms to particles 200 mμ in diameter; rod shapes and pleomorphic club shapes are common. Staphylococci have shown fewer shape changes, appearing generally as Gram-variable or Gram-negative spherical forms or short rods. Thread-like forms have been seen with all Gram-negative atypical isolates.

UNDERLYING PATIENT PATHOLOGY

Evaluation of cases from whom atypical bacterial forms have been isolated has shown that in a high percentage the patients have had underlying pathology. It is not known whether any of the particular diseases noted predispose to the formation or persistence of atypical forms, or whether this reflects a general susceptibility to all types of pathogens in that population. The types of pathology noted are summarized in Table 48.4.

COMMENT

In some cases the patient had received antibiotics prior to the recovery of atypical bacterial forms. In others, no antimicrobial therapy had been used prior to the isolation of atypical forms.

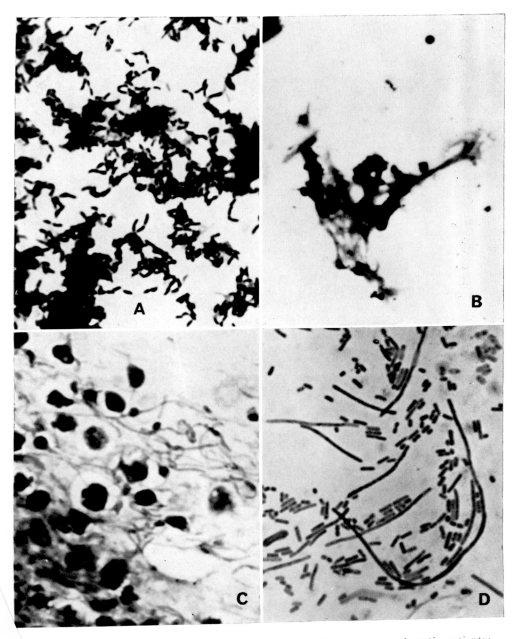

Figure 48.4. Atypical bacterial forms isolated from blood cultures of septic patients; × 1900. A: *Streptococcus viridans,* showing pleomorphic and rod-like forms. B. *Streptococcus ...mogenes,* showing tendency of atypical forms to grow in clumps adherent to debris. C: *...mophilus influenzae,* showing large spheres and thread-like forms. D: *Proteus mirabilis,* ...ving elongated rods.

Many factors have been shown *in vitro* to induce formation of fragile bacterial forms; these include leukocytic enzymes, low pH, inadequate culture media, lysozyme and antibody plus complement, as well as antibiotics. All of these factors have their clinical counterparts in patients with pus collections or with chronic infection. The presence of atypical bacterial forms in a patient who has not received antibiotics implies that a bacterial-host interaction occurred in order to produce the damaged bacterium.

In some cases (as in the patient with Whipple's disease cited in Case 5) the pattern of symptoms with recurrent fever, leukocytosis, arthritis and polyserositis most resembles that of serum sickness, or those diseases thought to have an immunologic etiology. We can speculate that in Case 5 and others like it, the bacterium is acting as a foreign antigen and that the same immunologic reaction which creates atypical bacteria results in the pattern of symptoms observed.

Such cases make it profitable to begin to re-evaluate our concepts of the clinical appearance of infectious disease.

SUMMARY

Media and processing techniques are being developed to permit isolation and identification of atypical bacterial forms in clinical patient material.

Rigid laboratory controls and criteria have been adapted and designed to demonstrate that identified atypical organisms came from the patient and were related to his disease.

In 41 cases, atypical bacterial forms have been identified. These include 21 cases with septicemia, seven with positive pus cultures, seven with one pyarthrosis, five empyema and one case of positive skin biopsies.

Organisms identified in atypical form include streptococci, staphylococci, *Herellae*, *Klebsiella*, *Escherichia coli*, *Proteus*, *Hemophilus*, *Listeria*, corynebacteria and *Candida*.

The appearance of the atypical forms

TABLE 48.4
Underlying Diseases Diagnosed in Patients from Whom Atypical Bacteria Have Been Isolated

Agammaglobulinemia
Aldrich syndrome

Lymphoma
Hodgkins' disease
Leukemia

Lupus erythematosus
Rheumatoid arthritis
Stills' disease
Sjögren's syndrome
Periarteritis

Uremia
Cirrhosis

Foreign body
Chronic urinary tract infection
Underlying heart disease

varied with the species studied and the nature of the specific isolate.

Clinical presentations of patients from whom atypical forms are isolated vary widely; patients tend to exhibit underlying pathology.

REFERENCES

1. Charache, P., Bayless, T. M., Shelley, W. M., and Hendrix, T. R.: Atypical bacteria in Whipple's disease. *Trans. Ass. Amer. Physicians* **79**: 399, 1966.
2. Chears, W. C., Jr., and Ashworth, C. T.: Electron microscopic study of the intestinal mucosa in Whipple's disease; demonstration of encapsulated bacilliform bodies in the lesion. *Gastroenterology* **41**: 129, 1961.
3. Gutman, L. T., Turck, M., Petersdorf, R. G., and Wedgwood, R. J.: Significance of bacterial variants in urine of patients with chronic bacteriuria. *J. Clin. Invest.* **44**: 1945, 1965.
4. Kagan, G. Y., Koptelova, E. I., and Pokrovsky, B. M.: Isolation of pleuropneumonia-like organisms, L-forms, and heteromorphous growth of bacteria from the cerebrospinal fluid of patients with septic meningitis. *J. Hyg. Epidemiol.* (Prague) **9**: 310, 1965.
5. Mattman, L. H., and Mattman, P. E.: L forms of *Streptococcus fecalis* in septicemia. *Arch. Intern. Med.* (Chicago) **115**: 315, 1965.

6. Nativelle, R., and Deparis, M.: Formes évolutives des bactéries dans les hémocultures.
Presse Méd. **68**: 571, 1960.

7. Nativelle, R., Deparis, M., and Sarrazin, A.:
Répercussions pratiques de la connaissance
des formes L et du cycle L des bactéries.
Rev. Praticien **11**: 1877, 1961.

8. Nelson, E. L., and Pickett, M. J.: The recovery of L forms of brucella and their relation
to brucella phage. *J. Infect. Dis.* **89**: 226,
1951.

9. Rosner, R.: Isolation of *Candida* protoplasts
from a case of *Candida* endocarditis. *J. Bact.*
91: 1320, 1966.

10. Wittler, R. G., Malizia, H. F., Kramer, P. E.,
Tuckett, J. D., Pritchard, H. N., and Baker,
H. J.: Isolation of a Corynebacterium and
its transitional forms from a case of subacute bacterial endocarditis treated with antibiotics. *J. Gen. Microbiol.* **23**: 315, 1960.

11. Yardley, J. H., and Hendrix, T. R.: Combined
electron and light microscopy in Whipple's
disease; demonstration of "bacillary bodies"
in the intestine. *Bull. J. Hopkins Hosp.* **109**:
80, 1961.

49

Discussion

Drs. George Gee Jackson and Robert G. Petersdorf,
CO-CHAIRMEN
Drs. Michael F. Barile, Abraham I. Braude,
Patricia Charache, Roger Cole, Monroe D. Eaton, Wolfgang
Epstein, Robert A. Fekety, Jr., Earl H. Freimer, Carl W.
Godzeski, Laura T. Gutman, Gary J. Haller, Morton
Hamburger, Benjamin M. Kagan, George M. Kalmanson,
Edward H. Kass, Raymond J. Lynn, Edward A. Mortimer,
Jr., Jack L. Strominger, Marvin Turck

DR. KASS: The very important studies of Dr. Freimer* raise a couple of questions that I am sure we all have in our minds.

First, of course, is how can we be confident that the difference between those patients who contracted rheumatic fever and those who did not was no more than a matter of total antigenic stimulation and, therefore, reflected in the total amount of antibodies. It has been an old observation that the total amount of antistreptolysin remains also high in people who are destined to become rheumatic compared to those who are not; the titers also persist longer, etc. So, are we simply measuring the same thing, namely total antigenic load leading to a large amount of antibodies, some of which have this interesting characteristic? One might also inquire about the specificity of the phenomenon, since it inevitably is related to the question of rheumatic fever in one's mind. Is there any cross-reactivity with comparable membrane areas in other animal species where rheumatic fever does not occur? What about the curious cross-reactivity with the sarcolemma of striated muscle?

* See pp. 279–292.

If the localization of antibody in the heart muscle were somewhat related to the late lesion, one would expect a similar lesion to occur in striated muscle. Or is there some specific reason why this does not occur?

DR. FREIMER: The first question has naturally occurred to many people. We have evidence, tabulated in Table 37.5, where you might have noticed that the average ASO responses of the two groups were also included in the last column. It is certainly true that the average ASO response of the patients who went on to develop rheumatic fever is more than three times higher than that of the uncomplicated group. But when you start looking at individual patients, we have some with ASO as high as 1500 who did not develop rheumatic fever and had, at best, only a minimal trace of cross-reactivity antibody in their serum at the time of their scarlet fever, or subsequently. So, it does appear from a limited series, perhaps a dozen of these patients, that parallelism is not the rule.

I might mention that the series from which the data were taken represents some 300 patients with scarlet fever during an epidemic in Great Lakes in 1944. The sera, the case histories, and the streptococcal strains of every one of these patients were preserved by Dr. Lancefield. All of the cases were documented. One could secure samples of sera obtained at any given time from the day of onset of scarlet fever and for the months the Navy followed them. I think the two antibodies do not follow in parallel.

As to the relationship of antibody to rheumatic fever, I think this is strictly gossip or fancy; we could talk for hours about it. There are no facts. The only thing I might point out, what we feel is most significant, is the staining of the media of the small arterioles, where we believe the antibody is deposited primarily. This is strictly without any further evidence. It is certainly true that, if this antibody were to affect the sarcolemma of skeletal muscle, there should not be any in the sera at all: it would be pulled out as fast as it is made. There must be something else involved; we do not know. This is just the first stage of this series of studies, and I think we tried only striated muscle of guinea pig and rabbit.

DR. COLE: I would like to ask Dr. Mortimer* if he has any evidence by direct microscopy, either phase or (preferably) electron microscopy, of whether there are actually L-forms in the peritoneal exudates from which he obtains the L-form colonies.

DR. MORTIMER: We have not even looked, Dr. Cole; you know what a mess that would be. We used culture instead.

DR. COLE: Dr. Haller, what was the shortest time at which the chambers were extracted and you found whether the implanted L-forms were or were not still viable?†

DR. HALLER: Five months was the shortest period after which we looked for the L-form, and about 22 days for the streptococci.

DR. COLE: Dr. Freimer, can you reproduce the effects you described with the membranes of stable L-forms of group A streptococci?

* See pp. 345–351.
† See pp. 352–355.

DR. FREIMER: We have not tried.

DR. EATON: Dr. Freimer, I would like to know a little more about the nature of the antigen. You mentioned defatting the antigen by extraction with lipid solvents; did you find any antigenic activity in the lipid solvent extract?

DR. FREIMER: No. The reason we defatted was primarily to see if the antigen was in the protein fraction. The defatted sarcolemma membranes are just as active as the untreated ones. The extracts that can be prepared from these membranes are just as active whether the membranes are defatted or not.

DR. EATON: What about the soluble extract?

DR. FREIMER: The lipid has no activity. Removal of the lipid does not seem to alter the activity.

DR. LYNN: In partial answer to Dr. Cole's question, we have shown fluorescent antibody results much like Dr. Freimer's with antisera against the stable L-forms, using both heart tissue from rabbits and heart valves from rheumatic fever patients.

I have a question for Dr. Mortimer: I wonder whether he has shown any of the extracellular substances such as hemolysins or DNase to be present in the streptococcal L-forms.

DR. MORTIMER: We have shown the hemolysins to be present, but much of this work has been done by other people, too— Dr. Freimer, for example. Most of the extracellular products, at least those that have been studied, have been shown to be present.

DR. STROMINGER: As I listened to Dr. Freimer, I found myself wondering whether any correlation could be made between those patients who developed the antibody and their immunological typing. There is so much interest now in the immunological typing of human cells as a consequence of interest in transplantation, that it might be possible to do some studies which might suggest why some individuals develop that antibody. One might guess that they must be individuals who do not have the cross-reactive antigens in their heart cells and would therefore recognize the streptococcal membrane protein as foreign.

Dr. Freimer: That may be so, but many of the sections we stained came from patients with rheumatic heart disease whose auricles had been removed at surgery. These people had rheumatic fever, and obviously rheumatic fever with cardiac damage, or would not have come to surgery. Those are the hearts that stain brightly. Normal hearts also stain as brightly. It does not appear as if there would be a distinction between their uptakes of antibody.

There are many other studies we have done, one of which is to show patients who develop carditis have a much higher level of this antibody than patients who just develop rather mild rheumatic fever with joint symptoms. But all of the patients do have some of the antibody, and in higher titer than patients who do not develop rheumatic fever.

Dr. Fekety: Dr. Godzeski,* how were your specimens obtained, and what type of antibiotics had the patients been receiving?

Dr. Godzeski: We assumed the patients with rheumatic disease had been on penicillin and/or streptomycin. They were on heavy penicillin-streptomycin before and during the operative procedure, but we did not get cultures except from the tissue homogenates.

Dr. Mortimer: Dr. Kagan,† in regard to the cystic fibrosis patient from whom you recovered staphylococcal L-forms, I wonder if you have ever recovered staphylococci from that patient or members of his family, and phage typed that organism and the revertant to show they were the same.

Dr. Kagan: We did not phage type the organism in that patient before or after. We have been somewhat discouraged about phage typing after work from other laboratories suggested that the phage type *per se* changes from time to time in the same known staphylococcus, though we probably will end up by doing it anyway.

Dr. Godzeski: I might answer that. We have phage typed before and after on one patient. The phage type we found after re-

version was the same as the patient had initially on entrance to hospital. Also, we ran antibiotic sensitivity patterns completely; they were the same.

Dr. Mortimer: Dr. Godzeski, it was not clear to me from your presentation whether you recovered typical macroscopic L-form colonies on the initial isolate. I think all of us have had experience with this sort of thing. The repeated transfer is fraught with a great many difficulties, and I would be much happier if you recovered such colonies on the initial isolate.

Dr. Godzeski: Yes, we have had an initial primary isolation of an L-phase colony, when we used solid medium. With the cultures we did obtain most of the time, though, we used broth for initial isolation; this is transferred after five to ten days incubation. We also can get typical L-phase type colonies, or at least abnormal-normal type colonies, on the second transfer away from the original inoculation. We had never seen some of these types of cultures in our laboratory before. This could still be contamination. However, it is inconceivable there would be such numbers, and I think we would run into more of them than we have.

I think perhaps the original damage from rheumatic fever is such that it may, in some as yet unknown manner, open the heart tissue to secondary infection by other organisms at a later time. I do not know that this causes the continuation of any clinical problem whatsoever. All we really know is that when we culture the tissue homogenates (we cut away the external tissue and aseptically take out a piece of the core, and this is put in a glass and diluted in 10% sucrose), we obtain those isolates. They are there, probably intracellular or intercellular, but not easily removed by the washing process. What they are doing there I am not able to say.

Dr. Hamburger: I would like to ask Dr. Gutman‡ a question. You introduced stable L-forms, protoplasts or spheroplasts, into the medulla of the kidney and found these reverted *in vivo* when they had not reverted *in vitro*. This again raises

* See pp. 379–390.
† See pp. 372–378.

‡ See pp. 391–395.

some very interesting possibilities for other experimental work. But my question is, how many passages or how many times had they been passed *in vitro* without reverting at the time they were injected into mice?

DR. GUTMAN: What we did was to take a sample from a central aliquot and use that for injection and, also, to sample for stability at the same time. A sample from this main aliquot could be passed for at least two months, and in some cases was passed for three or four months, without reverting, in the absence of penicillin.

DR. EPSTEIN: I would like to address some comments to Dr. Braude's presentation* about the formation of protoplasts in urine. First of all, he noted urea had apparently a protective effect and suggested it was an osmotic phenomenon. Ever since Fischer's earlier studies of the osmotic phenomenon, it is quite clear that urea is taken up by the cell extremely rapidly. I wonder whether the effect of urea might not be (a) partial stabilization of a fragile body, or that (b) like glycine, it has another effect, by which it promotes the development of the spheroplastic forms, not related to any osmotic effects.

A second point is that, using criterion of lysis on dilution to conclude that L-forms or things like L-forms are present may be misleading, especially in urine, because in urine there is a permanent solute, urea, in high concentration, and this is a protective solute. A trick has been to take an ordinary culture and add 1 M glycerol: if diluted rapidly in distilled water, the glycerol goes out a bit slower than water; a high osmotic effect is produced, and the cells can be torn apart and lysis produced in 90 per cent or more. In urine, the same occurs, i.e., urea is present. If it is diluted, one might expect quite a few perfectly Gram-negative organisms to lyse on this basis.

DR. BRAUDE: It is possible that the effect of urea that we observed was not so much a matter of failure to penetrate, to diffuse across the membrane, but was rather the result of the stabilizing effect, as Dr. Epstein suggests. If this is true, it is still in-

teresting, I think, in the fact that it worked only if some sodium was present. I would like to ask Dr. Epstein, in turn, whether or not the observations dealing with the diffusion of urea into the bacterial cell were studied with different bacterial strains, because we observed this only with some bacterial strains. And, second, whether or not these studies on diffusion were reviewed with respect to the presence or absence of sodium chloride.

As far as lysis of bacteria occurring as a result of the primary lytic effect of urea, I think it could also have been a possibility.

DR. KASS: Another problem I would like to offer for comment occurred in experiments such as the one Dr. Kalmanson showed.† We are all aware that in patients with bacteriuria, and almost invariably in patients with renal insufficiency, it is difficult to obtain urines of above 600 or 700 mOsm, yet some of these forms seemed to appear in that zone, and I am very hard put to decide what it was that kept them there. Certainly, attempts to study renal medullary osmolality in such kidneys have rarely shown levels above 500 or 600 mOsm. The same can be said about rat studies, merely as a word of caution. It is exceedingly difficult, even in the rat made hyposthenic by withholding all water, to raise renal osmolality above 800 mOsm. The rats eat so much, metabolic water makes such a large relative contribution to their total urine, that that is about the highest point they can achieve without deprivation of food as well. The ordinary rat, on ordinary hydration without extreme attempts, will rarely go above 700 or 800 mOsm in actual medullary measurements.

I would urge that an additional control that should be done in these experiments as one goes along is actually to dissect the medulla and measure osmolality. There are perfectly adequate methods for at least getting a reasonable approximation. One suspects the differential is not going to be nearly as great as that worked out in the test tube experiments.

As long as I am suggesting alternative

---

* See pp. 396–405.

† See pp. 406–414.

control of what should be done, I would like very much to see if someone, in studying operative specimens, would try to do a correlation between the length of the operation and the likelihood of obtaining the forms that were obtained, and also whether someone would take a look at the surgeon's gloves at the end of the procedure. The occurrence of transient bacteremias during surgery is so well documented, and the patients, of course, are almost always receiving antibacterial drugs during the procedure, that it might be that one is actually picking up transitional forms that have simply been attacked in the very brief period of time during the surgical procedure on the patient.

Finally, just a small, unimportant point to direct toward Dr. Turck* (and I am sure he shares the same skepticism, but I think it ought to be mentioned) is that, in the situation where *Proteus* is recovered after passage to the rat, I think we all would want to be a little careful about this, since *Proteus* is *the* common pathogen of the rat.

DR. TURCK: In that particular case, the *Proteus* was recovered from the rat in the L-form and subsequently reverted. I think anyone who does get *Proteus* from rats has to be very suspicious because it is a natural pathogen.

DR. GUTMAN: There was one potential *in vitro* reversion. This was not after passage.

DR. TURCK: This patient had multiple myeloma. Subsequently, another patient Dr. Gutman studied, a young girl with lupus erythematosus, was also found to have *Proteus mirabilis* in variant form. Dr. Gutman brought up the question, though really as speculation, as to whether or not certain immune mechanisms themselves that are operative in the body may not be responsible for inducing these forms, for we know gamma globulin can do it.

DR. BRAUDE: I do recall one control we did that rules out, I think, the possibility that simple dilution is responsible for lysis of bacillary forms. This is simply the inoculation of bacteria, the same bacteria, into the diluted urines, in the absence of penicillin. They do not undergo lysis, but grow in very heavy fashion.

DR. KALMANSON: Dr. Kass' remarks are quite cogent. While we did not time the length of the operation, we considered the question of whether the organisms recovered were transient visitors supplied by the surgeon. If it was so, they were all picked up in osmotically stabilized media.

Another point I did not bring out before and perhaps is worth mentioning, is that in two instances the same species was found in the urine and in the kidney. It was "protoplast" in the kidney but appeared as classical bacterium in the urine. I do not know how to explain that whatever factors might be keeping it as "protoplast" or osmotically fragile form in the kidney parenchyma apparently failed to keep it in that form once excreted into the urine. We could not obtain pelvic urine at the exact moment of biopsy. In our hospital the surgeons do not treat patients with antibiotics, at least not without some reason. These patients were not on antibiotics.

CHAIRMAN JACKSON: Dr. Barile, do you relate your observations† to *Mycoplasma*?

DR. BARILE: We were in fact, looking for *Mycoplasma*. We could find *Mycoplasma* in the throat scrapings, but we could not find them associated with the lesion.

CHAIRMAN PETERSDORF: I would like to ask Dr. Charache‡ a couple of questions. Hers is obviously a very important paper for the clinician who is dealing with infections every day.

First, how common is the phenomenon of finding atypical forms? Second, how many of her patients had antimicrobial therapy in relatively close temporal proximity to the time the forms were isolated? I think that, if many of them had antibiotics, I would not be too surprised to find what fundamentally looked like sick bacteria in cultures and on smears.

My third question concerns the Whipple's disease problem. You did not comment on it, Dr. Charache, but I seem to recall you also cultured bacteria, or

---

* See pp. 415–421.

† See pp. 444–456.
‡ See pp. 489–494.

atypical bacteria which reverted, from the intestinal biopsies of patients with Whipple's disease. Of course, this problem has been of considerable interest since it was found that many cases responded to tetracycline. Many have looked for these organisms and have not found them. What I would like to know is what you are doing differently from those who failed to find variants in patients with Whipple's disease.

DR. CHARACHE: I have no idea of how common this phenomenon is. We studied three groups of patients. The largest group were preselected, and they were chosen because we thought they were most likely to yield positive results or because they had a diagnosis which was of interest to the laboratory.

We have two other sources of cultures. One is the so-called laboratory referrals. Those are the ones in which the main laboratory thinks there is something in the culture but cannot identify it. In that group I think we have had a dozen, altogether. We have had a high percentage yield; I think there was one negative.

The third group came from a large screening study and in that, over an eight-month period, all pleural, joint and ascitic fluids from the Johns Hopkins Hospital were simultaneously cultured for both ordinary bacteria and atypical forms. In that study, and we have only evaluated the first three months, our controls were good. We had only one of 31 cultures positive when the source was a nonseptic patient. In those thought to have sepsis we had a high yield, and 24 positives; of these, at least half would not have been identified in the past.

So I think, when you choose your source and you choose your patients, the yield is probably in the neighborhood of 20 to 30 per cent. As for the antibiotics, in the first group we chose patients on antibiotics, as we thought they would be positive. Of the first group of ten cases, nine had been on antibiotics. In this group, our largest series of 41 now, I think no more than half had received antibiotics.

In terms of the biopsy material of Whipple's disease, we got a series of positive blood cultures. We did not culture intestinal biopsy. We cultured two adjacent lymph nodes removed aseptically at surgery. These were cut into about 19 sections. The ordinary heart infusion broth samples and all the solid media were sterile. We had, I think, one or two positive in thioglycolate broth and all but one of the hypertonic samples were positive. They have all grown streptococci. These have been thought by other investigators to be nonsignificant because they were not rods. I cannot explain what every other person is doing, but I do not think any of them is doing quite what we are doing.

We also have one other positive case with Whipple's disease which has yielded a streptococcus; it is alpha-hemolytic, but as yet I do not know whether it is an enterococcus.

DR. BARILE: In studies at the National Institutes of Health with Dr. L. Laster, a pleomorphic organism (strain 350) was isolated from a gut biopsy of a patient with Whipple's disease, thus confirming the reports of the European workers.[2, 3, 4] Electron microscopy studies of the same specimens revealed intracellular small rod-shaped microorganisms, a feature considered pathognomonic of this disease.[1] The morphologic, biochemical and serologic properties of strain 350 were consistent with a streptococcus: it produced a "mild-positive" precipitin reaction with reference Streptococcus Group M antisera. In the skin and oral mucosa of rabbits, lesions were produced by this strain which on histologic examination showed a PAS-positive staining reaction.

DR. CHARACHE: We find sometimes that, when the organisms have reverted, they do not make good agglutinin preparations. In that patient which I projected, we did get a good agglutinin reaction. With the second case of Whipple's disease, the organism did not agglutinate.

DR. KASS: A very small point. These isolations in osmotically protected medium make me concerned about the fact that enterococci are characteristically salt-resistant and grow very well in salt-containing medium; one begins to wonder about the differentiation and on what it is really based. I am very concerned that the variant forms grow in osmotically protected medium while the parent form cannot be that easily obtained from such a medium, and yet this is the method we use to determine enterococcus.

DR. TURCK: They also grow on medium that is not osmotically protected.

CHAIRMAN JACKSON: Dr. Charache, did you show antibodies in the biopsy lesion?

DR. CHARACHE: We will do it soon. We just made rabbit antistreptococcal antibody, and we have shown this works only on slide preparations of the streptococcus.

DR. KASS: It seems to me that this field, like so many other fundamental areas of inquiry, has received its primary sustenance from strange clinical observations and, like so many other fields, is now ready to take off on its own, more or less independent of the clinical findings. I am not certain how clinically applicable these findings are, and I am sure none of us is really certain. I know that this is a powerful and extraordinarily interesting tool for biological study, and I hope that the people who choose to study either these curious forms or their elegant derivations, such as the membrane work, will not feel any sense of compulsion to relate these to clinical experiences. I hope they will not fall into this trap—I am sure it is a trap right now. And I am equally confident that those of us who work with disease in patients will have a very interesting time trying to answer some of the questions posed here, and perhaps trying to relate the questions we are attempting to answer to what is being learned by those who I hope are studying this phenomenon for its own intrinsic, scientific value.

It is very much more difficult to move onward to what we are all going to do in expressing clinically the interest we all share. It is obvious we are going to have to do a lot of homework about just how we are to proceed. I would like to suggest that some of us remain in close touch with just the elementary question of what type of media and what type of approach we are going to use when we set about the problem of parallel cultures between the ordinary clinical experience and the cultures that we will want to take, and some

of us are taking, in materials that may conceivably harbor these deprived forms. I think of them as a sort of shards. The archeologists go around looking for little pieces of shard. We are almost at that stage. The reason, of course, is obvious. There have been so many indications that medium that is useful for the Gram-positive cocci, the staphylococci and streptococci we generally see in sucrose-containing media, will not be nearly so useful for the Gram-negative rods which more commonly may require urea-containing media or, perhaps, some osmotic stabilizer. It is quite clear that a given medium is not going to be useful for all organisms.

It is equally clear that in busy diagnostic laboratories it is not going to be possible to use a great array of potential stabilizers on all possible sources in which the problem may be interesting. So, either a very small number of specimens is going to have to be processed using a great array of possible stabilizers, or we will have to pool, and each one of us take one or two pieces and hope that we can get together in the not too distant future and see some sense. The ideal would be, as more fundamental studies develop, to find more uniform approaches that would solve the methodological problem.

Finally, I think, simply to reiterate that which has been intrinsic in so many of the questions, and that Dr. Petersdorf just listed again in his question, we ought to shy away from saying too much about isolations that have to do with patients who are right now, or have recently been, on antibacterial agents, because this tends to clutter up our thinking and may, in fact, give us so much difficulty in interpretation that the whole thing may begin to become a bit of a mess. This may, of course, help us no end in our practical rumination also.

CHAIRMAN PETERSDORF: If I have any remarks to make that pertain to the clinical aspects of this problem, they are that we have to be cautious and we have to be conservative.

From a number of papers, although stated conservatively, a number of clinical facts about microbial persistence, latent infection, could be derived. Drs. Kagan, Turck, Kalmanson, and others have been appropriately cautious. I would only urge this restraint be continued—not to the elimination, however, of active work in the field. I think this is a very active, exciting field, a field we are just beginning to clear; yet it is still a very murky field from the clinician's point of view.

I would like to echo Dr. Kass' remarks, that we have a great deal to learn, even at the very fundamental level, and this, to me, has been the most exciting part of this meeting. I learned something about the fundamental microbiology, structure and biochemistry of these forms that is going to help us go back into our clinical laboratories and perhaps make some better controls and some worthwhile observations.

REFERENCES

1. Chears, W. C., Jr., and Ashworth, C. T.: Electron microscopic study of the intestinal mucosa in Whipple's disease; demonstration of encapsulated bacilliform bodies in the lesion. *Gastroenterology* **41**: 129, 1961.
2. Kjaerheim, A., Midtvedt, T., Skrede, S., and Gjone, E.: Bacteria in Whipple's disease; isolation of a hemophilus strain from the jejunal propria. *Acta Path. Microbiol. Scand.* **66**: 135, 1966.
3. Kok, N., Dybkaer, R., and Rostgaard, J.: Bacteria in Whipple's disease. I. Results of cultivation from repeated jejunal biopsies prior to, during, and after effective antibiotic treatment. *Acta Path. Microbiol. Scand.* **60**: 431, 1964.
4. Levaditi, J. C., Prevot, A. R., Caroli, J., and Nazimoff, O.: Particularités histologiques de la maladie experimentale provoquée chez le Lapin par inoculation de maladie de Whipples'. *Ann. Inst. Pasteur* (Paris) **109**: 144, 1965.

Author Index

The boldface page numbers refer to specific chapters by the authors.

Subject Index

Because of the differences in usage of the terms Atypical form, Bacterial variant, Fragile bacterial form, G-form, L-form, L-phase, Large body, Osmotically fragile form, Protoplast, Spheroplast, Transitional form, Variant form, the author's preference has been followed, and the pertinent cross-references indicated.

A

Acetobacter, cell wall, 9
Acidity, *see* pH
Actinomyces, 82, 478
Adenosine
 diphosphate (ADP), 31–33, 37, 38
 monophosphate (AMP), 31
 triphosphate (ATP), 31–33, 37, 38, 163, 172, 176
 triphosphatase (ATPase), 33, 145, 171, 176
  of *S. faecalis* membrane, 163–172
Aerobacter aerogenes, 25, 397
 spheroplast, 397
Aerobacter chromobacter, 180
Agalactia, 74
Agar
 bacterial growth on, 118
 concentration
  in L-form medium, 47, 48, 77, 82
  in PPLO medium, 82
  in reversion medium, 49, 50, 225–228
 L-form growth on, 78–82, 84, 85, 217, 223
 PPLO growth on, 82, 84, 85
 spheroplast growth on, 223, 226, 228
Alcaligenes faecalis, 12
 cell wall, 12
 protoplast, 410
Alkalinity, *see* pH
Amino acid, 59, 76, 174, 179–181, 183, 187–191, 330
 of cell wall, 257, 282
 see also Large-body induced by; L-form induced by
Amphotericin B, 479
Ampicillin, 231, 236, 238, 307, 309, 417, 420, 478
 see also L-form induced by
Amyloidosis, 451, 452
Anaerobe, 343
Angina, 424, 429–431, 440, 441, 445
 Vincent's, 445
Animal cell, 186–188, 203
Anion, 132, 176, 178, 181, 189–191
Anthrax, 256
Antibiotic, 161, 203–208, 213, 230, 239, 270, 302, 308, 309, 373, 379, 386, 387, 396, 401, 404, 405, 412, 461, 466, 480, 489, 491, 493, 499, 500
 action of, 52, 55–61, 308, 309
 medium, free of, 221, 227, 228, 237, 238
 resistance to, 59, 217, 236, 270, 306, 309, 341, 345, 418, 467, 469, 480, 490
 sensitivity to, 306–309, 314–317, 341, 383, 420, 463, 475, 478, 490
 see also Large body induced by; L-form induced by; Protoplast induced by; L-form, inhibition by; and the specific antibiotics

Antibody, 24, 27, 76, 177, 302, 348, 350, 396, 496
 fluorescent, 338, 461, 474, 476–478, 480–482
 heart-reactive, 356–370
 protoplasmic, 147
 to cell wall, 106, 278, 281
 to diphtheroid, 276, 278
 to L-form, 377, 412
  membrane, 355
  of diphtheroid, 276
  of *M. tuberculosis*, 378, 474
  of Streptococcus strain LG1, 355
 to M protein, 362, 412
 to protoplast
  membrane, 365
  of *B. subtilis*, 24
 to Streptococcus, 274, 277, 356, 358, 360, 361, 365, 501
  Group A, 356, 358, 363
Antibody-complement, 261, 267, 268, 389
 see also Bactericidal action of
Anticomplementary substance, 23
Antigen, 219, 495
 cell membrane (of Group A Streptococcus), 369, 370
 cell surface, 27
 cell wall, 25, 278, 279, 285, 289, 291
 cytoplasmic, 147, 285, 286, 291
 E. coli, 415
 Gram-positive coccus, 292
 heart-reactive, 236, 361, 363
 L-form, 272, 423, 429, 468
  of diphtheroid, 277
  of *M. tuberculosis*, 473
  of Mycoplasma, 277
  of Streptococcus, 275, 343, 354, 355, 423, 429, 439
 M. pneumoniae, 343
 M protein, 362
 membrane, 25, 42, 149, 152, 278, 285, 286, 288, 289, 291, 292, 356, 363–365, 370
 S. aureus, 363
 somatic *O,* 30
 Streptococcus, 272, 275, 356, 361
  beta-hemolytic, 423
  Group A, 285, 288, 289, 355, 356, 370
  Group C, 289
  Group D, 42, 289
  Group G, 289
  M.G., 343
  S. viridans, 363
 Vi, 23, 26
Antigenic determinant, 24–26, 274, 278
Antiglobulin, 474